Cherished Memories

Tales from Perry County Storytellers

Volume 2

Compiled by Debra Kay Noye

Cherished Memories – Volume 2

Copyright © 2022 Debra Kay Noye

All rights reserved. No part of this book may be used or reproduced by any means, graphic, electronic, or mechanical, including photocopying, recording, taping or by any information storage retrieval system without the written permission of the author except in the case of brief quotations embodied in critical articles and reviews.

ISBN 978-1-945169-85-4

Orison Publishers, Inc.
PO Box 188
Grantham, PA 17027
717-731-1405
www.OrisonPublishers.com
Publish your book now, marsha@orisonpublishers.com

Disclaimer: No stories will be printed for other purposes beyond this book. We tried our best to preserve the stories as written, but technology definitely has a mind of its own, and human error may happen.

Photographer Credit Author's Photo: Edyn Noye (photo location: 1540 Room Restaurant, Desoto Hotel, Savannah, GA)

Other Books by Debra Kay Noye
The Treasurers in Great-Granny's Scrapbook
City Cousins Spend the Summer
Cherished Memories Volume One

Gracious Me!! There's Some Folks Who Need Thanking

Foremost, Flo Dunkleberger Loy from Pleasant Valley, stepped up to the task once again and was invaluable in formatting and double checking the stories. Her nephew, Jason Donson, brought to our attention programming which made sharing of documents smoother. Kudos to his expertise and advice!

First of all, to my husband, Fred, for undertaking many helpful tasks, which allowed me to freely read submitted stories, perform interviews and then write "growing up" stories on behalf of so many Perry Countians. He also stepped up to the plate interviewing and writing a special story on behalf of some baseball fans, a former classmate and former State Police Sergeant.

I knew Bill Lyons had enjoyed participating in *Cherished Memories*, so I presented him with a challenge for Volume #2. Bill also asked if more stories from the legendary McConnell Boys, up in Fowler's Hollow, would be welcomed. With his wife, Crista's help, he hit two stories out of the ball park.

These are some very important folks who participated in *Cherished Memories* and suggested storytellers for Volume #2, (Patty Campbell and Larry Reisinger), and some wrote new stories (Carol Gabel Ulsh, Steve Metzger and Lynn McMillen).

Not to be noted last by any means, a heart-felt **THANK YOU** to all the participants in Volume #2, whether you wrote your own stories (some in printed long-hand and beautiful cursive-style) or I interviewed and had the privilege of writing them for you. It was once again a pleasure and I learned so much from each and every story regardless of the story size.

Thank you for believing and supporting my efforts to preserve our Perry County way of life for generations to come.

Debby

PREFACE
THE WHERE FORES AND WHYS OF CHERISHED MEMORIES VOL. #2

If you read *Cherished Memories* published in 2021, you already know I'm on a mission to preserve Perry County's way-of-life and history.

The idea for *Cherished Memories* started in Bedford, Pennsylvania, when my husband, Fred C. Noye and I were antiquing. Long story short, I discovered the large volume, *Penny Candy and Grandma's Porch Swing, A Living History of North Central Pennsylvania,* lying on the floor of the antique shop. It was chock-full of "growing up stories" penned by the storytellers themselves. Yepper, that's how it all began and *Cherished Memories* became a reality.

Mercy Sakes! I had sworn I'd not do a second volume, but deep in my heart I also knew there were so many more stories that needed to be told before they vanished. The stories were deserving of being put to print, so generations to come would have something tangible to hold onto while learning about their Perry County ancestors.

I also wanted to make sure those in our society that would distort our past and re-write our histories, could not undo "how life really was in the 1920s-1970s in Perry County." Kudos, to those who believe in my mission and eagerly shared their Perry County stories for Volume #2.

With sixty-seven storytellers in my first book, Volume #2 tops out at ninety-eight storytellers. Some wrote their stories lovingly in beautiful cursive while others hand-printed. I received many emails with stories in the text bodies or as documents. And, the extra fun and challenges took place when I sat down and interviewed Perry Countians for three plus hours in one sitting. I was given the privilege to write their stories after volumes of notes or as some referred to my hand-writing as scribbling. There is so much information in both books that need to be read now! Don't forget to encourage and share with others, because that is how our true histories are preserved.

Cherished Memories Volume #2 is once again dedicated to you, Perry County!

CONTENTS

Gracious Me!! There's Some Folks Who Need Thanking iii

PREFACE The Where Fores And Whys Of Cherished Memories Vol. #2 v

A Lifetime In Liverpool, Perry County
Storyteller Richard Edward Miller 1

"A Century Of Modest Living"
Storyteller Florence Swartz with
Beverly (Swartz) and Robert Snyder, Gayle (Swartz) and Richard Fegley
Recorded by Debra Kay Noye 10

The Nulton Sisters
Storyteller Sabrina Nulton Gray 16

An Enterprising Perry County Farmer
Storyteller Clair E. McMillen
Recorded by Debra Kay Noye 19

Remembering "The View" In Duncannon
Storyteller Jane Sload Clouser
Recorded by Debra Kay Noye 26

'Twas A Safe Place To Live
Storyteller Jean Shearer Sanderson 29

Church Life Memories
Storyteller Jill Miller Seaman 31

Uncle Raymond Gutshall
Storyteller Pete Frownfelter 36

"Never Moved From The Same Spot In Ninety-One Years"
Storyteller Robert M. Flickinger
Recorded by Debra Kay Noye 39

Growing Up In New Bloomfield
Storyteller Donald C. Stoops Jr. 48

Life Growing Up On The Family Farm
Storyteller Barbara Ellenberger Hamilton 50

"Blessed With A Great Place To Live"
Storyteller Vicki Wilson Gainer 53

A Lifetime In The Perry County Courthouse
Storyteller Bonnie Weibley Delancey 59

"No Strangers To Hard Work"
Storytellers Lorena Rice, David Rice and Danny Rice
Recorded by Debra Kay Noye 64

Remembering The Neighborhood Grocer
Storyteller Sylvia Orris Hocker 70

From The Farm To Creating A Lasting Legacy
Storytellers Rena and Robert "Bob" Brunner...72

From One End Of Ickesburg To The Other
Storytellers Darlene Berrier Adams and Deloris Berrier Kitner
Recorded by Debra Kay Noye 75

Riding Bike All Over Duncannon
Storyteller Aloise George Gamble 81

"An Ideal Time To Grow Up In Newport"
Storyteller Sally Ann Myers
Recorded by Debra Kay Noye 84

A Whirl-Wind Of A Perry County Historian
Storyteller Harriet Berrier Magee
Recorded by Debra Kay Noye 88

Kids And Copperheads
Storyteller Sabrina Nulton Gray...97

Lyons General Merchandise And Post Office
Storyteller Tana Lyons Parrett 99

Another Perry County Country Boy
Storyteller Leroy Earl Fleisher
Recorded by Debra Kay Noye 102

Hunting And Other Memories
Storyteller Bob Nace..108

Carl Johnson's Memoirs From The 1940s-1950s
Recorded by Paula Johnson Davis 112

Memories Of My Home In Old Ferry, Perry County
Storyteller Wendy Jo (Wise) Campbell 114

An Enterprising Youth Influenced By His Grandparents
Storyteller David Magee
Recorded by Debra Kay Noye 119

Saturday Night Ritual
Storyteller Ted Loy..126

The Life Of John Reisinger
Storyteller Kerry J. Reisinger..127

Marysville Tales From A Perry County Artist
Storyteller Wanda Marie Reed Pines
Recorded by Debra Kay Noye 130

Growing Up In The Cove 1950-1970
Storytellers Judy (Cunkle) Johnson, Jerry Johnson and Robert Johnson 134

Cooper's Store And The Kanon Theatre
Storyteller Suzanne Cooper Brown 140

This Is Trooper Krammes Reporting In
Storyteller Stanley "Whitey" Krammes
Recorded by Fred Noye 143

All In A Day's Work
Storyteller Joe Baker
Recorded by Steve Metzger 148

Hidden Treasures In Pleasant Valley
Storyteller Sabrina Nulton Gray..151

County Dispatch, This Is Ambulance 59 Signing Off
Storyteller Nicholas E. Lemaster
Recorded by Debra Kay Noye 153

Little Pfoutz Valley Remedies And The Mail Route
Storyteller William Cameron 159

A Love For Preserving Trains And Perry County
Storyteller Woody Dyer...163

Growing Up With Hall's Ice Cream
Storyteller Peggy Hall Raub 168

Game Warden, Harold Russell
Storyteller Connie Russell Raffensperger..171

My Memories
Storyteller Jeanne Wagner Bender...177

Memories Of Back Hollow Road
Storyteller Sarah Ann Singer Herman..181

Harry G. Sheaffer – A True Perry County Legend
Storyteller Craig M. Sheaffer
Recorded by William G. Lyons 184

Blain Union School Days And Baseball
Storyteller David Rice..194

Growing Up In Kistler
Storyteller Nancy Myers..196

Growing Up On A Farm Outside Of Loysville
Storyteller Ethel Mae (Wilson) Mohler 200

"Kennedy's Corner And Crossroads"
Storyteller William K. "Bill" Kennedy
Recorded by Debra Kay Noye 203

The Kitner Family Of Perry County
Storyteller Cindy Jay 209

Falling Springs Farm
Storyteller Carol Janet Gabel Ulsh 213

The Tressler House Bed & Breakfast

A Bloomfield Star Was Born
Storyteller John M. Sanderson, Jr. 219

One Of Perry County's Oldest Families
Storyteller Grady Reisinger 222

Strawberry Fields In New Buffalo
Storyteller Marilyn Knuth Bankert...228

Life On The O'toole Farm
Storytellers Carol Ann Kling O'Toole and Frank G. O'Toole
Recorded by Debra Kay Noye 230

Benvenue
Storyteller Keith Hite 236

From Pulling Weeds To Checking Under The Hood
Storyteller Nancy Weldon Tressler
Recorded by Debra Kay Noye 239

"All In A Day Well Spent"
Storyteller Charles E. Magee
Recorded by Debra Kay Noye 248

My Experiences
Storyteller Marlin C. Raffensperger 253

They Came To Play
Storytellers Roger Hickoff and Myron Rohrer
Recorded by Fred C. Noye...256

Reflections On The Establishment Of
Storyteller Kate Matunis Wolfe
in conjunction with Suzanne Hoban Matunis..261

Growing Up In Blain, Perry County, Pennnsylvania
Storytellers Claudia Bower Barry and Belinda Bower Gemme 268

Duncannon's Local Gathering Place
Storyteller Peggy Hepfer Miller
Recorded by Fred C. Noye...271

Keeping An Eye On Bloomfield From The Barber's Chair
Storyteller Donald C. Stoops, Jr. 275

Family And "Perry County Home" Memories
Storyteller Shirley Sheaffer Nace..277

Great-Granny Didn't Need A Car
Storyteller Lynn D. McMillen 283

Childhood Memories Of Growing Up In Marysville
Storyteller Susan Spoonhour Rice 287

Spending Time With Grandma And Grandpa Lower
Storyteller Carl Johnson
Recorded by Paula Johnson Davis..292

"Adventures Of The Legendary McConnell Brothers"
Storytellers Larry & Jim McConnell
Recorded by William G. Lyons 295

"Baseball's In His Blood"
Storyteller Max Mohler 300

Hard Work And Family Fun On The Farm
Storyteller Ruth Fisher Reisinger..302

From Mechanic To Pinsetter To Preacher
Storyteller Rev. Donald W. Raffensperger
Including Ethel Raffensperger Mowery, Marlin and Gary Raffensperger..305

Loafing And Learning The Gossip At The Local Stores
Storyteller George Coldren...316

Delivering Mail From Back Hollow To New Germantown
Storyteller Vicki Wilson Gainer 318

Hauling Bananas And Race Cars
Storyteller Ray Franklin Campbell
Recorded by Debra Kay Noye 321

Never A Dull Moment Teaching At West Perry High School
Storyteller Patricia McAteer..326

"You Can Take The Girl Out Of Perry County But Not Her Heart"
Storyteller Janet (Ellenberger) Colborn 329

The Future Is Not Ours To See
Storyteller Wendy Jo (Wise) Campbell 336

"Big Jim's" Adventures In New Bloomfield
Storyteller James E. "Jim" Swenson...339

Memories Of Loysville From The 1970s
Storyteller Laura (Lyons) Guyer 343

Memories From A One-Room School
Storyteller Nancy Bower Brown 346

"Best Life In The World" From A Perry County Legend
Storytellers Charles and Pauline (Frownfelter) Lupfer and Tim Lupfer
Recorded by Debra Kay Noye 349

Surviving The Depression In The Cove
Storyteller Gerald "Jerry" Bell 356

"Those Were The Days – Where Have They Gone"
Storyteller Philip McKeehan 359

Kids Discovering Perry County History Series
Author Debra Kay Noye...361

A Frolicking Good Time At The Family Reunion 363

Lose A Bet - Be A Princess..365

Fun And Games At The Family Reunion At Liberty Hall 370

All Good Things Come To An End 374

Sharing Life's Journey 376

A Lifetime In Liverpool, Perry County

Storyteller Richard Edward Miller

My name is Richard Edward Miller and I was born in Liverpool, Perry County, Pennsylvania, along the beautiful Susquehanna River, on September 12, 1938. I was born in a house which became the parking lot for the Liverpool Methodist Church on the town square. My parents were Albert Schuler Miller and Esther Irene Lower Miller. My father's parents were John Davis and Flora Murray Miller. Benjamin and Sarah Lower were my mother's parents.

When I was one and a half years of age, we moved to the south end of Liverpool in the spring of 1940. Our new home was a saw mill converted into a house. This is where I was raised and lived until I was twenty-three years old.

"My mom always said she had two batches of kids!" which filled our one-story modest house. Sarah, John, Dorothy, Geraldine, Floranna, Fred and Nancy arrived first. Batch number two began with Ronald, Lewis, Gerald, Richard, Marilyn, Barry and Dennis. What a brood and mom never had a nickname for any of us. Just be aware if she called and used your middle name as well, "you knew you were in trouble"!

On my first day of school at the Liverpool Elementary, I remember it was a rainy day. My sisters took me to my first-grade classroom and left me in the doorway! I just stood there and cried my heart out because I was so scared. My teacher, Miss Ruth Brown, who was also my neighbor, showed me to my seat. I guess I calmed down and began to get to know my three classmates, Carrie Kline, Brian Billow and David Deckard.

We were taught cursive writing (note from Debby Noye: Richard presented his story in a well-penned cursive form), times tables, reading *Dick and Jane* and other subjects. We began each school day with the salute to the American flag and prayer. Miss Brown was loved by all.

In second grade, Brian Billow and I were asked to participate in a minstrel show, sponsored by the Liverpool Lions Club. The yearly event was held in the school auditorium which also housed the fifth graders. Brian and I were to sit in a tee-pee pretending to be American Indians. Needless to say, we never came out to dance around as instructed. We just peeped out the doorway and to this day I can not do any public performing.

The minstrel shows were very entertaining and well attended by the public. I can recall Howard Arnold, Walter Wert, Ed Freed, Oscar Tyler and several others who sang, played the tambourine and danced while performing old spiritual songs influenced by Black Americans. The school also hosted roller skating parties at Rheam's Roller Rink outside of Millerstown.

I came to like school and was an average student. The only teacher I had a problem with was English teacher Betty Rumberger. We had to do an essay on someone famous. I choose Walt Disney and did my research at the school library, filling out index cards showing my reference books and all the information. I put long hard hours into my essay and expected a satisfyingly great grade.

When Mrs. Rumberger returned my essay papers, all I saw was a failing grade written in red with a note. "It seems I graded these same papers written by your siblings a few years ago!" I was totally shocked and tried to tell her it was not true because I had worked long and hard hoping for a good grade. As I settled for the worst grade ever, I lost some respect for Mrs. Rumberger that day. All in all, she was a very good teacher, but I feel much better now that I've cleared the air and gotten this off my chest.

My dad never drove or owned a vehicle, so we walked everywhere unless a kind neighbor or relative offered us transportation. One of my dad's jobs was digging graves in the local cemetery. At lunch time, we kids would take a tin lunch pail and water carrier to where he was working. As dad enjoyed lunch, we would play "cowboys and Indians" throughout the cemetery. The black cast iron fenced grave sites served as jails. Summers were never boring for the imaginative Miller boys!

Once summer arrived, we looked forward to the annual Lower family reunion in August, which was the highlight of our summer. It was held above Dressler's Campgrounds, later at Krafts, Crows Ferry or Meadow Grove Park and was well attended. Grandpa Lower traditionally cooked his homemade chicken corn soup in a large iron kettle over an open wood fire. Everybody brought all kinds of foods to share. Home-style fried chicken, potato salad, baked beans and pickled eggs were some of the favorites. Remember, there were no fast or prepared foods back then! Specialty desserts like my mom's triple-layer chocolate cake or banana pudding cake topped off the picnic, along with an ice-cold watermelon.

Of course, we spit out the watermelon seeds as the juices ran down our arms and the games began. There were three-legged sack races using burlap feed bags. (Back in those days you saved and used everything.) Coins would be hidden in sawdust for the kids to uncover. It was a time when cousins were close and we all got along. Oh, how I wish our family would have reunions as we experienced!

We always had to wait till the thirtieth of May before we could go swimming in the Susquehanna River, which was straight across from where we lived. It was still a tad chilly and we did not have swimming suits like today. Practically living in the river during the summer, my mom would call us her "River Rats". Lucky for us, the Red Cross did sponsor swimming lessons at Crows Ferry or Wallis' pond. Otherwise, we learned by doing and following the lead of our older siblings.

In those days, Keller's Coal Company, from Port Trevorton, would be running coal barges on the river. They would create channels while digging up the river bed dredging for coal. We would be walking in the shallow water and suddenly drop down into a hidden channel or ledge. That's why you needed to be an extra good swimmer. And, that's why a lot of local folks, like us, used coal to heat their homes.

When the coal barges were anchored, we would climb aboard and fish from their sides. Using a bamboo pole, fishing line, and a hook holding a squirming fishing worm, we were tickled when the little sunfish were biting and we had a major catch. We were scared to wade out to the barges through the weeds and grasses, because we would be loaded with leeches or blood suckers on our legs. We had a difficult time peeling them off our skin.

At night they had a night watchman from town named Rube Sheaffer. He would catch huge snapping turtles and put them in wooden barrels. I think people would make snapper soup from them. I know we were scared of them!

The river had many swimming holes and the town favorite was Ring Rock, because it had a nice deep hole for swimming. There was Charlie Miller's Rock, the Little Ring Rock, Ritter Rock and others. All seemed to be named for the family living closest to that area of the river. But for a real challenge, we would go to Crow's Ferry to show off our skills on the log roll. You would climb up onto a chained log and spin it with your feet to throw off the other people, who were trying to do the same. It was a game of "King of the Log", that left you with brush burned bellies and covered in green slim from the moss that covered the underside of the submerged log. Oh, what fun!

Since we did not have the fifteen cents to enter the local movie theater, owned by the Taylors, across from the Canal House uptown, in the summer we would sit outside the open doors (no air conditioning) and be able to see and listen to the movies. We would be teased by the ten-minute Superman reels, so we would always want to go back and see more.

One summer a traveling circus or "traveling show of gypsies" came to town and set up right beside our homestead in an empty field. We were so excited but knew we wouldn't be able to afford to go to the circus. Occurring at the same time, a milk truck wrecked and our neighbor to our south, Herman Long, who owned a garage and small store, towed the milk truck to his garage. He offered some of the milk to the circus people. The circus owner asked us if we would carry buckets of milk from the garage to his circus animals. We did in return for tickets to see the circus. We were one bunch of happy kids. I was seven or eight at the time and still remember the horse that could count. When they asked the horse what one plus one was, he would stomp his feet two times. And, two plus two was four stomps from the well-trained horse. We were so amazed. There were monkeys and other tame animals, but no exotic animals. Oh, what great times, but we were always warned to be aware of the gypsies!

Summer days were not spent only on the river. There was a small creek south of us and "Bum Bum" George Murray would come down and ask if we would go with him to catch bait to be used for fishing. He would take us to the creek and we would lift up stones disturbing the water, while he held the net ready. We would stir up hellgrammites, crabs and stoneys, which were small two-to-three-inch catfish. "Bum Bum" had a pail for the cray fish and stoneys, but he would put the hellgrammites in his hat and place it back on his head for safe keeping. We could not imagine how he could tolerate them on his head, because we were scared of them. He taught us how to pick them up so they wouldn't pinch us. We also caught frogs, which we liked to eat. We'd cut off the legs, pack them in mud, and throw the mud ball into a hot fire until we figured they were cooked. Cracking the dried mud ball open, we'd enjoy the frog legs without any condiments. Once "Bum Bum" determined he had enough bait, he would take us home and reward each of us with a nickel or dime.

Carnivals were held on the Market Street Green where the white gazebo stands today. They were later moved to the ball field. I remember acrobats performing on high poles and wires near Glenn Billow's house, once owned by Tiny Thompson. It was very new and exciting to see the couple swaying from pole to pole. Besides food stands, penny tosses, fish bowls, and darts took any monies we managed to earn. We would actually smoke the thin bamboo sticks used to hold the balloons for the dart game. It was very bitter!

A highlight of the summer was the traditional town picnic held on Butter Crust Bread Day at Rolling Green Amusement Park near Shamokin Dam in Snyder County. We were given ride tickets, but we spent most of our time canoeing on the lake, watching the monkeys or the "Laughing Lady" by the fun house, and of course the hilltop arcade. Everybody packed a picnic lunch for the long enjoyable day. One year they canceled the picnic due to the death of one of the town barbers, Kirk Johnson.

During the summer we had a truck patch behind our home to raise vegetables for our table. We had to keep it weeded and control the yellow bean bugs and beetles. Dad would give us a tin can with gas or oil in it to hold the plucked beetles. One day we asked to go uptown to meet our friends. Dad replied we could go after the weeding was done. So, we made a deal with him that if we filled so many baskets with weeds we would be allowed to go. We took burlap bags and put them in the bottom of several baskets which were then topped off with weeds making them look full. It sure didn't take long to accomplish and we headed towards town. Only a short distance from home, we heard Albert Miller's distinctive shrill whistle from his first two fingers placed in his mouth signaling we had done wrong. I know we didn't make it uptown for several days.

One summer our house roof needed repainted and our brothers-in-law Bill Leach and Mark Reinard painted it green. Us boys made fun of them by calling them chickens and cream puffs, till they came down off the roof and chased us to the river. The older boys took off in the boat leaving me on the shoreline where they caught me, pulling down my pants and painting my behind green. I knew I couldn't pull my pants up and ruin my clothes, so I waited to be cleaned off with kerosene. I guess I learned a lesson!

An interesting person who came to town to collect garbage was Andy Stroup who lived out near Oriental. Andy reminded me of the performer Gabby Hayes. When we needed something to do on a Sunday, we would go out to Andy's just to be nosy. We would tell Andy we needed a part for something and then spend the afternoon looking for it. His house was so full of junk, papers, magazines and anything imaginable that there was barely a path through it. But it was a day well spent!

One summer day we were sitting on our porch and a strong storm suddenly came in from the west. We ran into the living room and all hail broke loose! Our windows were all broken out and water ran through our living room. Shortly after that, two more storms brought more hail and rain. Thank the good Lord the next day was bright and sunny. Our living room furniture lined the front walk. It was a very frightening storm system and to this day I cringe when I hear of hail storms. Our older sisters were visiting Aunt Mary Catherine and Uncle Hugh "Hot Dog" Johnson in Hunters Valley and missed all the excitement.

In the early 1940s in the evenings, we would be sitting in our living room when we would hear someone outside yelling for us to outen our lights and pull the blinds. The "black outs" air raid tests were conducted by the local Civil Defense volunteers, who maintained a small shed at the top of Key Hill to watch for possible enemy aircraft. We would sit in total darkness till they announced that all was clear. My sisters Dorothy and Sarah worked at the Middletown Depot. We collected tin cans to recycle and milk weed pods to be used for insulation in life preservers.

Rationing of foods and commonly used goods also occurred then. You had a government-issued booklet of stamps allowing you to purchase sugar, flour, and salt in white cloth sacks, or butter, coffee, shoes, clothing, gas, tires and the list goes on. Fred Zaring, who owned Zaring's Store, was kind enough to run a tab for us. His store was long and narrow with the candy counter in front of the register. Wooden barrels held pickles in brine and he would grind coffee. There was a small meat counter, fresh vegetables and fruits, canned goods and other staples. We also patronized the Weis Store, across from the gazebo, owned by Uncle Ernie Lower. Once in a while, we went to the A&P Store in Newport, where I enjoyed the smell of freshly ground coffee and purchasing celery.

Some evenings were spent playing cards and board games. We gathered in the living room to listen to radio shows like Amos and Andy, Baby Snook, Gildersleeve and others. Our favorite was the screeching door of the Inner Sanctum. I don't know who was scared more. Looking in the back of the radio and seeing the flickering tubes, I would imagine I could see people talking.

In the summer especially and I suppose year-round, the iceman, Ernie Zaring would bring us chunks of ice on the back of his truck. The blocks of ice were stored in sawdust and covered with a piece of canvas. He would carry the ice chunks into our closed-in back porch with his ice tongs. He would put it into our old wooden icebox. In the summer, he would take an ice pick and chip off small pieces of ice for us to suck on. I think we kids enjoyed that as much as a Good Humor Ice Cream Truck coming around.

No refrigeration in those days, as well as indoor plumbing. Coal and wood were used in the pot-belly stove to heat the house. Besides the truck patch providing vegetables, we hunted for rabbits, squirrels, ringneck pheasants and deer which provided us with meat. Many a meal of squirrel pot pie filled our bellies and the local game wardens provided us with venison roadkill. We did not raise any animals for food, but there was George Lesher's slaughter house above Kurtz's Garage.

Mom could make a meal to feed her large family with very little meat. Some of my favorites were beef and diced potatoes over homemade biscuits, sauerkraut dumplings and a white sauce with chopped hard-boiled eggs. Mom called it "Eat it and Like it" served on toast. We had to eat what we were served and never went to bed hungry.

Clousers from Hunter's Valley delivered gallon jugs of milk straight from the cow which could be full of garlic from free-range grazing. Later the milk delivered by Miller Brothers from Millersburg, across the river, was pasteurized. The icebox kept the milk and meats cold.

My brother, Fred decided to try and make sour cherry wine. He waited till mom took a break for the afternoon out on the porch before he got out her pressure cooker, filled it with cherries and put it on the stove. After a while we heard an explosion. Low and behold, the pressure cooker had exploded and the kitchen was a disaster area with cherries hanging from the ceiling and all over the kitchen. Just then, neighbor Isabelle Cook was spotted coming across the street to fill her water buckets because their well was dry. Fred yelled at us to go get the buckets and not let her into the house. Our running out and grabbing the buckets made Isabelle suspicious, so she barged in the door. "Esther, get in here!" she yelled. Needless to say, mom was shocked at the mess, which left stains that couldn't even be covered with paint for years.

Wash day was quite a chore as we had to carry buckets of water to fill our old wringer washer and washtubs several times. Fred and Ronnie usually stayed home to help as they were best suited for the job. Mom made her own lye soap for the all-day washings. Dot, Sarah, Floranna and Dean would hang them out to dry.

To earn money, we would cut up rags and sell them to the garages next door. We had to make sure we removed the buttons, snaps and zippers. Nylon and silky materials were not acceptable. We would also pick buckets of dandelion flowers for Muggsy Hoffman to make dandelion wine. Empty soda bottles were gathered for the deposit monies.

When I was old enough, I mowed and did yard work for Harry Ritter and Anna Leach. I also picked apples, putting them into a shoulder bag before being emptied into half-bushel baskets, for White's Orchard about a mile out on Route 17. I harvested tomatoes for Matter's also out on Route 17 about half mile. Strawser's at Oriental had me picking strawberries and black raspberries into berry baskets. I was paid per box. One day I was so hungry after picking berries, that I stopped at a local store and spent every cent I had made on chocolate milk and moon pies. What a special treat! There was always work available, you just needed to look.

On the south side of our house, Herman and Ida Long had a garage and a mini store. Herman would always have new toys to show us and Ida invited us over to watch the black and white television shows. I enjoyed the comedy shows of Sid Caesar and Imogene Coco, as well as Dinah Shore sponsored by Chevrolet "See the USA in a Chevrolet"! Dancing cigarette pack commercials appeared with other shows. We did not get a tv until I was a senior in Greenwood Joint High School.

Holidays were extra special to us, including Memorial Day with parades honoring our veterans. Church members would gather and march through Liverpool with the children carrying pink, violet and white bouquets of irises and wild phlox. Veterans' graves were marked with an American flag so the children knew where to place the bouquets. Flags were flown from the front porches of homes that lined the streets. Everyone was patriotic and proud of it! Picnics were held afterwards.

Every year at Thanksgiving we would get a live turkey from Taylor's out in Centerville. Dad would chop the head off and scold the bird in hot boiling water so we kids could pluck off the feathers. He used a flaming paper bag to singe off the remaining hairs. We saved the long wing feathers using them to keep the ashes cleared from around the living room coal stove. We also sifted the coal dust each year before filling up the bin under the back porch for the winter.

We always had a great Thanksgiving meal of bread stuffing, mashed potatoes and sweet potatoes from our truck patch, my mom's dried corn, canned cranberry sauce and pumpkin pie. Thanksgiving is still my favorite holiday and we had so much to be thankful for.

One year I went to a shooting match, using sixteen-gauge shotguns, held at the Liverpool ball field. I was too young to participate, so I asked Wayne Shuler to shoot for me. Wayne won a live turkey which was put into a burlap bag. I carried it home and tied it to the clothes line using binder twine around its legs. In the morning, I discovered the turkey had gotten loose and was running through the neighborhood. Needless to say, that turkey graced our Thanksgiving dinner table and I was one proud kid!

Christmas was coming and we needed a tree and decorations. Dad would take us out over Rubendal's Hill off Route 17 to find the perfect tree. Sooner or later, we would find a jack pine that was anything but perfectly shaped, but had a lot of potential. We would decorate the tree with old glass ornaments, homemade paper chains, and strings of popcorn. Tinsel would be applied by one strand at a time as sister Floranna, "Fuss" to us kids, would direct the decorating. We were so proud of our trees and never took them down till after New Year's Day.

We also gathered trailing pine, crowsfoot and red berries. Dad and mom made wreaths using the greens, bitter-sweet vines with orange-red berries and pine cones.

Mom was always busy in the "pre-holiday" kitchen baking lots of cookies which she stored in large metal lard cans. We loved to decorate the sand tarts which were cut out into different shapes. Sugar cookies, snickerdoodles, molasses and other varieties (pre-chocolate chip) filled the tin cans as well as fudge, divinity and taffy candies. One of my favorite Christmas gifts were clear toy candies, which were store bought.

The following Christmas after my dad died in 1950, mom told us "we were not going to get much". We went to bed early so we could get up around five o'clock to see what we were not getting. However, shortly after we had gone to bed we were told to get up because we had visitors. There stood Santa, Roy and Mrs. Bair, Hattie Hoffman and other people from the Liverpool churches. They had brought us candy, oranges and gifts. Another country church surprised us with bags of groceries and gifts.

One of the gifts was sweaters with reindeer and lucky me, one was my size. I was the happiest child alive and so proud. I would hope that you would donate to your church and community, so others may be blessed with a Merry Christmas.

We wore "hand-me-downs" so it was a tradition at Christmas to receive either a new pair of unlined rubber boots or a snowsuit. Uncle Wiggley, Monopoly, and other games were found wrapped bearing numerous names under the tree. We learned to share and played the games from sunup to bedtime.

Christmas generally meant snow and I remember how my mother loved to sit by the window and watch it coming down. Dressed in our wool clothing, we would walk up town to shovel snow off sidewalks to earn a little money. The snow stuck like glue to our clothes weighing us down and making it difficult to walk. We would scavenger wooden lids, old pieces of linoleum and anything that we could use for sledding down Rubendall and Key Hills. Crashes were frequent because we had no control.

As youngsters we attended church and Grandma Miller, who lived with us after a while, would lay out our Sunday School clothes on the back of the living room couch next to the pot-belly stove. Sunday morning, we got washed up, dressed, smacking our elbows against the hot stove pipe, and waited for Maurice

Schuler to arrive in his big car. Oh, what fun we had at Sunday School taking little pieces of paper, holding them over the heating grate to watch them float, until Gerty Schuler, our teacher, put a stop to it.

One year for the church Christmas pageant, they asked me to be a shepherd, but I felt I was too big, so instead I was to pull the curtain for the performance. Once I pulled the curtain, I had to slide down between the choir and the organ. Gertrude started the music by playing the keys and pulling the various knobs on the organ, but there was no sound! One of the choir members leaned down and told me I had knocked out the organ plug. With barely enough room to maneuver, I managed to replace the plug so the show could go on.

Easter meant five or six o'clock sunrise services, egg hunts, mom's homemade candies and coconut cake decorated with jelly bean candies. We used onion skins to color the hard-boiled eggs which were turned into pickled eggs after the egg hunt.

On November 15, 1961, I married Janet Knouse, daughter of Joanna Fisher Knouse and David Knouse from Oriental. Jeffrey Steven Miller was born the following year. Grandchildren are Ethan Edward Miller and Abigail Marie Miller, plus a niece, Amanda Knouse Majek we helped to raise.

I was drafted and served in the Army from 1961 to 1963. I was stationed at Fort Myers while on assignment at the Pentagon, Washington, DC., where my duties involved security, including making sure typewriter ribbons did not leave the premises. They were removed and placed in sealed envelopes at the end of each workday. It was a privilege to be chosen for duty there. I was discharged two days before the assassination of President John F. Kennedy. Fort Myers was the center for the funeral arrangements because the Army Band and horses were housed there.

Other businesses that existed in Liverpool throughout the years:

Lesher's Gas Station and Restaurant currently Mark Spade's home.
Evelyn Deitzler owned/managed the restaurant, and sister Nancy waitressed.
Loy's Clock Repair
Martin Sheaffer Shoe Repair Shop
Mary Wilt's Doughnuts
Stailey's Tin Shop
Annie Stailey's Candy Store
Chester Kerstetter's Vault Shop
Jack Lutz's General Store
John Lutz's General Store with sewing supplies
Ken Lower Ice Cream
Bill Sourbier's 5 & 10 where Shine Coffee is today
Bill Gebhart's TV and Shoe Repair
Bill Barner's Meat Market
Dr. Amos Kunkle
First National Bank of Liverpool
Kirk Johnson's Barber Shop later Wilfong's

Mrs. Wilfong's Dress Shop
Mrs. Moore's Gift Shop
Eugene Nichol's Insurance
Cordellia Shumaker's Sub and Soda Fountain in the Commercial Hotel
Miller's Store
Bob Regester's Garage
Ray Latchford's Ice Cream Parlor
Doc Kerstetter's Bar Room
Freed's Hardware and Paint Store
H. A. Long
Francis Spade's Beauty Parlor
Joe Lebo's Gas Station
Mag Murray Barber Shop
Eddy Mangle Store
Dress Factory that employed most of the Liverpool women
Snyder's, Terry Taylor's and Nipple Convalescent Homes

"It is my wish that all readers will enjoy my memories as I have written them. Just remember my memories are mine. Other people may have different memories of the same event or people and places of business. I hope that my grandchildren, Abby and Ethan Miller, and my great-grandson Mason Allen Stuck and great-niece Mackenzie Collins Majek find my memories interesting."

"A Century Of Modest Living"

Storyteller Florence Swartz with
Beverly (Swartz) and Robert Snyder, Gayle (Swartz) and Richard Fegley
Recorded by Debra Kay Noye

Florence "Gram" Swartz, who turned one-hundred years old in 2022, is proud of the hard life she lived. Now when she moved from Mifflin County in her mid-twenties, to a farm on Knisley Road off Buckwheat Road, she was very reluctant, because she did not know anybody and she was leaving her family of nine siblings. Her husband, Galen Swartz (1918 - July 19, 1993) whom she married in 1941 (fifty-two years of marriage) had lived on the farm prior and knew the local people. The farm they bought was known as the Roy and Blanche Burkepile place and there were not any close neighbors.

Having grown-up in an austere household, managed by her seventeen-year-old sister, after their mother died, Florence learned to keep a neat and clean home or experience consequences. She finds no excuse today for anybody to live untidy! Florence recalls scrimping to get by, but never wanting for a meal. Treats were unheard of unless you fell into the spring while getting a drink of fresh water. Florence was four years old at the time and her sister comforted her with a "Mary-Ann Cookie" which was like a large sugar cookie.

Christmas preparations included making fudge, popcorn balls (no strings of popcorn for on the Christmas tree, because that would cause too much dirt!) and hand-pulled vanilla taffy. Florence's eyes sparkled as she mentioned the taffy, a very special treat.

The family did splurge again, when Florence asked for a violin, because she loved to hear violin music. There was an old man who visited them on Sundays and he played the violin, "making it talk". Violins cost fifteen dollars, which was too costly, so they arranged to make one-dollar monthly payments. Florence practiced faithfully. However, it didn't take too long before her brother demanded she "put the screeching thing away!" She gave up her dream, but still has the violin, which hangs on a grandson's wall.

Her sister made sure the family went to church every Sunday. They donned their finest clothes and walked the three miles to the Spring Run Church of the Brethren at McVeytown where she is still a member. Florence really enjoyed her church family and had perfect attendance for three years. Florence was active in the Millerstown Methodist Church, where she helped with many church fundraisers.

Her family wore hand-me-downs and her sister sewed a lot of their clothes. When she married, Florence didn't like sewing so she ordered clothing from the Sears and Roebuck catalog to be delivered to her home. Once in a while, Florence would dress her family in their finest clothes, "just like going to church" and go shopping to Newport. It was a major event, a real treat for her children Beverly (b. 1941) and Gayle (b. 1944). They remember patronizing the 5&10 Store, Zuckerman's Clothing and Shoes, the A&P and the Weis Store.

They lived very close to Donnally Mills, so they also dressed up to go shopping at Logan Jones' Store. Jones sold a little bit of everything, even used items and hardware including stove-pipe which most folks needed for their cookstoves. Florence would buy groceries, such as canned goods, lunchmeats and cheeses, bread and cereal, from the long wooden shelves. There were not a lot of options (brands) to choose from like today. The girls would point their fingers and dirty the glass case, holding all the candy, which was right inside the door. They enjoyed their choices of penny candy. A small paper bag full cost one to five cents.

Richard Fegley (b. 1945), Gayle's husband can remember patronizing Gordon's Store, which previously was Jones' Store, looking for something warm to wear in the winter. Don Gordon told him to come into the back of the store where all sorts of items were piled and he pulled out a pair of heavy bib-coveralls, which had been worn by somebody else. They fit "Rich" and he was happy with the find.

The small wooden store, with wooden floors, right in the center of Donnally Mills, on the corner of Route 17 and now Creek Road, had a pot-bellied stove. Like most small "Mom and Pop" stores it attracted local loafers, who would sip a cup of coffee or a soda, and sit around "telling lies or big tales." Jones' daughter Shirley Gordon eventually took over running the store. The families lived beside the store. The store has since been demolished.

Just as she learned at home, Florence applied her housekeeping skills to her new Perry County home. She maintained a large garden and preserved the vegetables and fruits. She didn't always go to a store or place a catalog order to buy seeds for her garden. She would save some of the seeds, to preserve them for the following year's planting. She would dry them out in the open-air or in the oven of the cookstove at a very low temperature. She wanted to dry them, not to cook them! Afterwards she put the dried seeds, such as peas, green beans and pumpkins in a cloth sack and hung them up so air could circulate and keep them from molding. It was also to avoid rodents getting to them easily.

Florence had electric on the farm, but a hand pump supplied water in the kitchen and an outhouse stood outback. She used the clear glass and green canning jars to preserve her garden's bounty. Some required the rubber seals with wire to fasten the glass lids. She also used the metal zinc lids. In later years, the two-piece metal lids with the rubber seals like today were used to can even meats. If you didn't can, you didn't eat well!

When Florence wasn't busy hand-milking the cow, tending to the sheep, pigs and other cattle including the work-horses and chickens, she was taking care of her children and making sure the house was clean and food was preserved for her family to eat. They butchered the pigs, but didn't use some of the organs such as kidneys and they didn't eat the freshly cooked meat in the kettles. Instead, Florence always made a big full-course dinner for all the helping hands. She worked doubly hard that day. She said they used flour and cornmeal to thicken the broth from the cooked meats, but didn't add a lot of the cooked ground-up meat into the scrapple kettle. Lots of lard was produced which was a staple in everyday cooking and baking. Florence and Rich remarked about the "oleomargarine", which became a popular substitute for butter and lard. Florence did churn her own butter. They crop farmed with a more modern rubber-wheeled tractor.

In 1949, the family built a house on Knisley Road and left the farm. Galen began cutting paper-wood or pulpwood for the Glatfelter Pulpwood Company. Glen McNaughton was the driver who transported the cut timber. Once Galen quit timbering, he went to Precision Ware in Thompsontown and crafted cabinets.

Florence began working at the New Bloomfield Dress Factory, behind the Rhinesmith Hotel, during the school year. Yes, she hated sewing, but at the factory, she pressed off the "dusters" which women wore over their dresses to keep them clean. She used an electric steam-iron and was poorly paid by the piece. The amount of work varied, so did her paycheck. The garment factory eventually moved to above the A&P Store in Newport, according to Florence.

Florence spent twenty plus years working for the Greenwood School district in the cafeteria. That's where she really earned the nickname "Gram", from the thousands of students she prepared and served lunches to in the cafeteria line. Gram and her daughter, Beverly, who also worked in the cafeteria, took pride in preparing home-cooked meals for the students. Most dishes were made from scratch such as soups and the special holiday meals of turkey and stuffing. Gram giggles as she remembers the day she forgot to turn on the ovens. So, when the students were lining-up to come through the lunch line, it dawned on her what had happened. She quickly told the others and saved the day! She loved interacting with the students and they in turn loved her. It was a hard decision, but Gram gave up her spatula and tongs at the age of eighty-five.

Galen in the meantime decided to open Swartz's Atlantic Gas Station, where Amanda's Pure and Simple Gas Station is today, at the east end of Newport's bridge over the Juniata River. He managed the business first in the 1950s and then again in the 1970s. He ran a full-service gas station and garage performing car and truck inspections. Back in those days, when you pulled up to the gas pump, somebody pumped your gas, checked your oil and washed off the windshield. Vehicles were better maintained then. Once he quit the service station, he worked for Shuler and Alder Homes in the construction business.

Beverly and Gayle attended the one-room Locust Grove School at Donnally Mills. The school of forty students, in grades one through four, were taught in a divided room. Mrs. Eleanor Black taught grades one and two in one side, and Mrs. Harry taught three and four on the other side. The red-brick school was heated by a large dirty coal-burning furnace in the back of the room. There was a hand pump for water and the outhouses were outback. The girls carried egg sandwiches, cookies, bananas, and once a big pickle in Gayle's lunch box.

Bev giggles when she recalls a fellow student discovering a hot dog in his lunch thermos. It had swollen to the point he couldn't get it out and had to use a knife to cut it up. Her school experiences also left her hating eggs to this day. Again, a fellow student told the teacher he could eat a raw egg. The teacher told him to bring one to class and prove it. Well, he eagerly did in front of the class with the raw egg oozing out of his mouth and down his chin. This was a turning point in Bev's life.

The red-brick River School, beyond the Juniata River Bridge west of Millerstown, was where Bev attended fifth and sixth grades. Mr. Harry Bixler taught thirty students. While at River School, a male student who sat behind Bev and another girl complained to the teacher, about the girls' use of the perfume "Blue Waltz." They were instructed to go wash it off. Then in 1953, Gayle went to the new elementary school in Millerstown.

The sisters didn't participate in band or sports when they were in high school, because of living so far out in the country and lack of transportation. Gayle though was a cheerleader, sporting a skirt to her knees as part of her uniform. It was cheering on the boy's teams that sparked her interest in Richard Fegley, whom she married.

Rich grew up between Richfield and Mt. Pleasant Mills in Greenwood Township. He went to first and second grades at Millerstown. In third grade, he attended the one-room school Gilfillen on Seven Stars Road. Mrs. Helen Beaver was the only teacher. The school used a coal stove for heat and the older boys would carry coal in from outside. Rich decided to try his hand at carrying coal and when he tried to pitch it into the stove, it went all over the floor. Coal creates a lot of dirt! The school had two outhouses, one for each sex. There was a stream, which ran from the Brofee Farm, nearby for water and every day without fail one of the students would fall into it. For fourth through sixth grades, Rich attended Millerstown again.

Rich had a tough time growing up, because his father, who had worked at Snap-On-Tools in Newport while tinkering with farming, died Christmas Day in 1952. That left his mother to raise seven children with her pay from working at the Liverpool Dress Factory and Social Security of one-hundred-thirty-three dollars a month. She didn't drive till after her husband's death, but she made sure her children walked the one-mile to attend St. Peter's Church and Sunday School, regardless of the weather. Rich did that for fourteen years straight without missing a Sunday.

He did not have fancy clothes to wear to church, because he wore hand-me-downs and his shoes were often tattered with the soles flapping as he walked. His family lived on a seventy-three-acre farm with some woodland. They had a milking cow which produced two gallons of milk and enough extra for homemade butter. They raised pigs, butchering four to five every year. Rich said they sugar-cured the bacon, hams and shoulders before smoking them. They would be left then to hang in the dirt cellar, where his mother lined the shelves with all of her home-canned goods. They also had a fresh-water spring running through their basement. Rich had relatives from Sunbury who did not have children, so they treated Rich's family very well at the holidays.

Even at a young age, Rich would walk the five miles, along with his mother, to pick vegetables and fruits at Reverend Lengel's farm and orchard. He picked half-bushel baskets of tomatoes for ten cents per basket and green beans for ten cents a pound. Rich used a canvas bag over his shoulder to carefully pick apples. Then they were gently dumped into bushel baskets. Lengel was strict about bruising and no picking apples off the ground.

If Rich wanted to go anywhere or play sports, he walked, just like his teammates. He and his siblings did not have bicycles, because they were not affordable. It was eleven miles walking distance to Millerstown to play midget baseball and later the same playing high school baseball, basketball or soccer. Those cold winter evenings walking home after practice or a game, Rich often stopped at the Troup Brother's Store in the center of Seven Stars. It was a typical country store run by Butler Troup.

Rich found work at the BBQ Cottage in Harrisburg during the summer, so he was able to save some money for a car of his own. He knew an old gentleman from McAllisterville who sold old cars. He bought a 1941 Chevrolet for less than forty dollars. That beat-up car did not last long, because of the use and abuse it received from Rich and his friends. Gas at that time was eighteen cents a gallon. He then bought a 1937 Chrysler.

His mother also worked at Precision Ware in Millerstown hand-sanding cabinets to perfection. She would load the kids up in the car and they'd go to Mom's Place in Millerstown for a five-cent cone of ice cream.

After graduation, Rich went to work for John Bowers of Harrisburg installing carpet. Then he worked for Essis and Sons Carpet and S&A Homes installing carpets. Finally, he decided to go into business for himself, Fegley's Carpet of Millerstown. He was first established in the old print shop (Wagner's) then he moved to the old firehouse location on North Market Street.

He keeps busy these days volunteering with the Millerstown Fire Company, a fifty-year legacy, and as a paid Millerstown EMT. He had the hair-raising experience of rescuing, along with fellow EMTs, his mother-in-law, sister-in-law and brother-in-law from near death on 12/1/2019. It was a cold winter night and the electric had been off for many hours. Bev's husband had hooked up and started their generator, not realizing the choke had stuck and carbon monoxide fumes were filling their home. All three had succumbed to the fumes and luckily their son discovered them alerting 911. They survived due to everyone's training, quick thinking and actions.

Both Beverly and Gayle credit their jobs with the Pennsylvania Department of Revenue due to their typing proficiency, meaning no mistakes on the exams conducted. Bev worked in Motor Vehicles as a grapho-type operator which in turn aided in processing a new vehicle title. Gayle worked in Personnel as the secretary to the Director of Personnel.

Bev worked at the Montgomery Catalog Store in Newport which included Soutner's Gift Shop. Then she worked in Greenwood School's cafeteria. Gayle worked as a technician at the Newport Weis Store Pharmacy. She did everything to help make the pharmacy run smoothly, except fill prescriptions. She counted pills, rotated stock on cleaned shelves and waited on thousands of customers. She enjoyed meeting new people, but the rude behaviors of some left a lot to be desired. She retired after many years.

Beverly's husband, Robert "Chick" Snyder Jr., also grew up in Juniata County. Swartz Valley, between Richfield and Seven Stars, was his stomping grounds, including the one-room Swartz School. He graduated from East Juniata High School and went to work for the Department of Revenue. After leaving Revenue, he worked for several printing companies and retired from the former Strine's Printing of York.

In his spare time, Chick likes to do woodworking, but his passion is singing gospel songs as a tenor in local churches and church sponsored events.

As a funny note: Gayle's dad and his siblings decided to hitch the family's buggy to their bull, when the parents were away for the day. When the bull did not respond to Ben's "giddy up" commands, he used a horse whip. That startled the bull so much that he raced uncontrollably around the barn and jumped the fence. Galen decided to hide the damaged harness in the loose hay and cleaned off the muddy wooden staves of the buggy's wheels. That cured the boys of harnessing the bull ever again!

It's stories like Bev's and Gayle's dad that made for adventure during some really rough years. Children created their own fun when they weren't being as responsible as their parents and grandparents. Brought up with strong Christian values, the children worked hard and were determined to be an integral part of their family.

Florence is a prime example of the above, as she dismisses her turning one hundred years old. She hopes she has set a fine example for her four grandchildren, five great-grandchildren and three great-great-grandchildren. She'd still be on the cafeteria line greeting students, if only she could!

Florence's family would like to say that "she is the **best** mother and grandmother that they could have ever asked for...and they **love** her".

The Nulton Sisters

Storyteller Sabrina Nulton Gray

From early on I remember being very interested in learning about the Bible and God. While we lived in Pleasant Valley, we regularly attended the Mannsville Lutheran Church, across from Urich's General Store. I remember going to Vacation Bible School at our sister church Messiah Lutheran in Elliottsburg. Neighbor Diane Dunkleberger was my teacher. That was when I first felt God had a special purpose for even me. My mom gave me a coin tied into my hanky for the offering so I would not lose it.

I also remember a very scary Halloween party in the Mannsville Church basement, when one game required the lights to be turned off as our hands were immersed in bowls. We were told that the things we were touching were eyeballs! They were only wet grapes! To this day I do not like Halloween celebrations.

When we left the valley and attended another church, I remember our former pastor (Rev. Dietrich) saying he missed my mother's strong voice singing the hymns. Music was always important to our family.

Glenn Byers who showed us the new farmhouse invited us to visit his church, the "Village Chapel" in Donnally Mills, where we put down gospel roots. He expressed that the singing and music were great. He was right! Almost every church family would participate in the monthly hymn sings which drew others from all over.

Before my mom and dad were married, my dad bought a second-hand banjo that I now own. He would spend many evenings strumming and singing with his brother Sam and friend, Turk Haas. When we moved, we finally had enough room for an old upright piano. Many evenings after the milking my parents would play and sing together. Our whole family was excited to learn how to play the piano from our mother.

Mom played by ear while chording with her left hand and picking the melody with her right hand. Dad being self-taught only knew a handful of chords. I think I ended singing in a low voice because the key of C was the easiest to play. I remember them singing "Sweet Violets", "Don't Fence Me In", "You are my Sunshine", "Jesus is Coming Soon" and "Amazing Grace".

Every month, our church would hold a hymn sing. We would sing from the hymnbook or other gospel songs. Each family was encouraged to select and practice a special song to be shared at the hymn sing. Our church had a small congregation with more kids than adults; Glenn Byers (4), Glenn Strawser (4), Wanda Benners (5), Nultons (5) and Pastor Jim Strawser (2), whose daughter Ann became my best friend.

At a hymn sing is where I met my music mentor, Sammy Rothrock, the Pastor's nephew from Swartz Valley in Juniata County. He played the piano and sang like an angel, but best of all he had the patience to teach others what he knew. He soon became my brother's best friend and spent many hours teaching us how to use our vibratos and to "sing from the gut". Some might say that we learned to belt out the songs.

The "Nulton Sisters" (Sabrina, Gigi and Dixie) first experience singing at a public function was at a 4-H talent show. Our Wila 4-H leader, Resta Tressler encouraged us to participate in the talent show. We told her we would if we could sing a Christian song. She happily agreed and we sang three-part harmony to "Born to Serve the Lord". We were young (ages 8-11) and did not expect to win anything as we shared a gospel message. We were shocked when we won "Best in Show", which started our gospel singing journey. Perry County discovered us that night! A highlight was singing at the revitalization of the Perry County Fair in 1971 when we were invited to provide an evening of entertainment. Hence, we were asked to commemorate the fair's twenty-fifth anniversary where Gigi and Dixie along with the next generation sang as well.

In 1973, our home church became Newport Assembly of God on Fifth Street. Here we were asked to sing often and enjoyed the guidance of Ruby Bellis, piano instructor. She encouraged us to sing at the Teen Talent competition sponsored nationwide by the Assembly of God churches. Again, we expected nothing by singing for God's glory. We competed and won locally, state-wide and regional in New Jersey. We placed in the top eight at Nationals in Springfield, Missouri. This opened many doors for us to sing in Pennsylvania and beyond.

After singing for a Harrisburg Pastor's Conference, we became very busy traveling to various state-wide churches. Every weekend was filled with singing engagements. We still remained very active and grounded in our church, growing under Rev. Harry Vaughn and current pastor, Rev. Gary Bellis.

We recorded an album in 1974 at the Baldwin Studios in Mechanicsburg, Pennsylvania. There were 1,000 vinyl albums produced selling for $5 each. The album was titled "Today I'm a Branch" with a bright green and purple cover. Speaking of money, the "Nulton Sisters" never requested a fee for singing. We trusted the Lord to provide our needs which He did through love offerings and private donations.

Weekly we sang at a prayer and praise service at the Loysville Post Office, sponsored by auctioneer Chuck McGarvey, a converted honky-tonk singer from outside of Loysville. Frequently we sang at the Perry County Full Gospel Businessmen's Association monthly meetings at the West Perry High School.

Siblings Jeff and Barb joined us in performing in the early years. Losing their interest, the "Nulton Sisters" trio consisted of Dixie our percussionist who played tambourine, cabasa, and sang tenor. Gigi played the bass guitar and sang alto. Sabrina played the piano, sang lead and wrote songs. Through those few years of singing, some of our "groupies" became our lifelong friends.

We sang at the Living Waters Campground in Cherry Tree, Pennsylvania, in September 1975, where I met my future husband, Gary Gray. The "Nulton Sisters" disbanded in 1976 when I married and moved from Perry County. Today the sisters still get together and enjoy singing "Born to Serve the Lord". Some of our children are still singing and writing songs. Today I get to sing, tell stories, and teach quilting on the streets of Gatlinburg, Tennessee, where I reside and am known as "QUILTIN' GRANNY"!

An Enterprising Perry County Farmer

"A WORKHORSE FROM THE AGE OF SEVEN"

Storyteller Clair E. McMillen
Recorded by Debra Kay Noye

When you hear the name Clair McMillen several things come immediately to mind. Foremost is that Clair is a farmer, in the western end of Perry County. Kistler to be exact, where he has farmed between Ickesburg and Blain, all his eighty-eight years. Secondly, most farmers will think of him as a farm equipment dealer, McMillen Brothers, specifically selling and putting up silos throughout Pennsylvania, Maryland, West Virginia and Virginia. Thirdly, some folks associate Clair with the Pennsylvania Farm Show, where he has been in attendance for the seventy plus years the agricultural expo has been in existence. Quite a legacy with stories that need to be told.

That legacy goes back to 1785, which appears on a stone erected on the McMillen family farm, which is now owned and farmed by Clee McMillen, nephew to Clair, and his family. That makes the McMillen Farm the oldest in Perry County! The one-hundred-forty-acre farm sitting northeast of Kistler, just beyond the Sandy Hill Church, on McMillen Road, was where Clair Eugene was born on May 19, 1934, to Eva P. (Lesh) and Preston A. McMillen. He had siblings Meade, Perry, Lois, Clee, Max and Clyde, which are all deceased. Clair is the last of his family and still goes into the McMillen Brothers business office every day.

Clair has only known hard work since he was seven years old, especially growing up during the Depression years. It wasn't just working around the farm. He had to wash the breakfast dishes before he headed off to the one-room Sandy Hill School, not quite a mile away. When at the age of seven, he went outside at recess, it wasn't to play with classmates. His dad would have an extra team of horses or mules hitched to a plow waiting outside and Clair would plow the field on his break from classes. Their farm fields stretched to the school grounds. He was doing man's work, long before he became a teen. That's not all by any means, because he was put atop Polly, a gentle workhorse, and was responsible for guiding her in the barn while unloading loose hay by use of a hay-prong into the mow. This was a very important job.

Clair at least had some fun when he sledded to and from school in the winter. There are a number of hills around the properties to be able to do that. When Sandy Hill School was closed, Clair went to the one-room Pine Grove School for eighth grade. At seventeen, he was of the first class to graduate from Blain

Union High School in 1952. He didn't play sports, because he was quite small, a "shrimp" for his age at one-hundred-fifteen pounds, but he was obviously a "workhorse." Clair was the class president as well as president of the FFA (Future Farmers of America).

With his success in his FFA involvement, Clair should have received the Keystone Farm degree prior to graduation, but his class instructor was not familiar with the application process. Several years after graduation, it was suggested to Clair that he complete an application and with the help of Jack Glassburn, FFA instructor at Green Park Union High School, he received the award.

At the age of sixteen, he participated in his first Farm Show (1950) as a member of the Pennsylvania State FFA Band, playing the alto horn. He was part of the band for four years. Clair liked music and thought he might like to learn how to play the piano, so he rode his horse to Loysville for lessons from the Kleckner sisters. He soon tired of that and decided piano playing wasn't for him.

Clair also rode his horse to Lynn Irvine's Shoe Shop, nearby Kistler, to get his hair cut. It cost him fifteen cents.

He was slated to attend Penn State University, but while sprucing up the house and outbuildings with a new coat of paint, in the late summer, he developed a pain in his stomach. Doc Kistler of Blain, told him on a Sunday morning, he had appendicitis and he needed to get to the hospital immediately. The doctor who operated told Clair his appendix was extremely close to bursting. That same surgeon in later years, had an accident with a chainsaw involving his leg and did not survive.

When he was home recuperating, which took two months because he was extremely ill, Clair decided he didn't want to go to PSU, but instead wished to sell silos like his dad. Right then and there, his dad decided Clair would need a farm of his own and purchased the farm west of Kistler during a public auction. McMillen Brothers Farm was born.

Getting to that point in time, took a lot of hard work and intestinal fortitude on Clair's part. The McMillen farmhouse had electric but no plumbing. Clair smiles when he tells of the toilet, stocked with Sear's catalogs, out by the pear tree. There was a coal furnace for heat and a Kalamazoo cookstove where his mother baked homemade bread and many a mincemeat pie. He loved mincemeat pies made from venison (the neck was generally preferred because it was more tender), raisins and apples from their farm orchard. His mother would store the mincemeat in crocks in the cellar which had a dirt floor. Clair would snitch some mincemeat from the crocks.

His family locally hunted white-tailed deer, and in 2021 Clair bagged a doe and buck around the farms. Grinning as he tells the story about bagging two deer with one shot, goes like this. He was hunting and two-hundred yards away stood a herd of deer. He pulled up and shot the first deer right behind the neck and it fell to the ground. When he went to check on his kill, he found it to be laying on top of another dead deer which was also shot through the neck. What's the odds of that happening again? Well, ring-neck pheasants once populated Perry County, and Clair loved hunting them, especially during his high school years. They were all over the farm, probably because McMillen's crop farmed, along with the orchard, nut trees and wild berries. Clair once again took a shot and bagged two pheasants who were standing with their heads aligned. He didn't fish, except to catch a few suckers on his way home from school which caused him to be late for chores, so no tall fishing tales!

The cellar was also where his mother stored all her canned goods. Clair was responsible for spading the garden in early spring for the "spring onions," radishes, and carrots. He also put fresh manure around the rhubarb plants. His mother planted a large vegetable garden, because she had many mouths to feed. The potatoes were also stored in the potato bin in the cellar. Clair knew once spring came round, he'd have to sprout the remaining potatoes.

The apples in the orchard were eaten and made into cider. Clair says the family would find arrowheads around the orchard. It is a testament to the story about his great-grandfather's hired man being killed by an arrow as he carried half a hog into the butcher house. This was back in the day when the farm was first settled.

McMillen's raised hogs and butchered three a year. Clair enjoyed eating the meats from the kettles, especially the liver. He declares that to make good ponhaus or scrapple, you needed to use lots of meat along with the broth. Unlike most scrapple available today, which has little if any meat!

When Clair was a senior in the FFA, he had a Spotted Poland China sow, which produced thirteen female piglets. Well that skyrocketed into so many more piglets roaming free around the farm, that his father declared in a jealous tone that Clair had more hogs than he. The pigs would get into the family garden, so Clair had to put a fence around it. Talk about "free range" pigs, just goes to prove today's methods are not new by any means! He sold his hogs to Lehman in Cumberland County, averaging ten to twelve dollars a pig. Not bad for a FFA project, that didn't require any feed costs!

His mother was in charge of the three-hundred-fifty laying hens. Clair would help her grade and package the eggs so they were ready to be picked up by Emlet's from Loysville. His mother declared the egg money paid for the groceries. Clair, again in the FFA, raised broiler chickens and peepies on a hill-top peep house with three shelters, across from their farm pond.

Ten to a dozen cows were milked by hand and Clair did his share of the milking. He enjoyed "washing off the faces of the barn cats" as he milked. When you squeeze a cow's teat and aim, you can hit a target at a far distance. The cats enjoyed the milk bath. The heifers were bred and the calves were raised till they weighed 250-275 pounds. They were then sold as veal cattle.

Even though Clair's father was a well-known horse and mule trader and used those brutes in the field and around the barn, he also had a 101 Massey Harris tractor which he later hitched to the threshing machine. They still with a long belt used the horses on the barn floor to transfer the straw to the mow. Clair would tramp down the wheat straw to make more room in the mows.

A binder was used to cut the wheat which was then gathered into shocks before being threshed to release the grains. Clair said that if it was a wet summer, the farmer had to be careful that the wheat stalks didn't start to sprout and cause a build-up of heat in the straw mow. If that started to happen, the straw would be removed from the mow, taken apart and the green sprouts would be removed. Otherwise, there was a strong chance of the straw catching fire and the barn burning to the ground. As technology developed Clair was happy to be able to cut down on the amount of time that it took to get the hay and straw into the mows. He welcomed the baler which threw the bales onto the ground, even though he had to load them onto the wagons. And, the square baler that pushed a bale toward the wagon allowing Clair to use a hook to grasp the bale and then rank it on the wagon bed, still hard physical labor!

When Clair's brother, Perry returned from serving in WW ll from 1946-1947, and started farming, McMillen's purchased a 1949 A John Deere tractor. When McMillen Brothers started farming the two farms, Clair said, they'd run a two-bottom plow all day, sun-up to sun-down, to get the fields ready for planting.

It was not unusual to see forty to fifty horses and mules in the McMillen meadows. Clair's dad would buy, sell and trade horses and mules around central Pennsylvania, but particularly in Mifflin County's Big Valley, which boasted a large Amish farming community. Clark Adair, from Kistler, hauled McMillen's horses in his twenty-foot stock truck to Big Valley. One time to make a sale, Clair's dad offered an Amish farmer the opportunity to try out one of his horses hitched to an open-buggy, which he declared could out-do any horse in the valley. The Amish man took him up on the offer and off he went. The horse moved so fast the Amish man lost his hat and right then and there, he told Clair's dad to tie that horse in his barn. Done deal, horse sold!

Now their horses weren't raised necessarily for speed and racing, but once in a while Clair's dad put a horse in a race to prove a point. One year at the Juniata County Fair in Port Royal, Clair ended up riding a horse bareback on the dirt track. He had never participated in a horse race, but his dad insisted and off he went. He had trouble before the first turn when the horse would've preferred to jump over the fencing, but Clair was insistent and got the horse straightened out so it became a fast and furious race. Here's the kicker, Clair's dad had also hired a horse with rider out of Cumberland County, to compete in the race. Clair came within six inches, pretty much a horse's nose, to winning the race over his dad's entry. In essence, his dad bagged two wins that day!

It was Clair's job to help break the colts for riding and working in the fields or pulling buggies. He would tie one of the front feet up before mounting the colt and then he rode them through the plowed fields that had not been harrowed. The uneven ground caused the colt to pay attention to its footing and not try to buck Clair off. It was a clever way of avoiding being thrown to the ground by an unwilling colt. He once was out riding a brood-mare when a nasty stallion came up and bit him in his leg near his hip socket. Clair attributes that bite to the constant discomfort in his hip which he finally had replaced several years ago.

The horses and mules were trained to perform specific task around the farm. When using a spike-tooth harrow through the newly emerging field crops to cut down on the weed growth, mules were used because their feet were smaller than horses. They did not trample the vegetation ruining the new crop. Clair sometimes used three horses with a sulky-plow to till the soil.

When Clair decided to stay in Kistler to farm and sell silos, basically he took on two full-time jobs six days a week, with farming chores on Sundays. He would travel around central Pennsylvania and the neighboring states, starting out at four o'clock in the morning, arriving back in time to help finish plowing or making hay and generally late for supper. It was his dedication to "great customer service and follow-up on sales leads" that made him a top performer and salesperson, which was acknowledged by many companies throughout Pennsylvania. Some, like Hone Silos, tried to recruit Clair. They knew it would be a great move for them to have Clair on their sales team, because he was a top sales producer. The motto, "better to join them than fight them" didn't work for Hone because Clair decided to remain an independent salesman and work for himself. It certainly paid off and his business grew beyond selling silos to other farm equipment such as heated waterers by Ritchie; mechanical barn cleaners from Cornell, Berg, Jamesway and Gratz; Sharon Steel Buildings, Round Top Barns and Badger Equipment Company.

His longevity as a Ritchie dealer selling silos has spanned fifty-five years and his efforts were acknowledged by the company. Since turning eighteen and beginning his sales career, Clair has been associated with the following silo companies Marietta, Unadilla, Soltenberger, Lancaster, Motter, Renno, Ribstone, Star which was a poured concrete silo, Negley-Miller, Fickes, and Madison out of Ephrata, Pennsylvania where he was a top salesman for five years. In the 1970s-1980s, Clair sold forty-five silos a year in Pennsylvania, Maryland, Virginia and West Virginia.

Clair recalls the early days when silos would cost the farmer between two and four-thousand dollars, depending on the size. A ten-foot by thirty-foot high silo might run fifteen-hundred dollars, which nobody builds that size anymore because the demand for silos has reached to the height of one-hundred-twenty feet. Those super-sized silos now range from thirty to eighty thousand dollars and that is without the automatic silage unloaders, which require less hands-on when feeding the livestock. Van Dale is a Minnesota based company that Clair represented and successfully sold their silo unloaders. He served on Van Dale's Board of Directors for four years and twice a year the company flew him to their headquarters for board meetings, at no expense to Clair.

Some of his sales also involved getting the site ready for the new silo. That might even require taking sledgehammers to the old tile-silo, which was put together with mortar, and knocking it loose one layer at a time. What a feat of fearless super-human strength and determination to finally topple that silo to the ground. Clair calls this "throwing a silo." Cables were used to hopefully steady the silo till the workmen could stand aside, away from any harm. Clair was always wary because he knew someone in the business that lost his life. The farmer would salvage the steel and bury the concrete and tile debris somewhere on the farm.

Other times, he would oversee the placement of footers and the pouring of concrete for a silo base. If the job was in Perry County, he would arrange for Juniata Concrete, from Newport, to supply the concrete. Clair says the smaller twelve-foot diameter silos are only sixty to sixty-five feet high. Silos built with concrete staves are eighty to eighty-five foot high. The one-hundred-twenty-foot-high silos are twenty to twenty-four feet in diameter and can hold tons of silage in their round poured-concrete structure.

The method of getting the silage into the silo remains much the same, as it is blown-in through a silage spreader. In the past, the farmer after a while would have to climb up the sides of the silo then into it to level the squishy, slippery silage, by using a fork and tramping it down. This was a dangerous job in so many ways. Today, there are automatic levelers avoiding the old hazard and Clair sells them, too.

Back when Clair was a kid, he'd climb the rungs of the interior silo doors to reach the top so he could jump in and start to hand-fork the silage down the chute to the cart below. He might have to do this several times depending on the size of the herd of cattle he was feeding, because the cart could only hold a small amount. As the amount of silage went down in the silo, the doors would have to be manually removed and put somewhere close by out of the way. Once the silo was close to being empty in the spring, there might be a layer of not-so-sweet smelling liquid on the silo floor. This too would have to be removed by hand.

Fast forward, today Clair sells automatic silage unloaders and self-propelled feed carts that put the silage or Total Mix (haylage, corn silage and grains) right into troughs for specialized feeding. High-moisture (25-30%) snap-ledge has proven to increase production (60-65%) of milk in dairy herds. To top it off, the silo doors are now hinged and can remain intact. The new costly equipment has eliminated the need for manual labor, which is becoming harder to find.

Rissler is a Lancaster County company, who specializes in mixers and conveyors for automatic feeding carts. Val Metal is a special heavy-duty feed mixer that has a roller mill which rolls the grains before it goes into the mixes. Clair represents both companies. As Clair speaks about the new innovations in farming, he is excited about the new technology.

When the silos and all the new-fangled equipment became available but too costly for some farmers, that is when the landscape became filled with tarps held in place by used tires. "Bunkers" were formed on top of the ground to keep the silage in place. Deep "trenches" were dug into the ground which held tons of silage. The tarps protected the silage. They were cheaper solutions for the dairy farmer who was milking thirty-head of cows.

Livestock need a great source for water despite the weather and Clair fills that need by representing Ritchie waterers. He's sold over fifteen-hundred waterers with or without heat elements and thermostats in the watering troughs. They are made of a poly-compound that will not rust and deteriorate like metals when exposed to livestock manure and urine on a daily basis. They are generally red or yellow in color and easily spotted.

Speaking of manure, for the most part gone are the days of the farmer scooping and scraping manure and urine from the cow stalls, milking stations, and feeding areas. Clair carries automated alley scrapers, gutter cleaners and specialized chains for every animal waste situation. Some of the high-tech systems operate twenty-four hours a day to avoid any kind of build-up, because the cows are being milked three times a day. Some waste is pumped into holding tanks and the size of the holding tanks depends on the horsepower of the tractors the farmer owns. A heavy-duty tractor is needed to pull the bulk tanks filled with liquid waste even on hillsides. Ever wonder why you do not see manure being spread on the fields during the winter months? Duh, you say reminded of snow drifts! Wrong, the farmer can apply for government grants which dictate when the manure can be spread. And, in the winter months, the liquid manure runs off the fields. Clair likes to use Dry Hill Farms in Upper Dauphin County as his source for pumps for manure pits and lagoons. He supports local businesses when he can.

Clair almost forgets that he also sold DEKALB Seeds, especially corn seed, and also baler twine, the farmer's version of duct tape after it's cut or ripped from the hay or straw bales. His seed sales earned him trips to Hawaii, Spain, and Mexico, but his work-sales travels logged forty to fifty thousand miles on his pick-up truck per year. Clair had a display of seeds at the Farm Show along with equipment.

Besides spending a lot of time on the road promoting McMillen Brothers Inc., and making those sales calls, Clair has spent the last seventy years at the Pennsylvania State Farm Show in Harrisburg. His company sets up a booth and exhibit area where farmers and the general public can see what is new to the farm scene and learn about the life of the modern farmer. In past years, some of the companies he represented would erect silos, and several years there were eight on site. (There were times when he was asked by companies, he represented to stop selling their silos because they lacked the man-power to erect the silos on time.) That was in the 1990s. His company displayed the largest amount of farm equipment in 2020. He enjoys interacting with the public, the old farmers and the up-and-coming farmers, the milkshakes and even being snow bound during a vicious snowstorm. Even when he turns everything over to the next generation, Clair will still attend the annual Farm Show, because it's a tradition and it's in his blood.

Now going to the Farm Show is certainly fun for Clair, but for fun over the years he has actually sponsored a bowling team known as Madison Silos. They bowled at the Hi-Way Theatre in Ickesburg, where Clair once bowled a 600 game (3 games of 200), with a normal average of 180. Clair said Ty Zeigler would get after Clair because he often bounced (lofted) the bowling ball toward the pins. Clair also enjoyed playing pool at the famed theatre.

Clair might not have had the extra time to enjoy some relaxing sports or comradery with the local men, if McMillen Brothers hadn't hired Dale Adair of Blain, to help out around the farms. His hard work was invaluable as was his mechanical ability to keep the equipment running. There was a softball field built on the corner of one of the farm fields, which was used by the Kistler team. Players were Ray and Clyde McMillen, Pepper Shields, Richard and Harold Metz, Dutch Earnest, Jake Smith, Rev. Herd, Hugh, Bobby and Larry McMillen; "Bub," Jim and "Shrimp" Clark, Mark Hench and Bob Nace. Clair and "Shrimp" Clark were the pitchers. Clair was most times late getting back from his sales travels. They played Loysville, Landisburg, New Bloomfield, Ickesburg and Blain softball teams. When softball went by the wayside, the ballfield was farmed.

He kept Sundays free for family and church, attending Center Presbyterian Church off Robinson Road.

It isn't too often these days that one can sit down and talk with a farmer who lived and farmed through the days of using mules and horses in the fields to modern times, where those same fields are no-till and manure is sprayed instead of spread. Technology actually has eliminated, in some instances, the farmer connecting to the earth and getting his hands dirty! Clair speaks with pride about his accomplishments and is ready to turn over the helm to his nephew, Clee McMillen and family. Clee will become responsible for the McMillen Brother's property and upholding the legacy of McMillen Brothers Inc. There's a twinkle in his eye as Clair smiles!

Remembering "The View" In Duncannon

Storyteller Jane Sload Clouser
Recorded by Debra Kay Noye

Jane Sload, daughter of Dorothy Hartz Sload and Kenneth "Red" Sload, of Benvenue, the island from Clark's Ferry Bridge to Amity Hall, and Bob Troup of Duncannon were born on President Lincoln's Birthday in the Harrisburg Hospital. The hospital's newsletter referred to them as "two little patriots were born on February 12, 1930". In her early years, she moved around Pennsylvania due to her father's work, but Jane eventually spent most of her youth at 1016 High Street in Duncannon.

Jane remembers all the coal dirt from the passing trains that burned coal to run their engines. Her grandmother, Emma Lukens Hartz, lived beside them.

To Jane, "it seemed like there was a grocery store on every corner in Duncannon". Her Aunt Alice and Uncle Hen Hartz owned the Corner Store, where the Dale Maguire Insurance Agency sits today off East Market Street. It was similar to a modern-day Uni-Mart selling Pensupreme Ice Cream, milk, bread, snacks and everyday necessities. She worked there as a teen. The Aldon Product Company (named after Al Bixler and Don Taylor) workers from the factory nearby would come in for lunch. When the outhouse was added to the store, it was divided in two so it could accommodate both sexes at the same time.

Jane was "arrested after curfew" when her mother sent her to the store after dark to buy a lunch cake for her dad's lunch. While Harry Fritz, the town cop, was walking by he said "Good evening" to Jane. The next day she was told to report to the Justice of the Peace, Harry Belton. His office was behind the United Brethren Church. Needless to say, her mother was a little upset. Her "sentence" was that she had to attend Sunday School every Sunday for one year. She was already going to Sunday School and Church every week. In fact, Jane attended services twice most Sundays, because her family enjoyed the two o'clock service held at the "Chapel" on High Street, now owned by the Duncannon Lions Club. Jane's church evolved through the years, becoming Otterbein United Methodist Church.

Her home also doubled as a store and luncheonette after her relative's store was sold. Building onto the house, her dad created a one-room store and eventually served lunch. They had a two-burner gas stove and a griddle to cook hot dogs and hamburgers. Manbeck's Bread was delivered to the store by John "Chick" Charles, and Custer "Cussy" Leedy delivered Duncan & Herr bottled milk. Jane says in the winter months, the milk delivered at homes would freeze forcing the cream three inches above the paper bottle cap. Clyde "Badger" Allendar would bring fifty-pound blocks of ice for the metal soda cooler. Meats were delivered twice a week from Lebo's Meat Market in New Bloomfield. Jane still smiles at the thought of the penny candy. She helped in the store as needed, but doesn't ever recall receiving any payment. Maybe a handful of penny candy was more than a treat!

Her dad decided to build a restaurant and bar with gas pumps and later a six-unit motel beyond present day Maguire's Garage, at the foot of the mountain south of Duncannon. The original two-lane cement roadway passed by the property, prior to the construction of the current four-lane Route 11 & 15. "The View" opened on Halloween in 1947 and was open 24 hours a day. The restaurant was named for "the View Tower" where the railroad men took shifts to switch tracks for oncoming trains. Walking into the restaurant, a long counter ran the length of the building with booths facing the roadside. The small bar had a few tables, and a black and white television. "Fight nights" on TV would bring a rowdy crowd. Jane's Uncle, Ivan "Mick" Sload, was one of the bartenders. When Mick was off duty, the waitresses would have to fill in. They were instructed if a customer wanted a cocktail, to reply "Perry County takes their liquor straight!"

Her Aunt Francis Hartz Reynolds, who lived on Market Street, was The View's daylight waitress. Lottie Neff was the daylight cook. The midnight to 8 a.m. shift was handled by whoever was available when Charles Flickinger, from Duncannon, wasn't available to cook. Even though the waitstaff wore white uniforms with aprons, they were still responsible for pumping gas. Jane recalls Eva Morrison and Betty Rhinehart were also waitresses. Jane was seventeen at the time and she married John Dale Clouser (b. 1926) from Duncannon the same year, 1947. They owned a truck, "The Green Hornet", and would gather up the restaurant employees, transporting them to and from work.

Parents visiting cadets at Carson Long Military Institute in New Bloomfield frequently stayed at the View Motel next to the restaurant because it was one of the closest places to stay.

Her father realizing truckers needed a rest-stop, built onto the restaurant. The first floor was for truckers to rest and the second story a family home. To entice folks to stop by more frequently, he opened a walk-up ice cream window to serve soft custard.

Even though her family was immersed in store-keeping during her childhood, they made sure she was able to participate in Duncannon's Girl Scouts led by Ruth Swank. Her husband, Dick Swank, led the Duncannon Boy Scouts. It made sense that the two troops would join together in activities. Jane recalls hiking together and having to cross a creek using a single rope to hang onto while walking on a single rope. Unfortunately, the rope broke and Dick Swank fell into the creek making him an unhappy hiker.

While camping at Pine Grove Furnace Girl Scout Camp, Jane liked the camp so much she stayed for three weeks. Her cousin, Juanita Sload, was a camp counselor. They slept in tents and dined in the mess hall, which later became a prisoner of war interrogation camp during WWII. Jane had to take swimming lessons before she was allowed to participate in the camp's free swim. A swimmer was born and Jane went on to give lessons with Jean Wolpert, of Duncannon, when the YMCA opened a pool outside of Duncannon, currently the Perry County Recreation Association. Mrs. Adell Hughes insisted everybody wash their feet in a basin before diving into the YMCA pool. Back then, the pool's filtration system was not yet hooked up. The Red Cross also taught swimming at Gibson's Rock near Dromgold's Corner. The classes were conducted in the shallower cold water below the barn on the sharp turn. Jane recalls camping at the same location with the scouts. She received her lifesaving and instructor's certification from Lena Stoops, of New Bloomfield, at the New Bloomfield pool.

Duncannon boasted many swimming holes along the Susquehanna River. Jane's mother was raised near the old Clark's Ferry Bridge toll booth. In fact, her grandfather, Fred Hartz, manned the toll booth, collecting and selling tokens allowing vehicles to cross the bridge. Her mother, Dorothy, also took toll as a young girl. After the wooden covered Clark's Ferry Bridge was replaced with concrete, Jane and her friends would swim out to the first pier. A popular spot for car washing, picnics and swimming was where the campgrounds are currently located near the famed Duncannon Subway railroad crossing. Baptisms occurred near the Clarks Ferry Tavern by going under the arch. The dam on Little Juniata Creek and Shermans Creek located at the underpass of Route 11 & 15 on Creek Road, were favorite swimming spots.

Jane, her mom and dad were Civil Defense volunteers who watched for planes during WWII from the Penn Township School playground. There existed a small building about the size of a phone booth from which they called in sighted planes using the code "Longstreet One Nine". Jane recalls the "black-outs" when lights were off and the blinds pulled until they were notified it was clear to return to normal.

Jane's school memory begins in fifth grade with teacher Miss Spease at the Duncannon High School. Grades three through six were in the lower level of the brick school building with seventh through twelfth above. First and second grades were in a small white building close by. Years later when Jane got her first paying job as a secretary at the same school she attended in her youth, she would have to run over to the little white building and announce the "fire drill."

Fortunate to be able to participate in school activities, Jane remarks even though she was short she played guard on the girls' basketball team against teams like Marysville and Millerstown. But she loved parading with the band playing the clarinet. Oddly enough, Jane played the accordion and took private lessons at Troup's Music Store in Harrisburg. From Duncannon, Jane would take Valley Transportation to her accordion lessons. She, along with Bill Wills, also took accordion lessons in Steelton. Believe it or not, she still has that accordion!

"A big night on the town" meant walking to the square and back or to the cemetery or the "Chapel." Jane would go to the Markan Theatre on Market Street, watch the movie then cross the street to Sam Michener's Ice Cream Parlor for a homemade ice cream sundae.

Turning sixteen, she earned her driver's license in a '41 Oldsmobile and became her mother's designated driver.

Her marriage to John Clouser resulted in three children, Kenneth, Linda (Kutz), and Michael. Jane's devotion to her church remains true today, as does her volunteer spirit, like her family before her.

Jane beams and grins as she shares her cherished memories about growing up in Duncannon, Perry County.

'Twas A Safe Place To Live

Storyteller Jean Shearer Sanderson

My father, Dwight Shearer, was born on a farm in Dellville. His father was a teacher and had attended the Bloomfield Academy. My father also wanted to be a teacher, so after graduating from Duncannon High School he hitchhiked to Shippensburg to get his teaching degree. My mother, Pauline Umholtz was from New Bloomfield. After teaching a few years, they decided a teacher's salary was not enough to raise a family, so dad took a job as a letter carrier for the Harrisburg Postal Service, and they moved to Harrisburg. I was born in Harrisburg, and shortly after that the family moved back to New Bloomfield. Several years later my dad bought a small farm in Clouser Hollow.

In the late 1940s, Clouser Hollow Road was dirt, and there was very little traffic. I have four sisters and one brother. We could ride our bikes on the road safely. There was a small stream below our house and a "swimming hole" across the road. In summer we could play in the water and in winter we walked on the ice – I never had ice skates. There was also a big hill across the road that was great for sledding.

We had cows and chickens, ducks, geese and pigs, and I had to help feed them all. When I got old enough, I milked the cow before going to school. There were many chores to do. My dad had a large garden, and we picked the vegetables and helped with the canning. We picked cherries, grapes and crabapples, and mother made cherry pies and jelly. Dad liked to hunt so we also ate rabbits and squirrels. We made our own butter, and because we had lots of milk, we also made ice cream.

Encouraged by my Aunt Dorothy Umholtz, I started to sing solos in church when I was eight years old. She also initiated the duets sung by my cousin, Ida Umholtz and myself at various churches.

I attended school in the Bloomfield-Centre Joint which later became Perry Joint School District. In first through fifth grades, I went to one-room schools. Instead of the traditional one through eighth grades, by the time I entered school, the buildings held only one or two grades. I went to Comp's School for first grade with teacher Mildred Sanderson; Airy View for second and third grade with teacher Alice Gant and Jericho for fourth grade with Herman Heston. For the first half of fifth grade, I went to Center with teacher Frank Fry. Then for the second half of fifth grade, I attended Bloomfield Center with Edie Campbell and sixth grade with Florence Rice, who had also taught my mother.

We had bus transportation and Ernie Kretzing, from outside of New Bloomfield, was the bus driver. When I went to Jericho, I sometimes walked home across the field and down to my house. The school buildings had no running water, so it had to be carried there. They were heated by a big wood-burning stove. I remember when I went to Jericho, we built forts out of the wood pile. There were few swings, no slides, or jungle gyms. We played tag, jumped rope and had ball games. One time in third grade at Airy View, snakes came into the building.

There wasn't much to do in New Bloomfield in the 1950s. My cousin and I would go to Doc Book's Drug Store to drink a Coke, and we'd go to Sheaffer's store for penny candy. There was a movie theatre in town, and when we could get someone to drive us, we could go to Newport, Duncannon, or Ickesburg to the movies.

I went to Perry Joint Junior-Senior High School for seven thru twelfth grades. I was active in chorus, band, marching band, and some of us formed a sextet to sing in concerts. Known as the Glee Club, the sextet consisted of myself, Ann Morrow, Bonnie Ramer, Norma Pierce and Marie Weible. I was a cheerleader for football and basketball games. Until I learned to drive, I kept my parents busy driving me to various activities.

Living in the Bloomfield area we always felt safe. We could walk anywhere, keep our door unlocked and didn't have to be afraid.

Church Life Memories

Storyteller Jill Miller Seaman

As a child, our family's social life seemed to be centered around our little country church located about ten miles east of Newport in beautiful Bucks Valley – Bucks United Methodist. The church stands on a knoll amidst the fertile valley which lies between the Juniata River to the west and the Susquehanna River to the east.

Whether we were catching up with neighbors before or after church, talking with them on the phone or seeing them at the local stores, the topic of conversation at some point was about something that was happening at church. A lot of these chats ended with "See you on Sunday!"

Sunday worship service began at 9:00 a.m. Mom, Laura Knuth Miller, was the church pianist, so not going to church meant you must be very sick! If Grandma Blanche Evinger Knuth, mom's mom, was at our house, you REALLY better get ready for church on time! Dad was never a church goer, except on Memorial Day as part of the local American Legion's ceremony.

Imagine what it was like for six kids, a mom and a grandmother to all get ready to leave for church together! Let's keep in mind that there was one full bathroom and one room with a toilet and a sink. You worked quickly once you got your turn.

We would all somehow fit into mom's 1963 Chevrolet Impala, knowing that our youngest sister would always be the one to sit in the front between mom and grandma. Off we would go for the half-mile ride over the hill to the church.

Inside the church, every family had their own favorite pew where they would sit – not assigned seating, just a good spot for that family every week. There was no "children's church" then. Whoever was upstairs for worship only went downstairs if they had to use the restroom. Church was for everyone!

Someone would always light the candles before the service (the acolyte). They slowly walked up the center aisle carefully holding a long brass "stick" that split at the top with a wick (that was lit) on one side and a bell-shaped snuffer on the other side. Once they got to the front of the altar, they would stop and bow their head for a second or two. Then progress around the banister of the altar and step into the area where the actual altar was located (the chancel). On a table in the center of the chancel, there were two candles that needed to be lit for the service to begin. The acolyte would then pause in front of the center of the table as they did before. Then reach the candlelighter across to each of the candles, pausing again after lighting. They would slowly make their way back out of the chancel and stop one last time at the front of the altar before making their way to the back of the church. Only then was the wick outened by the acolyte using the slide that was part of the candlelighter. Oh, how I couldn't wait until I was old enough to do that! It would be an honor to be finally asked to light them.

We would progress through the service and sing at least three hymns each week. If you weren't sure of the tune of the song, no worries – Martha Sheaffer Rice would always be singing loudly to act as the song leader. Most times we knew the songs from repetition over the years, but there would be Martha's voice powering over everyone's voice for every song. While it may have been annoying, it was very helpful. It was also helpful that Martha had a half-decent voice and was also a pianist making reading the music an easy task for her.

The other "job" I was anxious about being asked to do was to be a collection usher. Sitting in the pew and watching that beautiful brass plate with the red velvet bowl inside come into the pew and be handed from person to person was a wonderful thing to experience. Sometimes I would be the lucky person to be at the end of the pew and, after putting in my quarter, I would turn and pass it back to the next pew.

Before we knew it, Rev. Mark Jordan was beginning the sermon. It was important then as it is now to pay attention to what he was saying to us during these weekly words. However, if you turned to look around behind you, there was a good chance that you may see that the farmers in the congregation have fallen asleep. Knowing that if you did the same thing that you would get in trouble from both mom and grandma, turning around and paying attention to Rev. Jordan would be a much better idea!

After our last hymn, the minister would close our service with a benediction. Then, mom would play one more song, which no one would sing along to, while the same acolyte who lit the candles would walk back up and outen them. They would follow the same pattern of stops as when the candles were lit, this time using the bell snuffer side. However, before putting out the second candle, the wick would be lit from the candle. The acolyte would once again walk with the wick lit and not put it out until they got to the back. Again, I couldn't wait for that to be me.

As soon as church was over, all of the children from toddlers to sixth grade would go downstairs for Sunday School. Our teachers also made their way downstairs with us. We would all come together for an opening song or hymn, a brief scripture, and then make our way to tables which were separated by age levels. The younger children were separated into two classes (preschool, first and second grades). Their classes would each sit around a wooden kidney-shaped table on little wooden Windsor chairs. The table was inset for the teacher to be able to sit at the middle on one side. It also had a drawer for the teacher to access.

The older children were separated into two classes (third and fourth grades, fifth and sixth grade). They sat at rectangular tables with regular sized plank bottom chairs.

The classes were separated into sections with the use of a bookshelf between the older two and the younger two. These bookshelves held Bibles, pencil and pens, paper, and of course crayons for crafts.

Each week, our teachers would present a scripture-based lesson that may or may not be followed up with a craft. Our time was well-spent learning the books of the Bible in order, the Lord's Prayer, and in sixth grade, the Apostle's Creed.

We would also learn a recitation and special songs for presenting to the entire congregation for Children's Day, Promotion Day and Christmas. Learning these "pieces" at home with the help of mom was a task at times. However, after a practice or two on a Saturday as THE day grew closer, our presentation days were always successful!

Of all of the Promotion Days, the one from sixth grade meant that you were literally promoted. The Junior and Senior classes for our preteens and teens were upstairs at the front of the church. The adult Sunday School class also met upstairs in the back of the church. I enjoyed being able to make that move to the upstairs.

Upstairs operated a little different than the children's classes downstairs. Haven Showers was our Sunday School Superintendent and would begin their class time with a hymn and a prayer. Then the various classes would start.

The other interesting thing that happened upstairs was that there was a secretary who kept track of the collection and the attendance. The classes downstairs each had a small envelope that their class's collection would be placed into. About ten minutes after things got started, the secretary went downstairs and brought all of these envelopes upstairs. She would record the amounts and the attendance into a special booklet made for this purpose.

The BEST part of the secretary's job (in my mind anyhow) was that she would update the numbers for the collection and attendance on a board that was mounted on the wall. The board has place markers for: Attendance Today, Attendance a Year Ago, Offering Today, Offering Last Sunday and Offering a Year Ago. There are black and white cardboard numbers that are used to show these figures. How fun it looked to be able to update this board. When I was a teenager, I finally was taught how to do the secretary job and became a substitute. Finally, I could make these updates and it was fun!

When there was ten minutes left until the end of Sunday School hour, the secretary would ring a bell. This was to let the upstairs teachers know to start wrapping up their lessons. At five minutes left, the bell would be rung again and that would mean the lesson time was over. It was now time for the closing portion of Sunday School. Haven would come back in front of the room and ask the secretary to present her report. She would stand and announce the same figures that she added to the register board. There would be one last song followed by a prayer, and that would be the end of Sunday School.

After church, we would pile back into the car with mom and head back over the hill to home. However, if it was a warmer day, we would be allowed to walk home. That was always a joy because of the freedom that it allowed. Sometimes another person who was also on their way home would stop as we walked and ask if we wanted a ride. I almost always said "thank you, but I want to walk."

Back then, we knew that we would see all of our neighbors with children when we got to church. We may be able to continue our discussion from Sunday School with them as we visited during the afternoon or on the bus the next day.

As the school year progressed, we knew that our summer would begin after school was over. We also knew that Bible School would begin the week after school was out. Bible School was held during the day then. A more in-depth study of the scriptures and a more relaxed atmosphere would bring all of those same Sunday School friends. It also gave some of our fellow church friends an opportunity to invite their friends that attended a different church.

Several other highlights of Bible School were getting a new pin each year (and wearing it along with any previous year's pins every day), getting to sing out of the smaller Bible School songbook, and the Friday afternoon wrap-up picnic that was held out at the old schoolhouse (now the Bucks Valley Community Club). The teachers would drive out to the schoolhouse that was about a half mile from the church and get things ready while the majority of the children would walk. My memory couldn't tell you one thing we ate at the picnic, but I sure remember how much fun to be trusted enough to walk out there!

The teenagers of our church would be able to join Youth Fellowship which was a combined group from our church and the United Methodist Church in the town of Newport. When my older siblings were in Youth Fellowship, my mom was the coordinator from our church. She would pile all the teens into her car and off they would go to Newport for their Sunday evening meetings. The teens would worship together, sing together, and enjoy each other's company while learning about God. Every once in a while, they may get to work on a project or two as well.

This was another church-related activity that I could not wait to enjoy. Once I was old enough to join, I sure did! We had wonderful meetings. Lots of fun singing! One year we went on a retreat to a hunting camp that one of our coordinators belonged to. It was a weekend full of the Love of God!

An annual Sunday School picnic was held at Deckard's Woods which was a lovely picnic grove. Preparation for this meant the clean-up of the area itself. Picking up broken branches of all sizes. Clearing any debris out of the small kitchen-type pavilion and then cleaning the built-in selves or covering them with tablecloths. One of the farmers would then mow the area so that folks could gather on that scheduled date. It was also a homecoming for those who had grown up in Bucks Valley and always was an event that everyone looked forward to.

Friends and families would gather bringing a dish or two to share. You would always count on certain folks bringing the dish that was your favorite from previous years. Two of mine were Mary Showers' baked beans and Edith Noll's hot milk sponge cake! Yum!!

Before long, the once empty, quiet grove was full of cars and groups of people seated in folding lawn chairs of all types. They would swap stories of yesteryear as well as current events. Sometimes the yarns shared would get pretty long but were apt to bring a smile to those listeners.

Games were enjoyed by both young and old. Laughter abounded by those participating and those watching from the sidelines. It was a good day all around!

A few times a year on a Sunday evening, we would all gather up again to head to the church for a hymn sing. Haven Showers would get things started by introducing the various guest singers. The talent of these musicians was an honor to have heard. Before the event was over, there was always a time at the end for the actual hymn singing by the full-house crowd. Haven would ask for suggestions to be called out by page number. Everyone would quickly turn to that page and mom would hope it was a song she was familiar with as she began to play. When the singing was completed, everyone would be invited downstairs for time of fellowship. The ladies of the church would bring cookies and make a punch for all to enjoy. Those evening were always a fun time to look forward to!

My mother was the piano player, which influenced why she made sure all of us were in church and Sunday School every week. I also had a grandmother who was very deeply religious – so much so that at one point in her early years, she contemplated becoming a missionary. In her aging years, she passed her time researching various subjects throughout the Bible and recording her findings by hand on notebook paper.

What makes us what we are as adults? The influence of the people we are surrounded with. Luckily, I was influenced by some magnificent folks. I am proud to say that each of these individuals molded me into a spiritual, fair, and quite happy grown-up person.

Uncle Raymond Gutshall

Storyteller Pete Frownfelter

The tranquility of Route 274 in the western end of Perry County becomes illusive considering the fast-paced world we live in today. Growing up on a small farmette, two and one-half miles from Blain and one-half mile from New Germantown, was peaceful at best and sometimes just down right slow.

I grew up there from the mid 1960s-1970s amid the turmoil of the Vietnam War, Watergate and other political upheavals. We were truly blessed with the ability to see this unfold nightly on the national news via any one of five tv channels. Most kids in the area had only one channel. Life in the valley went on mostly unaffected by such events.

Life consisted mainly of two things during my childhood. The chores at home and the leisure time in Blain playing sports with the guys from town and the surrounding area.

Chore
noun, plural noun: chores
1. a routine task, especially a household one
2. an unpleasant but necessary task

The second definition was more the way I looked at chores, but you couldn't play ball unless the chores were finished. With all of this said, we can proceed with the story of Uncle Raymond.

Raymond was an old man from the time I could remember him. He worked hard all his life in two occupations. The first being the sawmill industry, which he left due to loosing too many fingers. The last being a job at Frank Smith's Feed Mill in Blain. Our family knew Frank had given Raymond the job out of the goodness of his heart. It would've been hard for Raymond to find work at his age anywhere else. We knew his job would be safer and his remaining digits would probably remain attached. Raymond would retire from his job some years later. Mr. Smith came to my father one day and explained that Raymond had developed the habit of taking naps on the feed mill floor during working hours. Frank was not concerned about the naps, but was concerned that Raymond may be run over by a truck. My father had a talk with Raymond and persuaded him to retire without revealing the true nature of the episode. Dad, (John Frownfelter Jr.) was good at those things.

My uncle was a man of average height and lean of body. His standard apparel was green Dickies coveralls and work boots embellished with galoshes in case of inclement weather. He topped all of this off with a round, floppy, orange hunting cap which showed considerable disrepair and soiling. All his clothing would usually be covered with sawdust and in later years feed mill dust by the end of the day. This attire was normal at the time for working men as were the calluses on his seven fingers.

Raymond's dietary habits were simple. I only ever saw him eat one banana and drink one pint of chocolate milk daily. He always carried chiclets with him and bestowed them on us whenever we met. The chiclets were a substitute for chewing tobacco when amongst company.

Chewing tobacco was an art form to Raymond. If he offered you a ride to Blain, you knew his spit can would rest between your feet. He could hit it every time and never get any on your shoes. This was not my fondest memory.

My mother, (Winona Frownfelter) did tell me Raymond always had dinner. He knew when all the farmers on Route 274 had dinner. He would stop at their homes on alternating days at the prescribed time and be invited to eat. Raymond had never married, and I believe they knew his game, but made sure he had a place at their table anyway.

One day my brother, (John Frownfelter lll "Skip"), was mowing our lawn. It was not a normal lawn, it covered three acres. This small golf course was a constant source of consternation to my brother and I due to the work time it created. To our relief, our father purchased an "economy" lawn tractor with a very large mowing deck. It was the picture of modern industry. It was orange in color and presented itself as a real farm tractor, though it was about half the size. It even had tall wheels on the back. My brother had a great sense of pride as he drove it, as any thirteen-year-old would. I was not big enough to reach the pedals and was prohibited from its operation. I could only watch with envy as my brother rode it about the yard with head held high.

A small creek was situated at the one end of the lawn. After a heavy rain, this area would become very muddy. Skip was getting very close to this area with each pass of the mower. All kids knew that the more you mowed with the riding mower the less you had to do with the push mower. My brother was trying to forego the push mower altogether. The words, "maybe one more pass" probably entered my brother's mind shortly before the rear wheel got itself embedded in the mud. The more he tried to extricate it, the deeper it went. The mower was now officially stuck.

I'm sure that two truths entered my brother's head at this point. My father absolutely hated ruts and loved his tractor. He turned off the tractor and went for planking to sure-up the back wheel. Sometime during this feverish event, Uncle Raymond had appeared. He stood a small distance from the train wreck with hands in pocket emitting a small constant chuckle while wearing a faint grin. As my brother struggled to remove the great orange beast from the mud, Raymond's chuckle was permeating his mind. Unable to withstand it any longer, he inquired of my uncle, "how would you get it out?" To this my uncle replied without hesitation, "Well I wouldn't have gotten in there in the first place." My brother, knowing he was busted, went back to work.

My brother did eventually get the mower out of the mud. He fixed the yard and cleaned up the tractor. I don't believe he suffered any ill effects of it when my father got home. We used the push mower more often after that.

I could've told countless other stories but chose this one because it shows the way of thinking I grew up with. My Uncle Raymond passed many years ago but his and the wisdom of others stay with me always.

"Never Moved From The Same Spot In Ninety-One Years"

NEWPORT'S LEGENDARY BOB FLICKINGER

Storyteller Robert M. Flickinger
Recorded by Debra Kay Noye

If you're gonna talk about Newport's history from the 1930s forward, then you must go to H. M. Flickinger and Sons at 317 Market Street in Newport, where Bob Flickinger still hangs his hat. He hasn't ventured far from the house next door in his ninety-one years and he's mighty proud of his family's business legacy.

His life began simply enough on August 23, 1929, when he was born in the Harrisburg Hospital to Herbert M. and Margaret Flickinger. Bob grew up with all the modern conveniences of the time, electric, plumbing and a telephone. His father established H. M. Flickinger plumbing and heating in 1926. He would travel to homes and businesses in his Model A trucks, which had hand-painted signs on the sides advertising his business services. Flickinger's performed repairs and installations of new heating and plumbing systems.

Outside of town in the countryside most of the homes and farms did not have electric or plumbing, but like everyone else were heated with wood or coal. Flickinger's installed "hot-air or hot-water and steam" heating systems using cast- iron registers and furnaces. The supplies were procured from the Harrisburg, York and Lancaster area wholesale vendors. It was no easy task to transport and install a cast-iron furnace or registers. Some would be in pieces, but regardless of the weight, Bob's dad would "jack them up and roll them using pipes" onto his short or long-bed trucks and into houses and businesses.

Heating with oil was introduced in the 1930s, still using cast-iron furnaces. Bob says when automobiles and gas became readily available, that's when oil appeared for heating. Newport's gas and oil sources were Sinclair, Atlantic, Texaco and Standard. The Farm Bureau was added to the mix in the 1940s, delivering gas to the farmers.

To this day, Flickingers use the same "Vacuum Grip" tools given to them when doing repair work for the Forged Steel Products Company on Fifth Street, Newport. Bob remarks that they have "everything they ever made." The highly polished steel tools first manufactured in 1926 by local workers, have withstood the test of daily use over time.

Before mass produced "smoke" pipes, Flickingers would purchase large sheets of tin and make stove-chimney pipes for heating systems they installed and repaired. Wiley Davis had a Tin Shop, which made custom tin stove pipes, roofing, interiors for wooden ice boxes and every day household items like tin drinking cups.

Bob knows that the windows and trim on houses on Front Street in Harrisburg were manufactured at the Newport Planing Mill. The three-story building on Mulberry Street near the sewer plant was wiped out in the 1936 flood. They also made wooden cabinets. Before Bob's time, several brickyards existed as well as Marshall's iron ore smelting on Route 849 in East Newport.

When he wasn't running bases in a pick-up game of baseball in the alleys and streets of Newport, Bob was delivering messages to area residents about phone calls his family received on the townspeople's behalf. Bob's home was one of two that had a telephone in his immediate area. Folks would also come to their home to make calls, on the wall phone which was nothing more than a wooden box with a mouthpiece that folks talked into while listening on a short-corded earpiece. Their number started out as 22R to 224 to 224R, just as Bob has experienced all the changes in phone styles. Most people stopped by Flickinger's business if they needed work done.

The phone bill was paid directly to the phone operators. At the time, there were two phone companies in Newport. Newport Phone Company was in a house on Second Street between Catherine Alley and Mulberry Street and operated on limited hours. McKibben, who owned the Green Park Telephone Company, started the Perry County Phone Company on the second floor of the First National Bank of Newport building and made phone service available twenty-four hours a day. Those companies were merged into the United Telephone Company.

Another means of sending messages and communicating was through the United States Postal Service. Mailed letters cost three cents. Two local men, Harry Zeiders and "Pansy" Wertz were the borough's mail carriers, delivering mail twice a day, once in the morning and afternoon. Bob declares, "back then the post office paid their bills and made money all on three cents a letter!"

There were no playgrounds in Newport when Bob was growing up, so any open spaces were fair game used by the children. Bob said it wasn't uncommon for fights to break out when they were playing ball. In fact, he figured they sometimes "fought just to fight," but nobody got hurt.

It was the fashion for school age boys to be dressed in knickers. Bob said, "the corduroy swished when he walked." He was glad to finally graduate to long pants at the age of twelve.

Bob attended elementary school through sixth grade where the Schoolhouse Apartments exist today, between two churches, Reformed Church which became United Church of Christ and the Methodist Church which has become a lawyer's office. One of his teachers, who lived in his neighborhood, had also taught his father. If you lived close enough to school like Bob, students walked home for lunch. Allotted lunch time was a total of a half hour, so there was no dilly-dallying.

Country kids packed their lunches, because they either walked, even from Markelsville, or rode a school bus to high school. There were two buses hauling students to the Newport High School: Harry Gabel of

Gabel's Busing and Lewis Burd. Bob remarked, "a lot of country kids attended school only through the eighth grade," at their local one-room schoolhouses. Newport High School's location has been unchanged. Bob played football, basketball, and baseball in high school, because sports teams did not exist in the other grades like today.

Bob grew up in the Depression during the 1930s prior to World War ll, when there was little work for men and women. If you had money, you spent it wisely. You bought one pair of needed shoes, not two or three like today, and you needed a rationing stamp to make that purchase. Rationing books determined some of the commonly used items that could be purchased. Red stamps were required to purchase milk and meat. Groceries required blue stamps, while bread needed brown. Even children were issued books of stamps.

Most of the vacant lots in town where kids might play ball, became gardens. There were gardens everywhere to feed families, and everything including meats were canned because freezers and refrigerators did not yet exist. Bob says his family had a farm plot, which required a lot of picking. Stones and rocks that is, because after dinner Bob would be instructed to take a hoe and bucket to remove them from the soil. Bob recalls picking sweet cherries from their family tree and the season kept giving as his grandparent's and other relative's trees slowly ripened.

During the Depression, men referred to as "hobos" looking for work traveled from town to town by hitching a ride on the railroad cars. Some of them were highly educated and skilled, but there wasn't work in their respective fields. They traveled throughout the towns, knocking on doors, asking for handouts, food, and small jobs. Bob's mother always fed them.

The Flickinger's ice box was filled daily by a man named Byers, who traveled from house to house. Until the 1940s, the Quarry Dam on Buffalo Creek supplied the nearby three-story icehouse with blocks of ice, which were preserved in saw dust. In the winter, horses were used to pull large round saw blades over the frozen dam to cut the ice into two x four foot thick blocks. The dam needed repairs by the 1950s, but no funds were available. This led to the closing of the nearby Snyder's Flour Mill whose waterwheel on Buffalo Creek relied on the dam for a consistent source of water. Snyder's were known for their fine flour and freshly ground cornmeal. Farmers would bring their corn to the mill, located at the far end of Bloomfield Avenue by the bridge, not too far from the icehouse. Wentzel's Mill existed at their present location.

The Quarry was also where the roundhouse was located for trains from the Newport and Shermans Valley Railroad to turn around and head back in the direction they arrived. The actual railroad and a freight station were located where the Weis Store exists today. That's when the railroad chugged along on Third Street straight through town. Farmers would cut timber during the winter months sawing it into railroad ties to sell to the railroad. There was a stockyard at the freight station where farmers would bring their cattle to be shipped, and to purchase horses being shipped in from out west. Bob says at times Newport bustled like a scene from the wild west, with farmers driving their cattle and horses throughout the streets. Cattle trucks and trailers did not yet exist.

Bob recalls white-tailed deer being shipped in from Michigan in the late 1920s-1930s to replenish the declining deer population. People always relied on venison as a meat source. Bob remarks, "people survived on venison, shooting them all!" Licensed deer hunting season did not exist.

The trains not only used coal, leaving a trail of dusty coal dirt behind, but also delivered coal to the town. There were three coal yards in Newport; Snyder's where the firehouse is located, Smith's where the Post Office is located and Fickes located at the old feed mill on the north end of town. You could walk into those businesses and purchase coal by the bucket, wheelbarrow, or the ton. Remember coal was a primary source of heat when Bob was growing up. Newport was a "hub" for coal supplying the entire county for many years.

After the trains quit running, during WW ll, the Shermans Valley Transportation Company, owned by David Gring, traveled as far as Blain. Trucks transported all sorts of goods throughout the county. Gring owned the Gring Mansion in East Newport. Today the mansion is being further restored by Cheryl Miller, owner of Espresso Yourself Cafe located on the town square.

Bob recalls Newport's businesses from his younger years. "Every two blocks, there was a small grocery store," because people went to the stores daily to purchase common items. The Weis, A&P and American which became Acme, were big name grocery stores in town. Breads, rolls and cakes were also purchased daily at Noll's on Walnut Street and Berger's on Fourth and Market Streets. Both baked in brick ovens. Remember there was no means, including plastics, to keep anything from spoiling, so you used up everything and did not cook to create leftovers. The small groceries did not sell meat.

Newport had its own "Little Italy" on Second Street before Walnut. Boova's Produce Stand spilled from their living room onto the sidewalk. The sidewalk would be jam-packed with all kinds of fresh fruits and vegetables brought back from Boova's weekly trips to Baltimore. Bob says, "they had everything but the music." Boova's were enterprising enough to create banana vaults out of concrete in their basement to ripen the favored tropical fruit.

Butcher shops like Oren's next door to Flickinger's, Smith's on Market Street, and Harper's on Market Street, slaughtered cattle, and hogs for sale in their shops and for farmers. Back then butcher shops displayed hanging quarters of beef and hogs, which were taken down, placed on a wooden cutting table, and cut to order. They also used ice to keep the meats cold. Bob's grandmother would take a metal bucket to the butcher shop for lard, which she used in cooking, baking pies, and along with pan dripping lye soap.

Shull's Fish Market on Front Street traveled to the docks in Baltimore, Maryland, to purchase seafood for resale. Bob recalls how the owner would shuck oysters all night on his return. Throwing the oyster shells out the back door of his shop, creating a stink. The fish, oysters, crabs, and other seafood were kept on ice.

Raw milk was peddled door-to-door by various dairies, Reisinger's, Aucker's, and Blacks from Millerstown. Bob's mother patronized the local Boswell Dairy, owned by a black family that delivered milk and cream to the back porch seven days a week until the 1950s when pasteurization was implemented. Wilt's dairy delivered pasteurized milk. Every Saturday, a pound of freshly made butter was purchased from a lady peddler off Middle Ridge outside of Newport. If you had a sweet tooth, you could walk down to Smith's Newport Candy Company and buy some candies. Smiths also peddled their candies in labeled boxes throughout Perry County, even as far as Blain.

Bob's knickers would've been purchased at Zuckerman's, Lipsitt's, or Brandt's which became Benny Carl's and then Charlie Welfley's clothing and shoe stores. Women's clothing was sold by Memminger's in the old Citizen's National Bank building. Zuckerman's was on the square across from the Goodwill. Lipsitt's was on Market Street and Penn Avenue, now apartments. Steinberg's was on the first floor of the Moose building, which is now Brother's Pizza Shop. Leiby's Clothing Store was in the Leiby Buildng, on North Second Street where Sweet to the Soul is today. His sister, Beverly Shirk of Shermans Dale, and his mother patronized them.

"No woman would go shopping, visiting friends and family or to church without donning a fancy hat. It was the fashion of the day." Newport's Millinery or Hat shop was located on the second floor of the current Jacob's Insurance Agency, right on the square. Mae Wagonesler displayed mannequins sporting her well-made fancy hats. She cleaned, refurbished, and designed new hats.

Bob says, "it was a big deal back then, to go to tailor shops and have clothing custom-sewn after selecting the materials, being measured and properly fitted." Men's suits and trousers were handmade in Reibert's on Market Street and Butz's on Newport's square. Shoes and boots were repaired by Gibney's on Penn Avenue or Ditmer's on Walnut Street. The Elk Tannery existed until 1936 when the flood wiped them out.

Newport was known for clothing factories, which were a source of employment for the area's women. Page owned a shirt factory in a house on Third Street, where the hand and machine sewn white dress shirts were sold to the Arrow Shirt Company. The factory burned in 1936 and was rebuilt as a dress factory. Page also owned the Millerstown shirt factory, home of Stitch in Time today.

Women's slips were manufactured on Penn Avenue. The New Bloomfield Dress Company factory was above Gelnett's Garage and the Duncannon Dress factory occupied the building once home to Forged Steel Products. Smith's Hosiery Mill in Oliver Township made men's socks until the early 1950s.

Once you were all "duded-up" in your new suit, off you'd go to a hotel for a fifteen or twenty cent haircut, and shoeshine. Barber shops were in the local Newport hotels like the Hotel Graham now the Jacob's Insurance Building, another on Walnut and Third close to the railroad station which was torn down and the famous Newport Hotel on the square which is now senior apartments. All the hotels had dining rooms and bars. David Myers' aunt owned the Newport Hotel, which featured the popular Mingle House Dining Room serving fabulous home-cooked Sunday dinners that people traveled from all over to enjoy. A plateful of roast beef, fried chicken, turkey with the trimmings, or baked ham prepared by Mrs. Paden or Mrs. Adams cost one dollar and fifty cents. The business, which hired local people, was eventually owned by David Myers. Ray Hackenberger manned the shoeshine stand in the hotel. An alternative to hotel stays was the Clark Boarding House, across the alley from Flickingers. Robert "Bob" Clark played pro-baseball for several years.

When the hotels permanently closed, barbers who set up shop were Paul Wilson, Russell Cox, Martin Rowe, Dick Newlin and later years Alton Comp. Mildred Haines and Myrtle Knutson on Second Street had beauty shops in the late 1940s.

Except for the hotels and their dining rooms, all businesses were closed on Sundays. Most businesses were open from eight to five o'clock Monday through Friday. Pre-WW ll, Saturdays found the town bustling till midnight because all the farmers arrived in their horse and buggies, to conduct business. They dropped off grain or bought feed from Fickes' or Smith's Feed Mills, patronized the grocery stores, and had a night out on the town There were lots of loafers at Boserman's Drugstore Soda Fountain. Bob recalls the ice cream sundaes, banana splits and sodas. Boserman's became Earl Gowers then Welfley's. John Eby's Drugstore sat on the corner of the square where Goodwill is today. In 1941, Sam Myers purchased the property and demolished the building. The new building was built to house the 5 & 10 of J. J. Newberry. The second floor was the Newport Masonic Lodge. (J. J. Newberry had been located on Market Street next to Flickinger's Appliance.)

There were two bar rooms besides the hotels and later fraternal organizations, such as the Moose, Owls, American Legion and Veterans of Foreign Wars. Jake Sanderson's Bar was on the square and Geary's Bar is where the Hard Hat is today. The "speakeasies" were outside of the borough.

Ten o'clock curfews were mandated during the depression and enforced by two part-time police officers. Of course, during the summer months, the curfew was stretched a bit. Bob's parents made sure he finished his homework and was in bed by nine o'clock on school nights.

During WW ll, parents kept a closer eye on their children's whereabouts, because of the air raid drills and "black-outs" enforced by the local Civil Defense volunteers. When the sirens blew, Bob recalls seeking shelter, and pulling the blinds to darken the rooms, until the all clear was sounded. If the air raid occurred during school, students were dismissed for the day, so they could go to their CD assigned job posts. Volunteers were issued armbands and flashlights. Bob was a designated message carrier. He rode his bike to and from the twenty-four-hour manned "look-out" post above the cemetery. The volunteers recorded every plane passing through the area and telephoned an immediate report to Middletown. There were coded phone numbers assigned each town.

Newport's air raid "first aid" station was in the Reformed Church now the United Church of Christ. Bob's mother was the Red Cross warden in charge of setting up and manning a hospital. Doctor's offices were also designated "hospitals" as Bob called them. His father was responsible for the safety of the town's sewer and water during this time period. Newport's fire house was also manned round the clock.

This wasn't the first time in Newport's history that military preparedness took place. Bob recalls being told that during WW l, when the draft was instituted, there was a small Army encampment of twenty-five to thirty men, where the Newport High School stands today. That area of town was a large farm with open fields. The camp remained training men for two to three years. Bob figures they would've traveled around on bicycles or motorcycles.

Bob used to sit and watch the people come to a local movie theatre in half a house next door. Another movie theatre was located in the present-day Hard Hat Bar on Market Street. The theatre Bob best remembers was the Newport Theatre owned by Miss McBride, who also owned the Mifflin Theatre in Mifflin, Juniata County. The Second Street location is now a pet store. Newport Theatre could seat two hundred and fifty patrons on wooden folding chairs. Eventually, cushions were purchased. Movies were ten or fifteen cents and snacks were not available till years later. The last movie Bob saw was Shirley Temple in "The Good Ship Lollipop!"

If a commonly used home remedy or Vicks and Musterole didn't cure a cold or ailment, there were plenty of medical doctors available. Bob says, "doc always gave you a packet of pills!" Doctor's offices were Carl's on

N. Second Street and Dock Alley, Book's directly across the alley, Ulsh on Fourth and Oliver Street, Brunner at Second and Walnut, and Bartho on Market between Third and Second Streets. Green, another doctor of sorts lived on Front Street with his twelve children. His office was open only on Saturdays and Sundays. According to Bob, he reminded him of the traveling gypsies because of his swarthy complexion and the use of a fortune tellers' ball to prescribe medicines and predict one's future. Front Street would be lined with cars particularly Cadillacs from New York and New Jersey waiting their turn to see Doctor Green.

Bob relates how bands of traveling gypsies camped outside of Newport, in an area known as Gypsy Hollow Road today. Mothers gathered their children and wouldn't let them out of their houses when gypsies were in the area. The gypsies would come to the back door of residents and ask if they could paint their roofs or do any odd jobs. The painted roofs looked great until the first rainfall when the water washed most of the paint off. The paint had been diluted with kerosene by the gypsies. No wonder they had a bad reputation!

Newport's house painters were Beatty, Smith, and Sausaman. Bob speaks with pride about Howe Township resident Andy Loy, a sign painter whose talents went beyond simple business advertisements. He was an extremely talented artist who painted on canvas and did murals like the Clark's Ferry Bridge scene on the wall of the Newport Hotel. Loy was commissioned by the railroad to paint the murals in the New York City Train Station.

Needing a dentist, Newport residents could see Doctor Witmer on Market Street between Third and Second Streets. Hewling's dental office was where attorney Allen Hench's office is today, and Todd was on Market Street directly across from Flickinger's Appliance Store.

Bob recalls a veterinarian on Market Street who had built a concrete tub in his barn to bath cattle and horses. Public water and sewer were available as early as 1898 in town.

Furniture stores and funeral homes were synonymous in Newport through the years. Lee Kell, an undertaker, had a furniture store where Green Acres Realty is located today. Sam Myers was an undertaker and furniture dealer whose legacy was passed down through his son, Dave, to the current generation. The store and funeral home are located on Second Street. Back in the early days, embalming was performed at the "embalming house" in the beauty shop located beside Carpetbaggers. Bob grins as he tells about "the Texas Lunch selling their famous hot dogs in the same location," years later. Viewings were held in private homes and churches, with graveside funeral services. Dave Myers also opened the first laundromat on Second Street in 1958.

Smith's Hardware Store was located where Bitting's restaurant is today. In the back of the Newport Hotel, Rice's had a hardware store which they moved to where Soutner's Gift Shop is on the square today.

Besides the trucks used for business, Bob's dad had a Ford automobile, which was used only on Sundays. After eating Sunday dinner, Bob's dad would take them through the countryside to Ickesburg and Elliottsburg, sometimes visiting relatives. Remember this was during the Depression into World War ll when gas was rationed, and most women did not drive. Bob's mother decided to learn how to drive, so his dad would take her to the Perry County Fair's sulky-horse racing track to practice. Bob and his brother Herbert Jr. played ball and watched her go round the track.

Bob recalls the Perry County Fair was held the first full week in September. Schools were closed one day of the fair, so students could attend. The Perry County Fair was "a great thing back then!" Sulky-horse races could be watched from the grandstand, as well as entertainment performed by "hillbilly and gospel groups" which required a ticket for entry. There were also family sing-a-longs.

The fairgrounds were a grass field with a "fancy house." Cattle did not have much in the way of shelter either. Games of chance and some carnival rides existed. Granges, churches, and civic organizations had food and beverage stands. There were vegetables and fruits as well as agricultural related displays. Most townspeople walked to the fair. Bob thought a fee of one dollar was paid to park a vehicle.

In August of 1941, the polio pandemic shut down schools and all public gatherings for more than a month. The Perry County Fair ceased shortly thereafter when WW ll broke out.

Until WW ll, Robinson's Circus arrived every year on the train. The various railroad cars would be pulled into the sidings, where they would be unloaded. The circus would perform a matinee and evenings for two to three days. They set up a large tent for their three-ring circus acts. The circus paraded through town promoting their wild animals like lions and tigers. Young female circus performers rode the elephants through the streets. Bob says they had a few games of chance and cotton candy and popcorn. When the trains stopped running, trucks transported the circus to town.

A Carriage Shop repaired wagons and built carriages where the icehouse is located today. Some of the wheels made for the carriages could've been made at a local blacksmith shop. Smith's livery stable and blacksmith shop was on the lot that is at the rear of the Jacob's Building. Sunday's blacksmith shop was on Walnut and Ira Henry had a shop where Myer's Furniture Warehouse is today.

If you were in the market for automotive transportation, you had the choice of Gelnett's Ford on Market Street, Flurie's Buick, and Studebaker on Penn Avenue, Schill's Packards on Bloomfield Avenue, Shutter's Studebaker dealership on Penn Avenue, Brandhoffer's Studebaker on Second Street across from the Episcopal Church, Kell's Chevy and in later years Morrison's Chevy on Front Street. Bob declares, "at one time in Newport there were eighteen gas pumps, now there are none in the borough!" Most of the auto dealerships also did repairs or sold gasoline.

Delancey's had a Bicycle Shop on Walnut Street where you could get your bike repaired or purchase a new one.

When fires broke out in town or the countryside, people naturally banded together to help one another. An unorganized group of firefighting volunteers (1898-1910) was active using hand and horse-drawn fire fighting apparatus. It wasn't until 1925 that the Newport Fire Company was organized. The first bare-bones fire truck was purchased for three hundred dollars in 1927-1928. People back then wondered how they'd ever pay for the new truck. In the 1930s-1940s, the fire company ran a fire truck till it broke down and couldn't find parts to fix it. Bob remarked, "by the time you get one paid off through fundraising efforts, there's another that needs purchased!" Today, new fire trucks and equipment cost beyond seven hundred and fifty thousand dollars. To raise funds, the fire company held carnivals on the square of Newport. Then the carnival was moved to the old coal yards on Walnut Street. Bob tells of having to wash off his feet from all the coal dust once he returned home. The old tannery site and the playground hosted the carnival until today's carnival on the fairgrounds. The Lions Club also had carnivals.

Newport started an Ambulance Association in 1958-1959, transporting people to hospitals without charging a fee. They hoped for donations or gas money, but that did not work out as planned.

What parade wouldn't be complete without the Newport Drum and Bugle Corp! Newport Fire Company, which was in the current Newport Borough Building, formed a band in the 1920s, which was disbanded when WW ll started. Bob played the trumpet and marched in his wool uniform. The band boasted fifty to sixty musicians and they played Sunday concerts on Newport's square. After the war, the Newport Fire Company Drum and Bugle Corps emerged participating in county-wide parades. When interest waned by the younger generations, the corp was disbanded, donating instruments and uniforms to Carson Long Military Institute in New Bloomfield. Carson Long closed disposing of any remaining items.

You couldn't have a band without music and instruments. Back in the day, most everybody who was so inclined played an instrument or sung in a choir. Instruments, sheet music and lessons were available from Smith's on the corner of Second Street and Dock Alley, and Kough's on the square where present day Carpetbaggers exists. Kough's also tuned and sold pianos. "Music was really big back in my day!" Bob exclaims on a wistful note.

Bob has experienced many lifestyle changes and witnessed Newport's facade evolve through the last ninety years. But he still gets a gleam in his eye and a grin on his face, when he tells about "growing up in his town!" He is a true legend and a cherished "walking history lesson" from Newport.

Growing Up In New Bloomfield

Storyteller Donald C. Stoops Jr.

In 1945 when I was five years old, we moved from West Main Street in New Bloomfield to 409 West High Street. There were only three houses on West High Street at that time. The road was not completely paved, so of course, the house my father built was on the dirt part.

I went to school at the present-day Lutheran Parish House. A bicycle was my transportation in good weather. In spring and fall, mud would pack between the tire and fender and freeze tight. I would have to spend time knocking it out. Since there was no cafeteria, I walked or rode my bike twice a day to school and back. There was one hour for lunch. In bad weather, we brown bagged lunch and stayed at school.

With my father in the Barbershop (Stoop's Barbershop) on the Square, I would take advantage at times. I would ride home with him with my bike on the front bumper of his car. However, in ninth grade, while the new Perry Joint High School (present day Bloomfield Elementary School) was being built, classes were held in various buildings around town. My classes were on the stage of the Firehouse on High Street. We also had to endure a freshman initiation, which had us dressing in various costumes of various design. There was no physical action only degrading embarrassment. My class was the last one to endure such initiation.

In the winter, I would ride to the barbershop with my father. The shop opened at eight o'clock and the school at nine o'clock. I had an hour to entertain myself. I would at times be the first customer of Clyde Askins for a Rocky Fudge ice cream cone. Clyde's store was where the present-day Perry County Economic Development Authority/Tourist Bureau, and Perry County Chamber of Commerce is located. If I was lucky, at lunch, with fifty cents that I could beg from my father, I would buy my lunch at Gring's Restaurant. (Boyer Funeral Home today.)

Bicycles were the main mode of transportation. I would ride from High Street across the neighbors' yards to Main Street and down the lane to Dillman's farm (site of the present-day housing development) to buy a quart of fresh milk for a quarter and bring it home in a Kings Syrup Molasses can in my basket.

Many times, the trip was successful, but there were accidents. (A Kings Syrup Molasses can made a good carbide cannon for the 4th of July.)

There were three places I would spend a good bit of time in the summer: the state shed on West Main Street watching the mechanics, Rice's Memorial works watching Mr. Rice engrave the granite tombstones, and the Darlington's farm house watching a blind man, Davey Ale, making brooms in the summer kitchen of the house. (Darlington's house is now owned by the Eckert's on Cold Storage Road.)

In the evening, the kids would play bicycle tag through the streets and alleys of town. Tired of that, we would gather at the square at Dr. Book's Drug Store (building presently vacant, prior the Bloomfield Pharmacy) to pitch pennies. The monument was also an attraction. We would sit on it and name the make and model of cars that came around the circle. There were a few vigorous discussions.

Playing baseball behind the Firehouse on High Street or on the empty lot on McClure Street, where the first Catholic Church was eventually built, was another favorite pastime. We used the town baseball team's cast-off broken bats which we tried to repair with screws and tape, and old taped baseballs.

I graduated from a bicycle when I could drive. My transportation was a Cushman Motor scooter built like a small motorcycle. It was a pleasure to ride at that time. The rural roads were generally dirt with little traffic. I did cause a little attention when I modified the exhaust system to be a little more vigorous.

Life Growing Up On The Family Farm

IN THE 1950s AND 1960s

Storyteller Barbara Ellenberger Hamilton

Growing up on our farm in Duncannon, Penn Township, Perry County in the 1950s and 1960s was quite an experience. Our old farm house, built in the 1880s, had no heat upstairs. Yet we had our mother, Louise Ellenberger, in the wintertime, tuck my sister Janet and I into bed, saying, "Now lay with your backs together to help keep each other warm." In the mornings, we would run down the steps, out into our kitchen and onto the lid of our old green wood box behind the woodstove to change from our pajamas into our day clothes, that mother always had stacked to get warm for us to put on. Mother always had a good warm fire burning in the old woodstove. My sister Janet and I had many wonderful mornings waking up in our old iron-frame bed, climbing onto the footboard and taking somersaults onto our old mattress with the old springs underneath.

Breakfast usually included bacon, eggs and toast. I have always liked my eggs, "dippy," or for lunch, a fried egg sandwich. There were times I would go out into the garden and bring in loose leaf lettuce and make a lettuce and mayonnaise sandwich. Cocoa and toast were a good breakfast too.

In the summertime you could find Janet and I in the garden pulling the weeds. Dad always had Janet and I ride the planter to sow corn. Mom and dad always had a large garden growing cucumbers, peas, tomatoes, peppers, green beans, lettuce and onions. I remember one year dad planted peanuts and another field of potatoes. That sounds great, doesn't it? Just remember, they all had to be dug up and harvested. Fun work!

Being a farmer, dad always planted fields of sweet corn to eat and sell. Mom and dad would walk down the rows, pulling the ripe corn off the stalks and making piles for Janet and I to fill our yellow rubber-coated egg baskets with ears, which we carried out to the ends of the rows. Dad or mother would count the number of ears needed and put them in an old feedbag to transport back to our house. We learned very quickly to wear long sleeved shirts in the corn patch because if not, we would be miserable from the scratches and itching.

Back then, I attended school when I was five years old. We usually carried our lunches in our Roy Rogers lunch boxes. If we bought our lunch, which back then was twenty-five cents, we would bring our lunch back to our room on a tray. When finished, it was our responsibility to scrape the leftovers from the tray into a large tin can and stack our trays. Don't forget the nap time we were required to have after going out for recess. Whenever any of us opened our lunchboxes to see what our mothers packed for us, it was always a special day if we found marshmallow crackers! Yum! But I never traded them with others!

There was a period of time when our mother worked in the elementary school kitchen. I loved it, because when we went out for recess, I would run around to the other side of the school and call into the open cafeteria window asking for my mother. I then asked to have a popsicle. She always got one and handed it out the window to me. Yes, I was spoiled!

At recess time, we were very active outside, playing games such as Lemonade….when your team would decide on an occupation to act out. The two teams would line up opposite each other and the one team would say, "Here come three fat Dutchmen ready for work." The other side called out, "What's your trade?" Our team called out, "Lemonade," then the other team said, "Let's see some". We then pantomimed our work activity. When the opposing team named our occupation, we would turn and run, trying not to be caught. When the last person on your team was caught, it was the other teams turn to do just as we did. That game would last all recess. If we weren't playing Lemonade, you would find us usually jumping rope.

Growing up on a farm provided Janet and I with many moments of pleasure. Yes, we worked hard tending the animals, but we also had downtime which we spent either catching minnows or building dams in the creek. One day our father, Kenneth "Deitz" Ellenberger permitted Janet and I the ability to take our one tame mother pig's babies for a walk in our old doll carriage. At the end of our walk, we ended up under our large cherry tree in the yard, where we placed all of the piglets on the grass. When they decided to wander, it was fun catching and putting them back into the doll carriage. Then back with their mother, Snooty.

Harvest time on the farm was always a lot of work. Neighbors back then left their busy time to pitch in and help each other. Addy and Minnie Holman, and Ian and Wilma Smith along with my parents Louise and Deitz Ellenberger always helped each other with their harvesting. The men worked together, but mother, Janet and I were responsible for preparing their meals and taking them out to the fields on the back of our pickup truck, making it a tailgate picnic. June was the month designated for baling hay. Addie Holman and dad shared a baling machine. Dad was very particular about how the bales needed to be stacked on the wagon. When the wagon was full, dad would take it back to the barn and unload the bales into the haymow. Wow! Some of those bales were really heavy for a kid to toss into the haymow and stack just as dad wanted. You never complained, it was your job to do.

Life on a farm was a much slower pace back then. Friends would visit, especially on Sundays, or drop in to chat a while. Some evenings, friends with children, would drop in. That meant Janet and I needed to entertain the visitor's children. So, we got dad's flashlight and all of us went out to the barn to look for mice! We knew the best places to find them was in the feed bins. We would tell them, "Watch closely, when we open the bin door, if there are any mice in there, they will stand up on their back legs, look into the light, and then take off!" We always had great fun and the kids were entertained watching and counting the number of mice we found.

We grew up with ponies and horses. Spot was our first pony, then came our horses; Lady, Flossie, the palomino and Bruce, the paint. We spent many hours of fun riding over the fields and in the mountains.

At one point in mom and dad's farming career, dad decided to raise chickens. He needed to build three floors of coupes in the barn to house them. He placed his chick order and then began building. He had two completed and received the phone call saying the peeps were being delivered. He wasn't ready. I remember handing him nail after nail to help get the floor completed. But we didn't get finished on time. The peeps arrived! What would we do? All the sliding window screens were placed across every doorway in our upstairs hallway, including the stairway and newspaper placed all over the floor. Feeders and watering bottles were added. Then the one-thousand peeps were added. Janet and I were responsible for changing the nasty newspaper every day. To go to bed in the evening, we needed to step over the window screens, walk through the peeps to get in and out of our bedrooms. What an experience!

Faith in God was a must for mom and dad. We attended the Middle Cove Sunday School that originally was the Middle Cove Schoolhouse that my dad attended as a boy. Back then there were three schoolhouses in the Cove; Upper Cove, Middle Cove and Lower Cove. When they closed, they were sold. That is how Middle Cove became Middle Cove Sunday School, later changed to Middle Cove Bible Church located on the corners of Cove Road and Sawmill Road. Lower Cove school became the home of my mother and father after they were married.

Living on a farm is a learning experience of work ethics, life values, working by yourself to get a task done or with others while dunging out the stables. I believed it helped our faith in God grow stronger day by day. I'm so thankful for our parents instilling in us the importance of attending church and our Christian values.

Living on the farm was not always work. Janet and I each had our own used scooter to ride. When older, we both had bicycles. I remember when mom and dad brought mine home from Sears Roebuck.

One thing for sure, we never lacked food for our table. There were always pigs and chickens to butcher. My grandparents, Fremont "Bud" and Pearl Bitting always helped out with butchering our pigs. Mother, Janet and I cleaned and plucked many, many chickens. We were never hungry. Praise God!

In those days, we had a milkman, Sam's Ice Cream, Charlie Chips and a breadman delivering milk, bread and ice cream in their trucks. We would put a note in the milk box on our porch telling the milkman what we needed. The breadman came to our door, but we needed to go out to the ice cream truck to choose our flavors of ice cream.

I cherish all the memories I've gathered over my lifetime of farm living!

I never got off the farm. Mother and dad gave my husband, Harry and I land to build our home. They also gave my brother Kenneth "KB" Ellenberger, Jr. and sister Janet Ellenberger Colborn the same. Our feet are firmly planted in Perry County to stay!

"Blessed With A Great Place To Live"

Storyteller Vicki Wilson Gainer

D. Bernard and Fairy Flickinger Wilson were married on May 2, 1945, shortly after dad recovered from his wounds received in World War ll. Both mom and dad graduated from Blain Union High School in the same class. Mom had also attended the Turkey Tail one-room schoolhouse. Dad attended the one-room school in New Germantown.

Dad's parents were James Milton and Grace Welcomer Wilson. They lived on Lower Buck Ridge Road, where their house and barn still stand. They had six children; Gertrude, George, Robert, Mary and then 20 years later, they had my dad and Ruth. I have such wonderful memories of my grandparents. My Grandma Wilson was the kindest and most loving woman I knew. She would rock us on her green rocking chair in the kitchen. She had a cookstove that she kept fired summer and winter. She never had an electric stove. She never said a "cross" word to anyone. She had a great faith and always attended New Germantown Methodist Church. Grandma always wore an apron. She had a large garden and lots of flowers. She died at age eighty-nine and was never in a hospital.

Grandpa Wilson was our candy man. He always had orange marshmallow peanuts in the wooden cupboard for us. It didn't take us long to figure out what cupboard they were in. Before he farmed, he worked for the Sherman's Valley Railroad. His ways on his farm were primitive. He farmed with mules, raised his own hogs to butcher, milked by hand and built his own wooden-rail fences. I remember his snow-white hair and his beautiful blue eyes. He died at 83.

Mom's parents were Newton and Mabel Reber Flickinger. They owned a farm on Adam's Grove Road. Grandpa moved away, but grandma kept the farm. The barn and house still stand today. They had six children: Neil, Gale, Fairy (mom), Joyce, C. Leona and Phyliss. Grandma was a very hard worker. In addition to running a dairy farm, she had six children to care for. The three older children were a huge help. She used to have my sister Ginger and I help in her strawberry patch. I vowed on a very hot day never to pick another strawberry! That vow didn't last too long.

Grandma's home was a gathering place for twenty-one cousins to roam and play. What a wonderful time we had. We had the Shermans Creek to wade, a covered bridge to climb, a huge barn for playing in the loft and trees in the yard to climb. Seven of my cousins lived out of state and when they visited it was an exciting time for us. Grandma's big farmhouse was filled with the smells of her delicious cooking and baking as well as kids everywhere.

It was a big deal when grandma bought a brand-new Allis Chalmers tractor. It was made in 1948 and I still have it. On her farm she also had the Turkey Tail School where some of her children attended, and she taught. She graduated from Shippensburg Normal College with a teaching certificate. Grandma had a daughter and three great-grandchildren graduate also from Shippensburg and a great-great granddaughter attending Shippensburg University. Grandma died at age 89.

Dad served in the US Army in World War ll. He was wounded in his left foot and sent home to recover at a hospital in Virginia. Meantime my mom and grandparents waited anxiously for him to come home. Dad was honored with a Purple Heart and an honorable discharge. After his discharge, mom and dad married and rented several homes in the Blain area. My sister, Kathy was born in 1946 and passed away in 1948. I was born in 1948 in Harrisburg Hospital with Dr. Belmont, from New Bloomfield, delivering me. One of my earliest memories was when I was three and we lived at the old Blanche Maley place. Mom had a coffee pot sitting on the stove in a place that I should not have been able to reach. Somehow, I managed to reach and pulled the hot pot down with scalding coffee pouring on me. I still have a scar on my wrist from the burns.

For a time, my parents had to live with dad's parents. I remember my grandparents had a phone on the wall that we cranked. It was fascinating to me that I could talk to my aunt and uncle two miles away. My grandparents also had an outhouse. I was not fond of going into the outhouse. I was always on the lookout for spiders and snakes.

My mom also worked part-time for Gertrude Shumaker as a telephone operator. Gertrude lived with her daughter, Nellie in a home on what is now Toad Road in Blain. Mom took incoming and outgoing calls and plugged wires into a switchboard. She said it was an interesting job.

My sister, Ginger was born in 1949 and I finally had a playmate. My dad was working full-time for Clyde (Spike) Nesbitt at the Blain Planing Mill. I'm not sure if we were still living with my grandparents. My dad was unloading lumber at the mill and fell off the back of the truck. He hurt his back and had surgery. I can still see him lying in Harrisburg Hospital in traction. He was hospitalized for six weeks.

In the meantime, my family lost its income. My mom went to work at the Dauphin County Old Folks Home for a year until my dad was healed. Dad then went to work for the United States Forestry Department. By then we were living behind the old Buss Johnson farm above New Germantown. We loved it there with lots of room to play. Dad worked a mile from the house. At four years old, I had appendicitis. Dad was away on a job, so my Uncle Bob drove mom and me to Harrisburg Hospital where I had surgery. If I think about it, I can still remember the gauze pad filled with ether being held over my nose.

My sister, Jean was born in 1953. By then we had moved into the big house owned by the forestry department. I was five years old and started school at Blain Union. I remember mom teaching me how to wash dishes and dry them. There was a huge staircase in the house with a great banister for sliding when our parents weren't nearby. It was at this house that my sister Jean became very sick. My parents had her to many doctors and they diagnosed her with a brain tumor. She became an invalid. She had several surgeries on her head, but nothing helped. I remember going to Harrisburg Hospital, a hospital in Scranton and Children's Hospital in Philadelphia with Jeannie as my parents desperately sought help for her. As dad worked, my mom was devoted to her care.

One day mom was sewing as Ginger and I were playing on the floor. Mom told us she was going to take a nap on the sofa while we played. Mom put her scissors under her pillow as I watched. After I was sure she was asleep, I took the scissors from under the pillow. It took some coaxing, but my little sister, Ginger finally agreed to let me cut her hair. Being the three-year-old, untrained beautician that I thought I was, Ginger got a very uneven, short haircut! When mom awoke, she was quite angry with me. But as she really looked at Ginger, she started to laugh. I can still see my sister and her short hair.

We dressed in our finest to go to the Blain Picnic. It was a very big deal for us to attend. We were not old enough to be by ourselves, so our parents kept close watch on us. We usually got fifty cents a night and a dollar to spend on Saturday. If my Uncle Neil saw us, we got a lot more money! We didn't buy much food at the picnic because Grandma Flickinger had her own table. It was a very long table that probably would have seated forty or more. All my aunts and uncles, cousins and anyone else that was invited, gathered on Blain Picnic Day (Saturday) and ate together. Everyone brought food to share. The table was located by the Shermans Creek behind where the large fire company building is now located. It was a joyous time. Occasionally, one of us would get lost and then there was panic until we were found. We were allowed to ride the Merry Go Round and Ferris Wheel on occasion. The Blain Picnic was so important to us, that mom used it as leverage to get weeds pulled in the garden. We had a quota and if it was not finished, no Blain Picnic. The weeds got pulled! The Blain Picnic was always held in Blain, PA in August. Sadly the Blain Picnic was discontinued several years ago.

My parents found a farm that was for sale on Center Square Road and made the huge step to buy the farm. Dad bought it from Jasper Collins in 1955 for less than ten thousand dollars. Center Square Road was still a dirt road at that time. The farm had been in the Collins family for a long time. The farm had approximately one hundred and sixty acres of fields and woodland. It had a log home, log barn, pig pen, chicken house and shed. The house and barn dated to the early 1800s. The house had six bedrooms until dad added a new kitchen, bedroom and bathroom. We had an outhouse when we first moved. Shortly after we moved my youngest sister, Bernie was born. Dad later bought another sixty acres of woodland. It was a wonderful place to grow up.

Dad tore out the underside of the barn and built a dairy barn. For a while, we milked our cows by hand. I had my own cow, Switchy that I loved dearly. I used to wear a felt cowboy hat to the barn and when I was milking her, I would put my hat on her head. She got mastitis after delivering a calf and no matter how much dad and Dr. Anderson, from Loysville, did for her, she died. I was brokenhearted.

We continued with the dairy cows until new regulations from the government were implemented. Dad said no to the changes and sold the cows. He then filled our pastures with Black Angus beef cattle. They were an adventure, always trying to keep them inside a fence. We had fields of hay and grain. We also sold sweet corn. We raised potatoes for ourselves. Mom always had a huge garden. She canned and froze all our vegetables and meat. We churned our own butter and made our own cider. There were walnut and hickory trees on our farm, so we picked nuts and hulled them for mom to bake with. She was famous for her walnut cakes.

We had our own chickens and mom sold eggs. We had hogs that we butchered for our meat and we had our own beef. When the chickens were too old to lay eggs, we butchered them. Oh, how I hated that job! It was messy and I can still smell the stink from them. It was a big deal and a tiring day for mom and dad when we butchered hogs. Before we were old enough to help, dad would get some men to help. But then the day came when we were useful AND we got to take a day off school! Butchering is a long process, but when we had our own meat to eat it was all worth it.

My sister, Jean died in 1957. It was a sad time in our lives, but Mom was her caretaker and she was deeply affected.

My parents had no money to spare. They worked hard and did everything they could to keep us fed, clothed and pay the staggering medical bills they had. I remember dresses that mom made us out of decorative feed sacks. At Christmas, dad would take all of us to Carlisle to shop and see the lights. We would also eat at a restaurant. What a treat that was for us.

Mom never had enough money for Christmas, so my parents decided to open our home in deer season and board deer hunters. They would come on Sunday afternoon and usually stay until Wednesday. Mom would cook a big breakfast and supper for them. She also packed them each a lunch. We would have between eight and twenty-six hunters at a time. The time we had twenty-six hunters, we gave up our beds and slept at Uncle Bob's house. We almost always had the same men every year and they became like family.

My mom had the rule that there was never alcohol in our home. She was contacted by a couple men to see if they could stay in our home. They came in from hunting late one evening and she could smell alcohol on them. They were promptly asked to leave. As we got older, we were a big help to mom. I don't know how many years we had hunters, but we did it until my mom got older. She was featured in the Perry County Times at a time when she had hunters. Mom was a fantastic cook and baker. I learned a lot from her.

I think we got our first TV in 1956. That was such a big deal to us, but there was no TV until all our chores were finished. It was black and white, but we didn't care. We watched Howdy Doody, Fury, I Love Lucy, Gunsmoke, Wagon Train, Tom and Jerry, Bob Hope, etc. and our parents made us watch Lawrence Welk. There were so many wonderful shows.

My parents always made sure we all went to church. We attended the Blain United Methodist Church in Blain. We all juggled to sit beside dad. One of the funny memories I remember is what we did if we sat beside dad. He would put his arm behind us on the back of the pew. We would then take his big fingers and pretend we were milking. That always brought giggles from us until mom noticed. Can I just say mom was the disciplinarian in church! We did not have a youth fellowship at the Methodist church, so mom took us to youth fellowship at a church near Manassa. She also took Ginger and me to many tent meetings and to hear evangelist's passing through our area. It happened to be at one of those meetings that I accepted Jesus as my savior.

I was my dad's tomboy and I loved being outside with him. I helped him combine, cleaned cow stables, fix fence, make hay and just anything so I could be outside with him. Ginger and I always had to help with hay. As I got older, dad left me rake hay. Ginger and I were not fond of hay making. It was a hot, dusty and heavy job. Our younger sister Bernie "helped" on occasion. Sometimes we would beg dad to ask a neighbor to help us in the mow. Sometimes we got the help and sometimes not. Ginger and I would race to see who could get in the shower first.

Dad loved to coon hunt, and we loved to go with him. He always had coon hounds to raise. It was exciting to go with him, especially if the dogs would tree a coon. We always thought that dad only took us with him to carry food, water and lights. Dad also loved to play the guitar. He played by ear and picked up tunes easily. He could also yodel as well as sing. Ginger loved to sing with him.

Dad decided we should have a pond, so he chose a spot in our woods, about a half-mile from our house to build one. He cleared the area and made a wonderful picnic spot for us. We used water from a spring and had picnic tables and a firepit. We camped many times over the years and swam in the pond. They were wonderful summers and sometimes our only vacation. We would invite friends for corn roasts or to sing around the fire. As my own kids were born, they also got to camp at the pond. We played softball in the meadow with our parents, ice skated on the creek, got ice from the creek to make our own ice cream and built forts in the woods with discarded binder twine and pieces of boards.

If we were lucky, dad would take us to one of the stores in New Germantown. Lee (Hackey) Linard had a tiny store and if you wanted groceries, you asked him or his wife and they would go in the storeroom and see if they had it. They had a water soda cooler in one corner and sometimes we were allowed to get a bottle of soda. The other store in town was Bistline's. You could buy gas and shop for the groceries yourself.

Our parents also fostered numerous children through the years. Some stayed a week and some much longer. When I was fifteen, we had three siblings ages one, two and three. There were two girls and a boy. The oldest boy was in another foster home. We had them a year. During that year, we all became quite attached to them. I adored the baby and hated to even leave her to go to school. Dad and mom decided to adopt Denny at age four. The girls were assigned to other homes that didn't want a boy. Dad finally had his boy! Sadly, Denny died at age fifty-three of a heart attack.

My parents, especially dad, were very protective of us. There was no dating until age seventeen. If mom talked dad into allowing us to go to a dance, we had to leave the dance before it was over. We are probably the only daughters in the United States that had to call our dad the first night of our honeymoons to let him know that we were okay!

Dr. Frank Belmont delivered all five of us girls in the Harrisburg Hospital. He was so special to our family. He also helped care for us when we were sick. I remember one night dad took me to see Dr. Belmont for an illness. As we were sitting in the waiting room, there was an air raid drill and all the lights went off. I was so scared that I crawled under a chair. Dr Belmont also delivered both of my children as well as my nieces and nephew. His longtime nurse was Helene (Duck) Bower. She was always so kind to us.

In May of 1960, dad became a Civil Service rural mail carrier in Blain. Life got a little easier for my parents after dad got the job. He loved delivering mail. I became his sub in 1980 after taking the Civil Service exam. He retired in March 1984 on disability (from an earlier tractor accident). I took his place in March 1984 and retired with thirty-three and a half years of service. I have now been retired eight years.

We all went on to marry and give mom and dad ten grandchildren and many great-grandchildren. Dad and mom instilled in us a love of God and our country. Dad died in 1997. Mom sold the farm in 1998. She passed away in 2008. They had a lot of adversity in their lives, but there was never a doubt about how much they loved me. They left me a legacy of hard work, appreciation of all that I have and a great love of where I am blessed to live.

A Lifetime In The Perry County Courthouse

Storyteller Bonnie Weibley Delancey

My name is Bonnie L. (Weibley) Delancey and I am also a war baby born in 1943. My parents were Ernest E. Weibley and Idella M. (Minium) Weibley. I was raised in Saville Township and still live there today.

Larry S. Delancey worked at the Perry County Courthouse in the maintenance department from 1977 to 1984. We became close friends and were married in 1981. Commissioner Elwood Mohler hired him to run the Mohler's Service Station at New Bloomfield. After working there sixteen years, he worked at Little Buffalo State Park until he retired. He passed away in 2017.

My father worked at H. P. Dyson's Feed Mill in New Bloomfield and my mother worked for the Dyson family cleaning their houses. In later years, my father went to work for the Ford Garage in Newport and my mother worked in a garment factory in Millerstown.

My grandparents were B. Roy Weibley and Hulda M. (Peck) Weibley and Clarence W. Minium and Rebecca M. (Smith) Minium.

I was fortunate as a child to have both sets of grandparents live very close to my parents. I would help them mow the grass, help in the garden and other chores. I had a lot of good times riding my bicycle or walking back and forth to visit them.

I remember the ice truck delivering blocks of ice for the icebox in the kitchen and the man would give me a piece of ice to suck. That was a treat in the summertime. After my parents bought a refrigerator, I missed the ice in the summer.

We raised chickens and when the feed truck delivered the feed, my mother would ask for the bags with the flower print or plain colored. She would use the bags to make me dresses, sun suits, pillow cases, sheets and quilts. I still have quilts in my cedar chest that were made from feed bags.

My parents and grandparents also butchered pigs and beef every winter. It was my job to help mother make the food for the lunch for everyone who helped to butcher. My favorite part of the lunch was the pumpkin pie. I also helped my father to get the butcher kettles, the grinder and other butchering equipment ready for the day.

My first year in school was at the old school house in Ickesburg. Only the first and second grade classes were in the school. My teacher was Mrs. Nora Bixler who was my aunt. She was strict. She also tried to make me write with my right hand. (Well that never happened.)

My second year we moved to the Ickesburg High School Building outside of town. Grades one thru six and then grades seven thru twelve were moved to the new building (Green Park Union - GPU).

When I was eleven years old, my father told me I should ride my bicycle around the neighborhood to see if any of the older ladies needed help cleaning their houses. I was fortunate to get three jobs. Two were cleaning and some laundry, and one was laundry and mending the clothes.

I was paid fifty cents a day for cleaning. Later years a dollar a day and one gave me antique dishes, which I still have in my china cabinet. Another gave me dishes and a history book which I still have. My father told me he wanted me to learn responsibility of working for people. I will never forget those that I helped in their lifetime.

My father in later years worked for Karl Kennedy as a school bus driver. He was the bus driver the first day Debra (Freeman) Noye started to school. Her father was waiting to help her on the bus and said to my father, she is bashful, would you let her sit in a front seat. She sat with me. She was so cute and very bashful.

I graduated in 1961 from school and started to work in a garment factory in East Waterford. We made dresses that were shipped to New York for clothing stores. It was a learning experience for ten years.

I decided I wanted to find a secretarial position. I applied for a position that was in the Commissioner's Office in the Perry County Court House in New Bloomfield. I was contacted to come to the Commissioner's Office for an interview with the Commissioners Max E. Powell, Norman Pressley and Harry G. Sheaffer. A week or so later after the interview I was contacted to report for work on June 15, 1970. This was when my career began and after 50 plus years, I am still working at the courthouse.

I have worked with fourteen boards of County Commissioners:
1970-1972 - Max E. Powell, Norman Pressley, Harry G. Sheaffer
1972-1976 - Edwin B. Wallis, Jr., William A. Rohrer, Harry G. Sheaffer
1976-1980 - Harry G. Sheaffer, Edwin B. Wallis, Jr., Samuel R. Nulton
Note: Edwin B. Wallis, Jr. – Resigned in 1979
Lawrence (Larry) E. Beaver was appointed by the court to fill the unexpired term.
1980-1984 - Ralph Elwood Mohler, Lawrence (Larry) Beaver, Edward R. Kennedy
Note: Lawrence (Larry) Beaver Died May 18, 1982
Richard (Dick) Long was appointed by the court to fill the unexpired term.
1984-1988 - Ralph Elwood Mohler, Billy M. Roush, Edward R. Kennedy
1988-1992 - Ralph Elwood Mohler, Billy M. Roush, Edward R. Kennedy

1992-1996 - Billy M. Roush, Jeffrey A. Conrad, Edward R. Kennedy
1996-2000 - Mark K. Keller, John J. Amsler, Jr., Edward R. Kennedy
2000-2004 - Mark K. Keller, John J. Amsler, Jr., Edward R. Kennedy
2004-2008 - Mark K. Keller, John J. Amsler, Jr., Edward R. Kennedy
Note: Mark K. Keller resigned 11-30-2004
Warren R. VanBuskirk was court appointed to fill the unexpired term 1-24-2005
2008-2012 - John J. Amsler, Jr., Warren R. VanBuskirk, Stephen C. Naylor
Note: Warren R. VanBuskirk died 9-21-2009
Brenda K. Benner was court appointed to fill the unexpired term 11-23-2009
2012-2016 - Brenda K. Benner, Paul L. Rudy, Jr., Stephen C. Naylor
2016-2020 - Brenda K. Benner, Paul L. Rudy, Jr., Stephen C. Naylor
2020-2024 - Brian S. Allen, Gary R. Eby, Brenda L. Watson

I faced many challenges in my years of service, but there were many times of laughter.

In the early 1970s, the county had the paper ballots for voting that were printed at the Perry County Times Office known as Swank Publications. It was the responsibility of the three county commissioners to deliver the ballots and ballot box to the thirty-three voting precincts in the county.

The commissioners divided the county into three sections. Commissioner Max Powell took the eastern part of the county, Commissioner Norman Pressley southern part and Commissioner Harry G. Sheaffer took the western part of the county.

They would deliver the voting material to all the Judge of Elections in each precinct.

When the new board of commissioners came into office in 1972, it was the same procedure for delivering the voting materials. However, Commissioner Wallis was delivering the ballots to the eastern end of the county, when the ballots started to fly off the back of his pickup truck. He called the office and I told him to pick up what he was able to find and bring back to the office. He was on Route 11 & 15 near Liverpool when this happened and he said the ballots were on the road and in the Susquehanna River. I called Judge Kugler and explained what happened and that Commissioner Wallis was trying to get all the ballots possible and bring back to the courthouse.

When he returned, he had the ballots in a large black garbage bag with a big red bow tied on the bag. Judge Kugler said it is a nice bow on the bag. Commissioner Wallis never delivered the ballots again on a pickup truck without a cap on the back. Needless to say, the Perry County Times Office reprinted the ballots in time for the election.

Commissioner Rohrer delivered the ballots to the southern part of the county and never had any problems. Commissioner Sheaffer took the western part of the county to deliver the ballots to the Judge of Election at each of those precincts. In the fall, he would take his gun along to also look for turkeys. He delivered all the voting supplies with no problems. He also shot his turkey.

Later years, we upgraded the voting equipment to the punch card voting system. The Judge of Election picked up the equipment at the courthouse and returned the equipment after the polls closed at 8:00 p. m. in the evening.

The Commissioners and staff would then run the cards for each precinct through the card reader to record the votes for each precinct. Commissioner Kennedy almost knocked the plug out of the wall when we were reading the precinct cards. We all screamed at him and said don't move.

If that would have happened, the totals would have been lost. From that time, Commissioner Kennedy was not allowed to be near any electrical outlets in the room. None of us were laughing that night.

The county has the paper ballot system again. However, this system has been upgraded that you scan your ballot in a scanner and the votes are saved on a tape and a thumb drive. A lot easier than it was in prior years when they were counted by hand at the polling places.

On the lighter side of incidents that happened in the courthouse over the years there was a lot of laughter, these are a few things that occurred.

Percy Rodemaker was the Register and Recorder of Deeds and Wills. One day a lady came into his office to file forms. Percy asked her where she lived. She said I live in the New Germantown area and I raise chickens. These chickens were of different colors. Percy asked her if he could buy some of the chickens. She agreed. Percy told her to bring them to the courthouse in a crate and put them in the side entrance into the building. There was a small room and it was suitable for a chicken crate. The day she brought the chickens, there was another lady came into the building, heard the chickens crowing and she ran out of the building screaming. I believe every employee in the building was laughing.

Another time a lady was stuck in the women's restroom and screaming for help out the window. I came to the rescue and got the door open. She was not a happy person but we all had a good laugh.

Another time, I went to the lady's restroom and found goldfish in the commodes. I thought this was someone that thought whoever came in the restroom would scream. However, I was the one that went to the restroom and I did not scream. Do you know you cannot flush a goldfish down the commode? I went back into my office and did not say a word to anyone. Later someone else went to the restroom and there was a scream. Well, that called attention to everyone on the third floor of the courthouse. I never did find out who put the fish in the commodes, but I believe Dean McMillen and Glenn Keller had something to do with it. The look on their faces was somewhat suspicious.

One year, we were preparing to fill the jury wheel with names, which at that time were from the voter registration lists from each precinct in the county, Blain Borough through Wheatfield Township. We would cut the list of names in small slips of paper and put in the jury wheel. We were ready to start the process when we discovered we did not have the key to open the jury wheel.

Sheriff Marlin Raffensperger had the key. We called his office and was informed he was off for the day deer hunting. We found out where he was hunting, called his wife to get in contact with him to bring the key to the office. He did come into the office later with the key. He was not a happy hunter, but we always made sure we had the key before we started to add or pull names out of the jury wheel for court. Sheriff Marlin Raffensperger never forgot that day.

When George Frownfelter was Sheriff, he loved to play practical jokes on everyone. One day he came into the office to talk to the Commissioners and before he left the office, he poured salt in my cup of coffee. Needless to say, you know what happened when I took a sip of my coffee.

I thought do I pay him back now or later. I choose later. A month or more passed and I went to his office and asked if he was in the courthouse or out serving papers, etc. The reply from Deputy Donald Smith was he is out. I told Mr. Smith what he did to my coffee. I said it's now my turn to repay him. So, I emptied several of his desk drawers on the floor and left. Mr. Smith said I didn't see anything.

It wasn't until last year George Frownfelter and Liz Frownfelter came into my office and I told him that I was the one that emptied his desk drawers several years ago. I said you are not in office now and you cannot arrest me. We all were laughing.

I am so thankful that Max E. Powell, Norman Pressley and Harry G. Sheaffer gave me a chance to work at the courthouse. It has been a lifetime experience for me and also working with many wonderful people.

Bonnie L. Delancey, Director of Elections & Voter Registration

"No Strangers To Hard Work"

BLAIN FARMERS FRANK AND LORENA RICE

Storytellers Lorena Rice, David Rice and Danny Rice
Recorded by Debra Kay Noye

Frank Rice instilled a "can do" attitude in his three children, (David 1953) (Loretta Faller 1955) (Danny 1959), which was encouraged by his wife Lorena (Thomas). His energetic "jack of all trades" and enterprising prowess built the foundation for the coveted distinction "Rice's Century Farm" 1920-2020. Danny Rice is extremely proud that he has been able to carry on and continue the legacy after taking over the farms in 1998. Brother Dave's farming roots run deep pitching in as time permitted while pursuing his education and employment in Harrisburg.

Their dad was capable of "looking at something and being able to figure out how to fix it or create something new". He tackled mechanics, carpentry, plumbing and sewers, electrical and veterinarian issues while farming and trucking. He wasn't stingy with his self-taught, God-given skills using them to benefit his church, Zion United Church of Christ, just up the road in Blain.

Dave relates noticing the thick engineering manual full of engines and motors in their farmhouse basement bathroom. He eluded that his father did a lot of reading to enhance his skills. Well, it paid off but if he ran into a real problem he consulted his mechanics buddy John Frownfelter Sr. who owned a garage west of Blain. They would get their heads together. Frownfelter was an expert welder and between them "there wasn't too much they couldn't tackle!"

Frank attended public sales and flea markets throughout the years in search of parts, or machinery and vehicles that needed restored. "His energy knowing no bounds" even led him to discover an old truck chassis with a small tree growing up through the middle. Frank cut down the tree, took the chassis home and refurbished it creating a new truck. He took great pride in his restorations. It wasn't unusual to see Frank and Lorena showing off his prized, restored family milk truck in a county parade. Today, the family keeps the tradition going forward by parading through Blain Picnic Grounds.

Frank's love for farming and trucks, especially milk trucks, obviously began with his father, George F. Rice, who owned a milk truck and hauled milk from Landisburg area farms to Millersburg in upper

Dauphin County. Their farm was located very close to the Milltown one-room schoolhouse north of Alinda. As the story goes, in 1938, Frank's dad farmed with a Farmall F-12 steel-wheeled tractor. On a trip to Harry Keller's Farm Implements in New Bloomfield, Frank's dad was fascinated with the new modern rubber-wheeled F-14 tractor on display. The rubber wheels allowed tractors to maneuver more efficiently, accomplishing more in a farmer's work day. Bartering was very common so Frank's dad traded the old F-12 for the rubber-wheeled F-14. The swap was made on the Jim Bolze farm in Milltown where the F-12 was in a field hitched to a binder. The new F-14 finished the job. Frank's first tractor was a Farmall H. Before Frank passed, he and Danny restored a Farmall F-20 (another pre-WWll Farmall model).

Dan recalls attending the Pennsylvania Farm Show in Harrisburg, as a member of the Future Farmers of America at West Perry High School. He always marveled at the new farm equipment on display. As the size of tractors and equipment grew, Dan declared "they'd never appear in rural Perry County!" He changed his tune as he witnessed "the size and scope of the equipment increase farm production". From steel wheels on dirt roads to high-tech tractors with rubber wheels larger than inflatable pools, sharing the bustling narrow-paved country roads, has Dan pondering what new technology is next. Unfortunately, computerization of farm equipment demands high-tech experts, pushing aside the self-reliant farmer of Frank Rice's era.

Frank was always enterprising. He dairy farmed east of Blain, with his wife Lorena, hauling beef cattle, calves and pigs to the Carlisle Livestock Auction. This business was not new to Lorena, who would ride along in her father's cattle truck to the livestock auctions. Early in their farming career, they traveled from Blain by way of paved Sterretts Gap road, as the Waggoner's Gap road needed improved. Lorena loved stopping at Zorger's Store at the intersection in Alinda for ice cream bricks sandwiched between waffle wafers. "They really tasted good!"

When Lorena's father, Dean Thomas died, she inherited the 191 acre farm off Red Rock Road outside of Blain, adding to their 189 acre dairy farm. "They were very busy industrious people!" Lorena was heavily involved in managing the fifty dairy cow herd. "Over-seeing the herd, she was the first in the barn in the mornings to tend to the feeding and milking." Lorena tells the tale of when Dave was four years old. She would put Loretta (age 2) down for a nap at four o'clock in the afternoon, before they went out to do the evening milking chores. Loretta was as enterprising as her father and found a way to climb from the crib onto a bureau, walking outside in the rain across a bridge to make her escape, much to Lorena's horror!

Rice's purchased Holstein heifer calves from Alfred and Danny Albright's farm outside of Alinda on Route 850, which added to Lorena's farming responsibilities. Keep in mind, Lorena also tended a large garden, canning the vegetables as well as fruits and meats from butchering hogs and beef cattle. On a farm there is always extra laundry because of heavily soiled work clothes and toddlers added to the mix. Not to mention preparing meals three times a day to keep her busy family fueled. Dave, Loretta and Dan have a deep appreciation for their mother's work ethic.

Besides cows, Rice's raised beef cattle and grain farmed. Selling their first wheat crop in 1954 for one dollar and fifty cents a bushel paid the taxes. Back in the day, most farmers relied on the year-end sale of their grain crops to pay the taxes and the "tab at the local small mom and pop businesses".

Discharged from the Army in 1947, working at the Hershey Creamery in Harrisburg, Frank purchased a truck tractor "cab only" and hauled steel and sugar for other businesses. Long hauling cross-country came to a stop when he married and started farming.

Over the years, Frank purchased various trucks to perform varied tasks. He hauled coal for the Perry County Home east of Loysville - since torn down. Selling and hauling lime and fertilizer in dump trucks lead to custom spreading right onto the fields. His fleet of trucks consisted of two dump trucks and three specialty beds with spreaders. At one point, he and Harry Stambaugh of Green Park collaborated through a fertilizer dealership.

Frank's trucks were used to haul slate for the township and for the Pennsylvania Turnpike when the Blue Mountain tunnels were expanded and improved. Lorena recalls the days of hauling and loading sand and lime very well, because of the dirt drug into their farmhouse kitchen.

Family team work, Frank's ability to solve problems and a willingness to embrace new technology sustained the Rice farm going forward. Frank wasn't afraid to take solid advice and instruction from others. Veterinarian Burleigh Anderson from Loysville was one such person. Dan declares, "Doc Anderson was light years ahead of his time!" He credits Anderson with implementing the "Herd Health Program" for dairy cows in 1969. Nevin Rice at Blain, Milligans on Airport Road, Martins at Cisna Run, and Frank followed Doc's nutrition program for their dairy herds. Boosting milk production from twelve thousand pounds to sixteen thousand pounds of milk per cow per year was a life saver for the dairy farmer. According to Dan, "Doc didn't want to be a fire engine vet" racing off to fix something that the farmer could do himself. They were taught to be pro-active with vaccines and treating mastitis, an infection in the cow's udder with penicillium. Implanting embryos by artificially inseminating the cow was taught to Dan. He thawed purchased frozen embryos which he implanted in the cow's uterus, eliminating a "farm call" from the veterinarian. But Dave remembers when "Doc's coming was the highlight of the day." He was large in stature, well educated and read, a great teacher and good talker with a hearty laugh.

Dan likes to tell the story of discovering a cow trying to give birth around three o'clock in the afternoon. Upon physically examining the cow, Dan determined the cow had a twisted uterus and he couldn't remedy her situation. He called for Doc, who determined the cow's uterus was twisted twice, making for a worse situation ever! However, Doc told Dan to keep an eye on the cow while he went home for dinner. Maybe he needed a power boost for what he was going to try, to remedy the situation. On his return, Doc and Dan put a halter on the cow, lead her across the road from the barn, up the hill only to roll her down the hill, like kids playing a game. They did this a dozen times, before Doc decided to perform a c-section. He saved the heifer calf and the cow. Good thing it didn't occur in the winter months!

Hearty winters in the Blain area generally mean tonnage of drifted snow due to open fields along the roadsides. Lorena remembers as a kid that township roads, like Red Rock back in the Turkey Tail where she lived, were shoveled open, so when it snowed heavily you just stayed put and didn't even walk to the one-room Adams Grove Schoolhouse. The state used graders in the 1930s-1940s to open the main highways, which were then only passable. Lots of milk was dumped back in those days. The 1966 snowstorm drifted the entire area roadways shut. Always thinking and planning ahead, Frank already had in his possession a specially made bucket by Tressler's Welding from outside New Bloomfield, to fit his Farmall H tractor, which had a wide front end. The state highwaymen were having difficulties trying to open Route 274 past the farm, so Frank used his tractor bucket to help remove the snow, clearing the road for the milk truck to pick up his milk. Lorena remembers inviting Lawrence "Shrimp" Clark, who was plowing snow for PennDot to stay for dinner after a challenging work day. Winter also meant slick sledding on the hills across the road from the farm. Ice skating and pick-up games of ice hockey on Nevin Rice's pond in Blain or at Waggoner's Dam at Green Gates filled their Saturday and Sunday afternoons.

Dave recalls May of 1966 when Peggy Ann Bradnick of Shade Gap, Pennsylvania, was kidnapped by a local mountain man. It made national news on the Huntley-Brinkley Report on Channel 8, and a vinyl record "Eight Days at Sha-De-Gap" was produced, much to the chagrin of Dave, who can sing that song with gusto yet today! Rice's have a tenant property across the road from the farm and the lady of that house loudly played that popular song over and over and over. Irritating for sure, but amusing that Dave, a retired lawyer, doesn't miss a beat! His Grandfather Thomas influenced Dave's decision to become a lawyer, but Dave also realized he did not possess those mechanical analytical skills his father applied around the farm.

Like most rural farm siblings, the Rices played pranks on each other. Loretta and Dave were spanked after pushing young Danny into the farm pond. Dave locked Loretta in the cedar wardrobe and she proceeded to rock it back and forth till it required repairs! They like most farm kids had city cousins who visited every summer for several weeks. In this case, they were from Philadelphia and constantly taunted them with odd things like "when were they going to jump off the Tallahatchie Bridge" or eat black-eyed peas or sleep in the hay, all lyrics from the popular song "Ode to Billy Joe". The Rice siblings soon came up with a plan and told the city-slickers to beware of the ogre-like "Goon" who prowled upstairs in the barn. To make the prank seem more real, Rices would dare the cousins to venture out to the barn after dark. Dan and Dave would climb up into the hay mow and remain hidden while making strange noises to scare them off.

Lorena remembers going to the Ickesburg Hi-Way Theatre most Saturday nights when she was dating. There was a basement snack bar and bowling alley. Clark Bower, from Blain, would take her to Landisburg's Yankee Theatre and New Bloomfield's Perry Theatre occasionally.

Sandlot baseball was the most common form of entertainment for Saturday and Sunday afternoons. It wasn't just about the sport. It was about the rowdy cheering sections for their favorite town team or player. When the local teams would play a double header on most holidays, game one was played early around ten o'clock. The farm boys would go home to eat lunch and help with the chores. Returning to play the second game was a summer routine. Harvesting of crops, baling of hay and spreading manure was planned around the ball games.

Restaurants were scarce back when the Rices were growing up. Folks ate at home because there wasn't money to spend frivolously. Blain Hotel's Ernie Smith put out good fresh foods, according to Lorena. Reisinger Farm's Restaurant between Ickesburg and Blain served home-cooked meals. The Sun Bonnet Drive-In on Loysville's west end was known for soft serve ice cream.

Shopping locally meant a trip into town for dry goods from Glenn Smith's Store where Blain Market stands today. Lorena says the market was half the size then. However, the family enjoyed patronizing Earl Fisher's Store in Andersonburg. Right on the sharp curve, the store was in half of the Fisher's home. Walking in the front door, the long narrow aisles went from front to back of the store, with the check-out counter right inside the door. Lorena remembers getting molasses pumped from the barrel into a metal can so she could transport it home. She bought flour, salt and sugar in cloth sack bags. The Coca Cola pop dispenser located in the back was filled with ice water to keep the beverages cold. Dave and cousin Gary Thomas would meet and enjoy a pop and candy bar together. The store was open till eight or nine o'clock at night which encouraged local loafers to plop on the chairs inside or the front porch steps and "chew the fat" before heading home with a box of ice cream or groceries. Known loafers were Louie and John Moose, Dick Thomas, Bill Sheriff, Neil Flickinger, Dean and Ed Harris.

The second Saturday in August brought people from far and wide to the annual Blain Picnic held at Shermans Park commonly known as the "Blain Picnic Grounds". The grove of trees along Shermans Creek south of Blain hosted the Blain Picnic from the mid 1850s and was easily accessed as the Newport and Shermans Valley Railroad stopped nearby. (Noted fact: Lorena's family in the 1930s owned the grove and surrounding farm lands, beginning with Dean Thomas to Dorf Thomas ending with Dorf Thomas and Banks Rohm.)

The picnic was a "home coming" much like one huge extended family reunion. In the beginning, attendees would dress in their Sunday best. Ladies wore dresses and showed off their favorite hat. Men donned dress pants and suit jackets topped with derbies. Everybody wanted to make a good impression at the largest social event of the year! Everybody packed a picnic basket, dining on the blanket covered grass. Fried chicken, potato salad, cheese, homemade bread, fresh fruit, Montgomery pie and pound cake were enjoyed. Surely the youngsters played in the creek, games of tag and pick-up baseball. Through the years, the grove of trees was continually cleared to make room for concrete buildings and toilets, wooden buildings for food sales and vendors, pavilions with seating for dining, and parking. The Saturday afternoon home-coming became a Wednesday through Saturday event with a carnival atmosphere.

Lorena fondly remembers the picnic before it transitioned totally into a Blain community fundraiser. Her parents gave her fifty cents to spend riding the Ferris Wheel and Merry Go Round. She couldn't resist entering the Fortune Teller's tent and paying to have her fortune read. Lemonade and Orange drinks were available, but not food stands like today. When Lorena was very young, her father hauled their pony Rosie in his cattle truck to the Blain Picnic and the Shade Gap Picnic the first week-end in August. Parents paid for their children to ride Rosie, as Lorena dutifully lead her around the grounds. It was a way for the family to "make some money".

Dan remembers looking forward to Tom Shover of Paul Shover & Sons Inc. sellers of farm implements from Loysville, displaying farm tractors and equipment like hay balers. Tom always brought a red painted church pew so folks could sit and chat, creating "a loafer's paradise". Farm equipment and automobiles were displayed in the area where the large concrete building stands today. Bob Wallace, from New Bloomfield, salesman for N. E. Black a garage and automobile dealership in New Bloomfield where the Unimart is today, always displayed several new cars. The picnic was a way to meet and greet the public in the simplest form of advertising.

As the Blain Picnic evolved to a carnival atmosphere, Dave remembers being warned "not to waste your money on games of chance". "Faker's Row" as he called it offered all sorts of games like penny and dime pitches which left little opportunity to win any prizes. Dan recalls, "what's not to like about throwing rotten tomatoes" at local public officials or friends putting their heads on the line to benefit a local organization.

The popular Blain Fire Company chicken barbecue was started by Amos Sanderson, Dick Thomas and Emmett Shreffler among others. The wooden pavilions were then built for sit-down dining.

In the early years, gospel singing or hymn sings would've been part of the day. Lorena recalls live entertainment such as country music star Roy Acuff performing in the early 1950s. Local musicians and bands would've performed as well, especially on Friday nights.

The Blain Picnic no longer exists. The popular Shermans Valley Heritage Days held on the same grounds the second week-end in October attracts folks from all over. Farming equipment from those early steel-wheeled days is displayed and used in demonstrations as well as parading the grounds. The four day event is the largest fundraiser for the local fire company and organizations. The Rice families participate by volunteering and displaying Frank's restored tractors and trucks.

As Rices work around their family farm and travel throughout their community, they are constantly reminded of those who influenced them the most and laid the foundations for their legacy. Just driving a tractor through the fields brings many a fond memory for Dave of his Grandfather Dean Thomas, who would stop by most days to check on the farm and bring a refreshing cold drink as Dave was working in the fields. The tradition of a chat and a nice visit has passed. The memories live on despite technology and some like Dan have followed in his father's footsteps as a farmer and truck hauler. Lorena smiles and beams!

Remembering The Neighborhood Grocer

Storyteller Sylvia Orris Hocker

Growing up in Duncannon, Perry County, Pennsylvania, in the 1950s, I fondly remember the convenience of the family-owned neighborhood grocery store. From one end of High Street to the other, these friendly establishments provided for the essential grocery needs of their surrounding citizens. Starting downtown at the corner of Cumberland and High Streets was Cooper's Store, owned and operated by the Cooper brothers; Max with wife Doris and Paul with wife Flossie. Their father occasionally worked alongside as did some of the children when they came along. Friendly and hospitable, the Coopers were attentive to the needs of their customers.

Moving up High Street was the store of John Kennedy, established variety and grocer since the late 1890s and conveniently located near the Duncannon Elementary School on Church and Broadway Streets next to the Lutheran Church and in front of the Union Cemetery (now Pfoutz apartments). When school left out, we kids would make a "beeline" to Kennedy's and the large, well-stocked, wood and glass candy case. Friendly and capable, Miss Alice Wahl would wait patiently as I pondered what penny candy to purchase with my nickel and enjoy eating on my long walk home.

Our neighborhood on High Street was serviced by the grocery store owned by John and Emma Rohrer. Son Charles also worked with them and my mother would walk there several times a week for just enough groceries that she could carry home. Unlike weekly shopping of today, meals seemed to be planned on a day-to-day basis. The Rohrer's also lived at their store as did many shop owners at that time.

Uptown High Street folks frequented the variety and grocery of the venerable Miss Sarah White. Her business was also in the family home and shoppers would be greeted by the talkative, resident parrot. Her shop was quaint, old fashioned and smaller in comparison to others, but filled to overflowing.

As for the butcher shop, the Thomas Mutzabaugh family from the 1920s were a family of butchers. Aunt Annie and sons John, Tom, Dick and Joe continued to enlarge their butcher shop into the modern-day supermarket that the family finally sold in December 2021 to Karns Foods, after nearly one-hundred years of serving the community. Their butcher shop-grocery occupied many locations about town, including one on High Street, through the years.

Home delivery service was not to be overlooked as we were visited weekly by the cry "Bake-rrr" from Chick Charles, the Manbeck bakery man, stopping in with his large carrying case filled with fresh bread, rolls, buns and pastries. A sure sale!

Custer Leedy, the milkman from Harrisburg Dairies, would stop three times weekly with glass bottles of milk which were put into the insulated milk box that always sat on our front porch. Now days bread and milk, mostly in plastic or cartons, are purchased at a store and the lowly milk box might only be found at an antique shop.

Today three of the four grocery stores on High Street are private residences and Cooper's Store at the corner of Cumberland and High Streets has been torn down. Time marches on but fond memories remain.

From The Farm To Creating A Lasting Legacy

SHERMANS DALE, PENNSYLVANIA

Storytellers Rena and Robert "Bob" Brunner

Our story is much the same as everyone else who grew up in the early nineteen hundreds, specifically 1937 – 1938, and lived on farms.

Rena's Story
Rena was born in Carlisle Springs, Pennsylvania, and moved to our farm in Shermans Dale when I was three years old and lived there with my parents, Anna Pearl (Smee) and Ernest Kyle Hockenberry, and four sisters (Lois, Myra, Audrey and Wanda) until I got married. Farm life was very hard then with my father working long hours. I helped, or I thought I helped, to milk the cows when I was very young and of course we had no automatic milking machines. We watched cows in the fields to make sure they did not get into the corn and we helped to bring in crops in season. My sisters and I would ride the hay wagon and tramp the loose hay. We also bundled the wheat shocks to be put on the wagon. After which we would ride the wagon into the barn floor for the threshing of the wheat grains from the straw. Again, we would make sure the hay and straw were tramped down in the mows. A very dirty job, but it was life on the farm.

Our fields were plowed and harrowed by horses, as there was no such thing as no-till farming. We also made our own butter with a churn that separated the butter from the buttermilk which my father drank. We later got margarine from the grocery store with the yellow dot that we mixed with the plain white substance that looked like lard.

We used an outhouse and got water from a hand pump adjacent to the farmhouse. No refrigerator and cooled our milk, etc., in a spring house that is still visible from Route 34 on the farm where I grew up. No electricity and we used oil lamps when we did our homework and our chores. We heated water on a cookstove in the kitchen to do our dishes and for all our cooking. Of course, we always had a huge garden and picked cherries and blackberries in all of the fence rows around the farm.

A farmer neighbor had a couple of my sisters and I help to pick potatoes, which was my very first job to make money. My mother attended the market in Carlisle and we raised chickens to take there, plus eggs and some produce.

Church was always very important to our family and my mother was the one to go early and make the fire on cold mornings. My sisters and I would sometimes go along and stand on the big register in the middle of the room until we could feel the heat to get warm. We always looked forward to the Children's Day program held every June. We had recitations, songs, etc., and would decorate the church with flowers grown at our homes. The services were always in the evenings.

I went to Narrow one-room schoolhouse until I entered ninth grade at Perry Joint High School in New Bloomfield. My class was the first graduating class to spend a full year in the newly built high school. My years at the one-room schoolhouse were memorable as we had to walk one mile to school. No school bus to take us. But it was fun, as we got to walk home with many other kids. Two of us walked to McAlister's or Powley's with a bucket and got water from a mountain spring and brought it back to the classroom. On cold winter days, we had someone who lived close by come and start the fire for our teacher. There was a stove in the middle of the classroom that provided heat and where we could dry our gloves and coats when we got wet in the snow. Charles Shenk, who was an elderly neighbor, would arrive early and start the fire in the stove, so the classroom would be warm when we arrived. In later years, Steve Liddick made sure the stove was lit.

Our games consisted of playing baseball, tag and "tickley high over." We came up with the name since it consisted of throwing a ball over the schoolhouse roof with a group of kids on each side. Our teacher would also take us for walks in the spring and looked for arbutus and teaberries in the woods. After graduating from PJHS, I got my first job with the United States Department of Agriculture and stayed there until my husband and I started the Twin Kiss Ice Cream and Restaurant, which was a cornerstone in Shermans Dale in 1961.

Bob's Story
Bob was born in Shermans Dale on a farm and lived there with his brother and sister until he was ten when they moved to the family gas station. His parents, Goldie Marie (Stone) and William Charles Brunner, later added groceries and hardware items and it became known as Brunner's Community Store. We also added a pool table and a sandwich counter, which attracted a lot of business and lot of free labor from us kids. Our house was attached to the store so we were there full time.

My job on the farm was to milk cows, watch cows, and to plow fields with a tractor when I was about nine years old. That put me in a good position to drive an automobile when I turned sixteen years old. I also went from farm to farm helping neighbors making hay, husking corn and threshing barley, wheat, oats and also when we later got a combine. I went along from farm to farm riding the combine. Talk about a dirty job!

We had to use the normal outhouse of the era, pump water from an outside pump for washing clothes, bathing and cooking. We also had a Maytag wringer washer with a gasoline motor. No electricity so we used oil lamps for everything. We had a cook stove using wood for fuel and a wood stove in the living room for heat.

When visiting my grandfather's farm, I can remember going across the old bridge that crossed the Shermans Creek, just north of the current concrete bridge. At the time, there was a hotel along Creek Road at the end of the bridge.

While we were still on the farm, my mother was stricken with polio and the three of us kids went to live with our grandparents, uncles and aunts. I mostly lived with my Uncle Seymore and Aunt Sylvia Aughenbaugh. It was a rough couple of years with my mom away from all of us.

I went to one-room schools; Burnhill School for seven years and then at Shermans Dale School on Creek Road for the rest of my years till I entered Perry Joint High School in New Bloomfield. We played the usual ballgames and walked to school each day. There was no school bus. I attended PJHS and played football but no activity bus to take us home. We had to find a way to get home, walk or be old enough to drive. My first car was a 1947 Pontiac.

After graduating from PJHS, I worked in construction for a couple of years and then joined the United States Army to do my stint for two years. There was no war at the time, so I did enjoy traveling to other countries and being stationed the whole time with my brother. I was stationed in Germany and we traveled all over that country and also to Italy, Holland, Switzerland and Paris, France.

I got married while I was stationed in the Army and when I came home, I worked at Giant Grocery Store and in construction for a while. Then my wife and I decided to purchase the Twin Kiss Ice Cream building. It was a two-hundred and fifty square foot building that had been moved from Coatesville to Shermans Dale. It still stands as a landmark in the community. Over the years, we expanded the original building to a four-thousand square foot restaurant which is now a diner.

I saw a need for the community and my vision was to build a grocery store which became the IGA and opened in 1984. I worked at the Twin Kiss Restaurant for twenty-three years during the summer and construction during the winter and then after 1984 at the IGA Store. Then I decided to provide additional conveniences for the community by developing a sixty-four thousand square foot shopping plaza known as Village Square Plaza. Some of the original tenants included a new Post Office, a Ben Franklin Store, a White Shield Pharmacy, Farmer's Trust Company, a paint store and a hardware store.

In 1998, we added our next project which was Village Square West. It included the car wash, a laundromat, and a convenience store with gas pumps. After that was finished, we built twenty-four condo units. Our lives have been very busy, but now at our age, we're turning the day-to-day operations over to our sons and family. And to think, it all started as a dream with a two hundred-fifty square foot building known as the Twin Kiss.

From One End Of Ickesburg To The Other

Storytellers Darlene Berrier Adams and Deloris Berrier Kitner
Recorded by Debra Kay Noye

"Our parents were never concerned as to our whereabouts or who we were playing with all day long!" emphatically state the Berrier sisters who grew up in Ickesburg at the foot of the Tuscarora Mountains in Saville Township, Perry County, Pennsylvania. Darlene and Deloris Berrier just "needed to be back in time for supper" with their parents Kenneth Elmer (born 1908) and Nora Emma (Weibley born in1915) Berrier. They lived beside Bill Hoffman's Store on the east end of Ickesburg. In fact, their mother never went shopping anywhere with a large grocery list. She sent one of the girls next door or roller skating (back when the skates were buckled to the shoes) up the street to fetch a can of peas or freshly cut chunk of cheddar cheese. The family thrived in their small caring community.

In the winter, the girls would put on layers of clothing, maybe pants, long socks and unlined rubber boots to trudge up the roadway past the Hi-Way Theatre to sled on the snow crusted Kochenderfer's Hill. There was little traffic on the unplowed roads, as they set their Lightning Guider sleds on the top of the steep hill and flew down towards Saville. What a thrill and workout climbing back up to navigate the very slick hill again and again!

Delivered by Doc Kistler, from Blain, Deloris was born in 1947 in the house beside the grocery store. Older sister Darlene born in 1938 "didn't know we were expecting a baby and had no clue where she came from." She had spent the night at her Aunt Annie's arriving home to a baby sister.

Berriers had rented half of the Emmie Snyder property on the town square, when Darlene was born. That property has since been torn down and is now a Saville Township Park. Then they rented from Emma Berrier's twin sister, Anna and Ralph "Dip" Johnson, across the street from Hoffman's Store. The house had no plumbing, just an outhouse.

Their father realized he needed a steady income to support his growing family. He became Ickesburg's plumber using his truck for house calls. They also purchased the Lester Fuller property beside Bill Hoffman's Store in 1946 before Deloris was born. The Ickesburg Plumbing sign was hung on the garage between the house and the store. Their plumbing father converted a bedroom to a bathroom, so much for modern conveniences. Washday still meant using the wringer washing machine and the two rinse tubs to do laundry which was always hung out on a line to dry.

The property had a barn behind the house for several milking cows, which were hand milked daily. Deloris declared her dad would tell her to "pump the tail to get the milk to come!" The milk was strained and poured into bottles with paper caps. Family and neighbors would purchase the milk on the "honor system" from a cubicle on the back porch, leaving the empties behind.

Their dad also raised free-range hogs that roamed the old alleyway for six months till Bill Swartz, from town, hauled them to livestock auctions. One time their father had to bottle feed fifteen piglets that were runts. Satisfied they could go back to their mother's care in the lean-to, he smeared them with lard so they wouldn't smell like humans and be rejected.

Butchering of hogs occurred at Sweger's Butcher Shop, two doors up the alley from the firehouse. Everybody would come help scrape the hog and cut it up. Enjoying eating the cooked meats right out of the iron kettles was a special treat. Lard was rendered for the "best pie crusts" and scrapple from the cooked broth, pork liver and ground meats thickened with flour, cornmeal and seasonings. "That's when people really knew how to make scrapple!" declares Deloris. Their mother cleaned the pig stomachs, and the intestines which were used as ground sausage casings. The sausage was generally canned due to no electric freezers. (Aunt Anna, across the street, had an ice chest and would get ice deliveries.)

Their mother would roast the heart filled with a bread stuffing and pickle the tongue. Cracklings, hog rinds left from rendered lard, were placed on the back porch for everybody to nibble as a snack. The hams were cured, smoked and hung in a closet. Often, they would develop a green mold which was washed off before using. Darlene pointed out that King Syrup also molded which was skimmed off before use.

When the sisters weren't off playing and swimming in the nearby creek (crick as Deloris calls it), they were busy gathering eggs from their chicken house above the barn. Deloris hated gathering the eggs because the chickens would peck her. Eggs from the one hundred hens would be gathered from a long lidded wooden nesting box and individual metal coops. There was a roosting area too.

The sisters carefully carried the eggs to the basement. Then they were cleaned, put into cardboard boxes, to be picked up by Cecil Weller, the huckster for Emlet's Eggs in Loysville. The family ate the cracked eggs and Margie Murphy purchased the soft-shelled eggs, which occurred despite the chickens feeding on ground oyster shells. Darlene recalls a time when a hen seemed to not be laying eggs. It was decided they would eat her. Through the slaughtering process, it was discovered that she was full of eggs!

Farming and gardening go hand in hand. Their mother canned various vegetables and fruits on a kerosene stove in their garage. They had their own pear tree and their dad traveled to Adams County to buy peaches. He would haul them home in his truck and sell to the community. Local currants were picked at Mrs. Reisingers and turned into jelly. Their mother had her own grape arbors and turned them in to jelly.

Darlene recalls buying a new book promoting modern canning techniques. The suggested canning process used metal lids and rings, but the readied jar was placed into the oven instead of a stovetop "hot water bath" canner. Mercy sakes! Juices seeped out of the jars and all over Darlene's oven. Needless to say, Darlene conceded to the tried-and-true methods. However, her adventuresome spirit compelled her, in 1964, to purchase a "radar range" aka microwave of the future, after attending a demonstration by salesman Lee Kline, who lived across the street from the store. She thought cooking a hot dog in the bun was miraculous!

Raising and preserving their own foods, the family still relied on Bill Hoffman's Store next door. Deloris remembers witnessing local loafer Jim Swartz, from out beyond Greenwood Nursery, coming up to the store's meat counter, grabbing a hunk of fresh raw pork sausage and eating it. She was thrilled when ten cents would purchase a full bag of penny candy. Two cents deposit was added to all bottled sodas from the Coca Cola machine. Some folks made extra money by scavenging soda bottles and returning them for the deposit. Hoffman also owned the POS of A (Patriotic Order of Sons of America) building, formerly used as a dance hall, to expand his hardware and paint inventory.

A regular to the store was Willie Snyder. Crippled at birth, Willie was the daily newspaper deliveryman. He loaded his red wagon with the Patriot News and walked all over town selling the newspaper and collecting weekly payments. Deloris says, "he was a good-hearted soul."

The local barber, Piney Wallett cut their hair. While they waited a turn, the sisters played with his wooden puzzles.

Their "rotary dialed" telephone was on a party line controlled by a switchboard operator, Marion Frontz, who lived beside the Reformed Church. They paid the monthly $5 phone bill at the same location after receiving it in the mail.

The sisters attended church at St. Paul's Lutheran near the Ickesburg square. Their parents were married in the church parsonage. Deloris, who remains a faithful member, recalls the pastors over the years from Rev. Sharp, Rev. "Pappy" Gensler, Rev. Lau, Rev. Horick, Rev. Moore, Rev. Thompson, Rev. Seilhammer, Rev. Foulk, Rev James Gold, Rev. Karen Easterly and currently Rev. Elaine Moyer of Faith United Church.

The church has evolved over the years adding a Sunday School room onto the back in 1948. Fire in 1962 broke out the side windows, but the front's historical stained-glass windows were untouched. Nicholas Ickes, Ickesburg's founding family and Civil War Veteran's names, appear on the cherished windows.

A second addition was added to the back of the church in 1972 to accommodate the growing congregation. In 1965, Andrew's Lutheran Church of Eschol and Emanuel's Lutheran Church of Saville joined with St. Paul's Lutheran Church of Ickesburg. In October of 1967, Rev. James Gold was called to serve St. Paul's Lutheran and the United Church of Christ Churches, preaching two services.

Ickesburg's original brick schoolhouse was two stories with first through fourth grades on the first floor and fifth through eighth grades on the second floor. No indoor plumbing and you packed your lunch. Darlene fondly remembers her best teacher, Janet Davis, in second and fourth grades, filling her car with eight students and taking them to see the New Bloomfield Lion's Club Minstrel Show in New Bloomfield. She also cooked a dinner of sausages, potatoes and peas for them.

Darlene still giggles at the memory of Decker Foltz sneaking off to buy an ice cream cone and stashing the remainder in his desk, only to be discovered by teacher Mrs. Bixler as it dripped on to the wooden floor. "A really old" Mr. Snyder taught fifth and sixth grades when he wasn't sleeping the afternoons away. According to Darlene, "good looking" Mr. Hess read daily from the scary "Dr. Jekyll and Mr. Hyde."

Buses transported lunch-toting eighth and ninth grade students to Tressler Lutheran Orphans Home in Loysville, which is now the state operated Youth Development Center. Teachers that came to mind were Charlie Eaton and Mrs. Denton. The local Lion's Club sponsored school buses transporting children to swimming lessons at the macadam TOH swimming pool.

Darlene attended tenth grade at Landisburg High School. She recalls that was the year a lunch-sized plastic bag came into existence making it easier to carry a lunch.

Green Park Union High School opened with Darlene entering the eleventh grade. She graduated and married Gilbert Newlin Adams (born 1933) in 1955. They took up dairy farming west of New Bloomfield and established a "carousel milking parlor" in 1973. The Center School once stood on the Adam's family farm.

By the time Deloris was ready for school, Ickesburg boasted a new brick building known as the Ickesburg High School at the very east end of town. She walked down the street to attend first through sixth grades. Safety guards were posted to flag passing motorists to stop as students crossed the busy street. Her teachers were first grade Mrs. Brown, second Mrs. Crum who had Deloris help classmates with math, third Mrs. Bixler, fourth Mrs. Rice, fifth Mrs. Dillman and sixth Mrs. Morrison. Deloris loved the cafeteria lunches lovingly prepared by Anna Johnson and Catherine Kerr.

Deloris started seventh grade at Green Park Union High School. To catch the bus, she walked down the street to the Ickesburg School once again. She recalls Ken Morrison as a math teacher and Mr. Curtis taught her how to break down sentences properly. She was a member of the first graduating class of West Perry High School in 1964-1965.

The sisters were members of their school chorus and band playing the same saxophone. Their wool band uniforms were hot and scratchy, but kept them warm while marching in Harrisburg's holiday parades. Darlene remembers playing at the Forum in Harrisburg. Their band instructors were Clarence "Red" Hollinger, Choral director Walter Smiley who substituted, Baird Collins and Norman Harrison.

Deloris went on to graduate from Hagerstown Business School, while staying in the dorms, packing lunches and walking five blocks to attend classes. She then married and was raising twin sons when decided to move home. Her years in 4-H and Home Economics teachings from Lenore Trostle served her well as she sewed clothes for her family. She even made suits including neckties for the boys when she married Ronald K. Kitner (born 1951) in 1970. She even trimmed her boys' hair when needed.

Her business degree was put to use when Carl Sheaffer, co-owner of Sheaffer-Weary Chevrolet in Loysville, told her he needed more staff for the garage and car dealership. Hence, she started a lengthy career on January 2, 1977. Sometimes, one is blessed when volunteering, as the job offer came about while Deloris was stuffing envelopes benefiting Loysville's Perry Health Center.

Still today, the sisters attend the Ickesburg Fire Company and Lions Club carnival held on the fire company grounds. Their father and mother were the backbone of the chicken barbecue fundraisers benefiting both organizations. After their father put the chicken halves on the metal racks set over charcoal fired pits, he sprayed the chickens with their mother's signature recipe that included vinegar and butter. Both organizations had separate carnivals held on the Ickesburg school grounds, till moving to the firehouse location. Now their children and grandchildren enjoy the traditional Ickesburg carnival.

Darlene's family includes: Stephen G. (1956), Timothy C. (1962), Thomas L. (1964), Michael M. (1974), and Mary Ann (McCormack) 1977.

Deloris' family includes: son Richard (1970) and wife Heidi (1972) with children Noah, Miranda and Olivia; son Clifford (1970) and wife Karla with children Alec, Jacob, Kenzie and Ryker.

Deloris and Darlene can recall, for the most part, who and what existed on every street in town when they were growing up and beyond.

Entering the east end of town on the right side of the street the first house belonged to Mr. and Mrs. Brown, Marvin Campbell, Rice brothers, Janet Yingling, Sam Sheriff, Shotzbergers, Ethel Sweger and son Bob (owner of Sweger's Store in Millerstown), parsonage, Berrier's home, Hoffman's Store, Barber Shop owned by Piney Wallett to Charles Reisinger, Margie Murphy, Presbyterian Church was converted into a home by Stanley Dum, George Reisinger, Emmie and Zeno Snyder and Ickesburg Hotel owned by Pete Snyder.

According to the sisters, the Ickesburg Hotel was very nice inside back in its "hey day." Traveling salesmen and hucksters often stayed over in one of the hotel's upstairs rooms. Walking through the front door revealed a snack bar with booths and counter. Deloris and friends Ellen Snyder, Cathy Shiffer and Lyle Johnson would drop in for a bag of potato chips to dip in ketchup and a cone of Rakestraw's Ice Cream. You could enter the main dining room off the porch. Sunday family-style meals were cooked by their Aunt Lenore Irvine and served by cousin Fay Irvine. The hotel was torn down in 2021, revealing the original logs. The property is now a township park.

Entering the east end of town on the left side of the street the first property was Thelma and Charles Johnson, Elliott Reisinger (blacksmith for horses), A. B. Snyder, Hunk Rice, original schoolhouse, Jim and Naomie Boden (shoe repair, shoes were repaired as opposed to buying new), Anna and Dip Johnson, Alice Crawford, Alvin and Janet Fuller, Shotsberger (since torn down), Stanley and Jean Shiffer beside the crick, Faith United Church, two-apartment house where Mildred "Grammy" Fritz mother to Brownie Fritz, and Mrs. Fleming rented (torn down by Harry Campbell to build the current United States Post Office).

Entering the square going west (Route 17) left side of street Ickesburg State Bank, Church of God (currently owned by Faith United Church's "Gathering Nest"), unknown, Paul Loy (television repair), Phoebe Reisinger, Marion Frontz later owned by Rev. James Gold, United Church of Christ, Powells, John Kingsborough, Gordy Kell and Simonton farm back over the hill.

Entering the square going west on the right side of street Patterson's Store later Harry Campbell's store, John and Cass Lesh, Cloyd Bender, Leonards, Peg Lacey, Emma Hartman, Paul Sheaffer, Shulls, Bill Swartz, Hartmans, parking lot beside Hi-Way Theatre with bowling alley.

Entering the square going east on Route 17 on right side of street Ickesburg Hotel, Sam Sheriff's Garage, Pete Snyder.

Entering the square going east on Route 17 on left side of street Firehouse, Frank Dupert, Ricky Pike and parents, Charlotte Frederick, George Barns, Gerald Fritz farm with pond.

Entering the square going north on Route 74 on right side of street Nellie Bistline, Sweger's and the butcher shop, Kline's, Mrs. Rice, Harry Kerr (contractor, carpentry and lumber business behind his home in alley), Shulls, Arlene Rice, Tom Rice the mail carrier, Lincoln Reisinger, Anna and Dip Johnson (built in 1960 and every summer Deloris would go help pick rocks out of the newly tilled garden), Betty and Harold Nipple.

Entering the square going north on Route 74 on left side of street Harry Campbell's Store, Grays later Norman Maxton, Keith Stauffer, Hockenberrys (Tony according to the sisters made the best french fries for the Ickesburg Fire Company), Julius Rice and mother, Pearl (who penned the "Ickesburg News" column for the Perry County Times weekly newspaper), Harold Spotts lived in a converted chicken house, Harry Campbell's Store (needing to expand, closed the store on the square) building new structure, now Mountain Supply.

The facade of Ickesburg has changed, but the community continues rallying around the church, civic organizations and family-owned businesses. A glow surrounds the Berrier sisters sharing their cherished memories of growing up in Ickesburg!

Riding Bike All Over Duncannon

Storyteller Aloise George Gamble

My family:
Father - Charles Henry Gamble - Deceased
Mother - Isabel Sara Gamble - Deceased
Brother - Robert John Gamble - Deceased
Sister - Darlene Ruth Gamble (Duncannon)
Sister - Linda Alfretta Gamble - Deceased
Sister - Sharon Louise Gamble (Shippensburg area)
I reside in Enola.

I was born over the old post office north of the Duncannon square. I am not sure how long we lived there, but at some time we moved to a rental house for several years which was owned by Charley Gamber. My dad then bought a house in the lower end of Duncannon at 53 Valley Street behind the old Maguire's Garage.

Back then in the 1940s and 1950s, recreation time was quite different than it is today. My bike and I went everywhere without a second thought (my mom would have worried had she known my endeavors). At least once a day I would ride my bike down to see the shipment of new cars that came into Maguire's Garage. I would ride out to play in Shermans Creek at the first "singing bridge" on Dellville Road. My neighbor, Gene Foose, would take his car there to wash it, and since I was friends with his son Donnie, I would get to go along. Those times my bike would stay home.

I would also play at this end of Shermans Creek at a place we called Flat Rock (behind the new Maguire's Garage). We would ride our bikes off of Flat Rock as fast as we could to land as far out into Shermans Creek as possible. The bike would stop dead when it hit the water, we would fly over the handlebars into the air and be thrown into the creek as the bike sank behind us. That was fun! Playing in the Susquehanna River where Shermans Creek empties into the river was a great pastime. That section was called Six Arches because of the design of the railroad bridge. Years ago, the Susquehanna was full of coal. If you would stay on the coal bars, you could nearly walk half way across the Susquehanna River.

Another fun thing to do would be to ride my bike to the old train station and watch the trains fly by. The nearest train track to the station was only about ten feet from the platform. One day I got the brilliant idea of hanging onto the platform post, while a train went flying by at about 60 mph. For certain, I know I would not do that today and I also know my mother would definitely not have allowed me to do that had she known. I would have been in big trouble. When you heard the sound of a steam whistle, you knew the train was coming to exchange cars up at the Standard Novelty Works on Market Street in Duncannon. I would jump on my trusty bike and follow the train up through town.

When it got dark, a group of friends would quite often play hide-and-seek all through the lower end. (Donnie Foose, my brother and sisters; Lou, Mike and Mac Kenee, Tommy and Annette Loper, Linda and Ronnie Alleman.)

All the kids from the lower end had to walk to Penn Township Elementary School. We had to have crossing guards to cross over Route 274. I eventually got to be a crossing guard. At the end of the school day, "walkers" got to leave fifteen minutes early because the buses weren't back from their early runs. Some of the "bus kids" wondered where we went when we dropped out of sight off of Carver's Hill.

One of the best things about recess was a pick-up game of co-ed baseball. There were some girls that could play a pretty good game of baseball. Bill Morris had a reputation for hitting the ball and I for throwing the ball.

Moving through high school to graduation night, Gary Gutshall, Barry Lilley and I went cruising to Newport, Duncannon, then out of Perry County to Harrisburg. Then to Marysville where we met up with Sherry Sheaffer. They decided to jump the fence into the Marysville pool. I stayed with the car, probably because even after all that playing in the Susquehanna River and Shermans Creek, I never learned to swim!

One night Barry Lilley and I went cruising in Harrisburg and were drag racing a couple of cars from light to light. We won a couple and lost a couple. We then decided to go to the Bar-B-Q Cottage, circled the cottage a few times to find an opening to park and finally parked beside a little red Falcon. There were two cousins in it named Mary and Sue! We made a date to go to Haar's Drive-in the following Saturday. Barry was in the back seat with Sue and Mary was up front with me. Mary and I continued to date and on her birthday September 12, 1964, I married that girl. We were married twenty-eight days short of fifty years when she passed.

Even though I lived outside Perry County during my married life, memories and friends brought my life back to Perry County. In 2017, I went to a Susquenita High School class reunion to see the Buddy Holly Story. Ted Frisch and his wife were seated across from me and I was next to an empty seat, when a lady came in and asked if she could sit there and I said "sure." I had no idea who she was. Remember, it had been fifty-five years since graduation. I looked at the name tag to fit a face with her name and it was Janet Colborn (Ellenberger).

After the show, which was enjoyable and people were dancing in the aisles, many started saying their goodbyes under the overhang outside waiting for the rain to slow down. Janet happened to come by, stopped, and offered to share her umbrella. I declined the offer and told her I had been wet before, but she said the umbrella would help keep my suit dry. We actually stood by my car in the rain for about an hour talking about our dogs, cars, my Mary, her husband Clark who had also passed on, school memories and Perry County things. It was like we had never left. Janet was the first lady I talked to in-depth about my wife.

The next day, I sent her flowers for taking the time to talk with me, but I never heard a word for four or five days. It seems she seldom uses her front door and that's where the flowers were delivered. I went to a Hershey Region Antique Automobile Club meeting that Saturday night and when I came home there was a message from Janet. I called her back and five years later, we are still talking. Thanks to our Perry County bonds!

"An Ideal Time To Grow Up In Newport"

Storyteller Sally Ann Myers
Recorded by Debra Kay Noye

"You walked down the street and talked to absolutely everybody!" Sally Ann Myers misses those days of knowing everybody in Newport. Born in 1947 to David Mingle and Elizabeth "Bettie" Myers, Sally knew all her neighbors, most of whom were elderly and would sit on their porches chatting, coming and going as she pleased. Sally started her life on the corner block of Walnut and North Second Street in Newport. She remains there today in the same locations her parents resided and owned the David M. Myers Funeral Home and David M. Myers Furniture Store. These days Sally is proud to help continue the legacy started with her Grandfather Myers prior to 1895, making it Newport's and one of Perry County's oldest businesses.

Sally spent her first nine years walking up the street to attend the Newport Elementary School. She had to wear a skirt and blouse or a dress everywhere. In the winter months, she wore pants under her clothes and had to go into the dreaded cloakroom and change before she could take her seat in the classroom. She went home to eat lunch until a cafeteria was established.

Then she went to and graduated from a boarding school in Washington, DC. It was in the fourth grade that the "country kids" were integrated from the scattered one-room schoolhouses into Newport Elementary. Newport High School housed grades ten through twelve. Sally remembers playing "kick the can", hop-scotch and jumping rope in Newport's allies especially where the drive-through banking for Orrstown Bank, now the Jacobs Building on Market Street existed. Sally and her friends rode their bikes all through town and out into the country unattended. Of course, there was a lot less traffic because few people still owned cars or trucks.

She loved roller skating through the streets with her friends, but she would often loose her key. In those days, the skates were attached to the bottom of her shoes using a strap and locked by a key. Her dad would send her to Mathna's Hardware Store, on the square where Bittings is today, to purchase a new key for five cents. That was a lot of money to most people back then. On the weekends during school and in the summer, she would go to friend's houses and play card games while drinking the newest rage "Diet Rite Soda" from glass bottles.

Her family was one of the first to own a television in Newport. It was very small with a round screen. The picture was black and white but difficult to view. Myers also had a private telephone line, but they still needed to ask the operator to connect them to whomever they wished to speak. Sally said, "you'd pick up the receiver and tell the switchboard operator you wanted to talk to Anna Mae." The operator would then ring the intended party. Myer's phone number was 38. Most home's phones were on the "party line" system and folks could listen in on all the conversations.

Despite being allowed to roam through Newport with her friends all day, Sally could always depend on her mother's home-cooked meals. Bettie used whole milk delivered by Hall's Dairy, from outside of Millerstown, and "real" butter from a local farm lady. Ralph Kline, a farmer from outside of Newport, sold her mother capons and she proceeded to use every bit of the birds. Sally says her mother made the best chicken pot pie. Her mother was the "model homemaker" who made sure the family had what they needed, while their father worked twenty-four-hour days, every day of the year. He was always on call to not only pick-up the deceased, but in the early days the hearse was also used as the town's ambulance, transporting people to Harrisburg area hospitals. Dave Myers would change the side-panels of the hearse depending on what business he was representing. Some might imagine that he got them coming and going! But it is interesting to note, that Sally's parents first date was interrupted by an ambulance call.

You also might have assumed that Sally must have eaten her meals at the famed Mingle House Hotel's dining room, which her family owned. The Mingle House Hotel sat on the corner of North Second Street and South Market Street, right on Newport's square. It was a stately structure housing a hotel, restaurant, bar, barbershop and shoe-shine stand. There were hand-painted murals on the walls; one depicting the long-gone Pennsylvania canals and the other the Clark's Ferry Bridge at Duncannon, painted by well-known local artist, Andy Loy. The bar boasted a hand-made, cherry-wood bar, which can still be seen inside Humble Stitch today. A very popular Newport bartender was Billy Cox, famed professional baseball player for the Brooklyn Dodgers Baseball Team.

The Mingle House Restaurant was the most popular eatery for Sunday dinners, drawing long lines of folks who traveled from all over the county and beyond. The dining room could seat sixty, which was soon filled once church services were over. Mrs. Baker was the head cook, who prepared turkey, roast beef, ham and chicken full-course dinners, just like Sally's mother did at home. Still very young, Sally did not help a lot in the restaurant, but she did bus tables. She remembers the noisy automatic, tubular-metal, potato-peeler with the rough grooved tops resembling sand-paper that along with a slow water flow took off most of the potato skins. The potatoes still had to have some hands-on attention. So, the mashed potatoes for those dinners were real and not like today's powdery instant. But Mingle House's piece de resistance, were the freshly baked, homemade pies that lined the counters of Mrs. Baker's domain. Sally did say she would once in a while go down to the restaurant kitchen in the evening and grab a hamburger to eat in the dining room. She would often chat with Mr. Whitekettle, who lived upstairs in an apartment. Her Aunt Carrie Myers, who worked at the 5 & 10, also lived in the Mingle House.

Another essential long-time employee was Paul Leonard, who helped out where ever he was needed. Not only did he perform the embalming in later years, Paul was the "go-to-guy" for all kinds of repairs in all of the businesses owned by the Myers family. Paul and his sidekick, Charles Murphy of Newport, could often be seen in the furniture and mattress store which also sold wallpaper, paints and carpeting. They would cut the amount of wallpaper people wished to buy and mix the paints. Back then, wallpaper was very popular and Myers bought it by the truckloads. You probably guessed Paul also transported bodies to the funeral home and helped with the burials. He and Murphy delivered furniture to homes and businesses using a panel truck.

Now even-though, Myers Furniture Store is huge, they still needed additional storage space. Myers Warehouse on Front Street is the oldest standing building in Newport today. It has hosted several churches, a garage for the telephone company, and storage space for furniture, wallpaper, caskets and supplies. Sally also points out that most of the red-brick homes in Newport were built by local masons, who helped to found the Newport's Lutheran Church, prior to 1895.

Floods affected the businesses twice, but Sally recalls 1972 when her parents had to be removed by boat from the first-story of their home. The Juniata River swept through their living room and the businesses. The water was over eight-feet high in the furniture store. Neighbors helped neighbors and townspeople rallied round. The furniture was moved to the second story of their home and business.

David Myers believed in promoting his businesses. He started to award each young lady, who graduated from West Perry, Greenwood and Newport High Schools, a keep-sake replica of a Lane Furniture cedar chest, which was American made. It was prized by the recipients, who when they opened the small chest immediately saw David Myers Furniture Store on the underside of the lid. Today, it is considered a Perry County artifact and collected by those preserving Perry County's history.

Just like most professions requiring licensing, funeral directors, especially embalmers, need to attend continuing education classes. The time came when a need to fill Dave's shoes arose, so Sally became a licensed undertaker in 1992 and took over the embalming duties. Her brother, Jack, is also licensed and the business was incorporated. Sally attended Mortuary School at Northampton Community College in Bethlehem, Pennsylvania, in the late 1980s. Her internship, so to speak, took place in Carlisle. Mark Foor, of Newport, performs the embalming duties for the Myers Funeral Home today. Now, it is Sally's turn to be available twenty-four-seven when that phone rings!

Sally recalls traveling all-over with her father, who especially loved to be invited to area homes when they butchered pigs. He enjoyed every aspect of butchering, especially eating cooked meats and organs from the kettles. Their employee and friend, Charlie Murphy, hosted a butchering every Thanksgiving Day. Sally also enjoyed those adventures.

Dave was known to walk about Newport with his pet "weiner" dogs in tow. His well-behaved dachshunds were the prettiest bronze-red color and they trotted along side his left heel on a leash.

Sally's family at one time owned the entire block of buildings starting at the alley where Sweet to the Soul is today to include the current Goodwill Store, on the street opposite their businesses on North Second Street. In Sally's time, the Goodwill Store was a J. J. Newberry's 5&10 Store and her Aunt Carrie became a manager. Next was the United States Post Office, which became a laundromat started by Dave Myers. The original Weis Store, Sears Roebuck Catalog Store, and auto parts store with the massive glass windows, rounded out the businesses. Apartments were above most of the businesses, but the Masonic Lodge occupied the second floor above J. J. Newberry's. Dave Myers, in the 1930s, bought "Hill Home" from his uncle and the family would "get-away" to their retreat with a beautiful view. Sally enjoyed using the tennis courts in her youth and misses those idyllic times.

Sally recalls what businesses lined the streets of Newport in the 1950s. On North Second Street heading toward the square from the Myers Furniture Store was Lesh's Music Store, Alan Wolfe's Law office now Anita Kemble C. P. A., Zuckermans's Department Store with apartments above, Mathna's Hardware Store formerly Smith's Hardware Store, Nickolet Restaurant and Mingle House Hotel.

Across the street from Myer's businesses was Millie Haines Beauty Shop, Newport Auto Parts Store, Weis Store, Post Office, 5&10 Store, Borst Jewelers, First National Bank of Newport, a produce store and Comp's Barber Shop were all in the same building as the Citizen's Bank of Newport.

Following South Second Street on the left from the square, Ferster's Meat Market, now the Perry County Council of the Arts Gallery, Rice's (lived on the property as well as operating their hardware store which had been moved from South Market Street), Jess Thomas' News Stand which sold comic books much to Sally's liking, Bob Myer's Deli now Sharar's, Shower's Appliance Store, (Prior to Myers and Showers, the Smith Candy Company owned the buildings where they produced handmade chocolates and candy for distribution throughout the county and beyond. They also opened an ice cream shop where Showers existed. They also operated a restaurant in back on Penn Avenue.). Herm Harry's Restaurant - prior the PP&L Headquarters, and Kell's Funeral Home, now home to Green Acres Realty, completed the block.

Following South Second Street from the square on the opposite side of the street was Aumon's Jewelry Store (formerly the A&P) which is now Espresso Yourself Cafe, Reisinger Furniture Store now Carpetbaggers, Town Tavern, Gower's Drugstore formerly Boserman's, Western Auto Store, and the Newport Movie Theatre where Archie Dudley collected the movie tickets.

Following Market Street North starting with Citizen's National Bank of Newport on the square, Dick Newlin's Barbershop, to the American Legion which sponsored patriotic parades that Sally marched in as a Girl Scout, ending with a private residence now housing Allen Hench and Adam Britcher's Law offices.

Following Market Street North starting with a beauty shop became Dick Newlin's Barbershop, Magee's Drugstore with a soda fountain, Gelnett Ford car dealer, Newport Borough Office (Newport's original Fire House), ending with the Moose, which had a bowling alley in the basement.

Following Market Street South was Kauffman's Store (prior was Rice's Hardware and then the PP&L Headquarters). Crossing over the street was a candy store and Lipsitt's Clothing Store.

Strolling through Newport's square today, Sally is reminded of the changes that have taken place. It is now thriving once again after a respite and Mingle House is still standing having become senior housing.

Her family legacy is still intact, as the future generations have stepped up to oversee various business operations alongside Sally and her brother, Jack. They, too, strive to follow in their grandfather's shoes, greeting every customer with a smile, helping hand and respect.

A Whirl-Wind Of A Perry County Historian

GROWING UP ON THE "ISLANDS" ACROSS FROM PERDIX AND IN DUNCANNON

Storyteller Harriet Berrier Magee
Recorded by Debra Kay Noye

Harriet Magee and "Perry County History" are synonymous, especially history of the Duncannon area where she has lived all her life. However, her historical knowledge also extends to the battle fields of Antietam and Gettysburg where she conducts speaking tours for the United States Park Service. Her feet do not stay in one place for long, because she is continually sharing her vast knowledge which goes way beyond historical facts and places.

Ironically Harriet Louise Berrier was born on October 15, 1937 in the Polyclinic Hospital. She was the first C-Section ever performed at the Polyclinic, where she would in later years graduate as a nurse and go on to teach in the nursing program's "emergency room", for eighteen years.

Her parents, Mary Gross (b. May, 24, 1905) and Theodore B. Berrier (b. August 7, 1905) were living in Duncannon and already raising two of Harriet's cousins, who were much older than Harriet. Cousin Betty Berrier, who was twelve years older, helped to raise Harriet.

Her cousin, John Berrier was twenty years older and garnered quite a reputation as a football player, while attending Duncannon High School, William Penn High School (Harrisburg) and graduating from Temple University in 1940. At Temple, he played for the legendary coach "Pop" Warner. In 1955, he returned to Harrisburg where he began the Harrisburg Area Community College.

When WW ll came about, he joined the Air Corps and ended up instructing cadets at the Wright-Patterson Air Force Base on the operations of B-29 and B-17 air craft and bombers. Harriet didn't get to know him till 1943. John married Grace Markley in 1943 and Johnny was born in 1945. After the war, the family lived in Duncannon with his aunt and uncle for two years. In 1955, he earned a Doctorate Degree in Education from Temple University. While at Temple, he was teaching biology, running the ROTC program, serving as the registrar of the university, as well as coaching the freshman football team. In 1958, when Temple brought their university programs to the Harrisburg Area Center for Higher Education, John was appointed the administrator. In 1963, he became Dean of Instruction for the newly formed Harrisburg

Area Community College. In 1966, he was chosen the first president of the Lehigh County Community College in Allentown, serving until his retirement in 1983.

Betty, in the meantime, married Wesley Cassel of Marysville and became a housewife. They had a son Teddy, and lived in the same home in which she was raised. He joined the military during WW ll and was one of the first infantrymen on Omaha Beach. He also saw action at the Battle of the Bulge and helped in the liberation of Norway in 1945. He was wounded four times.

Harriet's home, when she was growing up, was like a "revolving door", because of all the relatives who needed a place to live for periods of time. Her Uncle Joe Berrier's family were some of the residents. He worked at Olmsted Air Force Base in Middletown. when he was deployed to help with the clean-up of Pearl Harbor. He was a tool and die maker, who made an actual cannon for Harriet's dad. Harriet's mother would hide the gunpowder on New Year's Eve so it couldn't be fired, because it lifted three foot in the air and made all the neighborhood houses rattle from the blast.

Five generations lived at their house at 630 High Street, which was beside the Duncannon Dress Factory and behind the Standard Novelty Works on Market Street. Since Harriet was so used to being around adults, it was only natural that she ventured inside the Standard Novelty Works along side the workers. She would go in a side-door and greet the workmen. One of her favorite work areas was the paint vats where the metal sled runners were dipped in a metallic red paint. They were then hung up to dry.

Today when you are visiting the Sled Works, which is housed in the old unchanged Standard Novelty Works factory building, and you go through the front door, the original factory is immediately to your left. This is where the process started and parts were gathered. The paint and shellac vats were in the middle of the long building. The slippery, shiny floor is a dead-give-away, because of the abuse it received from the chemicals used. The shellac was a protective covering on all the wooden sled parts.

The well-used, long, wooden steps to the left, that extend up to the second story are the same today as they appeared back then. YIKES! Well-worn is an understatement. The workers would have to climb them everyday and carry the sled parts and other supplies up and down those death-defying stairs, which was like going through a narrow cattle chute – no extra room. The second story is where the stenciling was done on the wooden sled's slats. (Harriet was gifted a big #144 sled bearing her name, in 1946, which she cherishes. Ira Wolfe did the stenciling.) The guide bars were also assembled and screws were adapted to fit the different sized sleds, scooters, swings and gates. The scooters could be adapted for all kinds of weather. Some workmen wore white or cream colored bib-aprons, which were stained from the paints and grease, over their work clothes. They wore "clod-hoppers", as Harriet put it, on their feet. The process of making sleds was very labor intensive until they modernized, which still required a lot of hands-on attention.

The north end of the building was where the sleds and other products were assembled and ready for shipment onto railroad cars. The factory's whistle would sound at noon for lunch and again at 4 p.m. quitting time. Harriet's Great-Uncle Bob Belton, who lived at the end of the block, was once in charge of blowing the whistle. Robert Clark Belton blew the whistle when Harriet was young. Workmen who lived close by went home for a quick lunch. Others carried tin lunch pails with a leather strap and ate outside when the weather was warm.

Some workmen that Harriet recalls were "Pud" Campbell who lived in the house directly across the street where the tower now stands, Ira Wolfe, John Boyer, Leroy "Jukie" Boyer, Josh Quigley and Raymond Gusler. The Duncan family, who owned the Standard Novelty Works, provided a house for worker, Earl Gusler. Paul Stansfield became a foreman after Jake Weaver, who died in 1954. Weaver was the keeper of the worker's time sheets (Harriet felt the workmen were paid a fair wage) and shouldered a lot of other daily responsibilities. He was Harriet's adopted grandfather, (Harriet never knew any of her grandparents, since they died before she was born.) and he allowed her in the factory. The factory workers were like one big family and looked out for one another.

Harriet remembers riding along with Stiles Duncan to pick-up supplies and having to cross the Clarks Ferry Bridge. However, the Duncan's were shareholders in the Clarks Ferry Bridge and did not have to stop and pay the toll. Harriet thought she was "big stuff" then!

Duncans had a unique advertising sales flyer which they distributed throughout the county and in publications. It featured local youngsters, on their sleds, on the brochure. (Dorothy "Dot" Hamilton and Dick Swank). Hamilton was a teacher at Susquenita for many years and following her retirement became a pastor, and Swank who later owned The Duncannon Record, which would've printed their ads in his newspaper. The factory operated until 1990 when the last Lightning Guider Sleds were built. It was the end of another Duncannon business which provided the townspeople with ready employment. Every child born in Duncannon received a Lightning Guider sled from the company.

Harriet really liked the Duncan brothers, who were also involved in the People's Bank of Duncannon. Pat Duncan, the father, was the bank president when the bank examiners turned up some improprieties after a review of the books. Somebody was needed to take the blame, so Stewart spent nine months in the Federal Prison in Lewisburg, Pennsylvania. Stewart was such a good guy to take the fall as he was probably not involved with the difficulty at all. The bank continued to do business as usual for a short time.

Today, the Sled Works maintains an adjoining building, which is to the right when you enter the huge antique and craft store. That building was made suitable for display areas in 1999, after the roof had collapsed during a heavy snow storm and was totally rebuilt.

Granny Get Your Gun
Harriet's grandmother, Margaret Catherine (Rader) Berrier was quite the character, according to stories she was told. Hailing from the hills of West Virginia, she could handle herself very well and that included firearms. It was said, that if she showed up to any shooting competitions and picked up her gun, you'd best just put your gun back down. She was that good, but also a hard worker and a great sportswoman! Harriet's grandfather, Joseph "Big Joe" Berrier discovered Margaret when he was visiting in West Virginia. Big Joe and Dr, Kalbfus, the first Game Commissioner, traveled to West Virginia to study and learn about their conservation procedures. He married her in 1887 and brought her to Harrisburg, Pennsylvania, where they lived in the area where the "sunken garden" is today.

Joe Berrier came to know Dr. Joseph Kalbfus, who was the first Pennsylvania Game Commissioner. Through this association, Joe became the first Game Warden in Pennsylvania. They set out to eliminate "poaching" in Pennsylvania, which was a huge task. They would go into communities encouraging them not to poach. This did not always go as planned and their lives were threatened by poachers they had arrested. A newspaper account in 1910, shows the men escorting a poacher, who threatened them with a knife in Allegheny County. Joe carried a pearl-handled pistol and a 63 Springfield rifle when he was out and about.

When Joe would come across bear cubs or other baby animals left behind after poachers killed their parents, he would rescue and bring them to his home. His wife would care for and raise the baby animals. Once they had two bear cubs, which were free to roam the house and decided that the huge punch bowl was an ideal place to curl up and go to sleep. The Harrisburg Hardware Store would also help him out with keeping and caring for the animals. They took advantage of the babies displaying them in their massive front window, which drew folks from all over to their store.

Game Warden Joe Berrier was instrumental in bringing the first importation of white-tail deer to Pennsylvania. They arrived in New Germantown from Michigan. This resulted in the continual increase of the Pennsylvania deer herd.

In the early days of 1895, because the Pennsylvania State Capitol had burned, the state Game Commission's Headquarters were moved to one of the three islands, across from Perdix and the Cove. There they held meetings as needed. The inception of the Pennsylvania Game Commission occurred on the Islands.

Harriet's grandparents owned the three Islands surrounded by the Susquehanna River. They are located in the Cove and actually in Middle Paxton Township, Dauphin County. The Berrier's had a large two-story house with a wrap-around porch. There was a well, but the water was used for cleaning only. All drinking and cooking water had to be carried by flatboat to the Islands. There was an outdoor privy. The same situation exists today. It took a lot of work and planning to live on the Islands, but they were mostly used in the warmer months. Harriet says "the Islands were a big part of her life".

Harriet's grandmother started an apple orchard on the Island. She enjoyed Summer Rambo apples for making pies and apple sauce, so that is what she lovingly nurtured. She also planted large "truck patches" and would transport the vegetables by flatboat to shore where they were transferred to horse-drawn wagons to be sold at the Broad Street Market in Harrisburg. Her West Virginia family would come to visit and large family reunions were held there over the years. The Berriers still hold reunions on the Island, and Harriet is now known as the "matriarch" of the family, as she is now the oldest.

Over the years, her grandmother sold the lower Island and gifted the middle Island, while keeping the upper Island in the family. The 1936 flood destroyed anything standing on the Islands (her grandmother had died so she did see her Island destroyed). WW ll left nobody around to care for the Island. The Island's condition deteriorated and in 1947 went up for sheriff sale. Harriet's dad purchased the Island and eventually built a shanty with a porch in the early 1950s.

Her dad also offered the use of the Island to the Duncannon Boy Scouts, whose dedicated leader was W. L. "Drummy" Drumgold. They would go camping and help to keep the Island cleaned. They used the Island till Agnes came in 1972. The devastation again was earth moving, because the Island was washed away leaving only 27 ½ acres remaining. A big Exxon gas tank had become dislodged from Inglenook and had slammed into the Island, breaking off chunks of land.

When the family went to assess the damage, they discovered Indian artifacts (arrowheads, hatchets, spearheads, bowls, paint pots, etc,), which had become unearthed. It turns out the Islands were used as a burial ground by the Tuscarora Indians, whose headquarters was located at the mouth of the Juniata River. It was customary to bury personal items belonging to the deceased, which is why so many artifacts were uncovered in one location.

Harriet also remembers all the coal dirt that covered everything. The Susquehanna River at Marysville and Duncannon was once heavily dredged or dragged for coal. The locals referred to the barges that came up the river from Steelton, as the "Susquehanna Navy". It was not a good quality coal but there was a market for it. (Side note: When the railroad's steam engines were fueled by coal, wash-day was planned around the railroad's schedule. The women certainly did not want their laundry hanging out to dry when the trains would pass by spewing coal cinders and soot.) Harriet discovered her grandmother's tin of silverware buried in the mire of mud and coal.

The Berrier family incorporated the Island in 1983. Today the Magee's Island cottage sits on piers in hopes of avoiding high water. A pavilion exists for family reunions and retreats, but Harriet can no longer lug the boats and motors. She must depend on others for help.

Her grandmother remarried Frank McKee, after Joe's death,. They had a little store "McKee's Store" in the Cove, across the railroad tracks at Burley Crossing.

The Duncannon Dress Factory
Harriet's other "playground" had actually been a Duncannon park before the Duncannon Dress factory was built. The same family that owned the Standard Novelty Works had developed the Duncan Park which was used as a picnic area.

The Duncannon Dress Factory, built by Julius Shapiro, at the end of the Depression, was a long nondescript wooden building. In the summer months, the windows would be open due to lack of air conditioning. (Since they lived close-by, Harriet's mother would make iced tea in the summer time and Harriet would sell it to the women workers during their lunch break for five cents a glass.)

The building was "a buzz" all the time, once the switch was flipped to start the sewing machines and the large iron presses. Bud Shultz was the machinist who kept all the machinery running smoothly. It was not easy work as the house-dresses, which were the common wear of the day, were pieced together following a pattern and pressed before being packaged in brown wrapping paper resembling paper bags. The packages were kept together by jute roping. Sometimes burlap bags were used instead of paper bags. It depended on materials available during WW ll, which caused many shortages including cotton. Most of the dresses were made from cotton, but there were instances when buckram, which is a stiff fabric similar to livestock feedbags, was used to make dresses. The finished products were shipped on trucks from the Susan Street dock.

Harriet says that the women worked very hard and were generally paid by the piece. So the more they accomplished, their paychecks would be higher. One thing she did not like was the constant smell of textiles (die in the fabrics) throughout the entire building.

The Growing Up Years
As a youngster, Harriet received an allowance which was unusual in the 1940s-1950s, but her father worked

for the Anchor Fire Proofing Company based in Washington, DC. He was a mason and the superintendent of the jobs in which he was assigned. His work required him to travel through out the country. Much of his work was on military bases and building Veteran's Hospitals. Harriet and her mother would travel with him and stay in the area renting cottages or apartments, during the summer time. Twice, because of his work and the fact that Harriet had made some new friends, they stayed on for the school year.

She was exposed to many different places and people at an early age. She soon found out that bias and prejudice existed, when the air-raid sirens sounded for people to take shelter and her black friends could not shelter with her. The separations due to color confused her, but she soon learned.

Her dad was a hard worker, who also built houses in Duncannon and could actually build a three-story chimney on a house in a single day.

She attended Duncannon Schools and was a Brownie and Girl Scout. Harriet, even though she is not tall by any means, must have been fast on her feet. She loved playing basketball and scored one-thousand points during her high school basketball days. There were only five girls and five boys in her academic class at Duncannon High School. During these years, she also took piano lessons from Ida Zerfing Barton and performed in many recitals at the high school. If she decided to go get cooled off with friends, she headed to just off "the point in the Juniata River" where she would wade out till it was deep enough to swim.

Still she found time, during her high school years, to work in Mary Barringer's Gift Shop on the square in Duncannon. It was a great location because Route 11 ran through Duncannon and brought many travelers to her shop. Mary had worked in Hershey for twenty-two years, before opening her boutique. Harriet remembers all the expensive glassware such as Fenton and Imperial Glass. There were Hallmark cards, M-Kay candles, Playschool Toys, ladies lounge-wear, hats and gloves, which were the rage of the times in women's accessories.

She earned fifty cents an hour working Friday nights and all-day Saturday. Mary taught her how to wrap gifts and make pretty bows. Men would patronize the shop, especially during any holiday, because their purchases would always be wrapped for no additional charge.

When Harriet's mother would go shopping for clothes or shoes, she would patronize Snavely's Clothing and Shoes on the square. For groceries, because it was closest to their house, she would go to Rohrer's on High Street. Sometimes, she would call the store and tell John Rohrer what she needed. Then she would put the money into a basket and send their Chesapeake Bay Retriever down the street to fetch the groceries. There was never a problem because the system worked and the dog Pal was well trained.

The Berrier family attended the Duncannon United Brethren Church which was established in 1911. Then in 1947, the Evangelicals joined them to become the EUB denomination. In 1968, they became United Methodists. The church was on High Street next to Glass' Bakery. Harriet liked the location, because she could sneak through the side door and purchase some "½ moon cakes". Present day the church is known as Otterbein United Methodist, located on Route 849 outside of Duncannon. When the church was first built, it fell victim to an arsonist. The church recovered and the weekly attendance averages fifty to seventy-five, which is remarkable. The other Duncannon area churches are Presbyterian, Lutheran, Reformed formerly the UCC, and the Assembly of God.

The Magees are quite fond of two paintings that hang in Otterbein Church. Harriet's mother commissioned the Reverend Dr. C. Guy Stambach, a former pastor at Otterbein to paint "Christ at Gethsemane". He was self-taught and also painted "Christ Knocking at the Door", which he donated to the church.

Harriet was a member of the youth fellowship and was married to Charles Magee in the same church.

Harriet's father built the Catholic Church, Saint Bernadette, on High Street and Father William Keeler from Our Lady of Good Counsel, Marysville's Catholic Church, conducted mass. He was ordained a bishop in later years. When Harriet's father went ahead and laid the cornerstone, Father Keeler was upset because he had wanted to bless it prior to being put into place. Her father told him, it had been blessed many times already!

Nursing and Teaching Career
After graduating from Polyclinic School of Nursing, she enrolled in Lebanon Valley College to earn Bachelor of Science Degrees in Nursing and Biology. She continued her education at Temple University where she received a Masters Degree in Nursing as well as one in Science and Education. She then attained the position of Chairman of the Medical Sciences of the Polyclinic Hospital School of Nursing.

Later while teaching at the nursing school, she received an invitation from Dr. Silvernail, a neurosurgeon at the same hospital to fly with him and five other nurses to Vietnam to bring soldiers with head injuries back to the states for proper care. Dr. Silvernail was the flight surgeon in the Pacific at that time. It was truly an experience never forgotten.

Harriet continued teaching nursing sciences at Polyclinic for eighteen years. She was also chairman of the Sciences. During this time, she was their dedicated basketball coach. Her student nursing team participated in the "Snap League", which is properly known as the Student Nurses Association of Pennsylvania. There were twelve teams which participated in the league. So there was a lot of traveling involved. The team won two State Championships and four Eastern Championships. Her love for basketball also led to refereeing girl's basketball games, which she did till she was seventy-three years old.

Harriet's capabilities did not go unnoticed and Bill Smith, the principal at Susquenita recruited her to teach at the school. She had all the credentials and then some. She taught biology, chemistry, anatomy, physiology, microbiology and humanities. But what she enjoyed the most was teaching "the gifted" students at Susquenita for twenty-two years. To Harriet, it was a real and most rewarding experience. Of course, they took advantage of the fact that she was a nurse, so she served as the school nurse too.

Today Harriet keeps her continuing education up to date, so she can still teach nursing where-ever she is recruited. She also serves on various boards where evaluations are performed on medical facilities. Nursing and teaching are forever in her blood.

Snippets of Downtown Duncannon
Originally to travel through Duncannon from the east, you would be walking through a lovely park called the Meadow, named for Alta Noye who lived in the area. Then crossing the iron bridge, spanning over Little Juniata Creek past the Duncannon Fire House on Cumberland Street.

There was a flouring mill, owned by Walter Raub and Frank Steele, which sat across from today's James B. Zimmerman American Legion. The mill was torn down when the new highway was built in 1957.

All the stone arches around Duncannon were built from left-over stones from the building of the Rockville Bridge at Marysville. Back then little went to waste.

The building that originally housed Zerfing's Hardware Store was purchased by Mary Barringer for her boutique. Lee Snavely, who owned the store across the street, decided to build Karl Zerfing a larger building in the adjacent lot next to Snavely's Store, which he rented to Zerfing. Snavely's Clothing Store later became Balsbaugh's Clothing Store. Zerfing's Store became the Hi-Lo Store.

Sarah White, who was "stone deaf" but read lips, operated a small store on North High Street about a block from Newport Road. Despite her challenges, she ran her store and was a deacon in the Presbyterian Church. The store was brimming with everything needed to stock a kitchen for meal preparations. Harriet and friend Helen Freet, when they were six years old, would go to the store for ice cream, and for the "entertainment". Sarah had a parrot which sat upon her shoulders and loved chatting with people. There was one problem though. Polly learned some colorful sayings and shared them with out warning.

"Philly" Glass, one of Glass' Bakery owners, delivered their baked goods to Sarah White's Store. As he was stocking the shelves with "½ moon cakes", individual pies, bread, rolls and other sweets, he would prank poor Sarah, without her realizing what was happening. Hence, Polly's exclamations of "Sarie, go to hell Sarie", were squawked quite often.

Sarah employed a spinster, Mary Refine, who according to Harriet was a "little jewel". She ran the meat slicer, cutting luncheon meats and cheeses to order. When Sarah closed up shop, John Rohrer, owner of Rohrer's Store down the street, hired Mary to work in his store. Mary's father, Johnny, did caning in his later years and was quite good repairing and caning chairs, rockers and foot stools.

Mercy Sakes! There were five millinery stores existing in Duncannon at the same time, which rivaled the number of bar rooms. That's a lot of hats topping off ladies' heads. It was the style of the day to don a hat before venturing out and about, even to pop into the local store next door. And, the wrist length or elbow length gloves were necessary to complete the "look" ensemble. You were expected to be "prim and proper"! It's no wonder Harriet's mother had their dog trained to do her shopping for her!

Duncannon like so many of Perry County's towns was flourishing and self-sufficient. You didn't have to venture elsewhere to find what you needed. Plus, there was always the catalogs to order from as well. There was a jewelry store, music store and ice cream shop. On High Street, Kennedy's Store, (which became the Duncannon Record office,) carried everything. Cooper's Store, on High Street, (formerly Sheller's Store) was a full-service grocery store.

On Market Street, Harriet thought Trimmer's 5 & 10 was a glorious place to shop. It later became Murphy's 5 & 10 Store. Logan's General Store was located next to the 5 & 10 (later became the Western Auto). Reenie Steele had a Baby Shop with a lot of nice things for babies and toddlers.

Cumberland Street boasted a corner news-stand, since 1886 when newspapers were sold by Seig for four cents each and the customers shared them because Seig only received three copies of the newspaper a week. The store was an American Store for awhile, before Fred Lauster reopened a news-stand. The Kanon Theatre was behind Cooper's Store and that is where Charlie Magee, Harriet's husband, was the youngest person to earn their projectionist license. He worked there for three months. Shiffer Brother's of Newport fame also had an appliance store. Grace Thompson operated a flower shop and sold glassware.

Travelers through Duncannon found lodging at the Doyle Hotel and Laird's Hotel.

Laird's Hotel was owned by Clifford "Shorty" Laird and had large windows which are still found today on South Market Street's Dance Studio and Senior Center Annex. It was a rather plain looking structure and not ornate inside or out. There were three doorways to the hotel. The lower doorway led to the barbershop and other small businesses. The large middle door was for the lobby, where guests registered. To the right of the lobby was the dining room and bar. It was a popular spot for alcohol. The door towards the square was for a millinery shop. The doorways have been altered over the years, but the windows remain. Beside the hotel was a butcher shop.

The Doyle, on the square, offered lodging, dining and a bar. However, it was known as the Johnston House before Jim and Ruth Doyle acquired the hotel in 1945. Pat and Vicky Kelly were the owners until 2022, when Don Failor bought and is restoring the entire property. The copper ceilings now sparkle. The woodwork gleams and the new bar looks like a piece of art. Appalachian hikers can still rest up over-night and replenish their bodies in the dining room and bar.

The stores flourished until Valley Transportation arrived on the scene providing people the opportunity to hop aboard and travel to Harrisburg especially in the evenings and on the weekends. It was a big adventure to pay a few cents to take the bus to discover new things. And, the old wives tale of the grass is always greener on the other side, reared its ugly head and took a bite out of Duncannon's commerce. Cars were also more readily available and people had more money in their pockets to spend, but didn't stop to realize their neighborhood store's still needed their patronage. Harriet remembers those days and is encouraged by the new businesses and the promise of revitalizing downtown Duncannon.

For those who have the opportunity to meet Harriet Magee, soon understand how she rightfully earned the moniker "Mrs. Perry County History" from friends and lovers of Perry County history. Her mind is chock-full of facts and experiences that few people have realized in their lifetime. And, make sure you have your jogging shoes on and pay close attention, in order to keep up with this Perry County fire-ball.

Kids and copperheads

Storyteller Sabrina Nulton Gray

Snakes and kids. It is not a desirable mix but that is what my mom had to deal with on our farm in Pleasant Valley during our very early years. We lived on our Great-Grandfather Samuel Swartz's farm, back over the ridge from Elliottsburg. Our Great-Uncle Bill Swartz rented it to our parents, David and La Wanda (Foster) Nulton along with the five of us kids: Jeff (8 years old), Sabrina (5 years old), Gigi (4 years old), Dixie (2 years old) and Barb (1 year old). After Barb was born, the hospital nurse said to my dad, "See you next year, Mr. Nulton". He turned and replied with a straight face, "No you won't. We finally figured out what caused them!"

This was the innocent time of the 1950s and 1960s when kids played outside and not on tv or electronics. While playing outside our mother taught us very early not to touch any snakes, but to come alert her right away - which we did. There seemed to be an endless supply of them on our farm. (As an adult I realize that copperheads are the most common of the dangerous snakes in Pennsylvania.) Mom kept a sharp shovel by each door to use to kill them. She wielded them frequently. I can still recount the many times we encountered the venomous copperheads.

One day our cousin, Steve Reisinger, who lived just up the valley with his mom and brother, Alberta and John, came to play. Alberta's husband, John, died while Steve was an infant. Steve and John spent a lot of time at our grandmothers since Alberta was a registered nurse and needed that extra help as a single parent. I believe Steve and John would have come more often to our house if my mom wasn't so busy with the house chores and taking care of five small children already. That day, Steve and Jeff decided to gather worms in a jar for later fun fishing in our small creek.

When dad came home from his job, he was alarmed because they had collected baby copperheads in the jar! Dad was not too happy and had to do some more snake education because baby snakes are venomous also.

For those who don't know, all venomous snakes have eye pupils (the black part) that are a slit and not round shaped. Also, when you find the snakeskin, if there is a single row of scales on the belly leading to the anal plate, the snake is venomous.

I remember well when our palomino pony, Tony, got a copperhead bite on the muzzle which was swollen for days. Then there was our beagle, Queenie, who died when she was bitten. The only other time that one of us came close was when Jeff was walking through the woods to get something from our grandparents (Elizabeth and Jonah Nulton) on the next farm over and he stepped on one.

Looking back, my mom was my hero. She protected us with the "trusty" shovels and prayed an awful lot for our protection. How did she do it with little toddlers running around underfoot? Well, she grabbed the twenty-two rifle and shot the snake sunning itself on the woodshed roof!

Through those years we saw many snakes in the yard surrounding our house. We moved in August of 1965 at which time our great-uncle decided to remodel and sell the old farm house. While doing the renovations, he discovered a copperhead den in the wall of the house at the base of the chimney! No wonder we saw so many! He dealt with them once and for all by pouring cement down and filling it up. They were sealed forever.

We then all realized that God had his protective miraculous hand on the five young Nulton kids. He was not done with us yet. God's plan for us was to move to a farm about three miles from Newport (now known as Windy Hill Road). Our closest neighbors were the George Delancy and Luther Burd farms. They became great neighbors and friends.

When we first went to see the new dairy farm, we met Glenn Byers from Millerstown who showed us the property and invited us to his church called, "The Village Chapel" in Donnally Mills (located a block off of Route 17 in the heart of Donnally Mills). Eventually, we also came to know Glenn as our milkman who picked up the cooled milk in heavy metal cans to be taken to the Sunnydale milk plant in Elliottsburg. The Village Chapel, pastored by James Strawser, is where our spiritual life took hold. We made many new friends with the church members and our new farmer neighbors.

Lyons General Merchandise and Post Office

WILA, PENNSYLVANIA

Storyteller Tana Lyons Parrett

For forty years, from 1945 until 1985, the Lyons Store anchored "downtown" Wila. The first fifteen years the ownership sign on the porch read "D. W. Lyons, Gen'l Merchandise." Dean, my father, passed away in 1960. The day after his death, my mother, Elizabeth (Lib) opened the store at the usual hour. And over the course of the next twenty-five years, changed the ownership sign to read "E. H. Lyons, Gen'l Merchandise." She continued the general store services (pumping gas, slicing lunch meat, dipping ice cream, weighing nails and packing groceries). She sorted mail and sold stamps as the postal clerk, and gave generously to and received generously from a very special community of good-hearted and hard-working folks.

Not only was the Wila Store the center of Wila, it centered our (Alice Jean's, Tana's and George's) growing up years. Some of our best life lessons were learned by living next to and working in the store:

The customer is always right. (Even if they are not!)

For many years, the annual D. W. Lyons customer appreciation calendar included this promise: *Be quick to kick if things seem wrong, but kick to us and make it strong. To make things right is our delight if we are wrong and you are right.*

Keep your ears open and your mouth closed.

A good day of work is a good day.

Greet everyone with a smile.

When someone needs help, offer yours. Good customer service extends outside the door.

By age five, we were trained to wait on those very serious penny candy customers – often quite a time consuming 1 or 5 or 10-cent purchase – and to make correct change. That was a fun task! Oh, as we grew, there were some unfun tasks – unpacking and pricing the weekly grocery order and rotating (old in the front, new in the back) stock; sorting, stacking, and counting the soda (7-UP, Ma's, Coke, Pepsi) bottles and handing back the 2 cent/bottle deposit. (Golly, the dirt and flies a sticky summer soda bottle could attract!) And there was sniffing out the bag containing the rotten potato or onion, tossing the bad one and washing, repacking, re-weighing and re-pricing the good ones. But, living, working, and growing up at the store and in Wila was the best!

Tick, tock, tick, tock, tick, tock…a sound I will forever associate with the store and ice cream. An antique Gem razor pendulum clock came with the store when my parents purchased it from R. C. Myers. We kids could hear the ticking when we went to bed and when we awoke in the morning from our upstairs bedrooms over the store. Near closing time, we were especially attentive to the big hand! When it read, 8:30 we knew we could lock the doors and turn off the lights – day was done. (Thanks to the fix-anything abilities of friend and Wila neighbor, Les Smith, when the clock needed a cleaning and tune-up, he would come to the rescue. I still go to sleep and wake up to its tick, tock, tick, tock, tick, tock.)

The clock hung in the center of the store on a post above and was anchored by the Sealtest Ice Cream sign that advertised the four featured hand-dipped flavors. Vanilla and chocolate were standard – freezer, right side; seasonal fruits cycled through cherry vanilla, black raspberry, strawberry, and peach in the third "position" (top left in the freezer) and bottom left flavors rotated between butter pecan, butter almond, black walnut, and vanilla fudge. Single dip cones were 7 cents, two dips 15 cents and if folks wanted hand-dipped family sized portions, that was sold by weight, covered by a piece of wax paper and the customer hurried home! As soon as we were tall enough to reach into the freezer, we kids were allowed to dip our own cones. With practice, we became quite adept at balancing large dips on small cones. A standard parental warning was, "do not mine the fudge vein out of the vanilla fudge." Although mother was a wonderful baker and usually had homemade cakes, pies, or cookies available, an ice cream cone was the perfect second dessert. In summer, three cones a day was not unusual. The favorite ice cream cone of the day, however, was eaten in the summer after the store closed and while cooling down on the front porch swing.

Every season provided unique opportunities for the Wila kids to entertain themselves or to play together. The store was often the communication hub for "who was doing what when". Winter offered sledding down Fosselman's Hill complete with minor and major accidents. A cold snap query was often, "Is the dam safe for skating?" When miller, Luke Toomey, decreed the ice on the dam to measure 4 inches, ice skating season was officially open.

Even though Wila kids attended and graduated from Newport High School, we all claimed allegiance to and prided ourselves in our Wila Tech educational origins. As such, the Wila Tech hockey team could be distinguished by its specialized equipment – a wiffle ball wrapped in black electrical tape, hand-built goal cage frames and personalized hockey sticks made from scrap wood and decorated with an official magic marker Wila Tech logo. Competition was quite serious, if not stylish. On the not too cold winter days, pick-up basketball in the Fosselman barn was usually an option. It amazes me to this day, that we were allowed unlimited access to the barn without adult supervision.

Spring meant that softball season could begin. No matter your age, size, or skill level, you had a place on the team. Early in our softball training we were taught to pop fly the ball onto the schoolhouse roof between 2nd and 3rd base. By the time the ball rolled down the roof and back into play, the hitter could safely be on first! Many a Sunday afternoon was filled with a softball double header. Although the store was officially closed on Sundays, the end of softball games meant that the Lyons kids left the field quickly to run down and open the store for the players to enjoy sodas and ice cream during the post-game re-cap on the front store porch.

Summer's activities were limited only by our imaginations. No part of town or surroundings were off limits, bike rides and woods explorations could last for hours (just be home by supper). The creek was our swimming, boating, fishing, and frog hunting water park – no lifeguards and often no adults. On particularly hot and lazy afternoons, a gathering on the front store porch might find a gang of us chewing wads of gum searching for the elusive Billy Cox baseball card. Unofficially, a Wila census was taken multiple times during those "what do we do now afternoons?" If the members of each household and the family pets were included in the count, we could declare the Wila population, on that day (pets came and went) to be approaching 100!

When September rolled around, it was back to school. Wila's school bus stop was in front of the store. Every school morning kids of all ages and grades would gather on the porch or in the store to wait for the bus. If lunches needed extras, candy bars were purchased and if lunch money was forgotten, Lib would supply.

Although there were many food perks of living next to the store, our favorite perks were the people (vendors and customers) who frequented daily, weekly, or monthly and who shared their lives and their stories. Vendors and their wares were varied. I am quite sure each delivery person had a perfectly normal sounding name, but we identified most of them by their product. There was the meatman, the mailman, the milkman, the Pepsi, Coke or Ma's man, the Morton Salt man (who always wrote a message in salt on the parking area beside the store), the breadman, the fruit-man and the potato chip man. The only exception was Ralph Kline. He was the egg man. But, because he was both a family friend and a customer, he, like all customers, was addressed by his first or nickname.

For forty years, the Lyons family was surrounded and supported by a sharing and caring community of customers who were also our friends. If fresh parsley was needed to finish the pot pie, Edith Reisinger's patch was available. Webb Asper helped us patch our very high shingled roof. Every spring, Leo Casner tuned up the lawn mower. If "relief store tenders" were needed, Verna Asper or Helen Reisinger or Jean Smith were trained and willing. Neighbors helped with painting, wallpapering, and emergency transport. We enjoyed the generosity of folks who shared freshly baked bread and sticky buns, quarts of wild black raspberries, homemade ice cream, and sweet corn for eating and freezing. There was not a soul in Wila who could not be counted on or trusted to come to our or any neighbor's aid.

Like most things precious, appreciation dawns slowly. At the time, little did those of us raised in Wila recognize our good fortune. We do now!

Another Perry County Country Boy

Storyteller Leroy Earl Fleisher
Recorded by Debra Kay Noye

Off Route 849 between Wila and Markelsville, Leroy Earl Fleisher made his debut at home in 1934. His parents were Clarence Wesley (b. 1902) and Rhoda Esther (b. 1903) Fleisher. He was the fifth of seven; Donald, Paul, Lester, Luther, Helen and Reba. The local ladies did assist his mother, especially Gertie Arnold Neely.

His farmhouse had no conveniences, so the family used an outhouse and the Sears Roebuck catalog served a dual purpose. Leroy said his siblings, "worked the catalog over pretty good", before using it as toilet paper. He enjoyed looking at the BB guns and bicycles. The boys had to share a bicycle, so his older brothers and father kept it fixed and in top shape.

There was a reservoir behind the barn which was fed by a well. Leroy's father had a gas powered "hit 'n miss" engine attached to the well to pump the water into the reservoir. From there the water was piped to the house and barn. There was also a thirty-foot high steel (Aeromotor) windmill, which was allowed to run at the well, only when the weather was not too brisk. His father was afraid a high wind would knock it apart. They had faucets in the kitchen, but water was heated on the wood burning cookstove.

Leroy said the single-cylinder hit 'n miss engine was used in many ways around the farm. It had a tank for gas and one for water to help keep it cooled down as it labored at the sawmill and grinding feed for the cattle. It needed to be hand-cranked to start.

Besides the little hit 'n miss, Fleisher's had a 1931 McCormick Deering tractor, and Leroy now has a 1930 McCormick Deering tractor in his antique collection of farm equipment. The steel-wheeled tractor was started by using gasoline which was then switched to kerosene. It was used to do the yearly plowing of the crop fields and for the belt-power to run other machinery. The 1020 McCormack Deering tractor was belted to the ensilage cutter to grind up the corn which was blown into the forty-foot silo for silage for the cattle. Fleishers used horses and wagons to bring the hand-cut corn out of the fields to the silo. Before they had the belt-driven-hammer mill, H. P. Dyson Feeds would come to the farm and grind feed for the animals. Leroy recalls gas rationing during WW ll, but felt the farmer was able to purchase a bit more gas than normal to be able to run his machinery.

Ed Tressler, from Wila, would bring his tractor and threshing machine to the farm to harvest the wheat and oats. Leroy really liked threshing days because his mother and the other farm women with their daughters, would all work together and would "cook the best meals" for the workmen. There would be platters of home-cured ham, roast beef, plus chicken and waffles with mashed potatoes and many side dishes. Homemade pies finished the meals. The men who generally helped during threshing were neighbors John Campbell and grandson John "Skunky" and Glenn "Shorty" Campbell, Alvin Fosselman, cousin George Fleisher who lived two farms from Leroy, and Roy "Tucker" Reeder.

Now Tucker had moved to Markelsville from Andersonburg to take up farming and he bought a new round hay baler which produced very small round bales. According to Leroy when it came time to make hay at Tucker's, he was obstinate and did not use his head. Tucker started to stack the round bales on top of each other when the wagon was not level. The bales started to roll to the other end of the wagon. The bales had to be loaded in layers. The wagon was then pulled to the barn by horses.

A horse was hitched to the rope which was through a series of pulleys in the barn and to the four-prong hay fork. Tucker stuck the hay fork into some of the bales, so when the horse pulled onto the rope the bales were lifted into the mow. Unfortunately, there were too many bales making a very heavy load and a rafter the pulley was attached to tore loose and moved to the next rafter. That in turn gave slack in the rope the horse was pulling. The horse, which Leroy was leading, fell on its nose. The helpers ended up tossing the bales off the wagon into the mows by hand! Leroy also commented on Tucker's unwillingness to partake of the fresh spring water, Leroy carried in a molasses bucket to the threshers in the fields. Tucker remarked he'd never drink after all those tobacco chewers!

But at Fleishers, they used their work-horses, Maude, Nell, Goldie and Dolly, to pull the wagons through the fields to bring in the loose hay to the hay mows. (They did not ride the horses, other than to or from the fields.) A dump rake was used on steep hillsides for gathering the hay into piles, which were then hand tossed onto the wagons. Otherwise, the hay was raked into rows by side-delivery rakes to be loaded onto the wagon with the hay loader hitched behind the wagon. It was Leroy's chore as a kid to guide the horses as they pulled the hay-fork loaded with hay into the mows.

Fleisher's ten cows were hand-milked into a bucket, which was carried one-hundred yards to the milk house where it was strained into metal milk cans. The heavy cans were put into a concrete trough of cold water. The milk was picked-up by Wilt's Dairy of Newport and later on Harrisburg Dairies. Elmer Gutshall was a driver for Karl Kennedy, from Green Park, who hauled the milk to Harrisburg Dairies. Once in a while, Leroy would ride along with them and get some free ice cream.

Leroy's mother used the raw fresh milk in her cooking and would skim the heavy cream from the top of the milk cans to make homemade ice cream. His father would get ice from Newport Ice Company, which was also used in their ice box.

Besides dairy cows, they raised a dozen or more beef cattle, pigs and chickens.

Once it became cold enough after Thanksgiving, Fleishers would butcher two or three hogs. The hogs were scalded and scraped in barrels and later Fleishers used a trough which was much easier because they could move the hogs around better. Leroy liked "butchering day", because there was lots of good things to eat. He enjoyed the cooked head-meat and various organs straight from the simmering kettles. His dad cured the hams, shoulders and bacon in a barrel of salt-water for four to six weeks, before smoking them. He would generally allow them to hang in the smokehouse till they were used. Leroy commented, "they were really salty!" For their evening meal on butchering day, they had fresh sausage. His mother would clean the intestines for rope sausage and the stomach for a special meal.

Beef cattle were also butchered on the farm and his family made their own dried beef. Because they did not have freezers, the wrapped beef portions were taken to the Newport Ice Plant, owned by Stewart Gibbs, and stored in their large rented freezer lockers.

Generally, Fleishers would order three-hundred peeps and raise them in the brooder-house, till they were old enough to lay eggs. The hens were fed ground oyster shells for better egg shell production. Leroy's mother was in charge of cleaning, grading and packaging the eggs to be sold. They would either eat the old laying hens or sell them. They made lots of kettles full of chicken corn soup.

As most farm families, Fleishers planted a large garden and his mother canned the produce. The canned goods were kept in the cold-cellar which had a dirt floor. This was where the potato bin was also kept. Leroy wasn't fond of having to sprout the potatoes several times throughout the winter and spring. The potatoes would start to grow sprouts and they needed to be removed by hand or the potato would shrivel and not be worth eating. He also disdained pulling weeds and picking the potato-bugs off the potato plants. His family also dusted the plants with lime to keep down the bug population.

Leroy's mother also maintained a flower garden and beds around the farm. She would plant various herbs which she used in poultices when someone caught a cold. Her herbal teas were also used to soothe a sore throat. It was rare that Doctor Bartho from Market Street between Second and Third Streets in Newport would make a house-call, bringing along his little black-bag from which he would produce packets and bottles of pills. They generally would see him in his office if someone was very ill. The Rawleigh Company representative also came around to the house selling spices which his mother incorporated in her special home-cures.

Fleishers had apple trees and would take of the apples to Clarence Smith's Lumber and Cider Mill on the corner of Route 849 and Fourth Streets in Newport, to have them pressed into cider. The cider was used along with peeled and cubed apples to make homemade apple butter. Once the apple butter was thick enough, it was ladled into gallon stoneware crocks and kept in the attic, where it was cold and dry so mold would not develop. But since Leroy and his brothers liked apple butter so much on their mother's homemade bread made from H. R. Wentzel Sons milled flour of Newport, there was never a chance of that happening. They would fight over who was going to clean-out what small amount was left in the crocks. Maybe this memory is one of the reasons why Leroy volunteers to stir the apple butter kettles when The Perry Historians have their fall fundraisers and demonstrate the art of apple butter making! Then again, he also gets to sample each kettle of the all-natural apple goodness.

Like most farm boys, Leroy liked to hunt rabbits, squirrels, ring-neck pheasants and grouse. He recalls his reaction the first time he shot his Uncle Harry Fleisher's 12 gauge shot-gun at the age of ten. It nearly floored him as he shot up in the air at the moving squirrel. He started hunting deer around the same age with all the local farmers who would put on a "drive" moving the deer into better shooting positions. All the venison was used by the families.

The deer hides were sold, as well as the beef hides from butchering. Leroy and brother, Lester would also trap in the Big Buffalo Creek which separated the two farms his father owned, totaling one-hundred-twenty acres. He rented out the other farmhouse. They mainly caught skunks, opossums and raccoon. He would skin out the animals, stretch the hides on board and wire stretchers till they were dry. Then he sold them locally.

To get cooled off in the summer time, Leroy would head to the creek, but in the winter he stayed in the kitchen. The wood-fired cookstove was the main source of heat. His mother would keep the doors closed to the rest of house to keep the heat in the kitchen area. There was a stove in the dining room too, but no heat upstairs. It was one of Leroy's chores to keep the wood-box in the kitchen filled. He says it was "a big job to cut enough of their own trees to have wood for the winter". They made sure their woodshed was well stocked, because cutting wood during the harsh snowy winters was not much fun. When Leroy would be out helping to cut wood, he would keep an eye out for wild teaberry.

In the winter, Leroy preferred to go ice skating on the Wila Dam by the Toomey Mill or the Markelsville Dam. Sometimes this was with his youth group from Wila EUB Church. He was once scared to death when some of the kids decided to drive a car onto the ice and proceeded to push it around. Leroy was afraid it would break through the ice and somebody would get hurt!

Luckily in the winter, he had snow pants to wear and buckle-style boots for over his shoes to help keep him warm. Otherwise he wore hand-me-downs or his family went to Zuckerman's or Lipsitt's Clothing Stores in Newport for clothing and shoes.

Shops in Newport were the destination on Saturday nights. Leroy would dress in his best navy peacoat with the insignia on the arms and his knickers to walk about the streets of Newport. His family would patronize Magee's Cut-Rate near the Mingle House Hotel, the American Store, the A&P Store where Leroy loved the smell of freshly ground coffee, and the Weis Store. If there was a suitable children's film playing at the Newport Theatre, they would take in a movie. His parents would go visit Olive and Ralph Moretz on Fourth Street, across from Guy Kepner's Farm Equipment. (His family generally patronized Frank Keller the International Farm dealer in New Bloomfield. Harry Keller, who took over the business was Frank's son.) Visiting was a normal past-time, even though Fleishers had a crank-type wall-phone. However, the phones were normally used for emergencies or to conduct business. They would listen for the two long and two short rings to know the call was for them and not another person on the party-line.

The Fleisher children couldn't wait to get home in their dad's 1938 Dodge car, because they knew he had gone into Gerald Bucher's Store between the now Jacob's Insurance Building and Comp's Barbershop, to purchase pints of ice cream. Once home, he cut the pints in half and the family shared them. Leroy drove a 1950 Dodge car once he got his driver's license.

Fleishers also patronized Flickinger's General Store in Markelsville, which Leroy called a "mini Walmart". The difference he points out is that everything was made in the United States in the 1930s-1940s. Part of the store was the local Post office.

The soda cooler was filled with ice to keep the bottles cold and the penny candy was held behind a domed glass display case. The floor was adorned with spittoons for the local farmers to loaf on the benches and "chew the fat", as Leroy put it. Another favorite store, after a Sunday game of baseball in Wila was Lyon's in the center of town. Leroy loved the Doughboy Soda which was bottled In Duncannon during WW ll. He claims it tasted similar to today's Coke.

His mother had him dress in knickers to attend church when he was little. His Sunday School teacher as a youth was Mrs. Allen Baker. Luke Toomey was his Sunday School teacher when he was in high school. Leroy would always learn Bible verses and special presentations to be recited on Children's Day and Christmas.

Fleishers would go out and cut down a Christmas tree off their property and adorn it with a mix of store-bought and homemade decorations. Every Christmas, Leroy's dad would get oranges, grapefruits and tangerines from the Orange cart in Harrisburg. It was a traditional treat! Leroy always got a special gift of his own and fondly remembers with a smile, the 32 Winchester Special Rifle he received one year.

For seven years, Leroy walked a mile to the Center School at the intersection of Center School Road and Walker Road, regardless of the weather. He would walk up the hill and sled down until he broke through the snow in the winter. There was a deep ravine up from the school and the students would dig tunnels through the high drifts during recess. They made sure they were vented, because it was their "smoke house". Students would bring pipe tobacco and paper to roll their own smokes. And, if they ran out of tobacco, they smoked the shavings from the pencil sharpener! Leroy comments there were a lot of pencils sharpened back then. The school would issue each student a tablet and pencils. Graffius Sheaffer from Markelsville, their teacher, happened to notice the smoke wafting from the tunnels one day, which put an end to their adventures.

These were also the years when a "snow day" was unheard of. Leroy recalls once he and Harry Rice were the only two students to show up for class, which was very unusual. They would've gotten a lot of special attention that day, but rarely did the students have home-work.

The one-room school had a wood stove in the center of the room. The teacher sat on a raised platform at the front of the eight-grade classroom. An organ, which Leroy said was never played also sat on the platform. The fifteen students packed their lunches of sandwiches, fruit and cake or cookies. If they needed a drink they walked to the gray crock with blue stripes and turned on the spigot for a cup of water. Students would take turns walking to the nearest farm for water to fill the crock. Of course, they used an outhouse.

The students played ball at recess in the warmer months and sometimes would walk to Oak Hall School north of Wila or to Markelsville for a scrimmage. The country schools were let out for the year before the "town kids". There was always a celebratory "weenie roast", (hot dogs) the last day of school.

Center School was closed and Leroy spent eighth grade at Wila School. Leroy played Newport High School football for four years. There were no activity buses, so Leroy walked the five miles home. Sometimes some local men, Raymond Stuckey, "Bee" Rice, Homer Wright, Charlie Dollier and Raymond Wright would haul the country boys home.

While attending Wila School for eighth grade, Leroy had the honor of participating in a "Wila Turkey Drive" for the Lawrence Fosselman Turkey Ranch. The drive consisted of going to a field where the turkeys were housed in shelters. The location was west of Three Square Hollow woodland on the former Smith place, now belonging to Edward and Bonnie Trout. Other boys in the school helped to drive turkeys east through the Three Square Hollow woods, through the fields towards Wila, then across the bridge, now the Luke Toomey Bridge on Route 849. Leroy remembers there were folks out watching as they proceeded through Wila on Route 849, past Wila's Lyons Store. Now every time Leroy sees the John Wayne movie "The Cowboys", it brings back memories of his turkey drive. At the end of the movie when the cowboys are driving the cattle through Belle Fourche it beings back the great 1946 "Wila Turkey Ranch Drive" to Leroy. What a memory for Leroy.

After graduation, Leroy worked at Snap-On Tools in Newport for six months, but he didn't like the confinement of working indoors. He was a file cutter working on pliers. He decided to sign on as a heavy equipment operator for a Harrisburg contractor. During this time, he married Lois Sheaffer (b. 1934), from Newport, and they set up housekeeping in one of his father's farmhouses. They had Roger Douglas, Randy Scott and Dana Fleisher (Siren), plus five grandchildren, six great-grandchildren and four step-great-grandchildren.

His experience and work ethic secured him a job operating heavy equipment for PP&l in 1962. The rest is history, because he spent thirty-two years with PP&L, and even served as an instructor for others to learn how to drive trucks and operate the equipment. At one point in his career, he was the line-pole digger and helped to set a lot of poles for electricity in Perry County. After an early retirement, he helped out his son, owner of Roger Fleisher's Excavating, part-time operating heavy equipment for seven years. These days, he volunteers with The Perry Historians and his church, Incarnation UCC of Newport in making candy Easter eggs as a fundraiser. A far stretch from the farm days!

Hunting And Other Memories

Storyteller Bob Nace

I was born in 1950, the youngest of four children born in three and one-half years to Frank and Maryellen (Rice) Nace of Stony Point, between Kistler and Blain. My Dad had returned from serving in WW II and didn't waste any time after he returned home! My other siblings were sisters. From a very young age, I was interested in the outdoors, animals and all outdoor activities.

My maternal grandparents, Bill and Corinne Rice and maternal uncle and aunt, Dale and Edna Rice lived near us and were involved in our family activities. My Uncle Dale and Aunt Edna lived beside us on the farm that had been my grandparents. I also had a maternal great-uncle and aunt, Leo and Helen Rice that lived nearby on another farm that our family was close to. We had lots of family interaction and fun memories.

My dad bought us a pony from a pony farm in Juniata County when we were young. I was probably six or seven at the time. His name was Buddy but we also called him Bud. He was a "sound" little pony that didn't spook easily. My sisters would always have our dad put a saddle on him to ride but he didn't like that at all. I always rode him bareback. My favorite places to ride were the fields around our house and on the logging trails up into the mountain. We would also hitch Buddy up to a two-wheel cart and go visit our grandparents and our Uncle Leo and Aunt Helen Rice.

My Dad worked at the Sunnydale Milk Plant in Elliottsburg. Sometimes he took me along to work with him, which was interesting, especially when he had to climb into the huge milk tanks to clean them. My best times with him though were roaming the nearby fields, ridges and Conococheague Mountain looking for wildlife. My Dad showed me how to safely use a firearm and the importance of that safety.

My first hunting experiences were with a single shot 22 that I used to shoot squirrels and rabbits. I also used a 410 shotgun. My Dad always had good hunting dogs too that would sometimes accompany us. He had everything from fox hounds to bird dogs to beagles and terriers. I greatly enjoyed hunting small game with our beagles and loved hearing their voices as they ran the animals. There were many times I didn't even shoot the rabbits. I just enjoyed the chase.

My very favorite dog though was Queenie, a fox hound. I was devastated when dad sold her to a neighbor in Liberty Valley. I was quite young at the time. One day I was in our yard and heard her barking. I looked up toward the mountain and there she was, coming toward our house! I was so excited to see her! The man who bought her had been hunting with her and she found her way back to our house! Of course, I couldn't keep her but it was so great to see and hug her once again!

My Mother always told me I had to clean anything that I shot or caught fishing (another thing I loved doing), so from an early age I learned how to do that so nothing went to waste. I taught the same thing to my two sons when they started hunting.

The first deer rifle I owned was a Remington 308 760 pump that I bought from Frank Smith in Blain. I remember asking him what kind of gun I needed to hunt deer and he said that gun was all I would need. Boy was he right! I paid $110 for that gun and also got an extra clip and two boxes of shells. I still have that gun fifty-five years later! My second gun purchase was a Model 12 Winchester Pump 16-gauge shotgun. I paid $30 to Harry Robinson at his store (Robinson's Store) in Loysville for it. I still own that one too! Over the years, I have also purchased other great firearms as well as bows. I started out with a stick bow, then several compounds, many bought from Bruce Markel in Loysville and finally a crossbow. Many fishing poles and equipment too!!! Love the outdoors!

I hunted a lot on my Uncle Dale's farm as well as on my Uncle Leo's farm. I shot my first deer in the briary meadow (that's what they called it) on my Uncle Dale's farm. My mom's friend Earl saw me from their house dragging the deer and called my mom. He said, "Mary, you're going to be eating venison tonight! I see him dragging one!!" Earl (we called him Doc) and Linda Hess were my parents very best friends. They would play cards and other games and we always had such great fun with them. One time we were going to Lewistown shopping in our small Renault. My dad was driving and Doc was in the front with him. My mom, Linda and I were in the back seat. We were slowly going up the Ickesburg Mountain and Doc turned around and said to Linda, "old lady, you'd better get out and push this thing!" They were great people but he died way too young.

We moved to Kistler in 1962. The house was much larger but was a change from living in Stony Point, away from the main road. Here the house was very close to the road and the closest neighbors were not our relatives. The plus was there was a grocery store within walking distance and an Atlantic gas station with a restaurant owned by Bob Wagner. Eventually my parents would buy that grocery store plus the gas station and restaurant. The gas station was eliminated and the whole building turned into a restaurant. There were many other owners of that restaurant after my parents and today it is a residence.

We came to be good friends with our neighbors and I eventually started working part-time for Clair and Clyde McMillen on their neighboring farm when I was fourteen. My mom told me I needed to get a job and earn money to buy my own clothes. I continued to work for them until I graduated from the West Perry High School in 1969.

I have been hunting for over sixty years and have hunted with some great friends who shared many memorable experiences. Just to mention a few were my dad, Charlie Reisinger, Carl (Punk) Middaugh, Wayne Sheaffer, Percy Harris, Rob Keck, Loy and Sally Nesbit, Marlin Fisher, my two sons Heath and Derrick and some of their hunting buddies. They have all helped me make those great memories that I will never forget. Some very exciting times, frustrating times and hilarious times! Sometimes hunting local, in other counties and sometimes out of state but all memorable and great stories to remember and tell about.

My very favorites are when my boys started hunting and got their first deer and turkeys. We hunted deer and turkey with rifles and bows, which were fun and relaxing times. We used to drive for buck on the north and south side of the Knob Mountain. When we hunted bear in Clearfield County and my boys drove him out to me through the thick laurel.

We hunted in New York's Allegany State Park different years with many different hunters and were always successful. The boys and I hunted in Illinois and I saw the largest ten-point buck ever in my hunting career. He was massive but wouldn't come closer than fifty-five yards. I waited him out for over twenty minutes and he just kept standing there. It was the hardest thing I ever did, but I did not feel I could make a clear shot, so I left him go. I've never seen another like him!

Heath and I went spring gobbler hunting and had an old gobbler going for two hours. We moved on him four times until an old hen came and brought him along. I was fifteen yards behind Heath and when he shot, I could see the leaves raise up six inches from the ground from the muzzle blast. He shot the gobbler.

We hunted in Ohio and one year Derrick shot an amazing ten-point buck. The look on his face was priceless. He hunted hard to take that buck. We have been very fortunate over the years in our hunting ventures and I wouldn't trade them for anything. I love my family and give thanks to my boys for all the great memories of hunting with them.

All my hunting mounts have special stories to them and hold special meaning in my heart. They will one day be passed to my boys; from the last turkey I shot hunting with my dad, the deer mount done by a local young man in Honey Grove who passed away from a fire only a few years later, the bear I was able to shoot because of the boys dogging him for me, and my largest buck ever shot on the very last day of a hunt in Ohio with my boys and their friend Justin Shull. They are all so very special plus the ones I didn't even mention!

My saddest hunting story ever. It was the first day of deer rifle season. It started out like a normal first day where I got up at 4:00 a.m. and headed for the top of the Conococheague Mountain where I had hunted for more than fifteen years. I was on the south brow of the mountain on a big flat rock with cover all around me. I liked to watch Blain and all the vehicles heading towards Blain on Route 274 and on Route 17 West from the Ickesburg area. I got to my big flat rock around 5:45 a.m. which gave me plenty of time before daylight to reminisce about the successes I had on that mountain.

While I was sitting there a shot rang out at 6:05 a.m. I remember looking at my watch because it was too early to be shooting at a deer. I thought to myself it was just someone whose gun went off while being loaded. About ten to fifteen minutes later, I looked toward Blain and saw, then heard the Blain Ambulance go out of Blain and head down Route 274 toward Loysville. When I got home later that day, I found out that my good friend, David Emlet had been shot by a careless hunter. I was very saddened and shocked to hear the news. I still think of David on opening day each year and the carelessness that took his young life. Many thoughts and prayers go out to his friends and family that were lucky to know him and the great person he was.

Other special times are more recent, when I hunted with my granddaughter Chelsea and her dad Heath in the same area. This past year, she shot a beautiful eight-point but I wasn't hunting with them. Her time had been limited due to attending college to obtain her Physician's Assistant degree. Sydne, my son Derrick's daughter is ten and has already bagged herself two nice bucks in her two seasons of mentor hunting with a crossbow. Brycen, her brother who is seven, hasn't quite figured out yet if hunting is his thing or not!

I dedicate these memories to my wonderful sons, Heath and Derrick Nace and to my beautiful grandchildren, Chelsea, Sydne and Brycen Nace. God Bless You All with Much Love.

Carl Johnson's Memoirs From The 1940s-1950s

"GROWING UP IN HUNTER'S VALLEY"
Recorded by Paula Johnson Davis

Hunting and Hiking

As a kid all I wanted to do was to be outside hunting or fishing. I started hunting rabbits at the age of nine with a 410 Single Shot Stevens shotgun. There were lots of rabbits, grouse and ring-necked pheasants on our farm that I started hunting as soon as the weather cooled in the fall. I shot my first deer when I was twelve years old, a 6 point on Buffalo Mountain, two miles south of home with an old 32-40 Winchester. I was barely big enough to hold the gun.

In the summer, I was always hiking and hunting groundhogs. There were plenty of them around. Our neighbor, Evan Hebel would pay me fifty cents for every groundhog I shot on his property, because they dug large holes in the fields which he would hit with the front wheels of his John Deere B tractor. Some days I would just climb to the top of the mountain, walk out along the top and see how close I could get to deer or other animals without them seeing me. We also had a few black bears in the mountains at that time.

The area where we lived was a V shaped valley (Hunters Valley) about four miles long with the Susquehanna River at the east end and two mountains as the sides coming to a point at the west end. At the east end of the valley was Crow's Ferry. A ferryboat hauling people and cars crossed the river east to the town of Millersburg. The ferry landed and docked near Liverpool on a beach where we went swimming.

A few hundred feet from the ferry landing was a field once the site of an Indian village where they camped, fished and hunted till the early 1700s. John Witmer owned and farmed the field. Often after he plowed the field, I would hunt for Indian artifacts. I found many arrowheads and spear points. After it rained, I would go searching, because the rain washed the soil away. I didn't think anybody else knew about the buried treasure trove of artifacts. I found it by accident and never told anyone. Then about 2005, I saw on the internet that a college found the spot and was doing an archaeological dig. They said it dated back to 10,000 years ago. I didn't do any digging, just found the ones on the surface.

Farm Hand Experiences
From the age of nine, I began to work for our neighbor, Evan Hebel, helping with the milking of about twenty-five dairy cows. I would help him make hay. He didn't have a baler so we pulled a hay loader behind an old wagon. We loaded the loose hay and hauled it to the barn to be unloaded by hand. That was the slow hard way, but we got it done!

Before 1950, a threshing machine would travel farm to farm. I also helped harvest the barley and wheat. We cut it with a binder, stacked it in the field and later hauled it to the barn. Then Jim Shutt, from nearby Bucks Valley, would come with his steam tractor and threshing machine to remove the grain from the straw. The engine burned wood that heated water to make the steam. One man operated the steam engine. One man pitched the bundles of grain onto the track which fed the machine. One man stood on top of the threshing machine and turned the blower chute directing where the straw was blown, sometimes into the barn's straw mow. The excess was blown into a pile, usually in the barnyard. It was a dusty job and usually done in the hottest part of the summer.

Another man, the bagger, stood by the grain chute. He'd fill burlap bags with grain, closing the chute to tie the bag. Grabbing another bag, the process was repeated until all the grain was threshed. Another man was standing by with a horse and wagon onto which were loaded the sacks of grain to be hauled to the granary and emptied in to grain bins. The grain in the bins had to be stirred daily to keep it from over heating. No matter how fast they worked the bagger was always knee deep in grain.

At noon the workers would break for lunch. The wives always had a large lunch fixed for them. Lots of fried chicken, ham, mashed potatoes, pies, cakes and homemade ice cream. The threshing went smoothly as everyone knew his job. All the men wore handkerchiefs around their necks to keep the chaff and dust out. It was an itchy job. Sometimes it took all day to do the threshing. I remember it well! After 1950, we had hay balers and combines that came by to do our baling and threshing.

After the first fall frost, we would pick about twenty acres of corn by hand. We would go down each row picking the corn and throwing it into a wagon pulled by a John Deere B Tractor with steel wheels and cleats. The wagon had steel tires with wooden spokes that had to be soaked in water to make the wood swell up so the steel tires wouldn't fall off. My hands would get so sore from all the picking. When the wagon was full, we took it to the corn crib and used a scoop-shovel shoveling the corn in to the crib. I could hardly hold a pencil in school after a day of picking corn. Later we would run it through a corn sheller, then mix it with wheat and barley grinding it into cow feed.

(My parents sold our farm when I was seven or eight years old and bought a house on Cherry Road, which is now the Hunters Valley Sportsmen's Club.) My farming experiences, in my teens, were on the Evan Hebel farm and with other area farmers, who taught me what farming was all about...hard work and perseverance.

Memories Of My Home In Old Ferry, Perry County

Storyteller Wendy Jo (Wise) Campbell

There are many memories of days gone by that hold a special place in my heart. While pondering what I would write about, I thought I would be remiss if I did not mention Mt. Olivet Church of the Brethren on Turkey Bird Road outside of Newport. That little church on the hill is how my family came to call Perry County home.

Back in the early 1900s, William H. Miller became the first minister of Mt. Olivet. He was very instrumental in the construction and establishment of Mt. Olivet. His daughter, Ada, would become the wife of Walter Brandt, son of Jay Brandt. The Jay Brandt family also played a big part and contributed many hours of manual labor to the church. Walter and Ada eventually settled in Old Ferry where they operated a greenhouse. Walter also had an ice truck delivering ice to local families (the days before refrigerators). Walter and Ada were my grandparents.

Walter and Ada had seven children. Two of their daughters passed away during childhood. My mother, Martha, was the only daughter who lived to adulthood, along with her four brothers. All of them, except one, remained in the county and raised their families here.

My mother would talk about walking to their one-room schoolhouse (Ferrell's School), no doubt in six feet of snow in the winter and uphill both ways! She would carry mustard and onion sandwiches sometimes for lunch. Her brothers would often take a shotgun in case they would encounter some small game on their way home. She said they would simply prop the gun in the corner at school when they got there!

The Juniata River provided entertainment and was a source of food for the family. My mom said that they would catch eels and then watch them flop in the frying pan when her mother would cook them.

Their home in Old Ferry was across the river from Mt. Olivet. Many times, when weather permitted, they would cross the river in the row boat, climb the hill and walk to the church on a Sunday morning.

They had friends that lived on a farm on the other side of the river. They would spend the day there and return home back across the river at the end of the day.

In the late 1950s, my grandfather became ill. My Uncle Lenus "Bugs" Brandt, who had a home on the outskirts of Millerstown, traded homes with my grandparents so he could take over the greenhouse operations. Grandma would still help out with the transplanting. In the early 1960s after my dad ended his Army days, he became a partner with my uncle in the greenhouse business. My cousins and I enjoyed carefree summer days playing in the dirt in the greenhouse, making mud pies and playing in the coal bin. Occasionally, a hobo walking along old Route 22 would stop at the greenhouse. My grandma or aunt would get them a cold drink and sometimes a sandwich.

I was fortunate to live beside Uncle Bugs, Aunt Helen, and their family. It has been said that cousins are our first best friends. This is so true. My cousin Kathy and I were inseparable growing up. We were in the same class at school and she even married one of my husband's best friends, Steve Hower, (In fact, my husband, Randy and I take the credit for getting them together almost fifty years ago!). Steve served in the Air Force for many years and their lives were spent far away from Perry County. Time and distance never mattered to us; we always and still can pick up conversation where we left off. We always said we were sisters in heart. If she wasn't at my house, I was at hers when we were youngsters.

Kathy and I also spent a lot of time with our twin Brandt cousins (Trudy and Judy—daughters of my Uncle Earl Brandt). They were a couple of years older than us and had a car! They would come and get us on the weekends and we'd go "running around." We spent many evenings at the bowling lanes in New Bloomfield or hanging out at their house in "Polecat." (Mahanoy Valley Road, Duncannon). We would look through Tiger Beat magazines and go "ga-ga" over the popular teeny-bopper bands of the day (Cowsills, Osmonds, David Cassidy, Bobby Sherman, etc.). Although those days are long gone, and we don't get together enough, the bonds we formed with one another will last forever.

The Juniata River was our playground in our backyards. My cousins and I built a tree house in one of the big old trees along the river where we would hold "club" meetings. We would swim, fish, catch hellgrammites, and just enjoy the lazy days along the river. There was a section of the river below my uncle's house that sort of looked like a pond and it was pretty deep. We were always told to stay away from there because there was quick sand in it and we would sink. There were also rapids out in the middle of the river that we called "the channel." Our folks said to never go near the channel because we would surely drown. We had an old row boat that we would row around and a wooden boat landing that we would jump off. My dad would also provide his shoulders as a diving board.

Our home had one TV, black and white, and we only got one channel. Uncle Bugs got a couple more than we did. I remember when the Beatles were going to be on the Ed Sullivan Show. I asked if I could go over and watch it. I was not allowed to watch those "long-haired hippies!" Our first experience with colored TV was when my folks purchased a plastic piece that fit on the TV screen. It had a few different colors on the plastic.

Our milk was delivered to our door. We would put money in the box and the box would be full of milk on the given delivery days. I even remember when bread was also delivered to the house. My grandma would help my folks "can" fruits and vegetables to prepare for the coming winter.

Brandt family reunions were held at Rolling Green Park or Willow Mill Park or the Liverpool Sportsman's Club. It was always exciting to get ready for the reunion in anticipation of seeing relatives that we only saw once a year.

Route 22 runs right through Old Ferry. It was the main route of the day. We would sit on our porch counting big rig trucks and see how many we could get to "honk" at us. Sometimes if we had an older cousin around, we were allowed to collect soda bottles that were thrown out the windows. We would then take them to the "beer joint" (Keystone Inn) where Bob Wright would cash them in and give us the deposit money. He had a soda machine outside where we would then use our earnings to buy a glass bottle of cold soda.

Kathy and I always had very short hair when we were small. Nancy Sweger would cut our hair and I remember giggling watching Kathy get her hair cut and she would do the same to me. We would pretend we had long hair by putting hand towels on our heads. I remember running out to the ice cream truck one time with these towels on our heads! In the winter time, if we happened to outgrow our snow boots from the previous year, we sometimes put bread bags over our shoes and tied them with rubber bands. We would slide down the hill in the snow on cardboard or the round lids off of wringer wash machines.

Wash day meant hanging clothes out on the line in all kinds of weather. I remember when my brother was small, I would help hang his diapers out on the line and then bringing them in at the end of the day frozen stiff! Then we would put them over the rack in the house until they dried. This was the case for all of our clothes. We froze our fingers, but oh they smelled so fresh! Once everything was dried, then the ironing would begin. We would dampen some of the clothes, roll them up, and then iron them. Heaven forbid if someone would leave the house with a wrinkled shirt! I must admit, I still iron my husband's shirts. Some habits, albeit fifty-year-old habits, are hard to break!

Many families in the 1960s and 1970s only had one vehicle and many of our mothers were stay at home moms, as was the case for my family. If my dad was at work, we didn't go anywhere. But, usually once every other week, my mom would borrow my step-grandpa's car and take us to their house in Millerstown. We would then walk to the Millerstown pool for the afternoon.

Mt. Olivet had a very active youth group when I was growing up. We would gather together often and go on hikes, ride the church bus for an evening of roller skating, Christmas caroling, camping and swimming at Ferry Boat Campsites in Liverpool, and sled riding on the Wayne Benson farm outside of Millerstown or the Mervin Gibble farm near Landisburg. Little did I know at the time we were at the Gibble farm that my future husband lived less than a mile away!

That brings me to the story of the Bill and Lois Campbell legacy near Landisburg. Bill and Lois were farmers and Bill worked for Agway in Newport for many years. They raised eight children of their own and fostered many children along the way. When I started dating my husband in the mid-1970s, I learned really fast that when you were at the supper table and the food passed by, you better get what you want because it wasn't coming back around! My husband, the fourth child in his family, was the oldest one at home when we started dating, but there were twelve children sitting at the family supper table. I only had one brother who was nine years younger than me. I found that life was quite different in the Campbell household where there were so many more children!

In the late 1970s, Bill retired from Agway, and he and Lois purchased a small gas station along Route 850. It was built in the 1940s by the Henry Brothers. Over the prior thirty years, not much had changed. When Bill bought the property, he renovated the building and operated a grocery store, deli and gas station. He would open at 5 a.m. and close at 9 p.m. seven days a week. As time went on, he built a service garage and sporting goods store. His two younger sons, Vernon and Elly, were still in high school and worked along with their dad and mom in the business.

In 1986, he sold the garage to my husband, Randy and the store to his older son Archie. Bill and Lois then opened Campbell's General Store in the old Robinson building in Loysville until they sold it several years later to son Brian. Bill and Elly then built the "big" sporting goods store where Shermans Valley Supply is now located. In 1991, Archie sold the store to Randy and me. We have been here ever since.

The store has had a few changes over the years since we have been proprietors. The changes have come about as a result of a combination of government regulations, big business (Walmart and Dick's Sporting Goods for example), and internet sales now the general shopping habits of consumers. At one time, we employed thirteen full-time and part-time employees. We operated a full-service garage, had a full-service gas station, grocery store, deli, plus Randy had a tire business "on the road" servicing Perry County and the surrounding areas. We also operated two pay-to-fish ponds on our home property for several years (Triple Creek Ponds). Needless to say, we were busy.

We would have our "regulars" stopping in for some cheese off the wheel, or a yummy freshly-made sub, or our famous chicken or ham salad from my folks' secret recipes. We always tried to sell the unusual and hard-to-get items. It was an incentive to get people to stop in and take a look around. Randy still tries to keep the odd hunting rounds of ammunition in the store. Our motto used to be "a little bit of everything, but not much of anything!"

Many of our regular customers would buy 'on time.' We had a charge box that got pretty big some months. Once we closed the gas pumps, we had to eliminate the personal charges. We could provide credit when we had a consistent cash flow that selling gas provided.

While the grocery store was booming, we would be open seven days a week. Sunday mornings would often see our coffee-drinking friends who would come and hang out and solve all of the world's problems! As time went on and the business evolved, we started closing on Sundays. We figured God intended for us to make our living in six days; if we couldn't do it in six, we weren't going to do it in seven!

We loved operating Triple Creek Ponds generally March thru May of each year during trout season. We especially enjoyed watching the youngsters catch a fish. We used to say "one cast and you're hooked" and it proved true most of the time. We closed the ponds after our daughter graduated high school and my dad passed away the same year. Randy couldn't be at the ponds and the store at the same time, so we had to give up something.

We've had many good employees over the years. Many of the neighborhood children were employees while they were in high school. Our folks, Bill and Lois Campbell, and, Gene and Martha Trout, all worked for us at some point. Our daughter, Sarah Campbell Columbus, spent many long days just growing up, working in the store and at the ponds. Our success and longevity are shared by the contributions of many.

The local community supported us in the early days, but as box stores became prevalent and people started shopping more "over the mountain," we saw the change. We would try to compete by providing personal service and convenience, but every time a new store or gas station opened in the area, a piece of our pie would be taken away. Randy and I have been in business for thirty-seven years this year. We have seen businesses come and go. As fast as one closes, another opens. We have stayed the course; we have endured many ups and downs, but have remained committed to our life-long dream of owning our own business.

Today, in 2022, we are still here, but operating on a much smaller scale as Triple Creek Rod and Gun. Randy has been working a full-time job elsewhere for the past five years. He has confidence in me to run the business when he is not here. We still rely on the support of our local community and welcome anyone who comes in the door. We enjoy what we do and are blessed that we remain standing after all these years. We are reaching the age where most people retire. We don't have retirement in our near-future plans, but realize there are many more years behind us than there are in the future. The business has been good to us; we have been able to raise our daughter here and now we have grandchildren who are spending time in the business and learning life lessons that can't be taught in a classroom. The future remains to be seen. One thing is for certain though, we are and will remain Perry County Proud and are thankful to all the people who have walked through our doors over the years. We like to think that they come in as customers and then leave as friends.

An Enterprising Youth Influenced By His Grandparents

Storyteller David Magee
Recorded by Debra Kay Noye

This story was partially written by "Dave" Magee, of Marysville. But as Debby reviewed his story, as usual, she had a lot of questions. The interview joggled Dave's memory and produced a plethora of pertinent information about Perry County.

"My memories of growing up in Perry County do not involve just one town. I spent many weeks with my grandparents in Center Township and Duncannon."

"I lived in Marysville, and spent a lot of my Marysville youth, from the time I was eleven years old till high school graduation, working at many part-time jobs."

Dave worked selling fresh fruits and vegetables for Raymond Fenicle at Fenicle's Produce Stand on Williams Street in Marysville. Every two weeks in the summer, he would travel along to the harbor in Baltimore, Maryland, to assist Fenicle in loading and hauling fresh cantalopes and watermelons back to be sold at the produce stand. When strawberries were in season and plentiful, Dave would ride along with Fenicle to Steelton and Middletown selling the boxed berries door-to-door. They did the same with peaches they trucked back from Adams County. When Fenicle's opened a produce stand in Enola, where the present day car wash exists on Route 15, Dave's dad would drop Dave and his brother, Roy, off at Fenicle's new location on his way to work at White Hill, a youth prison. They worked from 7 a.m. to 4 p.m., earning ten dollars a week each.

Now try to imagine, Dave making corsages for high school proms, Mother's Day or Easter, when it was customary for the women to be presented corsages to adorn their Easter outfits. He was taught to put wire around multiple flower stems then into tiny tubes holding water. Working from the outside with larger flowers to a center of smaller blooms, Dave created corsages of colorful carnations, which were mostly requested at prom time, because they were cost effective. Orchids were an Easter and Mother's Day favorite. He jokes about not being able to master making bows.

Albert and Cynthia Wynn owned Wynn's Greenhouse in Marysville in an alley behind the Church of God on Chestnut Street. They taught Dave the art of making corsages, wreaths at Christmas and arrangements for funerals.

The Wynns also planted bulbs in the ground, such as tulips, daffodils and hyacinth to sell for Easter flowers. However, Dave had to first dig them up after they emerged and plant them into individual pots. Then they were placed in the greenhouse and heat-forced to grow and bloom in time for Easter. One year, Dave recalls there was an overabundance of individual hyacinths remaining in the greenhouse come the Saturday before Easter. Dave took it upon himself to pot them into larger containers of three creating a colorful display. His ingenuity worked and they sold almost all of the hyacinths. To his surprise on Easter morning right before he left to go to church, the Wynns dropped by his home to present him with fifty dollars and a very large chocolate bunny to show their appreciation. He was thirteen at the time and worked seasonally with them till he graduated from high school.

Dave learned about planting, raising, transplanting, potting and selling plants and flowers in Wynn's Greenhouse, which carried a variety of gifts along with the flowers arranged for many occasions and plants for bearing vegetables. In fact, Dave took to getting his hands dirty in the soil and using his creativity to produce many works of flowering beauty.

Always searching for more ways to earn money to put clothes on his back and shoes on his feet, Dave kept the Galen Theater tidy, on the corner of Route 850 and Route 15. It has since been torn down. Not only did he get paid a whopping fifty cents an hour ($8-$10 week on average) for his work, he got to watch the 2nd and 3rd run-movies for free. There was a new movie every night and the projectionist (the movies were on large round reels) was Jimmy Roberts, who lived on Valley Street.

Galen "Bing" Fisher owned the Galen Theater and hired Dave after the man who performed the cleaning and stocking chores decided to join the Army. "Bing" treated Dave very well, even though he was very finicky about the cleanliness of the theater windows. Every Tuesday, Thursday, Friday and Saturday mornings or before the shows that night, Dave would run the sweeper, pick-up the trash, wash the windows and restock the candy and popcorn vending machines. In those days, the popcorn was dispensed through a chute into paper bags for five cents. Without fail, "Bing" would find fault with the windows and ask Dave to redo them prior to showtime. To alleviate the aggravation of doing the windows twice, Dave decided to eliminate the earlier cleaning and wait till evening. This worked out well.

The theater was not very large. The average cost per movie was twenty cents if you sat in the front rows of the theater which had unpadded seats. However, there were six to eight rows of soft padded seats in the back, which cost an extra twenty-five cents. Most of the movies would have some cartoons prior to the evening's feature. The biggest movie, which grabbed much attention, was "The Greatest Show on Earth", and Dave also loved the film, which came out in 1952. Directed by Cecil B. DeMille, the techno-color movie was a colorful behind the scenes look at the Ringling Brother's - Barnum and Bailey Circus. In fact, not only did Dave watch each night it played at the Galen Theater, he also went with his Uncle Ward and Aunt Ruth Rice, from Carver's Hill in Duncannon, to the Kanon Theater behind Cooper's Market. Ward Rice was a Duncannon Policeman along with Harry Fritz. Ward worked a full-time job at Olmsted Air Force Base. And, as luck would have it, Dave's Grandfather Magee, from outside of New Bloomfield, took him to the New Bloomfield Theater to see the same movie. The New

Bloomfield Theater was located near the current Veteran's Building on the square. He never tired of seeing that movie!

"The folks I worked for were very interesting people. Remember in those days, at least in my family, the word allowance meant go to work and earn it!"

"When I spent time with my Magee Grandparents in Center Township, that meant doing a lot of farm work, which they made seem like fun. We would paint the picket fences, milk the cows, churn butter, gather eggs, bale hay and weed the large garden."

Dave's grandparents, Charles and Myrtle Magee, lived on the original Magee homestead started by his Great-Grandfather Richard Magee on Jericho Road outside of New Bloomfield. It would be considered a 40-50 acre farmette these days. His grandfather was the first rural mail carrier for the New Bloomfield area.

His grandmother was a stickler for doing mental math, when neighbors would come to purchase eggs, butter, milk or veggies, when she had an abundance after canning. It was customary for Dave to stand beside her as she made the calculations. Dave was responsible for the transactions and informing the customer how much they owed and how much change they would receive. He was also required to read poetry and the Bible daily to enhance his reading skills. Her teaching methods involved calculating, reading comprehension and memory, plus being able to think on your own. (One exception though, she was a staunch Republican and expected you to follow her political lead.)

Hogs were also raised and butchered by his grandparents. Generally it occurred right after Thanksgiving when the cooler temperatures set-in. Dave enjoyed eating the cooked meats (various organs, head-meat, pig's feet, odd cuts) from the large iron kettles. That meat was ground and added back to the broth to be thickened for scrapple. Once the hog fat was rendered and pressed, Dave loved the cracklin's. His grandfather would sugar-cure the hams, shoulders and bacons, which were then smoked in the wooden smokehouse. The intestines were cleaned and stuffed with freshly made sausage. His grandmother would then cook the rope sausage, put it into large crocks and cover it with lard to seal. The crocks were lined up on the long benches in the cool cellar. When she would take some sausage out of the crocks for eating, she would always recover the tops with lard. They also raised their own beef cattle and butchered them right around New Years. The meat was left to hang in the cold barn for several days before portioning. His grandmother canned most of the beef in two-quart jars. The last time they butchered was in 1955 because his grandfather, who was very special to Dave, passed away.

Because they were very self-sufficient, his grandparents did not go to the local stores in New Bloomfield very often. When his grandmother did have need of flour or sugar and other dry goods, she would predetermine how much they would cost at Hair Brother's Store in New Bloomfield. Then she would get out the hatchet, wack off the heads, and "dress" the number of chickens, she would need to barter to pay her dry goods bill. This was not one of Dave's favorite farm chores. When she would take the chickens to Hair Brothers, Edna Hair would weigh them to determine a price for the birds. Then it would be applied to the groceries purchased and the "swap" was done.

"Saturday nights and Sunday afternoons in the summer, Granddad took us to New Bloomfield town baseball games behind the present day Post Office and Borough Hall. In the winter months, Carson Long

Military Institute opened their gym for the local youth to play basketball. The young men in New Bloomfield according to the season had pick-up games of basketball, football and baseball, where all ages and talent were welcomed."

A Lasting Christmas Memory
"Granddad Magee's last Christmas was partly sad, but a lot of happiness for two young boys ages eleven and twelve (Roy and Dave). We never remembered a Christmas tree in our Magee grandparent's house. So here we are with my parents visiting my grandfather who is dying of cancer. Roy and I decide he should have a Christmas tree. So, we hiked to the woods and found a three-foot tree, that was a little better than a typical "Charlie Brown Christmas tree", cut it down, brought it to the house and put it in a bucket of coal which held it in place."

"Roy and I figured out how much money we had in our pockets and walked a little more than a mile to Carmichael's Store on the town square of New Bloomfield. The variety store was right beside Stoop's Barbershop. We tell the owner what we are trying to accomplish and how much money we had to spend. Surprisingly, we had enough money for the tree decorations! We walked back to the farm and decorated the tree with small mercury glass balls, strands of beads and tinsel, while Granddad laid in bed watching us. I turned around to say something to him and all I saw was a smile on his face and tears in his eyes. I never spoke of this to Roy, but along with my own children's first Christmas, this Christmas was the best. The sad part of the story is Granddad died the next October."

Working and Attending School
Dave's mother became ill when he was young and that is one of the reasons why the four children were bounced around so much between grandparents and extended family. He attended Marysville Elementary School, riding Valley Transportation buses because school buses did not exist. He attended and graduated (six through twelfth grades) from Susquenita High School. He was a member of the first graduating class at Susquenita when it housed all six grades. Susquenita eventually had school buses and he caught the bus at the Penn Township building when he was living with family in Duncannon. He was not active in sports because he was always working so many part-time jobs or helping out his family.

Bob Holler of Duncannon, was the Holsum Bread man, driving a delivery truck throughout Perry County. He would take Dave along on his route on Saturdays. Holler picked Dave up by 4 a.m. and off they'd go to the breakfast buffet in Dauphin to fuel their bodies for the busy day ahead.

They started at the Holsum Bread Company docks in Harrisburg loading the truck. Then Holler would drive to the West Shore Plaza, where he dropped off breads and Dave at two grocery stores. Dave would stock the store shelves for two hours till Holler returned from the rest of his local rounds. Then they would head into Perry County restocking stores with Holsum Bread, wheat and rye breads, plus eight and twelve packs of hot dog and sandwich rolls.

Once in a while, Dave would convince the 7-UP delivery man, to let him go along to Duncannon and New Bloomfield. Restocking the store shelves was labor intensive, as Dave carried the heavy wooden crates loaded with full glass bottles of soda into the stores storage areas and restocked the shelves. There were also the empty returns to be carried to the truck and loaded to be taken back to the plant to be washed and refilled for the next delivery.

Even his Uncle Albert Magee, who lived across from the current day Karns Grocery Store in Duncannon, would hire sixteen year old Dave to help collate the booklets that needed to be put together. Magee's Print Shop was kept busy printing the Marysville Carnival books, which was a very large job, school yearbooks and other community booklets. It was there he started to learn the printing trade. Uncle Albert also taught him more about gardening and cultivating.

All his part-time jobs earned him enough money to buy new clothes and shoes at Snavely's Store in Duncannon. Later Snavely's became Balsbaughs, and Dave was allowed to "put clothes aside on a lay-away-plan". Otherwise, he wore hand-me-downs. Once, he decided to open a Christmas Club account and his goal was to save enough money to purchase a dress-suit. He was proud of his first suit purchased with monies earned and saved from his many jobs.

Time Spent with Family in Duncannon
"We were also fortunate to spend a lot of time in Duncannon with Uncle Ward and Aunt Ruth Rice on Carver's Hill in Duncannon, as well as John and Mabel Fritz, our mother's parents who lived in downtown Duncannon.

"It may seem strange today but then it was a general rule, that children's games played in Duncannon were on the ridge and meadow separating downtown from Carver's Hill. The Little Juniata Creek cuts through the "Meadow" at Noye Park as it is known today. The Duncannon Flour Mill was also there at that time. The games played by myself and cousins were War and we made up the rules as we went. There was also daylight hide and seek. We spent a lot of time there."

Dave's remembrances of Duncannon businesses start with none other than ice cream. Homemade ice cream from Michener's Ice Cream Shop on Market Street was his favorite. Owner Sam Michener's small shop had a few small tables to sit at, but most folks bought ice cream cones to go. Dave preferred a dish and one large scoop was five cents. The dishes were shaped like a waffle cone. They were metal with a paper liner, which was tapered. Patrons were given real teaspoons to enjoy eating their ice cream. Milkshakes were presented in the metal canister they were whirled in along with a paper cup. Dave was devastated when the price increased one day and he didn't have the ten cents for a dip. By now you're wondering, why didn't he get a job dipping ice cream. He tried! Maybe Sam figured he'd eat too much of the profits, because he knew Dave Magee loved his ice cream, except for coffee and coconut. Michener's also had an Ice House.

Michener's rival was the Juniata Dairy Bar further up Market Street. It was where the teens hung out, because of all the young girls (Donna and Janet Dietz, Susan Gelbaugh) dipping the ice cream. Plus, the size of the dips were much larger, but slightly higher at fifteen cents. Dave would often go there and eat a dish of ice cream, maybe even a large size for twenty-five cents, and be too full to eat supper. Jerry Wolfe owned the Dairy Bar, which did not feature homemade ice cream. The ice cream was manufactured by Harrisburg Dairies in Harrisburg. Side note – Harrisburg Dairies had their own brand "Hattie Harris" and eventually opened Hattie Harris Ice Cream Stores throughout Central Pennsylvania.

If he was hungry and had the money, he could go to the Sparkle Restaurant on the square and spend a whopping fifteen cents on a hamburg and fries. Dave declares aesthetically the restaurant hasn't changed much from his younger days. Huck Leonard eventually owned it and added a room onto the right side for a flower shop. The restaurant is now Goodies.

John Kennedy owned Kennedy's Store on High Street. It was a wooden grocery store which was very long and narrow with big windows. When you walked into the front door immediately on your right was the penny candy display and further down the check-out counter, where Alice Wahl, an employee would ring-up your order. On top of the glass candy display were three large jars filled with lozenges of peppermint, spearmint and wintergreen. The five cent candy display came after the cash register. The bread racks were on the left side of the store. Shelves filled with dry goods lined the walls. The milk cooler was in the back of the store, along with the Bird's Eye Vegetable freezer. Kennedy's did not sell fresh meats. People could go to Mutzy's Meat Market on Market Street or Cooper's Store on High Street for fresh meats.

Dave recalls his Great-Grandfather Beam lived with his grandparents, which was just five doors down the street from Kennedy's Store. Pap Beam was a tobacco chewer. He would give Dave twenty-five cents and tell him to go to the store for a fifteen cent pack of Silver Cup Chewing Tobacco. It took Dave longer to decide on what penny candy he wanted to purchase than to buy Pap's tobacco. Life can be sweet at times!

"We had Oren Watt's Auction House, where the Duncannon Beer Distributor is located today. Granddad took us with him sometimes. He gave us fifty cents and Roy and I would buy and buy things that no-one cared about but Grandma thought they were great! Mrs. Watts would give her husband, the auctioneer, a quick kick in the shins if she thought the prices weren't going high enough."

"Another thing we were able to experience was before my grandfather moved in to Dunncannon, he was a farmer for J. LeRue Hess on Sunshine Hill. There was a mansion and a farmhouse on the land. My grandparents lived in the farmhouse. The mansion was vacant. It made a great rainy day house to play in, exploring the rooms and making up haunted house stories. Outside the mansion's main entrance was a large willow tree that we kids hid under and played made-up games."

Fort Hunter Days
"When my grandfather left the farm, he went to work as the caretaker at the Fort Hunter Museum in Dauphin County. This was another great adventure for his grandchildren growing up in Perry County. We spent a considerable amount of time there and as we got older, we worked with him during the summer. He lived in the farm house for several years at Fort Hunter, before living in the stone-house across the road from the farm".

According to Dave, the Fort Hunter property was owned by the Meigs family, who were relatives of the Wisters who owned the Duncannon Nail Factory. Mrs. Meigs served as the director and tour guide for the museum and the property. Dave's grandfather was the caretaker for the entire estate. He used Doll, Fort Hunter's workhorse, to plow the fields and the large colonial gardens. When Dave went along to assist his grandfather in getting the grounds ready for an open house, he would trim various bushes and mow the grass. They would be served meals in the basement of the museum, cooked by Ralph Halter's mother, Anna, of New Buffalo. Mrs Halter was responsible for the inside cleaning of the museum and houses on the property. Dave enjoyed playing and exploring in the museum.

It was through meeting Mrs. Halter that Dave was first introduced to her son Ralph, who lived in New Buffalo all his life, until his recent passing. Dave and Ralph, who were life-long-friends, could not pass an ice cream shop or stand without stopping regardless of the time of day. The ice cream buddies would travel all over Central Pennsylvania in search of a new ice cream adventure. In later years, Dave took on the neighborly chores of providing Ralph transportation to purchase groceries. He would never tell Dave where he wanted to go afterwards, but if it was a choice between a bowl of soup or ice cream, a bowl of ice cream always won out. And, it wasn't unusual for him to eat his ice cream and order one more for the road, which he ate while Dave drove him home.

If there was an ice cream eating contest, Dave's other ice cream buddy from outside of New Bloomfield, would win spoons down. "Buzzy" Brunner, the Pumpkin Man, would attend church socials at Pine Grove, Roseglen and Ickesburg with Dave and ask for serving bowls heaped full of homemade ice cream. And, he didn't always stop at just one! He actually traveled with his own bowl if he knew the venue would not have a bowl large enough to fill his needs.

Buzzy and Dave had other interests in common and that was West Perry sports, especially the girl's basketball team. They traveled to all the games and to every state championship game. Buzzy always packed lettuce, tomato and cheese sandwiches for the events, but he did not like pizza. At the end of the girl's basketball season, Buzzy and Dave would always treat the team to pizza, but Buzzy did not join in.

"When I turned eighteen, I knew this would be my last Christmas in Perry County. Christmas meant nothing to me at this time as two of my heroes had died in my youth. Grandma Magee in early December 1959 and Uncle Ward days before Christmas. Often times when I think back on the times I had in Duncannon and western Perry County, 1959 comes back and sadly all the happiness goes away. The folks in these areas mentioned were so good to us, that it doesn't take long for all the good memories to return."

Dave went on after graduation to the Williamsport Technical School and completed his studies as a journeyman in four years instead of the normal six. He learned the printing trade from layout design, use of hot metal, linotype and various other machines used in all printing processes. He wasn't new to the industry, since he had helped out Uncle Al in Duncannon. He was ambitious and eager to be on his way. His work ethic for the Grit caught the attention of the foreman, who soon gave Dave as much over-time as he could handle.

One of the highlights of Dave's journey was when he was encouraged to run for Perry County Register and Recorder, by the widow and daughter (Doris and Suzanne) of Max Cooper, who had held the office. Max and Doris were also the former part-owners of Cooper's Store in Duncannon. He decided to run, vowing he would visit every municipality in Perry County.

Dave was recognized by his colleagues as a self-starter who didn't mind working. His grandparents helped him to build a foundation that carried him through his life. From mental math, to getting his hands dirty, to learning new skills, to learning how to treat the public, Dave absorbed their instructions and put them to good use. That surely was his grandparent's dreams for him and they would be amazed. He's still discovering new areas of Perry County to this day, most certainly on the trail of a new ice cream shop.

Saturday Night Ritual

Storyteller Ted Loy

Growing up on a farm, in Spring Township, Perry County, in the 1960s, might seem like a mundane existence to some. But not for the four Loy kids! With enthusiasm, we made due with what the country offered us. One experience that stands out vividly in my mind was born out of our proximity to Shermans Creek. As well as, the usual swimming, fishing and exploring of the creek, our family had a summer-time Saturday evening ritual. Most can relate, it was a Saturday bath!

Mom had her hands full, especially with three boys. Getting us all in the tub was probably like herding cats. She came up with a plan to make us want to get a bath. We would all head to Shermans Creek with towels, washcloths and a couple bars of Ivory Soap. It had to be Ivory, because it was the only soap that floated. Mom would make the rounds – looking behind ears and under arms – making sure we got most of the grime, so we would at a glance, appear clean at church the next day.

I never gave much thought to this summer-time ritual until many years later when I remembered the number of livestock doing their "business" in the creek from Germantown to Warm Springs. No harm came and it did make Saturday night lots of fun!

The Life Of John Reisinger

Storyteller Kerry J. Reisinger

John Edward Reisinger was born February 26, 1913 in Ickesburg to Charles and Phoebe (Rumberger) Reisinger. He was the fourth of nine children. He was educated through the eighth grade and as a youth worked as a farm hand.

He was in the first draft held in Perry County for military service in February 1941. He was sent to Fort Benning, Georgia and trained as a tank driver and gunner. He was made a Sergeant in the Second Armored Division known as "Hell on Wheels" commanded by General George Patton. He arrived for duty in North Africa on Christmas Eve 1942. During his service he saw action in North Africa, Sicily, Normandy, Northern France, the Ardennes, and Rhineland campaigns. He participated in the invasion of Sicily then was sent to England in preparation for D-Day.

In July of 1944, he was wounded in heavy fighting at St. Lo. His tank was hit by German fire that killed three of the five man tank crew. He and his other crew member were caught behind enemy lines and had to hide in hedge rows and an in an old farmhouse. While making their way back to his unit, he sustained a concussion and loss of hearing. After several weeks, he was back in action. John was awarded the Purple Heart and his battalion were awarded the distinguished unit badge for their advance at St. Lo.

He rejoined his outfit and experienced heavy combat through Northern France, Belgium and Germany where he once again was at the forefront of the fighting. John was assigned as the tank driver for the battalion commander. His tank took heavy fire and his commander was killed. In January 1945, in bitter weather, and some of the fiercest fighting of the war, at the Battle of the Bulge his tank took a direct hit. John was seriously wounded when the shell came through the front of the tank and exploded between his legs. He sustained shrapnel wounds from head to toe and lost parts of four fingers. He was able to crawl out of the tank and laid in the snow in sub-zero weather until members of his crew came back for him after the fighting had died down. The sub-zero temperatures and lying in the snow probably kept him from bleeding to death. The doctors were not sure if he would live or ever walk again.

The Second Armored Division's total destruction of the elite German Second Panzer Division at the Battle of the Bulge, was considered to be one of the most important actions of the war. It effectively secured the invasion of Germany and the eventual allied victory . As a result, John was awarded the Oak Leaf Cluster for being wounded in action for a second time.

After hospitalizations in Paris and England, he was transported back to a military hospital in Daytona Beach, Florida. During this time, he could not walk and had numerous operations on his legs. On his first state-side leave, he hitch-hiked home on crutches. In April of 1946, he was honorably discharged from the Army to continue his recuperation at home.

Around 1949, John started working part-time for the Millerstown Moose Lodge as a book-keeper and manager for the Lodge, using the skills he learned in the Army during his recuperation. Later on he became an officer and administrator of the Lodge. He retired in January in 1993 after forty-four years and was honored for his years of service and recognized for managing one of the most successful Lodges in the country and leaving them with a large surplus of funds.

In 1951, he started to work with his father-in-law (married Wanda C. Mumper) in the lumber business. He eventually took over the business in 1969 and he put in a fully automated mill in the old Breyer's Creamery across the Juniata River from Millerstown. His brothers George and Dick also worked at the mill. George was a truck driver and Dick was the sawyer. John operated the mill until 1984 when he retired and sold the equipment and building.

He was a good husband and father to Valerie J. Mitchell, Kim B. Reisinger, Lynn A. Reisinger and Kerry J. Reisinger as well as grandfather to six grandchildren. He was very giving to his children, and made sure his family was always well cared for. He had a wisdom that must only come from a long life and experiencing the things that he did. His family was always seeking his advice on various topics and, he always seemed to know the answer or the right thing to do. He was not a formally educated man, but was practical and knowledgeable on a vast amount of topics.

He seemed to know just about everybody in the county and everyone seemed to know and like him. With his many years of timbering, he seemed to know about every piece of property in Perry County and when it had been timbered and by who. He always was close to the land, whether in the woods or checking the crops. He kept a rain gauge and even at the very end of his life, he would ask his family if it had rained or what the temperature was outside.

John grew up during the Depression. He never cared much for material things, and even after he became successful in business, this did not change. He saved most of what he made and was generous with his brothers in the business. He was an extremely hard-worker, working six days a week at the lumber business, then evenings and week-ends at his part-time position at the Moose Lodge. He would do anything that needed done, including the most menial tasks like cleaning the ovens at the Moose or sweeping the floors at the sawmill. He used to say he never asked an employee to do anything he would not do himself.

He was a private person, content to be by himself in the woods or working with his hands, whether fixing something mechanical or making something out of wood. In his retirement years, he worked in his wood shop at his cabin making a lot of nice furniture for the family. He always had to be busy and never sat around and watched tv, except for the news. He was always on top of current events. John was a Republican, but didn't care much for politicians. He had no time for any type of bull or bragging. He could never understand how politicians could spend more money than they had. He used to say, if you don't have the money saved to buy something, you shouldn't buy it.

Maybe because of his war experiences, John had a very high tolerance for pain. He had the ends of two fingers taken off by a fan belt in a skidder. The Forest Ranger that took him to the hospital said he couldn't believe, how calm John was. Another time, he dropped a plate glass window on his arm that cut his forearm very badly. He calmly put a t-towel over it and drove himself to the doctors to get thirty some stitches. Once he flipped a bulldozer over on his leg at the sawmill and had to dig his leg out from under the dozer to get free. He never told anyone until his daughter noticed he was limping and saw it was bruised and infected, and made him go to the doctors.

John never complained, he always accepted his situation and moved on as best he could, whether it be the war injuries or the strokes he suffered later in life. He always fought to over-come any adversary and was as physically tough as anyone could be. He never wanted to put anyone out even as his physical condition deteriorated. He would say right up to the end, "I'm all right!"

He was asked if he had accomplished the things he wanted to accomplish in his life. He replied, he doesn't look back, he only looks forward! There will never be another one quite like John!

Marysville Tales From A Perry County Artist

Storyteller Wanda Marie Reed Pines
Recorded by Debra Kay Noye

Still a "spit-fire" today, Wanda Pines was born at home on October 9, 1926 to Leon and Madelene (Wolf) Reed who lived on Marysville's South Main Street, right along the Susquehanna River. Doctor Charles Snyder, whose office was on the alley at the corner of Front Street, helped in her delivery. Her grandmother, Grace Mae Keim Wolf, was a "practical nurse" who worked with Doc Snyder. Back in those days, new mothers took up to nine days of bed rest after giving birth. Her grandmother would stay and oversee their care.

Wanda lived a "bare-bones" life during the Depression, but it didn't stop her from learning how to draw by the age of five. Wanda would sing or draw pictures, hoping to make some new friends. She would gift them the pictures and pretty soon they asked her to do more. Wanda was enterprising enough to ask them to bring her some paper. She received her first paints when she was thirteen.

As a child running free through Marysville, Wanda was soon invited to play "ring-up" or hide and seek, sometimes under the street lights. Her grandmother Grace forbid any card games other than Flinch or Donkey. In the winter, Wanda would remove the lid from her grandmother's wringer washing machine and use it as a sled. She would fly from Broad Street through Lincoln which had a very steep hill. All the neighborhood kids would yell "donkey" as they sledded past on the dirt roads. Some had runner sleds manufactured in Duncannon (the Lightning Guider). When she was a bit older and was helping to do the family laundry, Wanda got her long hair caught tightly in the wringer. Her father helped to rescue her. That's when she decided to allow her father to cut her extremely long, straight hair.

She tells the tale about Monday's wash-day, whereby a dog was placed on a treadmill which was attached to the washing machine to keep it rotating properly. Wanda claims the dog soon caught onto the routine and disappeared Sunday nights. That didn't happen too often, as the dog was soon tied.

She remembers chickens running free through town, because most folks raised them for eggs and meat. As Wanda shares the story, a chicken fell through a hole in a local outhouse. Her brother, Norman, came to the rescue. He tied a rope around his middle, jumped through the hole and brought the chicken up to safety. Somebody reminding him to clean the mud off his shoes got a swift reply from Norman, "that ain't no mud!" Back then when the outhouses were cleaned out yearly, the human waste was placed on the gardens. That practice was banned because it was determined to cause typhoid. Wanda remembers not only using the pages of the Sears Catalog as toilet paper, but cutting out the pictures to decorate the interior of shoe boxes.

She wore "hand-me-downs," sometimes even her mother's. She remembers rayon fabric did not wear well. However, Wanda remembers Ethel Ashenfelter was a dressmaker, specializing in "odd shapes." Females had to wear dresses. Even if she wore pants underneath a dress in the winter to keep her warm as she walked to school, they had to be removed outside before entering the school building. She attended grade school at Marysville Elementary on Maple Avenue, which is now apartments. Her teachers were Phyllis Dissinger Detz and Mary Kass. Wanda always liked to read and everywhere she went through life, she would find the closest library. She remembers when Mrs. Detz started the first library in Marysville in 1943-1944. It was on the first floor of the red-brick Knights of Pythias building on Lincoln and Cameron Street. As the library's selection grew, so did the weight on the floor which caused great concern. The Marysville-Rye Library was incorporated in 1966 and built on Overcrest Road.

Wanda's grandfather fished in the Susquehanna River in the area where the ferry boats landed. His favorite fishing hole was at Ring Rock, so named due to a visible ring of iron embedded throughout the rock's structure. Her grandfather told of ferry boat operators using Ring Rock to tie up their boats. The family regularly dined on the carp and suckers he caught. When the river flooded, he would take his rowboat out onto the river and put a rope around a fallen tree or log and pull it to shore to be used as firewood.

The local taxidermist, Sherwood Little, lived on South Main Street and he would often get requests to mount a fisherman's catch. Fish lose their natural colors through the mounting process. He would take the dried fish skins, which were already mounted to Wanda to be hand-painted. She used a reference book on fishes to paint the natural colors. One time, she became creative with an extremely small fish. She painted a fishing scene on canvas, attaching a real fishing hook with line to the mounted fish. It was realistic and well received.

Her grandfather, Calvin Peter Wolf, would tramp through the Cove and Blue Mountains outside of Marysville into Rye Valley in search of wild ginseng. After he harvested the ginseng, he would dry it under the bed to be sold. It ended up in Philadelphia to be used for medicinal purposes. Ginseng (Sang) is very popular in Chinese cultures and commands a high price. Her grandfather would be very excited if he found a root that resembled a human being, because it was worth much more money.

Wanda's grandfather and father told her about Ted Tequichi, who at sixteen was encouraged by the Carlisle Indian School at the War College, to leave the school and find work. The Lawton, Oklahoma native, worked at the Duncannon Iron Works and lived with Wanda's family in the Duncannon area. The Native American Indian taught the local youth how to play football, which was a first for the area. The Carlisle Indian School was known for talented football players, including Jim Thorpe. Tequichi married Lily, a Mohawk from Michigan, and they eventually went back to his hometown where he became a Methodist minister.

When there was money for meat, they would go to Chauncey Benfer's Butcher Shop up from the square on Verbeke Street. He butchered beef and hogs and hung the sides in a large locker. He made scrapple and lard which he sold by the block. Wanda remembers a large wooden oxen yoke hanging over the display cases at the back of the shop. Benfer employed his nephew Hayward, who always sang "In a Little Spanish Town".

Wanda likes to remind people that Marysville was once known as Haley's Station, which was prior to the construction of the famed stone-arched Rockville Bridge. And, there were other bridges spanning the Susquehanna, prior to the Rockville. One was made of iron.

When Wanda walked along South Main Street, which was the main highway through Marysville prior to Route 11 & 15, she would begin at Bitting's General Store. (Her mother always told her a movie theatre was once in the back of Bitting's Store. Movies cost five cents.) "Bing" Fisher operated the Galen Movie Theatre on the corner of Valley Street, and Wheeler's Hardware which became Gault's Gun Shop, was across the street. "Pipey" Hench had a hardware store on Valley and Maple Avenue. Cox's had a grocery store. On the square was a photography store, Noss' Barbershop and a "confectionery/newsstand" as well as a pool hall, Gutshall's Hardware, a bar and Mader's Grocery Store. Wanda, always a storyteller, laughs as she remembers returning a dozen rotten eggs in a jar to the store. The clerk did not believe her, until she offered to remove the lid so he could get a good whiff.

She recalls Roth's Hotel on South Main Street, now the Waterfront Bar and Grill. Next to the hotel was a very tiny store which was also the residence of Mrs. Radabaugh and her son. Tony and Beatrice Radabaugh lived on the second floor. The Railroad Hotel, owned by Andrew Traver, was next door with an apartment building where railroad workers could sleep.

Wanda relates how the road was cobblestone past the railroad station. The train stopped once in the morning and evening. Workers started carving out the mountains on each side of Marysville in 1936 to build Route 11 & 15.

Wanda can visualize the red coffee grinder on the wooden counter of Keller's small grocery store, located on Lincoln and Lansvale Streets. The wooden shelving went to the ceiling and the storekeeper used a long handled "grab-it" to grasp items for the customers. Slanted glass display cases held coveted candies, especially hard candy which cost a penny for a small paper bag full. Baby Ruth candy bars were five cents and for one penny more you could purchase a candy bar new on the market. Wanda waited for the penny "grab bags" of assorted stale candy, which she shared with her family.

Further down the street was Uncle Norman Wolf's Shoe Shop, then the firehouse which also housed the local jail in the back. Wanda said the jail was mainly used for drunkards to sleep it off. William "Bill" Ashenfelter, Wanda's uncle, was the fire chief at the time.

The First National Bank of Marysville and George "Dordy" Kerstetter's beauty shop and barbershop were on Lansvale and Valley Streets. Wanda's eyes twinkle when she recalls, the owner of Shull's Bakery on Front Street, would donate cakes for church functions. They would always say, "these cakes were made to eat and be enjoyed, others were for sale." Jim White owned a grocery store on Front Street at the corner by the highway, which later was operated by his nephew, Percy.

Wanda giggles as she recounts a visit from the FBI, following a robbery at the local bank. It seems she had just conducted some banking prior to the robbery and the FBI was asking if she had noticed anything out of the ordinary. Of course, she was not aware of the robbery until the FBI came knocking on her door.

It was in the window of White's Store that Wanda's mother spied and fell in love with a china-head doll which had a leather body. She asked the owner if he would put the doll on layaway, till she could earn the money to pay for it. She did all sorts of odd jobs, ran errands and babysat, before the doll was hers. Wanda was allowed to play with the doll, but her brothers were somewhat jealous and taunted her by threatening to drop the doll out a second story window. They followed through with their threats and the doll was smashed to pieces.

Wanda was married after D-Day in 1945. Her husband, Thomas Roy Pines Jr., had been a prisoner of war during WW ll. He spent fourteen months 1943-1944 in a German POW camp, until the Russians liberated it. He was fed two potatoes a day, which was a lot less than his English counterparts. He was so thin, that he could take his fist up under his rib cage without any resistance. POWs were entitled to five hundred dollars as compensation for their service. Wanda's brother Norman was also a POW, during the extreme winter conditions only to suffer severe frostbite resulting in amputations in his legs and feet. Once the Russians liberated his camp, he was of the first to be evacuated due to health concerns.

Wanda's husband worked for the railroad while she raised four children, Thomas lll and Kevin (deceased at an early age), daughter Terrie and adopted son Danny. Her love of drawing led her to work for the Miller Furniture Store in Harrisburg, which was on the square next to the Senate Theatre. She drew pen and ink ads featuring furniture for the flexographic printing process.

She also liked to design houses and landscapes, including her own home. The front of the Bethel Independent Church formerly a United Methodist Church was designed by Wanda. A life-size picture of Christ painted by Wanda was also presented to the church.

Wanda and her father started the choir at Bethel Church in the early days. She sang alto and soprano (2 1/2 octaves), while her father sang baritone and tenor. They enjoyed singing and Wanda also sang for special events at the Marysville Moose and the "American War Mothers".

Wanda did do private commissioned works of art in various mediums. She also painted a lot just for the love of drawing and creating. She would donate painted items to her church for fundraisers. Her works of art are signed "WMR" which was before she married or "WMP" after 1945. Her works of art are featured in some of Roy "Rocky" Chandler's *Sketches of Perry County*, of which she is very proud.

Wanda Pines grew up in an era around Marysville that is rarely truly documented. She has created many works of art depicting Marysville's facade, preserving her "growing up" years as she freely walked throughout town.

Growing Up In The Cove
1950-1970

Storytellers Judy (Cunkle) Johnson, Jerry Johnson and Robert Johnson

Myself, Jerry Johnson (b. 1945-present) along with my brother, Bob (b. 1943-present) and my sister Jimmy Lou (1934-1966) lived at 1436 State Road with our parents James R. Johnson (1913-1988) and Winna F. (McMaster) Johnson (1913-1992). Our father was a cabinet maker, carpenter and house builder, but his specialty was making grandfather clocks. He would also refinish antiques for Bitting's Auction House (Tom and Portia Bitting) and Delancey's Antique Barn, on the corner of Linton Hill Road on Route 849. Our mother was a housewife and an active member of the Perdix Fire Company Ladies Auxiliary.

My grandfather, Archey Johnson (1885-1959) lived in the house with the elephants along the front porch steps, next to the Lucky Oaks Gulf Station. He was a member of the school board when the Susquenita School was built and opened in 1955. (He was a shareholder of the Perry County Railroad.) He loved to visit with us especially in the evenings once we had a tv. He loved to watch Covered Wagon Theatre and the Tuesday night fights. Bob and I would have to go out in the side-yard and turn the antenna to get a clear picture. If the picture was snowy, he would tell dad that he needed to clean out all the dead cowboys and Indians from the back.

In the backyard of our house, the gulf station-grocery store, and our grandfather's house, there were bird pens. From the houses to the railroad tracks, there were two acres of rare birds, owned by my grandfather. There were peacocks, pheasants, many unusual breeds of chickens and a variety of other birds. Bob and I would help to feed and water the birds. When we were in the pens, we would pick up feathers and sell them on the weekends when people would come to look at the birds. We would get five or ten cents for some, but get twenty-five cents for peacock tail feathers. It was a mystery how we always had three or four peacock tail feathers each weekend. I think Pap knew but never said anything.

One of the first guns we got was a Red Ryder BB gun. The bird pens were made out of pine. We would wait for the carpenter bees that came to drill holes and we would shoot them with our BB gun before they could get into the hole. They were the only thing we were allowed to shoot.

My first shot-gun was a .20-gauge action Mossburg. My Uncle George took me to Harrisburg to a pawnshop to buy it. I would hunt rabbits along the railroad tracks and hunt deer using pumpkin balls. Bob told me I'd only need six pumpkin balls and they would last for years. My first day of deer hunting I was out of ammo by ten o'clock. All I had to show for six shots was six dead trees. Jimmy Lou came and sat beside me with her .308 rifle and she missed another buck.

When Jimmy Lou got her car, she would take us to Dun-Mar Bowling Alley, which is now Leonard's Antiques on Route 11 & 15 in the Cove; the movies in Marysville or to Rheams Roller Rink outside of Millerstown or Heagy's Roller Rink near the Farm Show in Harrisburg.

Mrs. Helen Dersham, whose family owned the Decoven Diner, the Esso Station and Motel in the Cove, would stop in and buy pheasants for their tail feathers for the purpose of making "pill box" hats for friends. She would also stop in regularly to see if "Pop" had made any grandfather clocks. Sometimes if he had an order, he'd have to move it from the shop to the house or Mrs. Dersham would want to buy it. She eventually bought several grandfather clocks for herself and her children. The Dershams always had Doberman Pinscher dogs. The one male (Dobey) was trained to come out and sit at the gas pump. When you got done pumping gas, you would give your money to Dobey and he would take it into the station and give it to Jim Dersham, the owner.

Bob and I helped dad and Uncle George to clear and burn the brush when they were going to build. We dug cellar drains, mixed mortar, and carried blocks for the cellar walls. Back then there was no plywood. It was all one by tens or one by twelves for the sub-floors and roof. They would tack down the boards for the floor and Bob and I would finish nailing them. We would do the same thing for the drywall. When the plasterers were done, we'd have to clean the sub-floor of all the dropped plaster. Carrying the shingles up the ladder was a lot of work, but we were not allowed on the roof.

We also had chores to do around our house and the businesses. The Gulf Station was also a grocery store. I would pump gas and stock shelves on the weekend and some evenings during my sophomore and junior years in school. Part of my junior and all of my senior year, I worked for a concrete contractor in Camp Hill. We would set forms for curbing, steps, sidewalks and cellar floors before pouring the concrete. Then we had to strip the forms and clean them. Bob would run the backhoe for the curbing and for other work.

On some weekends, I would drive log truck for a trucker who lived across the street. I would take the load to Glatfelter's Pulpwood in York. I was paid twenty-five dollars a load. If I helped to load the truck Friday nights, sometime I could get two loads on a Saturday. I also helped him with some landscaping, raking and planting. One time he did not pay me, that was the end of that! You should have seen his truck windows the morning after Halloween!

I saved much of the money I earned to buy a car when I graduated in 1964. I was not allowed to have a car before graduation.

After Pap passed away, all the bird pens were torn down and burned. The backyard became our baseball and football fields. All the kids in the neighborhood would come to play ball and there were no umpires or referees. We would settle our disputes with fights. I was the smallest, but I'd get my licks-in and then run like the dickens for the house.

In the early days when the steam engines would go by on the railroad tracks, we had to stop playing and cover our eyes to keep out the soot. There were two water towers by the lower crossing at Burley Lane and Railroad Street. They were there to fill the steam engines. We would carry stones up into the tower and throw them at objects on the ground. We would take our bicycles up to Blacktop Crossing, and see how far we could ride on the rails. (I still have scars!)

We were either exploring in the Susquehanna River or on Cove Mountain. Dad built us a small eight-foot jon-boat and a larger twelve-foot. Mostly it depended on how high the river was as to which boat we choose to use. We had a dog named Hilda who rode on the front seat of the boat. One time, I had to turn the boat really quick to avoid hitting a rock and Hilda fell from the boat. Fortunately, she was a good swimmer.

A lot of times, we just waded but had to wear sneakers because of broken glass. Once we retrieved a picture-tube floating down the river. We took it onto shore, put it in the crouch of a tree and from about seventy-five feet shot it with a twenty-two rifle. The darn thing blew-up like a bomb went off! It threw glass and who knows what else for about thirty-feet. There was glass stuck in trees all around. That was the last tv tube we ever fooled with.

We always had 22 rifles and dad told us when we got our first 22 rifle that we would have to eat anything we shot. (That did not include rats!) To earn money for ammo, we would walk up and down the shoulders of Route 11 & 15 and pick up soda bottles. We could get two cents a piece deposit for them.

Harry Snow had a small sporting goods store in his basement in Perdix. We could buy twenty-two shorts for fifty cents a box of fifty. We had a shooting range behind the woodshop. We would use metal soda-bottle caps, that we got from the store's soda machine for targets. When we had extra money, we would buy Necco Wafers (a thin wafer-candy as big as a quarter) from the store and shoot them. In the evening, we would sneak down around the shop and shoot the mice and rats that came out from the building where pap kept his feed for the birds and to eat pieces of the shattered Necco Wafers.

We would also walk the railroad tracks to Perdix for our Boy Scout Troop 223 meetings. We would go early and shoot rats at the Perdix dump. The Boy Scouts would meet in the basement of Arnold's Grocery Store, which was next to the Perdix Fire Station. There was a small lot in back of the store, so we built a clubhouse and held our meeting there. Some of the girls in Perdix, formed a girl's club and used the scout building. It was fixed up really nice, but one night it burnt to the ground. The girls had a meeting that night and it was determined that they forgot to turn off the oven when they went home. Shortly thereafter the troop disbanded due to lack of boys, because most of the boys were older and moved on.

When heading south on Route 11 & 15, pap's house was attached to the Gulf Station and was the last house in the Cove. Everything south of there is considered Perdix. At the south end of Schoolhouse Road (we called it the back road) was the Garden Seat Tea Room Restaurant owned by Dick and Millie Novinger. Millie was the cook and baker. When the ladies at the firehouse would hold a soup and bake sale, Millie would always send some pies and cakes down for the sale. Millie and Dick always supported the local fire company. Unfortunately, the fire company is no longer in existence. The Marysville and Duncannon Fire Companies provide protection for Penn Township.

Another Cove business was Smitty's Junkyard and Fruit Stand which sat on the other side of the road from the Tea Room. I would go and help to burn out the old cars to be junked. When Sam brought the damaged cars from auction, we would go through them and sometimes find money, tools and about anything else you could think of. At the fruit stand, Sam's son, a neighbor and I would entertain ourselves by making blowguns with an old burned out "barn-burner" match and a needle. We used a loaded straw to shoot flies. We actually got pretty good at it! We would also have battles with old rotten tomatoes. Haldeman's (Tractor) Supply is there now.

Traveling north on Route 11 & 15 from Perdix, the first business on the right was our Pap's Gulf Station and across the street was his Dance Hall and Zoo. Perdix in the early years was a resort area for Harrisburg's wealthy and they would patronize the local businesses. There was a passenger train stop at the end of Firehouse Street in Perdix, and another at Burley Lane and Railroad Street during the 1920s-1940s. The kids that lived along Railroad Street would sometimes have to crawl under train cars to get to the school bus along Route 11 & 15 due to the train blocking the upper and lower crossings. Judy Cunkle's dad would call the control tower at Duncannon and try to have them move the train away from the crossings. It also prevented people from getting to work.

Judy Cunkle lived across the tracks and grew up in the Cove. Our sisters were friends and I was at her sixth birthday party. (We got married in 1965). I kiddingly tell everyone; she is from the other side of the tracks!

On the left just before Burley Lane was the King's Inn, a very popular restaurant and bar. We used to go to the backdoor and the cook (Mazzie Miller) would make us a pizza for fifty cents. The restaurant burned sometime in 2000 and never reopened.

At the intersection of Burley Lane and Route 11 & 15 was Bill Burley's Produce Stand, which closed in the late 1970s. Between Burley's and Rohrer Bus is a small cemetery. Rohrer Bus was founded in 1932 and is one of the largest school bus operators in Pennsylvania. Jim Rohrer drove our school bus on the first day of school. For me, I wanted no parts of getting on that bus. Pop finally picked me up and put me on the first step and Jim slammed the door shut. Hell of a way to start school. The next day I got that look from pop when the bus stopped. I knew the smartest thing I could do was to shut my mouth and get on that bus.

In 1952-1954, I was out of school off and on for two months due to illness. Missing that much school, my parents and the teacher decided to hold me back a year. In seventh through eleventh grades, I played football and was nothing more than a "tackling dummy." I did three practices my senior year and after a broken nose, dislocated shoulder and only weighing one-hundred and thirty-five pounds, I had enough of football. I went back to work for the rest of the summer.

Sometimes we would walk to school on the back road (School House Road). One morning when walking to school with Bob and some neighbor kids, I was bringing up the rear when I spotted a small monkey in a large tree, jumping from limb to limb. I hollered to the others and they thought I was crazy. They came back and watched for a while and when we continued past Mrs. Hammaker's house, she and her son were out hunting for the monkey.

We would ride our bikes on the back road to Cove Road and at Diffenderfer's Road there was a lane that led to an old farm pond. The farm was called Piney Perdix. We would swim there and sometimes camp out overnight. We spent a weekend or two camping out with the Boy Scouts. In the winter, we'd take our sleds to Bitting's farm along the back road. Across from the farmhouse, there was a lane that goes up into the mountain and we would sled down the mountain. We would sometimes do this at night. We put bicycle lights on our sleds.

The Bitting's would make and sell apple cider for fifty cents a gallon. We would buy two gallons and hide them along the back road in a wooden box for our walk to and from school. In a week or two, they got pretty good! We would walk down Bitting's Lane to Route 11 & 15 to Pop Steever's Store to get snacks and drinks. (It became the Quail Call Restaurant, which no longer exists.)

I left the Cove in 1965, but the memories remain.

Judy's Childhood Experiences in the Cove
Living next to the river is a wonderful experience, but it comes with risks. I grew up along the Susquehanna River and lived there all my life until 1965 when I married and moved to Duncannon. My parents, John and Viola Cunkle moved to the Cove in 1928 and raised three girls; Joan, Mary and Judy (b. 1946). All of us were born at home which was across the tracks and along the Susquehanna River. My parents survived three major floods, 1936, 1972 and 1975.

My dad was a driver for TastyKake for almost thirty years. Mom was a housewife and never learned to drive, so depended on dad to take us everywhere. We grew up learning to take care of a house and working in the yard and garden. One of our chores was yard patrol, which meant raking, picking up sticks and mowing the huge yard. We didn't have a power mower, so we used the old-fashioned push-rotary mower. Dad taught us how to mow in straight lines. There was no zig-zag or figure eights. We had a great many leaves to rake, so we would rake them onto an old blanket and pull them down to the edge of the property. We couldn't resist jumping into the large piles of leaves, but then we'd have to clean them up again.

We spent a lot of time in the river swimming, fishing or just exploring. Dad was a duck hunter and I remember one time when mom was hanging out laundry and a duck came flying over the clothesline and dropped dead on the lawn. Mom picked it up and cleaned it. Dad came off the river at dark and told her he didn't get too many and one flew away. Mom told him it didn't get very far and then told him the story.

With living that close to the railroad, you got used to the trains blowing their whistles at the crossing. We would wave at the engineers and they in turn would toot their horns at us. When it was nice outside, we used to sit on the swing on the front porch and wait for the "Broadway Limited" to go by at exactly 9 p.m., then we knew it was time to go to bed. The passenger train seemed to always be on time, so at 9 p.m., we knew that was it for the day.

We had to walk up the road and over the tracks to meet the school bus. A few times the neighbor kids and I had to crawl over or stoop under a stopped train to catch the bus.

As I got older, I was allowed to cross the tracks to get our mail or go across Route 11 & 15 to Pop Steever's Store to get mom some things. When we were little, mom would stick one of us in a baby buggy and we would cross Route 11 & 15 to Bitting's farm to get eggs. Occasionally, we would go to Duncannon for a movie for entertainment.

My older sister, Joan never learned to drive. Mary and I got our driver's licenses. When my dad took me out driving, he was really strict, but I learned a lot from him and was able to pass my test on my first attempt.

I was in seventh or eighth grade before we had a bathroom in the house. We had an enclosed back porch where mom did the wash with a wringer washer. She was always reminding me to keep my fingers away from the ringer. Finally, she gave dad an ultimatum to contact a contractor to convert the back porch into a bathroom. I guess he figured, she was serious and we finally got a bathroom.

I graduated in 1964 and was dating Jerry. We married in 1965. I was working at Nationwide Insurance and Jerry was working for PennDot. We lived in an apartment for a year and a half, and then bought our present house on Sunshine Hill in Duncannon. Six years later our son Jim was born.

Business Locations in the Cove from the 1940s -1960s

Heading south from Duncannon on Route 11 & 15 on the right side of the road:
Smith's Store was on the corner of Cove Road which leads back to Kinkora Pythian Home.
White and Wingate sawmill which is now Marstellar Concrete.
Decoven Motel to Decoven Diner to Dersham's Esso Station – all three were owned by Jim and Helen Dersham now recycling and auto repair.
Susquenita Junior and Senior High School
Dun-Mar Bowling Alley which became a skating rink now Leonard's Antique's.
Oyler's Tourist Park Motel and Cabins now residences.
Bitting's Auction House later Colonial Fair and now Big Bee Boats.
Pop Steever's General Store then the Quail Call Restaurant.
Burley's Fruit Stand now residence.
King's Inn Restaurant
Archie Johnson's Dance Hall and Zoo

Heading south from Duncannon on Route 11 & 15 on the left side of the road:
Hoffman Tire now Norm's Tire
Sam's Sporting Goods now rental property.
Gas for Less now vacant.
Scale House for weighing trucks now Pap's Sweets & Treats, DJ's Grill and food trucks.
Clair Miller's Row Boat Rental across the tracks along the river.
Archie Johnson's Rare Birds
Archie Johnson's Gulf Station which is now Dream Vacation Travel Agency and By Design Hair and Nails.
Smitty's Junk Yard and Fruit Stand now Haldeman Tractor Sales.

And, that was the Cove, between Duncannon and Perdix.

Cooper's Store And The Kanon Theatre

"MEMORIES OF DUNCANNON"

Storyteller Suzanne Cooper Brown

Growing up in Duncannon made my childhood a wonderful experience. During the 1950s-1960s, Duncannon was a very active and family-oriented community. The Duncannon Lions Club was responsible for creating so much of this family atmosphere. They promoted so many activities geared toward family life including holiday parades and carnivals right out my front door and talent shows.

My favorite was Friday night dances held at the Lions Club Chapel on North High Street. These dances were open to kids of all ages in the community. However, if you were twelve or younger, you were relegated to the basement after a certain time and lights were lowered upstairs. This was to allow the "real" teenagers to dance and socialize without the younger kids, especially their siblings who tattled. I'm sure they often went home and reported to their parents, who was dancing too close.

I believe Ken Delancey, our local jeweler, was responsible for spinning records. The main chaperone was Charlie Pennell, a very active Lions Club officer. He kept everyone under control and even interacted on the dance floor! I don't recall any serious disruptions or misbehavior.

At these dances, contests were held and prizes given. Once I won the twist contest and was ecstatic with my accomplishment, which is a small-town memory I cherish.

My parents, Doris and Max Cooper, were in partnership with my Aunt Flossie and Uncle Paul Cooper. They established Cooper's Market, located at the corner of High and Cumberland Streets, on Friday, May 23, 1947. Both Cooper families lived in apartments above the store, which really made it accessible but also time-consuming. The store became a daily gathering place for so many people.

It was a full-time family operation and one of my favorite childhood stories was when I was a small toddler. My mother would set-up the playpen by the cash register and put me in it to play while she waited on and checked out customers. It became problematic because it was located close to the candy rack. I'm not sure if the customers thought I was cute or felt sorry for me stuck in that cage, so they were continually handing me candy. My creative mother had to place a sign on the playpen, PLEASE DO NOT FEED ME! That took care of that.

I have so many stories and memories of growing up in the store, but another favorite was when Aunt Jemima came on a promotional visit for her new pancake mix. It was a very exciting day, because she came to our house afterwards and ate lunch with my family. Aunt Jemima made herself available for pictures at the store front.

One of the vital parts of the business were the workers, who are too many to mention for fear of omitting someone. But I must point out, we had the distinction of having two long-time employees both named Don Liddick. We appropriately named them "Town Don" and "Country Don." There were so many loyal life-time Cooper employees, who were all part of our "family!" Most are deceased, but their funny stories and experiences were extensive and I witnessed them making every single customer feel special.

My father was a generous and kind man who would help anyone. As I got old enough to actually work in the store, I realized this more and more. In Duncannon, most of the customers were hard-working laborers, who got paid once a month. My father would allow customers to charge their groceries until payday. On the first of the month, it was a big trip to the bank to make sure there was enough cash on hand to cash customer's paychecks and settle their accounts. Of course, there were a few exceptions, but the honesty and trust on both sides made it work even in some difficult times.

Coopers also had a very steady delivery service, similar to the ordering services in today's consumer world. People would call in their orders, which we filled and delivered on the same day. Many of these customers were elderly with no means of transportation. Often, they were very vague in their requests and I remember filling orders and choosing things we thought they'd enjoy and were an easy preparation. I don't recall any complaints. I do have fond recollections of these elderly folks' appreciation of not only their groceries, but the company and conversation of the delivery person.

The biggest reward in being part of this small-town business was getting to know and become friends with so many who passed through the doors. In a local store like we were, you knew everyone's name, their families and even their brand of cigarettes which were on the counter before they were ready to check-out. You came to know their shopping habits, their likes and dislikes. Most importantly, we knew their personal stories and hardships, and my family was there to assist any way we could.

My Cooper family also owned and operated the Kanon Theater, located behind our grocery store. This was such a contribution to the social lives of all the local kids. Friday and Saturday evenings, plus a Saturday matinee featuring movies was such a treat. I remember lines extending for a block, especially on Friday nights, to buy movie tickets. My Aunt Flossie was the "theater disciplinarian!" When she marched down the aisle with her flashlight, we all knew to sit up with our hands in clear sight! No one wanted kicked out or reported to our parents because in our small town everyone knew everyone.

We saw movies that were considered some of the greatest shows of all times. I was always there with so many friends laughing and making long lasting memories.

After giving their heart and souls to establishing and maintaining these Duncannon landmarks, my family sold the properties and business in 1973. The buildings may have been demolished, but the memories and experiences made in that block still live on today.

As I stated throughout my story, I am so blessed with so many wonderful memories and lifelong friendships made in the small town of Duncannon.

This Is Trooper Krammes Reporting In

Storyteller Stanley "Whitey" Krammes
Recorded by Fred Noye

The Pennsylvania State Police was founded in 1905, the first uniformed Police Organization of its kind in the United States.

However, there was no continual State Police presence in Perry County until 1950. Prior to that, if a State Police Patrol came to the county it would've come from Dauphin County, Carlisle or maybe Chambersburg. Then they would've probably come for a specific purpose.

Local law enforcement was left to "town cops" (if there was one) and in some cases the County Sheriff.

In 1946, a State Police detail or "Barracks" was set-up on the Island at Benvenue (Clarks Ferry). Not until October 1, 1950, did Perry County get its own State Police Barracks. It was located in the old Rhinesmith Hotel on the square in New Bloomfield and was staffed with six State Troopers.

The first Troopers were Cpl. Ludwig Jenkins, Trooper Stanley Krammes, Trooper James J. Convery, Trooper Edward Ruda, Trooper Joseph Devanney (Crime Investigator) and Trooper Stephen Stenpian.

The Troopers got one day off a week (hopefully) and two nights off a week. Their hours were 7 a.m. - 3:30 p.m. or 3:30 p.m. - 11 p.m. The Troop had three cars (Fords).

The accommodations at the Rhinesmith were two rooms upstairs and a small bunk in a room behind the front-desk room on the ground floor. They were paid thirty-seven dollars and fifty cents every two weeks and received a stipend of seventy-five cents for breakfast; one dollar and twenty-five cents for lunch; two dollars and fifty cents for dinner; seven days a week. The stipend was paid directly to the restaurant, chosen by the State Police Headquarters. Gring's Restaurant, in New Bloomfield located next to what is now Boyer's Funeral Home, was the chosen eatery. The restaurant got paid, whether or not the Troopers showed up for meals.

The Troopers were issued a .38 caliber revolver and they were issued three sets of summer uniforms and three sets of winter uniforms. With their shoes, they were issued black leggings.

The Barracks remained at the Rhinesmith until 1954 when it was relocated to the converted Towpath Motel in Watts Township, along Route 11 & 15 near New Buffalo. The force grew to an average of twelve Troopers.

While in New Bloomfield, Troopers did not have radios in their cars until 1952. The only communication was a radio tower located high on the hill over-looking New Bloomfield and a base-station in the Rhinesmith Hotel. To communicate while on patrol, a Trooper had to make stops at local Justice of the Peace offices and call into the desk for updates. There were also some friendly farmers who could be called and asked to turn on their front porch light to signal for a Trooper to stop and call the base. Some usually had the coffee pot on and fresh pie or cake ready if a Trooper might stop.

Stanley "Whitey" Krammes was born in 1928 in Landingville, Schuylkill County, Pennsylvania. He entered the State Police Academy in 1950, turning twenty-two during his training. Before being assigned, a Trooper trained for six months, including two months in-service training with an experienced officer. Of course, you had to pass a physical; had to be at least five-foot-eight, but no taller than six-foot-two and weigh between one-hundred-fifty and two-hundred-twenty pounds. You had to be single and remain single for three years. A Trooper had to receive permission to marry. And, that was no easy task! First you had to ask your superior officer and then it had to go up through the ranks to the regional commander and so on till it reached the very top, the State Police Commissioner. Then it had to find its way back down the chain of command. Oh, did I mention the background check of the intended bride.

Once commissioned you had a two year enlistment and had to re-enlist very two years. Mandatory retirement age was sixty.

"Whitey" remained at the Perry County Barracks from 1954 until 1961. The original New Bloomfield assignment worked out well for several of the Troopers. Four of the original six met their wives and married, so that long marriage process didn't intimidate them. "Whitey" decided to go to the Methodist church one Sunday and became enamored with the church organist, Arlis Wohletz, who also conveniently worked at Gring's Restaurant where the Troopers ate their meals. It was good fortune as they have been married for sixty-eight years.

However, Trooper Krammes' career almost ended before it began. While doing his two month in-service training with his assigned officer, tragedy struck. While out on night patrol, they pulled over an erratic driver near the old Harrisburg Drive-In Theater. When they motioned to the driver to pull over, the driver stopped quickly and didn't get the car completely off the road. After exiting the car, "Whitey" was told to stay back and direct traffic around the car while his superior walked to talk to the driver of the stopped vehicle.

It was then that "Whitey" noticed a large truck coming straight for them and he tried to signal the driver with his flashlight. When he realized the truck wasn't changing course, "Whitey" yelled to the other Trooper and tried to scurry between the cars, but the crash threw him some distance into a field. Trying to gather himself together, he finally found his hat and flashlight, and found his way back to the crash scene where he saw the officer lying under the car. He pulled him out but it was too late and the Trooper was dead.

"Whitey's" thirty-eight year career was quite successful. For most of his early years in Perry County, he was given the job as the Criminal Investigator at the Barracks. He was promoted to Corporal in 1961 and to Sergeant in 1966. He was assigned to Carlisle in 1961, but returned to New Buffalo in 1963 where he found that the barracks had been moved to the old Park Motel. He was assigned to State College in 1964 until 1966, where he became personal friends with Joe Paterno. He almost left the State Police when he was offered a very tempting job as head of security at Penn State, but after long consideration, he turned it down.

In 1966, he was assigned to the Hollidaysburg Barracks and then was given command at the Lewistown Barracks from 1967-1970. Then onto Harrisburg from 1970-1972 where he was placed in charge of the Traffic Detail. He finished his career back "home" in New Buffalo in command of the Duncannon Barracks, from 1972 until 1988.

In 1968, "Whitey" decided to quit taking tests for promotions. He knew if he was promoted to the next level it would take him out of the field and would place him into the headquarter bureaucracy. He preferred being in the field and the day-to-day law enforcement activity. He loved the comradery of the barracks.

When you have a career that long, you have a lot of memories and stories to share, and "Whitey" could've written a book. He remembers well about confronting a woman at Amity Hall who was trying to sell her children to travelers that had stopped there.

He remembers being called to help with the riots at Penn State during the Kent State uprising in 1968. Buses of protesters were brought to the campus from out of state and proceeded to wreck havoc to the Penn State campus. "Whitey" was asked to bring Troopers but to come unarmed. When he refused to allow his men to go unprotected, the local police in charge relented and the Lewistown Troopers were sent in.

He remembered a very snowy Christmas Eve when on patrol he came upon Cliff Sloppy and a group of people near Blain that heard what they thought was an airplane circling on the outskirts of the town, as if it were looking for a place to land. "Whitey" gave them his supply of flairs in an attempt to provide light and guidance for the plane to land. Wading in the snow, the locals hurried in hopes of averting a catastrophe. As it turned out, no plane landed and no report of missing planes were reported.

He was called into service to help track the "Mountain Man" at Shade Gap during the search for kidnapped Peggy Ann Bradnick in 1966. He provided assistance when an attempted jail break occurred at the old Perry County Jail and the sheriff's wife was assaulted. There was never a dull moment in this job.

But the case that sticks most in his mind, was a murder that occurred in Newport. A local man was constantly being arrested for being drunk and assaulting his wife. Police would respond to the wife's calls and pick him up. Time after time, she would then refuse to press charges and he would be released. This scenario was endless until one day when confronted by "Whitey" and Newport Policeman Kenny Crain, the man pointed a rifle point blank at Officer Crain. After a long confrontation, the man drove off to a local bar where "Whitey" and Crain picked him up without resistance. This time the wife could not drop the charges because the police charged him with resisting arrest. However, before his court appearance, he murdered his wife and attempted – unsuccessfully to commit suicide.

Not so many years later, the same scenario was played out with this man's son and his wife. The result was another murder and this time a successful suicide.

There was one other murder case that resulted in a big disappointment. The murder took place in front of the couple's child and when called to the scene, the child related what had happened. They felt they had an open and shut case until at trial, the child changed the story and the defendant was acquitted.

I asked "Whitey" if he ever had to deliver a baby. His response "came close once".

No story about the PSP in Perry County would be complete without one story about the legendary Trooper, "Moose" Lawlor. He remembered that Moose was six-foot-two and always wore platform shoes. He would always pull his seat in the police car forward and sit high on the back of the seat. He would take off his hat and drive with his head cocked to the side. As he drove, the seat would work its way back and by the time there was a shift change, the next Trooper found the seat so far back he could barely reach the accelerator.

Moose always fancied himself as a great driver, but "Whitey" noticed that the cars Moose drove always seemed to have little "dings" in them. The other Troopers denied they were responsible so "Whitey" devised a plan. He gave Moose his own car that no other Trooper would drive. When that car turned up with some "dings" the mystery was solved.

Moose was always prepared for any emergency. He was Canadian by birth, so he carried a pair of snowshoes in his car during the winter and went out and purchased his own shotgun to carry in the car.

"Whitey" was quick to point out that "Moose was a damn good Trooper". On several occasions, he was given awards for his life-saving heroism.

"Whitey" retired in 1988 at the mandatory retirement age. It should be noted that in this type of work, where lives are on the line everyday, a special kind of bond develops among the Troopers. Actually this environment becomes more like a large family with everyone depending on each other. The men who served under "Whitey" carried a special respect for him and came to look upon him more as a father figure. It was very difficult to see him retire, and many of his men continue to stop by to visit with him or to keep in touch. "Whitey" said he got along with everyone in his command except for one. In 2018, when "Whitey" turned ninety, most of his former colleagues showed up for his birthday party – even that one PITA!

However "Whitey's" law enforcement days were not over, when he retired in 1988. The State Police Pension wasn't that great, so when he heard that they were looking for part-time help in the Federal Marshal's Office in Harrisburg, "Whitey" applied. (1991) He would work a couple of days a week, or so he thought. Shortly after starting his new career, the man in charge of the Federal Marshals assigned to Harrisburg, left. In searching for a replacement it was noticed that "Whitey" had taken advanced training at the FBI Academy. All of a sudden, "Whitey" was working full-time and found himself in charge of the office. He remained in that position for twelve years.

The job mostly involved serving subpoenas and providing court security, along with transporting Federal prisoners. On September 11, 2001 the job took on a whole new meaning. The office was notified that the 911 hijackers could be targeting the Federal Building in Harrisburg. An immediate evacuation was ordered of the building as a precaution. Of course we all know, how that story played out.

Finally "Whitey" retired for good in 2003. So what does one do to relax when you are in a dangerous high stress job. Besides family adventures, with his wife, daughter and grandchildren, "Whitey" was one of the original members of the Dix Hill Hunting Camp. Founded in 1963, a group from the New Bloomfield area got together and purchased one-hundred-six acres of mountain ground from John Gantt. Over the years, the club has added over a hundred more acres to their holdings. It is located on the ridge between Meck's Corner and Montebello.

The driving forces behind the orignal purchase was "Red" Stoops, Doctor Frank Belmont and Harold Greaney. Other original members included, Don Stoops, "Red" Adams, John Sanderson, Bill Moore, Don Briner, Norm Black, Arden Shambaugh, Herb Baker, Dale Kumler, Henry Fehnael and Joe Darlington.

Today the camp still exists, but there isn't much hunting taking place. The club is limited to twenty members and is used primarily for social events for members and their families and a weekly card game.

Sure beats patrolling the highway looking for law breakers.

All In A Day's Work
OUTHOUSES TO SEPTIC SYSTEMS TO PORTA-POTTIES

Storyteller Joe Baker
Recorded by Steve Metzger

My name is Joe Baker, I grew up on Fourth Street in East Newport. My parents were Albert and Marianne (Rutkins) Baker. Almost everyone knew dad because of his business and nearly everyone talked to mom when they would call to have their septic tanks serviced.

Dad was a Newport native, having grown up in East Newport. The family business was started by dad and his father, who created Bakers Septic Service. During the Depression years, they cleaned outside toilets with a bucket on a long pole to reach the bottoms. Later my dad took over and began servicing more septic tanks and less outhouses. Even though I was still a kid, I worked with my dad washing the trucks and going along to help on service calls. Before I could drive, my dad would drop me off at someone's house to hand dig their septic tank open, while he worked elsewhere. Later, he would return and pump it out. The first pumps were slow and noisy, but throughout the years, we got bigger trucks, faster pumps and eventually used a vacuum system to clean the tanks.

My paternal grandparents were Raymond Baker and Mary (Sheaffer) Baker. My Gram and Pap Baker lived beside us. My Aunt Rhoda and Uncle Rod Saylor had the little store at the end of our block. My Aunt Catherine and Uncle Dave Bower lived three doors away, and my great friends Mike, Ed and Cindy Campbell lived two doors away. It was a good neighborhood where everyone looked out for everyone in those days. An unrelated, Baker family lived next to us. They were dear friends, that we considered family and I was lucky, I had two "Pap Bakers", one on each side.

Pap Baker (Raymond) was a little fellow who worked hard and chewed Silvercup tobacco. After retiring from PennDot, he was an Oliver Township supervisor and road worker, as I am today. It's almost a family tradition and I'm proud to serve the citizens of our township, many of which I consider lifelong friends, just like pap did. I have so many good memories of him, too many to mention. My Grandma Baker was a cook and baker at the Mingle House Hotel in Newport years back, who took pride in her pie baking until she could no longer do it.

A funny story that happened in East Newport had much to do with our business. A row-home fire broke out in East Newport in the 1970s. With limited ability to truck in water from hydrants far away from the fire, the fire company asked my dad to haul water. Thank goodness, the lines were similar and they were able to hook right up and take water from our trucks to run through the fire truck.

I swear, this is a true story! After hours of fighting fire and intense heat, one of the tired, parched firemen, unaware of which truck the hose was attached to, took a drink out of the hose and made a face saying "that tastes like (you know what)." It made everyone laugh for a moment. Dad had a quick wit and great sense of humor. It was hard for anyone to get one over on him. More than anything, he was always willing to give back to the community.

During the flood of 1972, I was eight years old and I can remember helping Abe Singleton take the live fish off the river bridge as the water went down. Our family was instrumental in the town cleanup, helping people in need where we could, pumping basements and hauling debris in our dump truck. Dad recalled the story of hauling the tainted liquor bottles, from the old State Store that sat along Market Street, after the flood. The bottles were tossed into the back of the dump truck and smashed, so that the liquor was destroyed, just like in the news reels about prohibition. Several of the liquor store "regulars" from town lined up to mourn the loss of the alcohol and watch it run out the bottom of the truck and down the storm drain.

My maternal grandparents were Ida (Kuhn) and Steven Rutkins. My Grandma Ida retired from Kinney Shoe Corporation. This lady was a hoot with a quick wit. I spent a week each summer at her place on Main Street in Landisburg. Eventually, she moved to Newport to be a little closer to us. Again, I have too many good memories of her to mention, but I love them all and the time we spent together when I was growing up.

My mother was originally from Bridgeport, Connecticut. My dad met her when she spent time on Great-Grandpa Sam Kuhn's farm near Cisna Run. She would spend summers there with her grandparents.

As a child, we all had chores. Mine were keeping our trucks clean. It thrilled me at age nine to pull a truck out of the garage by myself and wash it. My dad and his buddies, many of which were his lifelong friends from East Newport, did the mechanical work on the trucks. Dad worked long days, running the business throughout the day and maintaining the trucks sometimes late into the evenings. My job was to keep the shop clean, in order, put tools away and such. After my older brother left home, I took over grass mowing and many chores around the house too, since my younger brother was too small to be responsible for much.

Even though I worked hard, I had time to play. I had too many great friends in East Newport to mention. We did normal kid stuff, like bike riding, football, sledding in the winter and such. The East Newport playground was only a block away but we spent most of our time at each other's houses anyway. I didn't do school sports, because I was too much into helping with the family business, working with Dad on the trucks and doing what we did together. Still, I had lots of good friends and I love them all. We are all still good friends to this day.

My siblings are sisters Dawn Gerhart and Rox Maxwell. My brothers are George Demchak and Steve Herndon. About my sister, Dawn, she's a sister like no other in my eyes. She's been there for me all my life as a source of guidance, as a main part of my business office back in the day, and was always like a mother to me, whom I love.

When I was thirteen, my family built a new house and in 1980 we moved to Upper Bailey, outside of Newport. By then, it was just Steve and I living at home. We had a lot more space, but there was a lot more yard to mow, plus wood to split and lots of other chores. There was a much larger garage for the trucks. Dad and his gang of friends spent so much time working on things in there. It was hard to find a time when there weren't people around. Mom would brew coffee by the gallon. No one ever showed up that they weren't offered a cup, whether working in the garage or just sitting around the table "shooting the breeze." My younger brother and I made new friends living in the country and they often hung out at our place, swam in our pool or spent the night.

After a few years, we built a small barn and raised steers, hogs and chickens. My mom had a garden and we cut hay and grew corn. Along with that came blood and sweat but I don't regret a minute of the way I grew up.

In later years, dad and I decided to expand into the porta-potty business and at one time had 250 units to place and service. After my dad passed in 2006, we continued on until 2009 when I was diagnosed with a lifelong lymph node problem. I had choices to make, and needed to make them quick. So as much as I hated to, I gave up the business after having been involved in it for over thirty years. My career was as a wastewater treatment plant operator. So, at this point in life, I am semi-retired but I have been Oliver Township supervisor since 2002, chairman of the board and road master, just like my Pap Baker.

Speaking of family, I met my lady, Diana in 2010. Her parents are Donald and Nancy Robinson of 4th Street in Newport and she has a brother, Guy of East Newport. She and I do basically everything together. If she's cooking, I do dishes. If I'm cleaning the chimney, she's holding the ladder. She's been with me through the good, the bad and the ugly. That's hard to find these days and I am thankful to have her in my life. Shortly after I found out about my illness, I was run over on my motorcycle and she was there with me through it all. We reside on Harley Drive on top of Upper Bailey Road. Our property overlooks Newport and the general area. Between the two of us, we have two girls, two boys and five grandchildren.

We have many hobbies. Diana likes to cook, bake and use the Blackstone griddle. I swear that lady can find any three items in the pantry and make a Sunday dinner out of nothing - she's the best. She likes to toy with gardening and enjoys raising things you can't buy around here, like a crop of mini-corn.

My hobbies are basically what I did for a living, less the long days of driving and maintaining trucks. I enjoy running the backhoes and various equipment and I still have folks call for advice on sewer issues and I'm happy to load up my tools and help them out. I turned one bay of our shop into my man-cave with the tools I used all my life hanging on the walls, ready when I need them. My backhoe sits next to my chair where I enjoy opening the door early in the morning and having coffee. I also toy with sunrise and sunset photography, as the sun is coming up over the hills or setting behind the town of Newport. The town sure is beautiful with the colorful sky behind it.

Perry county folks are a special breed of their own! Many of my friendships are folks I've met through my growing up and working years in Perry County and I also want to say many of them have been an inspiration to me. I could go on and on, but the whole thing in a nut shell is "I'm so glad to have grown-up and had the pleasure of meeting so many great people in our community known as Perry County".

Hidden Treasures In Pleasant Valley

Storyteller Sabrina Nulton Gray

The Samuel and Carrie Swartz farm in Pleasant Valley, Pennsylvania, was my childhood home until I turned eight years old. My Great-Uncle Bill Swartz owned the farm and rented it to my father, David Nulton, who had a whole brood of youngsters with my mother, La Wanda. Farming was and still is the driving force in my dad's heart.

Dad ran his red Farmall tractor as often as he could but still needed to spend many hours away doing the job that paid the bills, as a toll collector on the Clark's Ferry Bridge in Duncannon. On May 15, 1957, he had the distinction of collecting the last token (at that time paper tickets) since tolls were no longer required. Later dad was the toll collector for the Pennsylvania Turnpike at the Carlisle Exchange.

We did not have modern conveniences while I was young. I guess that is why I can relate to an Amish lifestyle. We had no running water, only a hand pump. And you were never lonely in our outhouse because it was a two-seater. We would sit and browse through the Sears and Roebuck catalog as we were doing our business. We had no electric clothes dryer, either.

I can still remember our clothes line being full every sunny day and hearing mom's strong voice singing "Oh! What a Beautiful Morning" while hanging the laundry. During her lifetime she always hung her laundry outside to dry - even in the snow to "freeze dry". You see, after birthing four girls in four years she had three children in cloth diapers at the same time. So, all these diapers had to be cleaned and dried by hand. The water was drawn by pump, carried by bucket, heated on the cook stove and transferred to the two wringer washer tubs. One was for washing and one was for rinsing. Then the clothes were wrung out and placed into a basket to be carried outside and hung up to dry. We did have a few lines in the basement, just in case.

Raising five small children, mom had to come up with some creative ways to occupy our busy hands. When our dad plowed the fields above our house in the spring, there would be shining objects all over the fields after a new rain. We discovered quartz stones plowed up, washed new and shiny in the golden sunshine.

My mom gave us each a recycled baby food jar to keep our collected treasures. We would spend hours scanning the hillside looking for the little mirrors that sparkled. Keeping our eyes on the same spot until we reached it, lest we lose it. We discovered the world of quartz stones. Some were clear and others had a light amethyst color.

Once we ran out of the "shinies" then our father showed us the ground was also home to even harder to find treasures. Being dirt-colored, these small objects were very hard to spot. They were .25 inch to 1.25 inches in length but mostly in between those sizes. They were always round with a hole in it, like a bead. Through the years I have heard that they were petrified vertebrae of various animals. Whatever they were, we collected many. We cleaned out the debris from the middle holes with needles, washed them, and then strung them into necklaces. We instantly became Indian princesses! I still have some of those "Indian beads" at my current home.

Our treasure finding adventures came to an abrupt halt one day when our four city cousins Mike, Mitch, Michelle and Mark came for a visit. We all took glass baby food jars and climbed the hill to gather our treasures. It wasn't long until all of us came running to the house yelling for help. Cousin Mitch had fallen and his jar broke cutting the palm of his hand long and deep. There was blood everywhere! He was taken quickly to Dr. Belmont's office on West Main Street in New Bloomfield. After stitching Mitch, the doctor said, "Son, you came a half inch from never using your hand again". We all learned a lesson that day. Don't run with anything glass in your hands!

When we moved from Pleasant Valley in the fall of 1965, all the young ones missed our "hidden treasures" field. Though my mother would say "the real treasures moved with her". All five of us to our new home, a hundred-acre dairy farm three miles north of Newport, which sat in three townships, Juniata, Tuscarora and Oliver, but still in good old Perry County.

County Dispatch, This Is Ambulance 59 Signing Off

Storyteller Nicholas E. Lemaster
Recorded by Debra Kay Noye

Nicholas "Nick" Lemaster was a typical Perry County farm boy growing up in the sixties. He missed out on a lot of the "old fashioned" farming techniques, being born in 1958 to Shirley Markle and Clarence Lemaster on a farm in Perry Valley. His grandparents were Anna Bigler and Luther Lemaster, and Margaret Hetrick and Earl Markle. And, yes, just in case you are wondering, he is related to the famed Megan Markle, wife of England's Prince Harry. Nick's Perry County family consisted of Robert now deceased, Jeffrey, Pamela and Jamie. They obviously were a hand-full for his mother!

Nick remembers being told by his Pap about horses being used on the farm and the first cletrac tractor put to use on the farms (130 acres) owned by his Pap and farmed by his Uncle Robert Markle on Perry Valley's Ridge Road. He was twelve, when he was steering the farm tractor hooked to a wagon for the hay bales to be tossed on and stacked. He remembers the balers where he pulled the bales from the chute to the wagon bed, and later the kick-balers, which automatically threw the bales onto the wagon without ranking. His pap was really particular about the use of one of his corn cribs. All of the corn had to be totally hand-husked. He hated that job!

Nick also helped Warren Hetrick of Perry Valley on his farm, filling silo and hauling grain. Nick preferred farm work as opposed to pulling weeds in the family garden. His pap was always after him telling him, that the garden and strawberries won't get a chance to grow if you don't pull the weeds.

He was plowing and discing the fields by the time he was fifteen, which kept him off his dirt-bike, (which he purchased from R. E. Davidson and paid for it as he got paid for helping out on the farm), and from getting into trouble. It was nothing for him to be jumping the banks around the farms on his Honda 100, much to the chagrin of his mother. He eventually had a Honda 250 motorcycle, on which he sped up and down the country roads.

He and some buddies snuck-off on their dirt-bikes one day. Nick rode to Millerstown, crossed the river bridge, rode between the railroad tracks to Thompsontown and back home through the wood trails, thinking he had outsmarted his mother. She already knew where he'd been by the time he arrived home. The concept of people looking out for one another was still so true in the 1960s-1970s, especially among the country folk. Another incident occurred when he was "pulled over" on Route 11 & 15 by State Police Officer Norm Watkins, from the Newport Barracks, who lived along Route 11 & 15. He recognized Nick and his pick-up truck. They chatted about baseball and Trooper Watkins gave him a warning. Once again, his mother knew he had been "pulled over" by the Trooper, because someone who passed by the scene reported it to her.

Nick went to Liverpool Elementary School through sixth grade, graduating from Greenwood High School. He always drug his feet and didn't want to go to school. Once when he was trying to get out of attending school, his pap after fixing Nick some breakfast, told him, "enjoy yourself now, because time goes by so fast, as you get older!" Nick now agrees with his pap.

He played high school basketball and one year of baseball. He also played on the Liverpool midget team, riding his bike the three miles to the ball field which is where the Liverpool Pool is located today. Wayne Shuler was his coach. After practice, he would go over to Jay's Restaurant for a soda and sometimes a burger to tide him over till supper. His mother had arranged for Jay's to keep a "running tab" on Nick, and she would stop by and pay it. That's unheard of in today's business world. Coach Shuler arranged for the use of the Liverpool American Legion bus to take the midget team to see a Little League Game at Williamsport's Little League stadium, where the Little League World Championships are held. At that time, it was tradition to slide down the hill outside of the ballpark, on a piece of cardboard. Nick cherishes that day and the opportunity of a lifetime.

He recalls going shopping with his mother in Newport at the 5 & 10 Store. When Nick was growing up, Liverpool's booming businesses had all but disappeared. Today, the bedroom community is minus Miller's Grocery Store, the hardware store, the independently owned First National Bank of Liverpool is now Juniata Valley Bank, the local doctor, the rubber plant which had employed thirty people, and the three convalescent homes. Susquehanna Sprinkler, Chris' Pizza and Lowe's Restaurant still remain.

Nick tells the story of when he was helping with some auto repairs, when the jack slipped and cut him above his eye, laying the skin back. He went into Liverpool's Doc Minihan where he received five stitches and went on his way. Not in today's Liverpool could that happen.

However, if somebody needs medical attention, there is a Liverpool Emergency Medical Services, #59, it's own entity. Nick was instrumental in transitioning from the fire company ambulance to Liverpool EMS. He VOLUNTEERED, over forty years, serving as president and vice-president, commander and deputy commander, chief driver and assistant chief driver. The titles and accolades are not what Nick seeks. It is the satisfaction that he has helped his neighbors, Perry Countians and complete strangers when they needed life-saving, medial help the most!

To Nick it is so gratifying to hear that newborn's cry, and to immediately call that into county dispatch, so the time of birth can be documented for its birth certificate. That has happened twice to Nick as he drove the Liverpool Ambulance to a Harrisburg hospital. "That warm feeling came over him" just as the ambulance went under the Dauphin Underpass and the baby couldn't wait any longer. The attendants safely delivered that crying baby in the ambulance. Earlier years they used an old Cadillac-style ambulance, which quite frankly looked like a hearse. The second time, the crew assumed they were transporting a woman complaining of severe abdominal pain. Whoopsie! It was a shock to the ambulance personnel and to the woman when she delivered a healthy baby. The dispatch to county amazed everybody.

The Liverpool Ambulance had humble beginnings. And, if weren't for the cooperation of Liverpool's Good Samaritan Nursing Home (now Owen's House), it wouldn't have occurred. This was before the use of modern day pagers, which are used for communicating, when an ambulance and crew is needed. Here is how the early days were handled in Liverpool even before the use of box-style and modular ambulances, when somebody had a medical emergency. Some also applies to fires.

The person needing medical attention or in the case of an accident, the State Police might notify the Perry County Emergency Medical Dispatch team in the courthouse basement in New Bloomfield. The standard call for help was and still is 911. County dispatch would take the caller's information and then call Liverpool's Good Samaritan Nursing Home, which was staffed around the clock, and relay the information to them. The nursing home staff would then call the volunteers on ambulance duty for that time frame and tell them the situation. If it was a dire emergency and more help may be needed, they would automatically push the button to blow the fire company siren alerting the entire town and the surrounding area that a need existed for extra volunteers. A wire was run from the nursing home to the fire house, which enabled that siren to sound off. The same held true for a fire call.

The nursing home staff would give explicit details to the ambulance crew as to what medical attention was needed, where the patient was located, and what hospital the patient preferred if that was known. Sometimes that hospital preference couldn't be honored depending on the circumstances and the availability of the hospital. Nick remembers transporting a majority of patients to the Polyclinic Hospital in Harrisburg, which in most cases was the closest.

All the ambulance personnel, including the drivers, were trained in first-aid only. They also knew how to administer oxygen if needed and contain a bleeding wound. This was before EMT's, paid personnel who undergo more extensive training. Nick was the man behind the wheel for four calls in one day, and in one year's time he drove on over three-hundred calls. Liverpool is located along the extremely busy Route 11 & 15, between Duncannon and Selinsgrove. Many traffic accidents, particularly in bad weather, when people should have enough common sense to slow down and be mindful of roadway conditions, occur. When people use bad judgment, they can be thankful the modern-day trained medical personnel on the Liverpool ambulance is there to save the day.

Once the ambulance arrives at the scene, ascertains the situation, loads the patient and heads to the hospital, the driver notifies county dispatch of what has taken place and where they are headed. After they unload the patient at the hospital, they make county dispatch aware they are free for another call if need arises.

In today's world, with the uncertainties of what might take place when on an ambulance call, county dispatch keeps in radio contact every five minutes for an update. Today's driver and crew have to make decisions if the patient needs immediate medical care beyond what they can provide plus the length of time to transport. That's when Life Lion may be called to fly helicopters out of Hershey Medical Center to the scene for quick patient transport to Hershey Medical Center for acute care.

Nick had the unique opportunity to fly on Life Lion, out of Hershey to the scene of a motorcycle accident in Halifax. At first, Nick thought it was taking a long time as they flew over Indiantown Gap enroute to Halifax. But, they landed in no time. The very professional crew consisted of a pilot, the flight nurse, who happened to be Nick's neighbor Bruce, and another medical attendant. There are times a medical doctor would also be on board. It was a smooth ride, and definitely a ride of a life-time. Nick came away with a deep appreciation for the advanced services Life Lion provides.

Nick has had to help make those decisions as to whether or not to call for back-up help to save patient's lives. One case in particular, involved a multiple vehicle accident on 11 & 15, and three patients were flown by Life Lion and two were transported by ambulances. Some accidents were rather gruesome and one in particular has changed the way Nick drives today. It was a case where the driver would've survived any injuries, but was hanged by his mandatory seat-belt.

By now, you should've realized that Nick was driving that volunteer ambulance as much as if it was his part-time or nearly full-time job. Again, his employers were mindful of Nick's dedication to his community. N. O. Bonsall, of Old Ferry between Newport and Millerstown, hired Nick to help on the 1200 acre farm and drive truck. He hauled Bonsall's fertilizer and lime to farms around the area. Bonsall's also transported wood products for Meiser's Sawmill and Lumber Company in Millerstown. Nick hauled wood chips to Sunbury, cut lumber to Bethlehem Steel, pallets to Treen and lumber to New York.

In his ten years with Bonsalls, Nick also drove their sublet trucks for Camel Express. He hauled tons of bananas and Kraft products. Frank Campbell, President of Camel Express, knew of Nick's dedication to the Liverpool EMS. He made arrangements for Nick to take a flight out of Harrisburg to Philadelphia to Orlando, Florida, so he could drive a new ambulance ordered for the Liverpool EMS to its new home in Perry County. Other expenses were also taken care of. This saved the Liverpool EMS thousands of dollars in transport fees. Nick also traveled out of state to bring other emergency vehicles back to be put into use in Liverpool.

When Nick moved on to J. P. Russell and Son of Millerstown, he was delivering home heating oil and gas to farmers. He also delivered to gas stations. He sometimes had to take on extra responsibilities when delivering gas to businesses. Charlie Fuller owner of Fuller's Store on Route 104 would always pay Nick in cash for gas delivered. This occurred close to every two weeks, when Charlie would count as much as three thousand dollars out in front of customers and hand it to Nick. Each time he would deliver gas to the Oriental Store, owned by Lois and Denny Heath, Nick would change the price on the gas pumps for them. They did not know how to make the necessary changes in pricing. That's true customer service!

While working those ten years for J. P. Russell, Nick also drove for Camel Express at night. He would jockey loads from Center Hall for other Camel Express trucks, to take the loads further.

Hauling uneven cut 2 x 2 x 30" blocking to the Lebanon Steel Mill required a watchful eye on his load. The wood would easily slide out of place, once Nick left the sawmill from out back of Meiserville. The wood piles were chained to the truck bed. If he didn't stop and push them back into place, he risked loosing part of the load as he sped down the highway. He transported the lumber every two months for Bethlehem Steel in Lebanon. He liked hauling it in the winter, because the wood would get wet and freeze together, keeping them in place. Safety was a priority and he found that to be the same when he worked for other companies.

CLI Transport was a carrier for Sheetz and Nick drove tanker trucks for them for fifteen years. "Safety was their top priority", says Nick as he recalls the inspections and checking of computerized log systems looking for speeds that exceeded the speed limits. Even though, Nick had a vast knowledge of the trucking industry and many miles under his belt, he still had to attend a week of training in Altoona before he was hired. CLI wanted to make sure he knew what they expected of their drivers. Nick's schedule was six days on and three days off. Eventually that schedule allowed for six days off, but the drivers could pick up hours during that time period. His runs were from Harrisburg or Selinsgrove delivering gas to Sheetz Gas Stations.

By now you're realizing, Nick's life revolved around sitting behind a wheel, whether it be a truck or an ambulance. It was through the good graces of his employers, that when a call came in when he was working in Perry County, that off he'd go performing his civic duty. Of course, that meant showing up to help fight fires, too. His pickup truck was equipped with flashing lights and a siren. One time when he was speeding down the road to answer a fire call, he came upon a State Police car that was heading in the same direction of the call. Nick wasn't sure if he should pass the police car of not but then the Trooper had enough common-sense and courtesy to pull over and let Nick pass safely.

It wasn't till Nick was living behind the Liverpool Fire House that he got hooked on hearing that siren go off. The first call he responded to was when Barner's Carpet and Flooring on Front Street caught fire. His cousin Roy was involved in fire fighting, and Nick followed suit. The Fire Chief Glen Deckard asked Nick to drive the fire trucks, but he refused. He didn't want to be responsible for the lives of those volunteers hanging onto the back of the fire trucks. In the early days, fire trucks were built without extra seats, so the firemen in full fire-fighting gear had to step onto the bumper and hang on for dear life as the truck sped to the emergency. This was even in the harsh winter time. That stunt took guts, but those volunteers persevered saving many a property and lives at the scene of vehicle accidents.

Nick did become deeply embedded in the Fire Company. He served as Fire Chief and Assistant Chief. Just as important, Nick was the Liverpool Fire Police Chief, making sure traffic was directed around the scene of an accident, a fire close to the road and an ambulance call requiring the street to be blocked off till they could load the patient. This was night or day, because emergencies waited for no special time of day. On top of all that, Nick was Liverpool's Emergency Management Coordinator for twenty years. He was responsible for coordinating with the Perry County Emergency Management team in times of disasters, like floods, massive wildfires, and other incidents.

He also took a week off from work to make sure the Liverpool carnival (which was the largest money-raiser) ran smoothly. Yes, the carnival was at night, but there was a lot of work behind the scenes to get ready for the evening's events. The food prepared by the Ladies Auxiliary during the day, needed to be transported to the carnival grounds and set-up for serving to the pubic. The entertainment or show for the evening needed to be finalized and the staging area readied. It was just like having a full-time and part-job on his week of vacation. Now that's dedication! In years past, the fire company would actually borrow money from the First National Bank of Liverpool to tide them over the winter months, and be able to keep responding to emergencies. The carnival and fish fries would pay off that debt, but the vicious cycle would start all over again. Today they no longer have to rely on the bank to keep them afloat. Grant monies, financial support from Liverpool Borough and the outlying townships, and other fundraisers, ensure the fire trucks remain ready "twenty-four-seven".

Liverpool Emergency Medical Services is unique in that they maintain a Quick Response Unit (QRS). They have the only Mass Casualty Incident (MCI) trailer, ready to deal with mass casualty incidents wherever it is needed. Nick headed the process to obtain it through grant monies. It is a trailer stocked with enough equipment and supplies to treat thirty-two patients, alongside the attending ambulances and fire companies. It is designed to jump in and help out when there is a bus accident, apartment building fire, train accident, plane accident, or massive vehicle pile-up as witnessed in recent years due to hazardous weather conditions. The unit also has a 20' x 20' inflatable tent available for set-up. Liverpool fire and ambulance personnel have received extensive training in case such an emergency would arise. Luckily Liverpool has yet to put the MCI to use. The closest MCI unit to Perry County is in Dauphin and Cumberland County.

Firemen receive extensive fire training mostly at HACC, just like the EMT's who ride the ambulances. Their fire school had the capabilities to set-up actual demonstrations of what kinds of fire and rescue scenes they might encounter. The training is on-going and often times satellite classes are held at a local fire company. Besides learning how best to fight fires and rescue folks, the training is necessary for grant monies. That is why you have a fire fighter designated as a #1 or a #2 which has more training. It is based on the amount of training, and the training also reflects on the home-owner's insurance rates.

There are some fun times. The Liverpool Fire Company and Liverpool EMS treats the Liverpool area children at Christmas time, every year. Someone dresses as Santa and the trucks travel throughout the town and the outskirts delivering candy, oranges, and small gifts to families. Everybody has a great time and their kindness is rewarded. Most times they are out and about on Christmas Eve, delivering some joy.

Nick did manage to spend time with his son, Joshua and his two grandchildren, Chase and Shelby. Maybe it was having a son of his own, that made Nick insistent that the search teams did not give up on finding a young boy lost on the mountain in Buffalo Township, outside of Liverpool, in 1991. When others wanted to call it quits, Nick, who was the search coordinator of volunteers, declared "that baby needed to be found". The round-the-clock search, which was spear-headed by the State Police and included game wardens and forestry personnel, along with countless volunteers, was successful inside of twenty-four hours. The boy had ventured off while walking through fields of wheat.

Health issues have cropped up and Nick has decided to slow down, before he discovers he can't get back up and needs that ambulance called for himself once again. Maybe he won't take the 32 Winchester Rifle, he purchased at his Uncle Carl Umholtz's public sale, out hunting anymore. It's the same hunting rifle that his uncle laid on the ground and accidentally ran over. But he does enjoy, getting on his three-wheeled Can-am Spyder and riding cross-country with his best friend and companion, Linda Wilson.

Even though, he might have turned over the keys to the new-age ambulance, he sure speaks with pride about his forty years of serving his community. It's in his blood and truth be told, once Company #5 fire siren sounds through Liverpool and reaches his hill-top home, he's forever ready!

Little Pfoutz Valley Remedies and the Mail Route

Storyteller William Cameron

My name is William Cameron. I live on the farm called "Glencroften Shire" (Scottish for valley of small farms in the area), the area being little Pfoutz Valley. Big Pfoutz Valley runs from Millerstown to Liverpool. John Pfoutz had the first farm along Nekoda Road in 1755 and the valley was named for him.

I was born on our farm October 10, 1936, along with my three sisters, Reba, Nila, and Linda. They all got married and moved away, so I was left on the farm to work with my dad Leyder Cameron.

Previously there were six farms in Little Pfoutz Valley all owned by Aukers. Two brothers Caleb and John Auker donated a plot for the Auker Cemetery in 1795.

My grandfather Lednum G. Cameron bought the farm from George A. Zellers on April 2, 1927 for five thousand dollars. The sixth generation is now living on the farm; Ella Lednum, Madeline Leyder, Flora William, Bonita Perry, Alyssa Bradley and Layla Miles.

When my grandmother, Ella Cameron, was living in half the house, around 1944, my older sisters got the mumps. She told me if I didn't want to get the mumps, I should go down to the hog pen and rub my neck on both sides of the hog trough. Being a gullible boy of eight years, I did just that. I've never gotten the mumps to this day!

My grandmother would bake black cherry pie with the seeds in. Great taste but slow eating when you had to spit the seeds out. I think the older generation just chewed them up and swallowed them.

My mother, Madaline Cameron was a great cook (I did not like tomatoes, onions or broccoli). She could cook an appetizing meal with them in it and I ate it. Us kids would catch little sunny fish from the Cocolamus Creek. Mom would cook them with the bones in and that was a lot of picking to get a good bite of fish. When my dad encountered a bone, he'd just grind it up and eat it. What a good way to get calcium!

My wife, Flora Baker Cameron, worked in Harrisburg for Otis Elevator Company. I was a rural mail carrier out of the Millerstown Post Office. I would get home before her so lots of times I started to cook supper. One day I had those little pin-steaks from deer, marinated with onion salt, garlic powder and rolled in egg and flour. Fried in an old pan, already for her. She thought it was pretty good and asked what it was. I told her it was venison and she would not eat any more of it!

I've been a member of Perry Valley Grange for seventy-two years. Perry Valley Grange had a good reputation for serving meals at their grange hall for many years. The old cooks were getting tired and young people did not like that kind of community service. So, we sold the grange hall and hold our meetings at the Millerstown Community Park Building.

Pennsylvania State Grange printed a cookbook in 1925. Since then, twelve other editions have been printed, the latest being the 2021 issue. If you see a Grange Cookbook at a sale or auction, buy it! Could be well worth your while.

One-Room Schoolhouses
All country schools were three miles apart, so no kid had to walk more than one and a half miles to school. I walked with my sisters one-mile down Pfoutz Valley Road to Wardville School. We carried lunch in a metal lunchbox. We usually had home-cured ham sandwiches (hard to chew) and a bunch of concord grapes with seeds or maybe an apple. All eight grades were in one room.

My dad was on the school board for a few years and it was their responsibility to get the school cleaned and ready for the fall school term. The two outside toilets had to be cleaned out and lime applied to the inside seats and the catch tank. To sanitize the wood floor, they used old motor oil spread liberally over the whole floor to preserve the wood and kill any bugs and lice.

A big coal stove with a metal shroud around it heated the school. For drinking water there was a large ten-gallon ceramic urn with a spigot on the bottom. Two older boys were assigned the task of going to the nearest farm and bring fresh water back in a pail with a lid on it.

During WW ll, kids were told to pick milkweed pods. The silky threads would be used to make life preservers and parachute strings.

When my oldest sister, Reba finished eighth grade the teacher told her she can go to high school in Millerstown but had to find her own way there. My dad, Leyder Cameron had a 1940 Chevrolet four-door sedan so he drove her to Millerstown High School every day. Along the way, he picked up my cousins, Robert and Harold Cameron, and two Daughenbaugh girls.

The school board told him since he drove them in every day, they would pay him as a bus route. They gave him two (school bus) signs to hang on the front and rear bumpers. At that time, cars had real bumpers and running boards. That was my dad's first bus route with the Greenwood School District.

During WW ll, you could not buy new buses. He bought a panel van and took it to Swab Wagon Company in Elizabethville, Dauphin County, and had windows and bus seats installed. That was his first school bus. Eventually he had four bus routes in the Greenwood School District and two routes in the East Juniata School District.

Millerstown Post Office
Before rural free delivery, as we know it today, the Post Office hired men with horse and buggies to deliver mail to country stores with postal capabilities. The local people came to the store to pick up their mail. Millerstown had four such routes serving Wardville, Nekoda, Pfoutz Valley, Seven Stars, Knousetown, Centerville (which was called Burlee) Reward, Donnally Mills, Ickesburg and Eschol. In the 1940s-1950s, mail for addresses beyond Millerstown were sent and delivered by a railroad mail train. The outgoing mail was put in canvas pouches and taken to the Millerstown Railroad Station by Blake Seacrist and hung on a post with an arm extended towards the tracks.

The pouches were grabbed by mail train employees without stopping. For incoming mail there was a wooden chute to catch mail pouches thrown from the mail train without stopping. Mail was sorted on the train while enroute to the Harrisburg Post Office.

I got out of the Army in February 1962, having served twenty-seven months in Germany with an artillery company. The Russians started the Berlin Wall in August of 1961.

My cousin, Donald Cameron was rural mail carrier on Millerstown Route 2 and he needed a substitute carrier for Saturday deliveries and his vacation time. I was the substitute carrier on both Routes 1 and 2 for nineteen years before I got the job as full-time carrier on Route 2.

I was helping my dad with farm work and driving dump truck hauling stones to build black-top roads through the week. So, substitute mail carrying worked well on Saturdays.

Morris Kerstetter was on my mail route. He lived up a lane about a quarter of a mile long. Some days his mail would pile up in his mail box, so I would take his mail up to the house and check-up on him to be sure he was OK. When I did this, he would give me a bottle of his homemade wine. He had some older bottles that his father had made and we opened one. It did not smell very good and we were afraid to taste it. I told him to send a sample to the Agricultural Laboratory and get it tested.

About a week later, I noticed he had a letter from the Pennsylvania Department of Agriculture, so I took the mail up to his house that day. I was anxious to hear the results of the test. He opened the letter and stared to read; Dear Sir, we are sorry to inform you that your horse has diabetes.

Another time on the mail route in a mail box was a letter with just "Grandma" on it. I knew who her grandma was, so when I got to her mailbox, I put the letter in with her mail. Days later, her grandmother questioned me, how did that letter get from her granddaughter to her mailbox. I explained the situation to her and she was elated.

Milk Cows
In the 1940s-1950s, we had six milk cows and I did not like milking cows by hand. Sometimes they would kick and upset the milk pail. Dad had a pair of "cow-kickers" which when clamped on each rear leg with a short chain connecting them together, solved the kicking problem. Then there was the cow's tail sometimes covered with dirt or worse, cow dung! She would swish her tail and swat you in the face. It did not taste good.

We drank raw milk at home and occasionally dad would get sick. The doctor said it was "undulant fever" from drinking the raw milk. We bought a two-gallon milk pasteurizer and that took care of the "undulant fever" situation.

I started a deliver route in Millerstown and the surrounding countryside. So, we got pasteurized milk from their delivery truck. It didn't take us long to sell the milk cows and get black angus beef cattle.

Tractors
In 1940, my dad bought a Cletrac tractor. It had a continuous tract with cleats and didn't bog down like a wheel tractor. The neighbors were interested in it so my dad and Uncle Charlie started Cameron Brother's Farm Equipment. They sold Cletrac and Huber tractors, and farm equipment. Uncle Charlie was called to serve in the Army during WW ll.

You could not get new tractors during the war, so used tractors were in huge demand. The government put a ceiling on the price of used tractors, so at a farm sale you had to bid high on a pitchfork and you got a tractor along with the fork.

"Ingenuity, common-sense, hard-work, family and neighbor helping neighbor made the struggles seem worthwhile and helped preserve the Perry County farm community."

A Love For Preserving Trains And Perry County

Storyteller Woody Dyer

I am writing this only because some day people might want to know what we did before internet, cable TV, and mobile phones. I say I lived in Perry County most of my life, but I really didn't move there until I was in my late twenties.

I was born in Harrisburg in 1946 in the Polyclinic Hospital and lived in Harrisburg until I was four. After the death of my father's mother, we moved into her home which we were told was once a railroad house in Inglenook. The village is located just north of the Clarks Ferry Bridge in Dauphin County. In my youth, because no one knew where Inglenook was, I would just say where all the big (Esso/EXON) oil storage tanks are along Route 147 above the Clarks Ferry Bridge. Everyone knew where all the tanks were. They are no longer there.

In the "old" days, people came to this area to get away from the city, especially during the summer. There was also a YMCA youth camp located here. It had cabins (including a first-aid cabin), chow hall, recreation hall, baseball field, other athletic fields and a fairly large swimming pool. However, by today's standards, the pool would be classified as a health risk. I kind of remember a pump house but not the smell of chlorine. There was a small dammed stream behind the cabins which I believe fed fresh untreated water into the pool.

At one time Inglenook had at least one railroad stop, but I have never found any record of a station being there, but it did have a post office for many years. Also, before the railroad, the canal came and ran next to Route 147. There is a concrete aqueduct that once had barges passing over a creek that is now used as a bridge on Route 147. I remember the canal ditch, but over the years, almost all the canal has been filled in.

There were cottages and a Rod & Gun Club located along the river. Many of the buildings are still there.

Our house was on the other side of the railroad tracks, the middle house in a row of three. Originally all three houses were identical. The first house had burnt down at one time and was re-built on a luxurious scale compared to the originals. Our house had an addition built onto it, plus a washhouse/garage had been added. The third house remained "original" until it was torn down.

Now this was approximate 1950. Like many homes at the time, it had no running water, a hand pump was used. We had a very small two-holed outhouse (if you never used a privy, you have no idea what I am talking about). We cooked on a woodstove and the entire house was heated with a coal-burning stove in the living room. There was electric and a phone. The two-piece phone was stored in a wooden cabinet and it did not have a dial. The caller would tell the operator the party or number they wanted.

Soon after we moved in, the living quarters were modernized to a gas-cooking stove, running water, central oil-fired heating, and the phone service was updated to one with a dial and a party line. There were no private lines in the boondocks in those days. Also, the family grew over the years.

When I started to school things were always confusing. I lived in Dauphin County, had a Halifax address, a Dauphin phone number and I was going to a Perry County school. To keep things simple, I would just say I lived and grew up in Duncannon. It's really not a fib. That is where we went to school, church, scouts, movies, shopping, etc. Duncannon had everything a person would need, except for a hospital.

I can recall all the following growing up. There were at least six grocery stores (some no bigger than a large living room and one that roasted peanuts), two eating establishment (not counting taverns), a state store, post office, icehouse, a butcher shop, a clothing store (which handled everything from dress suits to rubber gumboots), an insurance broker, card and party store, two hardware stores, an auto store, jewelry store, drug store, flower shop, a paper/magazine shop (newsstand), barbers, a dairy with an ice cream bar, two car dealerships, coal and fuel oil delivery services, a bank, a TV store, farm essentials (just up the hill), VFW, American Legion, doctors, a dentist, two movie theaters, a bottling company, a twilight baseball team, a weekly newspaper and a large variety of churches and a funeral parlor. You really never needed to leave the town!

Note: In the first few years, we had to pay a toll to cross the Clarks Ferry Bridge and our local phone calls range (free) was from Harrisburg to Halifax. So almost all phone calls to friends and businesses were long distance and long-distance phone calls were not cheap in those days.

I did have some uncommon jobs in my life. My father was a milkman (delivered milk door to door) for Harrisburg Dairies in Harrisburg and I would help him on weekends (no school). I am sure this practice would be outlawed today. I did this from the time I was eight until I played sports in high school. It wasn't hard work, but you had to get up in the middle of the night, load the DIVCO (most milk trucks were DIVCOs), deliver the milk before breakfast, unload the truck (the empty bottles were washed and reused no recycling problem), then collect the money. There was no on-line banking in those days. Note about DIVCO trucks: They had an unusual characteristic. They could be (usually) driven standing up. Think about how that was done and they were all standard shifts. I was always amazed what goes on in the big city during the night.

Another job was staying at and working on my mother's uncle's dairy farm (York Springs) during summer harvesting season. They were highly religious people with six kids, but they always appreciated extra help doing the summer harvest. Everyone had chores no matter their ages. When I say worked, I mean worked. I got severely sunburned every year (we didn't know anything about suntan lotion or the relation to skin cancer) and a handful of blisters. Most days we worked from before daylight (milking the cattle), then harvested the fields to fill the silos and barn until the evening milking. The evening meal was usually the end of the workday. However, if it was church or hymn sing night, we milked and ate early. Of course, we didn't do any work on Sunday except to milk the cows.

They had no TV, books, magazines, etc. in their home. Sunday was for resting, visiting and swimming in the pond that the cows loved to wade in and relieve themselves. We should have all died from some kind of sickness. They did have a radio, but that was only used for the weather report and an occasional farm report. We worked hard and ate good. My aunt was a great cook and everything was from the garden or freezer. But, at the time, I hadn't realized how little money there was in farming.

In my mid-teens I started playing sports in high school. I was never a great athlete, but I was fortunate enough to get some playing time.

Also, at sixteen, I did get my driver's license. We were not poor, but we did not have the resources to get me a car and maintaining it. Thus, when not participating in sports, my summer career was at the world-famous Juniata Dairy Bar in Duncannon. The home of the fifteen-cent ice cream cone and I got paid real money for working there. Although it was not my favorite job in life, it did allow me to own a car and gave me spending money. I worked there for four summers and at the Harrisburg Dairies milk processing plant during the winter months while attending college and later an electronic tech school.

While at the electronic tech school, I got a job as floor manager at WHP-TV. Sounds impressive, but it was a part-time job. This was probably the most interesting job I ever had. We were responsible for preparing the studios and newsroom for the nightly live broadcast and any taped interviews or shows. I got the opportunity to meet many well-known people including Jackie Robinson, all the local politicians including the governor, race car drivers and anyone else that needed to be interviewed for the news.

With all jobs, there was always something that a person will remember. Mine was taping the Santa Claus show. It was unpredictable. The first time I helped to prepare the studio for the show, the director had me go to the basement and get a mop and bucket. I asked him why and he said you will see. The show consisted of very young kids that lined up to sit on Santa Claus's lap to tell him what they wanted for Christmas. The event was taped and televised at a later day and time. Sounds simple and easy.

Let me tell you what went on behind the scenes. First, the children are asked/told to go to the bathroom before getting in line. Of course, none had to go. Now there are twenty or more young kids standing in line doing the "potty dance." Most can do that dance until after they talked to Santa, but many can't. There were puddles on the floor everywhere, and if you watched closely, you could occasionally see Santa's face cringe when his leg suddenly got wet and warm. There are hazards in all occupations, but it was a fun job and maybe this is why the show is no longer broadcast.

Note: While working at WHP-TV, they went from televising in black and white to color and it was a big deal. The national network had been televising in color for many years, but the local channels were just starting to convert. It didn't matter much to many of us. Most of us couldn't afford a color TV.

In the spring of that year (1967), I graduated from Electronic Institute in Harrisburg and was fortunate to get a job as an electronic technician with IBM in Kingston, NY. I was able to stay with IBM though all the good years. I worked on the large computers that everyone talks about today. A meg (million bytes) of memory was the size of a very large room or a small gymnasium. Computer memory today is measured in gigabytes (billions of bytes) and is the size of a small candy bar.

Also, I got married to Crystal Laman from Marysville in 1967. We lived in Kingston, New York for twelve years. All three of our children were born there. Although it was a very nice area, the schools were very good and the pay was excellent, we decided to come home to Perry County.

I transferred to IBM Mechanicsburg in 1979. This facility was a distribution center for IBM parts and publications. It was definitely a career change. We bought a house in Marysville. This was really the first time I actually lived in Perry County.

While in New York, I started another unusual livelihood strictly by chance. During our early years both my wife's and my family had Lionel S model train layouts as part of the Christmas holidays. I especially enjoyed this tradition and looked forward to every year. It wasn't Christmas without the trains.

Unfortunately, my trains were twenty years old and were used hard and definitely needed a lot of TLC, but I couldn't find anyone that repaired Lionel trains anymore. The tradition almost disappeared and Lionel was making very few model trains and most were poor quality. There was no Googling in those days. Fortunately, I found some people that still played with and collected Lionel trains. They were able to direct me to finding parts. In the early days of this endeavor, I needed to buy donor engines, etc. to find the parts needed to get the host engine working.

In 1970, General Mills (the cereal company) purchased Lionel and started to give new life to model railroading. They also started making some of the parts required to keep the equipment running. As Lionel trains started to make a revival, other companies started to reproduce parts for old and very old trains. This sideline eventually turned into a fulltime job.

Starting in the late eighties, IBM's golden years started coming to an end. There are many reasons, but the collapse came quick. For those of us that had over twenty-six years or more of service, got a full retirement. Others were not so lucky. The distribution center needed to remain in operation. However, the operation was being taken over by a logistics company, so I was able to remain employed.

Unfortunately, I didn't age well. By the time I was almost sixty, I had two knee replacements, two open-heart surgeries and finally my spine needed to be reconstructed. I ended up on disability. There was no going back to working in a warehouse or any other job.

Fortunately, I had continued repairing and selling model trains from my home. Never was I real busy or made much money. Just something to do. But after back surgery, it turned out to be mental therapy (something I could do).

There were at least eight places in the Harrisburg area that you could get model trains repaired when we moved to Marysville. Two years ago, I was the only one that I knew that was still doing repairs in this area. I recently found a few people dabbling in it, but none are young. I am now in my mid-seventies and I really never ever expected to be this busy.

Part of the revival was triggered by COVID. People were encouraged to stay home, and many decided to get their old trains out of storage and start new memories. A large percentage of these repairs are between sixty and one hundred years old. And I have found Americans are not patient about getting things fixed. They expect the repair to be done immediately, not the six-to-nine-month backlog that I presently have. Unfortunately, I have advertised for several years for help and I am even willing to train someone that show a serious interest. However, there have been no takers that stuck around. Repair technicians quickly learn that model trains are toys when they are purchased, toys when they need repaired, but antiques when they are for sale.

I know people make fun about Perry County, but my family and I are proud to be Perry Countians. The county is big enough to offer us many opportunities, but small enough to have tight-knit and friendly communities.

Growing Up With Hall's Ice Cream

Storyteller Peggy Hall Raub

My first remembrance of Hall's Dairy, as a little girl, is going over to the dairy and talking to the drivers. They would come in from the routes, check their slips and receipts in the "office." (Now the mechanical room.) They worked from there until my grandfather, John K. Hall, built his house up the road from the dairy. He had a room with its own door for the men to come in and settle their books.

There were three milk delivery drivers then, Johnny Cox, Jim Cunningham and Dick Collier. I remember Dick didn't mind the cold and never wore a coat, even on the coldest days. Jim Cunningham had a daughter, Carol, and I would sometimes visit them. (Once when I was visiting, they asked me what I wanted to eat and I said a BLT. They said they didn't know what that was. I told them, they made it and liked it. We talked about that visit often.) Most of the milk delivery trucks were Chevrolets, but Johnny's was a Ford and they always joked that it meant "Fix Or Repair Daily". There was also a door-to-door ice cream salesman, Jake Jones. When Jake retired, Inez Leonard began delivering ice cream.

When the delivery men returned, the empty milk bottles were stacked near the bottle washing machine. There was a track that took the returned milk bottles from the milk bottle washing machine over to the bottle filler machine. They were filled and put into the milk cooler room, ready for delivery to homes and businesses.

When they put in the short-time pasteurization system, my mother, Sally, would make dinner for the men. It must have been around Easter, because I remember the meal on Friday had to be fish. At about the same time we changed from glass to cardboard milk containers. We also got a milk tank truck to pick-up the milk directly from the farmers and did away with the milk being delivered in cans. I remember going along with my dad, John Allen, to pick up milk in the tank truck. We would leave early in the morning, stop for a nap and a snack. We would deliver a tanker of milk to Rakestraw's in Mechanicsburg and get a cone of ice cream for the ride home.

My grandfather and I would sit on the porch of the farmhouse and he would make me do mental math. He would give me so much money, send me to the store to buy things, such as bananas at so much a pound, cheese, etc., then I had to tell him how much change I would bring back. No pencil, no paper. It was a fun game (I thought). If you wanted to drive and deliver milk, you had to be able to do math in your head. No pencil, no paper, or you didn't get hired.

When I was nine years old, grandpa asked me to work in the dairy store. I was paid $0.25 an hour. I really liked working there. The only thing I didn't like was walking home after I closed the store. When walking home I would often "hide" when a car came along.

The only ice cream freezer was a little room inside the milk cooler. I don't remember when the larger ice cream freezer was built. I do remember going into the "big" new freezer and not minding the cold. That is no longer the situation.

I remember trying new concoctions when we weren't busy. The one I remember best was raspberry ice cream with pineapple topping. I was pleasantly surprised at how good it was.

In the summer, when I wasn't scheduled, I was always "on call" if the dairy got busy during the week. I would sit and watch for the cars to come and hope that I would be called to work. Often when some of the farmers finished for the day, they would come to the dairy before closing. There was one that always came JUST before closing to get a banana split.

My grandfather had the policy that if you ate 5 banana splits, you got them all free. We had several people try and most did not succeed. There were a few that could eat all five. Once they knew they could do it, they would come back to try again. The regular banana split was chocolate, vanilla and raspberry ice cream with vanilla in the middle. The toppings were chocolate syrup, marshmallow, pineapple, peanuts, and a cherry. We use the same toppings today.

Milkshakes were always on the thick side and served in the milkshake tin with a glass, (if the customer was "eating in"), so the customer could get "the last drop".

For most of the time we only had one booth, a table with four chairs and six stools at the counter. I don't remember when they added the porch, which is now the office, but it allowed us to have an additional 4 tables and chairs for people to sit. One day a tire came off a truck, rolled down the driveway, through the windows and smashed into the refrigerator on the porch. I also remember there was a bench and two chairs that were in the yard of the farmhouse that people used to sit on in the summer.

Besides working in the dairy store, I loved to go to the carnivals to work. I looked forward to seeing the same people from year to year. We would take the box truck, with the freezer, milkshake machine, stainless steel table for the milkshake machine, and "saw horses" and boards for the stand. It was a chore to load and unload the freezer. Luckily, there were always people that would help. The New Bloomfield carnival was the start of summer and the Millerstown Carnival was the end. Almost every weekend we were at an event. I remember when a hurricane came through. We were at Thompsontown and had to quickly gather things up to get home before the rain came.

As they say, "Things change, yet they stay the same." We still do events, but in a self-contained trailer.

We deliver ice cream instead of milk to stores not individual homes. The banana splits, sundaes and milkshakes are made the same way and of course, the ice cream still tastes like it did when I was eating my then favorite chocolate chip. No matter what the flavor, I still enjoy ice cream and trying new combinations.

Game Warden, Harold Russell

Storyteller Connie Russell Raffensperger

The yellowed letter in the old cardboard box was addressed to Mr. Harold E. Russell, Route No. 1, Bedford, Pennsylvania, from W. C. Shaffer, Director of Game Protection, Office of the Board of Game Commissioners, Harrisburg, Pennsylvania. It was the letter that changed the course of my parents' lives. Dated June 17, 1937, it contained the welcome message that he had successfully completed the examination for admission to the second class to the Ross Leffler Game Commission Training School. He was to report to the Training Center at Brockway, Pennsylvania on Sunday, June 20, 1937 for the eight- or nine-month course. Hazel, his wife, also from the Bedford area, would stay with her parents during his training.

In the waning years of The Great Depression, it was indeed good news to receive. Dad was twenty-nine years old, had been married since 1934, and was more than ready for a steady job, especially one in which he was so interested. As it happened, this opportunity would launch him into a thirty-year career as a Game Warden and Land Manager in Perry County.

Even before his acceptance into the Training School he had worked part-time for the Game Commission. He had received a telegram and a letter in August, 1936, when he and Mother were working for Kohr's Frozen Custard for the summer in New London, Connecticut, telling him he would be appointed a Deputy and be in charge of some game lands and auxiliary refuges upon his return to Bedford County.

When his schooling was completed in February, 1938, he was assigned to Western Perry County at Blain. His predecessor, John Fenton was about to retire, but had not moved out of the newly-built Game Commission-provided home, so Dad and Mother lived just down the Back Hollow Road in a hunting cabin for a short time.

The "daily activities report" he was required to send in monthly to his superiors bear out what several men told my brother and me at his funeral in December, 1990: "Your Dad arrested me but he was fair!" From our perspective their observation pretty well summed up how he conducted his life, both professionally and personally. It was good to hear it confirmed even if not all those he arrested would agree! That is just the nature of law enforcement work. It was work that was in the "public eye" and open to criticism. Every now and then I was subjected to a few negative comments about my dad. In my early teens, I decided that I would not want to be married to someone who was vulnerable in that way. But about nine years after I married, my husband had a Call to ministry. Perhaps my upbringing in a similar situation gave me some preparation to be a Pastor's wife! I often think God has a sense of humor.

When he wrote his daily report, he usually included a few personal lines at the bottom of the page which he did not include in the report to the Commission. These comments were often the most revealing and poignant about our family life. Of my birth in 1939, he wrote, "At home rejoicing over the arrival of Connie Marlene on Sunday, August 13 at 12:55 p.m.". Mother had returned to her parents' Bedford County farm for my birth a few weeks earlier. He had gotten there from Blain just in time for my birth and now had come home for work.

It would be sixteen years before my brother, David, would arrive on November 1, 1955. I often requested a baby brother. One Christmas season when I was about three years old, Mother, Mrs. Bess Koontz (I called her Jane) and I were shopping in Harrisburg at Feller's Department Store. I wandered into their alterations area and the lady asked me what I wanted for Christmas. I quickly replied "a baby brother". It was a little late for that request to be granted that year, but I never stopped asking, and finally it paid off. Dad was just as excited as he had been when I was born. He was forty-seven and Mother was forty-two. They had long given up hope of having another child. They told me when they knew Mother was pregnant, and it was agreed upon that we would not tell anyone for a while to be sure all would go well with the pregnancy. But Dad could not keep the secret! I was happy, too, but did better than Dad and did not tell until he had let the proverbial cat out of the bag. I was at school the day David was born. I ran back into physics class after getting the phone call in the school office from Dad, and announced to everyone "It's a boy!" Since we were a small high school, chemistry and physics classes were offered alternate years, therefore juniors and seniors shared the class. Donald Raffensperger, who is now my husband, was a senior and I was a junior. He remembers Mr. Weigle, our teacher and high school principal, saying to me, "Now Miss Russell, when you are finished, we will continue with the class!"

In 2003, I sifted through photos and letters, diaries and other papers in that old cardboard box to assemble albums and some narrative to go with them. They were a treasure trove of Dad's thirty years of service. I discovered that along with his law enforcement and land management duties, Dad found time to trap. He caught weasels, skunks, raccoon, some of which he hoped to catch and others he would rather not. In his travels to check refuges, he shot crows and killed snakes, often writing down how many and what kind. He had a cardboard chart on the garage wall where he tacked up each set of rattlers from the rattlesnakes! (I think killing rattlers is now illegal.) He saw lots of red-tailed hawks, and checked on nesting turkeys which were in protected areas.

He patrolled for game violators, sometimes alone, and other times with his colleagues. They spent many "all-nighters" out on the roads, watching and listening for illegal activity. They arrested their share of poachers, some of which were contrite, while others were belligerent. One of the worst I recall was when he flagged down a vehicle at night and the man at the wheel purposely tried to run over him.

A comical incident happened when we still had the old crank phone on the wall in Dad's office. He called in a violation to his supervisor. Gertrude Shumaker, the telephone operator in Blain, came back on the line while the call was going through and told him that Rev. Gingrich's had a boy. The young pastor and his wife were serving in a local church and expecting their first child. In a small community everyone knew the arrival was imminent. But Dad thought Gertrude said, "Rev. Gingrich shot a boy." To which Dad asked, "Was it accidental or intentional!" We never let him forget that one.

Another time, he was out patrolling at night. Mother and I were in bed when we heard the put-put of an old Model A or Model T coming up the driveway. Mother was never afraid of whoever arrived at our home, so she opened the upstairs window and called out, "Who's there?" The gentleman driving the car replied, "Oh, it's just me and her." Finally, Mother had to ask for their name.

After Dad's passing, one of the Deputies related this story to my brother. It took place at a rural general store during deer season. A large group of hunters from a camp came into the store to purchase snacks while Dad and a deputy happened to be there. He asked them if they were all from the same camp. They said they were and Dad asked one of them with the deputy to go back to the camp and get their Roster so he could check it. Another fellow in the group walked toward Dad and told him that "something could happen to a young fellow like you working alone." The conversation ended when Dad opened his uniform jacket and revealed his revolver. The irony of the story was that the Roster was fine.

Deputy Sam Bender was with Dad one night on patrol to check out a tip on illegal hunting. They "cut" the lights on the vehicle, pulled off the road and waited. When the hunters drove toward their location when they were done hunting, Dad turned on the lights and started to ease out of his parking spot. The hunters, thinking it was another hunting group, rolled down their windows and began to tell Dad and Sam about their hunting success, and that some of their buddies were doing the same thing at another location. Also, they would be glad to share some tips. Apparently, they did not notice Dad's and Sam's uniforms since they did not get out of the vehicle. Dad and Sam just kept quiet and let them incriminate themselves. Those hunters were not arrested that night, but several weeks later that group and their buddies were all arrested.

C. V. Long, "Charley", the Fish Warden would ask him to help with law enforcement work during fishing season, and with stocking the local streams in the off-season. Dad also stocked rabbits, and later ring-necks, in his own job. C. V. always had a pocket full of candy. I soon learned to look forward to his visits. Charley was single and lived with his mother in East Waterford. She had a very entertaining parrot that I got to "talk" to occasionally. "Polly" was about fifty years old when she passed away. When Dad was in World War II, Charley often helped to mow our lawn.

Dad must have walked hundreds of miles doing his job. His daily records show him walking the refuge lines, etc. Sometimes it was three miles, other times two or four. He was in great shape. He also put many miles on our personal vehicle, and at times had a Game Commission pickup truck to use for the Land Management part of his job. His annual pay in 1939 was $1,380, and he was paid mileage when he used his own vehicle.

Mother often cooked for Game Commission personnel who were there on business, and sometimes they also stayed for a night or two so sheets and towels were laundered in the wringer washer. Students from the Training School came periodically and stayed for a month or so at a time, for on-the-job experience. She was paid for her efforts, and the men thoroughly enjoyed her Pennsylvania Dutch cooking. The one account I came across of her compensation was for $88, for "Overturf's and DeLong's board and room while on their field-trip to Western Perry County August 10 - 24, 1941." My parents told me in later years that by the time I was two years old my vocabulary was peppered with "expletives" I had picked up from all the guys who came through our home and Dad's office, which was just off the living room. These were men who were Game Commission employees, or someone paying a fine or turning in animal pelts to receive compensation. Dad was not exempt from the list. My parents were very happy when the "expletives" just went away after all their own efforts to squelch them.

The personal notes that I mentioned earlier included their trips back to Bedford County to visit their families. We crossed the Conococheague Mountain on our way to the Turnpike at Willow Hill to go to Bedford and Dad would have me spell it every time. Those notes mention that they attended movies at the CCC Camp (Civilian Conservation Corps) which was less than a mile from our home, and made homemade ice cream in the winter when neighbors would gather and hand-crank the ice cream freezer. Those neighbors included the Koontz's, Roy, who was the Forest Ranger, and his wife, Bess, and their adult son, North. They were like another set of grandparents for me and North like an uncle. Then there was "Smitty", Wilber Smith, who was the road supervisor. He repaired the dirt road and plowed the snow with a bull dozer. Sara and Clayton Amig and their daughter, Gracie lived nearby, too. Gracie and her dad worked in Harrisburg and were only home weekends. Some folks would come and play cards in the evenings. Roy Koontz was my buddy on those evenings if we were at the Koontz's. He would light their big stone fireplace and throw some kind of sparklers in it, to my delight.

The Game Commission house where we lived was only a couple years old when my parents moved in after Mr. and Mrs. Fenton retired. It had a bathroom, electricity from a generator, and a big coal-fired furnace. There was also a heater of some sort that heated the water. My parents were ever so grateful for those conveniences. I think it was 1948 when public electricity reached us. We also had a telephone. Some of the neighbors had telephones but many others did not. It was a "party-line" which provided some interesting situations.

World War II took Dad to Europe for 1944-45. I was four-and-a-half, and vividly remember when he left, his only furlough after Basic Training, and his home-coming. He was drafted in March of 1944 when he was almost thirty-six years old. He could have had a deferment due to the Land Management part of his job, but he did not want to be labeled a "draft dodger". The Game Commission allowed Mother and I to live in the house and pay rent. He did Basic Training at North Camp Hood, Texas, came home on furlough, and was shipped to England, then to Le Harve, France. His "meal ticket" for his overnight trip on the ship to cross the English Channel to Le Harve from Southampton, England is in the Family Album. Because of his law enforcement training he was assigned to the Military Police and helped to transport prisoners the U. S. A. had captured, to camps behind our lines. Like many who went to war, he did not talk about it very much. Thankfully he kept all his Army papers and every now and then Mother would give me some information. I know he was hospitalized with a stomach ulcer, which sometimes flared up after he was home. When the Army doctors treated him for the ulcer, they said they did not know how he had passed the physical to be drafted because he had Bell's Palsy in the left side of his face, which had occurred several years before the war. He was discharged in January, 1946.

I never felt afraid while Dad was away. Mother took care of the coal furnace and the mowing, except for C. V. Long's help. She shoveled snow, and killed snakes with one swift swipe of a hoe. She was rather reserved, but I always felt she was fearless and that made me very comfortable. We had wonderful neighbors who helped when needed. I recall my first day of school, standing at the end of the driveway, waiting for the bus. That day was a tough one without Dad but I was very eager for school and the company of other children. When we had enough gasoline, due to the rationing, we went to see family in Bedford, always picking up soldiers who were hitch-hiking along the Turnpike and dropping them off when we reached Bedford. Mother was an excellent driver and often drove for Mrs. Koontz.

Soon after Dad left for Basic Training, Mother applied for work at the U. S. Naval Depot in Mechanicsburg, Pennsylvania and worked from May through the end of December, 1944. She could not find a babysitter for me so she resigned. She traveled back and forth to work with Jim Mort and several others from the Blain area. Her pay was 62 cents an hour when she started and 87 cents when she resigned seven months later. That was adequate for those times. Her title was Packer III.

Finally the War ended and Dad was home and back to work in early 1946. There are certificates and photos of the Refresher Courses all the Game Protectors attended, and a letter of commendation from Dr. Logan, Executive Director of the Commission, for handling a game violation investigation well. He attended a Testimonial Dinner for Dewey Miller, who had a position with the Commission. He also was from Bedford County and had helped Dad prepare for the tests for the Training School. Another letter thanked him and "Mr. Utech" for a Wildlife speaking engagement for the Camp Hill Jaycees. That reminded me of the extensive knowledge Dad possessed of the outdoors – animals and plant life alike. He often shared that knowledge with Boy Scout Troops and Sportsmen's Clubs. He was a story teller, and enjoyed writing articles for the PA Game News. Those News Notes were comical more often than not.

Soon after he was discharged at about age thirty-eight, he began having heart problems. Chest pain came "upon exertion" and there was only nitroglycerin to help. I recall cardiology appointments in Harrisburg and times when he could not mow with the push mower due to angina (chest pain). He could still handle the duties his job required, and the years sped by. I understood enough to be concerned that I could lose my dad to a heart attack.

In 1953 he was transferred to New Bloomfield, Perry County, and became responsible for Game Law enforcement for the whole county. He had good deputies, so that was a huge help. David and I recall some of their names: Ted Latchford, Guy Morrison, Paul Rice and Sam Bender.

There was no Game Commission house so we lived in a second-floor apartment at the corner of South Carlisle Street and West McClure Street. Within a few months, a house came up for sale on West McClure Street across from the old jail. Through the G. I. Bill, my parents were able to purchase it. Unbeknownst to me, the location put me next door to my future husband. I was fourteen and not looking for a husband just yet. My brother was born in 1955. In 1957, Dad's heart problems escalated, and at age forty-nine, he had a massive heart attack in October. His heart was badly damaged. My brother was just two years old and I was eighteen and at medical secretarial school in Hagerstown, Maryland. If not for all that walking throughout his life, I suspect he would not have lived. He was able to return to work about six months later.

I dropped out of school and got a job as a Clerk in the Engineering Department at Bell Telephone in Harrisburg. Donald, that next- door neighbor, and I had dated off and on throughout our high school years and became engaged the summer of 1957. He worked for his dad at the New Bloomfield Auto Co. We planned to be married when I finished the fifteen-month medical secretarial course, but we pushed the date to December 27, 1957. Dad was not yet well enough to walk me down the aisle but could at least attend our wedding and stand to give me away. A year later, we had our first child and my brother, David, became a very young uncle at age three!

The damage to Dad's heart took its toll, and in 1968, eleven years after his heart attack, he retired on disability at age sixty. That concluded his thirty years of service. He faced another hurdle when Mother died in August of 1973 at age fifty-nine. She had been ill for two years, part of that time spent at home and then at the Memorial Building at Polyclinic Hospital. It was a sad and difficult time for all of us. David was seventeen and had just graduated from West Perry High School. By this time my husband had answered a call to Pastoral Ministry, completed college and was in seminary. Thankfully, we were just forty-seven miles away at New Oxford, near Gettysburg. Donald served as a student pastor and attended seminary in Washington D. C. We had three young children and I worked part-time. I got home as often as I could to visit and help out.

Following Mother's death, he cooked and took care of the house and made a wonderful home for my brother. The years passed. David graduated from college, found a job and married Debbie Reisinger. They lived in Newport. Donald finished seminary and our denomination sent him to Elizabethville, in the Lykens Valley, just thirty miles from New Bloomfield.

The organist at the Elizabethville Church had lost her husband and our son thought she and his Pap would make a good match. When the business where he worked part-time during high school gave him a ham at Thanksgiving, he asked if we could invite his Pap and Millie for dinner. That proved to be the beginning of a courtship which would culminate in marriage on January 1, 1981. But first Dad persuaded his cardiologist to do heart by-pass surgery for him. It improved his quality of life greatly. Millie retired from her organist position and moved to New Bloomfield following their marriage. They did some traveling and served as "chaperones" for juries which had to be sequestered for Perry County, and attended Masonic activities. Oh, and our son and Millie's granddaughter married even before Dad and Millie tied the knot! I often kidded Dad that he surely knew how to pick his women, since Millie, his new wife was a lovely person, just as Mother had been.

In 1990, Dad again had heart blockages and at age 82, he said "no" to more surgery, and passed away December 23 from a massive heart attack. When I sent our Christmas letter the following year I wrote "I was thrilled to have him till he was 82, but I miss him greatly. He was nearly always upbeat, lively, and interested in everyone and everything around him. Those of us who counted him as husband, father, grandfather or friend know we have lost someone vital from our midst."

My Memories

"WAGNER'S GROCERY AND BOB'S ATLANTIC IN KISTLER"

Storyteller Jeanne Wagner Bender

My story starts in the early 1940s. My father, Robert Long Wagner, and my mother, Mary Kathryn Noss (Katty) met at a very small country store (owned by Tommy Heckendorn), on Fort Robinson Road between Loysville and Kistler. It was directly across from the Centre Presbyterian Church. Dad had come to see Jesse Alexander, my mother's cousin. Mother was visiting Jesse and, well, it was love at first sight.

Shortly thereafter, they began dating, which was difficult since my mother lived in McCoysville (Juniata County) and Dad lived near Loysville. He traveled across the mountain to see my mother in an old Model A Ford. However, in 1941, Dad was drafted into the US Army Air Force and was sent to Jackson, Mississippi. Because of the war, they decided to marry so Mother road the train to Mississippi. After their marriage, Mother stayed with other war brides in an old southern mansion. She had many stories about her time there – the plantation house was very old, chilly and drafty.

Dad was reassigned to MacDill AFB in Florida and mother came home. While there he became ill and the Army notified the family that he was near death. Fortunately an observant nurse discovered his medications had been switched with his roommate. Once out of the infirmary, he was sent to Myrtle Beach AFB in South Carolina. Mom and my sister, Mary Ann, who was an infant, joined him there for several months. He was then sent overseas to England. Dad was attached to the 454th Squadron – and he frequently had the duty of driving General Dwight Eisenhower around. His unit was sent into Europe and he was in France, Czechoslovakia and eventually Germany. He earned a Bronze Star for his service.

While Dad was in Florida, Mom lived in New Germantown with my Aunt Marian Wagner Gutshall. Mary Ann was born in New Germantown. Doc and Minnie Kistler attended Mom at the birth. After returning from South Carolina, Mom and Mary Ann went to live with her parents (Irvin and Mary Noss) in Juniata County. They stayed with them until the end of the war.

Dad arrived home in 1945 and he and mother bought a farm near Green Gates from Ogden Rodgers. It was a farm with lots of hills, so Dad hung up a sign that said Rolling Acres Farm – it sure was! A year later

I was born, and in 1948 my sister Nancy arrived.

On the farm we grew lots of vegetables and had pear trees. Mom canned lots of the produce and she also canned our meat. We butchered hogs and steers. On butchering day I loved helping as we made scrapple from the head meat and other offal.

At Christmastime, Dad would go up on the hill and cut a pine or cedar tree – the house always smelled so good. He would cut some chunks of cedar wood and we would freshen up our dresser drawers. For our tree, we made paper chains and had a celluloid Rudolph. I still have it for my tree. It wouldn't be Christmas unless we pulled taffy and had a fruitcake wrapped in a whiskey-soaked cloth.

In 1952, my sister Doris was born on February 29th, making her a Leap Year Baby. Doc Kistler and Minnie were there, along with my Aunt Katherine Noss. We girls were sent to stay with "Aunt Ruth" Hess, a neighbor. She treated us girls like we were nieces and always made us treats. When we arrived home to discover a new sister, our cousin Patty was there. She did not want us to see our sister – she declared that Doris was now her sister!

In the early 1950s, Mother was busy with four little girls and then Dad purchased thousands of chickens for mother to tend. Dad was hired at Montgomery Wards in Carlisle selling tires. So the job of tending the flock, gathering the eggs, grading them and packing them fell to Mom and us girls. I can't imagine how hard her life was. She not only had to take care of us, the chickens, the eggs, the gardens, but she had to also press and iron a white shirt for Dad to wear every day for work. Mary Ann was a huge help to Mom. One day while gathering eggs, she reached into an egg nest and encountered a large black snake.

Once in a while Dad would come home, get one of our girls and drive to Bishop's Store in Center. He would get a half gallon of ice cream, and occasionally bring back a pack of soda. What a treat that Sunkist Orange, Cloverdale Grape and Sundrop was to us. If we had upset stomachs, we were given Ginger Ale and crackers. If we had a cold or sore throat, mom slathered our chests with Vicks VapoRub and put a hand towel around our necks.

In 1960, Dad and Mom purchased a grocery store/house from a friend, Howard Wyckoff. The store was in Kistler. When we moved, it was a much larger house with a big screened-in porch. Our general store was called Wagner's Grocery. We had wonderful neighbors like Mary Peck and Gracie Palm, Press and Eva McMillen, Baird McMillen, Sally and Leo Dobbs, Reed and Nellie McMillen and the Hess family. It was wonderful to live in this small community. Every week Eva would call down a grocery order, and I would carry it up to her home. She carefully checked off the articles before giving me a check for the groceries.

I loved living in the store – we sold everything from groceries, tobacco products, hardware, medications, paper products, etc. Our soft drink machine was water cooled, so each week we had to remove the bottles, dip out the water, clean the case (water would get slimy quickly), clean the bottles and refill the case. We had lots of penny candy, chewing gum and a big jar filled with peppermint sticks.

Our large cheese wheel required lots of muscle to press down and cut wedges. We sliced a variety of lunch meats and dried beef. Kessler's from Lemoyne came weekly and on Thursdays we had hamburger and assorted fresh meats delivered by Klings Meat Market (near Green Park). In the winter we got fresh oysters in large cans. Mother loved oysters but me, not so much! I liked eating the milk from oyster stew, along with the crackers, but not the oysters.

In 1960, Mary Ann married Nevin Rice and moved to Blain as a farmer's wife. She came on Thursdays to help price groceries and put them away. George Taleff from Steelton was the salesman from Harrisburg Grocery. Pap Weaver was the bread man from Capitol Bakers. Another man delivered Henry's Bread from Shippensburg. Soda delivery men came with Pepsi and Coke products.

When stock arrived, we carried the boxes to the top floor of the grocery store. The steps upstairs were very small and very steep. You had to be very careful not to fall. My sisters and I fell more than once going up and down those stairs. The groceries were placed in a certain order upstairs – we tried to keep them identical to where they were displayed on the main floor. It was very tiring work and, of course, someone was always on duty at the cash register, checking customers out. Our soda was kept in the basement and sorted out by brands. Those we had to lug up the steps to refill the display.

Nancy, mother and I were the sole operators of the grocery store until Dad bought the gas station next door – he named it Bob's Atlantic. Then I was "selected" to go there and help waitress after school in the small lunchroom. Mrs. Arlene Palm was our cook. She made the best ham bean soup. She used smoked ham and great northern beans, and she would add rivels (tiny lumps of dough dropped in the boiling soup). Male patrons loved Arlene's pies. She made apple, lemon meringue and blueberry. Several other waitresses helped out. We had Joan Palm, Joyce Latchford, Donna Jo Clark Shuman, and my sister Doris. Nancy stayed at home and helped Mom with the grocery store.

My father hired Bill Shuman to mount and balance tires, pump gas, and change oil. He also went out to farms and mounted tractor tires. If he was gone or busy, I sometimes had to go out and pump gas. Of course, gas was very inexpensive then.

In 1972, my parents sold the grocery store to Frank and Maryellen Nace. They then built a small ranch house near Kistler, right beside Don and Dori Hess. They remained there until the death of my father in 1991. Mother then sold the house and moved to Perlo Apartments in Loysville where she stayed until her health required her move to Perry Village Nursing Home.

A little about me, I graduated from Blain Union High School in 1964. We went a full day to school. There was no kindergarten at that time. At school I learned to cook, clean properly, and sew on a treadle sewing machine. My teacher, Mrs. Sarah Bower, was a real stickler. For my senior picture, I made a light-blue dress with pearl buttons and lace. Our neighbor, Shirley Dobbs Seiders helped me with it. After graduation, I wanted to enter the Nursing School at Carlisle Hospital, but after a field trip to Harrisburg Hospital, I accepted a job there working in the laboratory. I typed autopsies and pathology reports and worked for three pathologists. After a year of commuting to Harrisburg in my '57 Chevy, I rented an apartment on Second Street in Harrisburg with several other girls. I liked living there, but then I got engaged to Grant Shope (from Cisna Run) and moved back to Perry County after our marriage.

Grant and I adopted a daughter, Julie Ann through the Family and Children's Services in Carlisle. One day when I took her for immunizations, Dr. Joseph Matunis suggested I apply at the newly formed Perry Health Center as a medical assistant. The health center doctors were Dr. Blaine F. Bartho, Dr. Harry

Leonard, Dr. Orlando Stephenson, and Dr. Matunis. I absolutely loved that job and remained there for almost twenty-eight years. I answered phones, made appointments, scheduled surgeries, called hospitals and arranged admissions. Some days I felt like I was on a treadmill as I ran from the front office to the copy room. Over the years we had several amputations, one live birth and some burn victims. After leaving the health center, following the death of my first husband, I took a job at the Domestic Relations Office in New Bloomfield. I typed court orders, sent out notices of non-compliance, etc. My first day in this office, I arrived and wondered why the office was locked and there was bullet-proof glass in the small speaking window. It was a difficult transition from medical terminology to legal-speak.

In the 1970's, my sisters both married and left home. Nancy married Carl Myers and had two daughters. Nancy worked at the YDC in Loysville for eight years, then worked at the Sheriff's Office in New Bloomfield. She eventually made the transition to the West Perry District Office where she remained for twenty-three years. Doris married Dick Ernest and had two daughters. She worked as a cosmetologist in Carlisle. In her late twenties Doris developed headaches, and after many tests, it was determined she had a brain tumor. She had surgery in Hershey Medical Center and underwent radiation treatments for a long period of time. She never fully recovered and spent the last years of her life in Perry Village.

Grant, my first husband, was a diabetic and eventually lost a leg due to his illness. In his final years, he went into renal failure and I did peritoneal dialysis for him for several years. Sadly, he died of complications of this horrible disease. Several years later, I remarried Gary J. Bender of Cisna Run. We were blessed with two sons, Robert Joseph and John Drew. Sadly, after many years of marriage, Gary passed away suddenly following a heart attack. I now am blessed to have two grandchildren – a granddaughter Marlow (Rob's daughter) and Drew Mitchell (John's son). Drew and John now live with me in a small house near Blain.

Following Gary's death, I was hired by the Perry County Courthouse as a receptionist. I thoroughly loved this job and remained for seven years. During that time I developed colon cancer and following several surgeries, decided to retire. In my retirement, I took a course called Diakonia (through the Lutheran Church) and obtained an Associate's Degree in Lutheran Theology. I have written sermons and preached in various churches. I now enjoy spending time with my grandchildren, reading, quilting, baking and cooking. I also attend the Blain Senior Center, where I try to bake a dessert each week for their congregate meals. I also love to make meals and take them to my sister Mary Ann and her husband, Nevin.

I hope you enjoyed my story – there is much more, but suffice to say, I have had a wonderful life. It has been full and rich, and I have been truly blessed by the good Lord. I don't know how I would have made it through life without my children and my sisters, and my good friends.

Memories Of Back Hollow Road

Storyteller Sarah Ann Singer Herman

Although I grew up in Maytown, in Lancaster County, founded in 1760, our family frequently visited Perry County at least every one to two weeks. My father, Frank Singer married Myrtle Esther Keck on March 31st, 1934. They had two daughters, Audrey Esther (b. October 2, 1935) and Sarah Ann (b. December 2, 1936) born at home in Maytown. Our trips to Perry County were always to visit family.

We went first to 2214 Back Hollow Road, owned then by our parents. It was a beautiful location, seemingly going back in time, to a big log home with an outhouse, oil lamps and water from the spring-house. This log home and acreage was purchased in November of 1890 by Catherine Leiby, my great-grandmother. She and Jacob Leiby raised seven children nearby on Robinson Road.

Their daughter, Anne married Clark D. R. Keck and had two children, Catherine Elizabeth (b. August 19, 1888) and Niles (b. May 26, 1891). They lived at Cisna Run. Clark purchased a farm on Robinson Road when Anne passed away at age twenty-five, October 22, 1891. Niles was five months old at the time.

Catherine, Annie's mother, told Clark to continue farming and raise Lizzie. Leibys cared for Niles. Clark farmed the land with support from the family nearby. Then on March 16, 1899, Clark married Sara Hattie (b. June 20, 1873) Leiby, Anne's sister. The Lord blessed them with four more children; Mary Augusta (b. December 18, 1889), Myrtle Esther (b. October 11, 1902), Helen Janet (b. February 27, 1911) and Sarah Irene (b. September 23, 1914).

The children walked to Manassa to a one-room schoolhouse. Our mother, Myrtle Keck went eight grades to completion of her schooling. There were no high schools back then. Clark continued farming and Sara (Sadie) walked the back roads, to care for people in their homes and to deliver babies. The doctor was across the mountain, probably in Franklin County, and that is why the local people called on Sadie for help. They had a horse, but it was needed to do the farm work. Sadie and her older brother, Benjamin Franklin Leibey knew their herbs and how to use natural plants. Sadie would treat people and Ben treated the farm animals.

Lizzie, (Catherine Elzabeth Keck), married Jim Berrier when Myrtle was only six years of age and moved to Milton Grove in Lancaster County, where they farmed and raised eight children.

Mary Keck moved to Mt. Joy, where she worked for a dentist and their family. They entertained a lot and she served them well. Later, she worked for the shoe factory in Mt Joy. She walked to work, as she did not drive.

Myrtle moved to Lancaster County, near the Masonic Homes in Elizabethtown, where she served as a nurse to many of the residents. She would have been grandfathered in as a registered nurse had she not married Frank Singer, our father.

Helen moved to Elizabethtown as a teenager and graduated there from high school. Later, she married Dale Shope Lyons of Perry County and they had four children. Helen and Dale returned to Perry County, back to the Robinson Road property after Dale retired from the service. Later, Helen had Baird Collins build her a new home on part of the property that she kept on Back Hollow Road. Helen made all sorts of doll clothes and donated them to the Blain Senior Center. She made quilts too and taught a number of people how to quilt.

Irene was a teen when her mother passed away and only twenty-five when she lost her father. This was heartbreaking for her. After her father passed, she lived with her sister, Myrtle and Frank Singer, for a year in Maytown. She worked in the shoe factory in Mt Joy, five miles away. John McConnell grew tired of traveling from Perry County to Maytown to court her. They married August 21, 1941 in Elizabethtown.

They took up housekeeping at 3100 Fowler Hollow Road, Blain, Pennsylvania, where they raised three children. The family especially liked to pull practical jokes on family and friends.

After our father, Frank Singer, who was a carpenter and cabinet maker, passed in 1987, our home and contents were auctioned off. Jim and Larry McConnell, our cousins, purchased many of our father's tools, which they still use today to make furniture and other useful wooden items.

Not to be out done by his boys, Uncle John started making chairs, of which I have six oak chairs in our dining room. They are signed by him and dated July 2000.

My sister and I took turns going to visit John and Irene McConnell each summer in Perry County. He taught me how to milk a cow. We would play ball in the pasture with friends like Johnnie Frownfelter, Berdina Rowe and others. We would have to watch for "cow piles." This was near the Enslow Covered Bridge off the road towards Manassa.

Across from our place on Back Hollow Road was a church with a steeple. Sometimes we could hear the music and sounds from within. We were always curious, but we did not attend any of their services. We did however, go to Manassa Church on the Sundays we were visiting in Perry County.

In the summer, the Blain Picnic Ground, along Shermans Creek, always seemed to have events going on. One time we got to see Little Jimmie Dickens and the Grand 'Ole Opry bunch. It was truly amazing. Our cousin, Galen Keck and other friends often played their stringed instruments, entertaining in their homes and at special events around the county.

The Blain Picnic was always the second weekend of August. Families would bring picnic tables to set-up and our family usually had at least twenty to thirty people attend each year. Of course, there was always lots of food and entertainment. In later years once the Blain Picnic went by the wayside, Ron Keck and others started Heritage Days which is the second week of October. People come from all-over to see the antique tractor parades, quilt auction, and many other "heritage demonstrations" involving farming methods and equipment from years past. Sundays start off with a church service. It is always a huge event. I always returned home with some homemade scrapple and place McConnell's apple butter on top. Yum!

Ron Keck had the grocery store in Blain for some years. Ron was the son of Clark Keck. Clark was the eldest of Niles and Orpha Keck's family. Niles and Orpha Shoemaker Keck raised their seven children on both properties on Back Hollow Road and Robinson Road. The seven being Clark (b. 1916), Maxine (b. 1918), Grace (b. 1922), Willis (b. 1925), Jean (b.1929), Galen (b. 1935) and Velva (b. 1937)

Helen Lyons always prepared a meal for family and neighbors on the first day of trout season, often feeding thirty people. Her home was not far from Shaffer's Run. Today, Three Spring's Church sets-up tables and serves the fishermen along Mt. Pleasant Road. But I hear, this year 2022, topped them all. They sold ham bean soup, hot dogs, and other things like homemade chocolate and banana ice cream. They made thirty-two quarts of ice cream, and the only ones I know that make large quantities of ice cream are my cousins, Jim and Larry McConnell.

Catherine Phillips Leiby, Clark David Robert and Sara Hattie Keck lived out their days in the Back Hollow home. I've lived in Skagit County, the northwestern end of the state of Washington since 1965. My husband, Jack and I have raised four children and all of them live within thirty miles of us. Jim and Larry McConnell drove west to visit us in May of 1993.

I will always keep Perry County in my heart!

HARRY G. SHEAFFER – A TRUE PERRY COUNTY LEGEND

ICKESBURG BASEBALL & PERRY COUNTY POLITICS

Storyteller Craig M. Sheaffer
Recorded by William G. Lyons

Harry G. Sheaffer was born in Markelsville, Pennsylvania, on April 14, 1929 to Graffius and Effie Hoffman Sheaffer. Attending Newport High School, he was a two-sport athlete playing football and baseball, his favorite sport. He would often walk or hitch a ride home after practice. He graduated in 1947. Harry was becoming a man that would possess many fine qualities and would be known as a gentleman, leader, family man, friend, and a man of courage.

Harry first worked for the railroad for two years. Then he owned and operated the Ickesburg Beer Distributorship, located on Route 17 across the street from the firehouse between the old post office and the hotel recently removed in 2021.

He was drafted into the Army serving from 1951-1953 in Korea. Harry, a corporal at the end of two years, was asked to consider re-enlisting as a sergeant. While at home considering re-enlisting, his military base guarding fuel tanks, was blown up. He decided against re-enlisting, was discharged, and worked for the Pennsylvania Department of Transportation for four years as a laborer and truck driver.

Harry married Betty Jane Swartz on August 25, 1951. Betty lived in Ickesburg in the house below the Pennian Bank. Her mother, Vannie, died when Betty Jane was only fourteen years old. Her father, Clarence Leroy (better known as C. L. or Bill) hauled cattle and sold fertilizer and paint. He was known for his booming voice, especially over the phone or at an Ickesburg baseball game.

Discharged from the service, Harry, Betty Jane, and a very young Karen lived with Betty Jane's grandparents in Gratz. Harry played baseball in the Dauphin County League for one year, before moving to Newport and eventually to their life-long home near Ickesburg, in 1954. Together, they had four children; Karen Heusser (1952), Beth Reichenbach (1955), Craig (1957) and Brian "Chop" (1961).

Fortunately, two local girls, Linda Barnes and Perrietta McMillen, were available to look after their children when politics and social functions demanded of their time. Through it all, Harry was a devoted family man. The love and devotion of their parents bonded the family.

The family grew up with baseball. When the sandlot team had doubleheaders on holiday weekends, Betty Jane and her family would host cookouts at their home for the team between games. Son Craig hit .616 when he was in junior high school but health problems prevented him from becoming an active player. "Chop" was a member of the 1979 & 1980 West Perry state championship baseball teams.

In 1957, Harry, a Democrat, decided to run for Saville Township Tax Collector where the Republican Party held a 3-1 edge. He was considered a huge underdog, but he won by forty votes and was re-elected in 1961 by a large margin.

1963 was a year where all four candidates in the fall election for Perry County Commissioner were from Saville Township including Harry, Max Powell, Norman Pressley and Glenn Smith. This was the first of four terms won by Harry before bowing out in the 1979 election. He served as chairman of the commissioners from 1976-1980. These four years were the first time that two of the three commissioners were democrats since the nineteenth century. The other democrat was Sam Nulton of Carroll Township and the republican was Edwin "Bud" Wallis. He was appointed by the newly elected Governor Richard "Dick" Thornburgh to a state job with the Pennsylvania Department of Agriculture. Lawrence "Larry" Beaver was appointed to finish Wallis' term.

At the age of six, Craig has many memories of being on the campaign trail with his father, when they would be visiting with the voters. Craig would sometimes sit in the car for an hour while his father would be inside talking. While he waited, he would wrap his father's name on cigars and lollipops for handouts. Craig would ask, "What took you so long?" Harry replied, "They would want to talk and they know a lot of people." Some places were visited last, because Harry knew he would be offered a beer. He would be told, "Harry, you had a beer with me before you were commissioner, so if you can't now, I won't vote for you." Those voters were serious.

Harry was elected to Jury Commissioner in 1981 and 1985. He resigned in 1987 due to health reasons. His wife Betty Jane was appointed and re-elected the years of 1989, 1993, 1997, and 2001. Throughout the years, Harry and Betty Jane held a county office between county commissioner and jury commissioner for thirty-eight years. Harry also served as treasurer of the Perry County Democrat Party from 1968-1986, and chairman from 1986-1989. He remained active until democratic Judge Keith Quigley, from the New Bloomfield area, was retained for his second ten-year term.

Harry had friends in both parties and supported candidates that he knew could get the job done. Some included republicans like Representative Fred Noye, Senator Bill Moore, party chair Emory Stokes, Earl Rempfer, and Commissioner Elwood Mohler to name a few. Democrats, who strongly supported Harry, included George McAllister, Raymond Stuckey, Charles Lupfer, Bonnie McAllister, Dale and Rich Rohm, Stan Richard, Loy and Ruby Binger, Donald and Virginia McGowan, Flo Fisher, Helen Ruhl, Alfred Albright, Ralph and Gladys Albright, Dave Duncan, John Barrick, Roy Charles, Norman "Dipper" Rowe, Carl Maxwell, Em Shreffler, Ron Hampton, Keith and Shirley Watson, Chuck and Dot Jacobs, Chet Decker, John and Thelma Teats, Gene and Beatie Fritz, Dale "Brownie" and Joanne Fritz, Dean and Sally Fritz, Bob Sheaffer and Reynold Moose.

During these years he also worked at Stanley Jacob Weibley's, "S. J. Weibley Petroleum" and later Keystone Petroleum, who bought out S. J. Weibley. The business was located in Mechanicsburg, Pennsylvania where they would go out and install underground fuel tanks, pumps and do service work on the equipment throughout Pennsylvania. He also worked four years for the state Auditor General's office.

Harry's family owned the custard stand in Ickesburg from 1972-1976 (affectionately named "Hanks Place," using Harry's nickname). The stand was originally located on Route 74 beside the FBF convenience store and gas station. They sold soft serve ice cream, sandwiches, meals, Betty Jane's delicious barbecue, baked beans, and coleslaw. Her barbecue recipe is still used by the many that have it! The custard stand was a booming business for four years. The stand was sold to Jack Tracy in 1976 and renamed Tracy's Treat. At the time, Harry was commissioner, Karen moved, Beth worked in Harrisburg, Chop was in high school, and Craig was destined to hip surgery. Otherwise, "Hanks Place" would have remained in the family.

Bill Bunt, Perry County's longtime solicitor, was hired in 1976 by commissioners Harry, Sam Nulton, and Edwin "Bud" Wallis. Harry could always count on Bill as he made himself available all hours of the day or night. After Harry retired as a commissioner, he still showed support for Bill. He would talk with the newly elected board regardless of party affiliation and let them know how important Bill was to Perry County. Forty-six years later, Bill Bunt, with his knowledge and experience, continues to give Perry County his best. Bill has shared his sentiments about Harry with the following comments. He thought of Harry as a Thomas "Tip" O'Neil, a man who could work with both parties to get things accomplished. At the end of the day, the commissioners were still friends no matter what took place. Bill remarked that Harry was a loyal, decent, good, honest person that was able to unify the county government. He was always there to lead, faithful to the truth, and served with integrity for the people of Perry County.

Perry County's own, Fred C. Noye, was a renowned Pennsylvania State Representative who served the 86th District for ten terms from 1972-1992. Fourteen of those years, he was either the Majority or Minority Caucus Chairman. Paula Stiffler, who staffed the New Bloomfield legislative office, stated that "Fred is thought of as a great teacher and a lot was learned from him." With his love of baseball, particularly the Brooklyn Dodgers, Fred also served as President of the Perry-Juniata Sandlot League for three years. The following are some memories that Fred has shared about Harry.

"During the start of my campaign in 1971, I met Commissioner Harry Sheaffer for the first time. He was serving with Commissioners Max Powell and Norman Pressley. To my knowledge this was a historic first in that all three commissioners were from the same municipality, Saville Township, with all three serving two consecutive terms. Even though we were from different parties, I soon learned Harry was quite different from other members of the opposing party. In our dealings he was always kind and a real gentleman. As the years went by, we became good friends. I believe the common denominator that brought us together was our love of baseball. No matter what we were talking about, the conversation usually got around to talking about baseball. I soon learned that we had much more in common on issues than any political differences. Harry always displayed common sense on the issues and always kept a perspective of what was good for Perry County and its people. He wasn't swayed by big city politics or political ideology.

In 1971, there was a spirited campaign for the position of County Commissioner. Harry was comfortably the minority party member in the Commissioner's office. Perry County had a bedrock Republican majority and whoever won the Republican primary, would go on to being elected in November. The 1971 election brought change to the Commissioner's office. Two new faces were nominated by the Republican Party, with one of the incumbents losing and the other one retiring. The new commissioners were William Rohrer, of Marysville and Edwin Wallis, of Liverpool. Harry was easily re-elected to the minority post.

The new board of commissioners set forth a very active agenda. During the period of 1971-1975 the commissioners reassessed the county, closed the County Home at Loysville, contracted with a private nursing facility and finally approved an addition to be built on to the county courthouse. This was change that Perry Countians were not used to seeing and it occurred in a very short span of four years. While Harry didn't agree with everything, he was still being held accountable by taxpayers for these changes. It should be noted that the three commissioners worked extremely well together and became very close in their friendship. Even differences of opinion could not break their friendship.

When the election of 1975 rolled around, Harry received a strong challenge from within his own party for what was expected to be the minority position. But in the November election there was a huge upset. Harry found himself chairman of the board of County Commissioners. There were several factors that contributed to this upset election. First and foremost was the very active agenda that shook the foundations of the county. Reassessment led to tax increases along with more spending for nursing home care and the addition to the courthouse. Also, there were concerns by the Republican commissioners that Harry could lose the minority seat. Some Republicans set out to get Harry some Republican votes in asking people to split their ticket. That plan backfired and led to only one Republican winning re-election and the Democratic candidates winning control for the first and only time since before the 20th Century.

The chairmanship did not change Harry. He was still the same levelheaded, down to earth person that he always was. He treated everybody the same with respect and dignity. Character is what defined Harry Sheaffer, not politics.

In 1970 there was a position open in the commissioner's office for a clerk. Bonnie Delancey, from Saville, wrote a letter to apply for the position and a week later she had an interview. Bonnie met with the three commissioners from Saville Township, Max Powell, Chairman, Norman Pressley, Vice Chairman, and Harry Sheaffer, Secretary. They were now serving in their second consecutive term. About two weeks after the interview, she was to report to work on June 15, 1970. She is currently the longest standing county employee manning the Voters Registration Office. Bonnie is a wonderful, caring person who is very conscientious in her work and has been a great asset to Perry County. The following contains just a few past memories of her working with Harry.

The commissioners had the responsibility of the Courthouse, County Jail, County Home, Election Houses, Sixteen County Bridges, Agriculture Services, Extension Services, Soil Conservation, Court Services, Children and Youth Services, Tax Assessment, County Board of Elections, etc. With all these responsibilities, Harry worked closely with Max and Norman. Harry was always interested in working with the department heads, department staff, maintenance personnel, and janitorial staff.

Harry would help to proofread the paper ballots that were printed at the Perry County Times office and was excellent at that job. At that time, the county was divided into three sections for delivery of the ballots and the ballot box. Harry took care of the western part of the county and in the fall, he would take his turkey gun along. He actually did shoot a turkey delivering the ballots one year. Election Day and Election Night the commissioners would always be available to help the staff with the processing of the ballot materials. The poll workers would bring everything to the Courthouse after the polling places closed in the evening. Sometimes we did not leave the Courthouse until 1:00 a.m. on Wednesday morning.

In the spring, the schools would bring students in for tours of the county offices. One year Harry's youngest son Chop's class came to tour the buildings. Bonnie asked Chop to tell his classmates what his dad did as a County Commissioner. His answer was, he takes a trip once a year. Well, Harry quietly said a few words that Bonnie would not repeat. She replied, "No, you will just love that boy to death!" Chop was referring to the yearly County Commissioner's Convention. In this era, the commissioners met once a month in the Courthouse and a monthly meeting at the County Home. If we at any time needed information from them, they would come into the office to work with the staff.

In 1972, a new Board of Commissioners were elected. Edwin B. Wallis Jr., Chairman, William A. Rohrer, Vice Chairman, and Harry G. Sheaffer, Secretary. Again, new beginnings and working together with the county employees and taxpayers. In 1972, a reassessment of the county had to be done. Plans were discussed to add an addition to the Courthouse. The additional space was completed on December 6, 1975 and was opened to the public. The Commissioners worked at trying to update the County Home in Loysville to current standards with the Department of Labor and Industry. After many discussions with the architects, etc., it was determined the building was not up to state standards and the refurbishing costs were not justifiable. At that time the Commissioners looked for a new avenue and worked with the Department of Labor for a new building called Perry Village. The county reserved fifty beds for county resident's care in Perry Village, in New Bloomfield. In 1975, the old jail and the exercise yard were remodeled, after receiving sought after state grants. Harry, Bud, and Bill all worked together for the county and the taxpayers on the projects.

At the start of Harry's fourth term, in 1976, the Commissioners' Office changed to that of a Democratic majority of Harry G. Sheaffer, Chairman, Samuel R. Nulton, Vice Chairman, Edwin B. Wallis, Secretary. They faced new challenges including a new commissioner, more employees to be hired for various offices and changes involving the 911 center. They faced issues with employees wanting higher salaries and the Teamsters Union trying to become involved with the county departments. The commissioners tried working with all the departments in reference to union negotiations, but met challenges. The commissioners started to give meritorious service certificates to employees that performed outstanding work. An example of such was on February 20, 1978, when courthouse employees Larry Delancey and Sam Bender were presented certificates by county commissioners for obtaining food and medicine for a snowed-in diabetic. Among other things, they also participated in a mass snow removal at the courthouse.

The commissioners were under a lot of stress with different issues and on April 1, 1979 Edwin B. Wallis Jr. resigned. On that same date, the court appointed Lawrence E. Beaver, of Greenwood Township, to fill the unexpired term. Harry, Samuel, and Larry worked well together and respected the challenges that faced them working for the county taxpayers.

Bonnie has many fond memories of working with Harry for three of his terms in office. He always treated everyone fairly and if you needed help with anything, he was always there to finish the task. Bonnie is forever thankful to have been hired in 1970 and grateful for the experiences learned. She has good memories, over the past fifty-two years, of all the commissioners that she has worked for including the present-day board. Bonnie is pleased to be able to share some of her thoughts in this account honoring her dear friend Harry G. Sheaffer.

Sharon Charles, of Hunter's Valley, was hired as a secretary during Harry's fourth term and eventually became the chief clerk. She worked for the county from 1976-1991, left for a few years, and came back from 1996-2010 for a total of twenty-nine years. She worked for fifteen different commissioners. Harry went to bat for Sharon on a couple occasions because of her strong work ethic. She always considered Harry both a good man and a good politician. She reminisced that back in the 1970s-1990s, the political party's committee people would be checking with the watchers to see who had not voted. They would then call those people and offer to drive them to the polling places. Committee people took their jobs very seriously. Also, people who worked for the government, state and county, were eager to vote because their jobs depended upon it. After an election the party that won the majority also won the right to release the current employees and hire their own. In a way, the common practice was good because the people did their best at their jobs. Unlike today, many are not really interested in helping the public nor doing anything above and beyond for what they were hired, because their jobs are now secure. Sharon commented, "I guess that is how government got so big."

Hon. Keith B. Quigley (Ret.) was President Judge for Perry-Juniata County Court of Common Pleas in Pennsylvania. He was appointed to the bench by former Governor Milton Shapp in 1976. Quigley retired in 2004, after which time he served as a Senior Judge until 2017. Prior to joining the judiciary, Quigley had worked as the Perry County District Attorney for five years beginning in 1971. Before that, he had been a private practice attorney since 1964.

Judge Keith B. Quigley considered Harry a true-gentlemen and a joy to work with. He felt that Harry felt the same way about him. That is obvious considering that Harry stayed on as chairman of the Perry County Democrat Party to support the Judge for his ten-year retention before retiring. Harry was a wonderful man both professionally and a friend. The judge would often times attend the commissioner meetings and would be impressed with the way county business would get done without political intervention. In those days it was common in other counties for judges and commissioners not to get along well. This was not the case in Perry and Juniata Counties as the judge and commissioners had a great working relationship. Harry is remembered as "trustworthy and one of the good old boys."

As the gentleman that he was, Harry was known to be a man that would not degrade the character of others, including his opponents in the political arena and on the baseball field. The true value of Harry's leadership in both politics and sports is obvious from the many friendships he maintained and cherished throughout his lifetime.

Ickesburg's Harry Sheaffer and baseball have been one in the same for many years. He started playing on the Ickesburg Sandlot baseball team at the age of thirteen. At the age of nineteen, he had a tryout with the Pittsburgh Pirates at spring training in Florida. He commented that "you think that you are good, but there everyone is good, and you are a dime a dozen." He did really well in everything except throwing the ball from center field to home. His father Graffius was the manager for Ickesburg when Harry was first playing. When Harry did anything on the night before a game, his dad would always remind him "not to get home late and be ready to play!"

Harry took over managing the team in the early 1960s and told his father at the age of sixty-one that he should retire from the game. Harry's brother Arland was a pretty good ball player on the team. In the days before helmets, he was hit in the head by a pitched ball and was never the same again. When he got better, he still came to every ballgame to watch. Brother Dean also played when he returned from serving in Vietnam. Even though Dean was wounded twice and received two purple hearts, he was an outstanding baseball player. He could do it all despite losing one of his eyes stringing a bow!

Harry played center field, pitched, and in later years played first base. "Hammerin Hank" usually batted third in the order, hit a lot of line drives, and was known as a power hitter. He could hit the cover off the ball especially if it was a right-handed pitcher. Dale Reisinger, among others, have commented that Harry and Abe Shultz were two of the best players that they ever played with. Harry didn't care much for left-handed pitchers like Loysville's Ron Emlet with his knuckle-ball and drop. Harry always played with a big wad of chewing tobacco in his mouth.

In the 1970s, Harry becoming older didn't play much but would pinch hit with men on base. He would put on Craig's baseball shoes, step up to the plate and more times than not come through with a key base hit. Craig has been told over the years by many players throughout the county that no matter how long you live you will never be able to fit in your father's shoes when it comes to baseball. Harry was just that good and Craig considers it a huge compliment!

In the 1920s-1930s, a rough playing field existed off a road between Ralph "Dip" Johnson and where Jim Nipple lives. The Wayne Weibley Memorial Field located beside the Ickesburg Schoolhouse was where the team played till 1976 when the Willie Snyder Memorial Field hosted games. The bleachers were dedicated there in Harry's name on June 22, 1997, but the Ickesburg team had disbanded in 1979 after Harry's retirement.

Ickesburg took their baseball serious. Back in the day if farmers had hay ready, they would let it lay in the field until the next day because there was a game. At an Ickesburg game, fans would line their chairs along the schoolhouse to cheer the team on. Somewhere around 1950, Charlie Barnes was pitching in a game against Blain. He didn't like the calls from the home plate umpire. All at once, he marched onto the field, hitting the umpire in the face before he removed his mask. Charlie left the game with a broken hand.

On a couple of occasions, when the fans didn't like the umpire's call, they would charge right onto the field after him. There were times where fans may even hit the umpire and drag him around the field. Some memorable irate fans included Earl Rowe, Charlie Barnes, Les Simonton, and Wayne Kochenderfer. When a fight would start to break out, Harry would motion to 6' 5" Chuck Jacobs (a fan-good friend), who would take off his glasses and go out on the field to help in peace-making. A couple of players from Blain that would get fired up were Dale "Artie" Gray and Clyde Shambaugh. One year either the league or the umpire association suspended Harry from managing the team for a year, because of the ruckuses. Harry said if you think that I'm going to get in front of some of those fans when they were mad, you are crazy! People would say who won the game because we already know who won the fight!

Several times after a game someone would get a case of beer and the two teams would hang out and talk afterwards. Players were dedicated enough that they would go to the ball field to dig drains and sweep water off after it rained, getting the field game ready.

A few memories that need to be told
In 1970, it was the last game of the season at Newport. Ickesburg needed a win to make the playoffs. When the team arrived, there were only eight players and Harry looked to his son Craig. He said, "you are catching your Uncle Dean today!" Craig being only thirteen was quite nervous about catching in a game that meant so much. They won the game, made the playoffs and defeated Blain in the finals to win the 1970 playoff championship.

During a game played on Weibley field, Dave Fuller got tangled up in Harold Nipple's electrified barbwire fence in left field going back to catch a fly ball. The game was held up for more than ten minutes as several players tried to quickly rescue him from being continually shocked. He literally lost his shirt off his back! After this incident, the fence was taken down prior to a game.

Again, in Ickesburg's left field, a brand-new ball was hit foul and the opposing Blain left fielder told a ten-year-old boy to just throw the ball into the stream, which he did. That caused quite a stir from C. L. Swartz, Harry's father-in-law, whose voice carried well to the left fielder!

C. L. Swartz (Bill) would collect hat money from the fans for the team. He made sure he got to every fan! In 1976 at one of the first games at the new field, he collected a large sum of cash from a very large crowd. It was always nice when Harry could pay the umpires, other expenses and still have plenty of money left. David "Doc" Weibley and Dave Sheaffer would sell soda from a square metal tub filled with ice at the games to also raise money.

Back in the 1950s, the Ickesburg players would sometimes get together and scrimmage on a Sunday at the high school field. One day Harry stepped up to hit and drove a deep fly ball to right that cleared Snyder Lane, somewhere near 375 feet. Dale "Brownie" Fritz caught the ball and Harry said, "How dang far do I have to hit it!!"

Harry's last at bat in 1979, at the age of fifty, was a fly ball to right that struck the fence on the fly, 318 feet away. He made it to second base for a double. Youngest son "Chop" came in to run for him. During his last season, Harry batted five for thirteen for an average of .385.

Earl Rowe, 1892-1971, was a die-hard fan of baseball, the first Ickesburg team's catcher and became manager in the 1940s. Some people have said that he reached in front of the plate to catch the ball before the batter could swing. His glove-hand would show the damage when this didn't work. He was a fan who was very attentive of the play, voicing his opinion if a player or an umpire made a mistake. His voice could be heard above the crowd! Earl Rowe was the ultimate baseball fan, one of many in the Ickesburg area.

Earl once asked his grandson, Terry Urich, at the end of a high school game, if he had heard him yelling. Terry's mistake was telling him that he did. Earl replied, "You were not paying attention to the game if you heard me." When Terry was a senior, his grandfather told him to treat his bat with linseed oil over the winter to make it harder to break. Terry drilled a hole in the knob of the bat and applied the oil to let it soak in. After doing this all winter, he took the bat to his first game and the handle broke. Terry never tried that again.

Listed are many players from the 1950s forward: Dean Earnest, Harvey Swab, Harry Sheaffer, Don Reisinger, Gene Fritz, Paul D. "Srubby" Smith, Paul L. Smith, Warren Barnes, Dean Reisinger, Arland Sheaffer, Graffius Sheaffer, Bill Bistline, Abe Shultz, Max Powell, Kenny Orris, Dale Reisinger, Wayne Reisinger, Bob Bistline, Ronald Hampton, Charlie Barnes, Dale Haas, Charlie Smith, Charles "Chiz" Johnson, Chuck Shull, Jerry Spease, Jack Ulsh, Dave Fuller, Willie Reisinger, Harry Wilson, Steve Orris, Dennis Campbell, Les Bowersox, Stanley "Jake" Weibley, Dale "Brownie" Fritz, Bob Crawford, Barry Walborn, Bob Wolf, Steve Gold, Doug Albeck, Jim Rich, Mike Wilbert, Jim Bowersox, Bob Roth, Ezra Bupp, Monty Bupp, Dwayne Bupp, Les Simonton, Jacob "Jake" Simonton, Dale Rohm, Morris "Mort" Loy, Paul "Sipe" Stum, Bill Sheaffer, Kevin Sheaffer, Jan Reapsome, Jon Reapsome, and Dick Briner.

The 1976 Championship team: Harry Sheaffer, manager, Craig Sheaffer, Dean Sheaffer, Gary Walak, Kenny Campbell, Frank Kochenderfer, Doug Boeshore, Wayne Weibley, Mark Paul, Leon Hoke, Bill Lyons, Ron Bowersox, Brian "Chop" Sheaffer, Glenn Sheaffer, and Chester "Chet" Lesh.

Leon Hoke, an Ickesburg native, was one of Harry's players, who came out of West Perry High School where he started his senior year as a catcher, but could play many positions. To learn how to pitch, he threw balls to Craig Sheaffer countless hours and tossed balls at a barn wall. Two years later on a whim, he went to a couple of tryouts held at Shippensburg University, where he caught the attention of scouts from Cincinnati and Philadelphia. He was told that he needed experience at the college level. Shippensburg coaches were also impressed enough to offer him a spot on the Red Raider team. In his two years pitching, he lost only once and was named team MVP. He wasn't drafted into the major leagues. Instead, a Baltimore Oriole's scout offered him a tryout resulting in a contract. Leon played professional baseball, for his favorite team, over four seasons including the AA.

When anybody brings up Ickesburg baseball, Harry Sheaffer's name is always included in the same sentence. Harry played on the town team for thirty-seven years from the age of thirteen to fifty. He coached midgets, teeners, and the town team. He also served as Perry-Juniata League's president. As a player and coach, he helped to lead the club to a 1970 playoff championship. In 1976, he led Ickesburg to both the league and playoff championships. The team folded after the 1979 season when Harry hung up his spikes for good. "Hank" was the "Mr. Baseball" of Ickesburg. He was the glue that held the Ickesburg team together. His dedication and leadership were what kept this team together for all those years.

Lastly, this man was a man of courage. He lived with rheumatoid arthritis for fifteen years without complaining. With much pain and having to take powerful drugs with many negative side effects, he always tried to keep a positive outlook. While enduring his physical setbacks, he always smiled and looked to the next day. Harry had a devotion to his friends, and especially had his devotion focused on his family. The character of this man made it pure joy to have the privilege to know him and love him. Harry had a heart attack in June of 1995 and had several complications. He passed away on March 7, 1996 at the age of sixty-six. When Harry was buried, along with him was his Ickesburg uniform, a bat, glove, and a pouch of chewing tobacco. When one person came through the line at his viewing, he asked, who put that bat in his coffin. Craig replied that he did. The fella said your dad never used a thick handled bat in his life. Craig had to smile that someone would remember that.

A lot of information in this story came from Craig. Some of the things written here, the credit is given to Dennis Fuller for the kind words he spoke during Harry's eulogy. Also, Dennis's brother, Dave Fuller, had written a poem styled after "Casey's Revenge", and this is what Hank was all about.

All Ickesburg was in attendance, one-hundred fans had come
To see the pitcher who had put big Harry on the bum;
And when he stepped onto the mound, Hank's fans went wild,
The pitcher waved his cap, but Harry only smiled.

"Play ball" the umpire's voice rang out, and then the game began.
Unfortunately, there was not a single fan,
Who figured Ickesburg stood a chance; and with the setting sun
Hopes sank low because the rival team was leading "four to one."

The bottom of the ninth inning came up, with no change in the score,
But when the first batter up got on base, Ickesburg's fans began to roar.
The cheering grew and the echo off the Tuscarora Mountain was heard,
as the pitcher hit the second batter and carelessly gave "four balls" to the third.

Three men on base, with no outs and three runs to tie the game!
A triple meant the highest recorded in Ickesburg's hall of fame.
Unfortunately, the streak ended and the mood was dark as night
As the fourth batter fouled to the catcher and the fifth went out to right.

The fans were in disbelief and scowls covered their face.
Then Harry walked bat in hand to the plate, and took his time getting into place,
His piercing eyes and his clenched teeth were showing lots of hate;
He gave his cap a vicious twist and pounded his bat on the plate.

The pitcher grinned and let one loose; crossing home plate it sped,
The fans in total disbelief, "strike one!" the umpire said.
Like a speeding bullet, the second pitch curved just below Harry's knee
"Strike two!" the umpire shouted while Harry shook his head and made no plea.

But then the pitcher let loose again and it sounded like a shot,
but it soon was determined it certainly was not!
Above the fence in center field, the flying ball took flight,
and soon was totally out of sight.
Fans went wild throwing hats into the air, and cheering raised their clenched fists,
And, some fans hunted for the illusive ball that a determined Harry hit!

All the Ickesburg fans were ecstatic because Harry walloped that ball!

And there is no doubt that in Hank's life, he surely won the game!
To all those who knew Harry and loved him definitely consider him
"A True Perry County Legend".

Blain Union School Days and Baseball

Storyteller David Rice

Before the creation of West Perry School District for the 1964–1965 academic year, Blain Union School District served the extreme western end of the county. All grade levels, first through twelfth, (no kindergarten yet) housed in the building at the north end of town. Some of my favorite teachers were Margaret Nesbit (wife of Clyde Nesbit – owner of the Blain Planing Mill), Willis Smith, Dorothy Robertson, Wilson Shope and Amos Colledge.

It was in Willis Smith's fifth grade class on the afternoon of November 22, 1963, that we heard the first sketchy reports over the school PA system of the shooting event in Dallas, Texas. Before school adjourned for the day, JFK's death had been confirmed. I was ten years old at this time, and what struck me then, and still sticks out in my memory, was the palpable stunned disbelief and genuine anguish exhibited almost universally by the adult world (teachers, school staff, bus drivers, parents, townspeople, etc.). I never saw or experienced adults act so uniformly shaken up by any turn of events. How could an action so despicable occur in America, having our nation's young leader struck down in the broad daylight of a beautiful fall afternoon in front of a host of citizens? Many commentators have opined that America lost her sense of innocence that day, and I tend to agree, for in my opinion, while the nation has suffered through several national tragedies since then, nothing compares to the shock to the national psyche delivered that day.

In the 1964-1965 school year, my sixth-grade teacher was Amos Colledge, already something of an icon in the Blain area because of his status as the manager of the Blain sandlot baseball team for many years. Remember, this was a time when baseball was indeed the national pastime. Local sandlot games (doubleheaders on Memorial Day and the 4th of July) for instance always drew big crowds anxious to see the local guys play and, truth be told, to enjoy a 'good rhubarb' between opposing teams. These games provided a real form of entertainment for the inhabitants, especially the farmers, before satellite tv and the ability to jump in the car and head out of the county for entertainment.

Mr. Colledge was blessed with a slow, drawl-like voice that exuded knowledge and authority. One widely circulated anecdote about his managerial days has his Blain club (already not playing well), victimized by a bad call by an umpire early in the game, so egregious that Colledge stated that he would play the game under protest (appeal to the league president). Later in the game, after watching his club commit more errors, Colledge approached the umpires and informed them that he was withdrawing his protest, stating that: "We're playing worse than you are umpiring."

The absolute great thing for me, and other boys enthralled with baseball, was that Colledge would almost always in good weather have a softball game during recess. He would pitch, umpire, and break up skirmishes and then, back to the classroom and academics. For many of us, these recesses were the highlight of the day. In October of 1964, he brought into the classroom a small radio so we could listen to parts of the World Series games between the Yankees and Cardinals...no night World Series games yet. Our education did not suffer, as he dutifully saw to it that we fulfilled our academic tasks, including 'generous' amounts of homework.

Ah, what good and great times, and what good instructors we enjoyed! We did our academic work, we played enthusiastically, and we were disciplined (sometimes physically) when we rightly deserved it!

Growing Up In Kistler

Storyteller Nancy Myers

In 1960, Bob and Kathryn Wagner sold their farm at Green Gates, outside of Loysville, and purchased the grocery-store and house at Kistler. In the spring, our family (mother, dad, Mary Ann, Jeanne, Doris and me) moved from our small farm to Kistler.

I do have a lot of memories of those days on the farm; picking strawberries, thousands of chickens (and grading eggs for market), raising some beef cattle and helping with haymaking. We were carefree kids growing up in the 1950s; our swing set, jumping out of the apple tree pretending we had parachutes, riding bikes and hunting dandelion in the spring. One of my best memories involved our reward for picking and selling strawberries. That was the annual family trip to Myrtle Beach, where we had our first contact with racial discrimination. I vividly remember seeing signs that indicated "whites only" at motels and restaurants, etc.

So, now about living in Kistler. The grocery store had been closed for several years, so our family worked hard to prepare for the grand opening. Dad built a new front porch for the store. As you entered the store, the counter with a cash register was to the left with a meat cooler beside it and the soda cooler was to the right. There were several bays of groceries down the center. The walls were lined with shelves. We had a milk and vegetable cooler at the back of the store, along with an ice cream freezer. The store was rather small. At that time, there were various small family grocery stores scattered throughout the western end of Perry County. If you wanted a "large" store, you had to travel to New Bloomfield. Most people did their weekly shopping at local venues.

From the grocery store, a doorway led into our living area. We had a large kitchen, dining room, living room, library and "play room." Upstairs were three bedrooms, bathroom, and a large balcony which overlooked the old washhouse. We even had a screened-in porch – a luxury to us! The house was unique in that it had two attics (one over the house and one over the grocery store) and two basements. Coming from a small farmhouse, this place seemed huge to us.

I can remember the day of the "grand opening" of Wagner's Store. Borden's Ice Cream Company brought a large replica of Elsie the Borden Cow and placed it right inside the front door of the store. As you entered the store and stepped on the mat, the cow would "moo." It was a huge hit. As the grand prize for the store opening, we gave away ten dollars-worth of groceries. In 1960 that was a large grocery order! People from the Kistler area were happy to have a grocery store again. Our parents taught us to run the cash register, slice lunch meat, bag groceries and stock shelves. We were expected to work in the store and always helped carry groceries out to the customer's car. At times, we resented having to always "work," but in retrospect it was a wonderful life. We got to know the people from the surrounding area and many of them became friends for life. When we weren't in school, we girls were expected to walk up and down the aisles, making a list of items that needed restocking and then head upstairs to the "store attic" and get the needed items.

Our grocery supplier was Harrisburg Groceries. Their salesman, George, would stop early in the week and mother would place an order. Then on Fridays, the grocery truck would arrive. It would pull up parallel to the store porch and place a ladder-like device from the truck unto the porch railing. One man would shove boxes across the conveyor and the other man would pick them up and carry them in to the store. After they left, we girls were expected to cut open boxes and price the canned goods, etc. We then either stocked the shelves or carried the rest upstairs to the attic. It was hard, dirty work for us but we were all expected to help. We also took care of most of the housework and laundry, etc. since mother was always busy in the grocery store. Dad continued to work as a tire salesman at Montgomery Wards in Carlisle.

In 1961, Mary Ann married Nevin Rice and moved to Blain so now there were just three girls remaining. In 1962, dad decided the store was too small, so he built on a large addition, tearing down the old washhouse. He basically did all of the work himself. Sometimes a neighbor, Baird McMillen (an older gentleman) would "supervise." The interior of the store was doubled. We then carried a much larger selection of groceries, especially detergents, cleaning supplies, mops and some fabric, etc.

Once the grocery store was reopened in the summer of 1960, Kistler became a gathering place. Local men loved to "loaf" at the store. Many times, when we girls would wake in the morning and go downstairs, we would find three or four men sitting around our kitchen table drinking coffee, smoking and chatting. In the evenings the men and boys would hang out at the soda cooler or in nice weather sit out on the front porch steps and smoke. In the early 1960s, Kistler had a small ballfield just west of the grocery store and during the summer months these ball games drew large crowds. After the games, everyone would descend on the store to talk and drink soda. It was always noisy and smoky.

One early 1960s memory that stands out is, there were no "well-baby clinics" so the young mothers would bring their babies into the store and we would weigh the babies on the meat scales. Some of these babies grew up and remained in the local community. I sometimes smile when I think of holding a squirming infant on that scale or now see an adult that I remember as one of those we weighed as an infant!

After a bout of ill health, dad resigned from Montgomery Wards and then purchased the vacant service station and restaurant on the corner at Kistler from Clark Adair. Dad renovated it and about 1963 opened Bob's Atlantic. His right-hand man was Bill Shuman, a local man who worked hard. He was always pumping gas, changing tires and changing oil, etc. We were fortunate to have him throughout the years that my parents owned this business. The restaurant was run by Arlene Palm, a local lady who was a great cook. She soon had more business than she could handle, so dad added a waitress, Joyce Latchford. As the business grew, dad once again built a large addition onto the restaurant and added more waitresses, Joan, Donna Jo, Patty, Dorothy and Hazel. And of course, he expected us girls to help out after school. Jeanne was designated as the evening waitress and I was assigned to the grocery store. But in 1966, Jeanne married Grant Shope and left the family fold. That meant I was now the evening waitress. I can remember getting off the school bus, hurriedly putting on my uniform and heading down to the restaurant, carrying my school books. As part of my business course, I was expected to write ten pages of shorthand each night as schoolwork, so in between flipping hamburgers, dipping ice cream and pouring coffee, I would sit at a table writing shorthand. This always fascinated the men who came in to 'loaf.' They could not believe that I could read those "squiggles." I used shorthand in my first job, but now it is a lost art. One thing I did hate, however, was walking home at 9 p.m. always smelling like french fries and smoke! My cooking skills were pretty non-existent. I could use a flat-top grill, a deep fryer and a steam table, but I never really learned to cook from scratch, much to my new husband's dismay when I married in 1972.

Deer season was always very busy. At that time there were many hunting camps in the area. So, hordes of hunters from other counties descended on us. On Sunday before opening day of buck season, there would be a constant stream of traffic. The hunters would be buying cigarettes, Slim Jims, beef jerky, snacks and candy. And on the first day of deer season, we were all up at 3 a.m. and opened the restaurant and grocery store doors at 4 a.m. It was always a madhouse. The hunters all wanted a good breakfast before hitting the woods. But by 8 a.m., they were all gone, out hunting the elusive deer. For two weeks we worked like crazy, but we did a wonderful business and also got great tips!

By now dad had developed a reputation for the Sunday dinners we served at the restaurant. We always had a full house. He specialized in turkey dinners. Of course, that meant getting up early Sunday mornings and putting the turkeys in the oven and peeling mountains of potatoes. We hurried home from church and opened the doors to our customers. How I hated doing all those dishes by hand!

In 1966, I graduated from West Perry High School and started my first job as a steno at the Loysville Youth Development Center. That meant Doris now became the designated waitress. Most evenings mother would also go down to the restaurant, so when I got home from work, I took over being the evening grocery store clerk. Many times, I worked in the store still dressed in my good work clothes and high heels.

In the late 1960s, the war in Vietnam affected everyone in our community. I remember the day people from the Army came to the service station and asked directions to the John McGarvey home. We all immediately knew it was bad news. Their son Bill had been killed. He was such a fun-loving guy and the entire community mourned his loss. I have one memory of Bill. One Friday night I had to take the day's receipts to the bank in Loysville. I had just topped the hill near my grandparent's home, driving my little blue Ford Fairlane when suddenly a larger Ford pulled along-side me and Bill McGarvey gave me a big wave. Then he continued to just drive beside me. I panicked thinking that someone would come over the hill and then around the bend and hit us both head-on. Eventually he just sped up and passed me. It never fazed Bill, but it sure rattled me! Shortly after that he left for the Army and I never saw him again.

In 1970, Doris married Dick Ernest and moved away. That left me as the lone remaining daughter. I think dad thought I would be an old maid, but in October 1972, I did marry Carl Myers, my husband of now almost fifty years. In June 1972, my parents sold the grocery store and house to build a new small home near Kistler. They continued running the service station and restaurant until about 1982 (not sure of the exact year). At that time, dad received his first diagnosis of cancer and decided to retire and sell the business. Once he was in remission, he and mother started to travel and he loved building dry sinks, picnic tables and dog houses in his garage. As he gradually lost his sight to glaucoma, he slowed down and once again cancer reared its ugly head. Mom and dad were fortunate though to have wonderful neighbors, Don and Dori Hess. As dad built something, because of his failing sight, he would sometimes drive the nails in crooked. Don would come over and pull out the bad nails and re-nail it for him. Also, another neighbor, Amos Keller, would come to the house each morning and walk dad over to the restaurant where they would sit, drink coffee and tell tall-tales. Since dad was now legally blind, it was great that he got out most days to socialize. We lost dad in 1991 and a year later mother sold their small house and moved to Perlo Apartments in Loysville. She lived there until she was diagnosed with brain cancer. In June of 2005, we had to place mother at Perry Village and we lost her in January 2006. Unfortunately, my younger sister Doris had been diagnosed with a brain tumor in 1978 and had brain surgery at age twenty-eight. Following radiation, she lost her hair and it never grew back. She had quite an array of wigs and we never knew what she would look like! She eventually became a resident of Perry Village and we lost her on March 1, 2005. Now it is just Mary Ann, Jeanne and me.

Several years ago, the house and grocery store in Kistler burned down. I drove there the next day and as I stood there, I was overcome by sadness as I looked at the shell of what remained. Memories bombarded me and as I look back on these memories now, I realize we truly had a wonderful life in the small village of Kistler. Our family made friends, many of whom have remained for a lifetime. We girls were taught the value of hard work, the value of a dollar earned and the pleasure you can receive from doing good deeds. I wouldn't trade it for anything!

Growing Up On A Farm Outside Of Loysville

Storyteller Ethel Mae (Wilson) Mohler

I was born next to the youngest of eight children (Mary Ellen, Gertrude Elizabeth, Helen Lois, William Edgar Jr., Ruth Mildred, James Walter, Ethel Mae (1933) and Betty Kaye) on a little farm outside of Loysville, Pennsylvania. The farm was owned by Loysville resident, C. L. Lightner and my father, farmed it for 'the half.' In recent years, it was owned by veterinarian, Burleigh T. Anderson and presently Mr. Martin.

My father, William Edgar, would use his horses Tom, Dick, Harry, Nell and two mules to work the fields along with an old steel-wheeled tractor which my mother, Mabel would drive. Many times, in the hot summer days, my sister, Betty and I would carry ginger water, in a quart tin can with a wire handle, out to the field for them.

My father did not have a hay baler, so he would cut the hay and rake it into rows. Then, he used a hay loader which straddled the row, picked up the hay and elevated it onto a flat-bed wagon. My sister and I would spread it around until we had a full load. Then, we would pull it into the barn to unload. My father would get on top of the load of hay with a big hay fork with a rope which he would push down into the hay. My sister and I would then guide one horse, hitched to a single tree and rope, away from the barn to pull the hay up into the mow. My father would then pull on the rope attached to the hay fork to release the fork-load of hay into the mow. This procedure was repeated over and over until all of the hay was off the wagon and into the mow. Then back to the field for another hay load.

In harvesting the grain, (wheat and oats) my father used a binder which would cut the grain, bind it into sheaves and throw 3-4 sheaves out onto the ground. My sisters and brothers were in charge of putting the sheaves into shocks. We rented a threshing machine. We would load the sheaves from the shocks onto a wagon and bring them onto the barn. With a pitch fork, we would throw each sheave into the chopping blades of the threshing machine. The grain would come out of the machine into burlap bags which would be dumped and stored in the granary. The straw would be blown into a mow or outside as a straw pile in the barnyard.

We had eight to ten Holstein milk cows. My sisters Mary, Sis (Gertrude), and Helen would hand milk the cows. My brothers, Bill and Jim would do the barn work. My sister Betty and I had to throw down the silage from the silo to feed the cows. Sometimes, we would fight and throw silage at each other.

My father would always do butchering. We had a long wooden trough filled with hot water to scald the hog. It would be turned over and over then we would use metal scrappers to remove the bristles. Then the hog would be hung by its back feet on a high trussell and my father would cut it into different parts.

We would have two iron kettles. One for cooking head meats, liver, etc. and the other for cooking fat for lard. My sister and I usually cut the fat into chunks to put into that kettle. Sometimes, we would take a break and sneak around to pin the pig's tail on the back of someone.

My mother would always clean the pig's stomach and the casings for the sausage. My dad made the best panhaus!

We always had a huge garden with lots of vegetables. My mother and 'Mam', our grandmother, Laura Elizabeth Moretz, who always lived with us, prepared many things on our old iron cookstove. They canned meats, pickled tongue, souse, chow chow, corn relish, beets, beans, peaches, pears and cherries. We dried corn, snits, made sauerkraut, pull taffy (sal dic), walnut brittle and baked bread.

We never went hungry.

Our neighbors were, the Harry Wilson family, the Billy Bernheisel family and Minnie and Sammy Garber.

My older sisters Mary, Sis, Helen and my brother Bill walked or hitched a ride to Landisburg High School which is no longer in existence. My brother Jim, sister Betty and I walked, about a mile, to the two-room schoolhouse (now the Loysville Community Building) at Loysville, Pennsylvania.

On our walk to school, we would walk by an eight-story brick building called The County Home (demolished) which housed people without homes. Across the road was a big barn which is now the site of the Perry Health Center.

We made some connections to a few of the residents at the home. There was a gentleman who was always sitting on a swing on the porch. We would always wave to him and he would wave back. He had long blonde-gray hair which he pulled back into a 'plat' or braid. We named him 'Iky-Plat'. One time, we went to talk with him and heard the school bell ring. Obviously, we were late for school that day.

Another person, was 'Sim.' We were sort of scared of him. He was bald and chewed tobacco with juice running out each side of his mouth. He could not speak but would make slight sounds and wave his arms.

There was Nora Stone who helped out at the barn. She wore a long dress with several petticoats and burlap-bag like aprons. Under her aprons, she had pinned a small ragdoll and several one-dollar bills.

And finally, there was a small spring-house (no longer there) right along the road. In there was a little lady who would make butter in a churn. She would have pounds of butter on little saucers sitting on the stones at the edge of the spring.

After we passed our delightful friends, we would continue on to school. The school had two rooms. One room had grades one thru four. The other room had grades five thru eight.

Grades one thru four had students seated vertically from front to the back of the room starting with grade one to the right side of the room. Then moving left to the next vertical row for grade two and so on across the room.

Each individual grade level would be called, for its class session, to a long bench at the front of the room. You would have your lesson, sometimes using the long slate covering the front wall of the room. Lesson finished. You would be dismissed and the other grade levels would have their lessons. There would be recess morning and afternoon. Carrie Belle Hench was the teacher.

Grades five thru eight were also seated vertically. They did not go to a bench at the front of the room. Sometimes, individual classes would go to the front of the room to use the long slate. We would study Reading, Writing, Arithmetic, History and Geography. At the end of grade eight, there would be an Eighth Grade Test to enter into ninth grade.

Dorman Hockenberry was the teacher until he was drafted into the Army. Then, Frank Stokes took his place.

One day, the County Nurse, Helen Myers came to the school. We were all excited! There she was, in her navy-blue cape with gold buttons and a red lining! She came to check us for head lice. We didn't care, we thought she was wonderful!

At recess, we played tag, prisoners base, red rover, dodge ball, volleyball and softball.

Some of my classmates and friends at school were Judy Billman, Dick Briner, Lee Garber Briner, Marvin Emlet, Norman Metz, Delores Myers, Shirley Neff and Elinor Wise.

We may have been late for school some days, but our "friends" along the way made us smile as much as we brightened their day!

"Kennedy's Corner and Crossroads"

Storyteller William K. "Bill" Kennedy
Recorded by Debra Kay Noye

William K. "Bill" Kennedy began his childhood on East Landisburg Road above Landisburg's town square. He was born in 1938 to Irene L. (Ritter) and Karl E. Kennedy.

His father, Karl "Doc" was born in 1905 to Charles D. Kennedy (1866) and Anna E. Emlet Kennedy (1867). Charles was a farmer and lumberman, who cut many acres of timber in Kennedy's Valley, outside of Landisburg. His mother, Irene was born in 1908 to George H. Ritter and Margaret A. Bernheisel Ritter. George was in charge of the farming operations at Tressler Orphan's Home in Loysville. He was responsible for the dairy herd, vegetable farming and poultry production especially eggs.

Bill's immediate neighbor in Landisburg was Carrie and Aaron Morrison, who was a lumberman and owned a barbershop. The families visited each other and Bill played with "Honey Boy" Mose Morrison. Helen Fleisher, a student, stayed with the Kennedy family and helped with Bill's care.

In 1941, the family moved to the white house on top of the knoll at "Kennedy's Crossing" on Veterans Way between Green Park and Elliottsburg. Karl then purchased the one-hundred sixty-five-acre Harvey Bernheisel farm complete with a large red-brick house in Green Park, at the corner of Shermans Valley Road and Green Park Road. Karl was hauling milk, in heavy metal cans, for local farmers, while starting to dairy farm. Wanting to expand his farming acreage, Karl eventually purchased the George Coldren farm at Green Park and the Oliver Beard property on the north side of Shermans Valley Road at the crossroads of Shermans Valley and Waggoner's Gap Road. The twenty-five acres included all the grounds the West Perry School stands on today.

He also purchased seventeen acres across the road from the farm, north of Shermans Valley Road, known as the old Reeder property including a house and barn. Karl sold the house and barn to Miss Reeder, who opened a United States Post Office, where mailing letters cost three cents. The Jim Stum family lived with her in the back of the house. The Post Office was tiny, dark and rustic inside, with wooden floors, bars on the cashier's window and a few individual mail boxes, because Green Park's population was very small.

When Miss Reeder was busy elsewhere, her daughter, Bonnie Stum managed the Post Office, which was a hub for finding out what was going on in the neighborhood and close-by towns.

Across the alley from the Post Office, "Hen" Hess operated an antique business and the first house was the Noll property. The Reapsome property on the corner housed Edgar Stambaugh's General Store.

If you take the shortcut road through Green Park from Shermans Valley Road to Veterans Way, that is where the one-room Green Park School, now owned by the Historical Society of Perry County, is located in a grove of trees. Bill Kennedy knows this red-brick school very well, because he walked there every school day for eight years. The pot-belly wood stove sat in the front of the long room with wooden floors. Bill remembers, in the winter time, hoovering beside the stove after recess. Most of the boys would venture down over the small hill behind the school and play on the ice-covered race of the Bernheisel Mill near Montour Creek. More often than not, the ice would break and the boys would get wet. There were no snowsuits to keep them warm and dry. In fact, their boots were generally unlined rubber with five buckles to snap once the boot was forced over their leather shoes. Bill remembers wearing a winter hat with heavy earmuffs that once tied under his chin kept his head warm. Bill, like so many boys his age, hated wearing knickers.

Of course, the students would get cold in the winter as they dashed out to the outhouses located at each corner of the school grounds. The boys trotted to the west corner and the girls east, which was just beyond the hand pump. Bill would go out to the pump returning with a metal pitcher of water. The students would drink from the same tin ladle when they became thirsty. Sometimes, Bill's mother would include a metal thermos filled with iced tea in his lunch bucket. His lunch was usually a sandwich of jelly or peanut butter and jelly or a leftover meat from the previous night's supper. His mother also packed fruit like bananas and peanut butter crackers. Some times, he would also quickly walk the quarter-mile home for lunch. On warm days, the students would eat their lunch outside. Otherwise, they sat at their old wooden desks, which still had the ink well holes, regardless of their using wood or lead pencils. Some of the desks were double whereby students could sit on both sides, not just side-by-side. Some desks were single and folded.

His teachers were Miss Helen Briner whose sister Mryle Reapsome would substitute when needed. Miss Briner's home could be seen across the race and meadows behind the school. (His dad rented portions of the Smiley Briner farm where Miss Briner lived.)

Miss McCaulley, who Bill said was grumpy, also lived in a massive red-brick colonial house nearby to the east. Bill was made to stay after school as punishment for calling some of his classmates, kids. She made it clear the students were children and not kid goats!

Mrs. Gobrecht was another elementary teacher and her husband was the Landisburg High School superintendent, also teaching math and science. He encouraged students to locate rattlesnake dens and capture the "rattlers" for his dining pleasure. He was willing to pay twenty-five cents for each rattlesnake.

Other teachers were Grabowitz, Keener, Charlie Eaton and Dale Rice, who became a local rural mail carrier. Bill was bused to the Landisburg High School and then to the newly established Green Park Union High School for two years. He was in the second class to graduate from Green Park Union, located where the West Perry High School is today. He played soccer and baseball at Green Park, which was before football existed. Ray Buss taught history, and coached soccer and basketball at the school.

Since Bill was raised in the dairy industry, he decided to pursue an education in dairy husbandry at the National Agricultural College in Doylestown, Pennsylvania, which became the Delaware Valley Agricultural College. As a freshman walking early to a football game, he was stopped by the football coach, Tedd Gillman, who invited Bill to join the football team on the second string, which he did. His brother Edward R. "Ed" Kennedy (1940) excelled on the baseball team at the same college. (Ed Kennedy was a Perry County Commissioner for twenty-eight years.)

After graduation, Bill worked on the family farms for two years, before his father suggested he pursue a career in artificial insemination of cattle, especially dairy cows. So off he went to several weeks of classes conducted by Sam Flowers at the Curtis Candy Company, which had a large herd of stud bulls. His learning wasn't the sweetest deal, but he was taught how to store frozen semen in nitrogen at 360 degrees below zero. The semen needed thawed before implanting into an ovulating cow. Bill often implanted semen from the Curtis herd into Perry County bovine. He set-up a call system, whereby the farmers could phone, leave messages, and he would travel to the farms to inseminate the cows. He also purchased semen from other producers and purveyors like Harry Latchford, another artificial inseminator from Kistler. It was while he was out on the job, when he tightly lassoed a cow and she violently smacked him into a log. Veterinarian Burleigh Anderson, of Loysville, was in attendance that day. When Bill asked Doc Anderson how badly hurt he was, he soon learned he no longer had a nose. This ended his career, because he had to avoid dust and dirt for many years due to the reconstruction on his face.

He followed in his mother's footsteps and started teaching math and science as well as serving as the Blain Union High School librarian. After two years, all the schools merged into Perry Joint then West Perry School, where he taught science for three years in the middle school.

His agricultural background kept calling him back and Bill worked in the Perry County ASCS office in New Bloomfield, before finishing his twenty-one-year career with the Pennsylvania Department of Agriculture as an assistant to the deputy secretary, Regional Director/Chief of Poultry and Eggs, Bureau Director of Dog Law and as a State Milk Inspector.

Mercy Sakes!! What a career, but it wouldn't have been without the footsteps he followed. His father, Karl was very enterprising beyond the two dairy farms he eventually owned. He continued to haul canned milk from Landisburg's small dairy farms in his two flatbed trucks with removable wooden sides. The farms, which were still hand milking, produced five to ten cans a day, which held eighty pounds of milk. Now even though the Sunnydale Farms Milk Plant was close by in Elliottsburg, Karl hauled his and the other dairymen's milk to Pennsupreme, Supplee-Jones or Juniata Dairies in Duncannon or Harrisburg Dairies, in his open flatbed trucks. His trucks would travel across the Clark's Ferry, when it was still a toll bridge. Bill believes his dad invested in the metal plates which were attached to the truck front signifying the toll was prepaid. (A modern-day E-Z Pass.)

Eventually, through the years till 1950, as Karl added insulated trucks, all the milk was hauled to Harrisburg Dairies. Karl became good friends with Ben Wolf, Harrisburg Dairies' owner, who introduced him to Harvey Taylor, Harrisburg's infamous State Senator and they became life-long friends. (Karl was also Superintendent of Highways in Perry County for eight years.)

The Green Park Farm had seventy-eight head of cows and graduated from pail milkers to a pipeline and tank system. The second seventy-acre dairy farm (known as the Shearer farm), with a barn and red-brick house, was on Waggoner's Gap Road across from Mahanoy Ridge Road. The farms almost joined, if not for Stambaugh's Century Farm, to the south. Karl's hired man, Dick Shultz, lived on the farm and managed the thirty-head dairy herd. The barn has since burned down. Karl purchased feed concentrate to be added to ground corn and oats for feeding his dairy herds and other animals. Edgar Stambaugh, Karl's neighbor from Green Park, sold the additives at the abandoned Elliottsburg Railroad Station.

Between the farms and hauling milk, Karl employed seven men besides Shultz, who was originally from Mt. Joy, Pennsylvania. Elmer Gutshall, from Loysville, and Irish Gutshall, from Blain, helped farm and drive truck. They then shared the double-tenant house across the road from the farm.

Bill also helped where needed and would come home weekends from college to help out. It was a freezing winter night at the Carl McMillen farm, outside of Kistler, when Bill was picking up canned milk. McMillens had a wooden plank beside the large metal cooling tank for which to step on for better leverage to reach down into the tanks to grasp the handles on the cans. Some of the handles were rings that flopped. Others were stationary. Bill had pulled all of the cans, dripping with water, out of the tank, except for one that had frozen tight at the very back. He stretched and yanked hard to loosen it, only to lose his footing on the frozen water-covered plank. Into the cooler he went! He hated having to call his dad to bring him some dry clothes.

After he bought the additional farmlands, Karl decided to plant fields of red tomatoes where the West Perry Middle School stands today. He hired seven or eight people to help harvest the twenty acres of ripe tomatoes. They would hand-pick the tomatoes into half bushel baskets which were set along the rows of tomato plants. Often, rotten tomato battles would occur, according to Bill. Karl's flatbed trucks would be driven through the fields so the baskets could be loaded. They were then hauled to the old railroad station in New Bloomfield on South Carlisle Street. Other farmers did the same and Karl's trucks would haul the tomatoes to Newville for processing. The farmers were paid by the number of cans the tomatoes produced.

Yes, it is hard to imagine the fields where the Elliottsburg Post Office sits today, being covered in green shell-pea vines! The purple/pink and white blossoms would've been pretty in the spring, but no hand-picking this time. The ripe peas were mowed (like mowing grass for hay) using a swather which formed rows. Karl's trucks were driven along the rows and the pea vines were forked onto the flatbeds. They, too, were hauled to Newville for processing. There were several other farmers who did the same. Again, they were paid by the amount of product produced.

Karl preferred International Farm Equipment from Harry Keller, in New Bloomfield, but he also purchased an Oliver tractor from Kepner of Newport. He patronized the local farm dealers like "Tom" Shover's in Loysville and Sanderson-Fry in Elliottsburg. "Barney" Reapsome owned the farm implement and repair business prior to Sanderson. The farm implements were displayed where Resinger's Insurance and 1892 Unrefined exist today. The white outbuilding directly across the road was the repair shop. Karl also hauled New Idea, John Deere and Papeac Silage equipment for Sanderson-Fry. He simply backed his flatbed trucks up to their loading docks for easy unloading.

With farm equipment being so costly, Karl and some enterprising Green Park farmers joined together and purchased equipment used to share the harvesting workload. Joe and Lenore Trostle owned a pull-along combine with a seven-foot cut. Chester and Rachel Noll had a mounted two-row corn picker. Karl and Irene owned the baler. Boyd and Gertrude Reeder also brought their tractors and other equipment to the joint harvesting. While the men toiled in the fields with the crops, the women were busy in the kitchens preparing excellent dinners. Bill fondly recalls Gertrude's homemade hickory nut cake.

The hay baler was pulled behind the tractor, allowing the square bale to drop to the ground. Another team of men would follow with a tractor pulling a wagon and the bales were stacked onto the wagon bed. The load was taken to the barn where it would be thrown into and stacked in the hay mows. Once "kicker" balers came along, the bales were automatically thrown onto the sided wagons or hand-pulled from the baler, which eliminated a ground pick up, except for a few stray bales. "Baling or baler twine" was used to tie or bind the hay together and could be purchased at hardware stores. However, it was most readily available at farm implement dealers like Shover's, Keller's, Kepner's and later Agway in Loysville. Bill made it known even his sisters Trudy and Sue helped to make hay.

Adding a dump truck and bulldozer to his fleet of trucks, Karl started excavating locally. He hauled limestone from the Newport Quarry that "Shorty" Blosser, a well driller, blasted loose. Karl bought most of his trucks and cars from Clair Raffensberger, owner of New Bloomfield Dodge.

With his trucks in constant use, Karl needed a good mechanic to keep them in running condition. Clarence Pannebaker lived a stone's throw from Karl's Green Park farm. He became the all-round handyman and mechanic, who also built slide beds for Karl's trucks. Karl added a garage for his personal business use on the corner where the Kingdom Grounds Cafe stands today. Pannebaker eventually bought the excavating business. Bill remarks that gas was twenty-six cents a gallon when his dad put in an underground gas tank on the family farm.

By the time, Bill was in fifth grade, school buses were needed to transport the growing number of students to various small schools throughout western Perry County. Karl decided to seize the opportunity as did Lester Kell of Alinda and Mac Crull of Kennedy's Valley. Kennedy's fleet began with two buses, each capable of seating forty-eight students. Then he added four more capable of seating sixty students. The last three buses he purchased could seat seventy-two. Pannebaker was kept extra busy then!

Karl employed local people (Dick Wilt, Freddie Frey, Dick Shultz and Emma Russ to name a few) to drive the buses, alongside sons Bill and Ed and himself. The routes covered Green Park, Landisburg, Elliottsburg, Ickesburg, and Loysville including Tressler Orphan's Home which provided classrooms for the overflow of students.

Now after all that hard work seven days a week, some rest was needed, and "loafing" became a past time at the local stores and businesses. Kell's Store, heading into Milltown on the way to Alinda on Waggoner's Gap Road, was a hole-in-the-wall tiny country store. It was totally rustic and never changed through the years. The wooden floors might've been broom-swept because of all the farm-boot dirt, but it was too dark to see any! The wooden counter and shelves were accompanied by a few stools and dilapidated chairs. The air smelled of cigar smoke, hay and cattle, and there was a spittoon handy. Local farmers like Jim Stambaugh, Art and Tom Dum, Dick Shultz, the Naces, Karl and Bill would sit and "shoot the bull" with the owners, the Kell Brother's. Kell Brother's also harvested and sold lumber, like their counterparts in the area, Bolze Brother's. Bolze's (Lenus and Don) had a Planing Mill in Milltown and sold firewood. Don Bolze also owned the Loysville Feed Mill. The same crew would loaf in Reapsome's Store in Green Park and replenish their bodies with chunks of cheese off the massive cheese wheel and bottles of soda.

Other activities enjoyed by Bill involved his churches; Mt. Zion beyond Bridgeport and Messiah Lutheran in Elliottsburg. He, Ed and sisters Trudy Stum (1942) and Sue (1945) would go on church sponsored hayrides, Saturday night movies and roller skating at Rheams Roller Rink outside of Millerstown.

Bill's mother returned to teaching once the children were in school. She taught third grade at the new Green Park Union School system. But during the summers, she would prepare belly-filling meals for the work crews working in the fields and harvesting the crops.

Bill has witnessed a lot of changes in agriculture, and Kennedy's Corner and Crossroads. Times were simpler, yes, but hard work paid off and you had the satisfaction of a job well-done!

The Kitner Family of Perry County

SHERMANS DALE AND MECK'S CORNER

Storyteller Cindy Jay

Elizabeth (Kitner) Rinehart and her brother, Daniel J. Kitner Sr. related much of the history of the Hess and Abraham Smith Kitner families to their daughters, Carrie Rinehart Sunday and Annie Kitner Richey. It was direct knowledge from their homelife and related to them by their elders.

According to legend, the Hess and Lee families came to America very early as some members served in the Revolutionary War.

David and Violet (Lee) Hess came to Perry County from Lancaster County. They rented a farm from Mr. Hollinger, who apparently resided in Lancaster County. This farm was in Sandy Hollow, Carroll Township, Perry County, Pennsylvania. At some later date when their son, Joshua, got married, Mr. Hollinger built a large new barn and house nearby for Joshua and his new bride. They farmed while David and Violet lived in the original farmhouse.

Later, Abraham Kitner and wife, Anna Eliza (Hess) Kitner, bought the farm from Mr. Hollinger. It seems this took place about 1878. About this time or a little later, one of the Hess children, who was living in Lancaster County, took David to live with them. Violet continued to live in the old house while daughter, Anna Eliza and Abraham Kitner looked after her. As a result of this arrangement, David was buried in Lancaster County and Violet was buried in Snyder's Cemetery near Meck's Corner, Perry County.

The Hess family owned a lot of mules and horses. They were used to haul produce such as potatoes and apples grown on the farm, to Harrisburg and Lancaster. They also raised and transported live chickens, sheep, swine, ducks, eggs, butter, and apple cider, as well as lumber and wood.

The women obtained most of their household needs, such as pots and pans, sewing materials, etc. from a peddler who toured the country twice a year with a horse and loaded wagon. Otherwise, they had a carriage and horse for their use and occasional trips to the local town.

Abraham and Anna were farmers who bought the farm in Sandy Hollow where Anna was reared. They managed to buy three adjoining farms known as the Cook, Welsh, and Souder places. There was a large barn on the main farm where Abraham kept a great number of horses and mules. They were used for farming and hauling timber. As soon as their sons were old enough (six sons and five daughters) to handle a four-mule team, they were sent to haul lumber from the area's many sawmills. A lot of railroad ties were delivered to Newport and Carlisle in the late 1800s and early 1900s.

The men would leave at 4 a.m. They went in pairs to help each other to load, unload and assist if one or the other had wagon trouble on the road. They returned by 7 or 8 p.m. During the winter, bobsleds were used when the roads were snow covered. The hauling was in addition to the farm work. However, the women did much of the routine farm chores. It was their responsibility to tend the sheep, cows, chickens, and ducks.

Of course, the women raised, dried, and canned hundreds of quarts of vegetables and fruits. They made butter, cheese, and apple butter. Everyone was kept busy and didn't have time for mischief. The children all attended school but some only long enough to learn to spell, read, write, and do simple math. It is amazing how some of them became successful business men.

Abraham also bought two farms near Shermans Dale around 1912 or 1913. His daughter, Harriet Kitner and husband, Clinton Stambaugh, lived on the one 80-acre farm known as the Slough place in the early 1920s.

The other farm, 112-acres, known as the Robinson or Baer place, was sold to son Daniel Kitner Sr. and wife Jennie (Bornman) Kitner in 1914. Prior to that they lived on the Cook place in Sandy Hollow where oldest son, John Abraham Kitner, was born. Daniel and Jennie worked very hard and made many improvements over the years. The property consisted of a beautiful, well-constructed house and barn with a summer house, bake-oven, smoke house and many other out buildings. The house had nine rooms with a double fireplace, wooden floor basement plus a cold-storage cellar. The basement with the fireplace was an ideal place for laundry and butchering day. It was an excellent place for the children to play with no fire on rainy days.

Daniel and Jennie Kitner bought the Slough place from the Abraham Kitner Estate in 1930. They farmed this also. The house was in bad shape and never replaced. Daniel used the barn for storage.

Approximately 1947 or 1948, Daniel sold this place to his son, Raymond and wife Miriam 'Mim' (Barrick). Raymond and Mim also owned the adjoining farm that was called the Wilt Shearer farm (70-acre). (Today this property boarders Cottage Lane and Airy View in Shermans Dale.) The farm borders Shermans Creek.

Raymond's brother, Harry, purchased a small piece of land from this farm that sits on the banks of Shermans Creek. He constructed an enclosed cabin and pavilion with an outhouse and a hand-water pump. This became a cool get-a-way when the weather was hot and a wonderful place for family reunions. The kids would fish, play in the creek, and walk up the creek to Sheep's Rock. Sometimes you would even see a car pulled into the shallow part of the creek in order to give it a good washing. When the 1972, Agnes flood happened, the pavilion was tied to multiple trees in order to keep it from washing down stream.

The harvest of 1939 was done with the first rubber-tired tractor they owned. It was a F12 International. That same year in December, their son, John Kitner was killed when a falling tree struck him on a lot, they were sawmilling close to the bottom of Sterrett's Gap along Route 34. He was instantly killed leaving behind his young wife, Alva (Shatto) Kitner. They were only married for six short months when this tragedy hit the family.

In 1943, Daniel Sr. purchased a dozer to trail logs for his sawmill. When farmers saw what it could do, they called to get fence rows cleared, ponds made, and foundations dug. Business took off so much that the dozer never made it back to the sawmill and an additional dozer was purchased in 1947. Both dozers were kept busy working for farmers and townships.

Township roads were all horse and buggy roads and needed to be widened for modern traffic. In the wintertime, they could be seen pushing the snowdrifts off township roads. The equipment back then did not have enclosed cabs, heaters, power steering, or power brakes. It was hard work in very cold temperatures.

Four of Daniel Sr.'s sons, Raymond, Harry, Daniel Jr., and Boyd continued doing the excavating work. Business grew to where the brothers formed a partnership called Kitner Brothers Excavating in 1959. In 1960, they started paving parking lots and residential driveways. In 1966, Raymond was killed when the paving roller slid on a bank and rolled over at St Samuel's Church in Newport.

Raymond's son Gerald, Harry's sons Glenn and Barry, Dan's son Gary, and Boyd's son Kirby started working alongside their fathers and uncles to learn the business. The partnership became Kitner Bros Incorporated in 1988. In 1996, Glenn's daughter, Cindy (Kitner) Jay became the bookkeeper and secretary for the business. They were all raised to appreciate their customers and do quality work at the most reasonable prices until their retirement in the fall of 2015 when the business was then closed.

In 1949 Daniel and Jennie sold the homeplace to son, Harry Kitner and wife Alta Beatrice "Beaty" (Barrick). In 1958, Harry sold the farm to Texas Eastern Transmission Company who built a pumping station for their gas lines. The pumping station is just south of where the barn stood. Harry and Beaty moved to a farm they purchased near Meck's Corner, known as the Dyson Farm.

When Daniel and Jennie left the farm, they moved to a two-story house they owned near Meck's Corner on Route 34. In 1954, they built a brick ranch house just back of the two-story and moved there for the balance of their lives. They sold the two-story to their youngest son, Boyd Kitner and his wife, Ruby (Lyons) in 1954.

In 1982, Daniel and Jennie's grandson, William "Bill" Richey Jr. and wife Susie, bought the brick house and 5.8 acre of land from the Kitner Estate. They moved there in 1984 when Bill retired from the US Air Force.

Back to the history on the Slough place. Someone by that name owned the land in the 1800s and probably early 1900s. There were two farm buildings on the property that were vacated before the other one was built. One of the farms with a house and barn, was located on land now owned by the late William Bentsel and wife, Jane (Richey) Bentsel. The barn burned down in the late 1800s and the house was left to fall down. All that remained in 1930 when Daniel Kitner bought the farm was the barn foundation. The other buildings were a house, barn, chicken house, hog pen, shed, and a vegetable cave for storage of potatoes, canned goods, apples, etc. It was just off the east side of the house. As of 1992, three of Daniel and Jennie's grandchildren have built houses on the Slough place that has been in the Kitner family since 1920 when Hattie Kitner and husband Clint Stambaugh lived there.

Daniel and Jennie were very industrious people. Besides farming, Daniel owned and operated a threshing machine. In the late summer and early fall he went from farm-to-farm threshing wheat and oats in the area. The rig was powered by a steam engine. About 1926, he quit threshing and bought a sawmill. The mill was first powered by a steam engine and later by a power unit. In those days, sawmills were moved to wooded lots. Therefore, he moved the mill to many areas of Perry County cutting out a wood lot of 20 acres and sometimes 200 acres. He continued to saw lumber for buildings, railroad ties and coal mines as shoring and steel mills for forms, until 1955.

He was known as having a profitable farm (133 acres plus the Slough place, about 80 acres). When the children got around six years old, they helped. In fact, Jennie and the children were responsible for a lot of the farm work while Daniel operated the mill. His sons were also put to work on the mill at an early age. The parents were never cruel to the children, but they did teach them how to work. At one time they had dairy cows, but mostly the operation was fattening beef cattle and raising swine. Jennie was responsible for one-hundred or more chickens.

They had eight children; John, Annie (Richey), Raymond, Harry, Louise (Fisher), Daniel Jr., Bessie (Weller), and Boyd Kitner.

The days were long and work was hard but life was pleasant on the farm. In those days, children didn't demand so much such as entertainment, clothes, toys, etc. They made their own when they had time. They socialized with the large family of cousins, aunts, and uncles.

There were many family members who proudly served our country during peacetime and during wars: William Richey Sr., William Fisher and Harry Kitner (WW II), William Bentsel and Boyd Kitner (Korean War), William Richey Jr., Robert Richey, Glenn Kitner, Lee Kitner (Vietnam War), and Chad Richey. They all safely returned home.

As told by Daniel Kitner Sr. to Annie (Kitner) Richey and added upon by
Cindy (Kitner) Jay.

Falling Springs Farm

1976 – 1989

Storyteller Carol Janet Gabel Ulsh

Dave and I were married in June, 1960 and left Perry County in November when he reported to Ft. Benning, Georgia for officer training to serve in the U. S. Army. It was a tearful time for me leaving Perry County never knowing if we would return to live there again. Our son Keith was born at Ireland Army Hospital Ft Knox, Kentucky while Dave was a Company Commander on the training field.

After returning from the Army, we lived in Williamsport, Pennsylvania for four years where our daughter Joanne was born at Divine Providence Hospital, then moved to Simsbury, Connecticut, for two years with Aetna Life & Casualty. We returned to Camp Hill, Pennsylvania for six years where Dave was employed with M. Harvey Taylor & Son. Since horses have always been a favorite hobby for Dave and having a strong desire for fox hunting with horses, and wanting to board a second horse, we felt it necessary in 1975 to look for a farm.

Since my parents, Homer and Rhoda Gabel, were living in New Bloomfield we frequented Route 34 and happened upon a "Farm For Sale" sign at the intersection of Route 34 & 850 that sparked my attention. The small red-bank barn and large stone house caught my attention and the next thing we were buying Falling Spring property and moved there in February, 1976.

Falling Spring Farm – History tells us that in 1867 George Gibson established a post office, inside his general store "Falling Springs." The name of Falling Springs came about because several springs fed a small stream that flowed into the Shermans Creek after a sharp descent. Stagecoaches stopped at Falling Springs on their mail run. John Garman after the Gibsons, in 1885, opened a dry-goods, general store in the house at the intersection of Warm Springs and Landisburg Road, until 1904. A spring house was on the west end of the property which provided water and several springs were constantly running through the basement of the house.

Our friends, neighbors and relatives insisted on giving us gifts of animals to start our "Funny Farm" at Falling Springs. "Epstein", a Polish rooster, was gifted to us before we moved. Within the first year, we had

"Mitz and Dale" Red-Rock hen and rooster to provide us eggs, "Heckel" a Nubian goat who made friends for life with horse "Timber." Numerous cats and dogs occupied the barn over the years, but the most admired dog was Dutchess, a mixed St. Bernard and German Shepherd, who had to be put down for health reasons when we departed Falling Springs.

When we purchased the property in 1976, it consisted of nearly five acres located behind the house and barn, as well as a grassy portion across the highway to Shermans Creek. It was owned by Harry S. Stambaugh, of Green Park, who had converted the house into two rental apartments.

We proceeded to convert the house to a one-family dwelling by removing a wall inside to access the entire house and utilized the two-stall bank barn for our "Funny Farm." McAlister Bros., from Rye Valley, were able to close the third front door of the house with a stone fireplace, gathering stones off the hill behind the house. Obviously, that is where the stones were gathered to build the original house as they matched perfectly. We had a wood-stove connected on the inside to heat much of the house at that time. A huge barn beam was carved and erected as a mantel. After several years it dried out to the point of smoldering one Sunday morning and started to smoke. It had to be removed and brick was used to replace it. McAlister Bros. re-pointed the entire west end of the house at that time. Weller Bros., from New Bloomfield, installed a porch on the back and east end of the house that provided a place for much entertainment and relaxation.

The two-bay bank barn was in need of repair on the east end and a new roof which Weller Bros. completed, to house the horse "Timber" that we were previously boarding. We soon bought a second horse, "Doubles" a seventeen-hand chestnut hunter so that Dave could proceed to participate in the Beaufort Hunt in Harrisburg. A wooden fenced riding and pasture area was erected across the road.

Timber didn't jump previously, but Dave soon had him jumping most "any height," including the fence which he was known to do in the middle of the night if he wanted to go to the barn before dawn. It was quite scary waking up to a horse clopping down the road at 3 a.m.

Both our children at that time, Keith fifteen and Joanne twelve, participated in the Perry County 4-H Horse Club for several years. Carol's dad was able to open up hay mows and also built a pen in the wagon shed to house the lambs that our daughter Joanne raised for the 4-H Livestock Club, which were shown and auctioned at the Perry County Fair.

On the property was a smokehouse, outdoor privy, large double chicken house, as well as a wood house and small garage combined. Since Dave and Carol worked at full-time occupations in Camp Hill, we depended on our children to keep the place in order much of the time, especially in the summers. Fortunately, Keith soon knew that horses were not his favorite pastime. He especially liked to spend time playing high school football, cutting wood, hunting and fishing with local friends and relatives. Joanne on the other hand was active in school band and drama, 4-H clubs, and riding horses all over the countryside with her dad.

Unfortunately, my dad, Homer Gabel died Christmas, 1976, leaving my mother Rhoda, in her late seventies, alone in New Bloomfield. Even though she was in good health, she needed assistance with chores in her home and garden. At that time, I had just studied to become an electrologist. I set up an office in her house in New Bloomfield that offered me the time with her, as well as fulfilling my career in electrolysis. After several years enjoying life on the "Funny Farm," career changes involving long commutes, resulting in much time away from the farm, while both children were in college, it became necessary to sell the horses and the farm in 1989.

The Tressler House Bed & Breakfast

41 WEST MAIN STREET, NEW BLOOMFIELD, PENNSYLVANIA

1989 – 2001

It was 1989 when my mother, Rhoda Gabel, entered assisted living. Our son, Keith graduated from Susquehanna University, married, had a son Derek, and commuted to work in Lebanon. Joanne graduated from Hood College, but hadn't relocated. Dave and I were working from home; thus, we needed a sizable house to accommodate our family's needs. It was at this same time that the Hilda Tressler property at 41 West Main Street, New Bloomfield was for sale and we decided to look at it, never imagining its possibilities.

Bed and Breakfasts (B&Bs) were unheard of in Perry County at that time, but our daughter had spent the past few summers in the Berkshire Mountains, working and living in B&Bs that were popular in that area, and she was with us when we looked at the property. She immediately saw the potential for a B&B. The next day, we bought the house and the vacant lot across the alley that was also owned by the Hilda Tressler estate and proceeded to prepare to move there in February, 1989.

It is believed that the original portion of the house was built in 1833. The 1837 deed, which transferred the land from George Barnett to Abner C. Harding, contains reference to an 1831 agreement between Abner C. Harding and John Earnest, a carpenter, which would seem to pertain to the erection of the house. The deed mentions that Attorney Harding resided on the premises and practiced law from 1833-1837. He was married to Susan, a daughter of Dr. Jonas Ickes. On the same day that he acquired the property, he sold it to John R. McClintock, who opened a dry-goods store.

A deed recorded in 1837 indicated a two-story frame dwelling existed on the land then owned by George Barnett, the founder of Bloomfield. In 1871, the property was deeded to James Laird and William Tressler. The deed states that Dr. Laird was a tenant and had his office there. Later Dr. Laird transferred his share to William Tressler, who willed the property to his daughter, Julia Flickinger.

In 1928, Mary Shearer Bosserman, a widow, bought the house and grounds. For a time, Dr. Robert Stoner conducted his practice from this house. In 1939 his wife, Cora Stoner, bought the east end of the house, and Army General Frank E. and Hilda B. Tressler purchased the west end of the home. In July 1950, they obtained the remaining part from Cora Stoner. Until that time, there were two separate houses that were joined both inside and outside. Thus, two separate front entrances and two separate basements, one dirt and the west side concrete.

The lovely large yard at the east end of the property was sold by George Barnett, separately, to one of the early owners. The complete property lies at the extreme western property line of the original 1796 Thomas Grant named "Bloomfield" and adjoins the 1794 grant of land to Michael Marshall and Casper Lupfer named "Ryefield."

The plot to the east of this property's spacious lawn contains the "Town Spring" which supplied water to all the citizens of the early days. The spring overflow was called "The Horsewater" and supplied the needs of the town's animals. On the Tressler lawn was a separate and private spring covered by a spring-house.

In 1989, we proceeded to restore and preserve the character and charm of the dwelling and grounds. Inside of two weeks prior to occupancy, we were able to paint, remove layers of wallpaper and restore eleven of the twenty-two rooms on the east part of the house, with the assistance of local painter, Steve Umholtz. Later that year, an entirely new oak-wood kitchen was custom built by Weller Bros. (Charles, Leroy and Larry) in the rear between the two houses. The western end of the house had a two-bedroom apartment on the second floor with an outside rear entrance that accommodated Keith's family for the time it took for them to relocate and reconstruct an-original log home from Perry County in Lebanon County.

The first floor had a separate front door entrance and significant room to accommodate pleasant living-quarters, laundry room, enclosed porch and office space for my established Electrolysis practice that previously, I had at my mother's house on the corner of Barnett and Apple Streets. It was in this area that Hilda Tressler began New Bloomfield's Public Library before it was in its McClure Street location.

Little did we know, when we purchased the property, that General Tressler had collected old millstones with the intention of adding a millstone terrace, but never was able to accomplish this project. We uncovered fourteen stones near the alley and Weller Bros. were able to move and incorporate seven of them into a brick sidewalk from the house to the alley and a brick patio in the summer of 1989. The remaining stones adorned the landscaped gardens that became prize winners in the Pennsylvania Garden Magazine 1990 issue.

The Tressler House B&B, being a historic Federal Period home, was furnished in antiques that were acquired from both Carol and Dave's families and local auctions. One of the unique features of the house is a spider-web window transom gracing the front door. The entrance opened onto a large hallway carpeted with oriental rugs and accented by a huge mirror rumored to have come from a bar in Germany.

Guests were invited to relax in the living-room complete with double fireplaces (Hilda Tressler had a wall removed to expand the two small rooms into a gracious sitting area). It was able to accommodate our parlor grand-piano and many artifacts from Dave's parents, Dr. Leonard and Eleanor Ulsh's missionary experiences in Africa, in the 1930s. There were soft seats, a TV, games and interesting books for relaxing and entertaining.

The stairway in the hall leads to bedrooms furnished and redecorated in Waverly fabrics and matching wallpapers, carefully selected with the assistance of our daughter's college degree in interior design.

Visitors found gorgeous gardens, unusual trees including a two-hundred-year old oak tree near the house and flowers of many species in the fenced-in-yard with a duck pond. A covered porch accommodated vintage wicker furniture where guests could eat breakfast on warm days, relax and enjoy the quiet tranquility.

In less than two years, more than three-hundred guests from all over the world had enjoyed the peace and tranquility of this unique Bed & Breakfast. A full country breakfast was served every day to include a choice of four juices, seasonal fruit, different breakfast meats purchased from Ferster's Meat Market located next door, homemade pastry and hot tea or coffee.

In May of 1990, the families of Molly LaRue and Geoffrey Hood were able to rest, eat, talk and reflect in the comforts of the Tressler House during the murder trial of the Appalachian Trail killer, Paul David Crews. On September 13, 1990, at the Perry County Courthouse just a short distance down the street, the trial lasted more than two weeks until the guilty verdict was quickly announced after a short deliberation.

During the next several years, the Tressler House hosted many parents of the Carson Long Military Institute cadets, visiting gals from Linden Hall School, several New Bloomfield Open-House tours for the Garden Club and Civic Club, Class Reunions, birthday parties, Perry County Cooperative Extension Polish Exchange Tea, and our daughter Joanne and Milas Rose's Garden Wedding, as well as overnight guests from all over the United States and the world. In 1996, the Tressler House was written up in the January/February Issue of *Bed & Breakfast & Unique Inns of Pennsylvania*.

After twelve years of operating the B&B, all our family relocated out of Perry County. Dave traveled all over Pennsylvania in his sales job. We were following our grandson Derek in his favorite sport of ice hockey as a goalie on a traveling East Coast team. We found it necessary to move closer to our family in Lebanon County. Therefore, we sold The Tressler House in 2001, which remained a Bed & Breakfast.

A Bloomfield Star Was Born

Storyteller John M. Sanderson, Jr.

My name is John M. Sanderson, Jr. Marvin is my middle name, but I never particularly liked it, so I don't use it very often. I'm actually John M. Sanderson the 4th. My father was John M. Sanderson the 3rd. He was born in Roanoke, Virginia. His dad worked on the railroad and came north with the narrow-gauge railroad. My mother was Mildred K. Long Sanderson. Mildred (Mid) (Millie) was born and raised on the Long farm which is where Fred Morrow now lives.

I was born May 29, 1940. We lived at the sharp corner of Cold Storage Road that Fred Thebes now owns. Life was pretty rough back then, what with WW II getting pretty active. I can remember in my very early years of having food rationing stamp books with drawings of big, ugly, scary Japanese. I would try to hide them with stamps as soon as possible.

My dad worked for Hampton, Snyder and Seeds Planing Mill on South Carlisle Street in New Bloomfield. Then he and Ralph Fry bought the John Deere dealership in Elliottsburg in front of Sunnydale Farm's milk processing plant. The business was known as Sanderson and Fry, until Ralph died. My dad called the business Sanderson Farm Equipment, selling new, used and repairing tractors and machinery.

The Sandersons didn't have electricity until I was in first grade. Wood cooking stove was in the kitchen and coal-oil stove in the living room. No heat upstairs at all. My Grandmother Long would heat bricks in the oven, wrap newspaper around them, and put them in the bottom of my sister and my bed. My sister and I would put our PJs on in the living room by the stove, then run upstairs and jump into bed with our feet on the warm bricks underneath bed covers that were six inches thick. Best sleeping ever.

No indoor plumbing. In winter, we used a chamber pot. During the spring, summer and fall, we used the outdoor toilet which was about fifty yards out by the barn. Coming back from the toilet at night, I would imagine something following me. I would start to run and by the time I hit the wash house, I must have been breaking the Olympic record for the 100-meter dash. One of my most memorable times, was when I would visit the Stoops family on High Street and use their flush toilet. Lots of times, even when I didn't have to use the toilet, I would flush it just so I could see the swirl.

When we finally got electricity, it was only to heat a copper wire put around the outdoor water pump so it wouldn't freeze. Our phone number was a very simple 26R.

My mother's favorite pastime was a huge garden called a truck patch. I enjoyed planting and harvesting, but hated weeding and cultivating. The most fun was digging up the potatoes. It was like finding Easter eggs.

I think my mother brought me into this world to entertain. I was expected to sing in Sunday School and Church. My dad was a self-taught tap dancer. He taught me a few steps. When I was about seven or eight years old, dad and I put on "black face" and danced together in the old minstrel shows held in the Bloomfield Courthouse.

My mother was famous for singing the song, "I'm a Lonely Little Petunia in an Onion Patch," in the minstrel shows. She would actually cry. She must have been really convincing, because people in the audience would also be crying.

My mother enrolled me in the famous Marsha Dale Dance School in Carlisle. In the performance at the end of our lessons, I was a sunflower. My mother was bound and determined that I was going to dance on those variety shows on TV. So, she also enrolled me in a ballet school in Harrisburg. I walked into a large room with a brass railing along the walls and huge mirrors on every wall. I was the only male. The instructor had me holding onto the rail and doing knee bends with my left arm arched over my head. I cried the whole way home. My mother took pity and didn't make me go back.

My mother taught in a one-room school, Laurel Grove on Cold Storage Road. She didn't want me in class, so somehow, she had me go to elementary school in what is now the Lutheran Parrish House in New Bloomfield. I was the only country kid that went to the city school. However, before every Christmas vacation, my mother would take me out of school, and I would have to tap dance in front of all her students. I hated it, but you didn't say no to Mildred Sanderson.

Mother had me tap dance in lots of talent shows. I came in second lots of time, but I could never beat Bonnie Ann Ramer, who did ballet.

We had a huge wooden bob-sled that held up to ten people. We would take it to the top of Cold Storage Road, and if you could make it around the sharp turn where we lived, we would go all the way down to Main Street. You only made two runs a night at the most.

Mother enrolled me in a finishing school with Maryanna Rothrock. She taught us manners, politeness, etiquette, and different dances. We had to go to a young lady, take her hand, and say, "May I have this dance?" After the dance, you took the lady back to her seat, and said, "Thank you." At the end of our classes, we had a formal tea. For the first time, I had to buy a suit and tie. I didn't like it at the time, but now have come to realize that it's one of the best things I ever did. I love dancing at parties, wedding receptions, etc.

In High School, I participated in the class plays under the direction of Mrs. Grace Swan. After moving back on the Sanderson farm in 1974, Mrs. Swan called and wanted me to try out for the New Bloomfield Lions Club Play, "Mary, Mary." You didn't say no to Mrs. Swan. I was to play opposite a legend, Martha Holman from Carson Long Military Institute in New Bloomfield. I told Mrs. Swan I couldn't do that, but she said, "Yes, you can." The rest is history. It led to performing in approximately thirty Lions Club Theater productions, and some of the most enjoyable times of my life.

One Of Perry County's Oldest Families

Storyteller Grady Reisinger

The Reisinger tribe has been in this valley since about the 1750s, long before there was an Ickesburg or a Perry County. I thank my maker that he dropped me into the hills of Perry County to two hard-working parents on a farm. After sixty-nine years of life, I tell people I'm the luckiest man I know. My first memories are of pulling my sister around in my little red wagon (Deb Nyce). That little red wagon went everywhere with me and I eventually wore it out. Actually, it was my first pick-up truck! I hauled everything.

In the fall, Grandpap Reisinger and I would take my little red wagon and fill it with walnuts that we would gather. We put them in pot-holes in the township road and in the driveway hoping there would be enough traffic to smash the hulls off. Then they were put in attics or the granary to dry. Today we are lucky to get the walnuts before they are smashed on the road.

My dad, Robert "Dick" Reisinger was a dairy farmer and mother, Grace kept three to five hundred chickens for eggs. Needless to say, with all of the work, everyone in the family was brought into the work force. Didn't matter how young you were, there was a job for you and you grew into bigger things, that taught you a work ethic and responsibility. One evening at the supper table, Dad asked me if I had fed the hogs. That was my responsibility and when I told him I hadn't, then his reply was that I would do that after supper. It was cold and dark outside but after supper my barn clothes went back on and I went and did my chores.

Some of my youngest memories are with my Dad and Uncle Harold "Boots" baling hay together. "Boots" owned the next farm out the road; it was my grandfather's farm purchased in 1920. "Boots" was the father of Fred and Sue (Binger) Reisinger. Today the third, fourth and fifth generations, are on the farm. Outside my immediate family, Sue and I spent unaccountable hours together riding bike, building forts and tunnels in the hay-mow equipped with a communication system made from baler-twine and inflation tubing, throughout the big old barn.

I remember another neighbor, Wayne Weibley, coming to play and saying that our communication system was strung too high above the barn floor. It was strung twenty-feet above the floor and twenty-feet from mow to mow.

One winter, Wayne and I made chains for our bicycles from electric fence wire. That winter Wayne and I rode for a mile or more on Big Buffalo Creek without getting off the ice.

I played midget baseball for Ickesburg and my first manager was Dennis Fuller, winning all but two games. Wayne Reisinger coached my next two years. In the second year, we lost only one game and went undefeated the next.

In my early years my Grandpap Reisinger spent a lot of time at either my Uncle Harold's farm or at my dad's home. He and I would do hands-on, shoulder-to-shoulder work around the farm. In the spring of the year, we would make little dams in our pastures to create water holes for the cows and heifers. When the thistles got big, but before they went to seed, Pap and I would go out with a corn cutter and cut them off. Then Pap would dig down in the ground with his pocketknife as far as he could and pour old engine oil on the stem. My dad would run the harvesting equipment while Pap and I unloaded the wagons full of hay, straw and corn.

Pap chewed tobacco and kept a spare pack above the sun visor in his car. One summer my sister, Debbi and I took one of "Paps" spare packs. We took it up into the loft of the barn where no one would find it. In the summer evenings, when the work was done, and dad was in the house, she and I would go up in the loft and get a leaf of tobacco to chew. We would then go down to the big ole' water trough in the barnyard just in case we got dizzy or sick. We would dip our heads in the water to get straightened out. That first pack probably lasted about two years. But when we went for the second pack, we found that Pap was not as old and forgetful as we thought he was and we got caught! That was the end of the tobacco for many years. A couple of years later, my sister with her nicotine addiction was smoking straw in the outhouse and burnt it down.

At dinner time, when we were making hay, we would stop at a hydrant between the barn and the house to wash the dirt and chaff off. One day when Pap was washing his face and he straightened up, he had an eye in his hand. I did not know what had happened! And, he did not say anything. But when we got into the house, Mom and Dad could see the look on my face and knew I was upset. My parents and Pap explained that it was a glass eye, because Pap lost an eye in a blacksmith accident. My Grandpap Reisinger died suddenly in 1967, and I had a hard time recovering from that loss. My Grandmother Reisinger lived to be over one-hundred years old.

My mom's dad, Frank Shope, who lived close to one-hundred years, farmed at one time south of the Adair Covered Bridge at Cisna Run. And, I was allowed to stay with him for a couple of days. I would get a break from the work at home and he would teach me how to fish. He also worked for a time in the Forestry Department at New Germantown. There is or was a fire trail named for him on the Bryner Loop Road. Pap shared many stories, but my favorite was when he was clearing fire trails one morning and stepping across a log he landed on a rattlesnake. It was a cool morning and the snake could not strike fast enough to bite him.

His best farm story was about a pair of mules he farmed with. Pap Shope lived about five-hundred yards from the Shermans Valley Railroad, which arrived at Cisna Run about noon. Pap used the train whistle for his dinner bell. Unfortunately, after a while, the mules learned that if the train whistle blew, they got a break. Pap said if the train whistle blew, it didn't matter where he was on the farm or what he was doing, he might as well go for dinner because the mules stopped and were not going to move for a while.

In 1965, my dad sold his dairy herd and went to work as a sawyer for my Uncle John Reisinger. This meant that my brothers and I did as much work in the evenings and Saturdays for our dad as we could. It really taught us work ethic and responsibility. If we wanted to hunt on Saturday or do something else, we did more work in the evenings or very early Saturday morning. We all liked farming and seldom complained.

John Reisinger was severely wounded in WW ll and was left for dead in a tank. Luckily, he survived and worked the rest of his life. The Reisinger uncles were connected to a government road-builder during the great Depression. Therefore, they did not experience joblessness and hardship like so many. Fortunately, or unfortunately when WW ll started, they became tank or truck drivers.

During my high school years, the Hi-Way Theatre, built in Ickesburg by my Uncle C. K. Reisinger in the 1940s, was the starting point for a lot of late-night activities, that included barhopping, parties or trips to Carlisle. We could be at Dickinson College from the theatre in twenty minutes. That was all fly-driving one-hundred mph, with tires screeching through the curves. I tried to sleep five hours on Friday nights, so I could go all-night on Saturdays. We'd close down the Hi-Way, then Laurel Run Tavern and wind-up at Fleming's Truck Stop on the Carlisle Pike for breakfast on Sunday mornings. "Tricky Dick" Loy provided four of us, with a hair-raising experience, as we became airborne traveling east on Route 17.

C. K. Reisinger also built the garage beside the theatre, which has been run by Tom Powell for fifty years, his entire life. Powell now owns the garage, which is the longest standing business remaining in Ickesburg.

I graduated in 1970 and started farming for my dad. That fall, I lost my right hand in a corn-picker accident. That episode created a story of its own. I was in a field out of sight from the house. My mother knew where I was, but did not know I was in trouble. When I finally got out of the corn-picker, the closest help was old Glen Dobbs about two-hundred yards away. A fence row that you could not even see through, was between me and neighbor Dobbs. Somehow, I went through it and when I came upon Mr. Dobbs in the field, he got quite excited when he saw my hand dangling. We got in his car and he took me out to my mother. When I walked into the house, she about flipped out! We got in her car and she took me to Brownie and Gene Fritz's dairy barn. Gene finally took me to the Carlisle Hospital. I remember Gene telling my dad that he had a shimmy in his right front tire at seventy mph. I can still remember Gene was with me when they amputated my hand.

When I awoke that evening, I was told Sam Shields lost an arm in a self-unloading wagon that same morning. Sam and I had graduated together five months earlier. After a day or two, Sam and I would go through the hospital visiting people we knew from Perry County. They would announce over the PA system during visiting hours for Sam and I to go to our rooms because we had visitors. I didn't need to look very far to see someone with a worse condition than me because Sam was only three rooms away. We were both very lucky that day because we stood a better chance of dying than surviving.

!972 was a dry year, then later on we had Hurricane Agnes. It made things tough on the farm, so I went to work for my Uncle John Reisinger running a skidder dragging trees from the woods. This took my life in a different direction. I learned to work with other people, especially my Uncle John. I worked with two old hillbillies who taught me a lot of history about the upper-end of Perry County. Clair Gutshall was a timber cutter and a tough little wiry guy. He taught me how to cut timber, how to butcher and how to hunt turkeys. We had a lot of good times together, unfortunately like several other people I know, a tree killed him in 1980.

One of the great non-working experiences was a nine-day trip to the West Coast with my cousin, George Barnes. After much convincing, we were on our way, but George soon discovered that my love for history had us stopping at every historical marker we came across along the way. We drove seven-thousand miles in nine days, traveling twenty hours a day. When we reached the West Coast and the ocean, I snagged a piece of driftwood, which I still have, while taking pictures of sea lions. Sixty-six hours later we crossed over the Tuscarora Mountain and back home to Perry County. This is one historical trip everybody should take.

After working for my uncle, cutting firewood and part-time farming, I was ready to start farming on my own. In 1980, my brother and I bought out a neighbor, Larry Dobbs' dairy herd. It started a fifteen-year partnership. During those years, we put together a very large farming operation. We started with some smaller equipment that my dad and I had, and grew from about one-hundred and sixty acres to between nine-hundred to a thousand acres. We were milking in a neighborhood of one-hundred and sixty cows, when we dissolved the partnership.

Over the years, farming equipment and methods changed. We went from baling hay in small square bales to a large round baler. My dad used a two-row corn planter. I had a four-row and soon my brothers and I had a six-row corn planter. My dad had a single-row corn-picker and we eventually used a six-row combine. My dad had a thirty hp and an eighty hp tractor. My brothers and I farmed with a two-hundred-thirty hp, a one-hundred-thirty hp, a sixty hp and the thirty hp still owned by brother, Danny. My dad had a seven-foot sickles bar mower and we used a twelve-foot self-propelled hay-bine. Today there are thirty-foot mowers, six- hundred horse-power choppers and twenty-four row corn planters.

Many of the farms we rented were fifty-five to seventy-five acres, half in alfalfa and grains. We would try to mow or plant a couple small farms a day along with our other farm work. No-till farming was starting to become widely used, but was not perfected to our satisfaction so it amounted to a terrific amount of tillage work. Today with better equipment and techniques, it is far less labor and fuel intensive.

My dad really got a kick out of the bigger equipment. He had enough farming and sold his cows in 1965, but with the methods and equipment he was starting to get interested again. Then my dad died suddenly in 1984, which shocked our family. This caused my brothers and I to put a lot of deep thought into what we were trying to achieve. Eventually as with most partnerships, we decided to pursue our individual goals. We accomplished a lot in those years, but it took a terrific amount of long hours, sacrifice, hard work and determination.

1980 was a monumental year for me. My girlfriend Ruth Fisher and I decided to tie the knot and if that weren't enough later that year our first baby came along. We remember the night Lizzie was born as if it was yesterday. Ruth and I had done the milking, while my parents fixed Sunday supper. I was still sitting outside on the front steps, when Dad came and told me it was time to go. I asked where were we going and he said the baby is coming. The episode lasted all night and, in the morning, Elizabeth Grace Louise "Lizzie" was born. Two years later Robbie was born followed by Jim.

Neighbors around here always got a kick out of Lizzie being the boss of the kids. My kids were brought up as I was, doing chores, teaching them responsibility, educating them how to manage their time, and run and repair equipment. Most people tell me that I raised three good kids. And I tell them, that it's their mother's doing because all that they ever learned from me was how to work.

Because I was born in the prettiest valley in Perry County to two hard-working parents that kept us fed and clothed and taught us right from wrong. I was born among best friends, neighbors and relatives that anyone could ask for (Fred and Sue Reisinger, my cousin George Barnes, Wayne Weibley, and the Stone family from up the hollow). When we got to school, there were more friends than a person can remember. Once I got out of school and hit the new world, it was other friends, especially my brother-in-law Chuck Nyce. We spend a lot of time hunting and fishing together, among other things. I once went bay-fishing with a group of guys from Ickesburg. We did everything wrong, staying up all night drinking beer and eating a greasy breakfast. I got so sea-sick I wanted to die! After years of badgering, Chuck convinced me to go along with him bay-fishing. He said Dramamine was the secret to sea-sickness. This time I did everything right, but after an hour in the boat I was mad enough to kill him.

With friends of ours, John and Chris Sauder, we kind of raised our families together. John and I in our better days would work all day, do the evening chores, eat supper and then jump on our snowmobiles and ride half the night. Many years later, John would say, that it's no wonder we don't have backs any more, the way we used to have to pick-up those snowmobiles to turn them around.

One time there was a large gang of us hunting and driving deer on Perry's Ridge, which John now owns. John was on watch at the lower-end in his field when a nice buck came out and John missed it. When the drivers appeared, he just ranted and raved about missing the buck. One of the guys took an empty Pepsi can and placed it where the deer had stood. John proceeded to shoot at the Pepsi can two or three times, hitting it every time, but he missed a full-size deer.

Bob Weibley was another guy who hunted with us. Bob was big on carrying a handgun in a holster. After a couple years of this, I told Bob one day he had to be the smartest hunter in our group because he was carrying a five-pound revolver in a holster and the rest of us are carrying nine-pound rifles and none of us shoot that much.

Then there was Jack Palm, who was quick to come-up with a solution we were discussing. The guys were trying to figure out a way from keeping the deer from going across the Buffalo "Crick." Jack suggested that shooting them usually works! Jack and Bill were like my dad. They could really shoot. One day, three of us were walking up the Lower Ridge for the watch. Wayne Weibley was in front of me and Ron Weibley was behind me. I glanced out through the woods and noticed a buck standing looking at us. I tried to tell them where the buck was but they couldn't see it. So, I unwillingly pulled up and shot it! That was probably twenty–thirty years ago, so I guess I can admit, that it was the second buck I shot that day.

Harvey and Becky Reisinger were very helpful in raising our boys at a very critical time of a young man's life. In the mid 1990s, my cousin Fred, Harvey and my wife Ruth and I made a trip to Wyoming at the end of January. Ruth and I were looking at farms out there. We were finally able to buy my mother's farm, so we never moved west. Years later, Harvey and Becky did buy Wyoming property and moved there.

Our kids grew-up and started families of their own. In 2006, when our first grandchild came, it was Ruth's and my bleakest hour financially. That little boy, Reese made a huge difference in prioritizing our life. Our daughter, Lizzie, who teaches school in Juniata County, married Tim Fedder, who drives his own log truck, and they had Reese, Arden and Laural. Son Rob, who farms three-hundred acres part-time also drives his own log truck, married Angy Loy and their children are Sydney, Brody and Emmy. Son Jim, who normally runs two trucks of his own hauling logs plus moving a lot of equipment, married Kathy Sior and their children are Caleb, Alaina and Logan.

My farming experiences go back to about sixty-two years. My logging and sawmill experience goes back fifty years to my Uncle John Reisinger's sawmill. As a result of my experience in logging, my two sons, my son-in-law, and my brother Bob's son, Denny, are all self-employed log haulers. For fifteen years, son Jim and I ran a logging business after we rebuilt a skidder and I used a chain saw to cut down thousands of trees. We ran several skidders with grapples, a stroke-delimber, log loader and a couple of trucks. The largest chain saw was the two three-hundred hp with a heated and air-conditioned cab.

At the first grandson, Reese, I decided the true reward in life is in your children and grandchildren. I get great joy from teaching my grandsons about the outdoors and taking them hunting. They have developed great hunting skills and are very competitive with each other. I had more fun taking them hunting than the two boys put together.

The "Preach" asked me some time back, how I was. I said things are so good, I worry about what might be coming down the road. I have a wife, who is "stone solid" and a family I couldn't be prouder of. Pastor Elaine Moyer is one of the best things to happen in Ickesburg in many years.

After knowing many of these people in my story all my life, I can't believe how old they got. Glad that hasn't happened to me!

I'd like to thank Debby Noye for publishing these cherished memories, because the personal and family stories are irreplaceable to the "old" families in Perry County.

Strawberry Fields In New Buffalo

Storyteller Marilyn Knuth Bankert

"No need to worry. No need to Sparkle. No need to be anybody but oneself."

This quote by Virginia Woolf perfectly describes life in the 1950s through 1960s in New Buffalo, Pennsylvania. Life as a child growing up in New Buffalo, which was between Duncannon and Liverpool on Route 11 & 15, alongside the Susquehanna River, wasn't always idyllic but it was pretty close.

There were always chores; set the table for dinner and help to clean up afterwards, strawberries to pick, daily walks to Smeltzer's Store for a copy of the Harrisburg newspaper "Patriot News," then to pick up the mail at the United States Post Office. And of course, we went to the Hill Church in Watts Township on Sundays. As in most small-town families, these were our responsibilities. Our responsibilities, interests and actions were to define the foundation for who we would become and shape our values as adults.

Setting the table at dinner time meant that our family (my parents Alice and John Knuth, and siblings Byron, Wanda, and Robby) ate together. Even though we didn't think of it that way, being together at mealtime was a time for bonding, and for strengthening our family ties. We always knew we had the love and support of each family member. We knew that then and we know that even to this day.

Strawberry fields are ripe with berries in spring and summer and prime berry picking always seems to be when summer days are the hottest. Strawberries sweeten any celebration, especially in the summer. Our best celebrations always included our mother's made-from-scratch strawberry shortcake, our father's homemade strawberry ice cream, and sometimes even homemade root beer. My father's "hobby patch" of strawberries were so sweet they needed very little sugar. Of course, we topped off the shortcake and berries with fresh whipped heavy cream. It was an addiction! Many heartfelt thanks to my family who grew those strawberries that we had to pick in the hot summer sun. Looking back at that time, I am reminded of not only the high energy and hard work that went into my father's strawberry avocation, which grew from an enjoyable hobby to filling orders beyond the borders of Perry County. The delicious rewards and good times his strawberry patch yielded will be cherished forever.

We lived at the top of the hill, which is now 5 Knuth Road in New Buffalo. Daily walks along the paved streets (no sidewalks), to Smeltzer's Store, for the newspaper, was a chore shared among the older siblings. Then onward to the post office to pick up the mail from our dedicated postmistress, Kate Thompson, who served a lifetime in that position, seemed an impossible chore in the hot summertime. However, our grandfather's (grandparents Ada and John Knuth lived next door) vegetable garden was on the way to the store. How fortunate! Quite often he would offer us one of his plump, red, juicy tomatoes fresh off the vine and it helped to soften the arduous task of the journey. He probably watched each tomato grow and anticipated using that tomato himself but generously offered it to us. It was an extra bonus to have a few cuttings of our grandmother's majestic and colorful gladiolus from her flower garden, to take home for our mother. Daily trips to Smeltzer's Store were much nicer when he had these "little rewards." Sometimes we were even lucky to have enough to spend on penny candy or a new coloring book.

Summers were the best in New Buffalo. It was such a small town that everyone knew everyone else and many were extended family. (My maternal grandparents were Rachel and Melvin Dorman who lived in Watts Township.) For some reason there was an abundance of boys in town! Of course, this would bode well if you were a boy and future events like baseball games were favorable. These were "boys only" events and no girls were allowed! Girls always had bikes to ride, which we rode all over New Buffalo, transistor radios to listen to and helping out around the house.

Church at Hill Church on Sundays was a must! No getting out of it simply because we didn't feel well. No problem though, because it was a perfect opportunity to dress in our store-bought Sunday best and be with friends while fulfilling our Sunday obligations, which we all enjoyed. My mother was a self-taught seamstress and often sewed without using a pattern. She was excellent and I remember my fourth-grade teacher, Mrs. Hickoff, complimenting the dress I wore for May Day which my mother had lovingly made.

My father, along with his father and brothers, built the house that we grew up in. The house is still in our family and my daughter and her husband now own it as a summer retreat to get away from the city life. Sadly, there is no longer a strawberry patch. At various times, five generations of our family have called this house "home" including four of my great-grandchildren who currently live there.

Growing up in New Buffalo, like many small towns, instilled family values that I continue to find important today. The chores and responsibilities that we learned then helped to shape our values as we navigate our challenges in contemporary times.

Life On The O'toole Farm
HAND MILKING TO ROBOTICS IN THE BARN

Storytellers Carol Ann Kling O'Toole and Frank G. O'Toole
Recorded by Debra Kay Noye

Perry County country roads always bring the O'Toole family back home to their farm located east of Kistler off Fisher Hill Road. Milking cows has always been top priority for the modernized dairy farm, where Frank O'Toole at the age of seven began helping to hand milk 10 to 12 head of cows. Today the robotics milking system, which was the first in Perry County, handles the heavy duty milking chores saving Frank and son Bob six hours of hard labor a day and allowing for 60 to 70 in the milking herd.

Not always a dairy farmer, Frank was born in 1941 at Stoney Point, between Kistler and Blain. He lived back a long lane that started at the Leo Rice property and neighbored Wendell Smith.

His mother, Charlotte M. (Palm) O'Toole, trusted young Frank to walk up to the Leo Rice Farm and bring back a couple loaves of bread. Bread delivery trucks made their rounds through the county and stopped at the locals for the purchase of bread and or bakery goods. Four year old Frank ogled the baked goods this time and asked for cupcakes instead of bread. That opportunity did not arise again, as the family moved.

His father John F. O'Toole worked for the Letterkenny Army Depot and carpooled with Ted Latchford and others over the Conococheague Mountain to Chambersburg. Then he worked at the Blain Planing Mill, where he discovered his love of wood-working and life's vocation in carpentry. Eventually contracting independently, he remodeled more than forty kitchens, designing and building new cabinets. Carol Ann, Frank's wife, easily recognized his work upon walking into a home. His cabinets had a signature design and hardware. Frank and brother, Mike would help to move the big table saw from one work-site to another.

Frank's mother, Charlotte worked as a cook at the Carlisle Hospital, Wagner's Tire & Restaurant at Kistler, Sun Bonnet Drive-In and Tressler Lutheran Orphan's Home in Loysville. The O'Toole family members had their own line of work, but helped each other as needed with cars, trucks, and hands-on labor. Frank's father, John in his retirement, made grandfather and grandmother clocks for friends and family. Each year the family looked forward to something different made by Pap for Christmas presents. The grand-kids asked, "What's Pap making this year?"

In 1946, the family moved to their one-hundred-eighty acre farm of which ninety acres is woodland. As the brothers got older, the farm became John O'Toole and Sons Farming. Frank and Mike milked cows with milking machines. The buckets of milk were strained into heavy metal cans, then placed into the spring drain to be kept cold till the milk trucks would pick them up to be hauled to the Sunnydale Farms milk plant in Elliottsburg.

As milking techniques progressed through the years from bucket milkers to Universal systems with hoses to bulk tanks to pipeline systems, the farm changed names. Carl Baer, from Elliottsburg, installed the pipeline system, designed by brother, John "Mike" O'Toole in the early seventies and was very proud to do so. That milking set-up allowed for three rows of cows to be readied and milked, using a track carrying system that moved the milkers instead of hand carrying them from cow to cow. Carl Baer also solved the problem of young Bob sucking his thumb. He proceeded to demonstrate to him what might happen if he continued. Tucking his thumb under and into his fist, Carl showed Bob his hand, much to his horror. There was no thumb, ending Bob's habit.

When their father retired from farming, the brothers partnered as O'Toole Brothers and continued as dairymen. By that time, the family had acquired the adjacent Jim Rice farm of one hundred tillable and fifty wooded acres. Mike was also a DHIA (Dairy Herd Improvement Association) Milk Tester for the county collecting milk samples after weighing each cow's milk. The sample was checked for bacteria count, milk fat content, and a lot of other information to assist the farmer in the development of his herd. Technology is providing those services today right on the farm with the computer. Frank had the sole responsibility for their dairy herd and young animals.

When Mike retired from dairying, O'Toole Acres was born when Frank's son, Robert took ownership and the high-tech robotics system of milking cows twenty-four hours a day was installed. Bob is a Delaware Valley Agricultural and Science College graduate. His West Perry High School Vocational Agricultural teacher, Sam Wagner was instrumental in gaining access to computers for the FFA. Many other areas of the school did not have computers at that time. Bob learned how to best use his college prep and vocational classes to his best advantage. His advanced FFA (Future Farmers of America) studies and farming background and the unrelenting support of his mother proved instrumental in obtaining a full academic scholarship. Carol Ann learned of the opportunities at Delaware Valley during a high school visit and shared that with Bob. (As a side note - local baseball talent, Tom McMillen was playing that day.) Returning to farming, Bob has certainly applied his education in operating O'Toole Acres. Around 2010, he expanded the O'Toole acreage by purchasing part of the Paul Reisinger Sr. farm.

Weller's Dairy west of New Bloomfield on Shermans Valley Road was the second Perry County dairy farm to install the robotics system of milking large dairy herds. Gone are the days of any hand-on milking unless someone establishes a farmette! Today each cow is assigned a special collar and as the cow steps into the milking station, the computer system identifies her by the collar and the process begins. She doesn't have to wait for Frank to come around and put food in front of her. The computer determines the amount of specially formulated high protein feed to appear like magic in the trough. It keeps records of milk production and the cows are fed accordingly. An average O'Toole cow milked three times a day will produce at least eighty pounds of milk. There's a cow being milked every seven minutes, according to Frank.

They are also watered and have access to a "total mix feed" round the clock. No bales of hay given like the old days. There is also less waste with the modernized feeding system.

Wondering how long it takes to train a cow to automatically step into the milking station? Mother Nature dictates once the udder is full of milk, the cow soon learns and develops a routine to get relief. She's ready to drop that extra baggage! Cows that are "drying up" in the lactation stage are milked twice a day and fed less because there is less milk production. All this is monitored by Frank and Bob from the comfort of their home offices by simply watching their computers. Imagine spy cams in dairy barns these days!

O'Toole's grow one-hundred acres of corn, as well as barley, oats, alfalfa, soybeans, and sorghum to feed their dairy cows and heifers. Calves are housed in individual hutches away from their mothers and are bottle fed milk by Frank. Here is where that labor intensive work with the cows still exists, as Frank fills large plastic bottles fitted with a large nipple to individually feed each calf. As soon as he can, Frank will train them to drink from a bucket, being careful not to let them guzzle the milk, because Frank feels it affects their growth. He also switches totally to powdered "milk replacer" mixed with water over time and weans them at around six weeks. The heifers are kept for breeding to replenish the herd.

Of course, what goes in must come out, and the new robotics system for the most part also takes care of the manure and urine. There are two ways the O'Toole's get that out of their barns, each one being a different method. The flooring under the milking herd is continually being scrapped with a rotating chain drag with bat wing bars taken to one end of the barn and pumped each AM and PM into the holding tank. The barn where dry cows and heifers are, is slated under the area that the animals stand while eating their feed, with the majority of the waste materials falling through the cracks to the tank under them to be later pumped to manure storage tanks which are designed to hold a year's worth of liquefied cow poop to be sprayed onto the fields. No wonder one sees so many manure spreading tanks on the highways at one time these days. There are local farmers who do custom waste removal, just like custom combining of crops.

Frank proclaims he has two passions these days, collecting pocket knives and antique tractors. His tractor collection starts near the beginning of the farm tractor industry in 1930 with a "fly wheel". The massive iron monster on iron wheels, takes lots of arm muscle to spin the fly wheel which starts the motor. Watching one of these tractors roll sluggishly along a parade route reminds one of how far the industry has progressed. The highlight of his collection include his father's heavily used two cylinder John Deere tractor B and the first John Deere he has owned. Frank's knife collecting began as a good habit when he kept a pocket-knife handy. Carol Ann thinks a farmer's knife is the best multi-purpose tool that is always available in his pocket.

Hand milking all those cows certainly helped Frank develop a good grip on the baseballs as he whirled them past the batters, in his younger years. Throwing "cow patties" did nothing to enhance his baseball career, which began playing midgets and continued through high school. In 1959, playing for Blain High School, Frank pitched a "no-hitter" starting at four o'clock in Blain against New Bloomfield High School. Dave Wilt and George Smith were his high school catchers. The short one-hour game allowed him to get home in time to do the milking, before he headed off to his high school graduation. Later, Frank was encouraged to try-out for the Pittsburgh Pirates at City Island and before some scouts from another baseball organization which came to Juniata County. He felt that "the funds weren't good enough and decided to remain on the farm and milk cows".

Baseball was in Frank's blood, so he pitched ten years with the Blain town baseball team until 1969. His catchers then were Bill or Dale Gray and Dean Earnest, who originally played for Ickesburg. Blain team mates were Alan, Clark and Benny Bower who were getting up in years. Gene and Dave Wilt, Clyde Shambaugh, Dale Reisinger, Dale and Rich Rohm, Barry Sheaffer and Jim Nearhood rounded out the team. Blain's biggest rival was Loysville, followed by Millerstown, Newport and Ickesburg.

Frank's family was very supportive including his sisters Carolyn L. Zeiders, Nancy G. Rasmus, and Peggy K. Porter, and cousins Joseph O'Toole and Betty O'Toole Duffy. His maternal grandparents were Grace and Gardner Palm. His paternal grandparents were of Irish Catholic descent and lived in Philadelphia. (His grandmother died of the influenza pandemic in 1918.)

Frank's dad, "Jack or Red" (because of his flaming red hair) drove a truck for three years hauling supplies and workers back and forth between the Civilian Conservation Corp camps (CCC) in western Perry County. On Friday nights, it wasn't unusual for him to make some sly side-trips to pick up local young ladies to be dropped at Fowler's Hollow CCC camp's dance night!

Frank's wife Carol Ann Kling was raised on the Flickinger/Kling homestead not too far away off Rock Hollow Road, in an area off the "Buckeye", which is a ridge between the Tuscarora Mountains and Loysville. Actually the ridge starts outside of Erly, heading west toward Ickesburg and onto the Kistler area following Route 17. The one-thousand acres, named for the Buckeye Pipeline, still is a hunter's, hikers, and snowmobiling paradise. Flickingers and Klings harvested wood from the area. Carol Ann's mother, Carol G. Flickinger Kling told of riding horseback running errands, from the Flickinger farm to the end of Fisher Road which merges with Route 17. She would ride the long miles through fields and woods to drop off mail or shoes for repair.

Carol Ann shares about her family. "My grandmothers were tough ladies; one with a handicapped husband and the other raising five children alone, making sure they had the opportunity to graduate from high school. You toughed it out raising families, with family and friends helping each other!" Her grandparents were Will and Mary (Gantt) Flickinger. Pappy Flickinger became disabled when he fell from a barn loft and walked with a scissor gate using one or two canes afterwards. Arthur and Marion (Cooper) Kling were her dad's parents. Granddad Kling died in his thirties of complications from minor surgery. Money was scarce in both households, but her grandmothers managed to put food on the table without modern conveniences or fancy cuts of meat.

Her dad, Ray L. Kling grew up in the middle of two brothers and two sisters. Her mother, Carol was youngest of three sisters. Ray's family lived off Rout 74, north of Alinda. The Kling family operated a local butcher shop. Today, V. Art Kling, local auctioneer, lives in the family homestead. The children attended the one-room Milltown School a little more than a mile down the road. They walked, rode horses and sledded to school. The trek over Bell's Hill to Landisburg High School was much further.

Carol Ann's mother, in ninth grade, in the late 1930's, rode on one of the first two school buses used to transport students to the Blain Vocational School. Dewey Weibley was her bus driver. (In his later years,

Dewey dug out the O'Toole pond.) Local farmers would pick up extra work by driving school buses twice a day by juggling their farm chores. They had sensibility and were used to driving in all kinds of weather.

In first grade at Blain Elementary, Carol Ann received a note to her mother from her teacher Miss Clark. After seeing the school nurse several times it was determined Carol Ann needed to have her eyes checked further. On their many treks over Waggoner's Gap to Carlisle, Carol Ann's mother kept a granite basin under the car seat because Carol Ann would often become car-sick. Frequent stops were made at natural springs along the way to rinse out the basin. To try and distract Carol Ann, her mother would recite poems she had memorized during her school days like "Under the Spreading Chestnut Tree".

Centre Presbyterian Church, located near Fort Robinson on Route 850, became the Kling's house of worship in the late 1940s. Ray declared to his new wife, Carol, "Why are we driving five miles to a church when there is one just over the hill?" Carol's home church was in Loysville and Ray's in Landisburg. There were many Milligans, Morrisons, Loys, McMillens and other families but no Klings. Carol had attended Centre at times during her growing-up years with her childhood friend and neighbor Myrtle Keegans Fredrick. They could walk the short distance from their homes. Carol Ann remarks that "the church bells were usually ringing with the doors wide open as the Kling family rushed in at the last minute".

Sunday afternoon's jaunt meant traveling to Grandma Flickingers in Elliottsburg. Upon picking her up, grandma would decide where to go; check up on somebody or just take in the changing scenes of the countryside towards the Mannsville area. Grandma Flickinger never had a high school education, due to her mother's passing and being left to raise her eight to ten siblings. But she made sure, they attended the Bloomfield Academy, while boarding in New Bloomfield. Since this was the early 1900s, she would hitch the horse and buggy to take them to school and bring them home each week-end. On one occasion, the horse spooked and the buggy flipped over. Luckily nobody was injured.

In later years, Kling family trips to Carlisle included stops at Aunt Jean Keller's clothing store, Wengers, where clothes were already selected for the girls to try on. That was a treat for Carol Ann, because Aunt Jean was very generous. Her other Aunt Jean (Fox) made sure the Kling siblings received extra special Easter boxes every year. Toys were rare with the exception of Carol Ann's prized bisque doll. Her rambunctious siblings had torn it apart and hidden it at Grandmas. Carol Ann and Grandma found the doll while going through things for a later move. Grandma saved the parts and with the help of neighbor and friend "Cassie" McAlister, they brought the doll back to life and is cherished today.

The Kling Farm milked Holstein cows in their dairy herd. Chickens provided eggs and extra income. After they were washed and boxed, the eggs were picked-up by Emlet's from Loysville. A stray goat occasionally grazed the farm and pigs were raised for meat. Pigeons were caught and made into squab pot pie. Once the pigeons were caught from the barn's rafters, they were cleaned and cooked. The broth was used to cook hand-rolled squares of dough. It was cheap, belly-filling, tasty eats, enjoyed by all!

Paul Kretzing skillfully advised Carol Ann's dad how to butcher hogs. Miles Stone helped the John O'Tooles butcher. None of the men were trained to butcher. They learned from their fathers and neighbors as butchering time came round in the winter. The best part of butchering was enjoying the freshly cooked meats and organs straight from the iron kettles fueled by wood fires. Kretzing's daughters helped by cleaning up before and all through the butchering process.

Originally from Cherry Valley outside of Ickesburg, Paul Kretzing liked to visit with the neighbors on winter evenings. His bib pocket held his harmonica while his side pockets would be filled with his home-grown hazelnuts to share with all. He entertained while sitting on the steps, as all chairs were filled by the family finishing their supper. Carol Ann's mother always offered her chair but he liked the steps.

There were numerous older Kretzing daughters available to help Carol Ann's mother at different times during her early years of marriage and child-rearing. They scrubbed the white wains-coated kitchen each spring, after a winter of heating the house with a wood stove. Some of them became baby-sitters when new babies arrived. The Kling siblings are R. Lynn deceased, Carol Ann, Mary Jo Owen, Sally Mae Sweigart, Bonnie Lou Blumenschein deceased and Donna Jean Mummert deceased.

Like so many farm youngsters, Carol Ann was in 4-H and a member of the Perry County 4-H Dairy Club. A cow and calf halter was necessary equipment to handle a large bovine in the show ring and at competitions. Roy Snyder, from New Bloomfield, the Perry County Extension Agent taught the members how to make their own rope halters for their calves. And some fifty years later, Carol Ann is still propagating sweet potato starts originating from Roy Snyder. She learned how from her Grandmother Flickinger. The heirloom sweet potato is red skinned, white flesh inside, very sweet and can grow to the size of a small football. Carol Ann likes to thinly slice and fry it for breakfast or roast for enjoying at other times. Her mother's Candied Sweet Potato recipe is made for special holidays and still used at the annual Centre Church Turkey Supper.

Just like preserving the heirloom sweet potatoes, so has the O'Toole family sustained their family dairy farm. From working for and with his dad, Frank is now working for his son, Bob, keeping the dairy tradition alive. Bob has an older sister, Jo Ann O'Toole Raup who lives near Duncannon with her husband, Skip and father-law Ken. She works from home for Select Medical. Bob's wife is Stacy Hoffman O'Toole who is a teacher/reading specialist for West Perry School. They have two daughters; Grace, a junior in college and Emma, a senior at West Perry. Maybe one of the girls will follow her O'Toole family tradition of caring for god's creatures! Quoting Carol, "Not a word has been said about music in our or our granddaughter's lives. They grew-up around music, piano, dance, instruments at school, and Frank playing his guitar and singing." We'll close with verse;

Whatever will be, will be   The future's not ours to see   Que será, será

Benvenue

"A SPECIAL PLACE BETWEEN TWO RIVERS"

Storyteller Keith Hite

The good old days . . . that period in our lives when we hearken back to the simpler more gentler times. No computers or malls or cell phones. For me, it was growing up on the "Island," more properly known as Benvenue, located between the Juniata and Susquehanna Rivers, accessible from the south by the Clarks Ferry Bridge. Names like Dallago, Bornman, Grove, Miller and Williams were but a few who called the Island their home. Businesses included the Island Park Restaurant and Cottages, Holler's Restaurant, Groves Gas and Sporting Goods, the Del Marva Restaurant, Williams' Nursing Home and the Distelfink Drive-In which later became the Red Rabbit.

My family moved to the Island in late 1959 into the John Richter home, which was manufactured by Sears and Roebuck. It was a wonderful place to grow up. The house was on approximately five acres of land that was bordered on the west by the Juniata River and on the east by a branch of the Susquehanna River. There was a stretch of woodland across the eastern border where we immersed ourselves in all kinds of imaginary adventures.

One of my first memories in our new home occurred in the middle of the night during our first week there. My father was an engineer on the railroad and worked nontraditional hours. One night when he was working away, mother was getting the kids ready for bed when a bat unleashed its terror! My mother wasted no time in gathering up the kids and taking us to her mother's home for the night, vowing never to return until that monster was eradicated from the house!! I never knew whether my father removed the bat or it was my mother's hysterics that drove it away!!

In the summer, friends were always visiting and we would do battle in the Branch, on large inner tubes from an earth-moving Euclid supplied by a friend whose father worked construction. It was quite a feat to get on top of one of the tubes with ten or twelve guys all trying to get there first!

One summer, my father purchased a large World War II lifeboat that was over forty feet long and when you stood in the bottom of the boat you could not see over the sides. It was made of galvanized metal and

I think it was his original intention to have the boat scrapped for its metal. But some friends and I had a better idea and we launched it into the Branch. The boat provided hours and hours of fun and adventure for all of us, until it was washed down river by Hurricane Agnes in 1972. If you know where to look, you can still see the hull of the boat upside down near the confluence of the Branch and the main part of the Susquehanna River.

I remember the years when the Branch would freeze over and allow us to ice skate from shore to shore and for miles in both directions. A freeze that was so clear that you could see leaves and fish underneath. I remember taking an old car, that my father owned and unbeknownst to him, attempted to drive on the ice. Unsuccessfully I might add.

A couple of miles north of our home, there was a large pond that was created from an overflow of the Susquehanna River, that we aptly named the Artificial Lake. It was located a few hundred yards behind a large field and was virtually hidden from anyone who did not know of its existence. In the winter, the lake would freeze and became our private ice-skating rink where friends came during the daylight hours to play hockey and in the evening bring a date to ice skate and sit around a fire of burning automobile tires. The hockey was at times a war zone where high-sticking, tripping, slashing, charging, interference and roughing ruled the day. But at night, it was more serene and civil for figure skating with your friends and dates.

Each year, my mother's family would gather for a family reunion on the Island. It was a special time that was unique and enjoyable, especially for those who lived in the city. I remember one time when an aunt who lived in Philadelphia expressed concern to my father because there were no street lights on the Island!!!

A few houses from us was a large nursing home that was rumored to have been part of the Underground Railroad during the Civil War. Prior to becoming a nursing home, it was a hotel for tourists traveling through the area and known as the "Benvenue Inn." For my friend John and me, it was a place where we engaged in wheelchair races on the second floor!

We swam, fished, skated, hunted and explored.

Across the Branch is another island that we referred to as the Big Island. It was the home of the Duncan family for which Duncannon was named. At the point of the island was a large mansion that was home to the Duncans. When we first explored the Big Island and came across the mansion, it was as though the family just walked away one day, never to return. The house was completely intact and it was magnificent with curved stairways and door knobs that featured the Duncan family crest. There was a large barn, a smokehouse, underground cellar and numerous outbuildings. There were several other homes on the island that we presumed were for the workers who attended to farming the island. We spent a fair amount of time exploring the Big Island all under the pretext of being clandestine for fear of someone returning home! But no one ever did. The mansion, the barn and the outbuildings were subsequently torn down when the Pennsylvania Game Commission acquired the property and no trespassing signs lined the border for many years.

Growing up on the Island was a wonderful experience full of adventure and unbridled fun. But sadly, there were also some bad times, mostly because of the rivers. In the spring of 1963, I remember looking across the roadway in front of the house and seeing the ice stacked fifteen to twenty feet against the trees that lined the old canal. In a matter of minutes, the ice broke through the trees and flooded the island. Ice as thick as forty-two inches covered the yards and field and the damage was substantial.

I remember my grandmother had a large Chrysler automobile that was parked at my parents' home when the flood hit. When the waters receded and we were able to return, we found that grandmother's car had been carried nearly three-hundred feet from its original spot.

But the ice flood of 1963 was minor compared to what would happen in June of 1972 when Hurricane Agnes ravaged much of Central Pennsylvania. My father was working in New Jersey and my mother was attending a work-related convention in Philadelphia. As we listened to the news and the flood forecasters, we felt somewhat at ease because they predicted the waters would crest around seventeen feet in Harrisburg and we knew that our home would not be affected as long as the waters did not hit twenty-six feet. But seventeen feet became nineteen feet, then twenty feet to twenty-two feet and eventually nearly thirty-three feet! There was no time to remove anything from the house other than one car, the tractor and a boat that we put on the parking lot of the Red Rabbit Drive-In, which was not affected by the rising waters.

Two days later when the waters crested, my father, brother and I took the boat down to the house and pulled it onto the roof of the porch and entered the house through a second-floor window. As it turned out, we were one of the lucky residences. We *only* had seven and a half feet of water on the first floor while other homes had three and four feet on the second floor.

My mother had always wanted a large country kitchen. About six months before Agnes hit, work was completed on an addition to the house and she had her large country kitchen, complete with all new appliances, custom cabinetry and furniture. It was beautiful. But when the waters receded, we learned that it had been destroyed.

My mother had a large antique piano that had been handed down in her family. It was solid walnut and she loved to spend hours playing it. My father had the piano completely restored including new ivories, soundboard, rails and strings. When we returned, the piano was a mere pile of rubble with no possibility of being restored.

Everything inside the house and garage had to be thrown away. The Duncannon Fire Department pumped thousands of gallons of fresh water into the basement in an effort to remove the mud and muck that was left behind. To this day, I suspect you could rub your hand above a rafter and find dried mud from Hurricane Agnes.

My father grew up during the Depression and was raised by his grandparents just so his family could survive. He was a self-made person who was very independent. I only saw him cry twice in my life, once when my younger brother died and when he went into the house after the flood of 1972.

Agnes was devastating for tens of thousands of residents throughout the greater Central Pennsylvania. It was a time of reckoning I suppose against all the good times that had given us a lifetime of special memories of a very special place . . . the Island.

From Pulling Weeds To Checking Under The Hood

Storyteller Nancy Weldon Tressler
Recorded by Debra Kay Noye

It's very evident that Nancy Tressler's infectious laughter began with her childhood near Dellville outside of Duncannon. She was born at home in 1938 to Anna and Russell Weldon, who owned a small farmette on the corner of Dellville Road and now YMCA Road. Her home was surrounded by farms, not like the single homes that fill the landscape today.

Weldon's had some electric in their house, because Russell was an electrician, but no indoor plumbing existed. Nancy's mother maintained a dry sink with a granite basin of fresh water for the family to wash hands and faces as needed. There was a hand pump outside the back door, off the kitchen, which supplied the family with fresh spring water. Her mother kept a granite cup hanging at the pump for when they needed a long drink, instead of a quick slurp from the cast iron spigot. Water was heated on the old cookstove for bathing and doing laundry. The family used coal and wood to fire the cookstove.

Most times, Nancy, when she was young, would be sat on a chair beside the cookstove by her mother and given a quick washing off using a washcloth. However, if it was really bath time, her mother would bring in one of the wash tubs normally used for doing laundry, fill it with some hot water and Nancy would quickly bathe, particularly in the cold winter months, because the only heat in the house was supplied by the cookstove and others were waiting a turn in the then warm water.

Nancy's mother would bring those same wash tubs into the kitchen to do the laundry. They and the wringer-washing machine were stored on the back porch. Once the clothes were laundered, Nancy's mother would hang them out on the clothesline or sometimes, she would lay some onto the grass to dry. She would do this when she needed some help removing stains. The sun would bleach the fabric, especially anything white.

One day when their mother was out hanging up clothes, Nancy's brother, Myran, was playing in the house with his pull-behind wagon. He proceeded to get into the kitchen pantry and empty all of the flour, sugars, baking needs and other dry goods into his wagon. If that wasn't enough, he decided to add the dirty water from the wash basin. He stirred it all together, but had no obvious plan what he was going to do with his concoction. Neither did his mother when she discovered her "not-so-budding-chef!" There was not a lot of extra pocket money back in those days and the "wagon-creation" would've put a strain on the family's resources.

Nancy recalls one Thanksgiving Day, her mother had a huge turkey in the oven and was fixing all the trimmings, when the family became overcome with coal fumes from their Heatrola stove In the living room. Everybody was so ill that they could only eat some tomato soup, while their feast waited for them.

Prior to the Depression and through WW ll when the government encouraged it, people relied on their large gardens to feed their families and generally shared or bartered with neighbors. Nancy's family had a big "truck patch" where they raised potatoes and lots of other vegetables which her mother canned. They also had a strawberry patch, plus pear and apple trees. Like most kids, Nancy hated the chore of weeding, which was a weekly occurrence.

No farm was complete unless there was a milk cow, chickens for eggs and fried chicken dinners, and pigs for butchering. Nancy's dad always raised two pigs which were butchered on New Year's Day. The family used every part of the pigs and especially enjoyed the cooked head meat straight from the kettle. They made and ate lots of scrapple. Nancy would sometimes hold the pieces of pork for her father to cut into portions, and still has a slight scar remaining on her left wrist to prove that today. OOPS! The hams, shoulders and bacon trimmed from the pigs would be cured and then smoked in the family's smokehouse.

The family also raised most of the grains and hay to feed their animals. When it came time to cut the hay, Nancy's father would hitch the tractor to a wooden wagon. Nancy would be on the wagon, while Myran used a hay fork to pitch the loose hay onto the wagon bed. It was Nancy's job to tramp down the hay to make room for more, before it was hauled to the barn and pitched into the mows. Nancy and Myran liked to climb on the barn beams clear to the top of the roof and jump down into the soft piles of hay. Well, they had climbed to the top rafters, when Nancy decided the pile was too low and was afraid of getting hurt. She could not bring herself to climb back down, so her father had to get a ladder and rescue her.

To supplement the pork and chicken diet, they also hunted for squirrels, which Nancy's mother made into squirrel pot pie, made with hand-rolled dough. Rabbits were turned into "rabbit meat pies." They hunted around their property and enjoyed dining on venison.

As a specialty sideline, they raised Eskimo Spitz puppies and sold them. They would have been quite the novelty back then. Nancy's mother also wallpapered people's walls to raise a little extra money. Her talents were sought after and are very rare today. Nancy's dad did electrical work for other people and often bartered for his wages and goods.

Even though they used an outhouse, they had a modern wall phone which was a party line and shared with other families in the surrounding area. And, if one of them caught a common cold, her mother would tear up an old flannel shirt into pieces and heat one to apply to a layer of Vick's Vapor Rub which had been slathered all over their chest. The penetrating smell alone could open any clogged nasal passages. But if you scraped your knee, out would come the bottle of Iodine, which was applied to the affected area regardless of the extreme stinging sensation it might create. There was no ringing-up the local doctor, because their mother was equipped with an arsenal of home remedies. Not only that, children like Nancy soon learned to toughen up and take those common scrapes and bruises in stride. No whimpering unless you were really injured!

Their radio kept them in the know about their surrounding area and world events, particularly during WW ll. That is when local "blackout" exercises became common and even folks out in the country like the Weldons were expected to comply. They turned out their lights and pulled their window shades, (it was pitch black) till the "all clear" was announced on the radio. It was a national effort to be prepared for an enemy invasion should it occur. (Nancy's husband, Jim, as a teen, helped man the look-out tower behind Carson Long Military Institute in New Bloomfield. He was watching for and recording planes that would pass over New Bloomfield. He also picked milkweed pods so the silky fibers could be used as insulation in life preservers and to make parachute strings.) Weldon's did not get a television till Nancy was fifteen. It was during these dire times, that hobos roamed from town to town via the trains, and even appeared at the farmhouse backdoors way out in the country. Nancy's dad would allow the men to sleep in the barn for the night.

As was a tradition in most families, Nancy wore hand-me-downs from her cousins. Otherwise, her mother would fashion and sew dresses and skirts from the emptied sack-cloth feed bags, which generally had pretty colorful designs. The feed companies soon caught on and to entice the farmer's return business, they purchased the prettiest bags available. Not only that, but the farmer's wife was generally hoping for another similar bag to finish her sewing project. It was a common practice to use everything and not throw anything away. People made do with what they had and could afford.

Boots (Nancy would get boots from the Dellville General Store) and shoes were rationed during the war, but even before that time, children ran barefoot year-round. You owned one pair of shoes and Nancy so wanted a new pair of modern loafers. Her parents relented and Nancy would wear them with pride. However, Nancy and her brother liked to stand on the seats of the outhouse, reach out and grab the top of the door jamb and proceed to swing back and forth. Yep, you guessed correctly. One of Nancy's new leather loafers slipped off her foot and down through the outhouse hole. She retrieved her shoe and dutifully scrubbed it clean.

Winters when Nancy was growing up were much fiercer than today. Dellville Road would be covered in snow up to the top of the wooden fence rows that lined the edge of the fields. You would be snowbound from October through March, but that didn't stop anybody from going anywhere. Nancy's dad worked at Olmsted Air Force Base in Middletown, wiring planes. He and five other men from the area carpooled to work. When it was not his turn to drive, he would be picked up and dropped off at the start of the Dellville Road off Route 274. He walked from that intersection to their home in all kinds of weather. (The carpoolers were obviously a close-knit group and some of them helped out Russell when he needed to put a new roof on the barn.)

Nancy and Myran were bused to school, but when their road was not passable, they walked to the same intersection as their father to meet the bus, driven by Jim Rohrer. Sometimes a neighbor would hitch up the horse and sleigh and off they'd go for a fun ride to meet the bus. When they arrived home from school, Nancy was responsible for bringing in kindling and Myran to split wood to keep the cookstove fired. They were not allowed to play till homework and chores were done.

Nancy wore snow pants, a warm coat, gloves and boots to tramp around through the snow. She and Myran loved to play in the snow and would build snow forts, sometimes not in the best locations. The neighboring John Barrick and Paul Haas farms would be shut off from Dellville Road by the extremely dense snow. Since the roadway to their farms was impassable, it seemed a prime spot for Nancy and Myran to dig tunnels and carve out a fort. They would spend hours under the mighty drifts creating a secret world for themselves. Barrick's and Haas' would often park their vehicles elsewhere and walk just like Nancy's dad. They would walk right past the Weldon's following the deeply drifted roadway. One time, Paul Haas, as he walked up the road, suddenly disappeared. He had fallen through one of the snow tunnels. Nancy chuckles!

For the first (teacher was Jane Rohrer) eight grades, Nancy attended the Penn Township School then off to the Duncannon High School for nine through eleven and a half grades. She finished her senior year at the newly established Susquenita High School, which at first did not have a cafeteria. It was while she was in high school that Nancy participated in a "minstrel show." The yearly shows were held on the school stage on a Friday or Saturday night and drew large crowds. Nancy, along with school chums Mary Ann Pennell, Vonnie Doyle, Milly Jones and Carol Froggett, donned black faces and sang "Dem' Dry Bones." Nancy enjoyed performing and today takes in the New Bloomfield Lion's Club's productions, which were born out of Bloomfield's early minstrel shows.

Weldon 's attended the Dellville EUB Church with the Barrick, Ebersole and Bornman families. There were lots of children and her family would often load all the neighborhood children into their car and go to church and Sunday School. With all the children piled in the car everywhere, they never did a headcount, so it's no wonder Myran got left behind one Sunday.

Once they arrived home after church activities, Nancy's family would enjoy a large dinner. Afterwards, they would jump in the car and head off to their grandparent's homes for a visit. Yes, they went to both homes and it gave them an opportunity to see their visiting cousins. Nancy fondly recalls her mother's parents. Grandpa Reed was deaf, but could read lips, so the family learned to communicate by using sign language. Reeds had twelve girls and one boy, and one outhouse! Nancy flippantly remarks that it was said that Grandma Reed always had a child on the way, one nursing, one across her lap and one being rocked in the cradle. What a busy household, but not uncommon in those days. It was also not uncommon for families to lose babies and young children; such was the case of Nancy's parents.

Nancy's growing-up years reflected a time when folks interacted and would serenade "newlyweds." It was a time of joy in the bleakest of times, especially if belsnickelers showed up at your home during the Christmas season. Then Nancy and her family would try to guess who the mysterious guests were, while serving them hot cocoa and homemade sweets. The revelers would hand out candy to the children. Nancy remembers the freshly cut Christmas tree remaining bare until Christmas morning when she would awaken to it fully decorated with lots of icicles, her mother's favorite decoration. Nancy never knew ahead of time what she might receive as Christmas gifts, but recalls she and Myran shared a wagon one year. A large Christmas dinner was enjoyed and so were the oranges purchased by her father from the Orange Wagon in Harrisburg.

They were a musical family and would gather round to sing regardless of the time of year. They often visited friends on Friday or Saturday nights and have sing-a-longs accompanied by a piano. Saturday nights were also set aside to go to Duncannon for groceries at Rohrer's Grocery Store on High Street. Nancy would be given ten or twenty-five cents to walk down to Sam Michener's Ice Cream Shop on Market Street for an ice cream treat. She would sometimes babysit at her friend Peg Michener's (family owned the funeral home) house. If they decided they wanted some ice cream, they'd have to walk through the embalming room to the freezer.

Maybe that experience was a prelude to performing cosmetology on corpses for the Wayne Clemen's Funeral Home in New Bloomfield. Shortly after graduation in 1956, Nancy married James Tressler from New Bloomfield. One of the sidelines, Jim took on through the years was to transport the corpses and do the embalming for Clemens. He drove the hearse and did whatever was required. Tressler's were responsible for the funeral home when Clemens was on vacation. One time, they had seven bodies at once which kept them very busy. Nancy was responsible for answering the phone calls and delegating the responsibilities. She recalled a time when Jim was transporting a corpse from New York City when the brakes went out on the hearse. Now being a mechanic by trade, he knew what he could do to make it home safely. Tressler's son Randy would help Clemens to roundup the cards from the flowers and other items placed at the funeral home and cemetery. He would be dressed in a suit, tie and top coat to present the memorabilia to the bereaved families. When Clemens sold the funeral business to Bob Green, the Tresslers remained in their employment until it was sold to Doug Boyer and they decided to retire.

Jim also hauled "trotters" to the Poconos, New York and Maryland horse-racing tracks for James Stambaugh of Elliottsburg. Some of the horses were bred and raised in Perry County. Stambaugh's special breed did well on the dirt tracks.

As a teenager, Nancy worked alongside her mother at Snavely's Clothing Store on Market Street in Duncannon. She was responsible for keeping the store neat and clean, as well as waiting on the customers. When stock arrived, she would put the new clothes and shoes out for display. Nancy also joined a group of women from the Dellville area, who carpooled to Benvenue, the Island between the Juniata and Susquehanna Rivers, to clean seasonally rented cabins. Some of the women were Blanche Brandt and Bertha Barrick. Grace and Bob Hines, who owned the Benvenue Inn, learned of Nancy's work ethic through Catherine Stansfield, and they hired her to clean their home. Nancy said the house was very old and large. They asked her to stay on and help out with their newly adopted son, which she did. Nancy said the Pennsylvania State Police Barracks were located behind the Inn.

Like Nancy, James Tressler was born at home at 201 South Carlisle Street, New Bloomfield, to Ralph and Helen (Hubler) Tressler in 1934. His home was directly across from Tressler's Service Station, which his father founded, and Jim spent a life time in the grease and grime greeting customers as they pulled in for gas or a state inspection or a leaking hose. He, along with his sister Betty, attended various elementary classrooms situated throughout New Bloomfield's borough. He graduated from Perry Joint High School, just a stone's throw from his home. When he was just a youngster, Jim would take his toy cars along to the service station and pretend to fill them with gas. In those days, you didn't learn about the family business sitting listening to a class presentation like today. Jim practically lived in the gas station and definitely grew up with grease under his fingernails.

Ralph Tressler, Jim's father grew-up on the Tressler Farm outside of New Bloomfield and attended the Bloomfield Academy when it was in the Rhinesmith Hotel. He actually started his service station business on

High Street where the original fire house is located. Then, he moved his business to South Carlisle Street which later became a bowling alley, Perry Lanes. He was probably an enterprising man like Jim and felt the need to expand and have a place of his own, so he purchased an existing property further down on South Carlisle Street, which had been a cobbler's repair shop. When his neighbor indicated he would like to be able to sit on his front porch and see down the street, Ralph built his new garage further back from the highway by 1927.

Nancy recalls Jim telling her his Grandfather Tressler worked at Hampton, Seeds and Snyder Feed Mill beside the old railroad station directly across the street from the new garage. His mother would take the train from Elliottsburg to come and visit his dad in Bloomfield before they were wed.

Nancy and Jim took up housekeeping in a wing of the Tressler House on Bloomfield's West Main Street. At the time Jim was already working for his father in the garage earning twenty-five dollars a week. Their rent was twenty-five dollars a month. Nancy would go to the store with five dollars to purchase just what they needed like cleaning supplies and toilet paper. Nancy's parents maintained a large garden and that kept them in vegetables. It wasn't till Nancy was pregnant with their son, Randy, that Ralph decided Jim needed more income to support his family. His salary was boosted to forty-five dollars a week.

Jim and Nancy decided to buy his grandfather's house on South Carlisle Street for six-thousand dollars in 1957 and Nancy remained since. The property (house and fourteen acres) was established in 1865. The original four-room log house, was expanded by his grandfather, but still did not have sufficient electricity, especially wall outlets or sockets throughout. Nancy helped her dad to rewire the entire house.

When Ralph died in 1964, Jim took over Tressler's Service Station till he retired in 2010. Grandson Seth Tressler, a United States Marine, had just returned from Iraq and volunteered to help out which lead to him taking over the business. The original gas station was expanded by Jim to create a larger area where cars and trucks could be better serviced. By the time Jim took over, R. E. Smith of Newport was supplying gas under Esso then Exxon. Standard Oil gas was first pumped at the station along with a free oil check, windshield wash and a friendly greeting.

Nancy would often go to the garage to help pump gas while Jim worked on vehicles. She would take her children, and her grandchildren which she babysat, along to the garage to help out where needed. Everybody in the Tressler family regardless if they were a spouse or grandchild played a huge part in seeing that the customers were well taken care of. Of course, the children really enjoyed the treats offered at the station, and would sit behind the desk enjoying their lunch with Jim. Nancy would pump gas and take care of the other courtesies, so Jim could have some fun family time during his lunch break.

Son Randy (daughter-in-law Sherry Dum), daughter Judy (son-in-law Donnie Ricker) and daughter Tracey, all helped out and played important roles in the day-to-day operations of Tressler's Service Station. Randy and son, Chad also worked full-time at the garage for awhile. All the grandchildren, (Chad, Kevin, Seth, DJ, Derek and Danielle) at one time or another, had their fingers in the grease helping out their grandpap.

Nancy can remember when bottles of Coke were kept in a cooler full of cold water at the gas station. When the modern automatic machines were installed, it enticed thieves to break into them for the cash. Nevin Stroup from Millerstown delivered individually packaged pies, cakes and chips, to be sold alongside prepared sandwiches, Rakestraw's and Hall's Dairy Ice Cream, and an assortment of penny candies and candy bars. It was a dream come true for any child, who also enjoyed greeting the customers and filling their tanks, once they were deemed old enough.

It was the snacks, especially the penny candy selection, and the benches out front that drew customers to sit and chat awhile. Through the years, many adults returned to the station with their children, so they could experience the same friendly service and candy selection. But it was the local loafers, like Ralph Reisinger; Bussy, Fred, Eric and Keith Thebes; Eugene and Gary Eby; Paul and Leroy Comp; Jimmy Weldon and the Dum's, who made for a livelier day.

Eric Thebes would bring his nasty dog Jackson along with him to the garage and treat him to ice cream or cakes. The dog always remained in the truck and would not allow anybody to come near. One summer evening after a thunderstorm, Jim went to do "the stick test," to determine the amount of gasoline left in his gas holding tanks, and saw Jackson coming down the street. Jim was able to entice Jackson to crawl into his truck and he promptly took him home. The "stick gas" routine was nightly, so Tresslers could judge the amount of gas that needed to be replaced. Nancy remarks that the gasoline delivery companies became so strict that they had to leave a check to prepay for any deliveries.

Jim allowed customers to run a monthly tab. When Seth was young and pumping gas one day, he filled the tank and the customer drove off without saying a word or paying. He ran to his grandfather and told him, "Some Chinese dude just pulled in and didn't pay for his gas". Turns out, it was the local pediatrician, Doctor Chang, who had an account. However, there were two unknown shysters, who kept Jim occupied at the pumps on a summer day when all the garage doors were open, while the other robbed the cash register and the safe.

Then there was the call from Colonel Carson "Spike" Holman telling Jim he discovered several of his Carson Long Military Institute cadets in the wooded hills behind the school, with garbage bags filled with candy, tobacco and cigarettes from Tressler's Service Station. The cadets had broken out a window on the front door and were proceeding to grab as much as they could before Tressler's German Shepherd broke through the door separating the rooms. There was a trail of cigarettes leading from the front door as they made their mad dash.

There were years, when the gas shortages caused a lot of stress, and Tresslers actually had no gas. When a delivery did arrive, Nancy and Jim pumped gas till they ran out totally, and cars still lined the streets.

When Nancy was first married and wasn't helping out at the service station, she enjoyed walking through Bloomfield and remembers the businesses that existed in the mid 1950s.

Starting South Carlisle Street to Main Street on west side of street:
- Clyde Stroup's Gulf Gas Station which became Swenson's
- a mill to Tressler's Service Station to Cappy's Barbershop
- Meredith's Butcher Shop
- Restaurant run by Martha Roof and then Del Spease Weller - which would become the Perry County Sesquicentennial Headquarters where dresses, tickets for events, souvenirs could be purchased
- Margaret Bolze from Landisburg had a furniture store.

- 5&10 Store which stocked a bit of everything from soup to nuts to sewing needs.
- Dr. Book's Drugstore with deli and soda fountain

Starting South Carlisle Street to Main Street on east side of street:
- Hair Brother's and Myer's Store which carried groceries on the lower level and appliances, which they also repaired, on the upper level along with all sorts of hardware
- DWM Ford Dealership and Garage – Dyson, Weldon and McBride
- Perry Lanes Bowling Alley operated by the Raffenspergers
- Gerald Askins Plumbing and Electric to Dr. Chang, pediatrician
- Commonwealth National Bank

Starting on East McClure Street to shortcut road:
- on the right was Perry Joint High School which became Bloomfield's Borough Building housing the Post Office
- on the left across from the school was Gantt's Insurance Agency

Starting on West McClure Street towards South Church Street:
- Perry County Jail to Catholic Church to Bell Telephone Office Building

Starting on West Main Street on the south side of street:
- Dr. Book's Drugstore to Stoop's Barbershop
- Carmichael's Store (now Perry County Chamber of Commerce)
- Barton's Store (now Perry County Cafe)
- Movie theatre (Henry's Cobbler Shop)
- A & P Store to Harper's Grocery Store to the Town Well
- The Tressler House (Frank Tressler's Law Office)
- Hench & Lebo's Butcher shop (now Fersters) to Clemen's Funeral Home
- Norm Black's Garage (now Uni-Mart and the Central Perry Community Center)
- Frownfelter's Greenhouse
- Pennsylvania State Highway Department to Rice's Memorials

Starting on West Main on the north side of street:
- Rhinesmith Hotel to Bender's Restaurant (now Morrison's Law Office)
- Clouser's Hardware to Post Office to Dr. Belmont to Methodist Church

Starting East Main Street on north side of street:
Courthouse to Walter Rice's Law Office to Harry Kreitzer Law Office to Robb's Insurance Agency

Starting on East Main Street on south side of street:
- Commonwealth Bank to an Attorney to Joe Darlington timber sales
- Keller's Farm Equipment

Starting at North Church Street west side of street:
- Baker's Sign Shop
- East side of street was The Perry County Times Office

Starting at North Carlisle Street on east side of street:
- Eagle Nook Building which was a Carson Long Military Institute dormitory
- across the street behind Rhinesmith Hotel was Meredith's Butcher Shop
- the old Presbyterian Church to Doctor Rynkovitz, veterinarian
- entrance to Carson Long Military Institute

Nancy would like to "dedicate this story to my children, grandchildren and great-grandchildren. Many thanks for your help and love through my lifetime."

"All In A Day Well Spent"

FISHING, HUNTING, PRINTING, VOLUNTEERING

Storyteller Charles E. Magee
Recorded by Debra Kay Noye

At three months of age, Charles "Charlie" Magee arrived in Duncannon wrapped in a blanket in a clothes basket. His parents, Albert (b.1909) and Helen "Molly" (b.1908) Magee, first rented an apartment from Clyde Black, who had a barbershop in town. They soon purchased a house once owned by the railroad and moved it to the Dunkle property about two-hundred yards from Gamber's Corner on Route 274. Albert, who had learned the printing trade, opened a print shop beyond the house. The print shop is now gone.

The closest neighbor, Paul Woods, lived with his family on a farm at the bottom of the hill, across from the entrance to the Dellville Road. Woods had a son and two daughters, whom Charlie played with while visiting the farm. He was always warned to stay away from their two large horses. But like most children, Charlie couldn't resist. He went up to the horse, which stepped onto Charlie's foot. Everybody was afraid that his foot was badly hurt, but he was standing on very muddy ground and went totally unscathed. Now he did listen and stayed away from Wood's very mean bull!

One of Charlie's playmates, when he was in the first and second grades, was Ward Rice Jr., who'd come by the house and they'd play outside. One of their favorite spots was the woodpile. One time, Charlie's mom began to wonder where all the crackers were going, so she went to investigate. She discovered Charlie and Ward munching on crackers covered by worms or grubs. They were moving the piles of wood around to find worms, which "they thought were quite good." Must have been a new Duncannon delicacy.

He played cards with his friend Mike Raub and along with his older brother, Nevin and others played pick-up baseball games on Carver's Hill. One of his fondest memories was when little league baseball was started in the area. Nevin was an excellent first baseman and he was on the team that played in the first Little League World Series in Williamsport, Pennsylvania in 1947.

In the winter, he put his Lightning Guider sled to use flying down over the hills near his home, but he didn't like having to climb back up for another sled ride.

Magee's always had a large garden and Charlie recalls picking fuzzy yellow potato bugs. His father raised a few hogs which they butchered with the help of Paul Woods. Woods seemed to be the go-to-guy when local families butchered. Charlie recalls having to get up very early in the morning to get the fires going to heat water in the large iron kettles and then stirring the kettles once they were filled with meat and organs from the pigs. Scrapple required the most stirring, so it did not scorch on the bottom of the kettles.

Charlie had two beagles, King and Chief, that were registered with the American Kennel Club Association. He trained them to hunt rabbits, grouse and ring-neck pheasants in the hollow behind his home. His family ate all kinds of wild game. Charlie's mom was known for her squirrel pot pie, which she traditionally made every Thanksgiving. Deer were plentiful and Charlie's family used every bit of the animal.

Charlie says that his wife's grandfather Berrier was the first Game Warden in Pennsylvania. Her grandmother Berrier helped to raise the first ring-neck pheasants once they were shipped in from the Orient to New York's harbor. She raised them right along with her chickens, who became perturbed when the pheasants started to fly.

Charlie's mom bought him new clothes to wear to school, including pants. When he wore the pants to school, he was agitated because they were so scratchy and made him itchy. His teacher became concerned and sent him to the school nurse, who asked him to drop his trousers. When he did, his legs were covered in red blotches. That's when it was determined, Charlie was allergic to wool!

It's a wonder, Charlie's mom didn't burn the house down, with her winter "warming logs". Because they didn't have heat in the upstairs during the harsh winter months, Molly would warm wooden logs by the coal furnace, wrap them in newspaper and tuck into the bottom of Charlie and his brother Nevin's beds. It kept them toasty warm for a bit. But it didn't help when they had to dash to the outhouse.

Charlie was considered "an angel" while he attended the Duncannon High School. So, he was called upon to help out a lot with a variety of things. However, Charlie's friend, Denny Richards, who lived across the railroad tracks in the Cove behind the current day Sheetz, brought a skunk bladder to school one day. Before classes started, the boys put the skunk bladder on top of a heating register in the school auditorium. Well, it started to smell and nobody could determine where the smell was coming from. Charlie was in English class when L. W. Bell, the school principal, came into the classroom and asked for Charlie to be dismissed, so he could help to hunt down the mysterious smell. Being the "just wonderful" student that he was, Charlie obliged and walked innocently throughout the school with the principal. After a while, he pretended to find the skunk bladder and mystery was solved. Charlie notes that animal hides were worth a lot of money back in his youth and many men trapped the creeks. Richards was also an avid coon hunter, who went out nightly.

Having a father as a printer had its advantages, when Charlie was in Penn Township School. Paul Hurley became the Penn Township School Principal and he had a keen interest in learning about printing. He would get Charlie out of class to give in-class instruction to himself and several others. The "hobby" started to take Charlie away from his classroom enough so that his teachers complained. Hurley asked if there was a problem with Charlie's grades. Charlie's grades were fine. Point made! (Paul Hurley became the first principal at the newly established West Perry School system and he lived across the road from the high school. Hurley's were active in Tressler Memorial Lutheran Church in Loysville.)

According to Charlie, Paul Hurley was the best fly fisherman he ever knew and he taught Charlie a lot. Come the opening day of trout fishing season, April 15th, he and Charlie would skip school and go fishing. Bob Fox, from Duncannon, the school janitor, would tell Charlie he couldn't fib on his report card about being out fishing on the very first day. Hurley's wife, Gina, also liked to fish and would pack a lunch for them and tag along. Charlie liked to watch Hurley skillfully launch a line smoothly under a tree stretched out over the creek. It was a talent he envied.

They were fishing for Brook, Rainbow and Brown trout, from the Little Juniata Creek and Shermans Creek. Charlie would walk from his house across the fields behind Mutzabaugh's now Karn's Grocery Store out across the mountain to the former YMCA, to fish in Shermans Creek. He also walked to "Goose Pond," behind the former Herm Shearer Gas Station now Maguire's Garage, to fish near the mouth of Shermans Creek at the Susquehanna River. If he was bass fishing, he would take a boat out onto the Juniata and Susquehanna rivers from Benvenue on the Island.

The legal-size, eight-to-ten-inch trout were from state run fish hatcheries and stocked by the local fish warden and members of sportsmen's clubs or other volunteers. Once in the streams, they were fair game. Today most of the stocked fish average twelve to fourteen inches and fishing is prohibited for several days afterward, because fishermen became greedy. When Charlie fished, his catch ended up on the dinner table, after he cleaned them for his mother. The limit of fish per day per fisherman was ten.

Charlie says if you look real close rounding the mountain at the start of the stone wall towards Marysville, one can still see the "fish wall" in the Susquehanna River. It was an area of the river that formed a "v" with the rocks, enabling local fisherman to easily trap fish in their nets. Generally prohibited, this method was common during the Depression and the war years. Fishing meant food on the tables of many homes when meat was rationed and scarce, and jobs were hard to find. Charlie says Paul Woods had a "fish wall net" hanging in a shed.

The first Fish Warden was Charlie Long from East Waterford and Charlie, at the age of eighteen, got to know him very well. Being a fishing enthusiast, Charlie would help the warden stock fish with his old green military jeep. Charlie's "pride and joy" still had the gun mounts with a long windshield that folded down over the hood. You could be sure he also had his glove compartment stocked with snacks for all his fishing and hunting adventures.

Now Charlie even took Harriet Berrier, of Duncannon, who became his wife, for dates in his authentic military jeep. But the day he stopped in at Bender's Restaurant on New Bloomfield's square, turned out to be a hair-raising tale. As the story goes, Sam and Ed Bender, owners of the restaurant were "tried and true" bachelor brothers, who were obviously used to doing things their way. Their so-called eating establishment served ice cream, soda and sold cigars. If a patron ordered a sandwich by chance, they rushed across the street to the A&P Store and purchased what was needed to put a sandwich in front of the customer. It certainly would've cut down on the costs of housing inventory. On this particular day, Charlie was kind enough to hand over the keys to his jeep to Sam. As Charlie was drinking coffee with some fellow patrons, there arose such whooping and hollering on the street, that they went to investigate. John Brunner of New Bloomfield, was furiously driving Charlie's jeep through New Bloomfield's main streets. Sam was standing up in the jeep and wildly shouting as he waved Charlie's machete through the air. It was not a conquering moment!

Now the brothers also tried to pull a fast one, when they claimed to have hooked an exceptionally large fish out of the Juniata River, which they had frozen as proof. Their story reached the ears of a local man associated with a Harrisburg newspaper. The story was published along with a picture which drew a lot of attention. When the Fish Commission decided to check out their story, it was discovered to be none other than a Canadian Lake Trout they caught while on a fishing trip. Like their sandwiches, their story was full of bologna!

When Charlie was in high school and old enough to drive, he became the caretaker for his grandfather, Charles Sumner Magee, who had cancer. After school he would drive his jeep to their home on Jericho Road and spend the night helping his grandmother, Myrtle Catherine Magee. (His grandfather had a half-brother who was killed in the Civil War in 1865.) If she needed to run an errand to town, she refused to ride in Charlie's Jeep, so he drove their 1952 Chevy. Charlie finally convinced her to climb into the Jeep using a step-stool and she was "happy as a lark."

Charlie's dad, Albert, established Magee Brother's Printing in the shop beyond their house. He did all kinds of printing, such as business cards, programs, church bulletins, flyers and booklets. He used a letter press which was a hot type or lino type whereby he had to hand-set each character to be locked into the chassis of the press. It was a tedious job that required perfection. Al, as he was known, printed the school yearbooks and the Carson Long Military Institute's school newspaper. He also did printing for the Duncannon Novelty Works and for the Aldon Company products produced during WW ll.

Charlie learned the printing business from his father, especially during the summers. His brother, Nevin had started to work for Triangle Press in Harrisburg. Triangle had a need for somebody to learn how to run their Heidelberg Press, which was used for business cards and envelopes. They offered Charlie the position. Then they asked him to learn on the Miehl Vertical V50 Press, which produced newspapers, programs, etc. Triangle liked the quality work produced by Charlie, so they started him off "press-printing" and the ink caused Charlie to break out in hives on his arms. When he went to the doctor, he was told the ink was toxic waste, which caused health concerns. He continued to help with his dad's printing business, while he became the administrative assistant to Pennsylvania State Representative Fred C. Noye, of Duncannon.

Always a jokester of sorts, Charlie printed a special church bulletin for his fishing buddy, Reverend Henry Raub of the United Church of Christ on Second Street in Harrisburg. They would trout fish Laurel Run around Loysville. In one of the church bulletins, Charlie printed under the date "First Sunday after trout fishing." He made sure that bulletin was first on the stack, because Henry always read the top bulletin for accuracy. When he saw it, Henry thought it was very funny!

The Roseglen Methodist Church had a "Boy's Club," where local youth met once a week with Harry Billet for outings, similar to the Boy Scouts. They also played baseball. It was this group that inspired the Duncannon YMCA on the Paul Haas farm along Shermans Creek towards Dellville. Charlie served for many years on the board of directors, as well as the chairman. The group built the swimming pool and developed the grounds which allowed camping. Shirley Leedy and Peg Martz, local ladies, organized and instructed the swimming classes. Betsy Young Strayer also became an instructor in later years.

Charlie declares if "Doc" Morrissey, Duncannon's druggist on the town square, hadn't pulled out his wallet and handed the initial group of YMCA organizers a wad of cash, the pool would've been scraped, because there were not funds to pay the bills. Once the group got on its feet, memberships sustained it along with rental fees.

Charlie gives credit to Lester Nace of Duncannon, for helping with all kinds of tidying-up work around the grounds from mowing to snow shoveling. Bob Freeman helps to oversee the pool refreshment stand. The organization became the Perry County Recreation Association and Bill Stone is the current president. They permit swimming, camping, group functions and family reunions today. It is one of Perry County's hidden gems.

The Duncannon Sportsmen's Club is another organization that Charlie has a very long association. The sportsmen's group met all over in past years in churches, school auditoriums, the Martin Building behind the original Duncannon Firehouse and finally to their clubhouse and grounds off Montebello Farm Road. Carl Fox of Duncannon, has served as president for fifty years. Harlow Thompson of New Buffalo was a member of the Duncannon Sportsmen's and when in his eighties took a hunter safety course along with Charlie's son, Todd. Todd reported he and Harlow had the only perfect papers in the class!

Charlie was inducted into the Hall of Fame of the Pennsylvania Federation of Sportsmen's Clubs for his service and civic commitment to furthering outdoor education and activities in his community and beyond. Charlie was honored for over sixty years of documented sportsmen's activities, including hunter safety classes. His love of hunting and fishing found him purchasing a cabin in Potter County, which he still enjoys today. He has also served sixty years on the Boy Scout committee.

His father, Albert was known as "Mr. Nut of Perry County!" Charlie's backyard was a haven for Al's passion for growing and cultivating nut trees. His specialty was black walnut trees and he grafted trees developing an Elmer Myers Black Walnut, which when cracked open the nut was perfectly split in half revealing whole nut pieces. There were also a lot of edible chestnut trees on their property. Al exhibited nuts at the Perry County Fair and gave many presentations about his hobby to many groups including his home Grange Shermanata, in which he was very active, and the Perry County Pomona Grange.

He was even asked to consult about trees, especially on the New Bloomfield square, after some evil-minded prankster stripped the bark off them. He mended one particular tree, bringing it back to health. Harriet says, Albert was full of wisdom and his favorite saying was, "never put off till tomorrow, what you can get somebody else to do today!"

Charlie has been blessed to be able to pursue his love for the outdoors, and to preserve them for future generations, He became a very passionate civic-minded individual, who has left many a footprint in the Perry County wilds.

My Experiences
IN THE PERRY COUNTY SHERIFF'S OFFICE AND PRISON
Storyteller Marlin C. Raffensperger

My wife Kaye and I met while we were students at Lycoming College. After college, we were married in June of 1958 at her home church in Wilmington, Delaware. We then established our home in New Bloomfield and over the next few years become the parents of two boys, Brian and Greg. I worked in the family businesses, New Bloomfield Auto Company and later Perry Lanes, which was a bowling alley.

It was in December of 1965 that I was approached by a gentleman named William D. Smith who had been recently (November 1965) elected to the office of Sheriff of Perry County. He was to begin his four-year term of office in January 1966. He met with me in my parent's home across the street from the jail, to ask me to go to work for him. I was very appreciative of his intent, but I told him that I was not interested in that type of work and I was very happy being involved in the family business. He told me that he was aware that I had a degree in Business Administration. He just wanted me to run his office. I told him I would need some time to think it over.

Living near the jail as I was growing up, I was certainly aware of some of the responsibilities of the Sheriff's Office. I was not excited about working there. However, after prayer-filled discussions with my wife and family, I decided to take the job.

The beginning of 1966, Sheriff Smith and I became employees of the County of Perry. I do not remember too much about the early months of working there, but I do remember what happened the following year. Sheriff Smith began having health problems which lead to his inability to perform his duty and ultimately resulted in his passing in the summer of 1967. I was then "between a rock and a hard place." Long story short, I received Governor Raymond Shafer's appointment on December 13th, 1967 and was sworn in as Sheriff of Perry County. In the years that followed I become active in the Pennsylvania Sheriff's Association and in the years 1985-1986 become President.

Escapes
You have to understand that in the early years, the Perry County Prison was not a secure facility. We op-

erated basically the same as the sheriffs before us. Because of the lack of manpower and I assume funding, there was no one on duty at night after the inmates were locked up. There was an occasional escape. When someone escapes from custody, it's a good bet they will head for home. In one particular case, another officer and myself sat in the kitchen of the escapee's mother, who of course had no knowledge of her son's whereabouts. After the individual was taken into custody, we learned that he had been hiding on the rafters above the kitchen the whole time we interviewed his mother.

Attempted Escape
The most memorable event that happened while my family was living at the jail, was the night I went back into the cell block to secure the inmates in their cells. As I entered the cell block, I was hit on the head with a wooden scrub brush by one of the inmates. I went down on my knees but not out, as he had planned. I was able to contain the inmate with the help of my wife who was holding a loaded 9mm handgun pointed at us through the "pie hole." After the inmate was locked in his cell, I sat down and listened to what he and the other inmates had to say about the incident. The comments and language used cannot be properly printed here.

Nighttime Visitors
The house part of the building attached to the jail turned out to be a very comfortable home for my family and I for a number of years. One problem we did have however, was the occasional visit by a bat. The visits were usually at night, which sometimes consisted of scratching in the walls. They also made a physical appearance, specifically the bedroom. On these occasions, it would be necessary to call the "Bat Patrol." I would get fully dressed, don my football helmet, grab my trusty tennis racket and take my position at the top of the open stairway, where I would eventually make the kill. I don't remember whether my tennis talents at those times were considered offense or defense. The deceased would then be placed in the freezer for a later trip to the lab at Summerdale for rabies testing.

Dog
Those of us who have worked in the criminal justice system specifically dealing with the prison population, do not make many friends. That was certainly the case in the following incident. Some of you may remember the two-story white barn that sat on the north-west corner of the jail lot. It also served as the home for a German Shepherd, Brutus, which belonged to me. The dog, by his barking, would leave whoever was on duty know when someone was at the back or side of the jail. It was told to me in confidence by another inmate that an inmate made a threat that when he got out of here, he was going to kill that SOB, meaning the dog. Within ten days to two weeks after his release, Brutus was dead. If the person who is responsible for killing my dog is still around to read this, please give me a call and we will sit down and have tea.

Prison Personnel
I walked out to the prison office for the 11 p.m. - 7 a.m. shift change. Deputy Frownfelter was going off duty and an unnamed correction officer was coming on duty. When I went into the office, I found the correction officer and his two young children with him. Upon asking "what was going on" he said he was going to keep his kids with him for the shift. I advised him this was not a day-care center and sent him home. I asked Deputy Frownfelter if he would work a double shift to which he agreed.

Bloomfield Pharmacy Break-in
Over a period of several years, in the 1970s if I remember correctly, there were numerous break-ins at the

Bloomfield Pharmacy. So frequently were the occurrences that at one point, the owner gave a building key to Sergeant Stanley Krammes of the Pennsylvania State Police.

One of those break-ins was reported to me early one morning by my nephew, Steve Brought, who noticed the front door of the building was damaged. I went to the pharmacy, taking the on-duty deputy with me. I posted the deputy at the walkway between the pharmacy and the barber shop to guard the pharmacy's back door. I proceeded to the front and entered through the broken door. While searching the building, I found a perpetrator hiding in the basement. I placed him under arrest and put him in Perry County Prison until arraignment the following day before District Justice Jane Dyer.

For a note of humor: While guarding the rear door a huge chunk of ice broke loose from the roof of the barber shop and hit Deputy Frownfelter on the top of his head. He thought he was assaulted by the perpetrator.

You and I will all be a part of the history of Perry County and I appreciate the opportunity to share.

They Came To Play

A REMEMBRANCE OF DUNCANNON SANDLOT BASEBALL 1950s – 1960s

Storytellers Roger Hickoff and Myron Rohrer
Recorded by Fred C. Noye

After World War II young men returning to Duncannon found there was not a sandlot baseball team for them to join. In 1950 a group of fellows set out to form a team and received a sponsorship from the Duncannon VFW Post.

They were able to join the Dauphin League and it thus became known as the Dauphin – Perry League. They played teams from Dauphin, Halifax, Millersburg, Dalmatia, Herndon, Williamstown, Lykens, Elizabethville and Tower City. In fact, some of the Duncannon players played for the Dauphin team before the Duncannon team was formed.

Myron Rohrer was one of those men that played against his old teammates and he remembers meeting a "friend" of his near home plate. Myron was a catcher and a very good one. His Dauphin "friend" was on second base and the next batter got a hit. The ball was thrown to home plate and Myron had it before the runner rounded third base, but he kept on coming at Myron full speed with arms up. He sent Myron flying, actually knocking him out. Nothing like old friends!

The 1952 Duncannon team was a good team and they won the league championship.

After 1952, the team was on their own to raise the money for the season. They relied on small donations and collections from the games. Mayor Franklin Cook, "Cookie," was responsible for passing the hat among the fans at each home game. The "Mayor" was an imposing figure and he always had a big cigar in his mouth. He was usually able to "convince" fans to throw in a quarter or a half and an occasional dollar. After a few years, the ball club decided to have their own little carnival on Broadway Street in front of the old high school. Locals came out in full support for the food and games. They offered bingo, a watermelon wheel, a cake wheel, a penny pitch and a dunk tank. Of course, food was the primary draw. This is when Duncannon residents got a taste of Roger Hickoff's homemade ice cream and to this day it is highly sought after. That is what really brought the crowd. Local businessman and third baseman, Max Cooper, was the treasurer for the team.

Looking back from today, it seems it was inexpensive to field a team, but when you consider prices in the early 1950s, it was a challenge. You had to raise money for uniforms, bats, balls and catcher's equipment. And of course, you had to pay the umpires. In those days, bats were twenty-four dollars a dozen. Balls were twenty dollars a dozen. You had to pay both umpires five dollars a game, which later on went to ten dollars a game.

In 1953, Duncannon joined the Perry-Juniata league. The teams that they played in the P-J League were Newport, New Bloomfield, Millerstown, Loysville, Blain, Ickesburg, Port Royal, Thompsontown, and Mifflintown. During those years, Blain, Loysville and Newport were the dominant teams. There was real talent in the P-J League and it offered the fans good baseball. Of course, these young men played with lots of passion and there were numerous local rivalries.

In 1955, the Duncannon team decided to move to the West Shore Twilight League. The league was made up of teams from the Enola, Mt. Holly, Mechanicsburg, Dillsburg, New Cumberland, Lemoyne, New Kingston, Lisburn, West Fairview and the Army Depot in New Cumberland.

In the early years, Mt. Holly dominated as the team to beat. New Cumberland and Mechanicsburg were always a challenge, but the boys from Duncannon were in the thick of the race more years than not. In one five-year period (1956-1961), someone checked records and found Mt. Holly had a 148-67 record and Duncannon had a record of 147-68.

All in all, Duncannon played some of their best baseball as a member of the West Shore League. They won three regular-season championships and one playoff championship. In 1962, they won both the regular season and playoff championships.

Here is a review of some of the names of people who were part of Duncannon's baseball history during this time.

The first manager was Ray Russell who managed from 1950-1952. He was followed by "Bitty" Liddick from 1953-1955. Myron Rohrer 1956-1958. And Bernie Britcher until the mid 1960s.

Here are other names listed by the positions they played: (Some filled in wherever needed)

FIRST BASE: Warren Barton, Nevin Magee and James Zeiders

SECOND BASE: Vance Bolan and Sid Klinepeter

SHORTSTOP: Max Cooper, Sid Klinepeter and Vance Bolan

THIRD BASE: Max Cooper and Neil Hickoff

CATCHER: Myron Rohrer, Tom Bornman, Roger Hickoff and Earl Renshaw

OUTFIELD: Roger Hickoff, Ken Bornman, Bernie Britcher, Mel Wilt, George "Shake" Peterman and Earl Renshaw

PITCHERS: Frank Bornman, Percy Rodemaker, John Nearhood, Jim Nearhood, Paul Cooper, Abe Leiter, Don Rowe, Norm Rowe, Don Harbold and Myran "Mike" Weldon

Local resident, Tommy Beale, looked after the scoreboard. He served as the team's unofficial mascot. (Tommy was handicapped, but the team members looked after him and gave him odd jobs. They would even take him with them to away games.) Ernie Nearhood, the father of two members of the team, kept the scorebook.

Duncannon didn't always have a lot of extra players at each game. Sometimes their bench wasn't very deep (Roger Hickoff only remembered one forfeit in all the years that he played). Work schedules sometimes interfered with weekday evening games, so players had to be flexible and play wherever needed.

One evening Duncannon had a game at Lemoyne and they only had nine players and none of the regular pitchers could make it. Roger agreed to pitch, although he had only pitched on a few rare occasions. There was one slight problem. Roger's index finger on his pitching hand was broken. So, he pitched with his other three fingers on his right hand. The short version is that Duncannon won the game with Roger as the winning pitcher.

Baseball was king in the 1950s and 1960s. Everyone followed their local team with pride and passion. If they could not attend the game, they eagerly looked for the results and box scores in the local Harrisburg papers and the Perry County papers. Every game was not only played for fun, but the competition was intense. Many games had some memorable events that fans and players talked about for years. Sometimes those events got loud and rowdy. More than one game included a scuffle when tempers would flare.

One game that comes to mind was with Enola at Duncannon. There was no love lost between the two teams, but this one went to a new level. The Enola bench was really giving it to Myron Rohrer, Duncannon's catcher. He finally had enough and turned faking a throw into the dugout. The Enola bench scattered thinking the ball was coming. When they realized what happened, several players rushed towards Myron and the first one who attacked him was knocked out cold. The manager then came charging out and Abe Leiter threw a body block and sent him flying.

In those days batters did not wear helmets and there were a few scary moments when batters got hit by a pitch. Roger was one victim that got beaned in his first year playing. But he was back to play in the next game.

When an umpire was assigned to do a Duncannon game, they knew they had better be on their toes. The team was known for giving the umps a hard time, especially Rohrer, Britcher and Hickoff. They were very good at getting into the umps' heads and into the heads of some of the opposing players. Anything to gain a psychological advantage and it was amazing how well Roger could see from left field, much better than those umpires in the infield. That trio had their share of run-ins with umpires over the years and their share of early exits from games. When things got heated, Max Cooper was the peacemaker.

It is ironic that both Roger and Bernie became umpires when their playing days were over.

There was one umpire that everyone respected. Tony Kinn umpired many games for many years. He was a handicapped individual who had to call balls and strikes on one knee. He was always behind the plate, because he could not move quickly in the infield. When he missed a call and if confronted, he would admit he missed it. They respected that and usually did not give him a hard time. Although sometimes they couldn't help giving him a good-natured ribbing.

There were outstanding players playing sandlot ball in the West Shore League. Some names that came to mind were Bob Morehead from Lemoyne (who went on to pitch for the New York Mets); Paul Davies and Jay Evans played for Dillsburg; Bill Reichenbaugh of Mechanicsburg (who at ninety years of age is still managing the team); Ed Carl of New Cumberland and Perry Countians, Max Mohler and Ray Dillman who played with Enola.

It was thought that Jay Evans was probably the fastest man in the league. During one game he tried to steal second and Myron threw him out. He never tried to run on Myron again.

In talking about all the players, both Roger and Myron agreed, without hesitation on who the best ballplayers were that they ever played against. Without a doubt it was Max Mohler of Newport and Ray Dillman of New Bloomfield. They faced them in the Perry-Juniata League and in the West Shore Twilight League, when both players went to Enola to play. Both men had tremendous power and displayed it on a regular basis. There wasn't a window safe in the old Enola School building which was in right field. Another name they mentioned was Ken Holtzapple, who had a long career with Newport.

Duncannon had a lot of good hitters, but they were not power hitters. Cooper and Hickoff were free swingers. They did not take many pitches. One year they made a gentlemen's wager who would strike out the least. Hickoff struck out only three times, but Cooper did not strike out at all. Then there was Warren Barton. He probably knew the strike zone better than anybody and probably led the league in walks. But their real strength was their long list of pitchers.

The team played their home games on what is now known as Cooper Field. It sits above the town cemetery. It was a very hard shale surface and required regular maintenance. Besides being the left-fielder, Roger was also the self-appointed groundskeeper. You would often find him in his spare time raking the field of stones. He would also lime the field for foul lines and batter boxes for each home game. In later years, they played their games on the high school field in the Cove. That field was much better and had a grass infield as opposed to the dirt infield on the hill in Duncannon.

The left field area of the old ball field was very short and ended at the edge of several neighbor's backyards. One of those neighbors was the retired principal of the local high school, Wheeler Bell. He did not appreciate the balls flying into his garden and kept anyone from retrieving the balls that were hit there. So, the players decided to erect a fence. It was built quite high in an attempt to keep the neighbors happy and to save balls.

There were woods down the right field line, behind home plate and down the left field. A lot of foul balls were hit there so the team decided to pay ten cents to the youngsters that went in to retrieve them. The woods were full of bushes with thorns and there was a lot of poison ivy. It was a tough way to earn ten cents.

Both Myron and Roger agreed that some of the best memories were the years they won the championships. One of the most memorable games was at New Cumberland when they were playing for the league title. Duncannon came to bat in the last inning trailing New Cumberland by three runs. Vance Bolan came to bat with the bases loaded with two out. Vance was a good hitter, but not a power hitter. Then the unbelievable happened and he hit a grand-slam home run to win the championship for Duncannon.

Happy memories and a few scary ones. At the Duncannon field there was a high shale bank behind the backstop. You could drive your car in along the left field line and park on the hill behind the backstop. Many people would sit in their cars or on chairs high above the field to watch the game. One evening an unoccupied car drifted forward, down over the bank and passed through the opening between the backstop and the Duncannon players bench onto the field. It just missed striking a few of the players. Luckily no one was injured.

There was a set of bleachers that sat just beyond the Duncannon players' bench. In another scary moment a batter hit a "screaming" liner off the end of his bat right at the bleachers, striking the father of one of the players on the side of his head. It knocked him out and the ambulance had to be called. Fortunately, there was no permanent injury to the man.

For several years the team would travel on a weekend to Lewisburg to the Federal Penitentiary to play games with the inmates. They found it amusing that the nonplaying inmates would cheer for the Duncannon team against their fellow roommates.

Roger and Myron agreed they had a lot of fun over the years. But it wasn't just for the fun, they enjoyed the spirit of competition. And when the umpire yelled "PLAY BALL" you can bet those Duncannon boys CAME TO PLAY!

Reflections On The Establishment Of

DR. JOSEPH J. MATUNIS'S FAMILY AND PRACTICE IN PERRY COUNTY

Storyteller Kate Matunis Wolfe
in conjunction with Suzanne Hoban Matunis

My family's transition to Perry County began back in 1957 while my father, Dr. Joseph J. Matunis, was a resident at the Harrisburg Hospital, doing a rotation in the Emergency Room. It must have been mid to late winter when there was a commotion among several residents outside of one of the ER rooms. My father went to investigate. They were debating over who should go in to evaluate the patient's condition. No one wanted the task. Peering around the door frame, Dad spied a disheveled young boy seated on a chair. A raw odor emanated from the room. Upon entering, he hunched down, eye-level with the lad and asked, "When was the last time you had a bath?" The child's honest answer, "When the ice was off the creek." Later that day, he told Mom that these were the type of people he wanted to serve. (Years later, this child did become one of Dad's patients.)

At the end of his residency, Dad accepted a one-year post with the Public Health Service, to complete his required service time dictated by the G.I. Bill, which had paid his way through medical school. In June of 1958, with one year old Frank in tow and a second child on the way, the family moved to Kotzebue, Alaska, 300 miles north of the Arctic Circle, on the western coast, closer to Siberia than anywhere else. Dad was assigned to a local hospital, as well as to make rounds with the mail plane, bringing medical care to outlying villages of Inupiat Eskimos. (At that time, Alaska was still a territory.)

They returned to Mom's parent's home in Scranton, PA in June of 1959 with Frank and baby Mary Jo, while Dad searched for a place to settle down and start his practice. Through the Pennsylvania Medical Society, he was able to identify communities that were in need of a Family Practice doctor. Over the next two weeks, they visited several central Pennsylvania locations before deciding to settle in Perry County.

As members of a committee to locate a young doctor for the western end of Perry County, Mr. Paul Hurley, Superintendent of the West Perry School District, and William "Bill" Wilson, a local Boy Scout leader, drove my parents high and low around the county to help them find a home suitable for their growing family, with additional space for a medical practice. They searched the western end of the county from Blain to Ickesburg, from Loysville to Landisburg, and in between. Mom was enamored with a lovely stone house, back in the woods, outside of Ickesburg. However, it had very low ceilings such that she could touch them when she stood on her tiptoes. But more importantly, it lacked space and parking for a medical practice.

Finally, they found a house available for rent outside of Landisburg, with a back room that could serve as an office and adequate parking in the back. And, it was centrally located in the county.

A day or two after they moved in, there was a knock at the door. My Dad was away. He had gone to York to purchase equipment he would need to set up a medical practice in the house. Upon opening the door, Mom was greeted by a tall, good-looking blonde woman, elegantly dressed.

"May I come in?" Upon entering, she tipped her head back and proclaimed, "I am Lady Goosens. You may as well pack your bags, because as a Catholic, you won't be accepted here." And then she left.

[She was a Fetter, owner of the Fetter House in Landisburg, which was later donated to the Historical Society of Perry County. Her husband was Sir Harry Goosens, conductor of the London Symphony.] In time, Lady Goosens's prediction proved unfounded, as Dad's (and family) actions drowned prejudices of the time.

Dad's first patient at the house was a true shock to my Mom. She heard the sound of something approaching, reverberating louder than a car. It turned out to be a man on a farm tractor, in an odd, dusty blue attire. Being a city girl, she had never seen such an outfit… overalls.

All the man would say was, "Mary's got it in the back." It turned out that Mary was the man's sister and that she had severe arthritis in her back. Mary's attire was also an eye opener. She made her own dresses … from feed sacks. (In contrast, Mom had hand-made dresses growing up, made by her seamstress great-aunts who clothed the upper crust of Wilkes Barre.)

After being settled in for a while, Mom was invited to go on a bus trip with the Pocahontas Club. A few days later, the invitation was withdrawn. They were sorry, but the bus was already full. Apparently, word got out that we were Catholic. [Eventually, Mom did get invited on trips, because they needed more people to fill the bus.]

Being a city girl, Mom had never learned to drive and Perry County did not have public transportation. Warm-hearted people from St. Bernard's Catholic Church provided transportation to church events as needed, and Joan Anderson offered to drive her when other needs arose. Together, they served as her "taxi" for several years. Eventually, Dad decided Mom needed to learn to drive. They bought a second-hand stick-shift car. Dad tried to teach her how to drive. That involved one trip around the parking lot of the Church of the Living Christ, across the street from the house. "That's how you do it," he declared.

That proved to not be enough, so Dad pulled a connection with Martha Miller, the elementary school nurse in Landisburg. Her husband was the high school Driver's Education teacher. Dad told Mr. Miller, "If you want my wife, Suzanne, to stay on in Perry County, you need to teach her to drive." (If she wasn't happy here, they'd be moving elsewhere.)

The day Mr. Miller arrived to give Mom her first lesson, she came out of the house with three kids in tow and an infant in a table top baby seat. Astounded, he asked, "Do you need to bring all these kids along?"

Her response, "What else am I supposed to do with them?"

So, reluctantly, he allowed them to pile into the back seat. With three kids in the back seat and an infant in a baby seat (before the time of required seat belts and infant car seats), he managed to teach her how to drive a stick shift - much in spite of the romping of little kids in the back that distracted the instructor more than her.

When they got married, Dad had told Mom that his patients would always be his first priority, due to taking the Hippocratic Oath. That became clear through many occasions, but especially during Christmas Eve of 1961. This particular night, Dad got a call to deliver a baby. (Being a country doctor, he treated everything from the beginning of life to the end of life.) It proved to be a long night … for both of them.

Mom was on her own to put four excited kids to bed (ranging in age from ten and a half months to a week shy of four years old) and to tackle the Christmas Eve duties. As per their family tradition, Santa brought the decorated tree and gifts on Christmas Eve. Thus, at eight and one-half months pregnant with the fifth child, she was faced with the tasks of hauling in the tree, screwing it tightly into the tree stand, garnishing it with decorations and cleaning up, before finally bringing out the gifts. This year, that included assembling a bicycle for Frank, the oldest. The most challenging part however, was that the instructions were in Japanese or Chinese! By early dawn, when she finally got the bike together and was headed towards the stairs for bed, who should appear but little Frank, bounding down the steps exclaiming, "Santa was here!" No sleep for a weary Mom that Christmas morning.

My parents held fast to a financial agreement they made when they got married. They would not buy anything that they did not have the money to pay for. That was broken only twice. Both were out of necessity, and an investment in their future.

The first time was precipitated by their move to Perry County in 1958. Coming from the city, they had been able to make do without a car. However, in the country, a car become an obvious necessity. Holding to their vow not to buy beyond their financial ability, they would not take a loan through the car dealership. Instead, Mom approached Roger Blumenschein, loan manager at the Bank of Landisburg, about a short-term loan, explaining that they did not have enough funds to pay for a car out right at that time, but would be able to pay off a loan by the end of the month, in two weeks. Without hesitation, Roger cut them a check on the spot for the difference needed. Mom returned in two weeks to pay off the loan. No interest was charged.

The second time was five years later, in 1963. The family was stretching the limits of their rental home in Landisburg. With four little ones sharing one bedroom, an infant in their bedroom, a sixth child due in November, and half the first floor dedicated to the medical practice, they needed more space. They began searching for a permanent home, with room for a growing family, as well as adequate space for the medical practice. They were fortunate to be looking at the same time that Mrs. Wilson was seeking to rid herself of Perry County, after her husband's passing. She was never fond of the country life. Under her care, the old stone farm house (built in 1825), just north of the Youth Development Center, had been renovated and upgraded to bring in electricity, an oil heating system and running water. The three-quarter mile lane was dirt, as were most farm lanes and all but major county roads at that time. There was plenty of space indoors and out for their growing family and medical practice.

When my parents settled on buying the Wilson place, they turned again to the Bank of Landisburg for a loan. Old Mr. C. R. Egolf told dad, "Tell them what you need and come in once a month to pay whatever you can." They never signed any paper work. The county was keen on doing everything they could to keep their doctor. Such a thing could only happen with a locally owned bank. (When the house was finally paid off in the mid-1970s, Dad carved a space in the base of the banister and inserted an arrow head that he had found on the farm. His sign of ownership.)

Dad's patients jumped in to help when my family moved to the farm in October of 1963. They boxed up the house and office in Landisburg, carefully labeling each, pulling drawers from the dressers, then unpacking and reassembling everything in the new farm house, all the while my Mom, greatly pregnant, directed from a chair. The newest addition (Kate) arrived a few weeks later on November 16th.

A memorable first office visit came one Sunday, shortly after moving to the farm. Ben Barclay, a farmer two farms to the west of ours, was in need of some doctoring. His wife insisted that he first shower and dress acceptably to see "The Doctor." As a compliant husband, he followed his wife's directive.

When Mom answered the door, there stood Mr. and Mrs. Ben Barclay. Ben had put on the suit he had worn for his wedding (and was saving for his funeral). Mom had to call Dad in from the garden. Soon, Dad came tramping across the yard. "The Doctor" was a sight to see, dressed in a sweaty white undershirt smudged with mud, jeans with dirt caked at the knees and a piece of binder twine threaded through the belt loops to hold them up. Ben turned to his wife and adamantly proclaimed, "Never again!"

The community supported Dad and he wanted to support them in kind. He hired and bought locally whenever he could. With the growing family and business, he was in need of additional help. Fortunately, he found qualified help close by. Larry Kretzing agreed to continue farming the land as he had for Mrs. Wilson. He recommended his sisters Martha Crull, Thelma Negley and Catherine Noss for help inside and with the kids. They became like second moms. Jim Kuhn also stayed on as a grounds keeper to mow and keep the landscaping in shape. Lois Barclay, who lived at the farm house at the end of our lane, had some nursing training, but had never finished. Her skills proved to be just what the doctor needed in a secretary and nursing assistant, plus she was one more person to help mold the lives of his children with her patience, warm laugh and smile. There would never be a concern about her ability to make it in the lane to work. During snowy winter weather, her husband Jim (and later with the help of their daughter Karen), kept the farm lane cleared, at times plowing a second path in their fields, parallel to the road, to catch the snow, preventing drifting along the most vulnerable sections of the lane. People needed access to Doc, and he to them. They made certain of that.

Dad's dedication to his patients' needs went beyond pure medical care. He understood that their lifestyle was a big part of their overall health. One Sunday afternoon, just as we were ready to stick our forks into dinner, the phone rang. As always, Mom answered it. The woman at the other end was in tears. Her fence had been knocked over and the chickens had gotten out of the yard. They were in her neighbor's garden. The man was threatening to wring their necks! Dad knew these chickens were her livelihood. Without hesitation, he pushed back his chair and called on the older kids to join him. Off we went, leaving Sunday dinner to cool on the table. The chickens were gathered. Fence mended. Back home, Mom pulled dinner from the oven, a bit dried out, but warm and filling. What better way to spend a Sunday?

Several years after moving the practice to the farm, there was an unnerving encounter. It was late in the evening. Dad was at a medical meeting in Carlisle. Just having tucked the kids into bed, there was a loud knock on the door. That was not unusual. With the practice in the house, patients were apt to show up at any time if they were in need of Dad's services. He always obliged. Upon opening the door, Mom was greeted by a tall, thin man with a shot gun hanging at his side. He asked, "Is Doc here?" When Mom replied, "No," he turned and proclaimed, "I'll get him," then left.

Mom was stunned! She was a city girl, unused to seeing men with rifles. Alone in a house tucked almost a mile off the road, with a brood of sleeping children upstairs, what could she do? She called the police. They were located halfway across the county in Newport, thirty minutes away. When an officer finally arrived, she explained that she did not recognize the man (he wasn't a patient as far as she knew), but gave a description as best she could. After checking outside around the house, the barn and out buildings, the officer felt that the area was clear. He then headed over to Carlisle, pulled Dad from his meeting and escorted him safely home.

The next day, there was a phone call from the same man. Mom recognized the voice. The conversation was the same. "Is Doc in?" "I'll get him." At first, she was really unnerved. A police investigation found nothing. Time passed, nothing bad happened and as she became more accustomed to "country life" in Perry County, Mom settled on believing that the gentleman meant no harm, but was probably looking to ask permission to hunt on the farm, as many patients did to put meat on their table.

Dad was truly a country doctor. From the start of his practice in 1958 until he retired in 2007, he made his house call rounds on Thursdays to visit the elderly, or "shut-ins." His rounds took him through the back roads of Perry County from as far east as Newport, to Doylesburg in the west. Being a child of the depression, he liked to push the gas tank to its limit, putting the car in neutral to coast down hills and up the next. At times, one or two, or more, of us kids would tag along (and give Mom a bit of a respite). We provided company for Dad, and a distraction for patients from day-to-day life.

Arley Sweger of Landisburg, enjoyed telling one such story to her niece, Ruth Ann Kuhn, a classmate and friend of my sister, Mary Jo. The story goes as such:

One afternoon, somewhere in the late 1960s, Doc was making his rounds in his little green Vega. As soon as he pulled in beside the house, the car doors flew open and out spilled a pile of little kids, like clowns at a circus. They disappeared into the yard as he went inside to attend to his business. When he was finished, he called out, "It's time to go!" and the "clown car" scene reversed, with kids piling back into the little green Vega. A short time later, Arley heard a commotion outside. A small child was sitting in the middle of the driveway crying. She had been left behind. Arley quickly called up Doc. He calmly stated, "I'll be down shortly." Such was the rhythm of life for the country doctor with a brood of children. (Eventually to number a baker's dozen.)

On a personal recollection, I recall going on rounds once as a young teen in the late 1970s to stay with an elderly bed-ridden woman so her daughter and son-in-law could do some shopping. They were so grateful for the time to stock up on groceries. For my part, I learned a life lesson of how to light a gas oven.

These weekly, routine visits enabled many elderly to remain at home, or with family, for the duration of their life.

Being his own boss in the late 1950s and 1960s, Dad had flexibility in creating his own schedule, as well as billing patients. There were often times, before insurance dictated costs, that Dad would accept whatever form of payment people could provide, whenever they were able. At times that would come in the form of a chicken or two, a dozen eggs or more, pies or bushel of apples. (All such payments helped to feed his growing family.) He felt that no one should be denied services.

Speaking of Dad's medical meetings in Carlisle conjures up another tale. For years, he made weekly trips over the mountain to the Carlisle Hospital for required meetings, offering to give the other doctors, Jim Marakowski and Bob Gasull, a lift. They were more than happy for a chance to just sit and relax for the drive over. That was until one spring, as the weather warmed, they started to notice an odd, sour smell in the car. Trying to be polite, they would sniff the air, turn their heads and ask, "Joe, do you smell something?" Dad, in his typical manner, brushed it off. Smells didn't seem to bother him.

Each week, they would inquire again about an odd smell. Until one day, they decided they just couldn't take it anymore. His co-workers began making excuses about why they couldn't ride over with him. So, he checked again under the seats, but saw nothing amiss. He used the car to haul everything from kids with sweaty sports gear, to garden fertilizer and dented gas tanks to fill up the mowers. Never mind that sometimes he'd spilled a little (or more than a little) gas on the carpet in the hatch. It would evaporate eventually. But he had to admit that the car was getting a bit of a stiff whiff to it. On warm days, he would just roll down the window.

After a month or two of driving solo over the mountain, Dad decided that yes, there was a bit of a funky smell in the car. He decided he should check things out again. Under the seat were papers, wrappers, pens and pencils, some seed packs, dirt and crumbs, but nothing offensive. The carpet in the trunk looked like it could be used for a Rorschach inkblot test. So, out it came for a good airing. Then the source of the obnoxious, olfactory offense became clear. A greatly decomposed pile of black and green mush was festering in the wheel well. It turned out to be a wayward rutabaga.

Per his recollection, in the fall, he had taken a bag of rutabagas with him on house calls to deliver them to a shut-in patient in Doylesburg who had a hankering for some. One must have escaped the bag and nestled itself in with the spare tire for the winter. (Only, it wasn't meant to hibernate. Seems a worse fate than being eaten, in my opinion.)

Dad was resourceful, making use of opportunities (that are unfortunately unthinkable today). One morning (in the early 1980s) when taking kids out the three-quarter mile lane to the bus stop, the car died. The kids would get to school via the school bus. However, Dad needed to get to the Health Center, on the south side of Loysville, to see patients in half an hour. So, he took the "public transportation," climbing onto the bus behind his clan of kids. The bus driver dropped him off at the square in town, where he walked the rest of the way to work.

After school, my youngest sister, Emily, of early elementary age, confided to Mom that she was really upset about Dad riding the bus. He must have heard all the terrible language that some of the kids used! This was still at a time when kids of all grades rode the same bus.

Dad set up his practice with office hours in the morning and again in the evenings, after dinner, to best avail himself to his patients. Several afternoons were used for home visits, hours at the Youth Development

Center or hospital visits. Otherwise, afternoons were spent digging in the garden or foraging in the woods around the farm. His hands were roughly calloused and often stained with the season. Orange meant fall, the harvest of walnuts. Black was winter, with the pitch of pines from making wreathes. Brown was spring, in his gardens, on his hands and knees with his pocketknife planting, weeding and harvesting the cool weather crops of lettuce and spinach. Summer darkened the dirt stains, mixing in green smears of weeding and harvesting beans and broccoli, then, in late summer, tomatoes.

When Father Sharman come to St. Bernard's Catholic Church, Mom was prepared for the inevitable hesitant look from the new priest when Dad arrived at the front of the line for communion and put out his hands for the host. She calmly whispered that Dad's hands were not dirty, just stained from hard work.

His hands became the mark of acceptance in the community. Mom recalls a tale from Britta Harris about a comment made during a meeting she was in during which Dad's name was brought up. The person commented that Dad was for sure a member of the community, because he looked like everyone else – he had farmer hands. His deeds spoke volumes.

Growing Up In Blain, Perry County, Pennnsylvania

Storytellers Claudia Bower Barry and Belinda Bower Gemme

Our Bower family has a long rich history and linage. Christopher (Bauer) Bower was born in Baden, Germany in 1744 before coming with his parents to the Philadelphia area in 1748. He served in the Revolutionary War. One story that has been told is that during the war many colonists changed their names so as not to be identified as Germans thus Bauer became Bower.

The Bower Homestead (Established 1816) on Conococheague Road outside of Blain is a seventh-generation farm. Our father Claude (Bud) Averill Bower purchased the adjacent farm which our ancestors called "The Middle Farm" around 1949. Our parents were very much an unlikely couple. Dad was a farmer and our mother, Florence Isabella Jones, was a city gal from Wilkes-Barre. She was of English, Welsh, Scotch-Irish and Manx (Isle of Man) heritage. She came to Blain for her student teaching and was set-up on a date with our father to be. She was attending Bucknell University studying drama and English. After graduating from Bucknell, she married our father in 1949 and they took up residence at "The Middle Farm." She was a school teacher at Blain Union High School. She adjusted pretty well to farm life but there was one thing we remember that she never got used to and that was mice in the farmhouse. I remember if she saw a mouse in the kitchen, she would run up on the stair landing and bang a pot or pan to scare the mouse. It was quite amusing!

As Senior Citizens, now we look back at all the advantages we had growing up in Blain, although there were times, we didn't see it that way. Several times a year we would visit our grandparents in the "Big City" of Wilkes-Barre which was very exciting for us! Riding the city bus to shop, going to a community pool (not a pond!) and spending time in the Poconos where our grandparents owned a small cottage.

We believe Claudia was supposed to be a boy and that is why she was named Claudia after our father. Belinda came along about two years later and was named from a movie "Johnny Belinda" that our mother saw. Our sister, Bridget came along a number a years later and was given an Irish name associated with our Scotch-Irish background. Our father did not want a family name for Bridget so mother was reading Good Housekeeping and saw that Gene Kelly named his daughter Bridget and all of us really liked the name. Our father had to share one bathroom with four females, often hard to do!!

While a second bathroom would not be added until an addition was built on in 2001, dad and mother did do minor remodeling to the farmhouse when first married and again in 1960. The 1960s remodel was notable in that the Nesbit's Blain Planing Mill was instrumental in the cabinetry and it was possible to use native cherry and walnut found on the farm woodlands for kitchen cabinets and paneling. Another local business often visited was Stambaugh's Hardware Store.

Summers were always fun! We usually got out of school around Memorial Day! (Not anymore!). We spent most of our summer months in flip flops and bare feet except going to church on Sunday where Reverend Foulke would teasingly grab our chins and Uncle Pete who sat in the pew behind us would tug on our pigtails. We had lots of cousins from Iowa, Glenrock and Carlisle who stayed with either our grandparents or Great-Uncle Pete and Aunt Sarah on the next farm up the road.

We rode our bikes all summer. We swam in the pond with the Rohm girls, took swimming lessons at the Loysville pool and eventually went to the New Bloomfield pool. We also did a lot of fishing with our father, especially for bass in the pond with a jitterbug lure which was his favorite. Trout season was also a big deal when we would hike above Big Spring State Park with dad to fish for native trout.

Bible School and the Blain Picnic were THE big social events of the summer! We especially looked forward to the barbecued chicken and homemade ice cream provided by the Lions Club! Our family did a lot of picnics at Big Spring and Colonel Denning State Parks. We knew when dad suggested a Sunday drive it was most likely to get ice cream at Massey's in Carlisle or Hall's in Millerstown. Dad loved his ice cream!

Wintertime brought sledding and tobogganing on the big hill behind the barn in addition to ice skating. In the spring we looked forward to May Day, (Claudia was a member of the Court one year) dressing up and braiding the Maypole. Claudia had a lot of freckles and she hated them so dad told us if you wake up before dawn on May first, walk down the steps backwards, and then wash your face in the dew the freckles would go away. It didn't work!!

The Bower Families have always been huge baseball fans. Grandfather, uncles, cousins all played baseball for Blain. Our father was awarded a contract to play for the St. Louis Cardinals Farm League and went to Salisbury, Maryland for a summer. There he played with some future major league stars like Joe Garagiola. Though his future was not to be major league baseball, dad continued his love of the game as he participated in the Old Timers games and Donkey Baseball events often put on at the Blain School. Aside from baseball, other events at the school included school plays, square dances and cake walks.

While Dad never wanted "his girls" to work on the farm as perhaps he would have with sons, we did have chores and tried to help; gathering eggs, moving irrigation pipe, raising peeps, playing with piglets. We had fun playing in the stacks of hay bales, getting in the wheat bins only to discover, after terrible itching, that we were in the barley bins!

4-H was a big part of our lives. We learned to cook and sew and when Perry County restarted a Baby Beef Club, both of us won the honor of taking our steers to the Pennsylvania Farm Show. We had a horse, "Sleepy Joe," but he wasn't very sleepy especially when you turned him around to go back to the barn. We helped with wrapping and freezing meat after butchering by the spring-house in back of Grandpa Bower's house, and peeled peaches and prepared home-grown sweet corn for freezing. Our Grandmother Bower made the BEST Christmas cookies. She pasteurized our milk and made homemade butter. There was always a Jersey or Guernsey cow out back.

There were three especially memorable events in the 1960s. Celebrating Blain's Bicentennial in 1963 was really special. Our mother made all our period dresses and years later our niece Elizabeth and her friend were able to wear them again for a competition during Heritage Days. In 1964-1965 as members of the Blain Elementary School Band, under the direction of music teacher Dorothy Robertson, we performed at the New York World's Fair. And oh yes, little sister Bridget came along!

In conclusion, we feel fortunate to have been raised by wonderful and loving parents who instilled in us solid values, faith and patriotism. Our parents wanted the three of us to attend college and we all did and then some.

We could go on and on but it has been very gratifying reminiscing about our lives growing up in Blain, that we often took for granted when we were young, but no more.

Note: Some of the Bower family history information was taken from a publication "The Christopher Bower Story" compiled by L. Miles Bower in 1971 for our whole Bower family.

Duncannon's Local Gathering Place

FOR FEED, HARDWARE AND TALL-TALES

Storyteller Peggy Hepfer Miller
Recorded by Fred C. Noye

When you went to Hepfer's Feed Store, you knew it would not be a quick visit, but it would be fun. That is because you never knew who you would run into and the jovial owner loved talking and joking with his customers. Paul Hepfer purchased the business at the top of the hill on Route 274 leaving Duncanon in 1949, from Cliff Taylor of "Turkey Hill". At the time the business was primarily a feed business, but over the years it evolved into a seed, farm, garden and hardware store.

Paul was born in 1921 to Edward and Effie (Fortney) Hepfer. When his dad died, his mother eventually remarried Charles Horst in 1946. To help support her family, his mother raised, killed and cleaned chickens in her basement to sell at the Broad Street Market in Harrisburg. She also worked for "Jew" Frank, a chicken farmer who had a large operation in Roseglen.

Paul married Mary Raub, daughter of Oscar and Margaret (Taylor) Raub, in 1944 and they lived in Duncannon. Paul saw service during WW II in the Philippines. Following the war, Paul worked at the Clark's Ferry Tavern (which was not a tavern but a gas station and restaurant) on the Island and later was a familiar face to customers at Amity Hall.

One day while working on the Island, one of Paul's friends stopped by to show-off his motorcycle. Paul was enthralled so the owner suggested Paul take it for a spin. Things didn't go too well, as Paul and the motorcycle both wound-up in the Juniata River.

In the early days in business, Paul mostly delivered feed to local farmers. He had a fleet of two trucks and they were always on the go. In the fall, he would haul wheat and barley from the local farms to the mill in Highspire.

In 1954, the store was physically moved back from along Route 274 to its current location. That is when the seed and hardware section was added. As time went on, a truck scale and Atlantic Gas Pumps were installed.

As business increased, Paul added some local help that became long-time employees. Over the years, everyone got to know Paul's brother, Homer, and Calvin Kreiser. Of course, Mary helped out in the store when needed and she was the book-keeper that kept the business running smoothly and profitably.

Hepfer's just wasn't a business. It was a gathering spot for locals. Here you could find out all the latest about the weather, the crop market, talk sports and politics, and of course, learn all the juicy rumors around the area.

Paul and Mary had two children, Bill and Peggy, and that of course kept things lively in the early days of trying to run a business. There were all kinds of adventures for the kids in the "out buildings" and there was hay in the barn to play in. The Lepperd sisters, Martha and Miriam, along with Peggy enjoyed roller skating in the feed shed with their skates that had to be attached to their shoes and tightened with a key. It also offered lots of room to ride a scooter. However, one day a resident rooster decided to continually chase Peggy and was trying to flog her. Dad permanently solved that problem.

When Bill and Peggy were still in grade school, Bill told Peggy she was adopted, (being the sweet big brother that he was). Which of course, Peggy told anyone who asked if she was Paul and Mary's daughter. Their mother could have skinned them both, when she found out. Bill was in trouble for telling Peggy that, and Peggy was in trouble for believing him.

In the winter, there was sledding in Bill Gamber's fields, with neighbors Mary, Kay, Barry and Paul Foster including close friends, Martha and Miriam Lepperd. Sometimes their parents would take them ice skating in Montebello or on Shermans Creek behind Kisner's Garage, or to the pond down the road at Warren Snyder's.

One Christmas, Peggy's dad was going to go out and chop down their Christmas tree and he asked Bill and Peggy to go along. Both said no, but their mother said to put on all their snow gear (hats, gloves, snow pants, boots and coats) and go along. They got ready and their father told them, they were going out the cellar-way to grab a few things to take along. When they got to the steps to go outside, there sat a Christmas tree. Peggy figures her mom and dad were in cahoots on this practical joke.

If their parents were busy, Peggy would make the short walk down the road to their grandparent's home. They were regular visitors and enjoyed spending time with them. Playing cards was a favorite past-time for all the Raubs. Paul, Mary, and all the aunts and uncles came to play 500, Rummy or Pinochle.

The kids enjoyed going along with Uncle Homer when he made deliveries. Sometimes, they enjoyed riding in the cab of the feed truck with Uncle Homer driving over the bumpiest roads he could find as fast as he could. He would hold out his hand and tell Peggy he had something for her and when she reached for it, he would hand her his false teeth (Paul wasn't the only prankster in the family.). Bill and Peggy looked forward to when they took the trip to Lancaster in the truck to pick up feed from the Red Rose Company. She got to ride the conveyor belts that moved the bags of feed onto the truck.

Every stop was an adventure. Some of the customers would have cake, cookies and milk for the kids, and coffee waiting for Homer when he arrived with the feed truck. One stop that Peggy always enjoyed was where the lady of the house would take her to see her collection of hundreds of salt and pepper shakers.

They would try to eat dinner as a family, but many times business would interrupt. As a result, Peggy remembers, "we all became very fast eaters".

Even though the Hepfers made a lot of homemade ice cream, they did their share to keep ice cream companies in business. Paul would stop and buy a pint of ice cream, cut the square cardboard container in half, and he and Peggy would finish it off. Regardless, the Hepfer ritual was that almost every night at nine o'clock, they had a dish of ice cream before going to bed.

There were annual events that they looked forward to. Easter time was a fun time at the store. They always had colored chicks available and kids loved to come to see or buy the multi-die colored peeps.

The Pioneer Seed Company always hosted a spring event in Lancaster and Paul would take Peggy along. Lots of great food, prizes and free-bees.

Paul was always friendly, smiling, and jovial, but even he had his moments. Peggy remembers crossing the line on two occasions, when she was quite young. One time her dad was on the phone when she was playing with matches and one ignited. The other was at the Dairy Bar in Duncannon when she didn't listen to her dad about staying in the truck while he ran to get some ice cream. The parking lot was full of cars and she decided to get out of the truck and follow him.

Paul loved the water. He was a very good swimmer and enjoyed taking the kids to swim in the Shermans Creek at the first iron-bridge in Dellville and to Alter's Cottage above the second iron-bridge. Their parents saw to it that the kids took swimming lessons which were held at Gibson's Rock and every summer there was always time for a vacation. It was usually a camping trip.

The Hepfer brothers, Paul, Homer and Jim, all purchased lots along the Juniata River at Losh's Run. Paul and the kids enjoyed swimming in the river and Mary enjoyed "looking at the water". It was also a popular spot in the summer for church breakfasts and picnics that attracted eighty to one-hundred people.

When Peggy turned sixteen and was learning to drive, her parents decided that she needed to learn how to drive a stick-shift. So they went out and bought a new car with a gear shift. After she mastered that, about three years later, it was time to go back to an automatic.

In 1964, the family decided as a graduation gift for Peggy, they would drive west to California to visit relatives (she felt the gift part was just an excuse), but regardless, the trip was a life-time memory of seeing many wonderful sights, including a quick trip across the border into Mexico.

The Hepfers were very active in both the Shermanta Grange (fifty plus year members) and the Duncannon Reformed (now the Christ Reformed Church). But even the preacher was fair game for Paul. He would take a large pocket-watch along to church. If he thought the preacher was being a little long winded, he would stretch his arm out into the center aisle and swing the pocket-watch back and forth for the preacher to see.

One time for four weeks in a row, Paul told the preacher after the service, that "he had a warm service". Finally the preacher asked him why he always said that, and Paul told him, "it wasn't so hot"!

But sometimes the joke was on Paul. Everyone got a good laugh when at the church's Halloween party, while bobbing for apples, Paul lost his false teeth in the water barrel.

Hardware must have been in the Hepfer family genes. Paul's Uncle Paul Erb (his wife was a Hepfer) owned and operated a hardware store in West Fairview for many years. Later Paul's brother Jim joined him as a partner. Jim had two sons, Jim and John, who opened the large ACE Hardware Store in Lemoyne. John decided to go on his own and purchased the former Maguire's Hardware on High Street in Duncanon. Then, he opened a hardware store along Route 11 & 15 near New Buffalo and in the Karn's Shopping Plaza in New Bloomfield. He recently sold both stores to Luke Stepp, his nephew.

All good things come to an end and in 1982, after thirty-three years in business, Paul and Mary decided it was time to retire. Paul was experiencing some health issues and they turned the business over to the new owners, Clyde and Bonnie Pottieger. As usual, the Hepfers felt an obligation to help the new owners get through the spring rush, so they stayed on through the transition.

Hepfers, as a long-standing Duncannon business, is fondly remembered as a welcoming place to go for meeting good friends, friendly discussions and a place to catch-up on all the local news and "chit-chat" of the day. You could sit and "chew the fat", grab a snack or get a cold drink from the water-cooled 7-Up soda machine, while the friendly staff loaded your pick-up truck or car with your order. Talk was plenty, advice was cheap, remarks were humbling, but the experience was priceless!

Keeping An Eye On Bloomfield From The Barber's Chair

Storyteller Donald C. Stoops, Jr.

Stoops' Barbershop was opened in 1899 by my Great-Uncle Oscar Stoops. My grandfather Calvin Stoops took over the Barbershop when Oscar decided to grow apples.

The original shop and pool room was located on South Carlisle Street. Later it was moved to north-west of the square. After a period of time, moved again to the wooden building behind the current Perry County Café, which is in a brick portion that was added for a millinery store. In 1928, my grandfather then moved to 5 West Main Street, where the shop is located at the present time. The pool room was eliminated.

The shop was opened until the late 1960s from 8 a.m. to 7 p.m. on weekdays and 8 a.m. to 8 p.m. on Saturdays, closed on Thursdays. People asked why close on Thursdays. Most barbers close Mondays, so my grandfather decided to take advantage of that.

During the early days of barbering, shaving individuals who did not shave themselves was a large part of the business. In the 1950s, there were still several individuals who did not shave themselves. The last shave I did was on an individual who owned an establishment outside of Bloomfield Borough. He apparently was drinking the profits, because I shaved him while he was sleeping.

When the Post Office was located now where the District Office of the State Representative representing the 86th District is, there was generally a group of older gentlemen "loafing" in the shop discussing various events, (gossip) while waiting for the mail to be sorted. There was one time when two customers got into a verbal argument that escalated into a physical contest.

Military-style cuts for Carson Long Military Institute Cadets
We cut the hair of Carson Long Military Institute Cadets for years. They would come to the shop at the end of classes from 3:30 p.m. to 5:30 p.m. They needed to be present at line-up for dinner by 5:30 p.m. It was a challenge at times to get them all cut and be on campus for the line-up.

The regulation haircut was closely tapered on the sides, two inches on the top and crew cuts if the cadet wanted. Each cadet had an order-slip for a haircut which was then turned in to CLI for payment to the shop. You learn to be rather fast with the haircuts when you have ten to twenty boys in the shop. With cadets rushing down the hill to be the first haircut, several times a door window was broken.

My father, Donald C. Stoops Sr, took over the shop in 1946. I joined him legally in 1955 with an apprentice paper. Prior to that on a busy Saturday, I would put a customer on the chair and prepare him for a haircut, while my father cut hair of another on a second chair. When he was finished, he would move to the one I prepared. Then I would take off the cape of the one he finished and prepare another. It saved several minutes for a haircut.

Keeping a watchful eye on Bloomfield's Town Square
There is quite a view of the Square from the window of the Barbershop. Speeding traffic, cars backing out the same time from both sides of the parking area with the two meeting in the middle of the square with a thump. Cars backing out and crossing traffic. Cars and trucks cutting the monument short, all make for interesting viewing. People, also, do not use the crosswalks and walk directly across the square.

There were two major incidents on the square during my time in the shop. One time a disgruntled husband filled gasoline containers in his car and drove toward the Bloomfield Pharmacy, where his wife worked. The gasoline caught fire before he reached his destination about twenty-five yards short. He died in the fire.

Another time, a vehicle came down the hill (North Carlisle Street) straight across the square. The pickup truck hit a light pole, the corner of the pharmacy, and the barbershop. I was lucky to see it coming and exited the shop very quickly. The individual had a medical condition.

If the clippers could only talk, I wonder what stories they might tell!

Family and "Perry County Home" Memories

Storyteller Shirley Sheaffer Nace

I was born in 1951 the youngest of five children spaced over twenty-four years. Eight years, four years, eight years and four years between us. I doubt if it was intentional but always made for easy remembering of ages. Four girls and one boy, right in the middle. He always said he was the rose among the thorns! He and my sister next to me share the same birthday, eight years apart.

My Mother, Margaret was thirty-nine and my dad, Albert was fifty when I was born, and the only one born in a hospital. My mother and I were in the hospital for five days and the grand total for that was $82.00. My oldest sister was twenty-three, almost twenty-four when my dad had gone through surgery for a supposed brain tumor two years earlier. I was told by a distant cousin his surgery was "botched" leaving him paralyzed on his right side and disabled. (If it had happened today, he would have been a rich man.) As it was, that was not the case, and far from it.

Sheaffer's Valley Historical Figures
At that time, they lived in Sheaffer's Valley, which was named for my Great-Great-Grandparents, the George and Elizabeth (Shatto) Sheaffer family who had ten children. One of those children was named Wellington Merion Dallis Sheaffer born in 1845. He enlisted at the young age of seventeen during the Civil War in 1862. After serving in many different battles including Antietam, Fredericksburg, Mud March and Chancellorsville, he was discharged in May 1863, only to re-enlist in February 1864. In August of 1864, he was injured by a falling log and was wounded by a piece of shell during action. On May 4, 1865, he acted as Guard of Honor at the funeral procession of President Abraham Lincoln. The war ended, so in August of 1865, he was honorably discharged in Harrisburg, Pennsylvania.

He went on to marry a woman from Green Park, Pennsylvania, in 1875 and fathered seven children. He had a mercantile business, was a postmaster, and built a Fire Insurance business over the next twenty-six years until his death on July 31, 1925.

Back to My Dad's Recovery
My sister next to me was two at the time of my dad's surgery and year-long recovery. He and my mother traveled to Harrisburg weekly during his recovery period and to many doctor visits. My sister went to live with our aunt, one of my mother's sisters, who lived on a farm outside of Ickesburg. When I was born two years later, my sister continued to live with our aunt and uncle, who had no children of their own. She did so until she married.

My mother and I would go to visit her on Sundays and usually enjoy supper while there. This was where I acquired my love of home-cured ham!! My aunt and uncle would butcher their own hogs and cure their own meats. When my aunt would ask what we would like to have for supper, my answer was always HAM!! We had it fried with boiled potatoes that were browned in the pan's ham juices and usually corn.

When my aunt would give us some ham to take home to cook, mom would fry the ham, brown the boiled potatoes and make creamed lettuce. I loved that meal!! After I married and we butchered hogs with my in-laws, we would then sugar-cure and smoke the hams and sometime the shoulders. I would prepare the same meal as my mom had done. It is still a favorite of mine and became a favorite of our boys as they grew up. Ham pot pie also became a family favorite and I always served the same type of lettuce my mom used to make. Today my grandchildren request this lettuce side dish whenever they come for a meal. The tradition has lived on.

When I was six, we moved to Loysville from Sheaffer's Valley. I have very few memories of my early years living in the Valley. The one that sticks in my mind is gathering eggs from the chickens. We had a large chicken house and I can remember being told to gather the eggs. I didn't do a very good job though because the chicken's picked me and I ran from the chicken house crying! I think that started my aversion to chickens and any kind of birds. I like to look at them, but don't ask me to hold them or anything else!

My mother was the sole support of our household because of my father's disability. She had acquired a job as a cook at the County Home outside of Loysville. The move made it more convenient for her to travel to her job, which was less than a mile from our house. (It sat across from the present-day Family Practice Center).

My oldest sister and her husband, Joe and Betty Wilson lived in Loysville, so they were there to help my mom with anything needed. My brother lived with the Wilsons until 1957 when he graduated from Blain High School. It was more convenient than him living in the "Valley" and was a shorter commute.

In 1959, my brother Wayne and our cousin Lenny enlisted in the Army. On Valentine's Day in 1960, they took a train from Harrisburg to Louisville, Kentucky and a bus to Fort Knox, Kentucky for eight weeks of basic training. Next, they attended tank training and advanced armory training. I remember Betty and Joe drove my mom and I to Kentucky to bring Wayne home from the service. We stayed in the Army Barracks on base. To a nine-year old, this was a huge thing and very memorable.

My brother-in-law's family lived in Loysville and the surrounding area. We attended the same church, so they became like my adopted family. My sister and brother-in-law were like second parents to me as they had no children of their own. With me being the only child at home at this time, and my mom usually working seven days a week, they included me in their church and social life. They became my mentors and surrogate parents and did a wonderful job.

I remember always going out to eat after church on Sunday's and that was a big deal. I was baptized at and became a member of Tressler Memorial Lutheran Church in Loysville. I sang in the youth choir, attended Catechism, Sunday School, Luther League and Bible School there. I was also married and our first son was baptized at Tressler. I have wonderful memories of my former church and church family.

School Days
I attended first and second grade in the two-room schoolhouse directly across from our home. There were third and fourth grades in the second classroom taught by Carrie Belle Hench. There was no kindergarten in those days! My teacher for those grades was Mrs. Duncan, a fabulous teacher and so very kind. Some memories of those grades were air-raid drills where we had to crawl under our desks to take cover, playing on the huge playground equipment, going to the "other side" of the school for our lunches and then returning to our classroom to eat them and the huge cloak room where we kept our coats, boots, etc. The cloak room was also where you were made to go if you were bad. You stood in the corner with the door closed. Seemed scary to me!! Thankfully, I never had to go there! I considered myself lucky!

Third, fourth and fifth grade, I went to school in Landisburg and rode a bus, that being a first for me. My teachers were Miss Helen Briner, Mrs. Miller and Mrs. Stambaugh. All excellent teachers, but Mrs. Miller was very strict. I can remember her hitting students on the head with the wooden window opener pole, hitting their knuckles with a ruler and taping one of my friend's mouth shut with duct tape for talking! She actually put the tape the whole way around her head, hair and all! Our fifth-grade classroom and the cafeteria were both in the basement of the school and were a bit intimidating.

Sixth grade I went to Green Park High School as the classes were becoming larger and there was no room at Landisburg for all the sixth graders. I also attended seventh grade there. That's where I was when President John F. Kennedy was assassinated on Friday, November 22, 1963 at 12:30 p.m. CST in Dallas, Texas while riding in a presidential motorcade. It was announced to us over the loud-speaker. He was our 35th President. What a sad day. It's like remembering exactly where you were thirty-eight years later on September 11, 2001 when the United States was attacked by Islamic terrorists who had hijacked four airplanes and carried out suicide terrorist attacks. Nearly 3,000 people lost their lives in those attacks and more than 6,000 suffered injuries. May we never forget.

Perry Joint, Green Park and Blain schools consolidated in 1965 and became the West Perry School District. The Perry Joint High School and the Blain High School became known as Junior Highs. There weren't middle schools back then. Green Park High School became West Perry Senior High School. I'm not sure about the New Bloomfield Junior High, but I went to Blain and it housed first through ninth grades. Tenth through twelfth grades were then at the current West Perry High School where the ninth graders from both Blain and New Bloomfield came together in tenth grade. The two Junior Highs played against each other in sports and also against the Youth Development Center (the former Tressler Orphan's Home) in Loysville.

When attending high school at West Perry, I was a student worker in the school office after school during the school year and also in the summer. It was called the Neighborhood Youth Corp and we were paid for our work. I also babysat and cleaned for neighbors from the time I was eleven.

Remembering the Perry County Home
As I said earlier, my mother worked at the County Home. It was run by the Perry County Commissioners

and other county officials. The Matron and Steward at the home were Mr. & Mrs. Lee Leinaweaver of Donnally's Mills. Great people! Being six when we moved to Loysville, I was quite young and was able to go along to work with my mom sometimes. When there was no school, I was usually there with her most days.

She was one of the cooks, but also helped oversee the laundry duties, performed by some of the home's residents. There was a separate washhouse where the laundry was washed and hung out to dry. Then it would be taken to the laundry room on the Ladies Floor for folding, ironing, sorting and mending if necessary.

There was also a separate root cellar where the potatoes, onions etc. were stored. They called it the Cave. There was also a pond on the property which was used a lot in the winter for ice skating by myself and other family members, as well as people from Loysville. There were other outbuildings on the property, including a barn across the road, (which is now the Family Practice Center), several garages, an outhouse and a chicken house. The chicken house was a separate small building and had been used in the earlier years of the home, when it was called "The Poor House" or the "County Almshouse," as a place for the "crazy" people.

When the Home was originally built Perry County was still part of Cumberland County. Perry County was formed in 1820 and inherited the Poor House, which was completely destroyed by a fire in 1839. Samuel Shuman was contracted to build a new building. Later, the four-story brick County Home was built in 1871. It contained approximately seventy rooms. The Home was torn down in September of 2009. I only ever knew that small separate building as a chicken house in all the years my mother worked there.

My oldest sister and her husband, Mr. & Mrs. Joe Wilson were the Matron and Steward from November 1, 1963 to November 30, 1973, when the home was closed by the County and all residents were moved to Perry Village in New Bloomfield, Pennsylvania. There was and still is a cemetery that was part of the Poor House across the road and down over the hill behind the now Family Practice Center. I haven't seen it in many years but hear that it is not well kept. Maybe a future project.

There were four floors in the home and each floor contained an outside metal fire escape. The basement is where the furnace room was located, as well as the kitchens, storage areas with supply closets for canned goods, other grocery items and bathroom supplies. Also, there were two bathrooms, plus a dining room and kitchen area for the cooks and other kitchen workers. The Matron and Steward had a private dining area. Another dining room was reserved for male residents who helped around the Home doing various outside lawn care, farming, gardening, barn work or other chores.

The second floor housed the Boardroom as well as the personal living area for the Matron and Steward. (They were the overseers of the Home and its residents). One of the locked rooms on this floor is where valuable personal items, including money, was secured for the residents. There was also a suite of rooms for married couples. I can only ever remember one couple who lived there during the sixteen or so years I visited. A pump organ existed which I loved playing, or tried playing should I say.

The third floor was the ladies' floor. It contained its own dining room that included a sink to wash dishes, the laundry and sewing room, two bathrooms and the residents' quarters. There were a couple rooms where four women lived together but others were either single or double rooms. The hall contained a piano where local churches would hold some special services on Sunday afternoon and other occasions.

The fourth floor was the men's floor. It contained a Chapel for Sunday Services, dining room, a supply room, two bathrooms, and rooms for the gentlemen to sleep in. All the dining rooms, including the Boardroom on the second floor, contained dumb waiters for the food to be lifted up to each floor from the basement kitchen.

The dishes were washed on the women's floor and then sent back to the kitchen on the dumb waiter. The men sent their dishes down to the women's floor to be washed and put on the dumb waiter. The dishes used for cooking and storage in the basement kitchen were cleaned and stored there. There were no automatic dishwashers such as today. The ovens and stoves were huge gas appliances and there were large refrigerators and freezers. There were two sets of sinks in the main kitchen and another stove, sink and refrigerator in a smaller kitchen and dining room across the hall. This room was used a lot to peel potatoes as the cooks could sit down to do that chore at the two tables. They also used this room to make hooked rugs from old clothes that were discarded by residents or donated by local churches. My Mother and five other women that I can remember did the cooking, serving and cleaning up.

There were large metal staircases reaching from the basement to each floor above it and no other means of going to and from each floor. The Home's Chaplain at the time, Reverend Russell Kerns, Pastor at Tressler Memorial Lutheran Church in Loysville, spearheaded a drive to raise funds for an elevator. After a successful fundraiser spanning many months and involving many volunteers throughout the county and its churches, the elevator was dedicated with fan fair on June 12, 1971. The Perry County Commissioners at the time were Max Powell, Norman Pressley and Harry Sheaffer. The Dedication was a huge celebration consisting of a parade, of which Jack Glassburn was the Parade Marshall and included the Shriner's Mounted Patrol, Clowns and Calliope, the County Band, four Scout troops, numerous floats, a steam engine, antique cars, convertibles transporting the king and queen, Red Cross Ambulance, Hahn Pumper Truck from the New Bloomfield Fire Company and other fire apparatus from various county companies, Army jeeps and trucks, Pennsylvania State Police Honor Guard, Susquehanna Drill Team and the Gregg Family Pioneers. On the grounds of the Home were thirteen food stands, music by local Church Choirs, a local country music band, square dancing, a band concert by members representing all the Perry County Schools, and an old-fashioned hymn sing with favorite hymns chosen by residents of the Home. The song leader was Baird Collin, of Loysville, and the organist was Walter Smiley of Loysville. In all, there were more than 1,027 volunteers, businesses, churches, organizations, families, contributors and behind the scenes workers who helped make this Elevator Dedication possible!

The Dedication Service Program said it best:
"Even as much as ye have done it for one of the least of these your brethren,
ye have done it unto me."

Sadly, after all the efforts made, the elevator was only in operation for a few years until the County decided to close the home in November 1973. The residents were transferred to Perry Village Nursing Home in New Bloomfield. It was the end of an era. The Home and its contents were auctioned off later by the County.

Some other businesses including an Amish store resided in what used to be the old washhouse for a while but eventually closed up shop. There was even some type of a car repair shop which is still there. Eventually the old County Home was torn down in September 2009. What a sad day that was for those of us who had looked at that building our whole lives and personally knew someone who had worked or lived there. The only original things still remaining are the wash house (with an addition), the cave and the chicken house (which is now a home).

I have many fond memories of residents who lived there over the years. George Devinney would walk to the Loysville Post Office every day to collect the mail in his leather mail bag. I own and treasure that mail bag. He also helped out in the chicken house. He could not talk very well but could swear a blue streak that was very understandable! Mrs. Boyer was a kind soul who was like a grandmother to me, as I never knew mine. We used to sit on one of the porches on nice days and just visit. Other times we would sit on one of the porch swings that faced the main road and just watch traffic and talk.

Crawford Ross was a unique man who hailed from Ickesburg and could sit on a soda bottle and thread a needle. Hazel Page helped with the laundry in the wash house as well as the folding, mending and storing of it in the laundry room on the ladies' floor. She had the whitest hair I ever saw and couldn't speak plainly, but was a kind and gentle soul who always wanted to help in any way she could. She was in charge of washing the dishes in the dining room on the ladies' floor and always did a meticulous job. There were also others along the way that made me appreciate and learn from the older generation. Now I am of the older generation and appreciate all the kindness they showed to me as a child, teenager and then adult with a child of my own that they enjoyed. I wouldn't trade those years and experiences for anything.

I dedicate these memories to my wonderful sons, Heath and Derrick Nace and to my beautiful grandchildren, Chelsea Nace, Sydne Nace and Brycen Nace. God Bless You All with Much Love.

Great-Granny Didn't Need A Car

Storyteller Lynn D. McMillen

Today, in 2022, we can't even imagine living without a car. In fact, many residences I have driven past have three or four vehicles parked near the house. We have grown to depend on personal transportation to get us to our place of work or to retrieve needed items from the place of purchase to our homes.

I wonder what kind of car great-granny would have driven. It might surprise you to find out that great-granny didn't even have a car or a driver's license for that matter.

Obviously, things have changed, but how did great-granny get her stuff?

It's interesting to consider the changes that have taken place in communities as local customs change while the local economy evolves to adapt to the regional trends.

Some communities changed to the point that they disappeared. Center Square in Western Perry County is an example of this phenomenon. The last time I drove through Center Square the only remaining building of a once vibrant village was an old gray dilapidated building with faded letters spelling "Dance Hall."

The village of Center Square was centered around a Tanning Factory where many area people were employed. When you consider just how many horses and mules were pulling buggies, wagons and farm implements such as plows and planters, it's easy to understand that there was a definite need for tanned leather harness. (Several tanneries were near Center Square because the area's oak trees were rich in tannic acid.) Center Square was a fairly self-contained little village and everything the people needed to conduct their lives was available in the village.

Almost everything great-granny may have needed on a daily basis was available within walking distance. Most of the essentials related to food, clothing and shelter were available nearby.

The era of the tanneries and Center Square had already slipped into history when I came along in 1952, but I have had the opportunity to witness changes in daily life in Western Perry County.

I remember country stores in many localities while growing up. Nearest my home was a store owned by Wyckoff to Wagner to the Naces in Kistler. Down the road was Titzell's Store in Saville. I remember my dad buying the Sunday Paper at a little store "Alexander's" across Route 850 from Centre Church.

Bishop's Store was in Center. Goodling's and later Junk's stores were in Cisna Run. Up the road in Andersonburg was Fisher's Store. Further west in Blain were two stores I can remember (Smith's and Hench's), and Bistline's was in New Germantown. My point is that almost everybody was able to walk to whatever they may have needed, most of the time. To be honest with you, I'm sure great-granny took her horse and buggy to get needed groceries.

There was no real need for great-granny to have a car. Actually, the generation before me grew up during the Great Depression and buying a car was out of the question. (Then only a few years later World War II came along.)

As society moved onward and cars and trucks replaced horses and buggies, distributing goods to "country folk" involved a great deal of "direct selling" where traveling salesmen called directly on prospective customers.

Examples I recall include "The Fish Man" with barrels of iced-down fish in the back of his truck (my mother bought haddock). Seasonally we were visited by "The Peach Man" from Adams County. My mother would buy one or more half-bushels of peaches, then she would can them all. Each hot summer, my brothers and I would look forward to our mother buying a box of Fudgesicles from the Hall's Dairy Ice Cream truck (what a treat!). Hall's Dairy also delivered bottled milk to homes on a regular basis. From Cumberland County, we had Sam's Ice Cream and Valley Pride Bakery running sales routes too.

My mother would put a little orange sign in the front window of our home whenever she wanted the Eddie's Dry Cleaners truck to stop and pick-up clothing she needed to have dry cleaned. Later Mifflin Dry Cleaners made the rounds.

Other merchants that traveled the roads of Perry County included the local iceman and if you lived in the New Bloomfield area Lebo's Meat Market followed closely behind. The J. R. Watkins Company representatives came around selling spices and flavorings, such as cinnamon and vanilla, essential in baking. The Jewel Tea Company sold mostly to stores and they specialized in coffees, teas, silverware and dinnerware.

How did great-granny get eggs for her country kitchen you may wonder? It was very common in those days for each home in the country to have a "family flock" of laying hens (chickens). Great-granny would have ordered the baby chicks (peeps or biddies) early in the spring. When the little chicks would hatch at the hatchery in Millerstown or Liverpool, they would be "mailed" in a box immediately, arriving at their destination the next day. Great-granny started or supplemented her flock with chicks that were only one day old!

As you might realize, only the female chicks (pullets) developed into egg-producing hens. The male chicks (roosters) in about six months ended up in great-granny's kitchen.

Years ago, there were many (water-powered) grist mills in the county that ground locally grown grains such as wheat, corn, oats, barley, buckwheat and rye to improve the digestibility for both livestock and people. These local grist mills shrank in number as the market became dominated by mechanized feed companies who had trucks delivering layer-feed to great-granny and others. They also delivered feed for horses and mules, cattle and hogs, sheep and other animals. I can remember feed mills in Blain, Loysville, Bridgeport, New Bloomfield, Millerstown, Liverpool, Newport and Duncannon. These feed companies would call their customers on a weekly basis, get their order for the items needed and make deliveries the next day. In addition to feed products, their trucks would deliver salt blocks and animal health products, such as de-wormers, fly sprays for the barn and an assortment of other livestock aides. My dad, a dairy farmer, often purchased supplies from the IBA truck that would come by the farm.

In addition to being able to buy grocery items from route truck salesmen, great-granny could also purchase many dry goods and appliances. Many of these talented sales people would provide a certain amount of entertainment while they demonstrated all the attributes of their products. Every housewife had stories of seeing demonstrations from the Kirby or Electrolux vacuum cleaner salesman.

In addition to vacuum cleaners, I remember the Singer Sewing Machine salesman coming to our house. I'm sure great-granny relied on her sewing machine to enable her to make clothes for the entire family. Oddly enough, many feed companies began putting their feed products in sack-cloth bags and great-granny used them to make dresses, blouses and shirts. These "feed sacks" were often made with very pretty patterns which I'm sure were appreciated during the Depression!

The Fuller Brush Company marketed a quality line of cleaning tools, accessories and chemicals. My mother was always fond of Stanley Home Product's silver polish. You've probably used Avon products, a successful company.

Many salespeople would come to our home and want to sell to housewives in groups. That's how the "party" concept originated. You have probably heard of Tupperware (plastic kitchenware) who marketed through parties. Perhaps you have also heard of Dutch Maid clothing (made in Ephrata, Pennsylvania), who sold their products via drop-in parties at area homes, as well as Stanley Home Products. A few of these direct-selling companies have survived until today.

Mr. Clifford Sloppy, from Loysville, taught at Blain Union High School and later he worked at the Loysville Youth Development Center. In his free time, he traveled the local area selling Encyclopedias, Dictionaries and Bible Story Books. I know, because my parents purchased these books, plus others. (There was no reason we could not do our homework!)

An interesting side note about business communications before the era of car phones and cell phones. A very important person to local dairy herdsmen was the artificial inseminator. It was essential to secure the services of this technician in order for the cows to produce calves in a timely manner and thereby maximize annual milk production. But how could a farmer contact the "artificial breeder" as they were often called when Old Bossy was feeling romantic?

Here is the system Harry Latchford, from Kistler, used. Mr. Latchford had set up a call-center in certain locations, usually a grocery store. Any dairy farmer, with a cow ready for insemination, would notify their local call center of the situation. About every three hours, he would call each call-center to find out which farmers had cows that were in need of his services. This was all very important because each cow was in season only two to three hours each month! Oh well, just a side note to let you the reader know how we managed to operate before we all had cell phones.

Great-Granny and most everything from her time are gone with the wind. It's our responsibility to strive to preserve the best of that era and pass it on to our youth.

Childhood Memories Of Growing Up In Marysville

Storyteller Susan Spoonhour Rice

As I sit here contemplating what to write, so many special memories of growing up in Marysville in the late 1940s and 1950s come flooding back. During this time, Marysville was a self-contained small town where everyone knew everyone else by name, where the children were watched over and kept safe by the community, and where neighbors willingly helped their neighbors.

My parents, John and Mae Hummel Spoonhour, along with my older siblings Barbara and John, and I lived in half a double-brick house in the middle of Marysville across from Benfer's Butcher Shop. The other half was owned by our next-door neighbors, George and Emma Hain. Mr. Hain was the nephew of H. H. Hain who wrote *The History of Perry County*. The Hains, an older couple, kept a watchful eye on my sister, brother and me while we were growing up.

Most of our neighbors were older. John and Mabel Shull's backyard adjoined the back of our house. In the early 20th century, Mr. Shull opened a small bakery in his home. It was here that he created the original Ladyfingers and received a patent for them. He eventually added an extension to their home. For many years all of the baking, packaging and shipping occurred on the Shull's property.

When I was a little girl, I often visited the bakery to watch the assembly-line of women packaging the Ladyfingers. Everyone knew me and no one seemed to object. In fact, I was always asked if I would like a sample, which was probably my main reason for stopping in. According to my mother, on one such occasion when I was offered a Ladyfinger, I replied, "No, thank you. I just came to talk." (For those of you who know me, that shouldn't come as a surprise.)

Eventually a new facility was built and renamed Specialty Ladyfingers. After the bakery had moved, the extended building, along with the original gas bake ovens, remained. Mr. Shull still enjoyed doing some of his own baking. One spring afternoon in April of 1957, he turned on the ovens, became distracted, and sometime later lit them, causing the entire building to explode. Incredibly, Mr. Shull survived with only minor injuries. The entire building had exploded outward with only a few cement blocks holding up what remained. My dad was first on the scene and led Mr. Shull out of the rubble. The Shull's home remained untouched and still stands today.

For many years, Dr. Charles Snyder was the only physician in Marysville. No one needed an appointment to be seen at his office on Front Street. Office hours were 8:00 to 12:00 in the mornings and 6:00 to 8:00 in the evenings, or until every patient had been seen. We all had to sit and wait our turns until the door to the waiting room opened and Dr. Snyder said, "Next." He never had a nurse or receptionist. He dispensed his medicines into white envelopes from apothecary jars sitting on glass-enclosed shelves. The usual charge for a visit was one dollar with the exception of camp physicals which were almost always free. In addition to office hours, he also did home visits. Because of his unselfish dedication to the people of Marysville, Dr. Snyder was the first to receive the "Man-of-the-Year" award in our town.

As children we played outdoors as long as the weather permitted. I can still hear my mother say, "Just go outside and play for a while. It will do you good." (Translated that meant: I need some time without you kids under foot.) The little girls in the neighborhood often congregated on the wide sidewalk in front of the old Masonic Building and the Reformed Church next to our house. On warm summer evenings, we played such games as Hide and Seek, Tag or Mother May I. In addition, we liked to jump rope or play Hopscotch in the alley. The wide sidewalk was also a great place to roller skate. I learned to skate when I was three, probably because I wanted to copy everything my older sister and her friends did. No one had shoe skates at that time. Instead, our skates were clamped to the soles of our shoes and tightened with a key. Eventually the clamps holding the skates would loosen, and we would fall, hop up, and try again.

Backyards were also a great place to play. I spent lots of time at Ralph and Betsy Turner's, just up the street from where I lived. They had a big backyard with a wooden swing attached to an old pear tree. No one had a fancy swing set, but we could really go high on that homemade swing. Betsy and I liked to play with our dolls, but we were sometimes interrupted when the boys from the neighborhood, including Barry and Marlin Peters, and Steve and Mike Ritter, showed up. They would often have pear battles and someone would go home crying.

The boys in the neighborhood managed to find their own creative ways to play. When they were younger, many of them wore holsters complete with cap pistols and spent hours playing "cops and robbers" or "cowboys and Indians." Once my brother and his friend, Billy walked into the old Marysville Bank with their pistols drawn and said to the teller, "This is a stickup." The bank president made a deal with the boys, lollipops instead of money. By the time they arrived home, both mothers had already learned of their "misadventure."

Cathy Fesler and I spent many hours together growing up and were known to get in trouble from time to time. We liked to give her dog, Skipper, a bath and brush her teeth. For that we borrowed shampoo, as well as a toothbrush and toothpaste, from the family bathroom, putting them back before we were caught. When we brushed her teeth, Skipper looked like she was rabid with foam coming out of her mouth. Naturally she didn't realize that she was to rinse and spit. (She wouldn't even take a drink!) So one of us would hold her mouth open while the other one poured water down her throat, causing her to choke. She never tried to run away or bite us, amazingly after what we put her through. (I never did find out whose toothbrush we used, but am sure it wasn't Cathy's.)

Another time Cathy and several of the other first graders (I was five and hadn't started school yet) dared me to say, "Hi, stupid" to Mrs. Vera Carmichael, one of the first-grade teachers, when she walked by. Trying to impress my friends and not back down from a dare, I did what I was told. By the time I got home, Mrs. Carmichael had already called my parents, and I was in big trouble! It was a huge relief when I learned that my first-grade teacher would be Mrs. Telford!

Since there was no preschool or kindergarten at that time, in September of 1952 I started first grade in the old Marysville-Rye Elementary School, now known as the Clock Tower Apartments, on the corner of Maple Avenue and Chestnut Street. Grades one through eight were taught there. The first several weeks of school didn't go well. I cried every morning and feigned stomach aches, headaches, or whatever other ailment I could come up with so that I could stay home. My mother, however, didn't buy into this and would firmly take me by the hand, my pigtails flying, and drag me off to school.

To me the school day was incredibly long and I missed my freedom. Naps, which I had not taken for years, were required after lunch. It was so hard to keep still for 30 minutes.

And then the day came when we started to read! Even though we began with Dick and Jane, it was exciting to make stories out of words. A whole new world opened up that day, eventually leading to my becoming an English teacher.

School was so different then. Every morning we all stood for the Pledge of Allegiance to the flag, followed by our teacher reading from the Bible and all of us reciting the Lord's Prayer. When we were old enough, we students did the Bible readings, not always well, but we did them.

Our classrooms had old wooden floors treated with oil. The wooden desks had round holes cut into the top where inkwells once had been. We had a "cloakroom" where our coats, hats, gloves, and scarves were hung. It was a scary place because we all knew what happened when a student was taken there by our teacher, who was carrying a large wooden paddle. If we got in trouble in school, we tried to make sure our parents never found out, or we would be in bigger trouble when we got home.

Twice a day we lined up to go outside for recess, unless the weather was really bad. Sometimes our teacher would engage us in group play. I remember our standing in a circle singing Farmer in the Dell, hoping that everyone would be chosen to be a farm animal and not the cheese. Other times we played on the swings or the climbing gym. The entire playground was covered in blacktop and inevitably someone would fall and get hurt. One of our classmates, Roy Alander, fell from the top rung of the climbing gym while swinging by his legs. Several days later, he returned to school with a broken leg, walking on crutches. For a week or two he was the class hero.

Snow days were not nearly as frequent in the 1950s. Except for the two or three buses that transported students from Rye Township and Perdix, we all walked to school. However, when we had a major snowstorm and schools closed, almost every kid in town went sledding. The police would block off Lansvale Street at the intersection of Lincoln, providing us with a long ride down the hill, but also a long uphill climb back. Other times they would block off Broad Street at the Lansvale and Cameron Street intersections. This made for a shorter but faster ride.

Like Randy in *A Christmas Story* the younger children, so bundled up that they could barely move, came sledding with their mothers. However, as soon as we were old enough, the rest of us came with our friends. All types of sleds appeared. Some new, others, like mine, were old Lightning Guiders. Mine had belonged to my dad, who told us that he and his friends actually went sledding on Valley Street, starting at the top and ending on Main Street by the river.

The Marysville Lions Park pond was a great place to ice skate in the winter. The pond was only two or three feet deep, so if someone did fall in, there was no risk of drowning, however, frostbite was a concern. I learned to skate on double-bladed strap-on skates, advancing to my mother's old black single-blade skates. However, I was mortified to wear them because the other girl's skates were white. That Christmas I received my own white skates and immediately decorated them with yarn pompoms!

On cold windy days, the older boys would build a bonfire using old tires. The easiest way for them to start these fires was by carrying an empty gas can to Harper's Gulf Station at the top of the hill, filling it with gas, pouring the gas over the tires, and then striking a match to ignite the tires. Of course, the gas ignited quickly causing those closest to the fire to scatter as black smoke, along with the smell of burning rubber, permeated the area around the pond. Benches, constructed of discarded cement blocks and old boards, were placed around the fire. This made a good place for putting on or taking off skates, as well as getting warm, if we could stand the smoke.

Often the wind was so strong as it blew across the pond that it would carry us over the ice while we were standing still on our skates. On those same windy days, it was easy to become entangled with balls of wire that came from burning tires, causing quite a few falls. Late in the afternoon, with hands and feet numb from the cold, we would walk home. In fact, almost all of us walked everywhere we wanted to go.

The hustle and bustle of small-town life was most evident during the Christmas season, which began the day after Thanksgiving and ended when we returned to school in the new year. People began decorating their homes, the tree on the square was lit, and Bob Watts opened the upstairs of his Five and Ten, to the delight of all the children.

Each year Bob Watts created a toy land, a place we kids visited often before making our wish lists to Santa. This magical place was filled with all sorts of toys. There were trains, bicycles, dolls, baby carriages, toy guns, footballs, baseballs and bats, roller skates, and a large variety of games. I wonder if Bob ever realized just how much joy he brought to the children throughout the years.

On Christmas day, Bing Fisher, who owned the Galen movie theater in town, offered a free matinee from 2:00 until 4:00. We watched The Three Stooges, Ma and Pa Kettle, and LOTS of cartoons. One year I remember my older sister receiving a strand of pearls as a Christmas gift and my "borrowing" them, without asking, to wear to the matinee. During the show I started playing with the pearls when the string broke and the pearls began rolling down the sloped floor of the theater, many never to be found again. When the matinee ended, we all headed to the Moose where we were given a box of chocolates and an orange.

After we returned to school following the holidays, we had no breaks until Easter. This was followed by Memorial Day on May 30. On this special day of remembrance, the entire town would turn out for the annual parade. The soldiers and sailors from World War l and World War II, proudly wearing their military uniforms, marched or were transported in convertibles along the parade route. Flags flew and townspeople applauded these heroes as they passed by. The parade also included the high school marching band, the Scout troops, and girls carrying bouquets of flowers to be placed on graves. Others, especially the boys, would decorate their bikes with red, white, and blue crepe paper wrapped around the tire spokes, as well as small flags and streamers on their handlebars. Once at the cemetery, a military officer, often a Marysville native, would speak, followed by a gun salute and the playing of taps. I can still remember watching tears roll down the faces of some of those veterans. That memory will remain with me always.

Summer had arrived, which meant days spent at the Lions Park swimming in the dammed-up section of Fishing Creek. When we stepped into the cold water, which was probably knee-deep at the edge, our feet immediately started sinking into the mud. Once we were able to swim out a little farther, the bottom was covered with stones, and the water was not quite so murky. Some liked to enter the water using an old rusty sliding board. However, this really wasn't such a good idea because the seats of many swimsuits quickly developed holes. To get out of the water, we once again waded through the mud, often discovering that a leach had attached itself to us. Those were the good old days before the Lions Club pool was built!

The highlight of the summer was the Marysville Carnival, which was always held the first week of August. Our parents took us until we were old enough to go without them. After that, we walked to the park with our friends, arriving early each evening to the sounds of live music coming from the bandstand. For the next six glorious nights, we devoured junk food, rode rides until we got sick, and played games. Every once in a while, we even came home with a prize. What a great way to end the summer!

The only downside to the carnival was the realization that summer was almost over and school would soon begin. It would be another year filled with new adventures, and one day these adventures would become lifelong memories too.

Spending Time With Grandma and Grandpa Lower

Storyteller Carl Johnson
Recorded by Paula Johnson Davis

I spent much of my years from age six to twelve with my grandparents, Ben and Sarah Lower, on Front Street in Liverpool, Pennsylvania, a town of about two hundred at that time. Their house was only two-hundred feet from the Susquehanna River across the road and the canal. They bought just about everything they needed in town because Grandpa never drove or owned a car.

During his younger years, 1905-1928, my Grandpa Lower operated a ferryboat which crossed the river at Liverpool, hauling mail, freight and people. This was the only way to get to the other side of the river because few people had cars in those days. The ferry would take people from the Liverpool side of the river, to the east side where they could catch the train to Sunbury or Harrisburg. A few years before he died Grandpa gave me the compass from the old ferryboat and told me about his years of operating it. The last calibration date on the compass is 1928. I don't think the ferry operated in Liverpool after that date.

He told me of a flood one spring with very high water and lots of brush and trees floating down river. A child from Liverpool was hurt in an accident, but the bridges and roads were closed because of high water. The only way left to get to Harrisburg to the hospital was to cross the river and take the train. Grandpa took the ferry across, dodging floating logs and brush and saved the child's life. The other experience he related happened in 1910. He and two other men were on the ferry when there was a gas explosion. He was thrown from the boat and floated about a quarter mile down river, where he was rescued. He suffered extensive burns on his arms and face, but I don't remember him having any scars. One of the men stayed with the boat, the other jumped overboard. All three survived.

One night, before the new road was built, when traffic came down Front Street, a large tanker truck ran into the living room of Alma and Banks Nace's house next door to Grandpa's. No one was hurt. Grandpa said it really rattled his house as the houses were connected.

I can remember sitting on a glider on Grandpa's front porch in the evenings listening to him telling stories of his hunting and fishing trips. He always had a good time. I never heard him say a bad word about anyone.

Grandpa would take me fishing with him. He had a twenty-foot wooden boat and an Old Town Canoe that was eighteen-feet long. He liked the wooden boat best. He would pole the boat up the river a mile or two and we would drift back down fishing in every good hole along the way. He knew all the good fishing holes and named everyone.

In the evenings, Grandpa would take me to Lutz's store down the street from his house and let me pick out some penny candy. Sometimes we would walk down to his son, Ernie's Weis Store on Market Street and buy some groceries, talk awhile, and walk home. It was only two blocks but it seemed a long way to me.

He liked to hunt and fish. In the fall of the year, he hunted for ducks from a specially designed duck boat. In October when rabbit season opened, he would hunt rabbits and pheasants. Deer hunting was in December. Since Grandpa didn't have a car, he walked a few miles to go hunting. I went with him a few times. Usually my Uncle Harrison would go along, he had a car. In deer season most of his sons would come home to hunt, putting on successful drives. While Grandpa was off hunting or fishing, Grandma would nearly always stay home. She didn't like to be in a boat. She usually had my mom or my Uncle Herb's wife, Mary, help her with the cooking. They would have a good meal ready when the men returned.

I never saw them drink alcohol, but Grandma always had whiskey to put in her mince pies. Grandma made the best pies. She did most of the cooking on a coal stove in the kitchen. They had a 3 burner kerosene stove on the back-porch that they used as a summer kitchen. Sometimes grandma would send me across the street with fifteen cents, to the hardware store for a gallon of kerosene. Grandma would always have a pot of soup and hot water for cocoa on the stove in the winter time in case someone stopped by. They had a parlor coal stove in the living room.

They never had a dog or cat while I knew them, just chickens. Grandpa raised chickens for meat and eggs. He would keep about two dozen chickens and a couple of turkeys for Thanksgiving and Christmas dinner. They always had a nice garden, growing lots of vegetables, and a grape arbor outside the back door. In the summer, grandma was always canning vegetables and fruits or making jellies. Grandpa had a wooden barrel that he buried in his garden that worked like a root cellar to keep potatoes, cabbage and turnips in for the winter. He would cover the top with straw to keep it from freezing.

They had a big oak-wall telephone in the kitchen. It had the part you would speak into on the phone box and the ear receiver on a cord that you would hold up to your ear. It had a hand-crank on the wall box. They were still using it when I went in the Army in 1958.

In the 1920s-1930s, Grandpa Lower ran a pool room on the towpath of the canal. People would come from all over to shoot pool. The building was moved on rollers to its present day location on North Market Street in preparation for the construction of Route 11 & 15 in 1948. It is still in use as a private residence.

Grandpa worked for the highway department in the 1940s-1950s. Sam Fleisher was the supervisor who stopped by every morning, picked up grandpa and took him along to work. In the summer, grandpa would have to cut around the head-walls and culverts with a scythe where the tractors and mowers couldn't reach. They would also patch the holes in the roads. In the winter he threw sand on the icy areas.

I remember Grandma's breakfast called "coffee soup". It was crackers in a bowl with coffee poured over them. When I visited them, Grandma would make me cocoa and toast. The toast tasted so good made on the top of the stove. She always wore an apron.

Every year in August we would have a family reunion. Everybody would come. Grandpa Lower would kill some of his chickens, pick sweet corn out of his garden and we would have chicken corn soup. One hundred relatives would bring foods to share and there would always be homemade ice cream. We did this every year until Grandma Lower died, then we never did it again.

"Adventures Of The Legendary McConnell Brothers"

Storytellers Larry & Jim McConnell
Recorded by William G. Lyons

The lives and times of Larry and Jim McConnell were documented in detail in the first *Cherished Memories* Book that was published in 2021. Even so, it wasn't too difficult to learn more about these resilient brothers as they live their lives. We will begin with a few work-related stories and finish with a catastrophe that the brothers had to endure, but included many blessings as well.

In 1979, the Blain Methodist Church put out bids to have its deteriorating steeple removed and put on new siding. Not many contractors were interested in the job of removing a steeple. John, Larry, Jim and Paul McConnell won the bid and accepted the challenge. It was forty-five feet up to the bell and another eighteen feet to the top of the steeple. The men placed steel scaffolding up to the bell and had a twelve-inch-wide plank to walk on and work off of. They had the electric power lines below them. As John, Larry and Jim tore down the steeple, they had to throw the debris over the lines and onto the street. Paul had to direct the traffic. Putting on the siding was not nearly as precarious as tearing down the steeple.

Narrow Misses
Back in the 1970s-1980s, the McConnell's bought dead trees from the state to cut down and saw into lumber. Many of the trees were hemlocks, white pine and oak. One time they were checking out a tract of state land off of Union Hollow Road, back on the Second Narrows Road near Sheaffer's Run. As they were walking along John saw the head of a snake peering over a log. If he would've stepped over the log, he'd have been bitten. After the snake was killed, turns out it was a four-foot rattlesnake.

There are a series of ridges running south west of Fowler Hollow Road. Starting at Harry Book's to Dale Rohm's, it is known as the Beavertown Ridge. From there through the McConnell's land, it is known as Chestnut Ridge. Continuing west from Center Square, the ridge goes by the name of Center Ridge and then onto Shultz Ridge near Union Hollow Road. One spring morning, Larry was turkey hunting on the western end of Chestnut Ridge. He glanced down just in time to see a snake coiled up. He jumped over it, grabbed a rock and killed the twenty-inch copperhead!

Working in Doylesburg on a home back in their younger days, "the boys" hung a pair of women's panties on the house's electric service line and left them there. The following day, a man from a local garage came to pick up the ladies' car for inspection and service. The man kept looking up at something as he chatted. After he left, the lady noticed what he was looking at. She blamed her son for the prank as the McConnell boys looked on innocently. The son said it was the carpenters but the mother would not believe him.

The men were hired to replace the barn roof at Marlin Dillman's located just west of New Germantown. They had sixteen, ten-foot-long sheets of galvanized tin up on the roof with them. All at once the wind started to blow and Jim threw himself on top of the sheets of tin to keep it from blowing off. He held on to the lathe for dear life to keep it from blowing away or to turn him into a kite. The other three men worked feverishly to install the remaining sheets without incident.

Jim has always been known as a man with great strength. At one time he could squeeze bathroom scales with his hands until the scales would hit 200 pounds and just hold it there for a period of time. The brothers were working at Greg Bitting's house, west of Kistler on Route 17, and had to move an eight-inch-high steel I-beam forty-feet long to the center of the wall. As Larry was sliding the beam along, he looked over, saw that Jim had picked up the other end and was walking the top of the wall with it!

Another time, they were working on a holding area roof at Clark Bower's farm, on Seagertown Road west of Blain. There was a 6"x6" post 16' long, that was in the ground three and a half feet. The post needed to be moved and Clark offered to go get a tractor and chain. John McConnell said, don't bother with that as Jim proceeded to work the post out of the ground. Jim is known for tremendous strength and Larry is known for toughness. He claims he has fallen off more roofs or through barns, than the number of fingers on his hands, without being seriously hurt. Remember that the further west you go in Jackson Township, the tougher they get and these two fellas live in the last house west!

The McConnell's were working on a barn roof one day and Jim was wearing an old dress shirt with a stiff collar. That collar was driving him crazy and he just couldn't stand it any longer, so his dad cut the whole thing off. When they got home, Jim jokingly told his mother that he fell through the barn and caught it on a nail. When she learned the truth, she was not very happy about the collar being cut off!

It's common knowledge that these guys are as good at making ice cream as they are at eating it. Back in the day when the four of them were working together, (John, Larry, Jim and cousin Paul), they would often times flag down John Hall's ice cream delivery truck. The men would buy two half gallons of ice cream, split the boxes in half and eat it all since there was no way to keep it from melting. One time they were building Bill and Marie Gray's dairy barn on Bernheisel Road, with Eugene "Pepper" Shields help. Again, they flagged down the ice cream truck but this time they bought four half gallons of ice cream. Bill went to the house and brought out vegetable serving dishes to eat out of. After the six men were done eating, there still was some left for Bill's daughter, Marsha to have when she got home from school.

Another time in Doylesburg, they were building a chicken cage-layer house near the Catholic Church and its cemetery. A large group of starlings landed in a big tree near the cemetery. The owner of the new chicken house challenged Larry to shoot into the flock and see how many of the birds he could get. Larry had just purchased a new ten-gauge shotgun and was eager to try it out. He shot three times and the undertaker, who was in the cemetery, yelled to quit shooting as he hid behind a tombstone. The pellets were dropping from the sky but not one bird fell!

Larry's dad told him about making pine tar. First, you need the roots of a pine tree stump full of turpentine and knots in the log. You put this all in an iron kettle and boil. The turpentine will come out in the water. Keep cooking it down like boiling maple syrup until it becomes tar. Back in the day before grease, tar was used to lubricate Conestoga wagon axles. The McConnell Brothers have made some tar buckets to sell like the ones that hung on the rear axles of the Conestoga wagon. The sassafras buckets that they made are ten inches high, four inches in diameter with a telescoping lid and a rope handle.

In Civil wars times, during the 1860s, a black man escaped slavery from Maryland and ended up in Jackson Township in western Perry County. He went by the name of "Black Billy." It was assumed he was a family man, but not many details exist other than a baby is buried east of Uncle Vern's house on the north side of Chestnut Ridge. The McConnell brothers great-great-granddad, John Snyder, hired him to work on his farm. He wasn't a slave any longer, but a paid worker. "Black Billy" lived in a log house that is still standing today. It is located about a hundred yards north of Fowler Hollow Road.

McConnell's Forever Home
In the late 1700s and early 1800s, the property at 3100 Fowler Hollow Road, Blain, Pennsylvania, there was a log cabin home. It was approximately 20 feet by 16 feet with a dirt floor and was located behind where the present-day workshop is. A spring was located close by so it was easy to get water and safer for its inhabitants in case of Indians. The log cabin is long gone but some stone foundation can be seen.

The present-day workshop and butcher shop used to be a double house where two families lived. Former owner Clark Anderson moved into the current house in 1937. He needed some stones for a project at the barn and decided to take some away from the base of the huge fireplace in the old double house. When this was done in 1939, the whole chimney collapsed taking out the kitchen and two bedrooms, about fifteen feet of the building was lost.

The house that Larry and Jim live in was built by Clark Anderson from 1936 to 1937. The house does not have a stone foundation like many from that time period, but one of poured concrete. The cement was mixed by hand. The house itself is known as a "Sears, Roebuck and Co. House." At this time, there was a planing mill located in Sunbury, Pennsylvania that would cut out framework house-kits. The kits were numbered to put the house together. The boy's father, John lived across the fields from the house and helped to build it. In 1936, the house was framed but had no windows. John shoveled snow out of the house that winter and it was completed the following year.

John grew up on the neighboring farm and his future wife Irene was born and raised just west of Manassa on Robinson Road. They were married in 1941 and lived in the other half of his parent's house until they bought the current property in 1943.

On Friday, March 19, 2021 the day started off as any other. Larry had put wood in their outside wood stove and both brothers were busy working in their shop. Larry came out of the shop awhile later and saw flames at the east end of the house. There was a strong east wind that day and a glowing ember that had fallen out must have ignited starting the fire. He tried to pull open an unused door that they had screwed shut. He wasn't getting anywhere with that door and the fire was taking off. He ran and called for the Blain Volunteer Fire Company.

During this time, Jim was able to get in a door from the other end and save 33 guns before the fire took over. The volunteers arrived in eight minutes of the call and without their efforts the house would have been a total loss. Larry and Jim were safe but they had endured some heavy losses. Not only were the kitchen, laundry room, living room and half bathroom downstairs heavily damaged, there was smoke and water damage throughout the upstairs hallway, a bedroom and a bathroom. That was bad enough, but the biggest loss was in their gun room. Over the last six years or so they had been attending many gun sales and amassed around 280 guns. Jim saved as many as he could before it was too dangerous to go back in. Still, they lost 247 high quality rifles. There were many Remington Model 760s, Winchester Model 70s, 88s, and 94s. Also, there were some very nice Sakos and Rugers. Neighbor, Bob Good, gathered up all the ruined guns and soaked them in oil. He was able to get a little bit of salvage money for them to give back to the brothers.

The day of the fire, close by neighbor, Dennis Cauffman offered them his dad's brick house to live in as long as they needed. That's where Larry and Jim stayed until they could move back home. Travis McKeehan also had offered them a house.

The cleanup began the very next day, Saturday, when people came from all around to help. All salvageable contents were carried out to the barn and anything that was now junk was put on a pile. Jeff Smith provided a big shed for additional items to be placed in out of the weather, along with his dump truck to haul things away. A crew of Mennonite neighbors came on Monday and tore off the end of the destroyed part of the house. On Tuesday, about forty church people and neighbors continued to clean out the house, wiping woodwork, etc. Three Springs Church women's fellowship provided a big lunch for everyone working at the house.

Both Larry and Jim were in a bit of shock and dismay over all the events that happened in the last few days. Trying to decide what to do next wasn't easy and they felt very fortunate to have Ron Lupold step forward and spearhead the rebuilding of the house. He has a lot of knowledge in the different aspects of what was needed to be done. The men didn't have a good way to be reached by phone so Bill and Crista Lyons took them to an AT&T store. Larry and Jim carry I-Phones and now can be reached more readily.

As they settled in at the Cauffman house, they traveled back and forth each day. Many ladies from Three Springs made meals for them the first two weeks following the fire. Amish ladies washed all their clothes and dishes shortly after the fire. Bobbie Herr and Kim Boyer washed their clothes throughout the rebuilding process until they could move back home. Bobbie also wiped smoke off all their furniture that was saved. While the work at the house was going on, various people from the church (many women) pruned fruit trees at the same time.

Dave Stoltzfus poured footers and laid a foundation to replace what the fire took away (the laundry room and bathroom). During this time, Anthony Turner seal coated all the walls in the house. Ron Lupold drilled holes in the walls and then blew in insulation as Mike Trout and Bob Good fed the blower. Dan Cauffman measured and ordered doors, windows and other materials to build the addition, etc. He had some great help with his brother Donald, neighbors Dirks and Drayton Koser, along with Nick Campbell, Eric Smith and Jamie Boyer. They did a wonderful job of framing, roofing, drywall, etc. Scott Smith did the electrical work and Ron Lupold did the plumbing. Bob Good and Mel Lupold did the painting. Sam King provided beautiful stone work to the front of the new addition. Ron took care of lining up a company to install a new propane heating system to alleviate the need to burn wood anymore.

Dennis and Daniel Hoover hauled all the scrap metal away. Logan Bower had a tractor, big cart and payloader there. He hauled all the junk away and took care of its disposal.

The work continued to progress, but there were still some big items to address such as kitchen cupboards, wall coverings, trim, flooring, etc. The master cabinet makers and carpenters that the brothers are, then got to work. Using all their own wood, Jim proceeded to make beautiful oak kitchen cupboards with raised panel doors, that when you walk in, look and say wow! Larry used sassafras to make ship-lapped random width boards for wall paneling for the kitchen and cherry wood for the living room. He then trimmed the doors and windows with walnut facings and crown molding. Again, when you walk in, you say wow! They also laid a new kitchen floor. It was now getting into the month of August and it was time to move back home.

In a little more than five months, the McConnell's went from living their normal everyday life in western Perry County to a roller-coaster ride of hard work and emotions to that of being blessed beyond measure. The whole community rallied around the brothers from clean-up to rebuilding the home after the Blain Fire Company saved most of the original house. They went from being comfortable in their home to being uprooted, persevering and now living in their house with new amenities. No additional words are capable to express their appreciation for all the help that was given to them in a time of need. So many people helped and some that were not even known making it impossible to name everyone for fear of forgetting someone.

Larry and Jim are great friends to many as the support they received after the fire was overwhelming. To be able to move back home in less than six months is unbelievable. These two brothers have made many memories and continue to do so. With that said, anyone who knows them will think of them as the "Legendary McConnell Brothers!"

"Baseball's In His Blood"

Storyteller Max Mohler

"I HAVE ALWAYS LOVED PLAYING BASEBALL!"

Beginning at the Bloomfield Grade School on High Street in New Bloomfield, which is now The Lutheran Parish House, we would have 'pick-up' teams of nine or ten players and play 'scrubby.'

To play 'scrubby,' we would start with three players up to bat. When one player made an out, they would go to right field, then center field, left field and follow back through all of the infield bases to bat again and the game would continue. Sometimes, we would hit the ball over onto Carson Long's tennis court.

Some of our players were Ray Adams, Leroy Comp, John Dirst, John Fry, Dale Kepner, Max Mohler, Bob Morrison, George Morrison, and Maurice Shoemaker.

Also, every Saturday, all summer long, we would have pick-up teams and play 'scrubby' at the Bloomfield 'town team' baseball field back of the Bloomfield High School on East McClure Street, which is now the New Bloomfield Post Office.

Later, we had a Junior Teener Team coached by Jack Glassburn. The first year, we did not have uniforms. The next year, New Bloomfield Auto Company bought us uniforms.

We moved on and our Bloomfield High School Baseball Team, coached by John Weigle, played against other Perry County teams.

When I was a high school senior, my start with 'the town team' began. One Saturday, Bussy Thebes came to my house with a uniform and said, "Hey Mohler, we're playing Thompsontown today and we need another player." I had a couple of hits. We won the game and I was happy playing with 'the town team.'

The Bloomfield 'town team' was in the Perry-Juniata League with stiff competition between some of the following teams: Blain, Duncannon, Ickesburg, Loysville, Newport, Mifflintown, Millerstown, Port Royal and Thompsontown.

Blain always had a tough team. Their manager, Amos College said, "Give me nine or ten guys who want to play ball and that's all you need." Some of those guys were Alan Bower, Bud Bower, Clark Bower, Bill Gray, Dale Gray, Riley Neidigh, Dale Rohm, Rich Rohm and Gene Wilt.

We had some scrappy games ending in fights, many times instigated by Bussy Thebes. He always went to Blain, who was his biggest rival, with a chip on his shoulder. Overall, Blain usually got the best of us.

Loysville was good and sported a strong team. We always faced left-handed pitcher Ron Emlet in every game. He was tough on the six left-handed batters on our Bloomfield team. Some other top players on the Loysville team were Mort Loy, Dick Milligan, Ron Shambaugh, Bob Smeigh, Jim Stum and Paul Stum.

Duncannon always had a good team with top players Tom Bornman, Max Cooper, Paul Cooper, Neil Hickoff, Roger Hickoff, Sid Klinepeter, Jerry Rohrer and Myron Rohrer. They were very strong competitors and we usually had close games.

At one time, our Bloomfield team had six left-handed batters: Leroy Comp, Paul Comp, Ray Dillman, Don Mohler, Max Mohler and Jack Sill. Needless to say, there were many hits and home runs into the old oak tree beyond right field and several onto the roof of Bloomfield High School now the New Bloomfield Borough building. Our teams were strong and always gave our opponents a good battle.

Newport always fielded a strong competitive team with some top players like Bill Buffington, Herm Houtz, Ken Holtzapple, Bob Rice and Buck Wagner.

Millerstown was tough with 'Ducky' Thompson pitching every game. Along with other players Butdorf, Jim Crane, Hoffman, Dar Roush, Amos Miller and Paul Wagner.

One game, playing Port Royal, didn't end too well for me and my team. We had no pitcher that day. So, Tom Owen, our regular catcher, said, "I'll pitch," and then I took his place as catcher. In the game, Port Royal base runner, Skip Kepner, tried to score from third and came crashing into me. We got onto a fight. During our scuffle, my cleats caught and tore the umpire, Harry Becker's pants. He said, "Mohler, I have to throw you out of the game and besides, look what you've done to my pants." I said, "If I go, he goes." We were both thrown out of the game. Worse than that, my team lost!

Later, Ray Dillman and I went to play for Enola, managed by Bill Knaby, in the West Shore Twilight League. Some teams in that league were Dillsburg, Duncannon, Enola, Mt. Holly, Mechanicsburg, and New Cumberland. It was a good league with many top players and tough competition. Mechanicsburg, managed by Rick Rickenbaugh was usually the league leader followed by top contenders, Duncannon, New Cumberland and Enola.

At one time, I had three different uniforms to play for three different teams: Enola, Bloomfield and Berrysburg. Enola played Monday, Tuesday, and Thursday. Bloomfield played Wednesday and Saturday. Berrysburg played Saturday and Sunday.

Over the years, I have had the pleasure of meeting, playing with and making lasting friendships with many good baseball players. Obviously, I have not been able to mention all of them. However, based on my memory, I have tried to recall correct information to share with you.

Hard Work And Family Fun On The Farm

Storyteller Ruth Fisher Reisinger

My parents were William and Louise (Kitner) Fisher. My dad served in WW ll from 1941-1944 in the Second Air Force. My parents met when my dad came home on leave with my mother's brother, Harry Kitner, having served together in the Air Force. In 1947, my parents bought the farm where they raised four daughters and made a lifetime of memories.

I grew up on a small dairy farm outside of Shermans Dale that laid next to Shermans Creek. We lived in a big stone house, which was cool in the summer but could be very cold in the winter. We had about thirty milk cows and at one time had chickens and sold eggs. The egg check would buy the groceries. My dad raised some hogs for our own use and they would butcher every year between Christmas and New Year's, when us kids were out of school.

I had three sisters, Susan the oldest, Jennie then me and my youngest sister, Wilma, who was named after my dad and got the nickname "Willy". We all went to the barn and helped in the fields whether it was planting or harvesting. We loved to be outside helping but of course, there was housework. So, we all did learn to cook, do dishes and clean. My two older sisters learned to sew very well and still enjoy it today. But we did things as a family and always had fun even if it was a job we didn't care to do, like picking rocks off the fields after they were plowed and worked down for planting. This is how we learned to drive a tractor. We had a "Farmall BN" tractor, that we took turns driving to pull the wagon as we put the stones and rocks on. The tractor was small enough that dad could jump onto the back and help steer the wheel when we got to the end of the field. Some of those fields were very long. There were lots of rock piles at the edge of the fields.

The "Farmall BN" was the tractor my parents used to work the corn. Every summer after the corn was planted and was half knee-high, they would use the corn worker to work the ground between the rows to get rid of the weeds and loosen the ground. One summer when attaching the corn worker to the tractor, my sister, Wilma dropped the end on her toe, smashing it. Later in life, she had to have her toenail removed because it always got infected.

My mother enjoyed working the corn, but she preferred to do it after barn work and supper was over when it was cooler. One year, she was in the long field back by the creek and the fish warden stopped by because he saw this light moving slowly along the creek. He asked my dad who was back there fishing. We all got a good laugh after he left.

My two older sisters had to stack hay on the wagon when we baled hay. By the time Wilma and I were old enough to help, we had a kicker-baler that threw the bales onto the wagon. But we still got to help stack the hay in the barn. My mom loved to drive the tractor and she always raked the hay. My dad did the baling. Then my mom would pull the filled hay wagons from the fields into the barn. She could really back a wagon.

Then there were the barn chores which started with bringing the cows in from the pasture. They were usually waiting at the gate to come in and eat their silage and grain, while being milked. The silage was forked out of the silo by hand. We did not have the modern-day silo unloader. We got a lot of good exercise back then such as climbing the hay mows to throw down hay and straw.

At one time we put the milk cans in a can cooler, but in the late 1960s we built a new milk house and installed a bulk tank. A dumping station was used to put the milk into the tank, but we still used the bucket milker.

For fun we rode bikes and we had a big maple tree in our yard that had swings on. There were two smaller trees that we would climb and sit on just to talk about our day. We had two ponies that we rode, played with or sat on just for fun. We enjoyed brushing and combing them.

We always had kittens to play with and we always had a dog. It was a "cow-dog" and would help bring in the cows from the fields.

We had a big garden so we spent a lot of time pulling weeds and hoeing. We would help our mom to can and freeze vegetables. In late June or early July, we would go and help to pick cherries. In August, we went to the orchard to pick peaches. We had our own pear trees and a few apple trees. This was always a fun time and it was family time getting them canned and put away for winter. We grew up eating lots of fruit.

And, we also ate a lot of potatoes, because that was the vegetable my dad liked best. We always had a big potato patch and he liked to have them planted by his birthday which was April 21st. He would have the patch plowed and worked down, then used a potato plow to make the rows. We would gather together and cut the seed potatoes and drop them in the rows. Then they would have to be covered with soil. By this time in the spring, it was warm enough that we went barefoot. I still remember how good the warm ground felt on my feet! And then, there were the fishing worms that we would find, pick up and throw at each other.

My dad had a small sawmill and we owned timberland. Any time he needed any lumber, he would go to the woods, cut a few trees and saw them out. He also did some custom sawing for others, mostly neighbors. To this day, I love the smell of the wood and the fresh-cut lumber.

Sundays were a day of rest after the barn work was done in the morning. After lunch most Sundays we would go and visit our grandparents. My mother's parents did not have a phone, so a way to keep in touch was to visit. Of course, some of her brothers and sisters would visit at the same time, so that gave us a chance to play with our cousins. And, Grandma Kitner always had candy for us.

My husband, Grady and I were raised very similar. I guess that is why we hit it off so good. In our life together, we raised our children, our farm was our life and we did things as a family. Getting the work done and taking care of the cattle needed to be part of that. Milking was also a time for the kids to talk about their day at school or what might be troubling them. It could also be a peaceful time.

From Mechanic To Pinsetter To Preacher

"NEW BLOOMFIELD AUTO COMPANY AND PERRY LANES BOWLING ALLEY"

Storyteller Rev. Donald W. Raffensperger
Including Ethel Raffensperger Mowery, Marlin and Gary Raffensperger

In 1945, my parents, Clair and Agnes Raffensperger purchased the Dodge/Plymouth dealership in New Bloomfield from Harry and Polly Neisweinder. How did he get there to make such a purchase?

Prior to coming to New Bloomfield, my family consisted of my parents and four children: my sister, Ethel, older brother, Marlin, me, Donald, and my younger brother, Gary. We lived in Biglerville, Pennsylvania in Adams County. My father worked at York Chain and Cable Company, making chain hoists. On the side, he had a small auto repair shop, where he worked part-time, evenings and Saturdays. My mother worked at Musselman's Canning Factory near our home.

One day my father went to the bank in Gettysburg to make a deposit. While there, he was approached by the Bank President. During the course of their conversation, they were apparently talking about my father's brother-in-law, Glenn Bream, who owned the Chrysler/Plymouth dealership in Gettysburg. The president asked, "How would you like to have a dealership of your own?" My father replied, "I would like to have my own dealership, but I have no means of doing that." The president replied, "I know where there is one for sale that we can go look at and if you are interested, I will back you in purchasing it." He brought my parents to New Bloomfield and in a short time a deal was made and my family became residents of New Bloomfield.

When my sister, who was a teenager, was told that the family was moving to New Bloomfield, she replied, "I am not moving to New Bloomfield and away from my friends." Now, you would have a tough time getting her to move away from New Bloomfield.

Our family moved into the two-story house on the corner of South Carlisle Street and West McClure Street across from the Masonic Lodge. It was the ideal residence for our family, located just catty-cornered across the street from the dealership. The building lot was long and went clear to the alley making a fairly good-sized lawn for my brothers and I to mow with a "motor-less" push mower. At the end of the lot was the foundation of a barn that had stood there many years before.

Meredith's Butcher Shop was located next to our house. Some years later, when this business moved to the rear of the former Rhinesmith Hotel building on the square, my parent's purchased this property which also extended to the alley, where Mr. Meredith would park his truck. A short time later, my parent's decided to build a single-story house where the barn originally stood, with a two-car garage underneath. A retaining wall was built along the property line of the Meredith building, from the back of the building to the edge of where the new house was built. This section was filled in with dirt and topsoil, and seeded with grass, making the yard almost twice as large for the boys to now mow.

When my parents purchased the dealership, they named it "New Bloomfield Auto Company". At that time, it was known as a "sublet" dealership. By this I mean that all of the new cars that we received to sell were not delivered to our business directly from the factory, but came from the Brenner Motors dealership in Harrisburg. At times, this caused some problems for us in that we could not always get the particular vehicle that a customer wanted, so we would have to take whatever vehicles that Brenner's were willing to give us.

A couple from Millerstown, Mr. & Mrs. Charles Weiland, bought a new 1948 Dodge coupe and traded in a 1921 Dodge Touring car. Mr. Weiland had driven this car back and forth to Harrisburg to work. It was in very good shape for its age, so we kept this vehicle over the years and it was driven in a number of parades. One year, Mr. Bruce Dimmick, my class advisor in high school, and his wife, Joyce drove it in a Halloween Parade. A group of students from the school rode in the car, and standing on the running boards of the car, to portray "Cheaper by the Dozen." This vehicle was also used in the wedding procession for one of my daughters, and was finally sold at our parent's estate sale.

Recently, the son of a farmer from the Landisburg area, told my brother, that in 1948, his father went to a Ford dealership, a Chevrolet dealership, and to our dealership, and ordered a two-ton stake body truck. He did not tell any of the dealers that whoever got the truck first, that was the truck he would buy. Fortunately, our father was the first dealer to get the truck he ordered, so that was the truck he bought. This mostly all-original truck was still being stored on the family farm and my brothers and I were able to see it.

Late one evening, my father was called to bring his tow truck to pick up two vehicles involved in an accident in front of Homer Mullen's barn, on Route 34 south of Meck's Corner. A drunk driver in a dump truck had collided head-on with a passenger car. In the car were two reporters, a man and a woman from The Gettysburg Times in Gettysburg who were in the area covering a football game. Both of them were killed. My father towed in both vehicles. When the news came out, revealing the deceased names, my father realized that he had known the man when we lived in Adams County.

When we originally purchased the garage, there was an overhead door in the center of the front of the building where the vehicles were driven in and out for repairs, or they could be driven out the back door. In 1949, our dealership became a direct delivery dealership, instead of a "sublet" dealership. At that time, the whole front of the building was opened up and about one-fourth of the building became a showroom, with a side entrance into the alley. At the back of the showroom was the parts department and office area. Two overhead doors were put into the alley side of the repair shop area. The shop area was totally reconfigured with the addition of a twin-post lift and a pit area for the front-end machine. A new body and paint area was added on the south side of the building.

It was about this same time that Harvey Freysinger closed his welding shop on Barnett Street and came to work for us. He was instrumental in hand building the body for our new tow truck. It had an extendable boom, that also swiveled, and a heavy-duty winch, that could move almost anything, and boxes in the sides of the bed to store the chains.

There were some memorable experiences with that tow truck. Karl Kennedy, from Green Park, had trucks that hauled milk in cans. One of the trucks upset on the road between Landisburg and Gibson Rock. After the milk cans were unloaded, we had to get it back up on its wheels. On another occasion, a log truck was coming up the hill from Mannsville and, on the curve near the top of the hill, it slid off the side of the road and into a ditch. It was New Year's Eve, in a blinding snow storm, and my father and I were called to get him out of the ditch. In both of these occasions, the winch was instrumental in getting the job done. We would chain the front bumper of the tow truck to a tree or telephone pole, and use the winch to pull him partway up the hill. We would then unhook and move to another tree or pole and pull him a little further up the hill. We kept doing this until we got the truck to the top of the hill. I do not know how many hours it took us to do this job, but I know I was so cold I could barely move.

Some of the other employees, that I can recall, that worked at the garage over the years were: Carl Frye (Crums Corner) salesman, and Robert Mitchell (Cold Storage area), along with my mother, were the bookkeepers and Bob also served as parts man. The mechanics and other shop helpers were: Clarence ("Dutch") Baker (New Bloomfield), Jim Armstrong (Little Germany area), John Rudy (Duncannon), Bill Clouser, Carl Clouser, and Frank Miller (Newport area), George Mullen (Carroll Township) and Glenn Fisher (Dellville). George Reed (New Bloomfield area) was the body repair and paint man. Glenn Mitchell, Robert's brother also worked for us part-time, mostly during the off season for farm work.

From the time we moved to town, I was always in and out of the repair shop talking and joking with the mechanics. One day, when I was about nine years of age, I walked out into the shop, and on one of the work benches sat a Seven-Up bottle. Thinking it belonged to one of the mechanics, I grabbed it and took a drink. It turned out to be brake fluid and I made a quick trip to the bathroom. I then got my own soda out of the cooler to wash away the horrible taste in my mouth.

One another occasion, there was a fire at "Thebes' Dump", located in the woods below the Bailor farm. Dutch Baker, being a fireman, grabbed a couple of fire extinguishers and jumped into our pickup truck and drove to the fire. I ran down the street and down the old railroad right-of-way to the fire. When the fire was out, I thought I will just jump into the pickup and ride back to the garage with Dutch. When I opened the passenger door to get in, one of the acid/foam fire extinguishers upset and sprayed foam over the interior of the pickup. Needless to say, I did not ride back in the pickup and my father was VERY upset!

George Mullen was repairing a large truck tire one day. This type of tire rim had a steel retaining ring that had to be securely fastened to the outside of the rim after the tire had been installed. George had completed the installation of the tire and the retaining ring. He then turned the tire upside down and was leaning over the tire putting in air. He almost had the tire pressure too full when the tire exploded and went flying up in the air, and knocked George on his backside. The tire flew clear up and hit the ceiling, cracking the ceiling joists. Fortunately for George, his only injury was a broken arm and some sore muscles. If that tire had hit his head, it most likely would have killed him. Today they have a type of metal cage or framework to place the large truck tires in before airing them up to prevent such accidents.

When our business became a direct dealership, a transport company drove our new trucks in from Detroit. They were not delivered on a trailer like the cars. One time, they damaged one of the trucks in an accident; another time, they lost a driveshaft out of one of the trucks being piggybacked. My father said: "That is it! From now on we will drive in our own trucks." My father, and sometimes a second person, would fly to Detroit and bring back up to six trucks at a time. Later, my father purchased his own airplane and would fly persons to Detroit to drive back our trucks. My father's first airplane was a Stinson Voyager that had previously been owned by Arthur Godfrey. Later he owned aluminum bodied Cessna airplanes that my brothers and I would have to buff and polish every year. What a job that was!

Over the years, when my brothers and I became teenagers, we would work in the garage doing various jobs: sweeping floors, changing tires, doing oil changes and lube jobs, etc. One day, a customer came in who needed something checked quickly under his car. I was about fifteen at the time and already able to drive. I went out and got the car, drove it in on the lube rack, and stayed in the car.

The mechanic raised the rack, checked what needed to be checked, and put the rack down. It only took a couple of minutes, and I backed the car out of the garage and out the alley. It had snowed that day and the rear window of the car was covered with snow. Unbeknownst to me, another customer had pulled his car into the alley and I backed into the front of his car. Fortunately, both cars only had slight damage. One of the customers was a teacher at Carson Long and I do not recall the name of the other. Again, my father was VERY unhappy!

My brother, Marlin recalls a time when he was installing a set of seat covers in a car, a customer walked over and said to him: "You know installing seat covers like that can cover a multitude of sins!" During the 1950s, vehicles did not come from the factory already undercoated. This was a dealer installed option, and what a chore and messy job it was to do. Marlin recalls having to smear his face and neck with face cream, and wear a beanie cap and bulky shop coat while spraying the undercoating. It flew everywhere and newspapers had to be taped all around the bottom side of the car, and a tarp was laid under the car, to keep the undercoating from flying all over the shop.

After the showroom was built, each year at Christmastime, Santa Claus would come and deliver candy and oranges to the children and some household items for the adults, such as hot plate holders, food whippers, hot dog tongs, shoe horns, rulers, small pocket knives, etc. with the New Bloomfield Auto Company name on them. They have become quite the collectible items at local estate sales and auctions. We also had an L-shaped train display on two 4X8 and one 4X4 sheets of plywood. I was always responsible for setting up the train display and getting everything running, which often took several days. Then taking it back down and storing it after Christmas.

Due to my father making the numerous trips to Detroit to bring in his own trucks, he became acquainted with some of the employees in the Dodge Truck Factory Office. On one of his trips in the early 1950s, they told him that they needed a dealer, who had the financial backing, to go to the US Government Office in Philadelphia to complete a deal for forty-five Dodge Power Wagon pickup trucks. Most of these vehicles would be shipped directly to Saudi Arabia for the purpose of building an airstrip. My father came home and he and Raymond Egolf, president of The Bank of Landisburg, went to Philadelphia and completed the deal. We are not certain of the numbers, but we think it was between five and ten of these vehicles were shipped to our dealership. These vehicles all had winches behind the front bumpers as original equipment, so Harvey Freysinger built booms that were attached to the front bumper and frame rails. These booms were constructed in such a manner so that they could easily be taken apart and stored on the floor of the pickup. A false floor was constructed in the pickup bed, so the booms could be stored under them. On top of these false floors, we constructed boxes, and lined them with four-inch foam rubber. These were used to haul the delicate survey equipment.

The year that my father made the sale of this fleet of pickups, little New Bloomfield Auto Company was the top dealership in sales of Dodge Trucks in the entire Philadelphia Region, which included all of the Dodge dealerships in eastern Pennsylvania, including Brenner Motors in Harrisburg, from whom we previously had gotten our vehicles.

One of my joys was going with my father to New York City for the introduction of the new 1957 line of Plymouth and Dodge cars and trucks. I have pictures from this trip in my album. During the 1950s and 1960s, the New Bloomfield Fire Company had an ambulance. The businesses throughout the town supplied the drivers on a rotating system. At that time, there were no EMT's to provide any kind of medical care, other than trying to stop a profusely bleeding wound. You just went where you were called and put the patient onto the litter and into the ambulance. Most times there was not even someone in the back of the ambulance unless a family member went along. I remember two very important trips when my father was responsible for being the driver. The first was the night a young mother, pregnant with twins, was experiencing life-threatening complications. Fortunately, we got her to the hospital and things turned out well. The second was a tragic two vehicle collision on the curve near the former Perry Tool Building. In the one car were two drunks that we transported to Harrisburg Hospital. The driver of the second vehicle did not survive. I recognized this vehicle and knew who would have been driving it, but my father did not. I never told him who it was, until we had put the ambulance back in its garage. My father broke down and cried, for the driver was Lawrence Weston, who lived next door to the garage, where Bill Bunt's Law Office is now. He quite often came over to the garage and talked with my parents.

When I graduated from high school, my parents sent me to Detroit, Michigan for the Chrysler Corporation Dealer's Sons Conference, to learn about the ins and outs of the operation of a dealership. While there, I stayed at the Whitter Hotel, located on the shore of the Detroit River, which flowed into Lake Erie. The point of the river, where the Hotel was located, was where a tip of Canada comes down under a portion of the City of Detroit. So, every morning, when I looked out of my hotel room window, I was looking at Canada. I was at the Conference for five weeks and, direction wise, that fouled me up the whole time I was there! Canada to the SOUTH of me! My room rate was $5.00 per night with a continental-style breakfast. (A few years later, on his summer break from college, my brother, Marlin also attended one of these conferences.)

My first week in Detroit, I went to the Dodge Truck Plant and picked up a new 1956 ½ ton Dodge chassis & cab truck, (this was a truck with no bed) which my father had ordered and, which I was able to drive back and forth from my hotel to the Conference Center. There was a service station near the hotel in which I was rooming. I took the truck over there and had it washed and filled with gas. When I had nothing to do in the evenings or weekends, I sometime went over to the station and talked with the two employees. One time after I had visited with them, I got in my truck to leave, put the truck in gear, left out the clutch, and the truck would not move. I looked in the rear-view mirror and the two employees had lifted the back of the truck so the wheels were not touching the pavement. They had a good laugh over that joke they pulled on me.

When the five weeks ended, I went to Canfield Mounting Company and they mounted the front end of a new pickup truck that my father had also ordered, on the back of my truck, for me to tow back to Pennsylvania. I drove straight through from Detroit, without an overnight stop, which at that time was about a twelve-hour trip, due to the lack of freeways and four lane highways. Keeping up a 50-mph speed in those years was a real chore.

Late in 1957 and through 1958, the sale of new vehicles slowed for our dealership for a number of reasons. So, my parents made the decision to convert the building into a ten-lane bowling alley. The new car business was closed and the employees were left go. My father was going to continue in the used car business and he opened an auto repair business in the former Freysinger Welding Company Building on Barnett Street. He purchased a lot on Main Street to use as a used car lot. It was in front of what was then Henry Miller's Shoe Repair Shop and now is the parking lot for The Perry County Veteran's Building.

The conversion of the building and installation of the bowling lanes and pinsetters was a major project. An addition was added to the back of the building, the restrooms had to be relocated, the overhead door areas in the alley side of the building had to be closed, and an emergency exit door had to be cut into the side of the building near where the main customer flow of traffic would be located. Installation of the lanes and pinsetters took several weeks. During part of this time, I went to Paramus, New Jersey to a four-week Brunswick Corporation Automatic Pinsetter School to learn to be the mechanic who kept the pinsetters maintained and repaired. One weekend, while I was at school, my father flew my wife down to see me. He was always a good and very safe pilot, but on this day, he got off in his directions and landed at a Naval Base. He immediately was surrounded by several Navy personnel and vehicles. After a brief interrogation period, he was escorted back down the runway with instructions on how to get to his destination. This was very unusual for my father, because he was generally right on with his directions. He flew people to Detroit, me to Erie, Pennsylvania to get a used Soil Conservation pickup that he had purchased, and other people to various other places. My wife got quite a kick out of this and we had a nice weekend together.

Brunswick Corporation sent in a supervisor to oversee the installation of the bowling lanes and the automatic pinsetters. They hired local carpenters to do this work. I can only remember two of these carpenters: the Soule brothers, Harold ("Whitey") and John. There were others, but I do not recall how many there were, or any more of their names. One day when John Soule came to work, he bent down and looked down the lane that they had built the day before, checking to see if it looked level and straight. The supervisor, who was standing further over in the building, happened to see him eyeing up the work they had completed. The supervisor threw his hammer at John, and yelled "No one ever sights up my work!" He was a tall man with a Swedish accent and that really made him angry. The carpenters were always joking and doing tricks on each other as they worked. One day they nailed one of the worker's lunch boxes to the floor and he did not realize it had happened. When it came to lunch time, he reached down to pick it up and ripped the handle completely off of it. Another time they stapled somebodies sleeve shut and he could not get his hand down through his sleeve when he went to go home.

It was quite interesting to watch them build the lanes: they built them standing on edge and then lay them down and put shims under the entire length of the lane, to be sure they were level. Then the top was sanded smooth and coated with several coats of a special varnish that dried looking like glass and was super hard. Once the lanes were opened, they had to be cleaned almost every day and a special wax was put on them.

The Perry Lanes Bowling Alley finally opened in August of 1959. We had bowling team leagues on the week nights and Sunday evenings and open bowling week days, all day Saturdays and Sunday afternoons and evenings. My parents and my brother took care of the daily cleaning of the bowling alley and buffing and cleaning the lanes, and I was responsible for maintenance of the automatic pinsetters-weekly cleanings, lubrication, and repairs. If I did not clean the pinsetters as scheduled, then the pins would get dirty and need to be run through the cleaning machine, before it would normally be necessary. We always had more than two complete sets of bowling pins on hand at all times. It took many, many hours each week to keep up with these necessary tasks. No matter how carefully you cared for the lanes, if a bowler was having a bad night, they would usually complain to the person who was working the counter. Either there was too much oil on the lanes, or they were too dry or not clean, so their ball was not running correctly. Very seldom was it THEIR fault, because they were too tired or not releasing the ball correctly, etc.

We had a rotation system of who worked nights for the leagues and open bowling. But I was always on call in case there was a pinsetter breakdown or some pinsetter problem that they could not fix. The former garage parts department area was now the locker room. The former showroom area now contained a number of vending machines, pinball machines, pool table, restrooms, and eating tables. A bowling ball cleaner was in the locker room, and most of the above-mentioned machines were coin operated. In July of 1976, someone broke into the building and broke open all of the coin operated machines, and broke the glass in the display cases on the outside wall of the locker room. Why they broke the glass in the display cases, we never understood, since these cases were never locked. The burglars also attempted to break into the huge safe that was in the office and they were unsuccessful, however, they did enough damage to the opening dial that we could not get it opened. We wondered who we could get to fix it, so that we could get the money out of the safe. We finally thought about Ken Rice, an employee of The Landisburg Bank who also repaired clocks. He came and after several attempts, he was finally able to get it open. However, the combination on the lock had to be changed, because the old combination would no longer work. As far as we can remember, no one was ever arrested for this crime.

Brunswick Bowling Company had a contest to promote bowling that was advertised nationwide. The prizes were a fur coat and a Mercedes convertible. Persons were to come in and bowl and fill out a form about their bowling experience. These forms were sent to the corporate office by a certain date. After all the forms were sent in from throughout the United States, there was a drawing. Madeline Darlington, of New Bloomfield was the winner and the presentation was made in front of Perry Lanes. No one in our family can recall of her ever rolling a bowling ball down a lane.

Our entire family was eating dinner at our parent's home one Christmas Day when the phone rang and interrupted our meal. My father answered the call. On the other end of the line was an area business store owner. He had just gotten a new bowling ball and was calling to see what time the bowling alley was going to open. When my father told him that it was not opening on Christmas Day, he got upset and asked my father "Why not!" To which my father replied, "Is your store open today?" and the man replied, "No!" My father's next statement was, "Then why should my bowling alley be open," and hung up the phone.

With my parents, my brother, Marlin's family, and my family all drawing income from the business, it soon became apparent that there was insufficient income being generated to support all three families. My brother went to a bowling alley near Strasburg, Pennsylvania, that was looking for a manager, but was unable to get the job. I went to the Jewish Center in Harrisburg that was looking for a pinsetter mechanic, but they did not have the Brunswick automatic pinsetters. So those attempts to lower the employee costs failed.

I soon heard that Donald Clouser was closing the Atlantic Station at the east end of Main Street and it would be coming available for lease. I spoke with the Atlantic Refining Company area manager and was approved to lease the building. But I first had to attend a four-week training session on how to operate a service station. My training was held at Gabe Bretts Glenside Station in Ambler, Pennsylvania. I was in training during the week and was able to come home on weekends. There were two other new operators in training with me at the same time.

We held the Grand Opening of Raff's Atlantic Station in the spring of 1961, but the photo of this event does not have a specific date. When I would get my gasoline deliveries from Atlantic Refining Company, they would add a portion of the cost of my lease to the bill. Depending on how many times a month that I would purchase gasoline, the bill could be quite sizable. I worked at this station from 7:00 a.m. to 9:00 p.m. six days a week. My brother Gary worked almost full-time for me, and I had two part-time employees, Layton Sheaffer and Michael Sheaffer, who gave me some relief in the evenings and Saturdays. At the same time, I was still responsible for any repairs to the pinsetters. My father had taken on the responsibility of cleaning and the scheduled oiling and maintenance of the pinsetters. He had a maintenance manual and machine repair manual to follow, but not having the formal training that I had experienced, there were many tasks that he could not do.

Early one morning, Gerald Askins stopped in for gas. Gerald was a well-known local plumber. While I was pumping his gas, my business phone started to ring and I ran toward the office. When I rounded the back of his truck, a piece of copper pipe was sticking out of the right side of the truck about two feet. I did not see it in time to duck and it hit me just about one-half of an inch from the opening of my left eye and ripped the skin on my face open. Blood flew everywhere and I ended up on the pavement. I grabbed a rag I had in my pocket and held it tight to my face to squelch the bleeding. Gerald called my wife to take me to the doctor, and he stayed at the station until Gary could come and run the station while I was at the doctors. Luckily it missed my eye socket and I only needed a few stitches.

I had a regular weekly customer who drove a Falcon four-door sedan. He would step out of his car and say, "Fill my car with X gallons of gas, usually to the tenth of a gallon." And over ninety percent of the time he was correct. He drove back and forth to Harrisburg every day for work. He kept a very accurate record of every gallon of gasoline that was put in his car and figured out his gas mileage. He would reset the trip button each time he would fill up, so all he had to do was look at the mileage he had driven since he had last gotten gas, divided by his average mileage, and he would know how many gallons of gas he would need at that particular refueling. He would amaze me almost every time. His name was Humphrey Weston and he lived next door to Perry Lanes.

Unfortunately, I was only able to keep the service station opened for eighteen months until I ran out of money. A number of others had operated this station over the past years before me and they also only kept it open for a short amount of time. I think the main reason was that the Atlantic Refining Company was charging the same lease amount at this rural station as the operator of a station on a busy route like 11&15. They could generate a lot more business than I could at this rural location. What I lost was actually the amount of wages that I took out of the business in the months that it was open. It took me many years to pay back my loan to the bank.

About this same time, my brother, Gary went into the military, serving part of his tour of duty in Vietnam. When his time in the military ended, he went to Harrisburg Area Community College where he studied "Retail Sales." As part of his course work requirements, he had to work at a job in retail sales. His job was at Bowman's Department Store, where he was employed for a number of years.

My parents left me come back to work at Perry Lanes for a short time until I found another job. That job was as a parts man and service manager at Behney Motors in Middletown, a small Dodge Plymouth dealership. I was responsible for overseeing that the mechanics would have a reasonable amount of work each day, plus getting parts or maintaining a sufficient supply of parts that the mechanics would need. I also had to take inventory of the stock of parts which the dealership had on hand. Completing the workload necessary to do, what I felt was an adequate job for these two positions of both parts man and service manager, became a very stressful task and I left this job in nine months.

I came home one Friday evening and said to my wife: "I am very sorry, but I just cannot stand to work there another day." Here I was with a wife and three children and a debt from my ill-fated service station experience, and I had no job. What was I thinking?

I had some repairs to do on the car I was driving, because traveling back and forth to Middletown six days a week for nine months had taken its toll. I went to my father's Repair Shop on Barnett Street to do the repairs and soon needed some parts that my father did not have on hand, so I went up to N. E. Black's Dealership for parts. While I was sitting on a stool at the counter waiting to get my parts, Mr. Black walked in from the shop. He was a member of the Church where my family attended and knew me well. He stopped to talk with me, and during the course of the conversation he asked me how I was doing. I told him that I had just left my previous job and had no idea what I was going to do next. He said, "come back up this evening and talk to me." He offered me a job as a mechanic in his garage, so within one week, I was back to work. My wife and I both felt that it was God at work that I could find a job so quickly.

I had been working at Black's for about two years. One evening, my wife, Connie went to talk with our Pastor and his wife, Jay and Nancy Saxe. I had put the children to bed, it was getting late and I decided to go on to bed without her. I had just been in bed a short time and not yet real sleepy, when I happened to look out our bedroom window. There I saw a vision of a cross-shaped star, like one you see quite often depicted on Christmas cards. Just that moment my wife came in the front door. I called to her and she came up the steps and also saw the vision. We did not go to sleep for a long time that night, talking and wondering: what was the meaning of such an experience? We prayed about it and talked to our Pastor and we finally came to the conclusion, God was calling me into the pastoral ministry! This was not a big surprise for there were some previous inclinations.

Growing up in the garage, in the bowling alley, and through my high school years, I developed the bad habit of using swear words profusely. It was a part of my everyday conversations. Many times, my mother and my wife had to say to me, "Donald, PLEASE do not talk like that!" When I told the other mechanics at work that I had felt a call to ministry, they kidded me, "Well, you have the right words, you just need to get them in the right order!" Some months later on a very hot August day, I was doing a front-end alignment on an older model Buick that belonged to a farmer from up the valley. It had never gotten greased often enough, so I had to replace some bushings in the front-end before I could do the alignment! And everything was tight or caked with dirt. A couple of hours had passed by and I was soaking wet from sweat, covered with mud and grease, when I heard the owner saying to the shop foreman, Charlie Black, whose desk was right next to the alignment rack, "Do you realize, that mechanic has been working on my car for over two hours and he never swore once!" The Lord had worked a miracle! He had taken away my filthy language. On several other occasions, if a customer swore, the mechanics would tell them not to do that because I was going to be a minister. My response would be, "You do not have to answer to me!"

In order to be an ordained Pastor I needed to do a lot of schooling. I had only graduated from high school, and I had not gone on to college. I needed to have a college degree, and then go on to seminary to get a Master of Divinity degree. So, I started with some basic courses, part-time, at Harrisburg Area Community College, which at that time was located on Front Street in Harrisburg. My wife had been working as a telephone operator at Newport for some time, and I continued working part-time at Black's Garage. After some months, I decided to quit my job, and take a heavier course load. My home church, Keboch Methodist Church (now New Bloomfield United Methodist Church), hired me as a part-time assistant to the Pastor. This was an invaluable experience for my future position as a Pastor of my own Church. Within a year or so we decided that financially we were not making it. I contacted the Board of Ministry of The Methodist Church to see if I could receive an appointment to a Church as a Student Lay Pastor.

On July 1, 1967 I was appointed as Pastor of The Orangeville Parish consisting of five small rural churches in Columbia County. I would preach in three of the churches each Sunday morning, and a lay speaker would preach in the other two so that each church had services every Sunday morning. I had only preached three times before I was appointed to this parish, now I would preach three times every Sunday morning! I continued my education at Bloomsburg College, went on to Wesley Seminary in Washington, DC, finally graduating from there on May 3, 1976. It took me ten years to complete my college and seminary courses. I was ordained an Elder in The United Methodist Church on June 12, 1977. I served churches throughout the Central Pennsylvania and Susquehanna Conferences, and was Director of Red Bird Mission in Beverly, Kentucky for over a year, until I retired from full-time ministry in 2000. I continued to serve some part-time positions and did pulpit supply until I turned eighty years of age. I celebrated fifty years of ministry in 2017.

Back to the Bowling Alley: from the time I took over the Atlantic Station in the spring of 1961, until my parents sold the business in June of 1983, I was on call if there was a problem with, or break down of, one of the automatic pinsetters, and my father could not fix such problems. No matter where I was located, my father would call me on the phone and we would discuss the problem. We both had repair manuals to refer to, and if I could not help him to be able to correct the problem, I would get in the car and drive to New Bloomfield and help him solve the problem. I made many late-night trips, or all-day trips, from where I was serving in Orangeville, New Oxford, or Elizabethville, to help my father.

In January of 1966, my brother, Marlin went to work in the Perry County Sheriff's Office. He had been a huge help to my parents in keeping the Bowling Alley operating. He would help with cleaning, caring for the lanes, and working the counter at night. When Marlin left for the Sheriff's Office, my parents hired Sam Bender and Luther Comp (the father of Betty Shearer, Paul and Leroy Comp) to help. Sam mostly took care of cleaning, and Luther took care of maintaining the lanes. Luther had previously had an excavating business at the south end of Carlisle Street, next to the former Hair Bros. & Myers Store on the corner. Both of these men were very helpful to my parents in the closing years of their ownership of Perry Lanes Bowling Alley.

On June 1, 1983 my parents sold the Bowling Alley to Donald and Mel Liddick. They were from the Duncannon area and Don was a long-time bowler at Perry Lanes. The bowling alley has had five other operators since then and now has set idle for a number of years. The present owner's name is Donald Little, who I think is, or was from the Newport area.

And that is "the rest of the story!", as they would say.

Loafing And Learning The Gossip At The Local Stores

Storyteller George Coldren

About 1937, John Lincoln Coldren had a son George (Judge) Coldren who married Julia Hench. They had a son George in 1940. Growing up on a farm was an interesting experience. Always something to do. We'd get up at five for breakfast, dinner at noon and supper at six o'clock. Then we would go to the local stores for loafing and catching up on the local news. One night we would go to Edgar Stambaugh's Store in Green Park and the next night to Ike Billman's Store in Loysville. Making the rounds, we'd go to Dick Wilt's Store in Landisburg followed by Kell's Store at Milltown and Jake's Store in Elliottsburg.

Some of the old loafers at the stores were "Cracker" Clouse, Dean Shull, "Poodle" Foose, Bucky Weldon, Art Crull, "Shortly" Blosser, "Hen" Hess and John Stum. I learned over time that all they were saying was not always truthful.

While visiting at these stores, I would be leafing through magazines looking at guns. I had a particular interest in a Winchester Model 61 – 22 Pump Gun. One of the farmers asked me if I wanted the gun. He asked me how much it was and I told him eighty-seven dollars. He asked me how much I had saved towards it. I told him eighteen dollars. He said, "I'll buy you that gun if you work for me during your summer vacation." I hesitated about thirty seconds and then agreed. He told me he would get it in the coming week. I found that I agreed to getting up at five in the morning and getting home at seven at night.

I went back to school after summer vacation with my classmates Ed Neely, Ed and Bill Kennedy, Ken and Dean Pannebaker, Fred and Bob Reeder, and Grover Hildebrand. The teachers were Helen Briner, Bob Owens and "Pickle" Rice. When you misbehaved and had to stay after school, it was an automatic paddling.

On the farm, I decided to raise hogs. Not only slopping the hogs, I decided to feed them grass. One day I went to the pens and all the hogs were dead. My dad asked me what happened. I told him I fed them big leaves I cut from the bank. It was poisonous nightshade. OOPS!

Shortly after WW ll, money was scarce. One of our common breakfasts was "scalded" crackers and coffee soup. Sugar was rationed among other things. Gasoline was twenty cents a gallon.

The one-room Green Park School closed and another school was built that incorporated multiple one and two-room schools.

The local men gathered at various locations to play poker. Favorite spots were the Landisburg Quarry or Judge Coldren's garage, which was located in the fencerow between Route 274 and Route 233 in Green Park. Some of the local poker players were Boyd Reeder, Joe Trostle; Jake, Scott and Bill Weibley, "Cedar" Shull, Lee Shull, Dean Sheibley, "Skinny" Irvin, "Poodle" Foose, "Bear" Rice, "Shorty" Blosser, Jay McCoy and Judge. A good time was had by all.

The next summer, my dad offered me a job working for him. It was easier than working for that farmer.

I also helped build Green Park Union High School. Some of the teachers there were "Pickle" Rice, Charlie Eaton, Ethel Sheibley, Bob Owens, and Philip Cook, who became a veterinarian.

After graduation, I went to work at Masland's in Carlisle, then Gulf Oil on the Pennsylvania Turnpike. I decided to quit and go into the service.

My favorite sayings in life:
all that glitters is not gold
don't put off what you can do today
a bird in the hand is worth two in the bush
eat (….) and bark at the moon
don't spend good money after bad
a wise man should not waste time worrying

And, that's the end of this Perry County boy's story!

Delivering Mail From Back Hollow To New Germantown

Storyteller Vicki Wilson Gainer

My dad, Bernard Wilson had been carrying mail in Blain for many years, when his substitute carrier quit. This left dad without any relief and working six days a week. He stopped at my home one day and told me he needed a new sub and would I be interested. This required much thought because in 1979 I had a six-year-old son and four-year-old daughter. My husband and I had been living on his salary and we were always living paycheck to paycheck.

In 1979 a very nervous me went to Market Street in Harrisburg to take the Civil Service exam. Dad gave me all kids of instructions, including where to get a good breakfast before the test. The rest is history as they say. I passed the exam and became my dad's substitute in 1980. It was a balancing act with having two small children, but with the help of my family I was able to work. When the kids both started school, my schedule permitted me to be home in the morning when they left on the bus and I was almost always home when they got home from school. As a sub, I sometimes worked a day a week and sometimes no days at all.

Dad had been injured in a tractor accident several years previous and he nearly lost a leg. His knee continued to get worse and finally after twenty-five years carrying mail, he filed for disability. He received his approval on a Monday, and I had to take the route full time on Friday. It was a hectic time.

When I started, the route was 56 miles long with about 250 customers. Most times I was finished by 2:30 p.m. My day at work began with casing all my customer's mail. I then pulled it out of the cases and bundled it. I loaded the bundles and packages in the car and began my route.

For the first 25 years I drove vehicles (Dodge) with bench seats. I sat in the middle to deliver the mail.

It was only the last eight years of my career that I had a right-hand drive vehicle. I also drove on 16 miles of very dusty dirt roads every day. I should have had a warehouse of brake lining because I usually went through 3-4 sets of lining a year.

Back in the 1980s and 1990s our winter weather was much fiercer than it is now. There was only three times that I could not make it to the post office to work because of snow. There were a few days when I went into the office just to find out that a truck was not bringing mail from Harrisburg that day. I always used studded tires in the winter. They proved to be a great asset.

The days didn't always go as planned. There were flooded roads and roads under construction, which required detours. There were some vicious dogs on the route and trying to outrun them was useless. So, I began to carry dog treats with me. Soon all the dogs knew my car and were waiting for me. There was a day when I had three flats in one day. Bud came to my rescue with his truck, but then we had a flat with the truck! I had a flat on Upper Buck Ridge Road in a torrential rainstorm. In the time it took me to get the jack out, I was soaked. Before I had finished changing the tire two forestry workers came along. They said they would finish the tire and then there were three very drenched, muddy people.

I give much credit to my late husband, Bud and Blain Tire (Cory) for keeping my mail vehicles running in great shape. Several times they rescued me on the route, whether it be timing chains or brakes, etc.

I never quite knew what was going to happen when near a mailbox. As I was approaching a mailbox on Mt. Pleasant Road one sunny day, a big black snake was sunning himself on top of the mailbox. I sat there thinking, wow I wish I had a picture (this was before cell phones). I drove home and got my camera and got back to the mailbox in time to take a picture. And no, the customer did not get mail that day! That snake picture was published on the cover of our national union magazine. I also opened the lid of a mailbox on Robinson Road to find a perfectly coiled black snake in the box. The neighbors were feuding. Thankfully, the snake was dead. I think my boss Libby was more traumatized than me!

For many years I used front wheel drive Dodges on the route with studded tires. I was stuck once on Back Hollow Road and a friend dug me out. Another time on Red Rock Road there was a three-foot drift across the road. I stopped and considered if my car would go through the drift. I was quite daring as far as snow was concerned, so I decided to try it. I got three quarters of the way through the drift and got stuck. I called a near-by farmer and he pulled me out and took care of the drift.

I came close to hitting some mailboxes in my career, but I can say that I never hit one. I did have some on unstable posts that fell on my car several time.

I came very close to hitting deer on the route, but never did. In 33 years, I only saw one small black bear in the distance. Near the end of my career, I was in the Back Hollow and had just opened the lid of an unstable mailbox and before I ever had a chance to defend myself, I was stung 23 times on my face and scalp with bees. I was a terrible looking site by the next morning with one eye swelled shut and the other one not much better. Thankfully, I wasn't allergic. Six weeks later I was at a mailbox on Fowler Hollow Road and the very same thing happened. That time I did not get as many stings.

When we took our oath to become a US Postal Employee, we vowed to keep the sanctity of the mail. I took it a step further. There were things on the route that I saw that I will never disclose and many things in the mail itself. I took that vow very seriously.

One of my most rewarding situations that I encountered involved dismounting to deliver to an elderly lady. I took her mail into her home every day. She lived alone and could not drive. On a spring day I went to her house, but I had no mail for her, yet something told me to go to the house anyway. As a carrier doing the same route daily, you get to know the habits of your customers. I saw her door was open on a cool day, so I walked to the door. I called for her, but there was no answer. I walked into her house and called again and this time I heard a faint call for help. I found her upstairs on the floor nearly in shock and very cold. She had laid on the floor for 21 hours with a broken hip. Her call help button was on a downstairs table. I covered her, called 911 and stayed with her until the ambulance came. I was so thankful that I followed my instinct. For that I was awarded a HERO plaque in Harrisburg along with other carriers that deserved the award in 2006.

I belonged to a Quality Worklife Team for the Postal Service. I also participated in several Driver Rodeos in central PA. One thing I really enjoyed was being a Rural Carrier Academy instructor. I taught newly hired carriers in the classroom and on the street for three years. It was a rewarding experience.

My highest honor and the one I treasure the most occurred in 2010 when I was awarded the Million Mile Award by the postal service for driving accident-free for 30 plus years. My boss, Holly and I had a lot of fun preparing for the celebration. We knew the officials were coming from Harrisburg to give me the award, but the inside of the Blain office wasn't very presentable. So, we stayed after hours and painted the entire post office ourselves. Holly planned a great celebration for me. My family and guests were present. After everyone left, I did what I loved to do, I delivered my customers' mail.

I retired in June, 2013. I have so many memories that I treasure and there are still things that I miss. My customers were the most important part of my job, and it gives me joy when I go to Blain and see some of them. My job was to serve them, and I took great pride in my job. I've always been thankful that I could follow in my dad's footsteps.

Hauling Bananas and Race Cars

Storyteller Ray Franklin Campbell
Recorded by Debra Kay Noye

Ray Franklin "Frank" Campbell got his start on old Route 322 between Newport and Millerstown in Greenwood Township. He was born in 1948 to Benjamin and Jennie (Strawser) Campbell, across from the Keystone Hotel. He grew up with all the conveniences in an original log-house, covered in white siding, which had very uneven floors. He was the sixth child of seven who enjoyed swinging in the backyard.

His family also had a small farm in Perry Valley, but they maintained a large garden at their house, from which his mother canned many different kinds of vegetables. There was a cow for milking (his mother pasteurized the milk), pigs for butchering, and chickens for eggs and roast chicken dinners prepared by his mother, who was a tremendous cook. She would always have huge family Sunday dinners and hosted birthday dinners for the whole family.

At the farm, Frank, in his youth, grew sweet corn and sold three dozen ears of corn for one dollar. He also sold Christmas trees for $3.00 that he bought for $1.50 from one of the trucking company customers. Another enterprise when he was a bit older was catching pigeons and selling to Pontius in Thompsontown for $.25 each. He would persuade his older sister Shirley and Nancy's boyfriends to take him around to barns at night to catch the pigeons.

Since the Juniata River was just across the road from his house, Frank, his neighbor Jim Saylor, and his younger sister Kathy would go fishing for bass and carp. They and other local youngster would spend a lot of time down at the river and other places around Old Ferry. Frank says he can see the piers and the "lock" which was once the site of the rope-ferry-boat landing. A small island or "sandbar" still exists. He tells of his grandfather fishing for eels in the river, but that was before Frank's time.

His mother made sure he attended the Perry Valley Presbyterian Church. Frank was terrified of any church or Sunday School event that required children to perform or recite Bible verses. He did enjoy the full-course, homemade turkey dinners that the church hosted as fundraisers. The popular dinners were enjoyed by three-hundred people on the average. Those days are long gone. His church kitchen, at the old school house, had an old wooden ice-box, which Frank admired. Knowing they wished to rid themselves of the antique, Elizabeth Wright agreed to sell it to Frank for a donation to the church. He still cherishes that icebox.

Frank attended the Greenwood Schools. His mother had to keep after him to attend for the first couple of years. He recalls his Uncle Leroy Strawser was the principal in elementary school. Dana Gantt, Bill Jones, Jack Richards and Mrs. Beaver were some of the good teachers, according to Frank, who eventually grew to like school. His sister, Shirley came back to teach at Greenwood after college. His father, Ben was on the school board and back then the board would meet in the trucking company office. Graduating in 1966, he continued his education at Harrisburg Area Community College and Penn State Harrisburg earning a bachelor's degree in business. He also joined the Army Reserves and took basic training in between.

There was a reason Frank did not play in any sports in his youth. His grandfather, Harry "Pop" Franklin Campbell and his dad started a trucking business in 1933, when they bought their first truck. So, by the time, Frank was old enough to be running through the grease and oil in the trucking garage, they were known as H. F. Campbell and Son, Inc. That is where Frank's spare time was spent, as he learned the truck-hauling business.

So, it was only natural for Frank and his buddy, Jimmy Wright, son of Elizabeth from his church, to build from scraps "soap-box derby" cars and race them down the Perry Valley Road's hills. Good thing there wasn't much traffic back then! When he was at Jimmy's house, he helped to gather the eggs and Elizabeth prepared the cracked eggs for their lunch.

In later years, Frank hand-built an official sized "soap-box derby" car for his son Matthew to participate in the derbies sponsored by the local Jaycees. That car was converted to a table, which is now a show-piece in his son, Mathew's house.

Frank, "from the get go," was coming home from school and going straight to the garage to wash off trucks and trailers, or refuel them for their next run. Trucking was in his blood and it was obviously a topic of conversation at the supper table. Even his mother worked at the trucking company, maintaining the books. Frank has the typewriter and electric adding machines she used. Also, their caretaker at the farm, Charles Holley who milked their cow and brought the milk along for Frank's mother, worked daylight at the garage. Interesting enough, Holley didn't drive a vehicle, but knew how to drive a tractor around the farm. Maybe he didn't like the confines of a roadway but enjoyed being chauffeured to the garage.

It wasn't all work when he was growing up. Saturday was the day to go to town. His family patronized Zuckerman's Clothing and Bennie Carl's Clothing & Shoe Store as well as the grocery stores in Newport. It was the highlight of the week, especially to see a movie at the Newport Movie Theatre on South Second Street.

Even before the roads were paved, Frank's grandfather "Pop" and his dad built the Keystone Hotel in 1925, during the Depression. Frank's grandfather and his family lived in three rooms of the ten-room hotel. Rooms were two dollars a night and a hamburger with a cup of soup was twenty cents. They also sold gas. They built a dock on the Juniata River bank below the hotel for people to come ashore and enjoy a meal or rent a room for the night. They had sold the hotel by the time Frank was born.

While still operating the hotel, Frank's family started the truck hauling business by purchasing a 1931 Ford stake-body truck which they took turns hauling coal and lumber. When the WPA needed haulers for materials for roadway and building projects, they expanded their trucking business to include dump trucks. As their business grew, they moved their trucking operations to the old Ferry Pump-house, a hop-skip and jump from the hotel. The business name changed to H. F. Campbell and Son Motor Express to Campbell Express to the trendy version Camel Express. In 1979 when his grandfather died, the business office was moved into his home with the garage on the other side.

Along with the trucking business, it is believed that Pop had the first school bus in Perry County. Pop and some local craftsman build a wooden-body school bus on the chassis of a straight truck.

Campbell's began hauling dry goods but soon focused on refrigerated trucks as well. By 1956, they had a fleet of five tractors, five trailers and two stake-body trucks. The fleet increased to twenty-one trucks and thirty-nine trailers by 1977. With the need for refrigerated and temperature-controlled trailers, they topped out with sixty tractors, two-hundred plus trailers and twenty owner-operators in 2010. It was no small trucking business anymore and most everybody who was a direct relative worked and had responsibilities within the business.

Frank and his brothers were the third generation to be fully immersed in trucking. That grew to include the fourth and fifth generations.

Franks trucking family, aside from his grandfather, father and mother included Frank's son Mathew, and daughter Sarah (worked in dispatch like Frank), brothers Harry Albert "Abe"; Richard B. "Dick" and sons Mark A. and Jeffrey L., Donald L. "Dudley" Sr. and son Donald L. Jr., and grandson Tyler. Everyone had their own areas of responsibility.

Frank speaks with deep affection for young Jeffrey "Jeff," who passed away in 1991 due to leukemia. The Camel Express family established a yearly scholarship "HFC/JLC Memorial Scholarship" which awards two eight-thousand-dollar scholarships to Perry County students entering the medical field. Frank and his family are very proud to be able to assist Perry Countians in their collegiate endeavors and career goals.

However, Campbell trucking would not have been able to become the power-house in the trucking industry if it were not for all the dedicated employees maintaining the trucks and the truck driving. They employed ten mechanics and technicians in the garage to keep their trucks on the road. Without their due diligence and expertise, especially when computerization came along, Camel Express would've been hard pressed to fill their truck hauling contracts.

Most of the drivers were from Perry and Juniata Counties. Carl Saylor, from Millerstown, drove for Campbell's for forty-two years. He was partially the reason Campbell's established the "Million-Mile Hall of Fame," having driven truck the longest for the company. That's a lot of sitting behind the wheel of a tractor trailer, being diligent about your speeding surroundings and still meeting delivery deadlines. Forty-three drivers earned the distinction of being inducted into the hall of fame, but fifteen drivers attained two-million miles with a safe driving record. Harry Frantz, from Northumberland, topped them all by reaching the three-million mark. The Camel Express earned many safety awards from the Pennsylvania Motor Truck Association. Baney Benson and Donnie Dobyns, from Millerstown, who started in the 1950s were two of the early employees. Campbells at the height of their hauling business had ninety employees, which also included the office staff. Janice Shaw from Perry Valley became a mother, grandmother and great-grandmother while managing the office. Campbells was one of Perry County's largest employers.

Perry County owner-operators included Ken Bolton of Millerstown, and Ted Hockenberry and Johnny Bible, from Newport. These truckers owned their own cabs and pulled Campbell's trailers. They often hauled chickens from the Empire Poultry Plant in Mifflintown to Chicago and other points in Campbell's refrigerated trailers. Now since Chicago is a pretty long haul, Frank knew as the company's dispatcher he needed to back-fill the run. That meant putting feelers out to see if any production companies in the Chicago area or on the most direct route back to Perry County needed anything transported to Pennsylvania, Maryland, New Jersey, Delaware or New York.

In reality hauling of Kosher chickens turned out to be rather cheesy, as Frank was able to establish a good rapport with Kraft Foods. The initial backhauls were to Palmyra and soon Campbell's was hauling Kraft cheese products all over the east coast, in their costly refrigerated trailers and trucks. The refrigerated and temperature-controlled trailers and trucks required a lot more maintenance and up-keep. In the early days in the 1960s, Frank would travel to Lemoyne for dry ice in the summer to help keep the fish they were hauling frozen till they reached their destination.

Their dedication to Kraft earned them the distinction of "Kraft's Regional Carrier of the Year" in 2006, 2008 and 2009. The trucking industry is not a "nine to five" type of job, so Frank had to maintain the dispatch office twenty-four hours a day. Frank explains dispatching, "as constantly trying to put a puzzle together with all the parts moving!" A lot more challenging than washing off all those trucks and trailers in the early days. However, Frank really enjoyed his role in the family business.

So, you're thinking what could they have been hauling that needed so much attention to detail and precision deliveries. Camel Express went totally bananas! Yepper, their reputation garnered them contracts with Dole, Chiquita, and Del Monte hauling bananas from the docks in Manhattan, New York or Wilmington, Delaware and other ports to destinations all over the east coast. The trucks needed to be kept at a constant fifty-eight degrees. That is also when Campbell's hired some "New Yorkers" for the produce runs, so they could return home for the night, which for any trucker was a real plus. The New York State drivers also fit in good with the Kraft business.

Now you're probably thinking, hauling bananas had to be one of the easiest jobs in the world. In the early days of bananas, they were individual stalks of bananas that had been cut from the tree and shipped as is by boat to the states. When the trucks would arrive to be loaded, it was labor intensive to carry each large, heavy stalk of bananas from the boat or the shipping containers to the truck. You had to be careful to not bruise the green bananas too much. The same was repeated once the trucks reached their delivery destinations.

Through the years, the bananas were then cut into hands and placed in boxes, but those boxes were individually hand-carried from the boats to the trucks. Finally, the boxes were palletized, with forty-eight boxes to a pallet. That meant a lot less hands on. Finally, the boxes were put into containers which were put directly onto the trucks. All the efforts made sure the bananas were still looking good by the time they arrived on store shelves for the consumer. Frank says the bananas were gas ripened, not as people envision straight from the banana tree.

They also did a lot of hauling for Hanover Foods and Snyder of Hanover. Hauling produce would also take them into the Bronx in New York City, where fenced in produce markets were set-up, which became very challenging. There you were dealing with a whole new set of vendors and rules.

On November 27, 1985, Camel Express had the distinction of being the first vehicle to cross over the newly re-built Clarks Ferry Bridge. Their truck driven by Tommy Smith of Elliottsburg was carrying Jack Zogby, from Duncannon, who was the Secretary of the Pennsylvania Department of Transportation. Adorned with balloons, the truck ceremoniously opened the four-lane concrete bridge to a steady stream of motor vehicles, including tractor trailers.

Camel Express was also well-known on the "dirt tracks" throughout central Pennsylvania, which was the "hot bed" for sprint car racing. "Camel Express 26" was a 410-sprint car that won more than one-hundred feature races from 1977-1993, on the Williams Grove, Susquehanna, Lincoln, Selinsgrove and Port Royal Speedways. The trucking firm sponsored and owned the car that won eight track championships and the 1987 Central PA Pabst Championship right down to the last race of the series. Again, Camel Express had excellent and dedicated drivers; Barry Camp from Beaver Springs, and Jim Nace from McAlisterville. Jimmy Russell is credited for keeping the sprint car running smoothly. Like tractor trailers and trucks, a good mechanic is also needed to keep the cars flying around the tracks. Camel Express was inducted into the York County Sprint Car Hall of Fame.

Camel Express merged with S&H Express in 2013 and some of the Campbell family members stayed on in various capacities, but the legend was retired. Frank, who had never driven truck decided to try something new and did short-hauls and today he is back at it transporting milk in tankers.

Franks family always supported him. In 1969, he married Susan Hoke, who was a direct descendant of the Rider family that founded Newport, and they had two daughters, Laura and Sarah and son Mathew. Many of the company's customers were in the New York City area, so often Frank's family would accompany him on trips to the city and they would do some quick sightseeing. When they were on those trips or just going to Harrisburg, the children would watch movies in the back of the family van. Years later, now Frank enjoys going on trips and vacations with their children, and now he sits in the back of the van and watches movies. Laura turned out to be quite the trip planner and guide, especially navigating the New York subways and trips to Kentucky.

As he had spare-time, he became involved and spear-headed many community and county-wide endeavors such as the Newport Revitalization, Perry County Chamber of Commerce, and the Perry County Bicentennial celebration, that resulted in the placement of markers at historical places of interest throughout the county. Others involved in the physical placement of markers were Jeff Probasco, Fred Wertz, Rick Koontz, Doug Myers and others. They also helped to establish the Bicentennial Plaza at the Lynn Sheaffer Dum Memorial Park in Spring Township, outside of Elliottsburg. The Perry County Boy Scouts have been enlisted to clean the markers throughout the county.

Frank has received many accolades for his volunteerism, but he cherishes the Jefferson Award bestowed upon him by WGAL TV 8 for his commitment to his community and county.

Many a tread mark were left on the pavement as Camel Express trucked across the United States. Frank directed those routes and also mapped out a historical trail for people to follow, while learning about Perry County's history. Today on a snow-covered lane, he backs a quarter-mile to a local farm so the day's milking can be hauled to a local dairy processing center. That's all for now – "Ten 4 Good Buddy!"

Never A Dull Moment Teaching At West Perry High School

Storyteller Patricia McAteer

In August of 1971, my husband and I drove thirteen hours from Kentucky where he was stationed at Fort Knox for my interview for a teaching position at West Perry School District. When I arrived the principal, hearing that my husband was with me, had him come into the interview. It was the only interview that my husband attended. Questions on my ability to teach of course were discussed, but so were questions to my husband as to what would he do after the military. One cannot ask those questions today. When he said get a job here in Perry County, I knew we had scored points. I got the job and stayed at West Perry for twenty-eight years.

Thus, I started that September at West Perry High School teaching English while my husband went to Viet Nam. My class load was three sections of tenth grade and two of eleventh. But, wonder of wonders, also one section of driver's education (book work only.) Today we have induction programs for new teachers, teacher mentors, etc. I was given about eight English textbooks and one driver's ed textbook and told "have at it". I was also shown the ladies' faculty room which was a long room off the ladies' lavatory. The women did not go into the men's faculty room since it was full of smoke. (In 1973 the ninth grade was added to the high school and those ninth-grade lady teachers said we will use the main faculty room and that ended the ladies' faculty room.)

I soon learned how big in area West Perry really is during my first year. In April of 1972 we had a major snowstorm. The first day my husband (who had finished military service) and I dug out, so I would be ready for the next day. My landlord said you are not going in tomorrow, but "the roads are passable," I said. Next day the same conversation, so my husband and I went to Camp Hill shopping. By now I really am confused. My landlord called up the Assistant Superintendent Jack Glassburn and said to him, "tell this young teacher she is not going to school tomorrow," and Mr. Glassburn did just that. So, my husband and I decided to drive out to the school to see for ourselves. We were fine getting to the school and on to Loysville, but beyond the road was totally closed and the snow higher than the car. We were out of school for a week. Long-time Perry Countians know that the weather in Blain can be entirely different than weather in New Bloomfield. It was something I had to learn.

I thought having grown up in hunting country, Tioga County, Pennsylvania, I understood about the sport. But I was not prepared the day I heard this strange sound. Almost ready to yell at my class about the disturbance, I stopped and said, "That is coming from behind me, right?" The class said, "Yes." Behind my room was the faculty room, so I went in and there was a history teacher practicing his new turkey caller.

Indeed, creatures have played an interesting part in my teaching career. One day as I am teaching my eleventh graders, a spider the size of a pocket watch went scurrying along my blackboard tray. I yelped and by now the girls in the front rows are yelping, too. One of the boys in the back row walked up front, picked up the spider and tossed him out the window. Then in a quiet voice said, "Can we now get back to the lesson?" All of us girls then stopped yelping.

Another time a pet snake from the biology department got loose. We were all tense wondering where it was in the ductwork. The French teacher had to "float" (not having a room at the time) and went to teach in the science room. She put her books down and realized she was looking directly into the snake's eyes. Unlike me she didn't yelp, but called the science teacher to come get his pet.

Every so often, the Office would send out edicts to reinforce school rules. At one point, too many students were out in the halls during homeroom, so teachers were to issue no passes. This one student insisted he be allowed to go to the biology teacher. I said, "No passes." But he said, "I really have to go; they will die otherwise." I looked and he had a glass jar full of baby snakes. I never signed a pass so fast in my life!

As I mentioned earlier, many teachers had to float, so one very rarely got their main classroom during their preparation period. I came back to my room one day to find it full of dead squirrels. The science teacher was doing taxidermy with his students. For several weeks, I had half stuffed dead squirrels on my bookcase. Years later when I was assistant principal, we had the drug dogs in to check the school grounds. My job was to unlock any lockers the dogs hit. The German Shepard hit on the one locker and I opened it to be faced with one of the half-stuffed dead squirrels.

Teachers then and now are asked to cover classes when short on substitute teachers. My first experience was to cover girls' gym class. The principal said you just have to take attendance and do shower check; the male gym teacher will do the lesson. Did not happen. I ended up covering the whole class; I think it was basketball. A few days later the principal asked me to cover again. Lesson was now apparatus. Quaking, I said, "No." I would take the girls for a study hall, but I would not do apparatus. I doubt today, schools even get out the rings, horses and parallel bars.

Another class, I was often asked to cover was home economics. Today, we still have versions of this course in Family and Consumer Science, but often only a few weeks long. My first time the class was making an apple pie. No problem, I am a fairly good cook. Next time was sewing! Ugh! One girl came up to me and said would I help her put the facing in her dress. She was lucky I even knew the term. Just then the guidance counselor came to the door. She could sew so they pinned, tucked and pressed while I watched. Got to love guidance counselors.

Then as now we relied on AV materials, just not as sophisticated. Film strips, overhead projectors, 16 and 8mm movie projectors, and the purple mimeographed worksheets are gone, and not missed. I quickly learned how to work the movie projector as I was not trained for driver's ed. The other new English teacher and I shared films. He showed the film Tuesday and I did Wednesday. Even my department chair who had felt movies were a waste of time until she got a "rough class" was seen racing down the hall yelling, "Is that a movie I can show tenth graders?"

I also learned to never rely on technology and to always have a backup lesson because the bulb would blow, the film would break, or the power would go off. Even as an assistant principal my dot matrix printer went nuts, and in trying to get the printout stopped I got wrapped up like a mummy. The principal came by and had an awful time trying to help me, because he wanted to laugh like mad, but was afraid of upsetting my feelings. I shrugged and we both had a good laugh at my expense.

Perhaps surprising to some people, Perry County schools are often on the cutting edge of new educational trends. As part of IU 15 which includes Harrisburg, we had access to state sponsored workshops, pilot programs, and new materials. I was selected to score the PSSA state writing essays in Harrisburg. English teachers came from all over the state to grade the tests. (I have a button that says, "I scored 64,000 times in PA." Bad taste, but funny at the time.) What really surprised me was that in discussions with teachers from other parts of the state, I heard: What is that new initiative? I never heard of that program. Where do you get information on that idea? West Perry was indeed in the know on current practices.

Nevertheless, teaching is a tough profession. Both then and now. Teachers are expected to be counselors, instructors, referees, babysitters, and resources for most everything. As a teacher I had fun days like when I had my seniors acting out the death scene from Hamlet and bad days as I cried with students over the death of a classmate or the day the stunned history teacher told me the spaceship Challenger blew up. Every day was different.

I still subscribe to the theory that all you really need in education is a good teacher, determination and to always be teaching. I started day 1 and finished day 180. I taught in the freezing WP auditorium when we had a rash of students gumming up the door locks with chewing gum. I taught in the parking lot when cement dust started coming through my radiator during renovations. I watched the Vo Ag teacher do a phenomenal lesson on physics at a Burger King during an FFA convention. West Perry had many great teachers during my twenty-eight years there. They still do. As a result, we have graduates that are doctors, lawyers, bankers, soldiers, teachers, farmers, movie producers, architects and in too many other professions to name. Some things in teaching have changed, but some things still remain. Good teaching is good teaching no matter what generation. I was lucky to have spent much of my educational career at West Perry.

"You Can Take The Girl Out Of Perry County But Not Her Heart"

Storyteller Janet (Ellenberger) Colborn

You may take the girl out of Perry County, but you cannot take Perry County out of her heart. I am walking, living proof of that fact. If a genie came out of a bottle and told me I could live my life over again with no restrictions on wishes, I would choose to:

Be born to the same parents Kenneth and Louise (Dietz) Ellenberger, with the same sisters Barbara (Hamilton) Ellenberger and Linda Lee Ellenberger (deceased), and, of course my same baby brother Ken Ellenberger who I have always called K B (standing for Kenny Berger because he decided the name Ellenberger was too long to write on grade school papers, so he simply shortened it in his young wisdom to Kenny Berger which I then shortened further to K B).

Be taught the same social and moral values, whether the lessons were easy or hard.

Live in Perry County all over again and hope to experience those growing-up memories a second time around.

I certainly bring with me a heritage of first-hand stories and experiences not just from my years on this earth, but also from my parents. Living on a farm, we always had plenty of food in our 17' by 18' farm kitchen, which also served as our social center. It was an open-door and no-one or no thing was refused entry to our kitchen, although some were more welcome than others. Let's see…what did hang out in our kitchen? I remember a Shetland pony, a baby calf or two, baby pigs which would then get rides from Barb and me in our doll stroller, goats which escaped the kitchen and jumped onto the living room furniture which did not make mom happy at all, and the usual chickens, pet rabbit which ate leaves off mom's floor plants as high as it could reach, my cat named Cootie which mom referred to as Fleabag, and squirrels to name just a few. If we could lead it or carry it, chances were that it would enter our kitchen sometime.

Heat was confined to the downstairs in our farmhouse. The wood-box behind our kitchen cookstove gave us a warm place to dress in the mornings and a cozy place to read and do puzzle books. The cookstove oven was great for making food and pies and was also a fantastic place to warm your feet after playing outside in the snow. There was always hot water in the stove. I remember how mom and dad would bank the fire in the cookstove and we took many baths in the kitchen.

We learned to be creative in most of what we did. Farm life was fun and hard at the same time. Going out to the barn on freezing nights to scoop up bags of corn and grains to have them ready for the feed grinders the next day was not my favorite thing, but our animals needed to eat too and grinding our own was most cost effective. We did buy certain chicken feed and mash from Hepfer's Feed Store at the top of the hill on Route 274. The feed came in decorated bags which when empty went into the house where mom sewed them into pillow cases, curtains, aprons and tea towels. I am seventy-seven years old and still use some of those same pillowcases and tea towels today. For play, if I wanted an airplane, I simply broke a corncob in half, strategically pushed two or three perfect chicken feathers in the center, and that tail would twirl nicely on my plane. Any animal you can name probably lived on our farm at one time or another. Baby animals were always available for play, although we had one sow who did not want us touching her piglets.

As money was very, very limited, Barb and I were always thinking of creative ways to make some. When the Susquenita High School was being built in the early 1950s (1952-1954) Barb and I would pull our little red wagon down to the school and pick up soda bottles the workers discarded and then take them up to Joseph and Frances (Smitty) Smith's "mom and pop" store near Kinkora at the base of Cove Mountain, corner of current Cove Road and on the left side of Routes 11 & 15 as you go toward Duncannon. We got two cents for a regular bottle and five cents for a large size. Sometimes we spent some of the money right away on penny candy or saved it to spend on Monday nights when Joe would watch us at his store, called Joe's, while mom, dad and Smitty went to bible study at Middle Cove Church. Joe made us feel important because we beat him at checkers, could get and pay for our own candy, and sometimes we could even wait on customers. Dad frequently bought a pound of Joe's "wash-rubbers", ridged coconut cookies.

In reality, the world can be a small place and Perry County can make it even smaller with the intertwining facts of history. Joe's Store had its own history with our family because the store was originally located across the road, between Routes 11 & 15 and the Susquehanna River. It was owned by my grandparents, Clarence and Bessie (Fenicle) Ellenberger. It was also their home. When the railroad was being built up alongside Route 11 & 15, their home and store was in the way of the tracks. The railroad offered to move the structure over to the other side of Routes 11 & 15, which they did. It benefited all concerned. I believe the family only stayed there a short time thereafter.

Then my grandparents sold the store (which was the store Joe and Smitty bought and ran for so many years). Clarence and Bessie moved down to a storefront home on the "back road" (present Schoolhouse Road) less than a mile south of the Susquenita School. That storefront house is quite easy to spot, because it still has huge windows along the porch going across the entire front of the structure. My grandmother, Bessie, ran the store on the "back road" while at the same time the family was building a store property along the more heavily traveled Routes 11 & 15, which would eventually expand to include an adjacent picnic grove, along with an added gas pump. The store on the "back road" was eventually closed when only the business moved across the field to its new location, while the family still lived in the house on the "back road". In fact, some of the family continued to live in that same house until after the turn of the century.

Bessie was in charge of the store, helped by her children, Grace (Steever) Ellenberger and my dad Deitz Ellenberger, while my grandpa, Clarence Ellenberger, had a full-time job working for the railroad as a rail checker. He would walk up and down the tracks from the lower crossing up to the Duncannon mountain, walking only on the railroad ties, to check that nothing was loose and everything was in good order. Some who knew him said that he walked in a slightly stooped position later in life because of his many years of constantly looking down to check the rails.

Remember how I told you Barb and I pulled our red wagon to get money from soda bottle returns? Well, Dad told me he would pull his wagon along the railroad tracks from the store up to the base of the Duncannon mountain selling drinks and sandwiches from their family store to the railroad workers. Bessie made the front corner of her store into a cute little eat-in section with round, glass-topped metal tables and ornate metal chairs to match. You could buy everything you needed, run a tab and pay on your tab as you could, "a mutual honor system".

Bessie had decorative plates made imprinted with her name, the Cove name, and pictures of birds which she gave out to customers who frequented her store. These plates are quite pretty and still surface here and there today as a collector item. So interesting, these same plates which Bessie simply gave away for free can now cost $450 or more, if you can find one. Her store was later sold to Walter (Pop) Steever. For many years, the Middle Cove Church Ladies Aid had their annual Fried Egg Supper in Pop Steever's picnic grove in the summer. Barb and I never tired of riding our bikes down the "back road" to cut over to Pop Steever's, and I especially loved walking over that creaky, wooden floor, just to buy penny candy.

There was a lane connecting the "back road" and Routes 11 & 15 which people referred to as the "Lake" on my Grandpa's (Fremont W. Bitting—Walt's) farm which at that time partially adjoined our Ellenberger farm and currently is next to the Susquenita Elementary grounds on the south side. The "Lake" was so named because it had water on both sides of that lane which would freeze in the wintertime. They would cut ice blocks to be stored and used for people's refrigeration into the summer. That ice was stored in sawdust in ice houses at various locations in the Cove, one of which is at the base of Cove mountain off Holman Drive. My dad told me how he would help cut ice and "peddle" it for the old iceboxes (refrigerators). The "Lake" ran right down between the farm buildings, with the barn, pigpen, wagon shed, and saddle room (which to me had a wonderful, leathery, horsey smell) on one side, and the cider press and butcher shop on the other. All these buildings have since been demolished. In the summertime, portions of the "Lake" would dry out and my Grandpa and his brothers, Grover, Ralph and Thomas, would turn their many horses out into that "Lake" pasture, which could still be a bit swampy in parts.

There are so many memories I would like to repeat and reasons why I love Perry County. You can determine for yourself which of the following are good, bad or ugly. Regardless of how you view them, they have melded together to make me who I am today.

***

Visiting different churches in the area and singing in their musicals and services. Mom played the accordion, Dad played his mouth organ, and we kids and mom would sing.

Uncle Tom's (Thomas and Portia Bitting) Auction House which at some point became Colonial Fair and is now the site of Big Bee Boats and RV. When I was quite young, I got to take orders in the screened refreshment area and was always paid with a soda of my choice. I thought it was great.

The Dairy Barn became an auction site at the north end of Schoolhouse Road when my Uncle "Pete" (Fremont W. Bitting, Jr.) came on the scene. He was also a traveling auctioneer, who frequently took me with him to be a "runner" and allowed me to "rattle" for him when he wanted to take breaks, and I wasn't too bad. In fact, he said I got better prices than he did, a great ego builder.

Riding our horses in the Duncannon Centennial parade in 1965. Barb rode Bruce, our paint horse. I rode Flossie, our Palamino. KB (Ken) rode his pony, Penny and tipped his cowboy hat to the crowd all along the parade route.

Many opportunities provided by our creek such as making many dams to see just how high we could get the water. Also spending hours hanging over the side of the creek bank in order to catch minnows, look at them, count how many in the bucket, and then simply dump them back in the creek for us to catch another day.

When my Grandpa (Fremont W. Bitting, Sr.) would stop by the house and we would travel all over to orchards to pick up "drops" to make cider in his cider press. I loved my time with him. Later when we got back to the cider press, he wanted to know why I was so slow putting apples in the chute for him when he was pressing, and I said I was throwing out the bad and wormy ones. That was the wrong answer. He told me in no uncertain terms that every apple, no matter how ugly, goes up that chute because worms make it taste better!

Every June we would hop onto the drag-sled which dad pulled with his Farmall Super C Tractor and go up over the hillside to pick wild strawberries for jelly making and strawberry shortcake. We had to pick a lot of berries to fill our kettles because wild strawberries are extremely small (but very sweet). Nothing today comes close to the taste of those strawberry shortcakes mom made.

Grandpa Ellenberger (Clarence) stayed with Barb and me one day while mom and dad went to town. Grandpa told me not to play behind the bushes because of snakes. Sure enough, he saw a snake, grabbed me from behind the bushes, put Barb and me in the kitchen with instructions to stay there, got a gun and went back outside. Before long we heard a gunshot and so did mom and dad who were just getting home. Grandpa filled them in on what had happened. He told them he shot the snake, but not to get near it because it wasn't dead yet. He could still hear it hissing. On closer checking, he did indeed kill the snake, but he also shot a hole through our propane gas line!

Farmers helping farmers with harvesting their crops and anytime help was needed. Addison (Addie) and Minnie Holman and the Ellenbergers had adjoining farm property, owned farm equipment together and always worked together, even the kids, but we didn't have to work as hard. We mostly carried water or food to the workers or took on the role of "gofers" for whatever was needed. Every free moment we got during harvesting, Henry Holman and I would just hang in the cherry trees which grew by what is now named Holman's Lane. In season, we would eat cherries and save as many pits as possible in our mouths in order to shoot them at workers and equipment which passed by under us. We always thought they didn't know we were in the trees, but to this day I still don't know that answer. Other times Henry and I would laze in the huge mulberry tree near the Ellenberger barn, talk about nothing, and when mulberries were in season, eat all we could reach.

Homecoming at Middle Cove Church was a full Sunday with three services, morning, afternoon and evening along with really good food. When I was quite a bit younger, it made me wonder that so many older people crowded the afternoon outdoor service and had so much to say. Now I am one of those older people and understand it completely. Some of the men in the church would carry the piano out to the concrete by the road for the afternoon and evening services. The evening homecoming service was my favorite because it was under the giant oak trees with all the sounds of night insects high in the trees, and bugs flying all around the strung lights. Everything about it was special.

Friday night fireworks at the Marysville and New Bloomfield carnivals each summer. You would always find people you knew.

Getting excited in the mid 1950s to see the "New Train" go up and down the railroad tracks, every time! It was sleek silver with a red stripe and state insignia, streamlined and there was no steam engine to be seen! It was a big event for everyone.

Going to Duncannon on Saturday to do our grocery shopping at Cooper's or the American Store for the week. On occasions as necessary, we would also visit Murphy's Five and Ten, Mary Barringer's or Snavely's on the square, Zerfing's Hardware, the Drug Store, Lauster's and Barton's, later site of Western Auto. I know I am probably missing other stores we would frequent and we always stopped by the Duncannon National Bank, if for no other reason than to say hello to Charlie Pennell.

When crossing the Susquehanna River on the Clark's Ferry Bridge, Dad and Mom would give me the occasional privilege of handing the nickel toll out the window to the man at the toll booth. Dad told me when he was young, if you were horse drawn and crossed the bridge, you could cross for free if your horse had four white socks.

Grandpa Bitting had a huge, very old, white workhorse named Cap. My sister Barb and I and our neighbor friend across the field, Ronda Bender, would go down to grandpa's barn, put a halter on Ole' Cap (he listened so well and moved so slow that we did not even need a bridle), then position him beside the barnyard fence so the three of us could get up on his back which was extremely wide, and we would just go for a ride.

Some of my fondest memories were of outdoors. It was fun to ride the horse-drawn hay wagon at Grandpa Bitting's to gather the loose hay in the fields. That is practically a lost art today for the normal farmer.

Going to different church festivals, dinners, and fund raisers in the county.

Jumping into the pond and submerging to get rid of chicken lice from cleaning hundreds of chicken nests. We didn't have to do it too often, but the pond water worked.

After working in the fields or out at the barn or mending fences, Dad and Mom would sometimes take us to the Dairy Bar in Duncannon as a special treat for all we accomplished that day.

As soon as friends came, we would go to the barn to play in the hay and straw. Jumping from the rafters into a small pile of straw was forbidden, so that was one of the first things we did. As instructed by her mother (Rose Bender), my friend Ronda was not to play in the barn because her mom felt it was dangerous. (She also was not to swim in our pond because there were snakes in it. Of course, there were but snakes weren't interested in us as we swam.) So her mom wouldn't know, we carefully picked all the straw from her clothes. But Ronda went home with dust from the straw mow and dirt all over her arms and face, so she got in trouble for it. The next time, we were so careful, picked all the straw off her clothes and washed all the dirt and dust off. Would you believe, we missed one piece of straw in her shoe. Her mom was not happy and yes, of course, she got in trouble yet again!

Going fishing with Uncle Ken (Kenneth E. Bitting) on the Susquehanna River and coming back with fish and frequently snapping turtles. Some would be put into the cool waters of the spring-house, which also flowed over through the basement of the Bitting farmhouse. Sometimes a fish or two would show up in the basement trough.

Grandma Bitting's (Pearl Bitting) wonderful pies, cakes and fried potatoes, which were unmatched, as attested to by the fact she was a constant "baking" winner at the Perry County Fair. One year she did not win, though, because they disqualified her pie saying it was just too perfect and could not possibly have been homemade. That did not go down well with her! Grandma's pies should look perfect because she worked for years at Glass' Bakery on High Street in Duncannon. I loved to stop in to see her there. The smells were wonderful and she always gave me a baked treat.

Getting up on a Saturday morning, watching the dust dance in the sunbeams and then putting on my bathing suit and jumping into the pond (Barb too) which was pretty darn cold because of the creek water flowing through it. It was going to be a work day on the farm, but a fun day too.

Vacation Bible School in Duncannon every year for two weeks right after our school year ended.

Penn Township Elementary; decorating, practicing and performing for May Day; recess, double-dutch jump rope, and when it snowed sliding down that forbidden long hill at the edge of the playground; wooden stall bathrooms in the school basement.

Walkers who disappeared from view at the end of each school day; bus rides to and from Penn Township; the teachers (Mrs. Basom, Mrs. Beatty, Mrs. Minnick, Mrs. Ream, Miss Bryner, and Mrs Haas), and Penn Township Elementary School friends who are still friends today.

Dad made a ten-foot by ten-foot deer shanty with a tin roof to hear the rain, put in sliding windows on all four sides, and used a ladder to get up to it because he built it atop four cut off telephone poles, and placed it in the corner of our mountain field. He put two beds, one stool, a built-in cupboard, and a wood stove complete with stovepipe in it. Although Deitz used it only in hunting season, it actually was just as much for socializing as hunting, because hunters would stop by to get warm, socialize, and eat mom's homemade soup, pies, cookies, and other food he stocked. In the summers, Barb and I along with Bonnie (Smith) Simmons, and Betty Allandar, to name a few, would quite often sleep overnight in the shanty where, even though we pulled up the ladder, you could always count on someone or something coming by to scare us. Not much sleep, but lots of fun! After many years, the shanty was partially dismantled and carefully, but painstakingly, relocated up on the first flat in the mountain where, after more than sixty years, it still gets use each year during hunting season.

***

Writing this has brought back so many thoughts too numerous to list. I moved from Perry County to the Newtown Square area when I got married in 1967, but could never stay away. Every holiday found me home on the farm. I would come home to help in the fields if needed. Special occasions or church functions, homecoming, would draw me back. Family especially has always represented my strongest, deepest ties to Perry County. Memories and thoughts can transport me instantaneously to Perry County. I love that we lived in a farmhouse that was covered with yellow Indian paint and had huge green shutters (with live bats on the backside) which could be closed for both weather and Indian protection. I love the huge barn made with wooden pegs and so many stories and memories. I loved going to Sunday School and Church at Middle Cove, the neighbors, friends, and just people in general. I love that I got married at Middle Cove in Perry County with deer on the hillside. My parents had high morals, taught strong values, and lived their Christian faith in their rural, Perry County way, and always expected the same of me. I can lie down and watch the clouds go by overhead, and to me they will always be different and better in Perry County because I want them to be! My Perry County bonds are, now, and always will be, with me, for my life has been so very wonderful because of Perry County roots.

More than fifty-five years ago, I married Clark Colborn and he had me resettle in a different Pennsylvania county two hours away from my Perry County home. Even so, I still go back at every opportunity, and the memories and stories have not faded. My two children, Kathy and Ken Colborn, have heard my stories many times over and even suggested ones not included in this writing. Perry County is and always will be in the depth of my soul because you may take the girl out of Perry County, but you cannot take Perry County out of her heart.

The Future Is Not Ours To See

Storyteller Wendy Jo (Wise) Campbell

In 1955, Jay Livingston and Ray Evans wrote a song which was then recorded by Doris Day in May 1956 – "Que Sera Sera/Whatever Will Be, Will Be". The lyrics in the middle of the song are as follows: "when I grew up and fell in love I asked my sweetheart what lies ahead? Will we have rainbows day after day? Here's what my sweetheart said, que sera, sera, whatever will be, will be. The future's not ours to see, que sera, sera." A few weeks after that song was released, my mother (Martha Brandt) and daddy (Thomas Wise) were married on June 9, 1956. Little did they know then that the words to that song would be a theme for their lives.

I often said that my mom's love story could be the makings for a great romance movie. She was born to Ada and Walter Brandt in 1932 outside of Millerstown on the farm where Millie Rheam once lived (near the Cocolamus Creek). While she was in high school, she dated a young fellow by the name of Gene Trout. He left high school in twelfth grade, joined the Army, and soon was shipped overseas to Korea and the surrounding area. They kept in touch for a while, but lost track when he was deployed.

In the meantime, my mom quit school in the eleventh grade and eventually took a job as a housekeeper with the Sausman family in Thompsontown. The Sausmans had a son who was friends with three neighborhood boys, Tom, Paul and John Wise. My mom met Tom Wise while working for the Sausmans. She and Tom fell in love and were married, at Mt. Olivet Church outside of Newport, in 1956. They lived in a little trailer behind my Grandma and Pop Pop's garage (Mary and TK Wise) on Pine Street in Thompsontown.

Shortly after she became pregnant with me, my daddy, Tom was diagnosed with Hodgkin's Disease. For a little over two years, they traveled to Johns Hopkins for treatment. He came from a family of nine children. His one sister, Virginia Wise Sheets, and his brother, Paul, were tested to see if they would be a match for a bone marrow transplant. Ginny was a match. The night before the transplant was to take place in February 1960, my daddy passed away. He was twenty-eight years old. I had just turned two in January.

Sadly, I do not remember him. My mother made sure that his family remained part of my life growing up and they remain so today. I spent a lot of time with my Grandma and Pop Pop. Had he lived, I probably would not be writing about Perry County. I most likely would have been raised and lived in Juniata County! Because this story concludes with two people who grew up in Perry County, and their legacy continues in the county that they loved and lived in their entire married lives, I feel it is appropriate to share it as a cherished memory.

My mom was a young widow at twenty-seven years of age with a toddler. Her story did not end here. To fully understand the "love" story, we need to go back a few years….

Eugene (Gene) Trout was born in 1931 to Elaine Fry and Paul Trout. Elaine was from Millerstown and Paul was from Mifflin County. Elaine was only sixteen years old when she became pregnant with Gene. Of course, Paul Trout married her. The times were much different then for an unwed, let alone, teen-aged mother. After they married, Paul and Elaine moved to Thompsontown for a few years. Gene Trout and Tom Wise were the same age and became friends. My grandma Wise used to tell stories of Gene and Tom playing in their front yard. Gene actually got hooked with a fish hook while he was up in a tree in their yard by none other than Tom who was "tree fishing"!

Paul and Elaine's marriage did not last. As a result of their separation, Gene moved to Millerstown to live with his grandparents (Frys). He grew up in town, working for Butch Bortell in his butcher shop, playing baseball and singing in the minstrel shows at Millerstown High School. From stories my mom used to tell, he was quite the handsome young man and had girls on his coattails! As soon as he turned eighteen, he chose to join the call to service in his senior year. Most of the seventeen years he spent in the Army were spent overseas in Korea, Laos, Cambodia, and Japan.

During his high school days, Gene and my mom dated off and on. They kept in touch once he left for Fort Dix, New Jersey. My mom was smitten and probably would have followed him to the ends of the earth. Although he cared for my mom, Gene's focus was on the Army. He knew he was going overseas and his future was a bit uncertain. He wasn't quite ready to settle down. As time went on, he and my mom parted ways and lost contact.

Tom Wise also served in the Army and was stationed in Korea where he earned a Bronze Star. I have a letter that he wrote to my grandma stating that when he was on R&R while serving in Korea, he just so happened to run into some old friends, Gene Trout and Bob Sweger from Millerstown! This was long before my mom knew there was a Tom Wise!

When Gene Trout heard that Tom Wise had passed away and he was home on leave, he visited my mom and extended his sympathy. Evidently the embers were still smoldering from their high school days. They kept in touch, fell in love, and were married in May of 1962.

I had another daddy! He was not a replacement for Tom and he encouraged me to "remember" my daddy Tom; he was my bonus daddy. I often told my daddy Gene (as I lovingly referred to him) that he only married my mom so he would have me for his daughter! I rarely refer to him as my step-dad. He is the man who raised me and taught me my values. He loved me unconditionally and was proof that one does not have to be biological to be a father. He was my daddy on earth, all the while I was certain my daddy Tom was watching from Heaven.

When I grew up and had a daughter of my own, he was a wonderful, loving and doting pappy. He passed away in 2005 and we all still miss him dearly. One of my Wise aunts told me that she imagined the first thing my daddy Tom would say to daddy Gene in Heaven would be "thank you for raising and loving our daughter".

I never questioned his love for me and he never denied me the close relationship I had with my Wise family. In fact, the Wise family in Thompsontown welcomed my daddy Gene into their hearts and homes. My grandma Wise always referred to him as one of hers. The Wise family became his family.

For many years, daddy Gene did not see his parents. He kept in touch with his mother through the years he was in the service, but his dad left the area and did not make an effort to be a part of his life. When daddy Gene got out of the Army in 1964, he eventually went to work for Harrisburg Steel Mill and ran into a Paul Trout. This Paul Trout was his dad. They reconciled and had a very close relationship until grandpa Trout passed away some twenty years later. Because of the union of my mom and daddy Gene, I have a brother whom I am very close to. The day before our mom passed away in 2006 we promised her that we would remain close and we both cherish the bond we have.

As much as I would give to have known my daddy Tom, I understand and appreciate the way life worked out. Gene became part of two families (the Brandt and Wise families). He was denied the closeness of family growing up, but soon learned the blessings the gift of family brings. God knew the plans he had for all of us; and it is my belief that there is always a rainbow at the end of the storm, even though the end result may not be what we would imagine. My mom's life and my life is proof of that.

In closing, call it fate or coincidence or answered prayers of the faithful, life does have a way of working out. When one door closes, another window will open; we just need to have the strength, faith and determination to follow through and move on. We take the hand we are dealt and make the best of it with the support of loved ones and by the mercies and grace of God…que sera, sera.

"Big Jim's" Adventures In New Bloomfield

Storyteller James E. "Jim" Swenson

Growing up in New Bloomfield, my family lived on the corner of E. McClure Street and Barnett Woods Road. The elementary school where I went to school for 1st through 6th grades was across the street from our house, as well as the playground, basketball court and baseball fields.

Some of my earliest childhood memories are of my mother taking me across the street to the playground, where she would watch me walk down and across the ball field to meet my grandfather, Homer Weldon. He was one of the owners of DWM Ford Garage. In the showroom there was a hobby horse that I rode or I'd go talk with the mechanics or with Bonnie Lyons, the secretary. Everyone would call me "Little Jimmy", but I would tell them that I was "Big Jim." Grandpa would take me across the street to Tressler's service station to get a soda or popsicle and we'd listen to the loafers tell stories. Grandpa loved going rabbit hunting and he had a beagle named Smoky. I would walk behind Grandpa who chewed tobacco and I would chew raisins and spit when he would spit.

My Uncle Jim Weldon had a barber shop uptown where you got a haircut or loafed. One day I decided I wanted to be a barber like Uncle Jim, so I convinced my little sister Bib to let me cut her hair. I took her coat, wrapped it around her and cut her hair. Needless to say, mom was not happy.

Growing up, our neighbors were Frank and Catherine Fry, and Joe and Madeline Darlington Sr. Mrs. Fry would watch us kids if mom had somewhere to go and if you had trouble with any schoolwork, Mr. Fry, being a teacher, would help. As I got older Mr. Fry, when not teaching, would mow grass, trim bushes or rake leaves and he would get me to help. Being a teacher, he showed me different lawn tools and how to properly use them.

The Darlington's had a large garden and horse corral (Jacobs Insurance is there today) where you could pet or sometimes ride a horse. Mr. Darlington was nicknamed "Mr. Perry County" because of his knowledge of Perry County history, and this is where I learned a lot of New Bloomfield history. One other nice thing about the Darlington's home was their swimming pool.

Another memory about our neighbors was every evening in the summer, they would sit out on their porches and listen to Philadelphia Phillies baseball on the radio, like most people in New Bloomfield. At our house we had a big yard and even though we lived across the street from the ball fields, we played wiffle ball or kickball (nothing harder because too many windows were getting broken or cars getting hit), football or played army. Other games we played with neighborhood kids were hide and seek, and flashlight tag. When the fire siren would go off, we would stop playing and go up to the square to watch the fire trucks.

During the summer, the men's baseball team would play. For every foul ball you would find, you got a nickel and if they broke a bat, you could keep it. You'd take it home, put nails in it, wrap electrical tape around the handle and we'd use it for our games.

Come the 4th of July, the carnival was across the street on the ball field, and we had front row seats on our front porch to see the fireworks. The most fun game at the carnival was the men's baseball team's game. For a quarter you got three tomatoes and one of the players would put their head through a hole and you could try to hit their head.

When I would head out for whatever adventure I was up to that day, mom would come to suspect that I would probably come home with broken glasses. Mom got to be pretty good at fixing them but if it was on a Tuesday or Saturday, Dr. Silverstein was in his New Bloomfield office, and I would go to him for repairs. Other surprises for Mom would be when I came home with bumps, scrapes and cuts that would require stitches, or broken bones. One winter, the Boy Scouts went to Hidden Valley Scout Camp for winter camp, and we stayed at Ritter on top of the Ridge. Randy Tressler took his toboggan along. Randy and I were sure we could stay straight and go down the power line. Straight did not happen and we started down through the woods. Randy was able to roll off, but I stayed on. They gathered me up and dropped me off at my church where mom was. She took me to the hospital where they found out I had a broken nose and shoulder.

For us kids growing up we had Cub Scouts which led to Boy Scouts where I was very active. Another activity was Little League baseball, and my first coaches were Terry and Dutch Urich. Memorial Day was the first game of the season after the parade. I have been involved in the Memorial Day parades from when I started marching as a Cub Scout, in the Junior High Band, with the New Bloomfield Fire Company, up until present day with lining up and starting the parade.

Depending on the season, Sunday afternoons were always great. That's when the dads would come out and play ball with us, whether it was football, basketball, or baseball.

As we got older, we learned to ride bikes. This expanded our territory from the neighborhood to the whole town, where you could ride around, find other town kids playing ball, go to the many stores to buy candy, popsicles or soda. In the summertime, the best place to ride your bike was to the town pool that opened at 1:00 p.m., and swim until mom drove up and yelled for us to go home for supper. But after supper, we'd go back up until closing time or until your eyes were so red and sore from the chlorine, you had to quit.

Other activities the town boys would do is build soapbox racers. We would go down to the New Bloomfield Planing Mill's scrap pit, get lumber to build our racers, take wheels off wagons, go up to N. Apple

Street to Harry Keller's house and come flying down. I can't believe no one was seriously hurt. When not doing soapbox racing, we were racing HO cars and we'd go to different guy's tracks at their houses. The best track was at John Hair's. It was totally landscaped and had six lanes for racing.

During wintertime, we ice skated down at the New Bloomfield dam. On Saturday or Sunday there were ice hockey games and a lot of people would be skating. At night, you could burn fires to see for skating or sometimes the Fire Company would set up lights.

At Christmas break, the Carson Long Military Institute cadets would go home, and Colonel Holman would allow us to play basketball in the gym.

Every Sunday we went to Sunday School and Church. After Church, we went home for lunch and then headed out to play. In the summer, we'd have two weeks of Bible School. When we became teenagers, every Sunday evening we would have Luther League. We would have devotions and then have open discussions on any topic that we felt affected our lives as teenagers. Sometimes after we were done, we would go roller skating at the Rainbow Roller Rink, on Cumberland County's Carlisle Pike.

As a teenager, to make spending money, there were many odd jobs to do. Summertime help was making hay or straw for my Uncles Ben Dum and Bill Sutch on their farms or Frank Bailor's across the street from where we lived. We'd make hay or pick potatoes for ten cents a bushel. We would also mow neighbors' yards, rake leaves in the fall or shovel snow off the sidewalks in the winter.

Teenager activities were hanging out at Perry Lanes Bowling Alley to shoot pool, play pinball and bowl. Depending on the season, we'd still be playing ball and now hunting.

In the summertime, when we were done with doing whatever, we would meet at my friend Dave Russell's house and we would sleep out under the stars. In the morning we'd get up, throw our sleeping bag over the clothesline so it would be there for the next night and go on our way. During the night if we got hungry, we would go up to the laundromat, which was open 24 hours, because they had vending machines or we'd go raid Roy Snyder's cantaloupe patch.

One night we decided to try and sleep out in the New Bloomfield cemetery. It was very dark and we rolled around in our sleeping bags, trying to get settled in. We might have lasted half an hour. There were too many strange noises, so we got out of there in a hurry.

The summer of 1970 was the Perry County Sesquicentennial and a gang of us boys were helpers for the celebration. Whatever the general committee needed, we got it done. Hauling chairs and tables, putting banners up, hauling bleachers from all four school districts to New Bloomfield for spectators and helped build the stage for the pageant, "Hoop Poles, Brains and Buckwheat." We all had jobs for putting on the pageant: Chuck Good – stage lights, Scott Kumler and me – spotlights, Jim Sailor – rear projections, and Dave Russell, Dennis Askins, Lowell Briggs and Woody Sailor – backstage assistants. It was a fun summer.

The following summer was spent doing odd jobs and sleeping out at night with the guys. Towards the end of the summer, I turned sixteen, started to drive and joined the New Bloomfield Fire Company.

During my sophomore through senior years, I attended Cumberland/Perry Vo-Tech school in the mornings to learn plumbing, heating, and air conditioning. After morning classes, we would ride the bus back to West Perry for afternoon class. The summer of 1972, I got a job at Hair Brothers on South Carlisle Street, helping to do plumbing and heating. That year when the Agnes Flood hit central Pennsylvania, Mr. Hair sent us down to Newport to tear out oil burners and controls ahead of the flood. After the flood, I got sent back to put the furnaces back together and set up oil tanks that had fallen over. I got a lot of experience that summer. I graduated from Cumberland Perry Vo-Tech and West Perry then started my adult life working in the HVAC business.

This was just a small list of my experiences growing up in New Bloomfield. Being around the people was a very memorable experience.

Memories Of Loysville From The 1970s

Storyteller Laura (Lyons) Guyer

Growing up in Loysville, Perry County, and being a child of parents who worked close to home had many advantages. My mother, LouAnn (Wilson) Lyons worked at the Perry County Home located outside of Loysville. She was their nurse until it closed shortly after Perry Village opened in New Bloomfield. My Aunt Betty and Uncle Joe Wilson were the in-house managers of the County Home. My Aunt Dorothy Wilson (or Dort to everyone who knew her) was a cook. Margaret Sheaffer (Aunt Betty's mother or Ma'am as we knew her) also worked in the home. She was always kind and we considered her part of the family. In the summers, on days when no one was available to watch my brother (David Lyons) or myself, we would go to "work" with my mother. We never thought of it as "going to work." It was more like playing and visiting with family for the day. What a great time we had, acting out productions we created for the residents as only two young children could perform. They clapped and joined in with our antics. From what I can recall, there were thirty to thirty-five residents at any given time and were like surrogate grandparents to us.

One of the residents, Lee Clouser, would trap and fish in the pond located west of the building and catch snapping turtles. My aunt would make soup out of the turtle meat. Lee would clean the shell and when dried he would give it to us as a sort of keepsake. The shells did prove to be an interesting show and tell at Green Park Elementary School.

We would play in the brick outbuildings, which at that time were used for maintenance storage. We would climb up and down the old metal outdoor fire escape on the four-storied, red-brick County Home. The first floor was a kitchen and dining area plus a recreation room or common area. This is where we would visit, entertain and play with the residents. I recall the big old wooden rocking chairs the residents would sit and relax in. My aunt and uncle lived on one floor. The resident's rooms were on the other levels. We were not to visit the residents in their rooms because this was their personal space. I can remember the big stairways with steel-fronted steps that led to the different floors in the building. There were shared bathrooms on each of the floors.

When Uncle Joe had the time, he would help in our supervision. For anyone who remembers Joe Wilson, he was good at instigating and teasing. With that said, we received an education that we would not receive in school. It was a loving atmosphere and we always had something to do. Looking back, I'm sure my brother and I were an annoyance to the ones who were trying to get their jobs done, but we knew nothing of that at the time.

One of my most memorable events at the home was when the elevator was installed. It was dedicated Saturday, June 12, 1971, and I remember a ceremony with county commissioners (Max Powell, Norman Pressley and Harry Sheaffer) and many other "officials" attending. When the elevator was completely operable and all the pomp and circumstance was over, I remember thinking, what a great toy they had installed for us to play in. I estimate the elevator was big enough to place a stretcher in and could probably hold four to six people. We imagined being the elevator operators for so many visitors and residents. Unfortunately, our aunt, uncle and mother did not agree with our aspirations. We were not allowed to play in the elevator! I won't deny that we did try it out a few times, but for the most part, we knew to obey the orders from our supervisors!

My father Paul "Ed" Lyons worked at the Loysville Youth Development Center (YDC). Dad worked as a security guard along with Wendel Smith, Norm Kistler, Henry Anderson, and Maynard Weldon, all very pleasant gentlemen. He worked there when it was an open campus, not as it is now with fencing topped with razor wire. On the weekends when dad worked daylight, mom, Dave, and I would take our dog Fritz on a walk to meet him at the end of his shift. If we timed it right, he would be making his final rounds and we would walk along with him. We were also allowed to go into his office and wait if he was finishing paperwork. We thought we were very special to be able to do this!

I remember one evening our family was driving home from New Bloomfield and there were a couple of young guys walking by the side of the road. It was getting dark and my dad pulled over to offer a ride, which I found to be uncharacteristic of him. Finding out later, he recognized the boys who had gone AWOL from the YDC. The boys got in the car and dad returned them to the facility. Being unfamiliar with the area and in the dark, they seemed relieved to have been picked up and returned.

The YDC had a huge cement pool and dad would get us swim passes in the summer. I spent many a summer afternoon swimming with friends and relaxing by the pool.

In my teenage years, the director of the YDC, Mr. Williams, would contract with me to babysit his visiting young grandchildren. I remember him cooking a meal of Cornish hen for us. (He would stay at home but was not interested in entertaining the children on his own.) I didn't mind, as he was a great cook and a very interesting gentleman to talk with.

My dad also worked for Joe Nickel, the funeral director. When available, dad would be on call to pick up bodies and bring them to the funeral home. I remember one night he was called to receive a body from a hospital (I believe it was near Philadelphia) and we were all summoned to go along in Joe's station wagon. My brother and I, of course, had to sit in the back seat and unbeknownst to us until we picked up the body, we would be sitting with the deceased. Imagine what went through our minds as young children sitting with a corpse and the questions we presented to our parents – no wonder I consider this a memory!

There were two small grocery stores in Loysville. Emlet's grocery was located on the square, and Robinson's grocery and hardware was located at the west-end of Loysville. They were small in size but always had everything we needed from penny candy to lunch meat and cheese. As we got older, we were allowed to walk to these stores. Mom would give us a list and we were more than happy to independently walk to get the goods. Our families knew each other so it was not only a shopping trip but a visit as well.

Some other names and memories I recall of growing up within Loysville were Charlie and Ethel Clark. They were one of the first people I knew to have an in-ground pool. How exciting it was for us to be able to use this pool, if they were home. We had to either call or go to the house and knock on the door to make sure we had permission to swim. Charlie would let us swim whenever we wanted and didn't seem to mind our youthful behavior. Ethel was a bit stricter, never allowing us to make too much noise or splash or jump in and out of the pool too often. As we got older, we stopped going to the pool as often. Shortly before closing the pool for good, several deer jumped in and tore the liner. After Charlie passed away, Ethel had the pool filled in and paved over. As a side note, Charlie Clark taught my brother and I the song "The Old Gray Mare." He told us to go home and sing it to our mom, which we promptly did. She was amused but warned us to be careful whom we sang it to.

My memories of Loysville would not be complete if I did not mention our church, Tressler Memorial Lutheran Church, located beside the post office near Loysville's square. If you have never visited this red-brick church with its tall stained-glass windows, it is worth a look. If you do visit, you must remember this church was built over one-hundred years ago with no machinery - just man and horsepower. I know I am biased, but I find it to be one of the most beautiful buildings in the county. My Wilson ancestors helped to build this church and my family has attended consistently, serving on council, committees and singing in the choir. My brother and I were baptized, confirmed and married in this church. Growing up, Rev. Russell Kerns was our pastor and the most memorable for me. He was very active with Christian Endeavor and helped to organize a trip to Europe that my family was fortunate enough to enjoy. He also started our "clown ministry." This was a group of youth that would wear costumes and clown makeup. We would perform songs, sign language and create balloon animals among other talents at different venues. This was a great experience for all of us. Many fond memories cross my mind of the people and activities we have had (and continue to have) at Tressler Church.

Once school was out for the summer, my best friend, Lisa Clark and I would plan our summer vacation adventures. On the first day, we would always head to the Sun Bonnet Drive-In, on the west-end of Loysville, and treat ourselves to ice cream sundaes. We would also plan our itinerary for the Loysville Carnival, held on the Loysville Community Club grounds where the Loysville two-room schoolhouse still stands. What rides we would ride. The foods we would eat and the nights we would attend! After all this planning, the rest of the summer was spent riding bikes, swimming, playing badminton in our backyards and tennis on the Loysville Community Club courts within sight of the old County Home.

I grew up in the west-end of Loysville surrounded by close neighbors who watched out for us. Next door, Chester and Lucy Stahl always had an immaculate garden. The rows were perfect and the produce was plenty. We did our best to keep our kickballs, Frisbee, and other flying objects out of their garden. But if found in the garden for any reason, we would get a tongue lashing from Lucy. At the time I did not understand, but looking back I realize all of their hard work. Sara, Leroy, Marlin and Diana Rice lived on the other side of us. We always had a good time with them picnicking and partying on holidays. Other neighbors were Carrie Moyer, Dorman and Laura Hockenberry, Joe and Edna Nickel, Homer and Janet Stroup, Doc and Gretna Stine, Les and Grace Clark, Charles and Donna Morrison, plus Carl and Nancy Myers to name a few.

Our little section of Loysville was close-knit and I wouldn't trade any part of my growing-up in this little Perry County town!

Memories From A One-Room School

Storyteller Nancy Bower Brown

"RED HILL SCHOOL REUNION SEPTEMBER 26, 2018"

Many of the things we learned about life, we all learned from attending a one-room school.

First of all, it gave us a very good foundation in education, as well as some life skills, that we have been able to use throughout our lives.

Today we live in a different kind of world, and our children and grandchildren are receiving another type of education.

Back in our day, we weren't worried about self-esteem or having an identity crisis. In fact, we never even heard those words because we all knew who we were and where we came from. We knew each other's families and where we all lived.

We definitely went to a school in our own community. Most of us did not have indoor bathrooms, so it wasn't a big deal when we had to raise our hand and get permission from the teacher to go to the "outhouse" even in the rain and snow.

We all helped to carry water from the Anderson Farm spring-house to fill our water cooler. I do not believe we had a stack of "Dixie Cups" by the water cooler, so we could each have our own individual cups, but rather we shared a common cup or ladle to get a drink of water. Yes! We all survived!!

I can't remember that we ever had any serious outbreak of illness by sharing a cup. Perhaps it made us all stronger and we are still alive today! We learned to share at an early age and that was a good thing! No bottled water for us back then!

Remember the big black woodstove that sat in the middle of the room? Of course, you do!! It had a metal shield around it to keep us from getting too close and getting burned. It was a great place to get warmed up after a big snowball fight or sledding down the hill on a cold wintry day.

Another thing we learned from our education in a one-room school was that we were not confused by having different teachers for different subjects. We had the same teachers for all our classes, from grade one through eight and we all learned from each other.

Sometimes we learned by hearing what another class was doing, or just observing what was going on.

It seems to me I remember a few students shooting "paper wads" at some of us, not to mention any names. However, I never remember any of the girls doing that.

We were fortunate to live at a time before cell phones, E-mail, Facebook, TV and other means of communication which are so necessary in today's world.

Yes, we actually talked with one another and played games together. No one was walking around constantly looking at their cell phone to read their latest messages.

Anyway, the reunion is a special time for all of us to reflect on our education and friendships – that all began in a one-room school!

RED HILL SCHOOL MEMORIES

The school bus was waiting out in the front of our family farm home, west of Blain, Pennsylvania, to take me, along with my older sisters and brother to the one-room school several miles away known as Red Hill.

The year was the early fall of 1940 and I was going to be in the first grade. After we arrived at the building, we were greeted by one teacher, Mr. Frank Shannon, who lived in New Germantown.

We put our lunch boxes on a shelf in the cloak room. There were two cloak rooms, one for the girls and another one for the boys. It had a row of shelves where we put our lunch boxes and hooks on the wall to hang our coats and hats.

The front of the school had the blackboard behind the teacher's desk with the large and small letters of the alphabet above it. There would be a picture of a former president on the wall along with the American Flag. Back at that time we began our school day each morning with a student reading ten verses from the Bible, the American flag salute and repeating the Lord's Prayer.

The younger students sat in the smaller desks near the front of the room while the older students were towards the back of the room in the larger desks.

We always looked forward to our lunch time. Lunches usually consisted of cheese or peanut butter and jelly sandwiches, celery and carrot sticks, a piece of fruit, cookies or cake. Most of us did not bring our own beverage as we drank the water from the water cooler which was shared by everyone. Sometimes we traded sandwiches with another student, especially if they had bologna. Back at that time there were no prepackaged snacks available for us.

Back in those days the girls usually wore dresses or skirts. On cold snowy days we wore snow pants to keep warm along with winter jackets, hats, mittens and boots.

My early childhood education in a one-room school with grades one through eight was an excellent experience for all of us who attended.

That is why I was motivated to write the story "Memories from a One-Room School".

"Best Life In The World" From A Perry County Legend

Storytellers Charles and Pauline (Frownfelter) Lupfer and Tim Lupfer
Recorded by Debra Kay Noye

At the age of ninety-one, Charles Lupfer of Shermans Dale declares he's had "the best life in the world!" He was born at home on Mountain View Road during a fierce snow storm in 1931. Doctor Morrow from New Bloomfield ventured out in the storm only to find the roads were drifting shut. He managed to get as far as the #2 School. Charlie's father, Harry was determined to have Doc's help with the delivery. Hitching a team of horses to his car, with the reins through the front windows, off he went through the drifted dirt roads. His ingenuity paid off and Charlie was born without a hitch!

Charlie knows the WW 1 war stories told by his father, who trained three weeks in the Army before being sent to France, in 1917. Digging trenches at night played a huge part in a soldier's life. His dad was gassed during the war which greatly affected his health. During the victory celebrations, Charlie's dad, a member of the Military Police, was trying to calm a rowdy crowd when a whiskey bottle caused bodily injury to a participant. The ensuing trial delayed his return home.

His dad started farming in 1922 at the Lupfer farm that was located on Upper Pine Hill Road now Mountain View Road. The farm is still in the Lupfer family, owned by Allen Lupfer. Charlie's Uncle John joined his dad in purchasing the former Sheaffer farm on Route 850, currently known as Lupfer's Grove. They jointly farmed with John living at Lupfer's Grove.

Charlie's mother, Eleanor Owen, grew up in Dellville, between Shermans Dale and Duncannon. Her family operated Elmer Owen's Store across from Rice's Mill. They sold gas from the glass bottle reservoir pumps for ten cents a gallon. That's when the customer could actually see how much gas they were receiving. Charlie's family raised chickens and dropped off the eggs to the store every Wednesday night. His grandpap took the eggs to Harrisburg every Thursday when he made his grocery runs to restock the store. During the holidays, Charlie's aunt and mother would travel along to Harrisburg selling residents live geese and ducks off his twelve-foot flatbed Chevrolet truck with removable sides.

Like most farm women in the early to mid-nineteen hundreds, Charlie's mother was a "work horse." In 1943, she was hand milking twelve head of cows as well as tending to other farm chores, gardening and preserving, raising a family, and helping out in the family store. Unfortunately, their house burnt on Christmas Day in 1943. That's the same year, Grandpap Owens decided to purchase electric milkers for the farm – a time saver. The milk was strained into metal cans which were pushed on a cart to the spring-house to be kept cold till they were shipped off to Sunnydale Farm's milk plant in Elizabethville in Upper Dauphin County, prior to the Elliottsburg plant.

Eventually, Charlie owned and drove his own milk trucks picking up the metal cans seven days a week for Sunnydale Farms. If it was morning's milk, it was still warm. The full cans weighed one-hundred pounds with eighty-five pounds being milk. Lifting them out of the deep spring troughs or metal coolers was no easy task, nor was stacking them in the milk truck. Sunnydale would transfer the milk and wash out the cans for Charlie's return to the farmers. A milk tanker hauled the milk to New York. Clair Comp was Charlie's regular driver, but Charlie picked up his Sundays off.

Hauling milk for fourteen years, Charlie came to know many farm families from the Shermans Dale area; Millers, Comps, Sheibleys and Hockenberrys at the foot of Sterretts Gap where sisters Wanda (Cupp) and Rena (Brunner) Hockenberry often came out of the barn carrying their milking stools.

Interesting enough, Charlie's sons, Dennis and Allen, followed in their father's footsteps. They hauled milk for the family business, while they were attending West Perry High School. Tim Lupfer could look out the window of the West Perry Elementary School and see the family's milk truck sitting in the high school parking lot. His brothers, who were just old enough to drive, would pick up cans of milk in the Landisburg, Loysville and Blain areas on their way to school. The cans were dropped off at the Elliottsburg milk plant before the school bell rang. They repeated the route after school as well. Charlie expected his sons to help out where needed and it instilled in them a sense of self-worth, lasting a lifetime.

Tim also remarks about being told, when he was just an infant, his mother would go along with Charlie on his milk route. She'd wrap Tim in a blanket and lay him behind the seat on a wooden ledge, for the long ride.

Prior to 1941, the farm had no electric or indoor plumbing and an icebox held the sawdust covered chunks of ice carved from the creek in the winter. After the farmhouse burned, they did not rebuild until 1948-1949, moving in the year Charlie graduated from high school in 1950. By 1955, they expanded the barn to milk fifty head of cows. Implementing stable cleaners made Charlie feel "on top of the world." A pipeline milking system installed in 1994 transported the milk directly from the cow to a bulk tank.

Lupfers also raised heifers, chickens and pigs. Every year, they would order three to four hundred peeps, keeping them warm under a metal hood by using a coal brooder-stove. Raising peeps demands due diligence to make sure the peeps don't band together and suffocate. The peeps grew into laying-hens and the eggs were picked up weekly by Emlet's in Loysville.

They generally kept several sows (female hogs) around for piglets and for butchering. Once "fattened up," they were butchered on the farm. The family made scrapple using buckwheat flour and cornmeal to thicken the mixture of meat and broth. Lard was rendered, puddin' and sausage were ground. Sausage was also used to stuff the cleaned pig stomach.

H. P. Dyson and Sons, in New Bloomfield, and H. R. Wentzel and Son Feed Mill, at Bridgeport, came to the farm and ground feed for the animals. Otherwise, it was picked up or delivered in bags. Lupfers raised wheat which they sold. Oats and corn they fed to the animals.

Charlie remembers harvesting days when it took teams of two men to hand-cut the corn. He even used a cradle with teeth to cut the wheat and oats, which was then gathered into shocks and flailed on the barn floors allowing the chafe to blow away leaving behind the grains. Reapers and horse-drawn binders lead to the threshing machine which cut and shocked the grains. Lupfers bought a new threshing machine and did 'custom' threshing, along with his Uncle Warren "Buck" Jones. They threshed from Shermans Dale to Dellville for Dave Barrick, Charles and Howard Ziegler, Adam Fortney and Jasper Shearer.

The first binders were pulled by horses and then tractors, but still required some physical labor. Finally, augers ran the grains into combines, instead of using canvas and reels. Harvesting became easier but technology made the new farm machinery more costly.

Harvesting was more than a family affair. Neighbors helped neighbors. Farm wives baked and cooked huge meals keeping the strength up of the harvesting crews. The women would send the youngsters out into the fields periodically with cold beverages and snacks.

Farming and tractors go hand in hand. Charlie remembers the Fordson steel-wheeled tractor used by his dad, uncle and grandpap. In 1946, they bought an Oliver 70 tractor after seeing it at the annual Carlisle Fair. Ernest Shover of Paul Shover and Son of Carlisle, had a display of farm equipment. Besides discovering new farm machinery, Charlie enjoyed the horse races and the nightly entertainment.

Back in the day, anybody that grew up on a farm started helping out as soon as they could walk and follow instructions. And, most people walked or rode a bicycle everywhere, even to school. Charlie wasn't too fond of the store-bought knickers his mother had him wear to school and church. He was fortunate to have new clothes, because his grandfather bought clothing and shoes for the family when he went to Harrisburg to restock his Dellville general store. Charlie and his sister biked to church.

Charlie walked two miles to the Pine Hill School on Pine Hill Road. Raymond Brownawell bused students to the one-room Airy View School off Windy Hill Road. The school had no indoor plumbing. They used an outhouse. Drinking water for the students was carried by bucket from a neighbor. There were no drinking cups. The long-handled metal dipper in the bucket was used by everyone to drink water from. A wood-burning stove provided heat. Students carried their lunches to be eaten at their seats or outside. Mrs. Lester Sheibley who lived near the Lupfer's Grove farm was one of his memorable teachers, as was Ray Dunkleberger because "he slept a lot!" It's no wonder Charlie would rather be farming than sitting in class all day.

For four years, he walked or drove the old farm truck to the bus stop where Lind's Tree Farm stood on Evergreen Road. No door-to-door bus pickups in those days. There was only one bus load of students, from the Shermans Dale area driven by Carl Fry, transported to the New Bloomfield High School. Charlie's teacher, John Weigle, advised him to "stay home and sow your wild oats!" This was music to Charlie's ears, but his mother insisted he graduate. Marlin Zimmerman, from Halifax, was his Vocational Agricultural teacher. Other teachers were Bill Hornberger, Warren Morrison and Lois Smiley.

Charlie's stature came in handy when he played football for three years in high school. "Pretty big" Charlie played left-end wearing a uniform of canvas pants, numbered jersey with shoulder pads and a heavy leather helmet with straps. He walked home every evening after practice. New Bloomfield's opponents were Newport High School, Duncannon High School, Highspire, Millersburg and Elizabethville.

In the forties through sixties, many farmers were very enterprising and Charlie was no exception. When West Perry High School was formed, bus routes were established and put to bid. Seeing an opportunity to supplement his farming, Charlie became the winning bid on a single route, to see if it was a worthwhile investment. He purchased a sixty passenger GMC bus from Regesters for five- thousand six-hundred and seventy-five dollars. His route started in Pisgah to Fox Hollow to Dromgold's Corner to Carroll Elementary School to the West Perry High School.

When he bought a second bus, his run was very challenging starting at the top of Sterretts Gap to Carroll Elementary. Eventually he had a fleet of six buses when he bought out James Stambaugh of Elliottsburg and Shirley Sheibley of Landisburg. For the kid that was told he was better off staying home, Charlie's busing enterprise expanded to partnering on eight buses with Ronald Bolze of Loysville for twenty-one years. They sold their buses to Lauver's of Port Royal when Ron's wife died. Charlie's son, Allen, has taken over the Lupfer school transportation business, managing seven bus routes.

Charlie couldn't have managed all of his enterprises without the lifetime help of his hired-man and neighboring farmer, Jim Lowe. Another neighbor, Bob Diehl, was a diesel mechanic who often worked on Charlie's tractors and other farm machinery. Otherwise, he would take his equipment to Keller's or Stambaugh's in New Bloomfield for fixing. Tim Lupfer says, "it was a big deal getting off the farm to go to Keller's."

Lupfer's Grove
Gibson's Rock was where Charlie's great-grandparents, Charlie Lupfer and Emma Stauffer met and married. They began living at Gibson's Rock, which had a sawmill below the barn in 1890. They then bought Lupfer's Grove in 1892. Charlie's Uncle John was born at Gibson's Rock on Route 850. His father, Harry, was born at Lupfer's Grove in 1894. The barn at Gibson's Rock was host to Carson Long Military Institute cadet's yearly outings. The cadets would march from New Bloomfield to camp in tents and "rough it" for several days.

Old State Road was the original dirt roadway built along the west side of Shermans Creek. The current highway, on the east side of Shermans Creek, from Dromgold's Corner to Shermans Dale was built in 1926.

The fifty-five acres of Lupfer's Grove was all pasture land, with a house and barn. Charlie says, "there's a fair amount of swampy land close to the creek." It extends from behind the old Barnes farm to a small field prior to reaching Dromgold's Corner. The PWA (Public Works Administration) rented the land and barn from the Lupfers during the new dirt-road construction project. The barn was used to house and feed the horses, which were used to pull the wagons and haul the ground and stone. No fancy road-making equipment in those days. Pure hard labor from transient workers, who moved and stayed on-site with the jobs, forged today's roadway. The PWA needed a mess kitchen to prepare meals for the workers, so they built a small white building which today houses the Grove's kitchen, after it was rebuilt in 1952. The new road separated the barn from the house, and an entrance to Lupfer's Grove was created. Charlie's uncle lived in the house.

The Lupfer's farmed the land sowing corn and soybeans and baling hay. No farming is done on the land today. The Texas Eastern pipeline needed access through Lupfer's Grove in 1955. Lupfers were paid one dollar per rod (sixteen and one-half feet) for a lifetime right-of-way. Charlie claims the oil pipeline creates so much heat through the pipes that snow melts off very quickly. In the summer months, moisture is zapped away so any crops planted close to the pipeline will not do well.

The barn burned in 1973 and the house was demolished in recent years. Charlie decided to develop a small trailer-park and campground in the late 1970s. The campground is used today during the annual "Old Iron in the Grove" hosted by the Perry County Old Iron Club, whose mission is to preserve the county's agricultural legacy and educate the public about a forgotten way of life.

Dennis and Tim, Charlie's sons were instrumental in managing Lupfer's Grove. Since Dennis' passing, the responsibilities for Lupfer's Grove have fallen on Tim's broad shoulders, his brother Allen and nephew Scott. They are proud to continue with the family tradition of sharing their ancestral lands with others to enjoy.

Lupfer's Grove has served and benefited the Shermans Dale Community for years. Young's and Pisgah Churches always held annual festivals and hymn sings on the grounds. For eighty-four years, Shermans Dale hosted a Community Picnic complete with musical entertainment and lots of food.

Youth Sports and Vintage Car Shows
When most people think of Lupfer's Grove, youth sports and car shows come first to mind. Baseball has always been a focus of Tim Lupfer's life, as he "tagged along" with his older brother Dennis, better known as "Denny." The Lupfer's commitment went beyond playing baseball, as they took on the challenge of coaching youth baseball. Denny decided to coach Shermans Dale midget's and teener's teams on the baseball fields built by the Lupfers at Lupfer's Grove, but not without the help and support of the Shermans Dale community. Denny obviously saw a need for Tim to coach "pony-ball," so he asked him to coach the youngest players, setting them up with a good foundation and love for the game. For several years, Denny and Tim enjoyed coaching and had several successful teams along the way.

Tim's true testament came when Denny and Jerry Shreffler coached the West Perry All Stars midget team and won the Central Penn Midget Tournament in 1988, competing against thirty-five to forty teams. Tim and Ron Smiley repeated the same with the West Perry All Stars in 1991. Tim figures at least a thousand youngsters played baseball on their ball fields.

When the need arose for a field for girls' softball in 1990, Lupfers built a softball field along Shermans Creek, again with the help from the community. They also stepped up to the goal line when the midget football team was in need of a practice field. And, when Gary Shambaugh who headed up Shermans Dale's soccer program, contacted Tim about the use of Lupfer's Grove, Tim helped Gary map out a soccer field. Tim helped to coach one of the soccer teams as well. Tim's life revolved around Lupfer's Grove, where he also resided at the time. Tim and Denny made sure everything was in place for Shermans Dale youth and the community when they needed it.

Just like their father, the Lupfer boys appreciated old farm equipment and trucks, but they also loved restoring old cars. And, if you have a "pride and joy," why not show it off. Lupfer's Grove became host to the first "Car Show" in 1980, organized by Denny Lupfer and Dale Benner from Shermans Dale, the backbone of the Perry County Automotive Association. Some of the founding members of the car-club were Bill and Rich Speck, and Denny Horn from Marysville, Denny and Scott Rothermel, and Dale Wolf from Duncannon, Brad Reisinger from Ickesburg, and Tim. Their wives also participated and helped out with the shows. To advertise the car shows, the Lupfers would attend car races throughout central Pennsylvania and place fliers on parked cars. Tim says, "that was a lot of fun!"

The annual car show drew as many as over six-hundred novelty and antique cars and vehicles in the 1990s, making it the largest of its kind in central Pennsylvania for thirty-five years. Once it became too large for a small group of friends to manage, the Shermans Dale Fire Company hosted the car shows, till volunteers and local interest waned. Today, Tim has hosted a few "cruise-ins."

The Backbone of the Lupfer Family
Charlie Lupfer readily declares his wife of sixty-nine years, Pauline Frownfelter as the "backbone" of the Lupfer family. She was born at home in New Bloomfield in 1931 to Hazel and Luther "Mike" Frownfelter. Her parents had the greenhouse on West Main Street, even while her father worked for the railroad. At that time, they had one small greenhouse, adding two larger over the years. Eventually, Norman and Kay Harrison bought the property naming it Harrison's Greenhouse.

Pauline says New Bloomfield had sewer and water by the time she was born. Her dad also raised hogs which he sold to Hench & Lebo's Butcher Shop on Main Street. Her parents gardened with Pauline's mother preserving what they raised. Pauline carried on with the skills she learned once she had her own household and family. She had a sister Beatrice and brothers Clair, and Lester (who died at the age of twelve).

She walked or biked the three blocks to grade school beside the Lutheran Church on High Street for eight years, despite the weather. Her teachers, Mrs. Kingsley and Miss Noll from New Bloomfield, and Miss Rice from Blain, were strict. Back then, her teachers taught two grades in one classroom. Generally, there were ten to fifteen students sitting at individual wooden desks. Some walked home for lunch. Pauline was in New Bloomfield's Girl Scout Troop and recalls parading down the streets of town for Memorial Day celebrations.

Bloomfield High School, where the New Bloomfield Post Office is located, is where Pauline met fellow student, Charlie Lupfer. She asked him to the senior prom, but he was already invited by another. The prom was held in the decorated school basement with musical entertainment. Charlie says the school sponsored several weeks of dancing lessons for the boys prior to the prom. His dance partner was Mel Paul, the principal.

Pauline helped to manage the girl's high school basketball team by keeping score. She also took piano lessons from Mrs. McClure of Newport, playing the piano during services at the New Bloomfield Trinity United Methodist Church.

Earning a full dollar if she worked all day at the local 5 & 10 Store on South Carlisle Street, Pauline remembers receiving twenty-five cents an hour otherwise. She was not required to wear a uniform in the store. According to Pauline, there were counters all-round the store, selling all sorts of items except food.

Pauline remembers the south side of Main Street starting at the square heading west with Book's Drugstore and "Red" Stoops Barbershop. Clyde Askin's Store was a general store also selling clothing. Charlie remembers Flo Shatto from Shermans Dale was a clerk. The A & P Store was where the Veteran's Building is today. The movie theatre was two doors down.

After Pauline graduated from high school, she attended the Central Penn Business School in Enola and became a stenographer, learning short-hand. She worked for the Pennsylvania Department of Forest and Water before marrying Charlie in 1953. Pauline was always responsible for all the bookkeeping once she and Charlie married.

Obviously, Charlie was intrigued by Pauline's invite to the prom, so he hunted her up and they went on their first date to the Newport Theatre in a 1940 Pontiac owned by his Grandpap Owens. Charlie has always been a car and truck enthusiast, so he remembers driving a 1949 Pontiac, right after they were married to visit Pauline's brother, Clair, stationed in Texas.

They lived on Dellville Dam Road where Charlie farmed with his father. If they needed anything from a store, they traveled to New Bloomfield to Hair Brothers and Myers, which carried groceries and hardware. Charlie often went to town on Saturday nights to do the shopping, especially when the children were young. They moved to the farm in 1966 when present day "Creekview Farms" was begun outside of Shermans Dale. They liked to go out onto their property and cut a Christmas tree which they decorated with store bought ornaments. In fact, they even allowed a local fella to cut Christmas trees, which he then took to Harrisburg selling them for ten cents.

The Lupfers have always lent a helping hand to others and supported local organizations without asking for anything or much in return. Lupfer's Grove has become a Perry County tradition. The Lupfer name represents hard-work, love for family, friends and community, and a strong desire to preserve one's heritage. That's what legends like Charlie Lupfer are made of.

Surviving The Depression In The Cove

Storyteller Gerald "Jerry" Bell

Four score and six years ago (figure that out you math wizards), a son was born to Gerald and Louise Bell in Newport, Pennsylvania. During the height of the great Depression, it was typical to live with one's parents and it was no exception for my parents. They were living on Front Street with my dad's parents, Elmer and Rebecca Bell.

While living with my grandparents, my father picked up jobs around the area, most notably at Jack Benzel's, midway between Newport and Millerstown. When second son, Jim was born in April of 1938, we were on the move again, typical of the era in search of cheaper rent. What we found was worse housing, not a bathroom in sight, but oh, the two-hole convenience outside and Sears & Roebuck catalogs to wipe.

Finally in 1941, dad was hired on the PRR as a car inspector. Once more on the move, as we never had a car, we migrated to the Cove, outside of Duncannon. This move put my dad closer to Enola and bus service was available.

The house he rented (at five dollars a month) was an old railroad house next to the Cove station. Local trains stopped for local passengers in those days. Again, no bathroom – nice outhouse, white-washed, upper class!! Six rooms with a single light fixture dangling from the ceiling in every room. The house had running water but no faucets. Water came from the PRR spring up on Cove Mountain. This was the same spring that also furnished water to the steam locomotives, many of which stopped for a fill-up. Did I mention that we were seventy-five feet from the railroad tracks and at a grade-crossing. Whistle noise, brake noise, rail noise and after a while we never heard it!

I forgot to mention our first home in the Cove (on the other side of the tracks). In 1941, we had a fire. An oil can exploded while I was playing with matches. Dad saved me as he bravely fought the blaze and tore off my pants when they caught fire. I had second- and third-degree burns, and spent three months in the hospital. I was a very lucky boy, but our home was a total loss.

I went to school at Penn Township Elementary. I had good teachers and a great principal, Paul Hurley (later became county superintendent of schools). I was lucky to be able to ride the school bus, which was an old Brockway, owned by John Rohrer. It had side seats with a middle seat section. However, it took five gear changes to get-up "Legion" or Carver's Hill. Thus I never had to walk that proverbial mile with snow up to my fanny!

Most of my early years were spent helping my mom and dad around the house. Dad was an avid hunter, trapper and fisherman. (Sadly none of that rubbed off on me!). I did try my hand at skinning out muskrats, being careful not to slice the fur. I would then put them onto stretchers. Dad would do the mink which we caught a lot of from the surrounding area. My first trapping episode was my first – and my last. Dad laid out a line for me and sure enough the first day I caught a young muskrat, but it was still alive. Dad gave me a hickory stick and told me to hit it over the head to kill it. Three swats – still alive! I will never forget those pleading eyes of that animal – never again! But dad provided us with many a meal of pheasant, rabbit, squirrel, deer, fish – even snapping turtle soup.

My mom was a superior cook. What she was able to make out of nothing was a miracle, bread soup, coffee soup and cracker soup. One of the Bell legends that will live forever is when dad caught an opossum. We were fortunate enough to have a pressure-cooker, so dad told mom to do it in that. After a couple of bites, dad tossed it out. Mom said no more – the grease ugh!

We had a rather large vegetable garden of which dad was very proud – no weeds in that garden – thanks to me. I hated picking potato bugs. I would throw them into a can of kerosene – die you buggers! Mom canned everything we grew. I also picked wild strawberries. They made the best jelly ever. Mom always wanted to know why my berry can did not hold more – yum, yum!

We also raised chickens (roast chicken every Sunday) and rabbits which dad sold to the market in Harrisburg.

Granted this was considered spartan, but we didn't know what we didn't have; as a family of five we did pretty well. I went barefoot in the summer and loved running on the cinders along the railroad bed. We wore shoes in the winter with galoshes in the snow. The shoes had better last till spring.

We did own a radio. Mom was into soaps - Guiding Light, One Man's Family, Stella Dallas, and As the World Turns. I enjoyed Inter-Sanctum, the Bob Hope Hour, Jack Benny, Bob & Ray, Mr. Keen Tracer of Lost Persons and on Saturday, Sky King, Sergeant Preston of the Yukon, and Gun Smoke. For me, they were the good old days.

Another thing we had were good neighbors. I especially enjoyed the Scrignolis, who every Sunday would gather family for Italian food and vino followed by a rousing game of bocce ball. I learned some Italian (I think some were bad words!).

There was not much to do as far as industry or stores from Kinkora down to Archey Johnson's bird show in back of his small store, gas station and restaurant. There was a small ice cream store where Kings Inn is now. I made my first paycheck there when I was seven. I cleaned out the ashes from the boiler. Just up the road was Burley's Fruit and Vegetable Stand. Here I earned my second paycheck of fifty cents weeding flower beds for Memorial Day flowers. I worked from 8 a.m. until 6 p.m. – was I nuts?

Next up the road was Pop Steever's Atlantic Gas and Grocery Store, and Bitting's Auction House. I would go there with Mom and on special nights, they had homemade ice cream at five cents a scoop – yum, yum!

One afternoon, at Pop Steever's, a man pulled in with a new car and I knew it was a new Tucker. While standing there and admiring it, the driver offered me a ride and what a thrill it was! Could you imagine that happening today?

Not to mention many other events in my years in the Cove and elsewhere. I didn't realize what a great life and fun I had along with my brother, Jim and sister, Mary, and lots of friends.

Thanks, Deb, for letting me reminisce.

"Those Were The Days – Where Have They Gone"

Storyteller Philip McKeehan

I remember when I almost knew everyone that lived from the Conococheague Mountain above New Germantown to Loysville via Route 274, Route 17 and many back-hollow roads. My dad was a dairy farmer and many other neighbors were farmers as well and everybody knew everyone.

I went grades first through ninth at Blain Elementary School. West Perry was then only a three-year high school.

Each town or village had a general store selling groceries. New Germantown had Bistline's Store. Blain had two stores, Smith's and Hench's. Andersonburg boasted Fisher's Store right on the turn. Cisna Run had Junk's Store. Center had Bishop's Store and if you blinked while passing by, you'd miss it. Nace's Store sat on the crossroads at Kistler. Robinson's Store was on the west end of Loysville and Emlet's Store was on the town square. This was from the 1970s as I graduated from West Perry High School in 1975.

Being a farmer, we always had repairs to be made and John Frownfelter Sr. had a weld repair shop just a half mile west of Blain. Also, Marlin Dillman had a weld repair shop at his farm in New Germantown. John Frownfelter Jr. had the hardware store at Blain where he also sold guns. My brother bought his first 243 Remington there.

Most farmers that I remember milked an average of twenty to thirty dairy cows. Today, farmers are milking six to seven hundred head of cows. There were many more small family farms and help was more accessible than today. A teenager would work on a farm to make a little "spending" money for what they wanted like a car, motorcycle or other fun things. In turn, the farm equipment has gotten so much larger than the farm equipment we farmed with and not as much help is needed to harvest the crops.

One thing that I remember, my mom and dad called our daily meals breakfast (morning meal), dinner (noon meal) and supper (evening meal). Now a lot of people call it breakfast, lunch and dinner. We ate our largest meal of the day at dinnertime on Sundays after church.

The school busing situation for our very rural county was easier too. Many farmers, such as my dad and myself, drove a school bus. Some farmers and small businessmen owned one, two or three buses. Drivers were easier to get and ownership of buses was small. Everything today is large scale. Contractors own thirty, forty or fifty school buses, plus small passenger vans to transport students.

Home phones (landlines) were almost in every home. Cell phones were not around or if they were we didn't know much about them here in the country. Home phones had party lines, where more than one home was on the same line. When you would pick up the phone to use it, you may hear other people on the party line talking. Sometimes they would say, "we're on the phone, hang-up" or "I guess we're going to have to give the phone to someone else."

Churches and church-going was also what I've seen decline in later years. In Blain alone there was the United Church of Christ, a Methodist church, Zion Lutheran Church and just outside of town was Three Springs Church of the Brethren.

Family reunions were part of my life. They still are today, but a lot of families don't have reunions any more. I go to the reunions on my mom's and dad's sides of our family every year.

Another tradition I see disappearing is the taking of food to a friend or neighbor who has lost a loved one. My grandmothers and mom would make a covered- dish, such as scalloped potatoes and ham, and take it to someone they knew who had a death in their family. The sending of a birthday card and sympathy card was very prevalent also. These practices are also disappearing.

When I was growing up, people lent a helping hand without being asked. We connected and communicated without using an emoji or LOL. And, we actually laughed out-loud!

Kids Discovering Perry County History Series

Author Debra Kay Noye

Because everybody was over-looking our youth in their historical publications, I sat down in 2019 and penned *The Treasures in Great-Granny's Scrapbook*. I wanted Perry County youth, particularly ages ten to twelve, to have something tangible in their hands to read about Perry County history. A book they would enjoy and belly-laugh through without realizing they were getting a great history lesson. To further enhance the topics, I included full-color pictures of artifacts and memorabilia to demonstrate what the characters were talking about. It was the first of its kind in Perry County.

The Treasures in Great-Granny's Scrapbook is a fictional story about two cousins living on the family farm, in western Perry County, with their grandparents. Great-Granny also lives with them and she is a "hoot" as she shares her history and that of Perry County, after the boys discover her scrapbook in the woodshed, of all places. The boys love history and especially learning more about their county. They ask if the family can go on a Perry County road-trip to visit some historic places and start a Perry County museum in the den of the century-old farmhouse. The road-trip even involves singing "Dead Skunk in the Middle of the Road" and everybody, including Aunt Bitty, pitched in to help the boys start their museum.

The favorite segment of most youth and their grandparents involved an egg battle in the hen house. Mine is where Pap gets out his wallet and hands the boys money to pay the bill at the Red Rabbit, which is a Perry County tradition. Andrew and Jeremiah thought Pap was playing a joke with funny money, because it was for twelve and a half cents, actual currency issued by Perry County in 1837.

My first book focused on farm life and what people should know in general about Perry County. Great-Granny, with her country ways and sayings, is the matriarch of the farm family and the book.

My sequel, *City Cousins Spend the Summer*, published in 2021, features the boy's city-slicker girl cousins coming to the farm for the summer. The girls soon learn there are daily farm chores and they too become engrossed in learning more about Perry County history. They get to experience a family reunion, Perry County style, in the farming valley of Liberty Hall. Mercy Sakes! They start off for the reunion not

realizing Great-Granny is still snoozing on the porch and Pap forgot about the pistachio dessert on the van roof! And of all people, Great-Granny starts a food fight with the girls.

City Cousins Spend the Summer is focused on Perry County businesses and manufacturing with full color pictures of products made in Perry County. It also features various artisans with pictures of their works. Some of the highlights are *Early Morning Gobblin'* with Perry County turkey calls, finally fixing the old worn cellar door using Forged Steel Products' tools, discovering Aldon Products and using a Slice a Slice to cut bread, and bathing Jeremiah's and Andrew's 4-H Baby Beef projects. The summer is crammed full of adventures, life's lessons and Perry County history.

In *City Cousins Spend the Summer*, I did not go into great detail about the reunion and what happened at the Perry County Fair. I planned a second sequel to bring the reunion to life, but have decided to do that on these pages. One of the original city-slicker girl cousins, granddaughter Katarina (Kata) Noye-Losada, has helped me to bring the reunion and Perry County history to life. Kata penned the segment, *Lose a Bet – Be a Princess*.

So if you remember what I said above and even if you didn't read the books, please enjoy the end to **Kids Discovering Perry County History …** *A Frolicking Good Time at the Family Reunion.*

A Frolicking Good Time At The Family Reunion

Lars and Pat had planned for a talent show as part of the reunion festivities. They figured it would be nice to give everybody the chance to rest up after eating so much delicious food. Now our city-slicker cousins love putting on skits and had secretly prepared for the event. When Lars announced it's time to prepare for the show, the girls disappear beyond the wash house.

Lars starts the talent show with Aunt Jayme singing the Star Spangled Banner, our national anthem, and God Bless America with Great-Uncle Grumpy joining in with the soulful harmonica. Once they were finished, Gram jumps up and challenges anybody to sing Perry County USA, written and recorded by Bill Fleisher of Marysville. Aunt Myrtle, who could pass for an opera singer due to her size, rises to the occasion and comes up the steps onto the open hay wagon. Lars figured he would have a country stage for his talented guests.

Gram tells Myrtle she has the recording ready if she would like to sing along with it. That brought a smile and Myrtle does a few warm-up "me-me-mes." Without warning, she lets loose with some earth shattering yodels which echoed throughout the valley. This got the audience all fired up clapping for more. Taken by surprise and enjoying the encouragement, Myrtle starts to yodel and dance a jig on the wagon bed. She was moving from one end of the wagon to the other, as her audience hooted and hollered for more. Without warning, the wagon begins to roll right along with Myrtle's dancing.

Stunned she manages to remain upright, as an equally surprised Lars shouts for help in stopping the rolling stage. I yell to Jeremiah to grab one of the large landscaping stones as I sprint to help Lars as some of the menfolk steady the wagon. Gram grabbed Myrtle by the hand and helped to keep her on her feet as we gently pushed the wagon back in place. I shouted to Jeremiah to place the large heavy stone in front of one of the wheels. It worked and the wagon was secure. Lars gave us bear hugs, and admitted he had gotten side-tracked when he was putting the wagon in place for the show. Jeremiah and I decided to be extra cautious and place a second stone under another wheel.

There is a sigh of relief as the men take their seats on the straw bales. Lars thanks everybody for their quick thinking, then bellows "Let the show go on!" Gram starts the recording and Myrtle sings right along with Bill Fleisher and the Dog Patchers. The crowd goes wild, stomping their feet and clapping to the music. Myrtle finishes with her own rendition of Perry County USA. The standing ovation brought tears to her eyes!!

Lars introduces Cousin Lucas who performs a juggling act with baby watermelons. He soon has all three watermelons circling in the air above his head. The variegated striped green melons whirl round and round as he plays catch and release. I thought it odd Lucas seemed to be moving toward the table Lars had set on the stage for props. Everybody figured he was going to quit and lay the melons on the table till he caught the last one.

Instead, Lucas picks up a large butcher knife and slices a melon in half in mid-air. Lars stealthily dashes to the save, as Lucas' aim proves true once again. Jeremiah jumps on stage and manages to catch those melon halves before they hit the wagon-bed. That left one lone melon, which Lucas tosses higher into the air before welding his blade splicing the melon into four chunks! He catches two pieces and I dash in saving the remainder, while keeping a watchful eye on the whereabouts of the butcher knife. Pretending he is Zorro, Lucas makes a z-slash in the air as he takes a bow! Lars shouts out to the audience, "Meet Perry County's answer to Gallagher, the fruit and veggie smasher!" Lars motions for Pat to bring him some trays to place the melons on till the watermelon seed spitting contest. He wants them kept nice and cool. Kidding Lars tells everybody they should practice puckering up if they want to win.

Gram announces that if anybody needs a cool drink, they should go to the beverage station. Pat has made fresh-squeezed lemonade and strawberry iced tea. Uncle Jasper jumps up shouting that the last person to reach the beverage station would have to eat a raw egg! Kids and adults start rushing everywhere, trying to get around straw bales and beach chairs because they thought it was a real contest. Cousins were screaming they'd never eat a raw egg even if someone held their nose shut forcing them to breathe through their mouth. In the meantime, Jasper, a former sprinter in college, is leaping over straw bales and strewn chairs trying to catch up. Liberty decides to join in the fun and races alongside Jasper. Too close for comfort, their legs tangle leaping over the last straw bale. Jasper's toe catches on the baler twine and down he goes. He puts out his hands and ends in a hand-stand. He continues to walk using his hands towards the beverage table.

His cell phone slides from his pocket and a handful of coins glisten in the sunlight. The kids spying the coins scurry around picking them up, just like earlier during the peanut scramble. Pap had purchased fresh roasted peanuts in the shell from Wentzels Mill in Bridgeport for the occasion. Even the adults had a peanut scramble and Aunt Susie used her large apron to hold her stash. She had emptied it onto the picnic table to share with everybody.

When Jasper made it to the table, he was greeted with a glass of lemonade. Catching his breath before taking a gulp of lemonade, Jasper is reminded that he lost. He stammers that it was only a joke, and he wasn't swallowing no yolk! Tipping the glass to his lips, he chugs the yellow liquid only to discover too late that there was something bright orange floating in the bottom. Lars realizes that Jasper has spied the raw egg. He quickly strides to Jasper's side and pats him on the back while tipping the glass further. Down the hatch it went, and Jasper took his prize like a gentleman. The crowd cheered and told Jasper he was a good sport!!

Lose A Bet - Be A Princess

Andrew and Jeremiah walked out of the house towards Grace, Vallie, Edyn and I who were harvesting some baby red beets to make pickled-eggs for the family reunion. "Still doing your chores? We were done like 30 minutes ago," Jeremiah teased.

"Oh, so ya come here to brag?" tested Grace. Then arguing broke out between them. "Stop! Stop!" I yelled. "If we can beat you boys in a game, then you guys have to do a punishment and if you win it's vice-versa," I proposed.

"Fine but we get to pick the game!" Andrew shot back. "It seems like someone had trouble with their chores," taunted Edyn. We all giggled, but Grace knew not to aggravate too much. She scolded the rest of us. "Let them be. They will soon see that it is wrong to underestimate the city-slickers, plus Edyn."

"Do we have a deal?" I asked. I put my hand out and Jeremiah shook it, sealing a "done deal." The boys went to a little corner of the garden and discussed their plan. "What if we lose?" Vallie worried.

"We won't and we will crush them no matter what!" Edyn exclaimed heroically. "And if we do not, we will go down like brave warriors," proclaimed Grace. Holy guacamole those two do have a flare for dramatics. Now I don't say that a lot except when the time is right. The boys finally decided on a game to play. "It's who can kick the ball the farthest," Andrew started to explain. But Grace interrupted him, "It's pretty self-explanatory Drew, don't ya think."

"Don't call me that!" shouted Andrew. "Drew-Drew-Drew" sing-songs Vallie. "Everyone focus!" I yelled. Everyone looked at me like they had just seen a ghost. "Let's just get on with this," I muttered.

Jeremiah and Andrew decided to go first. "Oh and you only get one try each," added Edyn. Jeremiah grabbed the soccer ball and kicked without hesitation. It wasn't too bad a kick but it was a small challenge.

Vallie retrieved the ball for Andrew's turn. As Andrew started to kick, Liberty came bounding out of nowhere and knocked the ball behind Andrew. "Wait what!" he exclaimed throwing his hands in the air in total frustration.

"You only get one try!" Grace said dancing gleefully. We were all laughing so hard we were bent double. Vallie was rolling on the ground laughing. "You let Liberty loose!" accused Jeremiah shaking his finger at us. "NO! We didn't," I shot back.

"Sorry lads I was taking Liberty to get a doggie-bath but he got out of my grip," yelled Lars. "See we didn't sabotage," Edyn pointed out to Andrew and Jeremiah. "Sorry," they mumbled., but were still very upset.

"Anyways can we get on with the game?" I asked. Since it wouldn't be fair if the girls got four turns and the boys only two turns, we decided that Edyn and I would kick the ball and we were ready. "Go Edyn! Go Edyn! Go Edyn!" we cheered. She kicked the ball in her bare feet way past where Jeremiah's ball ended. I went even though I already knew we won. I didn't make it quite past Edyn, but I passed Jeremiah.

"Woohoo!" we yelled. Edyn and I did cartwheels to celebrate our victory. The boys were looking even more sulky than ever. I motioned for Edyn, Grace and Vallie to come over to discuss their punishment.

A few moments later we went up to the boys. Andrew noticed the smirk on Edyn's face. "Can we just do your chores instead?" he pleaded. "Nope. Your punishment is that you have to get up on stage during the reunion and dress up as princesses and sing a song of our choosing," I replied with great satisfaction.

"NO! Anything but THAT!" they begged. "You have to," said Vallie. "Now come with me, I am going to show you how to make yourself look pretty by using some make-up and styling your hair." Vallie was grinning from ear to ear.

"We should probably help," I whispered to Grace and Edyn. "Goodness knows what Vallie might do."

Let's Play Dress Up
Now Andrew, who is the spokesperson in *City Cousins Spend the Summer*, has kindly let me continue telling this story so here we are in the boy's bedroom at Liberty Hall.

"You boys wait here," indicates Grace, as she turns to Vallie saying, "I need you to stay here while we go get the costumes, because you are not going to be able to carry everything up the stairs." Vallie starts to whine because she wants to help. "How about this, you get to watch the boys and make sure they don't try to leave. Also you can holler if something's up," suggests Edyn. Now Vallie isn't that young but sometimes we baby her a little. She is a loveable, stubborn ten year old. "Well, do I get permission to make the boys do pushups if they are up to anything suspicious?" she asked. Even the boys couldn't help but smile for a bit. "Sure you can," I said. Now Vallie was all business. She actually made me want to stay in line.

Pat had told me where some of her costumes are stored, after I shared with her what we were thinking about doing. Pat was trying to remember about her collection of really old dresses and accessories, hoping they are what we are looking for. Of course, I love fashion so I was super excited. "I hope there are some things that are more antique. It would be very interesting to see some very old clothing," I express to the girls.

As we go down the stairs to the basement, Edyn flips on the lights. We all gasp. There were a bunch of old costumes, cool hats and feather boas hanging in see-through plastic garment bags. But upon opening up a steamer trunk, there was a bunch of well-kept vintage clothing.

"It's like these clothes don't even need to be tailored to look like a costume. They already are!" said an astonished Grace. As our eyes scanned the room, a voice behind startled us. "Well what are you girls waiting for, do you want to take a look?" asked Pat. "Pat! Please, we are super excited to take a look. I think we are just soaking up the beauty of these clothes," I blurted out.

We started sorting through the pieces of clothing. I was totally geeking out on everything. "Now I wish we were the ones dressing up," I moaned. "Oh yes, your sister was telling me in more detail about your plan. But when I went inside the boys bedroom, she was making them do pushups. I wonder what that was all about," inquired Pat. "Oh, that was nothing," replied Grace.

"Well if that is nothing, how about a little bit of history time?" asks Pat. "Of course, I would love to learn more!" I respond as I was eager to learn about these amazing outfits.

"Well some of these delicate outfits were from the theater. Some of them were the outfits that Marie Doro wore, so they are one-hundred years old." We eagerly asked Pat to tell us more.

"Marie Doro's given name was Marie Katherine Stewart. She was born in Duncannon, in 1882. She came from a very wealthy family. Her father, Richard, was a part-owner of the Duncannon Flour Mill in the 1870s."

"At a very young age, come to think of it your ages, Marie started to show-off her talents in the chorus of musical comedy shows and as a theater actress here and in England. Imagine if you can, by the age of thirteen, in 1915, she was starring in two shows. She was well on her way to becoming an American "silent-film star." Marie was a notably gifted, natural actress. She was a striking brunette and was declared the most glamourous, talented, beautiful actress of her time. Now, many don't know about her fame because she performed so long ago, and a lot of the silent-films were lost or destroyed over the years. She is actually buried in her hometown of Duncannon. Marie is truly one of Perry County's historic treasures."

"WOW, that is amazing," Edyn remarks. "I'd like to learn more." I agree.

"Well now that we learned some more Perry County history, do you ladies need help sorting and carrying these outfits up-stairs?" Pat wonders. "Yes. Thank you," I replied. We decided, out of respect for the vintage costumes, to not use the ones worn by Marie Doro. We knew they were priceless.

Once we finished putting all sorts of things gently into a few bags, we walk up all the steps to the boy's bedroom. "HOLY MOLY! That's a lot of clothing!" exclaimed Andrew. "Do you ladies need some help?" asked Jeremiah. "Actually we do," I said, handing over a stack of dresses to Jeremiah, who is always lending a helping hand with people even if they annoy him.

"Well, I'll let you youngsters to your fun. I have to go finish preparing some dinner for y'all. Holler if you need me." said Pat. "Okey Dokey," replied Edyn.

I was still looking through some outfits we had grabbed, when I came across a piece of clothing wrapped in paper and plastic bubble wrap. "Wait!" I yelled. "Pat, is this yours?", as I show her the package. "Mercy Sakes Kata! You gave me quite a fright!" replies Pat as she sat down and gingerly opened the package. "Kata, this was my favorite dress when I was a girl. It also was my mother's dress."

"It's beautiful," gasped Vallie. It was a lovely white dress with big poofy sleeves. There were little flowers embroidered on them. "These flowers were hand-embroidered," Pat shared. "Wow, that looks like it takes a lot of time to make," Vallie remarked. Pat laughed, "Yes, it did. Thank you so much for finding this. I thought that I lost this dress forever."

"No problem," I said, while looking at the beautifully designed outfits which were very precious. My sisters and I tried on clothes till we just couldn't anymore and then selected the ones for Jeremiah and Andrew. "I think this one will be the best," Grace announced. She held up a beautiful indigo-blue dress with purple lace threaded throughout the dress. "Ohhh, it's so pretty," Vallie breathed. "And this one can be for Andrew, " I added. It was a green and white dress with dark green ribbon representing vines.

As much as the boys didn't want to dress-up, they couldn't help but admire the dresses. "These are wonderful!" exclaimed Edyn, prancing around the room modeling the dress she chose. "I want one, too!" Vallie whined as usual. She started to see if there was one that might fit her without being altered too much.

"Wait a second, I have an idea," I said. I called all of the girls over. All of us huddled together while I whispered my idea of a "Treaty" with the boys. "Okay," I announced. "We have a proposition," started Grace, but was soon cut off by the boys whirling around and scaring the crap out of Vallie. "Sorry," they chorused sheepishly while putting a comforting hand on Vallie's trembling shoulder. "Anyway, Kata was thinking since these dresses are beautiful and hard to resist, that we would perform with you," finished Grace in one breath.

Quickly the boys agreed and we sort out all the details. For this huge family reunion there would be a special performance featuring all of us. Grace and Edyn started planning things out loud and I could hardly keep up. "OKAY! Hold your horses, let me get some paper," I yelled. We restarted and I began to make a checklist of everything. Finally after planning things, we flopped on the bed. The boys pulled up some chairs and sat down as well, as we explained our next plan. "Now we just have to wait," Edyn sighed.

"Ladies and gents! Time to set the table and have dinner!" Pat called up the stairs. We all finally realized there was a smell of food coming from the kitchen. We ran down the stairs almost bumping into Pat, who was carrying the salad. "Mercy Sakes! You almost ran me over!"

"Sorry," we chorused. "Grace, would you please take this out to the dining table and keep an eye on it, so Percy doesn't swoop in for a bite," she asks while passing the salad over to Grace. "Vallie please quickly set the picnic tables."

"What about us?" Edyn asked, always eager to help. "Can you go roundup everyone and the boys can grab and rearrange chairs and benches since we are eating outside today. Kata, you can come help me in the kitchen?"

As everyone sets off to do their chores, I followed Pat into the summer kitchen. There I was greeted with the aroma of the delicious food being prepared. There was chicken in the oven as well as some freshly picked green beans. "Kata you are going to make the mashed potatoes," Pat declared. As soon as she said that, I got right to work pulling out butter and fresh cream from the fridge to add to the cooked potatoes, which I was going to mash. After all, I LOVE potatoes so this was the perfect job.

As we carried all the hot food outside, I had the pleasure of serving everyone mashed potatoes, after we said a blessing. "These are delicious!" squealed Vallie shoving potatoes in her mouth. As everyone else followed her lead, they all said the same thing. "How did you make them?" asked Jeremiah. "Well, I could tell you now and if you want I'll write it out for you in Great-Granny's scrapbook which you keep in your Perry County museum. "Perfect!" he replied as some mashed potatoes slid down his chin.

Reunion Day
On the reunion day, everything was already set-up , because we had worked hard at Lar's and Pat's the previous days, and we were free to greet family as they arrived. There was lots of chatter, introductions and hugs plus a huge variety of food on the buffet and games of tag among the younger children. I decided to locate my sisters, Edyn and the boys motioning for them to come with me. "It's time," I whispered. It was soon time to perform, after some formal introductions by the older folks and singing to begin the talent show.

When we were finally changed into our costumes and quickly practiced one more time, I alerted Lars that we were ready. Instead of using the steps, I climbed up the haybales onto the wagon, with all the performers following. I got everyone's attention. "Hello! It's nice to meet so many people we did not know before today. Let me introduce you to my sisters, Grace and Vallie. We're the city-slicker cousins staying for the summer. These are our cousins, Edyn, Jeremiah and Andrew. We would like to sing a song and perform for you. I hope you find it entertaining." Then, Gram started the recorded music. We sang with gusto and danced with zest. When we finished a great deal of laughter and applause echoed off the hilltops, as we took our bows. Even Liberty howled his approval along with the guests and Percy did a fly over.

We were all laughing as we changed to our regular clothes. "To be honest that was really a lot of fun," confessed the boys. I almost flipped my wig at their remarks. "See our idea was good!" We carefully put the vintage clothes away.

Pat rushed up to us, with her arms waving, and started gushing, "You all chose the most amazing outfits ever. You used these dresses and costumes that I have had for so long. I'm so glad you put them to good use. Your performance was breathtaking and made a nice addition to our family reunion. You make sure you add a write-up about it in the scrapbook."

"Thank you!" we sang. "Now, let's go have some more fun," Vallie declares.

Fun And Games At The Family Reunion At Liberty Hall

HOW MANY WHOOPIE PIES CAN YOU EAT?

Thank heavens there was a break from eating before games that involved eating began! Pat was wise holding back on the desserts, because some of us ended up with a sweets overload!

Somehow Pat had managed to find the time to make miniature whoopie pies for a whoopie pie eating contest. When Lars announced the contest, kids magically appeared at his feet. Even our older cousin Lucas, from Markelsville, stepped up to join in the fun. Lars took one look at Lucas wondering about his age, but nobody objected to his participating. Each of us received a plate of five chocolate vanilla-cream-filled whoopie pies. They were a little larger than a silver dollar. I knew Jeremiah could wolf them down as fast as Liberty when he caught a boneless chicken thigh falling from Aunt Sara's plate. It didn't have time to touch the ground. Liberty gulped it down even before taste testing.

Lars suggested a glass of cold milk nearby to help wash down the mini- sweets. Gram was standing by if anybody wanted some of Jenny's morning milk. Lars spelled out the rules. We had two minutes to eat as many whoopie pies as we possibly could. No playing tricks like knocking into a competitor causing them to spill their plate. Pat and Aunt Bessie will keep the refills coming our way.

Pap does the honors to start the contest saying, "Shove 'em in till they reach your toes. Remember to save some for me!" Whoopie pie frenzy was unleashed on Liberty Hall. Grace tried to shove an entire whoopie pie into her mouth, following Jeremiah's example. That didn't work, so she bit it in half, still having trouble swallowing. She motions for Aunt Bessie to bring her milk to help wash it down. The whoopie pies were moist and stuck to the roof of our mouths.

We watched in awe as cousin Lucas tosses a whoopie pie high in the air as if eating popcorn. He maneuvers underneath opening his wide mouth and catches it. The audience gasps and claps egging him on to try it again. Being a ham, Lucas throws another higher overhead. This time Percy was the receiver swooping in and snagging Lucas' whoopie pie. "No fair!" shouts a stunned Lucas, as the relatives laugh. Lucas doesn't realize he's wasting time by throwing a tantrum.

Jeremiah is on his third plate of whoopie pies, and second glass of milk. I decided that maybe I'd save room in my tummy for another eating contest. Grace did the same. Everybody slowed down.

Furious Lucas crams three whoopie pies in his mouth at the last five seconds. This shuts him up and he struggles to swallow. I notice Lucas' face is becoming blue and he's having trouble breathing. Rushing to his side, I grasp him around his belly and give a giant squeeze releasing the mass of whoopie pie from his throat. He spat it into paper towels provided by Gram. "Looks just like whoopie batter to me!" exclaims Kata. Everybody is relieved.

Lars walks over to Jeremiah declaring him the winner. He had scoffed down thirteen whoopie pies in two minutes. That's one every nine seconds. He awards Jeremiah a Hain's hand-carved owl from his collection of carved birds. Lars also commends Percy on a mighty fine catch.

Frisbee Competition!
Now we all know Lars has a great sense of humor. When he devised the next competition, Pat tried hard to talk him out of it, to no avail.

We'd rested our bellies a bit before Lars announces another game, "extreme Frisbee". We followed him to a freshly mowed field close to the main house. Jeremiah and I thought it was a strange move but figured he wanted to make sure everybody would be safe from a rogue flying Frisbee. Lars tells us to scatter throughout the field. This seemed even more odd.

Lars had recruited Uncle Johnny to help. Uncle Johnny spells out the rules. He and Lars will throw a Frisbee towards us and we're supposed to catch as many as we can without pushing and shoving one another. Johnny's wife, Susie, will keep a tally of the catches to determine the winner of the most caught.

Pap arrives on the four-wheeler with wagon in tow hauling two large cardboard boxes. They open the mysterious cardboard boxes.

Reaching in Lars and Johnny quickly grab Frisbees launching them high into the air. Whirling at us so fast, we didn't have time to think about the odd shape and color as we competed to catch them. Cousin George, from Perdix, was the first to catch one. Using his hands to firmly clasp each side of the disc, it collapsed into several pieces like one of Great-Granny's delicate homemade sand-tart cookies. He stood there shocked and confused.

Jeremiah burst into laughter snagging one with his right hand. By this time Lars and Johnny had launched more Frisbees. Being odd shaped with irregular thicknesses, the rest of the cousins were having to make difficult decisions as to their game plan.

When Kata finally catches one and it cracks in two, she examines it further. "Yuck!! Is this a dried cow patty?" she wonders. The gleeful adult audience couldn't keep a straight-face any longer. Uncle Benjamin spills-the-beans by shouting out, "Cow patty Frisbee is the ultimate test to see who'll do their best!"

"Lars how could you!" exclaims Kata noticing an unharmed cow patty in the grass. She swiftly bends down, picks it up and whips it straight at his head. Lars ducks just in time to avoid the hard-thrown dried cow manure. He stands there laughing, along with the onlookers.

All the cousins are checking out their hands and clothing for cow poop residue. They're in absolute shock over the Frisbee competition. Aunt Sara announces the winner who turns out to be fast-footed cousin, Speedy with three complete catches. Honestly, we didn't care when he was awarded a Perry County t-shirt!

Adults and Their Eggs!
Lars and Pat announce it is time for the kids to relax and the adults to have a little competitive fun. He asks that people pair up and form two lines about eight-feet apart. Some had already figured he was planning an egg competition of some sorts. Pat asks Grace to hand each participant a plastic soup spoon. Vallie and Kata distribute an egg to one player on each team.

The instructions were simple. The egg was to be cradled in the soup spoon. The object was to carry the spoon by the handle to their partner across from them without dropping the egg. They had to transfer the egg onto their partners' spoon without mishap and no hands-on. Once the egg is transferred, that person had to rush to the opposite line and return transferring the egg once again. That person had to rush back to the starting point. The first team to complete the task would be announced the winners.

Looking over the teams, Lars decides the men should be in one line facing the women and they would be given the eggs first. He asks Great-Uncle Grumpy to signal the start of the race. Grumpy in a loud voice announces, "On your mark, let's scramble!" Uncle Pete takes long strides, while using his extra hand to steady the spoon. Grumpy takes note and bellows, "Use only one hand or take the penalty!" Uncle Pete had forgotten the rules.

The transfers go smoothly and the ladies are headed for the opposite line. Uncle Pete's wife Nancy had just had knee surgery and was taking it slow and easy which aggravated Pete because he really wanted to win. He shouts at his wife to get a move on just as she reaches the line turning to return. Well, from the look on Nancy's face at Pete's remarks, one could see she was really ticked off. She puts her left foot forward and takes the egg in her right hand throwing it straight at her husband. Pete had forgotten about Nancy's softball pitching days and was taken totally off guard. Thinking it was a hard-boiled egg, he whipped off his hat using it like a lacrosse net. It was a game saving catch!

Great-Uncle Grumpy immediately shouts, "Fowl!" Everybody stops in their tracks wondering what they did wrong. Looking around, they discover Nancy is back at the line pointing towards Pete laughing uncontrollably. Probably the yellow ooze draining from Pete's hat caught their eye first as Grumpy declares, "Out! You're disqualified!"

"By dang!! This is one of my favorite fishing hats!" Pete exclaims. "Who's bright idea was it to use real eggs?"

"Pete quit your whining! You're lucky she didn't hit you smack dab between the eyes," chuckles Lars. He walks over to Nancy and whispers something in her ear. Before anybody realizes what was happening, Nancy launches another egg courtesy of Lars towards Pete. Still examining his egged hat, he didn't know another missile was honing in on him. Nancy hollers at Pete as the egg meets its target, "Take it like a man," as the egg runs out of his ear and down his chin.

We thought it was the start of WW lll as Pete grabs the closest egg and whips it at Nancy who had enough sense to sidestep it. Liberty was watching the fun and made the save of the day. Otherwise, Great-Uncle Grumpy would have become the next egging victim.

Nancy and Pete started to slowly walk toward each other and everybody watched with concern. Pete reaches out to Nancy grabbing her into a bear hug. He kisses her while apologizing for his actions. The relatives clap and shout for more hugs and kisses as if they were at a wedding. Pete vows to be more patient and less competitive in the future.

Great-Uncle Grumpy declares the game over since there were so many disruptions.

All Good Things Come To An End

I'm so full I could bust!" announces Vallie patting her belly. Of course, this was after her third dish of homemade raspberry and vanilla ice cream. She loved to swirl the two flavors together before shoveling them into her wide-open mouth. Lars and Pat are master homemade ice cream makers using the fresh cream that formed on top of the milk from their Brown Swiss dairy cows. We had helped to pick the fresh black raspberries from their berry patches for Pat to cook down and squeeze out the juices, leaving the seeds behind. The berries were plump and delicious eating them right from the canes. I was wondering if Vallie was trying to get out of helping to clean-up the grounds at Liberty Hall after all the reunion guests had left. Everybody had been mindful and had placed their trash in the barrels Jeremiah and I placed around the picnic areas earlier in the week. So it shouldn't take us too long and we might even have time to spray off the picnic tables and the pavilion floor before we head home to finish up the evening chores. I hear Gram calling me to come and help with putting away all the Perry County memorabilia we had brought along to show the family. Jeremiah and I really had a lot of fun educating and sharing with everyone. Now to take them home and in there rightful places in the museum. As I approach the display tables, I can see Great-Granny pouring over the scrapbook, looking at all the pages of the attendees and even wondering who some of them were. She was giggling at some of the comments made by the younger generations.

After all the hugs from Lars and Pat, the ride home was full of reminiscing and hopes of holding another reunion next year. The city-slickers even hoped they could return too, because it was so much fun and they got to meet a lot of family they didn't even know about. Great-Granny was so exhausted that she napped and missed all the chatter. At least we didn't forget her this time and Gram made sure the goody baskets and coolers stuffed with left-overs and ice cream were safely stored in the back of the van. No mishaps this time, unless you count Vallie running after the van as we are leaving, because she was admiring all the colorful calendars on the walls of the outhouse one last time!

Arriving at the farm, Gram and Pap gave everybody their instructions, so all the farm chores could be completed in a timely manner before dark. Before Vallie headed to change into her barn-clothes before heading to the hen house to gather the eggs, she asked Jeremiah and I if we wanted to bath our 4-H Baby

Beef. We told her we would do that one more time before the city-slickers returned to their home at the end of the week. Kata chimed in when she heard Vallie's request and let us know she would gladly shine the hoofs again. It was going to be another busy week on the farm.

Jeremiah and I never thought we'd miss those city-slickers who fit right into our farm life and enjoyed so much of what we loved. When we were prepping and showing our 4-H Baby Beef, Caesar and Titus, at the Perry County Fair in August, we sure could've used their help to style the tails, poof the tufts of hair around their ears and do a spit-shine on their hooves. None the less, Jeremiah won Grand Champion and I garnered blue ribbons showing the forever contrary Caesar. There were no tears shed when our Baby Beef were auctioned, but Jeremiah did cartwheels for both of us as our well-filled-out Baby Beef brought extremely high bids. We would put the sales checks into our savings and offer Pap a fair share for the feed they ate. We had already been discussing where we would start looking for Baby Beef for next year.

The summer had come to a close and we were saddened, but then we do like school and we had a lot to share with our classmates. Jeremiah and I are going to ask if we can start a Perry County History Club during the afternoon study hall at school. We're also going to volunteer to help The Perry Historians with their annual Apple Butter boils at Shermans Valley Heritage Days and at Little Buffalo State Park's Apple Fest in October. We're going to be really busy keeping after our homework and chores, harvesting the corn and soybeans, then heading out to help The Perry Historians preserve a way-of-life in Perry County's history. Come to think of it, that's what Jeremiah and I are all about…Preserving Perry County's history.

Sharing Life's Journey

Thanks for joining me and all the Perry County Storytellers, who were so eager and willing to share their cherished memories of how life *truly* was in Perry County, during the last century. We hope you not only learned a lot, but were able to relate and bring to your mind cherished memories. The storytellers hope you take to heart their Cherished Memories!

Debra Kay "Debby" Noye
debrakaynoye.com
dknoye@pa.net

www.ingramcontent.com/pod-product-compliance
Lightning Source LLC
Chambersburg PA
CBHW080457240426
43673CB00005B/222